GROUP WORK:
A COUNSELING SPECIALTY

GROUP WORK:
A COUNSELING SPECIALTY

Second Edition

Samuel T. Gladding
Wake Forest University

Merrill,
an imprint of Prentice Hall
Englewood Cliffs, New Jersey   Columbus, Ohio

Library of Congress Cataloging-in-Publication Data
Gladding, Samuel T.
      Group work : a counseling specialty / Samuel T. Gladding.
          p.   cm.
      Includes bibliographical references and index.
      ISBN 0-02-344123-2
      1. Group counseling. I. Title.
  BF637.C6G5334   1995
  158'.35—dc20   94-42715
                                           CIP

Editor: Kevin Davis
Production Editor: Linda Hillis Bayma
Copy Editor: Colleen Brosnan
Cover Designer: Proof Positive
Production Buyer: Deidra M. Schwartz
Electronic Text Management: Marilyn Wilson Phelps, Matthew Williams, Jane Lopez, Karen L. Bretz
Illustrations: Jane Lopez

This book was set in Garamond Book ITC by Prentice Hall and was printed and bound by R.R. Donnelley & Sons Company. The cover was printed by Phoenix Color Corp.

Printed in the United States of America

10 9 8 7 6 5 4 3 2 1

ISBN: 0-02-344123-2

Prentice-Hall International (UK) Limited, *London*
Prentice-Hall of Australia Pty. Limited, *Sydney*
Prentice-Hall of Canada, Inc., *Toronto*
Prentice-Hall Hispanoamericana, S. A., *Mexico*
Prentice-Hall of India Private Limited, *New Delhi*
Prentice-Hall of Japan, Inc., *Tokyo*
Simon & Schuster Asia Pte. Ltd., *Singapore*
Editora Prentice-Hall do Brasil, Ltda., *Rio de Janeiro*

To my wife
    Claire
and my children
    Benjamin, Nathaniel, and Timothy
Who have all taught me anew that
    sensitivity is a strength,
      listening is a skill,
        love is an action, and
          life is a gift to be shared.

Preface

Groups are a part of everyday life. We are born into a family group, and many of the most important events of our lives transpire in our educational, recreational, and work groups. Almost everyone is influenced daily by some type of group. Sometimes just the memory of a group experience or the attraction of an upcoming group event can have a powerful effect on individuals. Whether or not you consider yourself to be attracted to groups, the fact is that virtually everybody is affected by the groups with which they directly and indirectly associate.

The helping professions, from medicine to counseling, have been active in working with people in groups since the early 1900s. Professionals realize that groups have not only the power to help heal, but also to harm. Working with persons in groups (i.e., group work) has become an increasingly popular and viable means of promoting positive change and accomplishing tasks. There are many special considerations to take into account when working in a group setting. Each population served and each group is different. Theories and models of group work abound. The contents of this book examine those factors comprehensively and clearly.

The first part of this work concentrates on the history, dynamics, leadership, and development of groups. It traces the evolution of this specialty from its formal origin as a helping approach to its present-day development. Group work currently is utilized in a variety of settings, especially those involving education, counseling, psychotherapy, and task accomplishment. In order to work effectively with groups on all levels, it is crucial to understand group dynamics as well as needed leadership skills. Part I of this text examines these areas. In addition, chapters in this part of the book are devoted to universal considerations in the development of groups such as forming, making transitions, working, and terminating. Leaders must be cognizant of not only the basic life cycle of a group experience but also the appropriate way to work with individuals in such configurations. A final chapter explores the area of ethical and legal aspects of group work.

Part II of this book consists of chapters on the use of groups throughout the life span. These chapters cover issues and procedures for working with groups that focus on children, adolescents, adults, and the elderly. Each of these groups has special needs that should be addressed in a group setting. Different types of groups and their advantages and limitations for these populations are discussed.

The final part of this book concentrates on theoretical approaches to leading groups. Ten theoretical models that have evolved are explored in regard to their premises, practices, leadership emphases, outcomes, and strengths/limitations. The specific group theories covered here are psychoanalysis, Adlerian, person-centered, Gestalt, rational-emotive, transactional analysis, behavioral, reality therapy, psychodrama, and self-help. This section of the book also contains a chapter on current trends in the field of group work and brings the book full cycle from a developmental perspective. It appears that groups will continue to be a strong presence in the 21st century and beyond. *Group Work: A Counseling Specialty* includes a good mixture of theory and practice. It contains practical information that can be universally applied to groups in various settings. It is user friendly in providing illustrations, charts, and brief examples of skills in many areas. The exercises at the end of each chapter will help you expand your personal and professional knowledge even further. Overall, this book is enjoyable, as well as informative, and easy to comprehend.

In reflecting on why I decided to write this work, I realized my own history in groups played a large part in the process. In 1971, one of my professors at Wake Forest University, Dr. Wes Hood, taught a course on groups. It was theoretically based and complemented the experiential course, "Basic T Group Experiences," that I had taken the year before at Yale. The Wake Forest class led me to see more clearly how group structure and purpose influence function and dynamics. Important aspects of group leadership went from mystery to understanding. It was during this time that I also attended the University of Georgia group symposiums and was exposed to major personalities in the field such as Virginia Satir, William Schutz, George Gazda, Jack Gibb, and Haim Ginott. All had a major impact on me as a young professional.

The educational experiences that followed, including further graduate study at the University of North Carolina at Greensboro, heightened my awareness and skills in conducting and participating in groups. Dr. Larry Osborne was especially helpful. At Rockingham County Mental Health Center, where I began my professional career, I was fortunate enough to be involved in a number of group experiences ranging from those involving adolescents to those with hospitalized patients. I gained even more experience in leading groups through the North Carolina Group Behavior Society and through teaching at the college level.

At Fairfield University, one of my colleagues, Peg Carroll, assisted me in getting involved even more in group work through joining the New England Association for Specialists in Group Work and its parent organization. My interest and participation in groups continued during my tenure at the University of Alabama at Birmingham. It was here that I edited the *Journal for Specialists in Group Work,* engaged in private practice with Adult and Child Development Professionals, and occasionally led college retreats. All of these activities helped keep me abreast of new ideas in the field. Now back at Wake Forest, where my journey in groups began, I continue to teach in group settings, work with volunteer groups, and chair the university's total quality group effort. I have realized anew through these experiences the importance of group workers having skills in task as well as therapeutic settings. Colleagues John Anderson and Marianne Schuber have been wonderful resources for reworking and refining my ideas. My term as president of the Association for Specialists in Group Work has further exposed me to new and exciting ideas, innovations, and people in the field of group work as well.

In the writing of this book, the past and present have emerged and blended. It has been an exhilarating experience. Besides professional colleagues and group members, my family has played a major role in the accomplishment of this task. My wife, Claire, has been especially patient and helpful to me during this time. During the writing of the first edition of this text, she was both pregnant and dealing with the stress of handling two children under the age of two. During the completion of this second edition, her life has been calmer but still demanding. It is not surprising then that the book is dedicated to her and our children, Benjamin, Nathaniel, and Timothy.

Others who have been of great assistance are Jo Spradling, my former graduate assistant at UAB, who proofed the original pages of the manuscript, and professional colleague, Paul Myers, who read the drafts of this work and made valuable suggestions. Then, of course, there is Vicki Knight, my former administrative editor at Merrill, and Kevin Davis, my present editor. No one ever had more congenial persons with whom to work. Their encouragement, genuine interest, and support helped keep me on time with this project, and their humor actually made it fun. Others to whom I am indebted for reviewing manuscript and providing insights reflected in this text are Robert Conyne, University of Cincinnati; Thomas Elmore, Wake Forest University; Stephen Feit, Idaho State University; Richard Hawk, Tuskegee University; Bernard Nisenholz, private practice, California; Sally E. Thigpen, Northeast Louisiana University; and Charles Weiner, Henderson State University.

I am more aware than ever of the importance of collaborative efforts in accomplishing tasks. John Donne was correct in reminding us that we are not islands. All are a part of the mainland, and each of us has some uniqueness to bring and share with others. It is in that rich mix of personality and process that the heart of group work lies. Together, participating in groups makes life better.

Samuel T. Gladding

Contents

CHAPTER 3

Effective Group Leadership   49

CHAPTER 4

Beginning a Group   79

CHAPTER 5

The Transition Stage in a Group   103

CHAPTER 6

The Working Stage in a Group   123

CHAPTER 7

Termination of a Group   145

CHAPTER 8

Ethical and Legal Aspects of Group Work 169

CHAPTER 11

Groups for Adults   245

CHAPTER 12

Groups for the Elderly   273

PART THREE
LEADING GROUPS FROM A THEORETICAL
PERSPECTIVE   291

CHAPTER 13

Psychoanalytic and Adlerian Groups   293

CHAPTER 14

Person-Centered and Gestalt Groups   317

CHAPTER 15

Rational-Emotive Therapy and Transactional Analysis Groups   339

CHAPTER 16

Behavioral and Reality Therapy Groups   361

CHAPTER 17

Psychodrama and Self-Help Groups   385

CHAPTER 18

Current Trends in Group Work   407

Appendix A   Ethical Guidelines for Group Counselors   427

PART ONE

HISTORY, DYNAMICS, LEADERSHIP, AND GROUP DEVELOPMENT

CHAPTER 1

History and Models of Group Work

> *Nathaniel joined a band of rebels*
> *and from that colonial action*
> *a nation sprang and a government grew.*
> *I, seven generations removed,*
> *ponder the boldness of his group*
> *wishing for such courage*
> *in my deepest interactions*
> *And knowing on some level at times*
> *his resolve is mine.**

The history of groups is as old as the history of people. From the beginning of humankind, individuals have gathered together to create, achieve, and resolve matters not possible otherwise. The legacy of group actions carries over generations and either inspires or suppresses behaviors. Groups are a natural way for people to communicate and interrelate with one another. There is no written history to indicate when or where the first groups were formed, but all cultures have made use of groups in their growth and development. "Since ancient times people have speculated about how certain groups such as communities and social systems shape human behavior (e.g., Plato's *Republic* or Thomas More's *Utopia*) and have experimented to see how they can devise groups . . . to change human behavior and thus the social system" (Luchins, 1964, p. 5).

Groups are defined in many ways, but the following definition adopted from Johnson and Johnson (1991) encompasses the main qualities of most forms of groups. A **group** is a collection of two or more individuals, who meet in face-to-face interaction, interdependently, with the awareness that each belongs to the

*Source: Gladding, 1988.

group and for the purpose of achieving mutually agreed-upon goals. From family councils to town meetings, groups are an important component of everyday life. They have the power to influence in healthy and unhealthy ways.

The concept *group work* encompasses all types of activities performed by organized groups—for example, task/work, guidance/psychoeducational, psychotherapy, and counseling/interpersonal problem solving. "In earlier days many similar activities performed by social workers were called 'group work'" (Lifton, 1972, p. 13). Today, the concept is more specialized. The Association for Specialists in Group Work (ASGW) (1990) defines **group work** as "a broad professional practice that refers to the giving of help or the accomplishment of tasks in a group setting. It involves the application of group theory and process by a capable professional practitioner to assist an interdependent collection of people to reach their mutual goals, which may be personal, interpersonal, or task-related in nature" (p. 14).

This chapter examines significant events in the development of groups and group work. It also focuses on major group models and ways of conceptualizing groups. By understanding these factors, practitioners are more likely to use group forms appropriately and realize the rationale behind the connection of group form and outcome more clearly. As Claiborn (1987) contends, "The past has a nice way of getting us to think about the present . . ." (p. 286). It guides people in assessing where they are, as well as where they want to be.

USES OF GROUPS PRIOR TO 1900

Prior to 1900, groups were generally formed for functional and pragmatic reasons. Most groups were large, and the primary emphasis in working with groups was to distribute information. Instruction and/or correction of behaviors were focused on mainly through a psychoeducational means. Immigrants, the poor, and the mentally ill were among those populations receiving special attention in large groups. Social workers and physicians used group structure to help these individuals gain knowledge about themselves and others (Shaffer & Galinsky, 1989). Group formats were also employed to help patients in hospitals and the needy in social agencies discuss problems and share experiences.

In England, a movement in the mid-1800s, called *moral therapy,* housed mental patients in rural settings and prescribed for them fresh air, the fine arts, and humane care (Gladding, 1992). The success of this treatment was outstanding. It showed how therapeutic groups could be structured and tailored to meet common and individual needs. Although expensive, this model was emulated in the United States by placing state mental hospitals in agrarian environments where patients could receive proper care in a healthy setting.

A more urban experiment, which focused on immigrants and the poor, was the work of Jane Addams at Hull House in Chicago. What she did would be classified now as the beginnings of **social group work** (Pottick, 1988). She organized individuals, new to the American culture or alienated from it, into purposeful and enriching groups that engaged in reading, crafts, and club activities. In addition, she discussed with group participants matters such as hygiene and nutrition that helped them make needed personal changes. The focus of Hull House was on promoting reciprocal relationships and increasing "individual self-determination and self-respect" (Pottick, 1988, p. 24). The model of group work set up by Addams emphasized "the larger social community" in which group members had common origins, goals, and needs. It was a forerunner also "to later therapy groups emphasizing the participants' membership in a common social system or organization (e.g., the Tavistock, T-group, and theme-centered models)" (Shaffer & Galinsky, 1989, p. 2).

Overall, the actual development of groups in the late 1800s was a dynamic movement which included contributions from the emerging disciplines of psychology, sociology, philosophy, and education (Bonner, 1959). The group movement developed, not because of one individual or discipline, but rather because of the need for social reform and education. The use of large groups for mainly instructional purposes evolved to the use of small groups for various purposes. By 1900, a group movement began that would slowly emerge during the first half of the twentieth century. It is to these developments over the decades that attention will now be focused.

GROWTH OF GROUP WORK—1900 TO THE PRESENT

1900 to 1909

Joseph Hersey Pratt is credited with having organized the first formal group experience that was not primarily psychoeducational or task/work oriented. He started a psychotherapy group for tuberculosis outpatients in 1905 at the Massachusetts General Hospital in Boston. He was one of the first to write about the dynamics that occur within group settings, and his work served as a model for other leaders exploring processes within their groups (Appley & Winder, 1973). Pratt started his group primarily for humane and economic reasons. The group served as a source of support and inspiration for tuberculosis patients whose conditions were chronic and cyclical and whose circumstances often led to personal discouragement and depression (Seligman, 1982). The group saved both Pratt and his patients time and effort in treating this disease by providing information and encouragement in a common setting—that is, messages did not have to be repeated to each patient one at a time (George & Dustin, 1988). Furthermore, Pratt noticed that the patients in the group not only became more concerned with each other over time but also had a positive influence on each other. It is to Pratt's credit that he recognized the therapeutic power of groups.

At about the same time Pratt was forming his hospital groups, efforts were being made to establish groups in the public schools. In 1907, Jesse B. Davis, principal of Grand Rapids High School in Michigan, directed that one English class per week be devoted to "Vocational and Moral Guidance" (Glanz & Hayes,

1967). Davis later repeated this effort in other Michigan public schools. Unlike Pratt, however, Davis did not emphasize the dynamics of the group process. Rather, he stressed the functionality of a group as an environment in which to learn life skills and values.

After the death in 1908 of Frank Parsons (who is credited as being the founder of modern-day counseling), counselors in many guidance settings, such as the Vocational Bureau of Boston, began to see vocationally undecided individuals in small groups, as well as on a one-to-one basis (Brewer, 1942). The emphasis at such agencies, as in the schools, was to use groups as a way of dispensing information and providing educational and vocational guidance.

1910 to 1919

The initial progress in group therapeutic work slowed from 1910 to 1919. However, soldiers were instructed in groups during World War I. During this conflict, psychological group tests, such as the Army Alpha and Beta intelligence tests were developed and administered. Groups were also used in a limited way to treat combat-fatigued soldiers. Furthermore, teamwork was emphasized during the war for both civilians and military personnel. However, new methods for conducting groups were not being developed.

Except for the period from 1916 to 1918, the focus in the United States during the 1910s was on the individual and individual achievement. Part of the reason was the legacy of American history on the importance of the individual as exemplified in Western lore. A reinforcer for this mind-set was the influence of Sigmund Freud's individual psychoanalysis theory. Although Freud was interested in groups, the major emphasis of his work and that of his followers was on intrapersonal dynamics. Therefore, attention was focused on the therapeutic work between clients and therapists on a one-to-one basis.

An exception to the focus of American society on individuals during this decade was the growth in select schools and organizations on group guidance and psychoeducational approaches to learning in groups. In Europe, J. L. Moreno published a significant, philosophical paper on group methods, written under the name of J. M. Levy (Milman & Goldman, 1974). Moreno would later have a major impact on the development of group theory and practice in the United States as well as Europe. His writings stressed the psychoanalytic and social psychological perspectives of individuals working together.

1920 to 1929

Several important events in the development of group work occurred in the 1920s. First, group guidance and counseling efforts were initiated in a new form. Dreikurs and Corsini (1954) attribute a major breakthrough to the systematic use of groups in counseling to Alfred Adler. Adler's form of group counseling was referred to as *collective counseling* and is reported to have been used as early as 1922. He employed it with both prison and child guidance populations (Gazda, 1989). In the child guidance clinics he established in Vienna, children were interviewed by a team of helping specialists, such as psychiatrists, psychologists, and social workers. Parents and children were helped by the team to realize that problems with children usually are related to problems in the family. Families, especially parents, became more motivated to find solutions to family problems by employing this principle. Family group meetings or family councils were devised by Adler and his associates as a means of getting input from everyone in the family on how to resolve difficulties and improve family relations. Adler's work was a forerunner of what later became a major form of group counseling. He applied group techniques to a natural group: the family.

A second major event in the 1920s was the formulation by J. L. Moreno in 1921 of the "Theatre of Spontaneity" *(Stegreiftheatre)*, a forerunner of psychodrama (Vander Kolk, 1985). Moreno's ideas would later influence other theorists, such as Fritz Perls "in his founding of Gestalt technology and William Schutz in his formation of encounter techniques" (Shaffer & Galinsky, 1989, p. 9). Some of the ideas stemming from psychodrama, such as role playing, the taking of "stage center," the emphasis on here-and-now interaction, the promotion of catharsis, the focus on empathy, and the encouragement of group members helping each other, are incorporated in many forms of group experiences today. Moreno helped promote the growth of group work by his decision to employ theatrical techniques with people who were psychologically disturbed. His innovations in the field of group psychotherapy/personality reconstruction challenged old methods of working with those experiencing mental turmoil.

The final significant occurrence during the 1920s was the investigation of small group phenomenon by social scientists. Researchers began to learn what types of interactions were the norm in small group settings and how individuals were influenced by groups (Allport, 1924). Individual versus group performances were also evaluated (Gordon, 1924; Watson, 1928). These studies grew in number and importance during the 1930s and 1940s. Because of this scientific approach, the concept of groups became more respected, and the power of groups became more recognized.

1930 to 1939

The 1930s are noted in group work history for five major events. First, there was an increase in group guidance and psychoeducational publications and practices (e.g., Allen, 1931; McKown, 1934). Second, J. L. Moreno continued to write and make creative presentations. Furthermore, there was an increase in the number and quality of fieldwork studies by sociologists, such as Muzafer Sherif (1936), Theodore Newcomb (1943), and W. F. Whyte (1943). A fourth event during the decade was the founding of the first major self-help group in America, Alcoholics

Anonymous. A final noteworthy phenomenon of the decade was the movement of psychoanalytical treatment into the group domain. Each of these events will be examined further.

Group guidance and psychoeducation in schools centered on vocational and personal themes. Initially, guidance and psychoeducational activities were the responsibility of homeroom teachers. Some schools even referred to homeroom as "the **'guidance hour'** or 'guidance room'" (McKown, 1934, p. 53). Whatever it was called, the responsibilities of the teacher were "to establish friendly relationships, to discover the abilities and needs, and to develop right attitudes toward school, home, and the community" (Strange, 1935, p. 116). Group guidance continued in this fashion until the 1950s.

The most productive writings and presentations of J. L. Moreno started in the 1930s and continued for several decades. Moreno introduced the terms *group therapy* and *group psychotherapy* into the vocabulary of helping professionals in 1931 and 1932 (Corsini, 1957; Moreno, 1966). He also devised one of the earliest forms of group treatment: *psychodrama* (Moreno, 1945). Psychodrama is an interpersonal approach where participants act out their emotions and attempt to clarify conflicts. This type of therapy and the emergence of therapy in small groups, which became more prevalent in the 1930s, opened the way for the theoretical conceptualization of group counseling (Gazda, 1989). Although R. D. Allen (1931) used the term *group counseling* at about the same time that Moreno used *group therapy,* he was referring basically to group guidance procedures. It was not until the 1940s that group counseling, as it is known now, appeared.

The third major event of the decade—studies of groups in natural settings—used various investigative methods to gather data. Sherif (1936), for instance, studied the influence of groups on the establishment of social norms by charting the response of individuals inside and outside a group setting to a particular stimulus called the *autokinetic movement.* He found individuals who had been a part of a group tended to view this light phenomenon within the range established by their group. Likewise, Newcomb (1943) found students from politically conservative homes tended to become more liberal because of the prevailing norms of their peer groups at Bennington College. Finally, Whyte (1943) studied larger social systems by moving into the slums of Boston in 1937 for 3 1/2 years. He found that gangs, clubs, and political organizations had a dramatic impact on individual's lives.

Alcoholics Anonymous (AA) was established in the late 1930s by founders who came to realize "the potency of individuals meeting together and interacting in a supportive way to produce change" (Posthuma, 1989, p. 3). It evolved into an organization that continues to help alcoholics gain and maintain control of their lives by remaining sober. Many of the techniques used in AA are similar to those found in other groups—for example, listening, empathizing, supporting, and teaching.

Psychoanalytic group analysis also emerged in the 1930s (Gazda, 1968). One of the leaders of this movement was Trigant Burrow, who studied how social forces affect behavior and stressed the biological principles of group behavior, a process he called *phyloanalysis.* Other pioneers of psychoanalytic group analysis were

Louis Wender (1936) and Paul Schilder (1939). Wender's work resulted in the model for group psychoanalysis that is used today. Schilder's efforts focused more on the interaction between individual group members (Appley & Winder, 1973).

1940 to 1949

World War II and the 1940s are often seen as the beginning of the modern group work period (Posthuma, 1989). Two major directions in the formal development of groups took place during this time: (1) the theoretical writings and practices of Kurt Lewin and Wilfred Bion and (2) the establishment of group organizations. Lifton (1972) observed that the climate in which group work developed during this time reflected American and British society's reaction against authoritarian dictatorships and showed a major concern with promoting democracy.

Kurt Lewin (1940, 1951) is generally recognized as the most influential founder and promoter of group dynamics during this era (Johnson & Johnson, 1991; Luft, 1963). A refugee from Nazi Germany, Lewin worked tirelessly to research and refine group dynamics and surrounded himself with energetic and brilliant people. He began writing in the 1930s, but the major impact of his work emerged in the 1940s. Lewin's approach, *field theory*, emphasizes the interaction between individuals and their environments. It is based on the ideas of Gestalt psychology, in which there is an interdependence of part/whole relationships. For Lewin, the group is a whole that is different from and greater than the parts that compose it.

It was Lewin, "the practical theorist" (Marrow, 1969), who was instrumental in establishing a workshop on intergroup relations in New Britain, Connecticut, in 1946. The workshop led to the formation of the **National Training Laboratories (NTL)** in Bethel, Maine, and the growth of the **Basic Skills Training (BST) Group,** which eventually evolved into the Training Group **(T-Group)** movement. Lewin discovered through his collaborative research that group discussions are superior to individual instruction in changing people's ideas and behaviors. His emphasis on a here-and-now orientation to the environment and his point that changes in group behavior depend on an "unfreezing" and "freezing" process of human behavior are major contributions to the group work field. It was Lewin, with his engineering background, who first applied the concept of *feedback* to group work.

Wilfred Bion (1948), a member of the **Tavistock Institute of Human Relations** in Great Britain, also stressed the importance of group dynamics. Bion was psychoanalytically trained but broke away from Freudian concepts, such as the idea that the family is the basic group model. Instead, Bion stated that group phenomena may be radically different from those within a family (Mackler & Strauss, 1981). His focus was on group cohesiveness and forces that foster the progression or regression of the group. Bion found that he could characterize the emotional pattern of a group as either a **"W" (work group)** or a **"BA" (basic assumption) activity,** which was an antiwork group. BA groups could be broken down further into three subpatterns: *BA Dependency* (where members are overdependent on the group leader), *BA Pairing* (where members are more interested in being with each other than in working on a goal), and *BA Fight-Flight* (where members become preoccupied with either engaging in or avoiding hostile conflict).

During the 1940s, two major group organizations and publications were founded. The first organization was the **American Society of Group Psychotherapy and Psychodrama (ASGPP)**, which was established by J. L. Moreno between 1941 and 1942. The second was the **American Group Psychotherapy Association (AGPA)**, a psychoanalytically oriented organization established by Samuel R. Slavson in 1943 (Gazda, 1968). Two pertinent journals started during the 1940s were *Sociatry* in 1947, which was changed to *Group Psychotherapy* in 1949, and the *International Journal of Group Psychotherapy* in 1949. Each journal reflected the philosophy of its founder, J. L. Moreno and Samuel R. Slavson, respectively.

1950 to 1959

The 1950s were characterized by a greater refinement in all aspects of group work. In regard to group behavior, Bales (1950) noted that in most groups stereotyped roles tend to emerge over time. He listed 12 broad categories from positive reactions (e.g., shows solidarity) to negative reactions (e.g., shows antagonism). At the same time, Karen Horney, Harry Stack Sullivan, and Carl Rogers developed distinct theoretical perspectives to "different clinical settings for different types of clinical problems" (Yalom, 1985, p. 504).

During the 1950s, group procedures began to be applied to the practice of family counseling. Among the pioneers in this area were Rudolph Dreikurs, who began working with parent groups (Dreikurs, Corsini, Lowe, & Sonstegard, 1959). Driekurs employed Alfred Adler's theory and ideas in setting up these groups, which were primarily psychoeducational. Another clinician, John Bell (1961), also started using groups in his work in family therapy. Beginning as early as 1951, he conducted family therapy sessions like group counseling sessions. Bell treated families as if they were strangers in a group. He relied on stimulating open discussions in order to solve family problems and, as in group counseling, he encouraged silent members to speak up and share ideas. A final trio of practitioners—Nathan Ackerman (1958), Gregory Bateson (Bateson & Ruesch, 1951), and Virginia Satir (1964)—were significant in this decade, too. Their independent but similar focus was in modifying the psychoanalytic model of group therapy to working with families. Ackerman and Satir were more clinically oriented and developed techniques for treating dysfunctions in families. Bateson concentrated more on research, especially group dynamics within families.

The last major development in groups during the 1950s was the implementation of new group concepts. A group "vocabulary" was developed to describe phenomena within group sessions. For example, the term *developmental group* was initially used during this decade by Richard Blake and Jane Mouton (Gazda,

1989). The first textbook in group work was published in 1958: *Counseling and Learning through Small-Group Discussion* by Helen I. Driver. Terminology for working with groups mushroomed in the 1950s.

As language and terms for groups increased, a shift occurred in the type of groups that were created. Group guidance began to wane in the late 1950s and was replaced by group counseling as a major way to bring about behavioral changes, especially in educational settings (Gazda, 1989). Group psychotherapy also increased in popularity as tranquilizing drugs made working with groups in mental health settings viable. A number of new types of groups called "quality groups" were implemented by the Japanese under the direction of work/task group master W. Edwards Deming (Hillkirk, 1993). These types of groups would later influence American industry in the 1980s.

1960 to 1969

Group work, especially group counseling and psychotherapy, was popular in the 1960s. Some of the most creative leaders in the history of group work came into prominence during this time. Group practice became so popular that *The New York Times* designated 1968 as "the year of the group." Many forms of group work were invented and/or refined during the 1960s, including encounter groups, sensory awareness groups, growth groups, marathons, and minithons. It seemed to be a decade in which there was a group for everyone and everyone was in a group.

Two of the most popular groups were encounter groups and marathon groups. Carl Rogers (1970) coined the term **basic encounter group**, later shortened to **encounter group**, to describe his approach to group work, which was basically an extension of his theory of individual counseling (Rogers, 1967). Encounter groups are often known as *personal growth groups* because the emphasis in these groups is on personal development. Encounter groups are sometimes also referred to as *sensitivity groups,* a term that focuses on individuals' awareness of their own emotional experiences and the behaviors of others. In encounter groups, emphasis is placed on the awareness of and exploration of intrapsychic and interpersonal issues (Eddy & Lubin, 1971).

Marathon groups were first devised by George Bach and Fred Stoller in 1964 as a way of helping people become more authentic with themselves and switch from "the marketing stance of role-playing and image making" (Bach, 1967, p. 995). Marathon groups are usually held for extended periods of time, such as 24 or 48 hours, and group members are required to stay together. Fatigue is an important factor in this experience. As time goes by, members become tired and experience a breakdown in their defenses and an increase in their truthfulness. Self-growth through interaction with others is the hopeful result of such groups.

With the popularity of groups came abuses. Many well-intended individuals and some charlatans established groups with no clear ideas on how to run them. As a result, some individuals became casualties of the popularity of the group movement. They were instructed to do such things as yell at others, physically attack those they disliked, or simply disrobe and lay all their defenses aside. The publicity seekers and entrepreneurs who set up such groups received reams of publicity—most of it bad. By the end of the 1960s, the group movement was under attack, and the field had been set back considerably. Many individuals made cults out of groups and impaired the functioning of those who participated in their activities (Landreth, 1984).

However, many good and important events occurred during this period as well, especially in the development of group theory and practice. Among the most popular theorists/practitioners of this decade were those who took a humanistic-existential orientation. Six will be briefly mentioned here: Fritz Perls, Eric Berne, William Schutz, Jack Gibb, George Bach, and Carl Rogers.

Fritz Perls (1967) conducted numerous workshops at the Esalen Institute in California demonstrating his Gestalt theory through the use of a group setting. Perls never claimed to do pure group work, but rather saw the individual as a figure who stood out against the background of the other group members (Frew, 1983).

Eric Berne (1964, 1966) was another major theorist/practitioner to highlight his therapeutic approach through the use of groups. His Transactional Analysis (TA) concepts of Parent, Adult, and Child were readily displayed and dealt with in group settings.

A third and very influential professional, William C. Schutz (1967), illustrated through group work that individuals can take care of their interpersonal needs for inclusion, control, and affection through groups. It was Schutz who stressed the use of nonverbal communication, such as touching or hugging, in groups (Appley & Winder, 1973).

A fourth influential theorist/practitioner of the 1960s was Jack Gibb, who studied competitive versus cooperative behavior in groups. Gibb (1961) found certain behaviors associated with competitive and cooperative orientations to group work. Furthermore, he discovered that competitive behavior in one person fostered competitive behavior in others, as well as defensiveness.

A fifth powerful humanistic practitioner of the 1960s was George Bach. It was Bach (1967) who described the power of and need for group marathons. He also devised creative ways to help individuals in groups and marriages resolve conflict by learning to fight fairly.

Probably the most influential theorist of the 1960s was Carl Rogers (1970). Rogers primarily applied his individual person-centered approach to groups and focused on interpersonal and intrapersonal dynamics. In effect, he took the T-group concept and made it more personal. This format caught on primarily because Rogers was based in California at the Center for the Study of Persons in La Jolla and because of the national social climate of the time. Since many Californians of the 1960s were uprooted transplants and felt alienated from their environment, Rogers's group concept worked well in promoting a feeling of community and connectedness. The same dynamics held true nationally during this period when the alienation of the Vietnam War and a sense of impersonal coldness in corporate America attracted people to encounter groups. The disadvantaged and college students were two populations that captured the attention of group therapists during the 1960s (Appley & Winder, 1973).

1970 to 1979

In the 1970s, group work continued to grow, but not without controversy. The term **groupthink** was created by Janis (1971) to emphasize the detrimental power that groups may exert over their members to conform. Janis showed that a groupthink mentality can be devastating to the growth of individuals and the problem-solving ability of the group itself.

Lifton's (1972) book of this period reflects the turmoil and concern surrounding the use of groups that had begun in the 1960s. He cites Jane Howard's (1970) book, *Please Touch,* as an example of an attempt to answer the critics of group work, who basically characterized sensitivity groups as antidemocratic and morally degrading. Howard's description of her movement from one encounter group to another debunked some popular misconceptions of these groups as "hotbeds" for junkies and addicts, but her book raised other issues, such as the importance of group leadership and the screening of group members. The controversy surrounding groups in the 1970s was due to their rapid, almost uncontrolled, growth in the late 1960s and the fact that guidelines for leadership and the conducting of group experiences themselves were not well defined.

In partial answer to this need for more professionalism in the conducting of groups, the Association for Specialists in Group Work (ASGW) was formed in 1973 as a divisional affiliate within the American Personnel and Guidance Association (now the American Counseling Association). The association grew rapidly during the 1970s and was active throughout the decade in promoting responsible group leadership and setting up standards under which group leaders should operate (Carroll & Levo, 1985).

Group research also came into prominence during the 1970s. Particularly important work was conducted by Irvin Yalom and George Gazda. Yalom (1970) analyzed group methods and processes and described eleven **"curative (therapeutic) factors" within groups** (e.g., altruism, instilling hope) that contributed to the betterment of individuals. Yalom and Lieberman (1971) found that leadership style in groups greatly influences how individuals fare in such settings. Aggressive, authoritarian, and confrontational leaders and those who are most distant and cool produce the most group casualties. Gazda was largely responsible for collecting primary accounts of how different group workers, especially psychotherapists and counselors, conceptualized and practiced their approaches (Elliott, 1989). He helped link group leaders together and later developed a rationale for developmental group counseling in the 1980s.

1980 to 1989

In the 1980s, the popularity of group work for the masses increased, as did the continued professionalism of the group movement itself. The American Group Psychotherapy Association (AGPA) was one of the associations that continued to refine group theory and practice. For instance, in the early 1980s, AGPA published a collection of articles edited by James Durkin (1981) that examined how general systems theory (a theory that emphasizes circular causality as opposed to linear causality) could be utilized in groups. Although general systems theory was not seen as a panacea for solving all problematic areas in examining group dynamics, the publication of these articles broadened the perspective of how group therapy was viewed. This scholarship helped explain the reasons that the three critical dimensions of any group—individuals, group members, and the group as a whole—operate in concert or apart from each other.

In addition to the expansion of theory, the number of different types of groups grew, too. Self-help groups, in particular, mushroomed. It was estimated that in 1988 there were between 2,000 and 3,000 self-help groups in the United States. These mutually supportive groups usually did not include professional leaders but were led by paraprofessionals or group members. Examples of such groups are Alcoholics Anonymous (AA) and Compassionate Friends (Schwab, 1986). Psychoeducational groups also received increased attention during this decade. Noted leaders in the group work area, such as George Gazda (1989), the first president of ASGW, proposed the use of **developmental group counseling** with multiple populations for teaching basic life skills.

Another sign of the refinement of groups during the 1980s was the continued expansion in the number of research articles being published. The number of research articles on groups had reached 20% by the mid-1970s, as compared with 5% of all such articles in the 1950s. In the 1980s, the percentage continued to increase (Stockton & Morran, 1982). A code of ethics for group workers was published by ASGW in 1980 and revised in 1989 (see Appendix A). Standards for training group leaders were proposed by the same organization during the decade and adopted in 1990. By the end of 1989, ASGW had attracted over 5,000 members and was the fourth largest division within the American Counseling Association (ACA). The American Group Psychotherapy Association and other group organizations also increased their memberships in the 1980s.

In summary, by the end of the 1980s, group work was recognized as a viable means of helping individuals in a variety of settings. More types of groups were available than ever before, with a new emphasis on self-help and social skills. More care was being focused in evaluating the effects of group experiences, and the number of research articles on group work showed an increase at the end of the decade.

1990 to the Present

In the 1990s, group work continued to flourish. The American Group Psychotherapy Association celebrated its 50th anniversary in 1992. A number of new books were published as well as a plethora of scholarly articles. Group work became increasingly utilized in school settings, especially as a way of influencing educational endeavors and social skills (Hudson, Doyle, & Venezia, 1991). However, group work also focused on groups for special populations, such as those in the midst of divorce (Addington, 1992) and adult offenders (Zimpfer, 1992).

The number of individuals interested in working with groups increased in the 1990s. For example, membership in the ASGW exceeded 6,000 members by 1995. This association was instrumental in increasing the number of courses required in group work for professional counselors. More emphasis was also placed on specialty areas in group work. In 1990, the ASGW approved and published professional standards for the training of group workers. Specialty areas covered were (a) task/work groups, (b) guidance/psychoeducational groups, (c) counseling/interpersonal problem-solving groups, and (d) psychotherapy/personality reconstruction groups. In addition, a distinction was made for core group competencies and group work specialists (Association for Specialists in Group Work, 1990) (see Appendix B).

In addition to these developments, more training and educational opportunities were offered in group work by almost all professional associations. For example, the ASGW held national conferences on group work in 1990 and 1994. The association also set up training institutes in 1992 to offer a variety of group continuing education courses around the country.

Furthermore, the 1990s were filled with a wide variety of self-help groups and support groups. Parenting groups became more popular, and the number of **cooperative learning groups** increased. In addition, focus groups, composed of representative samples of individuals concerned with issues, products, and/or outcomes, provided important information for businesses and politicians. Probably the greatest growth in the use of groups was in work settings where quality groups were set up among workers to promote teamwork, increase morale and efficiency, and ensure that more attention was paid to how tasks were completed (Crosby, 1984; Zeithaml, Parasuraman, & Berry, 1990). Quality groups empowered workers to positively affect their work environments. Quality groups also helped management personnel address human concerns as well as product integrity.

MAJOR MODELS OF GROUP WORK

Four models used to view groups are examined here with particular attention being focused on group standards. The different ways in which groups are viewed make a difference in how they are led and how they operate. The models presented are not mutually exclusive on many points but do offer some overall guidelines on certain aspects of groups. Hybrid types of groups are discussed in this section, too.

General Systems Theory

General systems theory is seen as a major way of explaining groups and their processes (O'Connor, 1980). From this perspective, "a group is a set of single organisms, commonly called members, which over a period of time or multiple interrupted periods, relate to each other face-to-face, processing matter-energy and information" (Miller, 1971, p. 302). In this systemic context, group members are always deciding between their needs for differentiating themselves (i.e., taking care of their needs to do things by themselves) and integrating with others (i.e., doing things with others) (Matthews, 1992). In this way, they are similar to a family (Bowen, 1978). From a systems perspective, group leaders must orchestrate their efforts in helping members and the group as a whole achieve a balance of these needs as the group develops.

A major thrust of the general systems model is the health of the group itself. The group may work in a functional or dysfunctional way depending on multiple factors, such as interpersonal relationships, the mental health of the individuals involved, and the skill of the group leader. There is no one single cause for assessing how the group works as in a more linear perspective. Therefore, the dynamics within the group and its complexity are highlighted.

Contact-Focused Group Theory

In **contact-focused group theory,** the focus is on the purpose of groups instead of their dynamics as in general systems theory. Three primary contact groups are described in this model: group guidance, group counseling, and group psychotherapy. In some cases, it is difficult to distinguish the differences between them. In fact, Ohlsen (1977) states that the difference between group counseling and group psychotherapy is more a result of the people involved than the process itself. Mahler (1971), however, has differentiated among these three major types of contact groups as follows:

1. the initially defined purpose of the group
2. the size of the group
3. the management of the content
4. the length of the group's life
5. the responsibility of the leader
6. the severity of the problem
7. the competency of the leader

A further means of distinguishing the differences among group guidance, group counseling, and group therapy has been proposed by Gazda (1989). In examining differences and similarities, Gazda places the emphases of these three types of groups on a continuum. Overlapping goals, professional competencies, and unique distinctions can be visually highlighted in this conceptualization (see Figure 1.1).

The TRAC Model of Groups

A third model of groups is known by the acronym **TRAC** (tasking, relating, acquiring, and contacting). Each letter represents an area in the total picture of group work (see

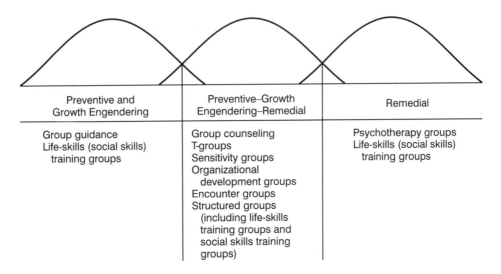

Preventive and Growth Engendering	Preventive–Growth Engendering–Remedial	Remedial

Group guidance
Life-skills (social skills)
   training groups
	Group counseling
	T-groups
	Sensitivity groups
	Organizational
	   development groups
	Encounter groups
	Structured groups
	   (including life-skills
	   training groups and
	   social skills training
	   groups)
		Psychotherapy groups
		Life-skills (social skills)
		   training groups

Figure 1.1
Relationships among group processes.
Source: From *Group Counseling: A Developmental Approach* (4th ed., p. 9) by George M. Gazda, 1989, Boston: Allyn & Bacon. Copyright © 1989 by Allyn and Bacon. Reprinted with permission.

Figure 1.2) (Saltmarsh, Jenkins, & Fisher, 1986). It is possible by using this model to explain how groups that start out in one major area (e.g., tasking) may move into other areas (e.g., relating). The TRAC model clearly delineates group process and management and the types of specialty groups found in each of four areas.

Overall, "the main characteristic that distinguishes one type of group from another is the focus. *Tasking groups* are focused on task achievement. *Relating groups* achieve objectives to increase the options for movement within the life of each person. *Acquiring groups* are directed toward learning outcomes that members can apply to others. In contrast, *contacting groups* are focused on the individual growth of members" (Saltmarsh et al., 1986, p. 34).

Specialty/Standards Model of Groups

A final model useful in conceptualizing groups is the **specialty/standards model**. In this approach, groups are defined according to their purpose, focus, and needed competencies. The ASGW (1990) has developed standards for each of four main types of groups: guidance/psychoeducational, counseling/interpersonal problem solving, psychotherapy/personality reconstruction, and task/work. Within these standards are similar core skills, such as working to build cohesion and resolving conflict, and specific skills particular to that specialty, such as a knowledge of sound teaching practice techniques in psychoeducational groups. Each of these four groups will be briefly examined.

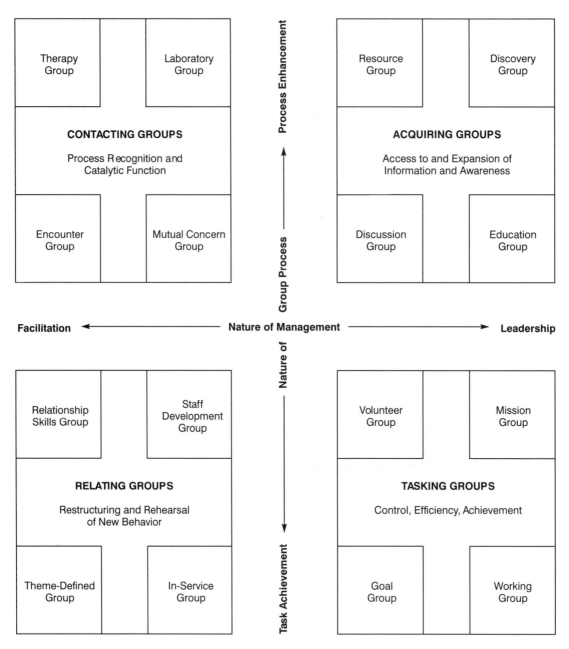

Figure 1.2

The TRAC map of group process and management.

Source: From "The TRAC Model: A Practical Map for Group Process and Management" by R. E. Saltmarsh, S. J. Jenkins, and G. L. Fisher, 1986, *Journal for Specialists in Group Work*, *11*, p. 32. Copyright ACA. Reprinted by permission of the American Counseling Association.

The first type of group, a **guidance/psychoeducational group**, was originally developed for use in educational settings, specifically public schools. Sometimes these groups are known as "educational" or "guidance" groups. The primary function of the group is the prevention of personal or societal disorders through the conveying of information and/or the examining of values. Guidance/psychoeducational groups stress growth through knowledge (ASGW, 1990). Content includes, but is not limited to, personal, social, vocational, and educational information. Preventive/growth activities can take many forms but usually are presented in the form of nonthreatening exercises or group discussions (Bates, Johnson, & Blaker, 1982).

Guidance/psychoeducational group activities are offered throughout the life span in a variety of settings. Sometimes these groups take the form of **life-skill development**, especially for those who have a deficit of behavior (Gazda, 1989). This type of emphasis is a "how-to" approach that may include the use of films, plays, demonstrations, role plays, and guest speakers. The size of the group varies with the setting (e.g., whether the activity is in a self-contained classroom or not), but the typical number in the group ranges from 10 to 40 individuals. The leader of the group is in charge of managing the group and disseminating information and usually is considered to be an expert in the area being discussed. Guidance/psychoeducational groups are designed to meet the needs of generally well-functioning people.

Counseling/interpersonal problem-solving groups, the second major type of group in this model, is preventive-growth and engendering-remedial (Gazda, 1989). The focus of group counseling and interpersonal problem solving is on each person's behavior and growth or change within the group. Therefore, the interaction among persons, especially in problem solving, is highlighted (ASGW, 1990). There is an emphasis on group dynamics and interpersonal relationships in these groups. Although guidance/psychoeducational groups are recommended for everyone on a continuous basis, group counseling and interpersonal problem solving is more selective. It focuses on individuals experiencing "usual, but often difficult, problems of living" (ASGW, 1990, p. 14) that information alone will not solve.

The size of these counseling/interpersonal problem-solving groups vary with the ages of the individuals involved and will range from 3 or 4 in a children's group to 8 to 12 in an adult group. The number of group meetings also fluctuates but will generally be anywhere from 6 to 16 sessions. The leader is in charge of facilitating the group interaction but becomes less directly involved as the group develops. Usually, the topics covered in group counseling and interpersonal problem solving are developmental or situational, such as educational, social, career, and personal. They tend to be of short-term duration. This type of group is a more direct approach to dealing with troublesome behaviors than are guidance/psychoeducational groups. A major advantage of group counseling and interpersonal problem solving is the interaction, feedback, and contribution of group members with each other over a period of time.

Group psychotherapy is sometimes referred to as a group that specializes in "personality reconstruction" (ASGW, 1990, p. 14). It is described in the professional literature as remedial (Luchins, 1964). It is meant to help people who have serious psychological problems of a long-term duration. As such, this type of group is found most often in mental health facilities, such as clinics or hospitals. As an entity, psychotherapy/personality reconstruction groups may be either **open-ended** (admitting new members at any time) or **closed-ended** (not admitting new members after the first session).

One of the primary aims of the group psychotherapy process is to reconstruct, through depth analysis, the personalities of those involved in the group (Brammer & Shostrom, 1960; Gazda, 1989). The size of the group varies from two or three to a dozen. The length of the group is measured in months, or even years, and the group is led by an expert in one of the mental health disciplines (psychiatry, psychology, counseling, social work, or psychiatric nursing) who has training and expertise in dealing with people who have severe emotional problems. The responsibility of the leader is to confront as well as to facilitate.

Task/work groups are the last of the major types of groups from a standards perspective. There are as many types of task/work groups as there are kinds of tasks and work. Saltmarsh et al. (1986) list the major types of tasking groups as volunteer groups, mission groups, goal groups, and working groups. Task/work groups also take the form of "task forces, committees, planning groups, community organizations, discussion groups, and learning groups" (ASGW, 1990, p. 14). Regardless of type or form, all task/work groups emphasize accomplishment and efficiency in successfully completing identified work goals (a performance or a finished product) through collaborative efforts.

Unlike other groups examined, there is no emphasis in task/work groups on changing individuals. Whether the group is successful or not depends on group dynamics—the interactions fostered through the relationships of members and leaders in connection with the complexity of the task involved. Since task/work groups run the gamut from informal subcommittee meetings to major Hollywood productions, the number of members within a task/work group may be large, but this type of group usually works best with fewer than 12 people. The length of a task/work group varies but most are similar to other groups in that they have a beginning, a working period, and an ending. A difference in task/work groups compared with others is that these groups may disband abruptly and little attention is paid by members or leaders to the termination stage.

Hybrid Groups

Some groups defy fitting any category, so-called **hybrid groups.**. They encompass multiple ways of working with their members and may change their emphasis frequently. For example, some groups are instructive and simultaneously or consequentially therapeutic. The prototype for such a group is a self-help group. This type of group will be briefly described here and examined in greater detail in the chapters to follow.

Self-help groups take two forms: those that are organized by an established, professional-helping organization or individual (a **support group**) and those that originate spontaneously and stress their autonomy and internal group resources—"self-help" groups in the truest sense (Riordan & Beggs, 1988). Although there are distinctions in support groups and self-help organizations regarding leadership and control (Silverman, 1986), these groups share numerous common denominators including the fact that they are composed of individuals who have a common focus and purpose. They are psychoeducational, therapeutic, and usually task driven. In addition, members of these groups frequently employ counseling techniques, such as reflection, active listening, and confrontation.

The civil rights movement of the 1950s and 1960s laid the foundation for the support group movement (Vander Kolk, 1985). Minorities, especially African-Americans, realized during this time that they would have to band together and rely on their own resources if they were to make substantial gains and obtain major changes in American society. Other factors (e.g., the success of earlier self-help and support groups such as Alcoholics Anonymous and Weight Watchers, and the failure of federal programs to take care of needs they were targeted to address) also contributed to the momentum behind this movement.

Many support and self-help groups seem to be successful in assisting their members to take more control over their lives and function well. Some that lack professional leadership make up for this deficiency in terms of experienced lay leaders. The narrow focus of these groups is both an asset in achieving a specific goal and a deficit in helping participants expand their horizons in many areas. In 1980, over 10 million people attended a self-help group (Yalom, 1985), and the number continues to grow.

SUMMARY AND CONCLUSION

Group work has developed differently throughout its historical growth. During its initial stages in the early 1900s, the emphasis on groups was mainly on functionality. For example, Joseph Hersey Pratt first used groups to teach patients ways of caring for themselves, and it was only accidentally that he discovered groups had a healing effect in and of themselves. Similarly, during World War I, groups were used strictly for their utilitarian benefits. In the 1920s and 1930s, natural groups were studied more closely, and the first major theorist in the group movement, J. L. Moreno, emerged. An equally powerful figure in laying the foundation for group theory was Kurt Lewin, who was a contemporary of Moreno. It was Lewin who influenced the development and growth of the National Training Laboratories and the Tavistock Small Group movement in the 1940s.

In the 1950s, the distinctions between group work and family therapy began to be formed. Theories that distinguished between working with individuals and working with groups also began to appear. In the 1960s, amid societal unrest, group work became very popular with the general population in preventive and remedial ways. It was seen as a viable alternative for individual counseling, especially in educational settings. Many different forms of groups were developed; indeed, the 1960s was a decade of groups. Group work research and the growth of self-help groups were refined during the 1970s and 1980s. Task/work groups became more important and influential from the 1970s until the present. Psychoeducational groups reemerged in importance during the 1980s and 1990s. Professional standards and ethics for group leaders were adopted at this time, and group organizations began earlier continued to flourish.

Many models of groups have been proposed during the history of group work. In this chapter, general systems theory, the relationship treatment model (group guidance, group counseling, and group psychotherapy), the TRAC (tasking, relating, acquiring, and contacting) model, and the specialty/standards model (guidance/psychoeducational, counseling/interpersonal problem solving, psychotherapy/personality reconstruction, and task/work groups) have been highlighted. Special attention was focused on the last model because of its pragmatic usefulness and current use. Hybrid groups were examined, too.

Overall, the history of group work gives those who study it an indication of where this movement has been and where it will likely go (i.e., become even more professional and consumer oriented). By studying the trends of the group work movement, it becomes obvious that not all groups are the same and some may be potentially helpful or harmful. Groups are popular in a variety of settings, such as schools, businesses, and community organizations. By knowing the development of this special way of helping and working, group leaders can use groups more effectively and beneficially, both for themselves and their constituents.

CLASSROOM EXERCISES

1. Discuss with two other classmates the types of groups in which you have been and your experiences in each group. Concentrate on the factors that made some groups better than others and share your conclusions with the class as a whole. Concentrate as much as possible on the qualities of work/task groups.

2. In groups of two, research a major figure in the history of group work, for example, Jane Addams, J. L. Moreno, or William Schutz. Note the contributions of this individual to the development of group theory and/or practice. Report your findings to the class in the form of an oral report.

3. Make an informal survey of your campus in regard to the types of groups that are offered. Assign two classmates to gather information on selected groups, such as study groups or fraternities. Examine the advantages of such groups and their development. How does knowing the histories of these groups help you understand their functioning now?

4. Plan with another classmate a guidance/psychoeducational group for a population in which you are particularly interested. Your focus can be on any topic that you and your partner think would be beneficial. Have class members give you feedback in regard to your plan and what other materials you might include in it.

REFERENCES

Ackerman, N. (1958). *The psychodynamics of family life.* New York: Basic Books.

Addington, J. (1992). Separation group. *Journal for Specialists in Group Work, 17,* 20–28.

Allen, R. D. (1931). A group guidance curriculum in the senior high school. *Education, 52,* 189–194.

Allport, F. (1924). *Social psychology.* Boston: Houghton Mifflin.

Appley, D. G., & Winder, A. E. (1973). *T-groups and therapy groups in a changing society.* San Francisco: Jossey-Bass.

Association for Specialists in Group Work. (1990). *Ethical guidelines for group counselors and professional standards for the training of group workers.* Alexandria, VA: Author.

Bach, G. R. (1967). Marathon group dynamics: Some functions of the professional group facilitator. *Psychological Reports, 20,* 995–999.

Bales, R. F. (1950). *Interaction process analysis.* Reading, MA: Addison-Wesley.

Bates, M., Johnson, C. D., & Blaker, K. E. (1982). *Group leadership.* Denver: Love.

Bateson, G., & Ruesch, J. (1951). *Communication, the social matrix of psychiatry.* New York: Norton.

Bell, J. E. (1961). *Family group therapy.* Public Health Monograph No. 64. Washington, DC: U.S. Government Printing Office.

Berne, E. (1964). *Games people play: The psychology of human relationships.* New York: Grove Press.

Berne, E. (1966). *Principles of group treatment.* New York: Grove Press.

Bion, W. R. (1948). Experience in groups. *Human Relations, 1,* 314–329.

Bonner, H. (1959). *Group dynamics.* New York: Ronald Press.

Bowen, M. (1978). *Family therapy in clinical practice.* New York: Jason Aronson.

Brammer, L. M., & Shostrom, E. L. (1960). *Therapeutic psychology.* Englewood Cliffs, NJ: Prentice Hall.

Brewer, J. M. (1942). *History of vocational guidance.* New York: Harper.

Carroll, M. R., & Levo, L. (1985). The association for specialists in group work. *Journal of Counseling and Development, 63,* 453–454.

Claiborn, C. D. (1987). Science and practice: Reconsidering the Pepinskys. *Journal of Counseling and Development, 65,* 286–288.

Corsini, R. J. (1957). *Methods of group psychotherapy.* Chicago: William James Press.

Crosby, P. B. (1984). *Quality without tears.* New York: McGraw-Hill.

Dreikurs, R., & Corsini, R. J. (1954). Twenty years of group psychotherapy. *American Journal of Psychiatry, 110,* 567–575.

Dreikurs, R., Corsini, R., Lowe R., & Sonstegard, M. (1959). *Adlerian family counseling.* Eugene: University of Oregon.

Driver, H. I. (1958). *Counseling and learning through small-group discussion.* Madison, WI: Monona Publications.

Durkin, J. E. (1981). *Living groups: Group psychotherapy and general systems theory.* New York: Brunner/Mazel.

Eddy, W. B., & Lubin, B. (1971). Laboratory training and encounter groups. *Personnel and Guidance Journal, 49,* 625–635.

Elliott, G. (1989). An interview with George M. Gazda. *Journal for Specialists in Group Work, 14,* 131–140.

Frew, J. E. (1983). Encouraging what is not figural in the gestalt group. *Journal for Specialists in Group Work, 8,* 175–181.

Gazda, G. M. (1968). Group psychotherapy: Its definition and history. In G. M. Gazda (Ed.), *Innovations in group psychotherapy* (pp. 3–14). Springfield, IL: Charles C. Thomas.

Gazda, G. M. (1989). *Group counseling: A developmental approach* (4th ed.). Boston: Allyn & Bacon.

George, R. L., & Dustin, D. (1988). *Group counseling: Theory and practice.* Englewood Cliffs, NJ: Prentice Hall.

Gibb, J. R. (1961). Defensive communication. *Journal of Communication, 11,* 141–148.

Gladding, S. T. (1988). *Ancestral thoughts.* Unpublished manuscript.

Gladding, S. T. (1992). *Counseling: A comprehensive profession.* New York: Macmillan.

Glanz, E. C., & Hayes, R. W. (1967). *Groups in guidance* (2nd ed.). Boston: Allyn & Bacon.

Gordon, K. (1924). Group judgments in the field of lifted weights. *Journal of Experimental Psychology, 7,* 398–400.

Hillkirk, J. (1993, December 21). World famous quality expert dead at 93. *USA Today,* B1–B2.

Howard, J. (1970). *Please touch.* New York: McGraw-Hill.

Hudson, P. E., Doyle, R. E., & Venezia, J. F. (1991). A comparison of two group methods of teaching communication skills to high school students. *Journal for Specialists in Group Work, 16,* 255–263.

Janis, I. L. (1971). Group think. *Psychology Today, 5,* 36–43, 74–76.

Johnson, D. W., & Johnson, F. P. (1991). *Joining together* (4th ed.). Englewood Cliffs, NJ: Prentice Hall.

Landreth, G. L. (1984). Encountering Carl Rogers: His views on facilitating groups. *Personnel and Guidance Journal, 62,* 323–326.

Lewin, K. (1940). Formulation and progress in psychology: University of Iowa studies. *Child Welfare, 16,* 9–42.

Lewin, K. (1951). *Field theory in social science.* New York: Harper.

Lifton, W. M. (1972). *Groups: Facilitating individual growth and societal change.* New York: Wiley.

Luchins, A. S. (1964). *Group therapy.* New York: Random House.

Luft, J. (1963). *Group processes: An introduction to group dynamics.* Palo Alto, CA: The National Press.

Mackler, L., & Strauss, C. (1981). Bion's bibliography. In L. R. Wolberg & M. L. Aronson (Eds.), *Group and family therapy.* New York: Brunner/Mazel.

Mahler, C. (1971). Group counseling. *Personnel and Guidance Journal, 49,* 601–610.

Marrow, A. J. (1969). *The practical theorist.* New York: Basic Books.

Matthews, C. O. (1992). An application of general systems theory (GST) to group therapy. *Journal for Specialists in Group Work, 17,* 161–169.

McKown, H. C. (1934). *Home room guidance.* New York: McGraw-Hill.

Miller, J. G. (1971). Living systems: the group. *Behavioral Science, 16,* 302–398.

Milman, D. S., & Goldman, G. D. (1974). Introduction. In D. S. Milman & G. D. Goldman (Eds.), *Group process today.* Springfield , IL: Charles C. Thomas.

Moreno, J. L. (1945). *Psychodrama.* New York: Beacon House.

Moreno, Z. T. (1966). Evolution and dynamics of the group psychotherapy movement. In J. L. Moreno (Ed.), *The international handbook of group psychotherapy.* New York: Philosophical Library.

Newcomb, T. (1943). *Personality and social change.* New York: Dryden.

O'Connor, G. G. (1980). Small groups: A general systems model. *Small Group Behavior, 11,* 145–173.

Ohlsen, M. M. (1977). *Group counseling* (2nd ed.). New York: Holt.

Perls, F. (1967). Group vs. individual therapy. *A Review of General Semantics, 24,* 306–312.

Posthuma, B. W. (1989). *Small groups in therapy settings.* Boston: College-Hill Publications.

Pottick, K. J. (1988). Jane Addams revisited: Practice theory and social economics. *Social Work with Groups, 11,* 11–26.

Riordan, R. J., & Beggs, M. S. (1988). Some critical differences between self-help and therapy groups. *Journal for Specialists in Group Work, 13,* 24–29.

Rogers, C. R. (1967). The process of the basic encounter group. In J. F. Bugental (Ed.), *Challenges of humanistic psychology.* New York: McGraw-Hill.

Rogers, C. R. (1970). *Carl Rogers on encounter groups.* New York: Harper & Row.

Saltmarsh, R. E., Jenkins, S. J., & Fisher, G. L. (1986). The TRAC model: A practical map for group process and management. *Journal for Specialists in Group Work, 11,* 30–36.

Satir, V. (1964). *Conjoint family therapy: A guide to theory and technique.* Palo Alto, CA: Science and Behavior Books.

Schilder, P. (1939). Results and problems of group psychotherapy in severe neurosis. *Mental Hygiene, 23,* 87–98.

Schutz, W. C. (1967). *Joy: Expanding human awareness.* New York: Grove Press.

Schwab, R. (1986). Support groups for the bereaved. *Journal for Specialists in Group Work, 11,* 100–106.

Seligman, M. (1982). Introduction. In M. Seligman (Ed.), *Group psychotherapy and counseling with special populations.* Baltimore: University Park Press.

Shaffer, J., & Galinsky, M. D. (1989). *Models of group therapy* (2nd ed.). Englewood Cliffs, NJ: Prentice Hall.

Sherif, M. (1936). *The psychology of group norms.* New York: Harper.

Silverman, P. R. (1986). The perils of borrowing: Role of the professional in mutual help groups. *Journal for Specialists in Group Work, 11,* 68–73.

Stockton, R., & Morran, D. K. (1982). Review and perspective of critical dimensions in therapeutic small group research. In G. M. Gazda (Ed.), *Basic approaches to group psychotherapy and group counseling* (3rd ed.). Springfield, IL: Charles C. Thomas.

Strange, R. (1935). *The role of the teacher in personnel work.* New York: Bureau of Publications, Teachers College, Columbia University.

Vander Kolk, C. J. (1985). *Introduction to group counseling and psychotherapy.* Columbus, OH: Merrill.

Watson, G. (1928). Do groups think more effectively than individuals? *Journal of Abnormal and Social Psychology, 23,* 328–336.

Wender, L. (1936). The dynamics of group psychotherapy and its application. *Journal of Nervous and Mental Diseases, 84,* 54–60.

Whyte, W. (1943). *Street corner society.* Chicago: University of Chicago Press.

Yalom, I. D. (1970). *The theory and practice of group psychotherapy.* New York: Basic Books.

Yalom, I. D. (1985). *The theory and practice of group psychotherapy* (3rd ed.). New York: Basic Books.

Yalom, I. D., & Lieberman, M. (1971). A study of encounter group casualties. *Archives of General Psychology, 25,* 16–30.

Zeithaml, V. A., Parasuraman, A., & Berry, L. L. (1990). *Delivering quality service.* New York: The Free Press.

Zimpfer, D. G. (1992). Group work with adult offenders: An overview. *Journal for Specialists in Group Work, 17,* 54–61.

CHAPTER 2

Group Dynamics

Emotions ricochet around the group
fired by an act of self-disclosure
in an atmosphere of trust.
I, struck by the process,
watch as the feelings penetrate the minds
of observing members
and touch off new reactions.
Change comes from many directions
triggered by a simple sentence. *

This chapter focuses on group dynamics. The term **group dynamics** was originally used by Kurt Lewin (1948) to describe what went on in small groups. Lewin was especially interested in how group climates and processes influence the interactions of group members and ultimate outcomes. He thought many factors contributed to the overall concept of group dynamics, for instance, group purpose, communication patterns, power/control issues, and member roles. For instance, if the group's purpose is to fight a common enemy and save a country, the intensity, roles, communication procedures, control issues, and interactions of its members are quite different from those of a group formed to study the influences of modern art in conservative communities.

One of the most encompassing definitions of group dynamics has been given by Cartwright and Zander (1968). These researchers describe group dynamics as an applied field of inquiry "dedicated to advancing knowledge about the nature of groups, the laws of their development, and their interrelations with individuals, other groups, and larger institutions" (p. 7). A shorter definition is given by Jacobs, Harvill, and Masson (1994) who simply describe group dynamics as "the

Source: Gladding, 1989.

forces that are operating in a group" (p. 23). By understanding these forces and their interplay, group specialists are able to discern the nature of groups and how interactions between members and leaders impact the group's development.

It should be pointed out that group dynamics (i.e., forces within a group) lead to **group process** (i. e., interactions of group members). It is often difficult to separate these two concepts because of their interrelated and reciprocal influences. For example, if there is a struggle for power in a task/work group, interactions between members will become more adversarial. This will lead to an intensified struggle for power which will lead to more hostility until or unless new ways of relating are introduced into the group (e.g., negotiating or compromising skills). Basically, the development of groups is one affected by multiple factors and should be thought of as *systemic* (i.e., circular) rather than *linear* (cause and effect) (Matthews, 1992).

The complexity of working with and in groups as distinct types of entities must be properly understood to promote healthy atmospheres within them (Korda & Pancrazio, 1989). Persons who are uninformed or ignore how groups function may become extremely frustrated and may behave inappropriately. Potential group leaders who do not have a good understanding of group dynamics will risk being not only ineffective but also possibly harmful and unethical.

One method of assessing what types of factors most influence certain group situations is by studying the research in such journals as *Small Group Behavior,* the *Journal for Specialists in Group Work,* or the *International Journal of Group Psychotherapy.* Good research that is clearly and concisely written can convey a considerable amount of information. Direct group observation and/or participation is a second means of comprehending the evolving nature of groups and how members are influenced by each other and external forces (e.g., cultural surroundings). This method can give firsthand knowledge about how the group is operating, but it may become subjective. A third way of assessing group influences is feedback from outside objective observers or a critique of videotapes of groups. This last means of obtaining data, especially if the outside observers use video, allows a thorough examination of the group as it enables one to both see and hear what is occurring within a group.

THE IMPACT AND INFLUENCE OF GROUPS

Groups, as dynamic entities, have direct and indirect influences on their members (Bion, 1959; Yalom, 1985). The presence of others may improve or impair the performance and development of persons depending on their background preparation (Zajonc, 1965). For example, if athletes are well prepared and rested, their performance will usually improve in the presence of an audience. On the other hand, if they have had only minimal preparation, their performance will probably deteriorate over time.

Every group functions in a social context, that is, a **social ecology** (Conyne, 1983). Individuals are affected by group associations and, in turn, significantly affect the functioning of the group. Internal and external events, as well as the passage of time, influence the lives of group members and the life of the group itself. For example, a study of the Beatles during the 1960s shows how each member of the band—Paul McCartney, John Lennon, George Harrison, and Ringo Starr—changed not only himself but also the outward appearance, musical style, and performance of the others and the group as a whole. The Beatles of 1969 were not the same group in the way they operated (or even looked) as the Beatles of 1964. The point is that groups are systems with many parts interacting in a complex and interrelated fashion (Toseland & Rivas, 1984). They are constantly in a state of flux.

Research taken from three separate disciplines—individual psychology, social psychology, and sociology—focuses on explaining the interaction in groups and how they exert an influence (Munich & Astrachan, 1983). Basically, people act differently in groups than they do by themselves. There is a type of **social influence** when in the presence of others that has a way of altering actions, attitudes, and feelings (Asch, 1951; Festinger, 1954; Sherif, 1937). For example, Solomon Asch found that individuals might make one judgment about the length of a line when alone and another when they were in a group. This phenomenon was especially prevalent if these persons were the last members in the group to be asked their opinion about the length of the line and all other group members had been unanimous in agreeing and publicly stating an opinion. In these situations, group pressure was prevalent. As a general rule, **primary affiliation groups** (i.e., those with which people most identify, such as a family or peers) exert greater pressure on individuals than **secondary affiliation groups** (i.e., those with which people least identify, such as a city or confederation).

Persons often work hard to break into groups because of a desire to obtain a special affiliation or identity. Specialized groups are often popular for this reason. College fraternities and sororities, for instance, provide some people with a sense of security in being recognized as belonging to a particular organization. The same can be said for country club membership. Because of the personal investment made to join such groups, people who later decide to break out of the influences of the group may find it difficult or even impossible. Acquired behaviors, thought patterns, and emotional experiences gleaned from groups are difficult to break (Trotzer, 1989).

The power of group dynamics was one of the first concepts studied in group research. "The origins of group dynamics are largely in social and industrial psychology and stem from the efforts of experts in these fields to understand group influence on individual behavior and on productivity in the workplace and in other human groups" (Friedman, 1989, p. 46). The landmark study of the influence of groups was conducted by Elton Mayo and his associates at the Hawthorne Plant of the Western Electric Company (Mayo, 1945). This research group tried to study the effect of manipulating physical features in the work setting. They discovered that physical aspects of the work environment were not as important as social factors within the work group itself. Changes in behavior as a result of observation/manipulation conditions under which a person works became known as the **Hawthorne effect.**

Whether a person likes groups or not, the power of groups must be respected. If an individual can anticipate possible influences of a group, he or she can plan ahead and set up groups or work within groups for the good of all.

PREPLANNING AND GROUP DYNAMICS

The dynamics of a group begin before the group ever convenes. In the pregroup stage, the leader(s) plan for what type of group to conduct, in what setting it should be held, how long it will last, who should be included, and how it will be evaluated. All of these considerations are an essential part of facilitating a successful group (Glaser, Webster, & Horne, 1992). If leaders are not sure of the type of experiences they wish to set up and for whom, the group will most likely fail.

Therefore, the first factor that must be taken into consideration in the preplanning is **clarity of purpose**, i.e., what the group is to accomplish. The title of singer James Taylor's song, "That's Why I'm Here," is a reminder of the importance of clarity of purpose. The lyrics describe both serious and light-hearted reasons for one's existence. Most groups could use Taylor's song as a guide for determining what their group will be about before they begin. For a group to be successful, it must be relevant and meaningful for all of its members. Otherwise, they are likely to withdraw or disengage. For instance, a psychoeducational group focusing on careers may have great appeal to senior high school students but not be relevant to primary school children unless it is modified to their level and presented so that they see a connection between themselves and future careers.

In addition to clarity of purpose, a group's setting (i.e., its environment) will influence how well it runs. Settings should be rooms that are quiet, comfortable, and off the beaten track. The type of environment which promotes positive group dynamics is not found by accident. It must be carefully selected because the functioning of the group is ultimately dependent on it. Members who feel secure in an environment are more willing to take risks and use themselves and the group to the fullest.

A third factor that must be considered in preplanning a group is time. The length of a group session should not be too long or too short. Sessions running more than two hours may cause members to become tired and lose interest. Likewise, with the exception of some children's groups, most groups need about 15 to 20 minutes to "warm up" before they start working. Therefore, groups that meet for less than half an hour do not have time to accomplish much. The ideal time frame for most groups is between an hour and an hour and a half. A few groups, such as marathons, use extended time periods to help lower defenses through the effects of fatigue. In this way, they promote identity and change. Most groups, however, meet weekly within the time period just prescribed. Such a time schedule allows group members and the group as a whole to obtain a comfortable pace or rhythm.

Even in a small group, size makes a difference in the dynamics of the group. Research indicates that increasing the size of a group (beyond 6 to 14 members) decreases its cohesiveness and member satisfaction (Munich & Astrachan, 1983). One study indicated a significant reduction in interaction among group members when the group size reached 9 and another marked reduction when the group size reached 17 or more (Castore, 1962). In such cases, subgrouping tends to occur, and some members become silent because the competition for conversation becomes more intense (Shepherd, 1964). Likewise, groups with fewer than 5 members (except those composed of elementary school children) tend not to function very well because too much pressure is placed on each group member to perform or contribute (Hansen, Warner, & Smith, 1980). There is virtually no opportunity in a group of 5 or less to choose not to participate.

Another component of a group that affects its dynamics is membership, both in regard to the mixture and number of people in it. **Heterogeneous groups** (those composed of persons with dissimilar backgrounds) can broaden members' horizons and enliven interpersonal interactions. Such groups may be helpful in problem solving such as in psychotherapy and counseling groups. Yet, **homogeneous groups** (those composed of persons with similar backgrounds, such as engineers or widows) are extremely beneficial in working through specific issues. Task/work groups are often homogeneous for this reason. The nature and purpose of the group usually determines what its member composition will be.

The race and gender of members are factors in group dynamics as well. Some groups, such as psychoeducational groups, do best when they have members with diverse backgrounds who can react to the guidance material that has been presented. On the other hand, group members of underrepresented or disenfranchised groups may bring issues to the group that divert attention from its original purpose.

Other factors affecting group dynamics that must be preplanned are the fit between members' goals and group goals, the level of membership commitment (i.e., whether members are joining the group voluntarily or because of external pressures), openness of members to self and others, commitment to take or support risks, members' attitudes toward leadership and authority, and the leader's attitude toward certain characteristics of members. The point is that group dynamics are a result of interaction patterns that develop due to careful or careless preplanning. The planning of a group and its importance will be discussed in more detail in chapter 4.

GROUP STRUCTURE AND GROUP DYNAMICS

Group structure refers to both the physical setup of a group as well as the interaction of each group member in relation to the group as a whole. Both types of structure influence how successful or harmonious the group will be and whether individual or group objectives will be met. Leaders and members have an ability to structure a group for better or worse. In this section, the physical structure of a group will be examined with the essence of group interaction following in a later section.

The **physical structure** (i.e., the arrangement of group members) is one of the first factors to consider in setting up a group. Physical structure has a strong influence on how a group operates. If members feel they are physically removed from the group or that they are the center of the group, they will act accordingly.

The seating arrangement can be very important. Many groups, regardless of purpose, use a **circle** format. In this configuration, all members have direct access to each other (Yalom, 1985). They have implied equality in status and power. The disadvantage of this arrangement is the lack of a perceived leader in the structure unless the identified leader is active and direct. Overall, the circle lends itself to being a democratic structure for conducting group work and is probably the best structured way for ensuring equal "air time" for all group members (see Figure 2.1).

However, the circle is not the only way to set up a group. Other formats yield different types of interactions. Leavitt (1951) conducted an experiment to determine the effects of various structures on group performance. He devised three communication networks in addition to the circle (see Figure 2.2). These were the "chain," the "Y," and the "wheel."

In the **chain** arrangement, people are positioned or seated along a line, often according to their rank in a group. Communication is passed from a person at one end of the configuration to a person at the other end through others. The chain is a popular way to run some group organizations. For example, the military conceptualizes its command structure as "the chain of command." However, a chain is seldom used outside of a hierarchical association. The reasons are the indirectness of communication, the lack of direct contact with others, and the frustration of relaying messages through others.

Figure 2.1
Optimal group
structure/interaction.

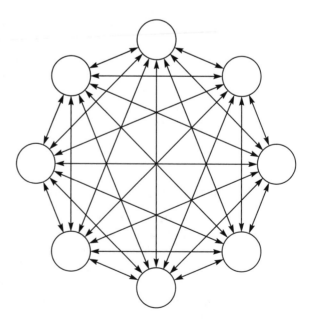

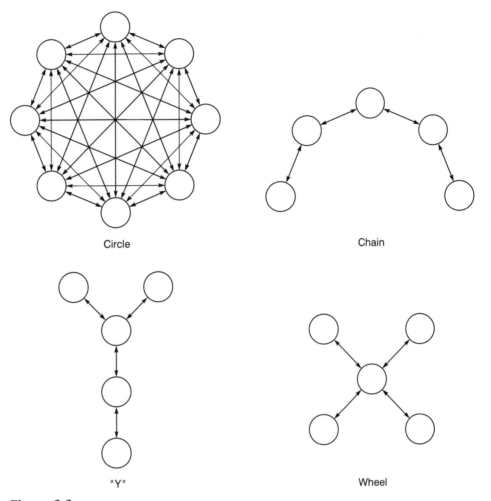

Circle   Chain

"Y"   Wheel

Figure 2.2
Effects of group structure on group performance.
Source: Adapted from "Some Effects of Certain Communication Problems on Group Per-
formance" by H. G. Leavitt, 1951. *Journal of Abnormal and Social Psychology, 46,* 38–50.

Another way of organizing groups is the **wheel**. In this arrangement, there is a
"center spoke," the leader, through which all messages go. Although members have
the advantage of face-to-face interaction with the leader in this structure, they may
become very frustrated by the inability to communicate with another group member directly. In the wheel configuration, some members are not informed about
what their colleagues are doing. For example, supervisors in a factory may work as
the center spokes in a wheel formation and have different personnel report to
them. If they do not give, as well as receive, information, their workers will not
know how the plant is operating or what issues need to be addressed.

The final type of group structure Leavitt experimented with was the **Y**. The Y combines the structural elements of the wheel and the chain. In this arrangement, there is a perceived leader. The efficiency of the unit is second only to that of the wheel in performance. Like a chain, however, the Y may frustrate group members who wish to have direct contact and communication with each other. Information is not equally shared or distributed.

In most groups, the importance of structure will vary according to the type of groups being led. For instance, in a psychoeducational/guidance group, members may be arranged in yet another structure—**theater style**—where they are seated in lines and rows. Because of the emphasis in many psychoeducational groups on obtaining cognitive information, this arrangement may be useful. On the other hand, if psychotherapy groups are to work well, they should be structured so that members can easily interact with one another verbally and physically, such as in a circle. Similarly, positive dynamics are crucial to the success of most task/work groups. Some of these groups will employ a more hierarchical structure such as a "chain of command" in order to operate efficiently. However, there is a move in many organizations to flatten hierarchies and use group circle formats. This trend is prevalent in businesses and associations that operate according to a quality management style (Walton, 1991).

Group Interaction and Group Dynamics

Group interaction can be described as the way members relate to each other. It consists of nonverbal and verbal behaviors and the attitudes that go with them. Group interaction exists on a continuum, from extremely nondirective to highly directive. For example, in some psychotherapy groups, members may be quite reserved and nondirect in their interactions with others, at least initially. In many task groups, however, members may be very direct and verbal. The type of group interaction (i.e., verbal, nonverbal communication) as well as its frequency make a difference in how or whether the group develops. Each factor will be examined separately, even though none of these components operate in isolation from the others.

Nonverbal behaviors make up "more than 50 percent of the messages communicated in social relationships" and are usually perceived as more honest and less subject to manipulation than verbal behaviors (Vander Kolk, 1985, p. 171). The four main categories of nonverbal behavior, according to Vander Kolk, are body behaviors, interaction with the environment, speech, and physical appearance. Group leaders and members have many nonverbals to watch. For example, when Sue wraps her arms around herself, does it mean that (a) she is cold, (b) she is imitating Heather, or (c) she is psychologically withdrawing from the group? The meaning of nonverbal behaviors cannot be assumed. In addition, it must be remembered that the same nonverbal behavior from two different people may not convey the same message. Walters (1978) has charted behaviors frequently associated with various group members' emotions. Nonverbal behavioral expressions should always be noted (see Table 2.1).

Table 2.1

Behaviors frequently associated with various group member states.

	Head	Face	Mouth	Eye Contact	Hands	Posture
Despair/Depression	Down	Sad frown (eyebrows down at outer ends)	Tightness	Little or none; may cover eyes with hand	Autistic behaviors; body-focused self-stimulating movements	Approaches fetal position
Excitement/Euphoria	Mobile movement	Mobility of expression	Smiling; laughing	Tries to capture and to hold eye contact of all other persons ("Look at me.")	Sweeping, expansive movements	Frequent change; seductive
Fear/Anxiety	Stiff movement; chin down	Flushing	Tightness; clenching teeth	Darting glances to others; wants to keep watch on others by not meeting their gazes ("I'll watch you.")	Tightness; gripping; sweaty palms ("clenched and drenched")	Frequent movement; crouching; hunching shoulders
Hostility/Rejection of another person Active/Overt	Head, and often chin, thrust forward and/or tilted upward	Angry frown (eyebrows down at center)	Lips tensed and pushed forward slightly	Defiant	Clenching; fist; thumping (symbolic hitting)	Poised on edge of chair
Passive/Covert	Down; turned away slightly	Squinting of eyes	Closed; normal	Aversion; blank staring	Body-focused movements; self-inflicting behaviors	Infrequent change
Dependency/Attraction toward another	Head slightly down while making eye contact ("Poor Me")	Mirrors expression of other	Frequent smiling	Frequent	Reaching motions	Quasi-courtship
Resistance to Learning	Turned; rolled back	Rigidity of expression	Tightness	Avoidance	Clenched; looking at watch; body focused movements	Held in; stiffness of limbs

Source: Adapted from "Nonverbal Communication in Group Counseling" by Richard P. Walters. In *Group Counseling: A Developmental Approach*, 4th ed., by George M. Gazda (Ed.). 1989. Boston: Allyn and Bacon. Copyright © 1989 by Allyn and Bacon. Used with permission.

Verbal behavior is also crucial in group dynamics. One of the most important variables in group work to track is who speaks to whom and how often each member speaks. On a formal basis, there are ways to chart such interactions, such as on a sociogram (i.e., a type of diagram that records the number of group member interactions). For example, by using a sociogram, it might be learned that Melissa addresses most of her comments in the group to one of three people. However, most leaders operate informally and map in their minds an awareness of how group members speak and to whom. They also pay attention to silence and how it is observed and respected. It is difficult for some groups to deal with silence but less likely to be bothersome in certain psychoeducation and task groups where members are not especially attuned to it.

Group discussion is usually important to the functioning of any type of group. In task, psychoeducational, counseling, and psychotherapy groups, discussion allows members to process information relevant to making decisions (Forsyth, 1990). Alternative courses of action can be considered more thoughtfully when they are discussed by the group as a whole. The amount of time spent in an active discussion of issues influences the quality of the group's decision (Laughlin, 1988).

Sometimes groups will not use their time wisely and will collectively engage in what is known as the **Law of Triviality** (Parkinson, 1957). According to this law, the time a group spends discussing any issue is in inverse proportion to the consequences of the issue. For example, in an hour-long task group, 50 minutes might be spent talking about whether a group celebration should be held on a Thursday or a Friday and 10 minutes might be spent in planning the activities and considering a budget for the event.

It should be noted that rarely will information alone help groups in making decisions. Large quantities of information are not generally helpful because they cannot be adequately digested. Rather, decision making is a process. It is based on members having an opportunity to relate to an ample but limited number of facts as well as people. Process, not content, is at the heart of decision making.

MEMBERS' ROLES AND GROUP DYNAMICS

A **role** is conceived as "a dynamic structure within an individual (based on needs, cognitions, and values), which usually comes to life under the influence of social stimuli or defined positions" (Munich & Astrachan, 1983, p. 20). The manifestation of a role is based on the individual's expectation of self and others and the interactions one has in particular groups and situations. For example, a reflective and introverted person might take the role of a "group observer" in an active counseling group. By so doing, the person could give feedback to the group as a whole without exposing personal feelings. Every person has multiple roles he or she can fulfill. When groups change or when people change groups, roles are frequently altered.

Roles are usually different from the overall identity of individuals. For example, persons may play certain roles in their vocational life, such as being a sales clerk or computer operator, but not envision themselves exclusively as their occupation. Therefore, although Terri sells shoes, she does not consider herself as just a salesperson. Nevertheless, roles strongly influence how individuals act in the group (Shepherd, 1964). For instance, entrepreneurs may want to push their point of view regardless of how it affects their acceptance into the group. Sometimes roles may become so strong that persons have a difficult time separating themselves from the roles they play. Such a situation may be enacted if an individual mainly sees himself or herself in terms of a role played in childhood. For example, adult children of alcoholics (ACoAs) often play one of four roles in order to adapt to their environments: hero, scapegoat, lost child, or mascot (Harris & MacQuiddy, 1991; Wegscheider, 1981). Unfortunately, in such circumstances, the persons may become trapped in dysfunctional ways of relating that will detrimentally affect them in all but psychotherapeutic groups.

Types of Roles

One way to conceptualize most roles in groups is to view them as primarily functioning in one of three ways: facilitative/building, maintenance, and blocking (Capuzzi & Gross, 1992).

A **facilitative/building role** is one that adds to the functioning of a group in a positive and constructive way. Members who take on such a role may serve as initiators of actions and ideas, information seekers, opinion seekers, coordinators, orienters, evaluators, or recorders. Group facilitating and building focuses on helping everyone feel like a part of the group. Those members who function in this way help the group develop while keeping conflict to a minimum. Group facilitators and builders do their best work during the initial formation of a group. For instance, in a task group, Jane may take the role of being an opinion seeker. Before the group moves on its decisions, she makes sure all views are heard by asking more quiet members for their input.

A **maintenance role** is one that contributes to the social–emotional bonding of members and the overall well-being of the group. When interpersonal communication in the group is strained, there is a need to focus on relationships (Wilson & Hanna, 1986). Persons who take on such roles are social and emotionally oriented. They express themselves by being encouragers, harmonizers, compromisers, commentators, and followers. For example, in a counseling group, Ned may help by serving in the role of a harmonizer as he assists members in seeing the differences they have and pointing out how these differences can give each group member a new perspective on the world. In group maintenance, group members are encouraged to openly express "both positive and negative feelings, supportive responses to member concerns and contributions, and acceptance of differences" (Shaffer & Galinsky, 1989, p. 25).

A **blocking role** is essentially an antigroup role. Individuals who take this role act as aggressors, blockers, dominators, recognition seekers, and self-righteous moralists. For instance, those who perceive themselves as outsiders, like

Tim who has been placed in a psychoeducational group for punishment, may actively attempt to keep the group from discussing a proposed topic. Such a member may also seek to divert attention away from the group goal by being negative and preventing the group from accomplishing anything.

Fortunately, few members act out a pure role. Hansen, Warner, and Smith (1980, pp. 442–446) have compared two of the most prominent classifications of group member roles as described by Benne and Sheats (1948) and Bales (1951). Figure 2.3 summarizes the work of Hansen et al. in this regard. Their classification differs slightly from that just described, but the basic roles and concepts they outline overlap considerably.

Problems in Carrying Out Roles

Sometimes there are problems in the fulfillment of roles (Hare, 1962). Both internal and external factors contribute to these problems, and there is seldom a simple cause. Four major forms of role difficulties are role collision, role incompatibility, role confusion, and role transition. In **role collision,** there is a conflict between the role an individual plays in the outside world (such as being a passive observer) and the role expected within the group (such as being an active participant). In **role incompatibility,** a person is given a role within the group (such as being the leader) that he or she neither wants nor is comfortable exercising. **Role confusion** occurs when a group member (or members) simply do not know what role to perform. This often happens in leaderless groups where members do not know if they are to be assertive in helping to establish an agenda or to be passive and just let the leadership emerge. Finally, in **role transition,** a person is expected to assume a different role as the group progresses but does not feel comfortable doing so. For example, in self-help groups, experienced members are expected to take on leadership, rather than "followership," roles. Yet, some group members do not feel comfortable doing so.

In most groups, there needs to be a balance between maintenance and task roles. "Too much attention to socioemotional functioning can cause the group to wander and lose sight of its goals; in similar fashion, overemphasis on task can result in disruption and dissatisfaction if members have no outlet for their grievances and no way to resolve their conflicts" (Shaffer & Galinsky, 1989, pp. 25–26).

THE EFFECT OF POSITIVE AND NEGATIVE VARIABLES ON GROUP DYNAMICS

Many group specialists (e.g., Corey, 1990; Jacobs et al., 1994; Ohlsen, Horne, & Lawe, 1988) have listed a number of variables within groups essential to their lives and functioning. Psychotherapeutic and counseling groups seem to have been especially targeted by experts in this regard. Yet, the factors generally noted

**Group Building and Maintenance Roles
(Positive Social-Emotional Roles)**

- *Facilitator or Encourager*—In this position, individuals play the role of a counselor's helper. They make sure everyone feels comfortable. Their motive often is to keep the focus off themselves.

- *Gatekeeper or Expediter*—Individuals in this role make sure the group operates within its proposed norms. They act like a counselor assistant and may generate hostility from others if they become too active.

- *Standard or Goal Setter*—This role is similar to that of gatekeeper, and individuals who take it push for establishing group norms and lofty goals. They are often unsure of themselves.

- *Harmonizer or Conciliator*—These are group mediators who seek to keep conflict down and emotionally control the group. They are afraid of the group getting out of hand emotionally.

- *Compromiser or Neutralizer*—Persons who assume this role suggest cognitive solutions/alternatives for group member differences. The same internal dynamics are probably occurring within them as with harmonizers, that is, they are afraid of too much emotion.

- *Group Observer*—These people provide feedback to the group by summarizing content or process within the group. They rarely participate directly in the group though because of the risk of exposing their thoughts and feelings.

- *Follower or Neuter*—The individuals who assume this role express a lot of agreement with the group, but are so unsure of themselves that they rarely offer their own opinions.

Group Task Roles (Instrumental or Task Roles)

The tasks undertaken by group members at this time help the group move toward accomplishing its goals.

- *Initiator-Energizer*—Individuals who assume this role prod the group to move and take action. They may be seen as hasslers.

- *Information or Opinion Seekers*—This role involves gathering more data, both affectively and cognitively, so the group may act. Persons who assume this role may push other group members to disclose before they are ready.

- *Information or Opinion Giver*—Persons in this role seek to give information, advice, or opinions to others in the group. They assume they have correct facts and proper attitudes. They are often annoying, but can act as a catalyst to spur the group on.

Figure 2.3
A classification of group membership roles.

Figure 2.3, continued

- *Elaborator and/or Coordinator*—Group members in this position are reality-oriented, and they make sure that the group is, too. Their logic often gets in the way of creativity.

- *Orientor-Evaluator*—The individual who assumes this role acts as the group's judge in evaluating how well it is doing in achieving its tasks, both quantitatively and qualitatively.

- *Procedural Technician*—One or more followers in the group may take this role, which involves concentration on the achievement of group goals. As such, this role is similar to the gatekeeper role previously discussed in the group-building section.

Individual Roles (Negative Social-Emotional Roles)

Individuals who assume these roles are self-serving rather than group-oriented. They lack solid interpersonal relationship skills and can benefit a great deal from a group. Yet, their presence within the group makes it difficult for the group to operate. Several of the most prominent of these antigroup roles as described by Vander Kolk (1985) are as follows:

- *Aggressor*—This person disagrees with most group members' ideas and behaviors. He or she may try to impose his or her ways on others.

- *Blocker*—These individuals are very rigid about what should be discussed, and often they resist the wishes of the total group and impede its progress.

- *Recognition Seeker*—The role consists of bragging and calling attention to self at the expense of others and the group in general.

- *Playboy/Playgirl*—The behavior of this person, for example, nonchalant or cynical, lets other group members know he or she is not invested in the group.

- *Help-seeker/Rescuer*—People who assume the help seeker role elicit sympathy from the group and are dependent. Rescuers meet their own needs but do not really help members function better.

- *Monopolist*—These individuals talk incessantly (because of their anxiety) about issues only tangentially related to the group. They alienate other group members and must be controlled.

- *Do-gooder/Informer*—The do-gooder wants to do what is right for others, whereas the informer wants to share information about someone in the group outside the group session. Both seek to enhance their image.

- *Withdrawn/Hostile Members*—These individuals seek to avoid group interaction and participation by being silent or intimidating. Both behaviors result in greater self-protection.

---

are applicable to most psychoeducational and work/task groups, too. These variables include such things as member commitment; readiness of members for the group experience; the attractiveness of the group for its members; a feeling of belonging, acceptance, and security; and clear communication. These factors are often collectively conceptualized as **positive group variables**. For example, if group members speak from an "I" position, everyone in the group becomes clear about what they are saying and can respond appropriately. Positive forces within the group, when expressed to the fullest extent possible, can lead to a group that is both cooperative and altruistic (McClure, 1990).

Yalom (1985) was among the first to delineate positive primary group variables based on research he conducted with others on therapy groups. He has called these positive forces within the group **curative (therapeutic) factors**. These variables are expressed in successful groups through a variety of means. They often impact the interactions of members and the group as a whole in complex ways. For counseling and psychotherapy groups, these therapeutic factors are:

1. instillation of hope—that is, assurance that treatment will work
2. universality—that is, what seems unique is often a similar or identical experience of another group member
3. imparting of information—that is, instruction about mental health, mental illness, and how to deal with life problems usually through group discussion
4. altruism—that is, sharing experiences and thoughts with others, helping them by giving of one's self, working for the common good
5. corrective recapitulation of the primary family group—that is, reliving early familial conflicts correctly and resolving them
6. development of socializing techniques—that is, learning basic social skills
7. imitative behavior—that is, modeling positive actions of other group members
8. interpersonal learning—that is, gaining insight and correctively working through past experiences
9. group cohesiveness—that is, the proper therapeutic relationship between group members, group members and the group leader, and the group as a whole
10. catharsis—that is, experiencing and expressing feelings
11. existential factors—that is, accepting responsibility for one's life in basic isolation from others, recognition of one's own mortality, and the capriciousness of existence

It is Yalom's (1985) contention that these variables constitute both the "actual mechanisms of change" and "conditions for change" (p. 4). The interplay of the factors varies widely from group to group.

Yalom's conceptualization of group dynamics is extremely useful for conducting group counseling and psychotherapeutic sessions for it gives group leaders and members conceptual ideas and experienced-based realities on which they need to focus. Such variables are like a map that can guide the group process. For instance, if a group member refuses to work through past family impasses and treats a group member as if he or she were a rejecting parent, the leader and other members can take steps to correct this behavior. In this case, the group might confront the troubled member with how he or she is acting and role-play situations to help the member recognize and resolve previous dysfunctional patterns that are interfering with his or her present functioning.

In addition to positive variables and therapeutic forces, there are **negative group variables** as well. These variables include, but are not limited to, avoiding conflict, abdicating group responsibilities, anesthetizing to contradictions within the group, and becoming narcissistic. If most or all of these variables are present, a group will become regressive and possibly destructive (McClure, 1990, 1994). In such cases, the whole group and the individuals within it lose.

Avoiding conflict involves the silencing of members who expose the group's shortcomings or disagree with the majority's opinions. Silence is often done through coercion or through acts of domination. For example, whenever Debbie tries to tell the group that she does not feel understood by the other members, she is belittled through comments such as, "That's touchy/feely stuff, Debbie, get real," or "You are being oversensitive." After awhile, Debbie learns not to speak. By avoiding conflict and silencing dissent, a destructive dynamic is set in motion. If it remains unchallenged and unchanged, the group becomes unhealthy.

One of the most destructive behaviors for groups to take is to become narcissistic. "**Narcissistic groups** develop cohesiveness by encouraging hatred of an out-group or by creating an enemy. . . . As a result, regressive group members are able to overlook their own deficiencies by focusing on the deficiencies of the out-group" (McClure, 1994, p. 81). In the process of projecting their feelings onto others, group members create an illusion of harmony that binds them together. For example, a student newspaper is launched with the intent of attacking the president of a university. Within the group, members focus on "digging up dirt" and disregard any positives they find. A bunker mentality develops in which the president becomes the enemy and the student newspaper, the source of all truth. Member disagreement is handled by dismissing anyone from the paper who does not agree with the party line. Cohesiveness is developed through rewarding member writers who can find the most damaging material to print.

Occurring in regressive groups along with the avoidance of conflict and the development of a group narcissism is **psychic numbing**, in which members anesthetize themselves to contradictions in the group. In the student newspaper example, writers may break and enter an office to get information they want and not feel guilty about breaking an ethical or legal code. Overall, in a regressive group, there is an abdication of responsibility for the group and a dependency on its leader. Members do not take on the role of being leaders or facilitators of the group, but rather become obedient followers. They do not take risks and, in effect, give their power away to influence the group. In such cases, the group is left without means to correct itself and will continue to be destructive unless a crisis occurs that influences its members to behave differently (Peck, 1983).

GROUP EXERCISES AND GROUP DYNAMICS

The outcome of a group is dependent not only on the variables present at the beginning of the experience but also on the amount and kind of group leadership displayed throughout the stages in the group's life. In chapter 3, issues involving leadership will be discussed in detail. Chapters 4 through 7 will deal with four important stages in the life of any group: beginning, transitioning, working, and terminating. The concepts of leadership and stages will not be covered here, but the effect of using exercises in groups will be.

The question of the place of prepackaged activities in groups is one that group leaders and members must deal with constantly. Gazda (1989) and Jacobs (1992) state that there are certain advantages and disadvantages to employing exercises in a group setting. For example, if the leader knows that a particular game or exercise is most likely to result in a positive outcome, the leader may wish to use it as a catalyst, especially early in the life of the group, in order to bring people together. In this capacity, games and exercises can play a vital part in promoting group dynamics.

Overall group exercises can be beneficial through promoting a positive atmosphere in a group. Jacobs et al. (1994), for instance, state that exercises have seven benefits (which will be condensed to five here):

1. They may generate discussion and participation. In this way they stimulate members' energy levels and interaction.
2. Exercises may help focus the group on a particular topic or issue. This is particularly true in task groups.
3. Group games help shift the focus from one area to another. Although effective group leaders should be able to shift the focus without employing games, some exercises provide a natural bridge to important group topics.
4. Games and exercises promote experiential learning. This means that members will probably go beyond their thoughts in self-exploration. Furthermore, exercises, such as "rounds," provide the group leader with useful information about his or her group and what needs to be done in order to move forward.
5. They increase the comfort level of participants and help them to relax and have fun. Learning takes place best when it is enjoyable.

Basically, group exercises and games can be used anytime in the group process and may consist of different types, for example, written, verbal, art, movement, and joint. The important point to remember in using game techniques in groups is that timing and instructions are everything. A poorly timed event with unclear instructions may do a great deal of damage to the group instead of promoting cohesion, insight, and group movement. If employed too frequently, group exercises can be a negative influence on the group by taking the focus off the purpose of the group. There are also some ethically questionable games/exercises that will promote anxiety and do harm. Gazda (1989) advises that group leaders who use games and exercises do so cautiously.

GROUP, INDIVIDUAL, AND FAMILY DYNAMICS

Working with groups is similar to and different from working with individuals or families. Individual, group, and family approaches to helping have some parallels in history, theory, technique, and process, but because of the unique composition of each, the dynamics of these ways of working are distinct (Gladding, 1992). The number of variables and interactions differ as well as the focus. A skilled group worker who has knowledge of individual and family helping dynamics is able to compare and contrast what is occurring in the group with what might be happening in another setting and, more importantly, to assess what may be needed. Awareness of individual and family helping dynamics assists a group worker in realizing if a referral of a member is in order. The complexity of working with others is a process that involves knowing what to do, when to do it, and what the probable outcomes may be. In this section, the dynamics of individual, group, and family work will be discussed in regard to persons and processes.

Persons

In examining the entities of groups, individuals, and families, one immediate common denominator is apparent. All are bodies, singularly and/or collectively, with defined boundaries and interrelated parts. An intervention cannot be made at any level without affecting other aspects of the body. However, in working with individuals, only one person is the focus of attention. The influence of others may be discussed, but they are not a part of any direct form of helping. In addition, single individuals may or may not be behaviorally or emotionally connected with others. Therefore, attention is almost always centered on intrapersonal issues.

With groups and families, the focus is on more than one person. Trotzer (1988) points out that groups share many similarities with families. For instance, both have hierarchies (power structures) associated with them. There is an interpersonal emphasis as well. Groups are distinct in that the members come together initially as strangers for a common purpose (Becvar, 1982; Hines, 1988). Therefore, there is a need to help members connect with one another and become a group before much assistance can be given. Families, on the other hand, have members with a shared history of interactions. This history may hinder or facilitate any actions taken in trying to offer assistance. Thus because of the differences in the composition of the persons involved, the dynamics of working with these different bodies varies. Overall, as Becvar (1982) concluded, the group is not a family and the family is not a group.

Process

The process of working with individuals, groups, and families is both similar and unique. One similarity involves theories. There are some common theories used as guides in individual, group, and family work, especially related to counseling and psychotherapy approaches (Horne & Ohlsen, 1982; Patterson, 1986). For instance, person-centered and behavioral theories have both been translated to working with people in all three formats covered here. However, theories that are utilized in all three domains have unique and common ingredients. They can be compared to a pie with filling covered by and joined to a crust (Becvar & Becvar, 1988). Underneath the crust is material that is specifically blended for a certain population. An individual theory of helping may not be appropriate for use in some group and family situations, just as some approaches created by group workers and family therapists are not geared for individually oriented helpers. In family therapy and in group work, a systemic theory (von Bertalanffy, 1968) prevails, so there is greater emphasis on interaction among individuals than there is on content.

Besides theory, the process of working with individuals, groups, and families is influenced by the helper's view of development. Helping in any of these three areas is similar in that the processes have a beginning, a working phase, and an ending (Gladding, 1992). However, outside of that broad-based similarity, there are a number of differences in development. Individual work is intensely personal, and its development is between the professional helper and the individual. Group and family work, on the other hand, are shared between participants and the helper. If the group process does not work well, members may be disappointed, but with the exception of some work groups, they can leave the persons involved and the experience behind them. Family groups, however, live together through any attempts at helping, and change may be a more tension-filled process because of the pressures from others in the family. As Virginia Satir (1972) has stated, "Troubled families make troubled people" (p. 18).

Overall, individual, group, and family approaches have processes that move in stages. However, the role of the leader in each differs in regard to theoretical issues such as how to induce change and what to emphasize. In chapter 3, specific leadership skills needed to make use of group dynamics will be discussed.

SUMMARY AND CONCLUSION

This chapter has focused on group dynamics (the forces within groups that influence the interactions of their members). In most groups, it is crucial that group leaders and members be aware of these dynamics because such forces help influence group development for better or worse.

In this chapter, several key areas of group dynamics have been discussed, for instance, the power of groups to either facilitate or hinder individuals in their performance and development. Group pressure and the social influence of groups on how people behave was examined. Individuals work hard to either enter or exit groups because of what groups can do or are doing in their lives.

In considering the dynamics of groups, leaders must preplan and be clear about the purpose of their groups. This type of action before the group begins can be instrumental in positively influencing the way groups function. In addition to a clear purpose, leaders should plan for a quiet, conducive environment for their groups. Planning groups with regard to time, size, mixture of people, and goals is crucial to this process. Group structure in terms of member positioning and group interactions, especially verbal and nonverbal behaviors, must be taken into account. If groups are to prosper, they must spend their time wisely and be as inclusive of as many members as possible.

Members' roles must also be considered. In healthy groups, members may switch roles and be facilitative or supportive. Antigroup roles, such as being aggressive, must be dealt with to prevent groups from being regressive and destructive. At the same time, positive group variables, such as clear communication and acceptance, must be promoted. Ways of helping the group include the limited use of group exercises. In working with groups, leaders are best able to understand and make appropriate interventions if they are aware of the differences and similarities in group dynamics compared to those of individuals and families in helping situations.

In summary, groups are a unique way to work with individuals in resolving past problems or accomplishing present tasks. Those who wish to participate or specialize in them are wise to realize that groups are dynamic entities with lives of their own that differ from those of their members. Those who are knowledgeable about how groups operate know what to expect and can help facilitate positive action in themselves and others. Before leading groups, it is important to plan ahead and understand how groups differ from individual and family situations. Through such means, leaders and members can assist leaders and members in utilizing the powers within the group effectively.

CLASSROOM EXERCISES

1. In groups of three or four, discuss what you consider to be the most important positive group variables. Are there some variables that are more important for some types of groups than for others? Which ones does your group think would be most crucial in the following types of groups: (a) a group for troubled adolescents; (b) a social skills learning group for mentally retarded adults; (c) a grief group for those who have lost loved ones; and (d) a work/task group planning for a lecture series. Compare your discussion with those generated by other class members.

2. Pick a role that has been mentioned in this chapter that you feel comfortable with. What is it about this role that you find attractive? Think about whether you have played this role in groups before. Discuss your findings with another class member. Also describe to the member what role in the group you consider least desirable and why.

3. This chapter mentions a pie analogy to describe theories associated with individual, group, and family work. In groups of three or four, draw a pie that represents group work. Think of what ingredients go into making a functional group, especially concentrate on the importance of factors that affect group dynamics. Discuss your pie with the class as a whole.

4. Observe a group that you are already involved in and notice what factors mentioned in this chapter are prevalent in the life of the group. How do

you think the group could be improved? What is your feeling after this observation about the influence of groups on people and people on groups? Discuss your impressions with the class as a whole.

REFERENCES

Asch, S. E. (1951). Effects of group pressure upon the modification and distortion of judgment. In H. Guetzkow (Ed.), *Groups, leadership, and men* (pp. 177–190). Pittsburgh: Carnegie.

Bales, R. F. (1951). *Interaction process analysis.* Reading, MA: Addison-Wesley.

Becvar, D. S. (1982). The family is not a group—Or is it? *Journal for Specialists in Group Work, 7,* 88–95.

Becvar, D. S., & Becvar, R. J. (1988). *Family therapy: A systemic integration.* Boston: Allyn & Bacon.

Benne, K. D., & Sheats, P. (1948). Functional roles of group members. *Journal of Social Issues, 4, 2.*

Bertalanffy, L. von (1968). *General systems theory: Foundations, development, application.* New York: Braziller.

Bion, W. (1959). *Experiences in groups.* New York: Basic Books.

Capuzzi, D., & Gross, D. R. (1992). Group counseling: Elements of effective leadership. In D. Capuzzi & D. R. Gross (Eds.), *Introduction to group counseling* (pp. 39–57). Denver: Love Publishing.

Cartwright, D., & Zander, A. (1968). *Group dynamics: Research and theory* (3rd ed.). New York: Harper & Row.

Castore, G. (1962). Number of verbal interrelationships as a determinant of group size. *Journal of Abnormal and Social Psychology , 64,* 456–457.

Conyne, R. K. (1983). The social ecology of group work. *Journal for Specialists in Group Work, 8, 2.*

Corey, G. (1990). *Theory and practice of group counseling* (3rd ed.). Pacific Grove, CA: Brooks/Cole.

Festinger, L. (1954). A theory of social comparison processes. *Human Relations, 7,* 117–140.

Forsyth, D. (1990). *An introduction to group dynamics* (2nd ed.). Monterey, CA: Brooks/Cole.

Friedman, W. H. (1989). *Practical group therapy.* San Francisco: Jossey-Bass.

Gazda, G. M. (1989). *Group counseling* (4th ed.). Boston: Allyn & Bacon.

Gladding, S. T. (1989). *Group dynamics.* Unpublished manuscript.

Gladding, S. T. (1992). *Counseling: A comprehensive profession* (2nd ed.). New York: Macmillan.

Glaser, B. A., Webster, C. B., & Horne, A. M. (1992). Planning a group: An instructional project for graduate students. *Journal for Specialists in Group Work, 17,* 84–88.

Hansen, J. C., Warner, R. W., & Smith, E. J. (1980). *Group counseling: Theory and practice* (2nd ed.). Chicago: Rand McNally.

Hare, A. P. (1962). *Handbook of small group research.* Glencoe, IL: Free Press of Glencoe.

Harris, S. A., & MacQuiddy, S. (1991). Childhood roles in group therapy: The lost child and the mascot. *Journal for Specialists in Group Work, 16,* 223–229.

Hines, M. (1988). Similarities and differences in group and family therapy. *Journal for Specialists in Group Work, 13,* 173–179.

Horne, A. M., & Ohlsen, M. M. (1982). *Family counseling and therapy.* Itasca, IL: Peacock.

Jacobs, E. (1992). *Creative counseling techniques: An illustrated guide.* Odessa, FL: Psychological Assessment Resources, Inc.

Jacobs, E. E., Harvill, R. L., & Masson, R. L. (1994). *Group counseling: Strategies and skills* (2nd ed.). Pacific Grove, CA: Brooks/Cole .

Korda, L. J., & Pancrazio, J. J. (1989). Limiting negative outcome in group practice. *Journal for Specialists in Group Work, 14,* 112–120.

Laughlin, P. R. (1988). Collective induction: Group performance, social combination processes, and mutual majority and minority influence. *Journal of Personality and Social Psychology, 54,* 254–267.

Leavitt, H. J. (1951). Some effects of certain communication problems on group performance. *Journal of Abnormal and Social Psychology, 46,* 38–50.

Lewin, K. (1948). *Resolving social conflicts: Selected papers on group dynamics.* New York: Harper.

Matthews, C. O. (1992). An application of General System Theory (GST) to group therapy. *Journal for Specialists in Group Work, 17,* 161–169.

Mayo, E. (1945). *The social problems of an industrial civilization.* Cambridge, MA: Harvard University Press.

McClure, B. A. (1990). The group mind: Generative and regressive groups. *Journal for Specialists in Group Work, 15,* 159–170.

McClure, B. A. (1994). The shadow side of regressive groups. *Counseling and Values, 38,* 77–89.

Munich, R. L., & Astrachan, B. (1983). Group dynamics. In H. I. Kaplan & B. J. Sadock (Eds.), *Comprehensive group psychotherapy* (2nd ed., pp. 15–23). Baltimore: Williams & Wilkins.

Ohlsen, M. M., Horne, A. M., & Lawe, C. F. (1988). *Group counseling* (3rd ed.). New York: Holt, Rinehart & Winston.

Parkinson, C. N. (1957). *Parkinson's law and other studies in administration.* Boston: Houghton Mifflin.

Patterson, C. H. (1986, April). *Gimmicks in groups.* Paper presented at the annual convention of the American Association for Counseling and Development, Los Angeles.

Peck, M. S. (1983). *People of the lie.* New York: Simon & Schuster.

Satir, V. (1972). *Peoplemaking.* Palo Alto, CA: Science and Behavior Books.

Shaffer, J., & Galinsky, M. D. (1989). *Models of group therapy* (2nd ed.). Englewood Cliffs, NJ: Prentice Hall.

Shepherd, C. R. (1964). *Small groups.* Scranton, PA: Chandler.

Sherif, M. (1937). An experimental approach to the study of attitudes. *Sociometry, 1,* 90–98.

Toseland, R. W., & Rivas, R. F. (1984). *An introduction to group work practice.* New York: Macmillan.

Trotzer, J. P. (1988). Family theory as a group resource. *Journal for Specialists in Group Work, 13,* 180–185.

Trotzer, J. P. (1989). *The counselor and the group* (2nd ed.). Muncie, IN: Accelerated Development.

Vander Kolk, C. J. (1985). *Introduction to group counseling and psychotherapy.* Columbus, OH: Merrill.

Walters, R. (1978). Nonverbal communication in group counseling. In G. M. Gazda (Ed.), *Group counseling: A developmental approach.* Boston: Allyn & Bacon.

Walton, M. (1991). *Deming management at work.* New York: Putnam.

Wegscheider, S. (1981). *Another chance: Hope and health for the alcoholic family.* Palo Alto, CA: Science and Behavior Books.

Wilson, G. L., & Hanna, M. S. (1986). *Groups in context.* New York: Random House.

Yalom, I. D. (1985). *The theory and practice of group psychotherapy* (3rd ed.). New York: Basic Books.

Zajonc, R. B. (1965). Social facilitation. *Science, 149,* 269–274.

CHAPTER 3

Effective Group Leadership

Before me is an opening in time
        behind lies a lifetime of training,
At both sides, and strategically located around a circle,
        are those who depend on my skills
        as they wait in anticipation.
Within me there is measured anxiety
        outside I show a calm facade;
The group begins
        with the soft sound of words,
                quiet nervous laughter, and a few faint smiles,
        all deft attempts to join with others
        and create simple trust in a blue-room environment.
"Growth becomes most likely" I think
"when introductions turn to actions."
So I start with hope and alertly trained eyes
        as thoughts and attention are carefully focused
        to the present experience. *

Leadership and groups are eminently connected. "Leadership is necessarily concerned with group activity" (Gardner, 1990, p. 80). There have been hundreds of research studies conducted to identify personal or professional attributes of leaders (Johnson & Johnson, 1991; Napier & Gershenfeld, 1989). Although some characteristics associated with group leadership (e.g., caring, openness, strength, awareness, warmth, flexibility, and sensitivity) have been pinpointed, there are still many unknown dimensions. In fact, leadership is probably "one of the most observed and least understood phenomena on earth" (Burns,

Source: Gladding, 1989.

1978, p. 2). Nevertheless, the role of the leader is crucial to the overall functioning of the group. "A group is a mirror of its leader. A group draws definition from its leader. It will be only as good as the leader, as good as his or her skills, and as good as the leader's own being" (Bates, Johnson, & Blaker, 1982, p. 73).

Many issues surround group leaders and leadership. Some of them deal with style and substance; others center on personality. There are different types of leaders, just as there are distinct types of groups, and the appropriateness of an individual to a particular group is dependent on many complex and interrelated factors. The way a leader functions in one group may be totally inappropriate in another (Forsyth, 1990; Kottler, 1994). For example, a **transformational leader** (i.e., a person who empowers group members and shares power with them in working toward the renewal of a group) may be needed when a group is floundering. On the other hand, a **traditional leader** (i.e., a person who is controlling and exercises power from the top down as an expert) may be appropriate in running a hierarchical group that is diverse and whose members are physically separated.

In this chapter, the multiple aspects of leadership will be examined. Particular attention will be paid to generally helpful and harmful actions of group leaders and what behaviors seem to work best in particular circumstances.

LEADERSHIP: A DEFINITION

The word *leader* first appeared in the English language in the early 1300s and the word *leadership* in the early 1800s (Johnson & Johnson, 1991). Yet despite the long history associated with defining leaders and leadership, a review of the literature shows much disagreement among social and political scientists on exactly what a leader is.

There is no one definition of either word. Indeed, "the concepts 'leader' and 'leadership' have been defined in more different ways than almost any other concept associated with group structure" (Johnson & Johnson, 1991, p. 145). For example, McGregor (1960) delineates two types of leaders: those who operate according to so-called Theory X and those who function according to what he describes as Theory Y. A **Theory X leader** is autocratic and coerces because he or she basically believes people are unambitious and somewhat lazy. A **Theory Y leader** is nondirective and democratic because he or she thinks that people are self-starters and will work hard if given freedom. Both styles of leadership assume someone (an identified person or persons) is in ultimate control. They are just the opposite of Theory Z (Ouchi, 1981), which stresses that a group will manage itself through the participation of its members. A **Theory Z leader** is, therefore, a facilitator who helps encourage group members to participate in the group and trust that individual and collective goals will be accomplished through the process of interaction. Clearly, there is disagreement about the concepts of leader and leadership in both the theory and practice of group work (Napier & Gershenfeld, 1989; Stockton, Morran, & Velkoff, 1987).

In spite of definition disagreements, some common factors in leadership can be distinguished. Forsyth (1990), for instance, defines leadership as "a reciprocal, transactional, and transformational process in which individuals are permitted to influence and motivate others to promote the attaining of group and individual goals" (p. 216). This definition encompasses many of the most important factors of leadership (i.e., reciprocity, legitimate influence, motivation, and cooperation for the achievement of common goals), and distinguishes leadership from control (Parsons & Shils, 1951) and power (French & Raven, 1960). It will be the basis from which leadership is conceptualized in this chapter. It is assumed that a leader is one who implements a number of facilitative qualities in a group, such as envisioning goals, motivating people, and achieving a workable unity, in an appropriate and timely way (Bates et al., 1982; Gardner, 1990).

GROUP LEADERSHIP STYLES

The style that a group leader displays has a direct effect on the behavior of group members (Sampson & Marthas, 1981). Leaders who operate exclusively from one point of view are more likely than others to influence members' behaviors in a specific way, either for better or worse. For example, leaders who are always telling their group members what to do may get immediate tasks accomplished but at the price of membership flexibility and innovation. Most effective group leaders show versatility (Kottler, 1994). They modify their leadership pattern to coincide with the purpose of the group and its membership. Usually they function between the polarities discussed in the following paragraphs.

Interpersonal Versus Intrapersonal Leadership

Shapiro (1978) states that group leadership is often focused on either the interpersonal or intrapersonal aspects of a group. The **interpersonal style of group leadership** focuses on transactions between individuals in the group, whereas the **intrapersonal style of group leadership** concentrates on the inward reactions of individual members of the group. Both styles of leadership have their place in a group, and effective group leaders use both styles at times. For instance, as a group leader of a counseling group, Don may ask Phyllis to reflect on her last outburst directed toward Mary Ann. Later, Don may solicit opinions from the group on how Phyllis could relate more positively with Mary Ann. Ideally, counseling group leaders begin by concentrating on the interpersonal dimension of the group. Later, when members are more comfortable with one another, the leaders integrate intrapersonal material into the group. Other types of group leaders, such as those who lead psychoeducational groups, may engage in the process in an entirely different way.

Leader-Centered Versus Group-Centered Leadership

Group leadership may also take the form of being leader- versus group-centered. A **leader-centered group** is autocratic, and the leader instructs the followers in the "right" way. It is sometimes referred to as the guru-oriented style (Starak, 1988). Adolf Hitler and Mao Tse-tung are leaders who have exemplified this style on a national level. The leader-centered group is based on obedience from followers. The **group-centered group** focuses on members and interpersonal processes. Leaders who have exemplified this approach to a group facilitate conditions to "promote self-awareness and options to develop the guru within" (Starak, 1988, p. 104). Mohandas Gandhi and Martin Luther King, Jr., led using this style. A simple way to distinguish the differences between these two styles is that, in the former, answers are given by leaders to followers, whereas in the latter, answers are derived from members' individual and collective introspections.

Whether a group is leader-centered or group-centered depends on who set it up, under what circumstances, and for what purpose (Gardner, 1990). Most leader-centered groups place a strong emphasis on the personality of one individual and give that person a great deal of power and trust. In these groups, there is chaos when the recognized leader is absent. Some religious and civic groups operate this way. On the other hand, a group-centered group emphasizes the members. For instance, almost all self-help groups are group centered and concentrate on assisting participants to resolve various personal problems. The broad continuum of leadership in groups is represented in Figure 3.1.

CHOOSING A STYLE OF LEADERSHIP

Choosing a style of leadership depends on a multitude of factors, such as the leader's personality and the purpose of the group. Lewin (1944) identified three basic styles of group leadership: authoritarian, democratic, and laissez-faire. Lieberman, Yalom, and Miles (1973) identified six basic styles: energizers, providers, social engineers, impersonals, laissez-faires, and managers. Hansen, Warner, & Smith (1980) contend that most models are either refinements or elaborations of Lewin's concepts; therefore, the focus of this section will be on Lewin's three styles and what the choice of each yields.

Authoritarian group leaders envision themselves as experts. They believe they understand group dynamics and are, therefore, able to best explain group and individual behavior. These leaders interpret, give advice, and generally direct the movement of the group much like a parent controls the actions of a child. Authoritarian leaders are often charismatic and manipulative (McClure, 1994). They demand obedience and expect conformity. Frequently, they use the wheel model that was explained in chapter 2. All information is filtered through them, and they decide what information to share with the group (see Figure 3.2).

This style of leadership is preferred by many group leaders with psychoanalytic backgrounds or by group leaders with strong teaching backgrounds who equate group leadership with instructing or control. The authoritarian leader

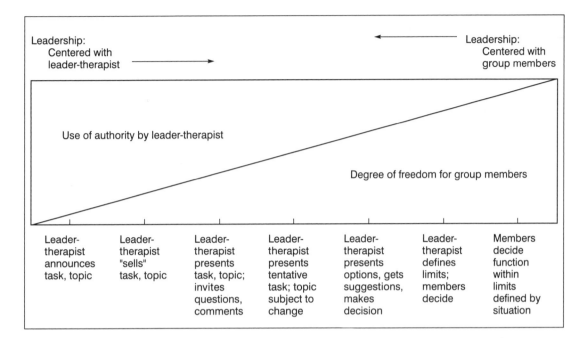

Figure 3.1

Leadership continuum.

Source: From *Small Groups in Therapy Settings: Process and Leadership* (p. 77) by B. W. Posthuma, 1989, Boston: College-Hill. Modified from "How to Choose a Leadership Pattern" by R. Tannenbaum & W. H. Schmidt, *Harvard Business Review,* 1958, *36,* 95. Copyright © 1989 by College-Hill Press, Boston, a division of Little, Brown and Company. Reprinted by permission.

may achieve much during periods of crisis, such as war, because of their commanding style and the needs of followers. Authoritarian leaders are powerful and usually safe from exposure of any personal vulnerabilities. They direct action and yet are protected by structure and function from self-disclosing.

Democratic group leaders are more group centered or nondirective. Leaders, such as Carl Rogers (1970), operate from this perspective and trust group participants to develop their own potential and that of other group members. These leaders serve as facilitators of the group process and not as directors of it. They cooperate, collaborate, and share responsibilities with the group. Those who embrace this perspective are more humanistically and phenomenologically oriented (see Figure 3.3).

Leaders who are comfortable with themselves and trust group members to take care of themselves often use this approach. The advantage is that they share power and responsibility and group members can interact openly. Trust, once established, is also fostered under this type of leadership as is calculated risk taking. The disadvantage to this type of leadership is that the group as a whole may be slow to establish agendas and to achieve goals.

Figure 3.2
Authoritarian leadership.

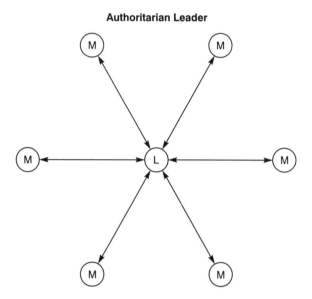

Source: From *Group Counseling: Theory and Practice* (2nd ed., p. 391) by J. C. Hansen, R. W. Warner, and E. J. Smith, 1980, Chicago: Rand McNally. Reprinted with permission.

Laissez-faire leaders are leaders in name only. They fail to provide any structure or direction for their groups. Members are left with the responsibility of leading and directing. Some inexperienced group leaders choose this style in an attempt to be nonthreatening; others pick this style to avoid making any hard decisions and thereby increasing their popularity. (Being liked or popular is not a key characteristic of being an effective leader, by the way.) However, a third group of leaders believes that this group style works best because everything is completely unstructured and the group must take care of itself from the beginning. Unfortunately, many laissez-faire group leaders and their groups do not accomplish anything because no clear purpose and goals are generally voiced in such groups. Interactions within a laissez-faire group are represented in Figure 3.4.

LEADERLESS GROUPS AND LEADERS

Laissez-faire groups are not the same as so-called **leaderless groups**, i.e., groups that rotate the leadership role among their members. One type of leaderless group is the self-help group covered in chapter 1. In these groups, leaders emerge as the group develops. In some forms of these groups, such as Alcoholics Anonymous or Parents Anonymous, this style of peer leadership works very well. Nonprofessional leaders in such cases develop as their groups progress. They usually end up creating a leadership style that feels comfortable for them, such as

Figure 3.3
Democratic leader.

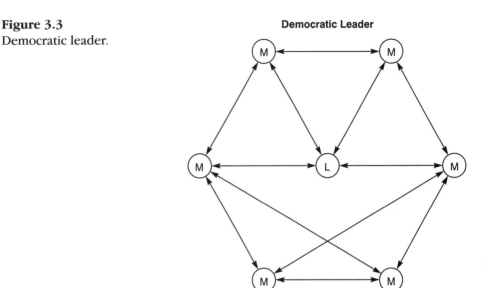

Source: From Hansen, Warner, and Smith, 1980, p. 391.

being confrontational, or they undergo brief leadership training by reading manuals or taking courses (Shaffer & Galinsky, 1989). Although some leaders of leaderless groups are effective, this approach is basically developed through trial and
error. It can be destructive as well as constructive.

Another type of leaderless group meets alternatively with and without a
leader (Mullan & Rosenbaum, 1978; Wolf, 1963; Yalom, 1985). Such groups may
increase the creativity and participation of individuals and the group as a whole.
However, notable group specialists (Gazda, 1989; Yalom, 1985) warn about the
dangers of these groups, especially when composed of moderately and/or
severely disturbed individuals. In such cases, if a leader is not present, the group
may get entirely out of hand and do considerable damage to its members. As a
result, the group regresses, and everyone ultimately suffers (McClure, 1990).

LEADERSHIP STYLES FOR DIFFERENT GROUPS

Different types of groups demand specific styles of leadership (Kottler, 1994). For
example, in psychoeducational and task/work groups, leaders usually do best
when they are directive and keep the group focused on the topic or job at hand.
Psychotherapy and counseling groups, however, require that the leader provide
support, caring, and sometimes confrontation and structure. They are more person oriented. Whether a leader exercises task or relationship leadership depends
on who he or she is, what is happening, and when (or if) goals must be accomplished. The different contrasting styles are characterized by Hersey and Blanchard (1969) as diagrammed in Figure 3.5.

Figure 3.4
Laissez-faire leader.

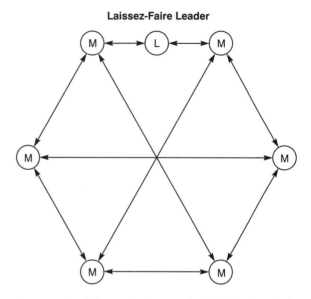

Source: From Hansen, Warner, and Smith, 1980, p. 391.

In the Hersey and Blanchard model, leaders choose an emphasis depending on whether they are people- or task-oriented. In reality, most group leaders will consider both aspects of a group. Their orientation to working with the group will be based on both personality and skills. In all types of groups, however, leaders need to be attuned to and utilize "core mechanisms of group process and change" (Polcin, 1991, p. 10). These **core mechanisms of group leadership** are emotional stimulation, caring, meaning attribution, and executive function. They were first described by Lieberman, Yalom, and Miles (1973) who distinguished these universal central factors from a group leader's orientation, i.e., theoretical approach. In all different types of groups, leaders must promote sharing on an affective as well as intellectual level, i.e., **emotional stimulation.** Feelings, as well as thoughts, need to be expressed. Furthermore, group leaders must show **caring**, i.e., a genuine concern for others, through their openness and honesty with group members. **Meaning attribution** refers to the leader's ability to explain to group members in a cognitive way what is occurring in the group. For instance, the leader might say, "Members of the group seem reticent to talk today about themselves. It appears the group is having a hard time trusting one another." Finally in the **executive function** role, the leader manages the group as a social system that allows the group and its members to achieve specific goals (Polcin, 1991).

PERSONAL QUALITIES OF EFFECTIVE GROUP LEADERS

Every group leader brings his or her personal qualities to a group, including preferred ways of perceiving the world and experiences in relating to oneself and others. Group leaders must ask of themselves such questions as, "Who am I," and "Who am I with you," and "Who are we together" (Hulse-Killacky, 1994).

The way the questions are asked, as well as the answers that are derived, play a strong part in determining how one's personal qualities translate into leadership. For example, if a person does not have a strong sense of self, it is doubtful he or she will be effective as a group leader. Similarly, if an individual cannot keep his or her identity while appreciating others, it is unlikely that this leader will exert a strong influence in the group. Personal qualities of effective leaders have traditional been explained through examining their personality traits or their learned skills. Effective group leaders probably utilize the strongest aspects of their personalities and knowledge and combine these with experiences in their leading of groups (Johnson & Johnson, 1991).

The Trait Approach

A traditional school of thought in human history is that some persons emerge as leaders because of their personal qualities. This point of view was advocated by Aristotle, Thomas Carlyle, and Henry Ford (Forsyth, 1990) and remains popular today. Some group work specialists have compiled long lists of ideal qualities

Figure 3.5
Life-cycle theory of leadership.

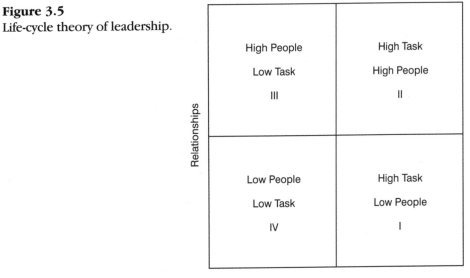

Source: From "Life Cycle Theory of Leadership" by Paul Hersey and Ken Blanchard, 1969, *Training and Development Journal, 23,* pp. 26–34. Used with permission of the American Society for Training and Development.

they believe are essential to the personality of an effective group leader, a so-called trait approach to group leadership (Johnson & Johnson, 1991). The proponents of this viewpoint believe that specific personality characteristics are essential for successful leadership (Latham, 1987).

Two examples of this approach are those given by Slavson (1962) and Corey and Corey (1992). Slavson advocates that the personal qualities of group leaders include poise, judgment, empathy, ego strength, freedom from excessive anxiety, a desire to help people, tolerance of frustration, imagination, intuition, perceptiveness, and an ability to avoid self-preoccupation. Corey and Corey include such qualities as courage, willingness to model, presence, goodwill and caring, belief in group process, openness, nondefensiveness in coping with attacks, personal power, stamina, willingness to seek new experiences, self-awareness, humor, and inventiveness. The ideal number of qualities appears to be almost infinite, and it is unlikely that many potential group leaders will possess them all.

The trait view of leadership, although popular and appealing, has little support in research. There is no one personality type best suited to be a group leader. Rather, effective group leaders possess a combination of certain personal qualities, a "personality profile," (Stogdill, 1974) that facilitates their communication with group members. These qualities promote the successful integration of the leader and the group and help the group work more efficiently toward common goals (Stogdill, 1969, 1974). Although research indicates that some personality qualities correlate with leadership, it is the combination of factors working in interaction that makes a difference (Stogdill, 1974) (see Table 3.1).

Table 3.1
Some personality correlates of leadership behavior.

Personality Characteristic	Type of Relationship
Achievement drive	Positive
Adaptability	Positive
Alertness	Positive
Ascendance	Positive
Attractiveness	Unclear
Dominance (bossy)	Negative
Emotional balance	Unclear
Energetic	Positive
Extroversion	Unclear
Nurturance	Unclear
Responsible	Positive
Self-confidence	Positive
Sociability	Positive

Source: Reprinted with the permission of The Free Press, a Division of Simon & Schuster from *Handbook of Leadership: A Survey of Theory and Research* by Ralph M. Stogdill. Copyright © 1974 by The Free Press.

Personality and Specific Groups

As indicated earlier, studies point out that persons who are effective in some groups, such as those that are relationship oriented, may not be skilled in other groups, such as those that are task oriented (Forsyth, 1990). For example, Stockton and Morran (1982, pp. 70–71) found that those who conduct encounter and counseling groups are most effective when they are:

1. moderate in the amount of emotional stimulation they give the group (e.g., challenging, confronting, emphasizing the disclosing of feelings)
2. high in caring (e.g., offering support, encouragement, and protection)
3. able to utilize meaning-attribution skills (e.g., clarifying, interpreting)
4. moderate in the expression of executive functions (e.g., setting rules, limits, norms)

The research also indicates that ineffective group leaders are characterized as aggressive, authoritarian, pressure oriented, disrespectful of members, confrontational, egocentric, inappropriate self-disclosurers, and poorly timed interveners (Lieberman, Yalom, & Miles, 1973). Experienced leaders act more like each other than inexperienced leaders do (Kottler, 1994).

It is often assumed that leaders who have been well trained in personal counseling will automatically be able to transfer their relationship skills to conduct groups. However, such is not the case. The dynamics associated in working with individuals, as opposed to groups, differ considerably. Just wanting to be a good group leader is usually not enough (Hansen et al., 1980). One has to have experience. In counseling, for instance, many individuals are better suited by temperament and skills to operate either with individuals or groups, but not both. Bates et al. (1982) recommend that potential group leaders examine their own personalities by using Jungian-based instruments, such as the Myers-Briggs Type Indicator (Myers, 1962), to understand how they might function in a group. Other group experts recommend both formal and informal ways of assessing oneself (Kottler, 1994).

THEORY AND EFFECTIVE GROUP LEADERS

The principles by which group leaders are guided is known as **theory.** The word *theory* receives mixed reactions in the field of group work because the word is often misunderstood and overused. Basically, a theory is "a way of organizing what is known about some phenomenon in order to generate a set of interrelated, plausible, and, above all, refutable propositions about what is unknown" (Blocher, 1987, p. 67). A theory guides empirical inquiry and is useful in testing hypotheses. It is different from a *philosophical assumption* (which is largely untestable and focused on values) and a *process model* (which is a "cognitive map" that provides a "direct and immediate guide for counselor action") (Blocher, 1987, p. 68).

On one hand, there are individuals who believe that theory is of minor importance and has little effect on practice. This position was especially prevalent in the 1960s when many new types of groups sprang up without solid theoretical foundations (Ruitenbeek, 1970). On the other hand, there are those who think knowledge of well-developed theory is essential to becoming a competent practitioner (Lewin, 1951). The place of theory in group work depends on the type of group being conducted, but effective group leaders are guided by proven theories.

Most major theoretical positions "consider the use of groups as a preferred mode of treatment" (Peterson & Nisenholz, 1987, p. 210). Since the late 1960s, almost all counseling and psychotherapeutic groups (and some that are task/work oriented) have been based on theories.

Operating from a theoretical base has definite advantages, but choosing a theory or theories can be problematic, especially in group work. Among the advantages of theories is that they are practical. A good theory helps a practitioner understand and find meaning in experiences by providing a conceptual framework. "Like the scientist, a counselor [or a group worker] uses scientific theory to organize his or her knowledge of behavior" (Claiborn, 1987, p. 288). The lack of a theoretical framework can result in confusion.

A second advantage of theory is it serves as a guide to expected behavior (Van-der Kolk, 1985). In group counseling, for instance, there is always a **settling-down period,** where members test one another and the group collectively, before the group unifies. Group leaders guided by such theoretical knowledge are better prepared to respond appropriately to settling-down times than those who are unaware.

A third advantage of a theory is its **heuristic** (i.e., research) **dimension.** Theory is the foundation on which research is built. Research, in turn, strengthens the quality of theory. It is difficult, if not impossible, to have a theory without a research component.

A fourth advantage of knowing and operating from a theoretical perspective is that the practitioner and group may make more progress than they would otherwise. As Corey and Corey (1992) state, "Group leaders without any theory behind their interventions will probably find that their groups never reach a productive stage" (p. 6).

A fifth advantage for the employment of theory in groups is that it helps practitioners formulate their own personalized approach to the groups in which they work. Patterson (1985, 1986) has made the point that some practitioners continue to repeat mistakes of the past or rediscover events of past decades because they are ignorant about how theories developed. Leaders who are most aware of what has been will most likely be skilled innovators of new methods and more highly developed in their ability to integrate and personalize information and process.

Finally, a knowledge of theory generally helps group leaders formulate a specific approach for each group member. It is the leader-as-scientist's task to enhance the fit between the hypothetical group member and the actual one. Theory allows the making and testing of predictions about how the group member will behave in response to particular environmental conditions, including select interventions (Claiborn, 1987).

Group leaders may have difficulty choosing a theory because many theories tend to be "either too specific or too general to account for all the elements involved in the complexity of human behavior" (Ohlsen, Horne, & Lawe, 1988, pp. 48–49). Theories are incomplete, and a practitioner who sticks with only one theory may be hard-pressed to explain certain actions in his or her group (Kottler, 1994).

A second problem in selecting a theory is that theories may become political. Practitioners of specific approaches tend to reinforce each other and to exclude others. Although this practice may produce theoretical enrichment, it often sets up a **we/they mentality** in which practitioners of other points of view are seen as "uninformed," "naive," or "heretical." In such cases, potential contributions to a theory from outside sources are never made, and questionable assumptions are not examined thoroughly.

A third drawback of theories is that there are many overlapping dimensions in theoretical approaches. For example, terms originated by Alfred Adler and Carl Rogers, such as *empathy, acceptance,* and *inferiority complex,* have essentially been incorporated into most major leadership theories. Other concepts, such as *reinforcement,* which has a behavioral base, are used frequently by people from various disciplines. The language of theories is not pure and can be confusing to the novice practitioner as well as to the general public.

A fourth troublesome aspect about theories involves research. There is some research (e.g., Korchin, 1976) that supports the premise that theoretical orientation and outcome are unrelated. Basically, this research states that experienced therapists tend to be more effective and similar in what they do than inexperienced therapists. If research continues to uphold this finding, then group leaders, especially those with a counseling background, may pay less attention to theoretical orientations.

A fifth limitation of theories, and a potentially dangerous one, is that group leaders who use theory may notice only select aspects of their group members (Kottler, 1994). In such cases, both members and leaders are placed in potential jeopardy. For example, if Kathy ignores the more angry side of Russell and other group members because her theory is based on emphasizing positives, she may find that she is unable to deal with the group's collective anger.

Related to this limitation are group leaders who become locked into a theory so tightly that they become rigid, inflexible, and mechanical in practice. These types of leaders have poor interpersonal relationships skills because they are focused on what the theory directs rather than what their group members need. For instance, if a theory directs leaders to simply reinforce and not confront, group members will find select behaviors are influenced positively, and other actions and considerations are stunted.

SKILLS OF EFFECTIVE GROUP LEADERS

The skills of a group leader are displayed in different ways and at various stages during the life of a group. Skills are most often demonstrated through the timely and appropriate use of select techniques. There are a variety of group techniques from which to choose, but effective group leaders use themselves, other group members, theory, and the group process itself in helping facilitate change. There is no "cookbook" detailing when to use specific interventions (Corey, Corey, Callanan, & Russell, 1992; Kottler, 1994). The group leader must determine what to do, when, and how.

In making such decisions, it is essential for group leaders to be well educated in group dynamics and to know the advantages and limitations of their decisions. This is important in the employment of theory and in the utilization of technique and group process.

In using technique, it should be recognized that a number of group skills are the same as those displayed in working with individuals. For example, group leaders must be empathetic, caring, and reflective. At the same time, there are a number of special skills that are unique to group leaders. Corey (1990) has formulated a chart based on Nolan's (1978) ideas about group leadership (see Table 3.2).

Among the skills that differ significantly between group and individual work are the following:

1. **Facilitating**—In groups, the leader facilitates by helping to open up communication between group members. In individual counseling, facilitation involves a more personal focus, i.e., opening people up to themselves.

2. **Protecting**—This skill involves the leader safeguarding members from unnecessary attacks by others in the group. It is not a skill used in individual counseling, but it is vital in group work in case group members are combative with each other, especially in the early stages of the group.

3. **Blocking**—Blocking is related to protecting. In blocking, the leader intervenes in the group activity to stop counterproductive behavior. This intervention can be done on a verbal or nonverbal level. In individual counseling sessions, the leader will block a person from counterproductive behavior, such as rambling, by confronting.

There are four other skills not included in Corey's chart that are also vital in some group work settings: linking, diagnosing, reality testing, and delegating.

1. **Linking**—Linking consists of pointing out that one person's concerns may be shared by other group members. For instance, in a psychoeducational group, the leader might link Matthew and Cheri together by stating, "I hear that both of you have a concern about what to say to other people after you have said 'hello.'" Through linking, interaction is promoted within the group. This skill is used by leaders who stress interpersonal communication in the group.

2. **Diagnosing**—In this activity, the leader identifies certain behaviors and categories into which a person or group fits. Diagnosing in groups does not usually include psychological instruments but is based more on leader observations. For instance, in a task/work group, a leader may notice that the group has a tendency to blame rather than to develop constructive ideas on different ways of doing things. In order to help the

Table 3.2
Overview of group-leadership skills.

Skills	Description	Aims and Desired Outcomes
Active Listening	Attending to verbal and nonverbal aspects of communication without judging or evaluating.	To encourage trust and client self-disclosure and exploration.
Restating	Saying in slightly different words what a participant has said to clarify its meaning.	To determine whether the leader has understood correctly the client's statement; to provide support and clarification.
Clarifying	Grasping the essence of a message at both the feeling and the thinking levels; simplifying client statements by focusing on the core of the message.	To help clients sort out conflicting and confused feelings and thoughts; to arrive at a meaningful understanding of what is being communicated.
Summarizing	Pulling together the important elements of an interaction or session.	To avoid fragmentation and give direction to a session; to provide for continuity and meaning.
Questioning	Asking open-ended questions that lead to self-exploration of the "what" and "how" of behavior.	To elicit further discussion; to get information; to stimulate thinking; to increase clarity and focus; to provide for further self-exploration.
Interpreting	Offering possible explanations for certain behaviors, feelings, and thoughts.	To encourage deeper self-exploration; to provide a new perspective for considering and understanding one's behavior.
Confronting	Challenging participants to look at discrepancies between their words and actions or body messages and verbal communication; pointing to conflicting information or messages.	To encourage honest self-investigation; to promote full use of potentials; to bring about awareness of self-contradictions.
Reflecting Feelings	Communicating understanding of the content of feelings.	To let members know that they are heard and understood beyond the level of words.
Supporting	Providing encouragement and reinforcement.	To create an atmosphere that encourages members to continue desired behaviors; to provide help when clients are facing difficult struggles; to create trust.
Empathizing	Identifying with clients by assuming their frames of references.	To foster trust in the therapeutic relationship; to communicate understanding; to encourage deeper levels of self-exploration.

Table 3.2, *continued*

Skills	Description	Aims and Desired Outcomes
Facilitating	Opening up clear and direct communication within the group; helping members assume increasing responsibility for the group's direction.	To promote effective communication among members; to help members reach their own goals in the group.
Initiating	Taking action to bring about group participation and to introduce new directions in the group.	To prevent needless group floundering; to increase the pace of group process.
Goal Setting	Planning specific goals for the group process and helping participants define concrete and meaningful goals.	To give direction to the group's activities; to help members select and clarify their goals.
Evaluating	Appraising the ongoing group process and the individual and group dynamics.	To promote deeper self-awareness and better understanding of group movement and direction.
Giving Feedback	Expressing concrete and honest reactions based on observation of members' behaviors.	To offer an external view of how the person appears to others; to increase the client's self-awareness.
Suggesting	Offering advice and information, direction, and ideas for new behavior.	To help members develop alternative courses of thinking and action.
Protecting	Safeguarding members from unnecessary psychological risks in the group.	To warn members of possible risks in group participation; to reduce these risks.
Disclosing Oneself	Revealing one's reactions to here-and-now events in the group.	To facilitate deeper levels of interaction in the group; to create trust; to model ways of making oneself known to others.
Modeling	Demonstrating desired behavior through actions.	To provide examples of desirable behavior; to inspire members to fully develop their potential.
Dealing with Silence	Refraining from verbal and nonverbal communication.	To allow for reflection and assimilation; to sharpen focus; to integrate emotionally intense material; to help the group use its own resources.
Blocking	Intervening to stop counterproductive behavior in the group.	To protect members; to enhance the flow of group process.
Terminating	Preparing the group to end a session or finalize its history.	To prepare members to assimilate, integrate, and apply in-group learning to everyday life.

Note: The format of this chart is based on Edwin J. Nolan's article, "Leadership Interventions for Promoting Personal Mastery," *Journal for Specialists in Group Work,* 1978, *3*(3), 132–138.

Source: From *Theory and Practice of Group Counseling* (3rd ed., pp. 71–72), by G. Corey, 1990, Pacific Grove, CA: Brooks/Cole. Copyright © 1990 by Wadsworth, Inc. Reprinted by permission from Brooks/Cole Publishing Company, Pacific Grove, CA 93950.

group grow, the leader must be a good observer who knows how to overcome distractive or disruptive behavior.

3. **Reality Testing**—This skill is used when a group member makes an important decision, such as changing jobs or taking a risk. At such moments, the leader will have other group members give feedback to the one who is contemplating a change on how realistic they see the decision. Through this process, the person is able to evaluate more thoroughly his or her decision.

4. **Delegating**—In delegating, the group leader assigns a task to the group or one or more of its members. The task can be as simple as observing and sharing impressions of what is happening in the group. Delegating can be complex, too, such as asking a member or members to lead the group. The idea behind delegating is to share the responsibility for the development of the group with the group.

Overall, there are more than two dozen leadership skills that can be utilized in various types of groups. The implementation of these skills will be examined more thoroughly in the chapters on group stages. Nevertheless, it is important to be familiar with the skills and how they are employed so they can used effectively at appropriate times in the life of the group.

GROUP LEADERSHIP FUNCTIONS

An effective group leader must be able to function in a variety of ways at different times. Experience, coupled with training, permits leaders to operate in such a manner. Each skill has a distinct function and is appropriately displayed by leaders at various stages of the group. At the beginning of the group, a leader is much more likely to function in an active and direct way than during the middle phase of the group process when group members are busy with their own activities. Obtaining proper closure at the end of the group calls for additional group leader skills, such as the ability to summarize.

There are both content and process functions that the leader must address throughout the life of the group. **Content functions** involve the actual words and ideas exchanged between leaders and members. For example, in the pregroup screening process, the leader must concentrate on potential group members' myths and misconceptions about groups (Childers & Couch, 1989). Some of these misunderstandings include "groups are for sick people," "groups are artificial," and "groups force people to lose their identity." As groups develop, less time generally is spent on content material, and more is focused on process functions.

Process functions are identifiable sequences of events over time that influence the development of a group (Johnson & Johnson, 1991). For example, interactions between group members that inhibit or enhance feelings of trust and confidentiality are those related to process. Group leaders focus more on process and the achievement of process goals as the group continues because the interactions and events within and between group members determine whether group goals are achieved or not. In other words, interpersonal dimensions of a group take on increased importance as the group moves toward its objectives.

Main Functions of Group Leaders

Leaders operate in certain ways in groups whether they are relationship, educational, or task/work oriented. It is vital that leaders recognize what functional strategy will work best and when. Bates et al. (1982) characterize four main functions that group leaders need to display at various times:

1. traffic director
2. modeler of appropriate behavior
3. interactional catalyst
4. communication facilitator

Each of these roles takes specific skills. For example, as a **traffic director,** the leader "must help members become aware of behaviors that open communication channels and those that inhibit communication" (Bates et al., 1982, p. 96). The role is both proactive and reactive in the prevention of certain behaviors (e.g., blocking "why" questions, focusing on the past, and gossiping) and the promotion of others (active listening, responding in a nonjudgmental way). In a similar manner, as a **modeler of appropriate behavior,** leaders must consciously pick and choose actions they think group members need to learn through passive and active demonstrations. These ways of modeling can include deliberate use of self-disclosure, role plays, speech patterns, and acts of creativity (Kottler, 1994). For example, if group leaders employ voice tones that signify happiness or sadness, they are directly and indirectly helping their group members learn ways to express their feelings.

The **interactional catalyst** role requires that leaders promote interaction between group members without calling attention to themselves. It is a functional process that continues throughout the group and can take various forms such as questioning whether two or more group members have something to say to one another and then being silent to see what happens. Finally, as a **communication facilitator,** group leaders reflect the content and feeling of members and teach them how to do likewise. This process focuses on both the expression of words and the emotion behind these communications. In addition, the leader stresses the importance of speaking congruently, that is, using "I" messages to state what one wants or what one thinks.

Leaders and Group Conflict

In addition to the four tasks just described, a primary function of group leaders is the management of conflict. The display of conflict is normal within a group and is especially prevalent in certain group stages such as "storming" (Tuckman, 1965). Five specific techniques for managing conflict in groups have been proposed by Simpson (1977) and elaborated on by Kormanski (1982). These are withdrawal from the conflict, suppressing the conflict, integrating conflicting ideas to form new solutions, working out a compromise, and using power to resolve the conflict.

1. **Withdrawal from the conflict**—This strategy involves leaders distancing themselves from conflict and postponing interventions. It has the advantage of letting leaders gather more data and observe longer without becoming excessively involved. It also allows leaders to consult and use resolution strategies later if issues are not settled. The disadvantages of this approach are that conflict may escalate and withdrawal is completely ineffective in dealing with a crisis situation.

2. **Suppression of the conflict**—As a strategy, suppression consists of playing down conflict. It is often used when issues are minor. It keeps emotions under control and helps group leaders build a supportive climate. Suppression is most effective when conflict issues are unimportant or when focusing on a relationship is more important than concentrating on an issue. The disadvantages of suppression are that it fails to resolve conflict and allows feelings to smolder and possibly erupt later. In addition, leaders may be perceived as weak or insensitive when using this strategy.

3. **Integrating conflicting ideas to form new solutions**—The idea behind integration is consensus. In using this strategy, group leaders try to get all parties to reexamine a situation and identify points of agreement. The goal is to develop new alternatives, to learn how to open up lines of communication better, and to build cohesive unity and commitment. One example of integration is **mediation**—having a third party hear arguments about a situation and then render a decision. The disadvantages of the integrative approach include the large amount of time it takes to implement and the unwillingness of some individuals to set aside their own goals and work for the good of the group.

4. **Working out a compromise**—In this method, each party involved gives up a little to obtain a part of what they wanted and to avoid conflict. The result is a win–win situation where cooperative behavior and collaborative efforts are encouraged. This approach is extremely effective when resources are limited, for example, in a work group where little money is available to spend on research and salaries. Compromising is a good strategy to use in avoiding win–lose situations. Negotiation is a good example of compromise. The disadvantages of compromise are that some parties may inflate their wants to get more, and the eventual action taken may be ineffective or less than desirable.

5. **Using power to resolve the conflict**—The power strategy involves "the imposition of someone's will on someone else" (Kormanski, 1982, p. 116). The source of power may either be derived from a person's status or personality. **Position power** is most often used when there are immature relationships between individuals (Hersey, Blanchard, & Natemeyer,

1979). Position power is derived from the status of people's titles, such as "group leader" or "group facilitator." *Personal power* is employed more frequently in mature relationship situations. The source of power in such a situation is from the individual and his or her ability to persuade others to follow a select course of action.

By using power, a leader is able to resolve a crisis quickly. However, the use of power creates a *win–lose atmosphere* where the losers may harbor feelings of resentment or powerlessness and may seek subtle or blatant revenge on those who have won. Arbitration is an example of a typical use of power. Table 3.3 shows what techniques are most preferred under certain group circumstances.

Overall, a prerequisite to becoming an effective leader is learning what strategies and roles to employ and when. Part of this knowledge is gained through studying the theory and practice of group work. The other part is obtained through experience, such as observing or co-leading actual groups. It is to the experiential side of co-leading a group that attention will now be focused.

CO-LEADERS IN GROUPS

A **co-leader** is a professional or a professional-in-training who undertakes the responsibility of sharing the leadership of a group with another leader in a mutu-

Table 3.3
Contingency assessment guidelines.

Preferred Technique	Contingency Factor
Withdrawal	Important information is lacking. Choosing sides is to be avoided.
Suppression	An important relationship is involved. The issue is unimportant.
Integration	Group commitment is needed. The group will put group goals first.
Compromise	Resources are limited. A win–win set is desired.
Power	Time is limited (crisis situations). A continued deadlock persists.

Source: From "Leadership Strategies for Managing Conflict" by C. Kormanski, 1982, *Journal for Specialists in Group Work,* 7, p. 117. Copyright ACA. Reprinted by permission of the American Counseling Association.

ally determined manner. The use of co-leaders in groups occurs often, especially in groups with a membership of 12 or more. The efficacy of using co-leaders depends on many factors, including economic considerations, advantages to the group, and the compatibility of the leaders (Vander Kolk, 1985).

Advantages

The strengths associated with co-leading a group, according to experts such as Corey and Corey (1992) and Jacobs, Harvill, and Masson (1994) include:

1. *Ease of handling the group in difficult situations*—When two leaders are present, they may help each other facilitate the movement of the group by one leader shifting the topic or the focus of the group if the other leader gets bogged down. Before and after group sessions, co-leaders can plan strategies and discuss problems that either they, members, or the group as a whole are experiencing.

2. *Use of modeling*—With co-leaders, group members are exposed to two models of human interaction. They see how individuals can relate to each other in positive ways and how they can disagree and still cooperate. When co-leaders are of the opposite gender, members may grow by more fully realizing and reliving earlier family dynamics and working on any unresolved issues that are brought up (Alfred, 1992).

3. *Feedback*—Whatever issues members discuss, they usually receive twice the leader feedback when the group is co-led. This input helps them realize more fully how they are perceived by others and gives them a different perspective than they would receive otherwise. For example, one co-leader may comment on intrapersonal aspects of a group member's behavior whereas the other focuses on interpersonal relationships. In such situations, leaders may also stimulate each other more and take corrective measures to avoid **burnout**, i.e., becoming physically and emotionally exhausted. Leaders, like members of the group, may grow more than they would if they were leading the group alone.

4. *Shared specialized knowledge*—In groups with co-leaders, there is a primary advantage for all concerned when the leaders share specialized training with each other and the group. This type of sharing can come in response to a situation in the group, such as dealing with anger, and can be done in private or in public forums. In these cases, everyone benefits because information is presented and discussed in a more dynamic and expanded manner than is possible in a one-leader group.

5. *Pragmatic considerations*—In a co-led group, it is possible for one leader to cover for the other if a group session must be missed because of illness or professional considerations. Coverage allows the group to continue and evolve.

Limitations

The limitations of co-leading a group are also important to consider. The disadvantages this effort entails have the potential to be very destructive. "Unless partners can work as a complementary team, much group time can be wasted in power plays, bickering, and mutual sabotage" (Kottler, 1983, p. 178). Among the potential liabilities of co-leading are the following:

1. *Lack of coordinated efforts* (Posthuma, 1989; Stockton & Morran, 1982)—The degree to which a group grows is dependent on the coordination of its leaders. When leaders do not meet to process what has occurred in the group or to agree on where they want to lead the group, destructive conflict within the group may occur, and the outcome of the group may be less than desirable. In such situations, the leaders may knowingly or not work at cross-purposes.

2. *Too leader-focused*—The old saying that "too many cooks spoil the broth" may be applicable to some groups with two leaders. In these cases, the presence of two leaders, especially if both are strong personalities and leader-centered, will work against the good of group members because too much attention is concentrated on the leaders. One leader may also dominate another and call attention to the leadership role instead of the goals of members. In such cases, the impact of both group leaders is eventually diminished (Alfred, 1992).

3. *Competition* (Posthuma, 1989; Trotzer, 1989)—Competition may be manifested in several ways—for example, through trying to gain the attention of the group or through using opposing theories. The point is that competition between group leaders will cost the group part of its efficiency and productivity. Leaders may also lose respect for each other in such an atmosphere.

4. *Collusion* (Corey & Corey, 1992)—In the collusion process, a co-leader establishes an informal alliance with a group member in order to address disliked qualities of the other co-leader. The result is an unloading of unexpected emotion onto the nonaligned leader and a splitting of the group into fractions.

Overall, when leaders decide to lead a group jointly, they must work as a team. Such an approach takes considerable preparation, and it both relieves and promotes stress on occasions. Co-leading requires that both leaders be competent to begin with and that they be able to express a wide range of facilitative skills (e.g., self-disclosure and timing) in an appropriate manner. It also demands that co-leaders be consistent and noncompetitive (Stockton & Morran, 1982). The three main models of co-led groups are those where the lead is:

1. *alternated*—that is, one leader takes responsibility for a specific period of time or a session, and the other leader provides support
2. *shared*—that is, where each leader takes charge momentarily as he or she sees fit

3. *apprenticed*—that is, a more experienced leader takes charge of the group in order to show a novice how to work with groups.

Gazda (1989, p. 64) states that "supportive feedback, mutual trust and respect, and a liking for each other appear to be at least minimal requirements" for co-leaders to have if they are to work well together and be of benefit to the group. His point is well taken. Co-leading can either be a bonus or a bust to group members. When co-leaders "develop a positive relationship in their group approach, they have a greater capacity for helping individuals and the group than a single leader" (Trotzer, 1989, p. 237). It is the development of the right conditions that either makes or breaks co-led groups.

GROUP LEADERSHIP TRAINING

Most people are not natural leaders of groups (Gardner, 1990). It takes time and training to perfect group leadership skills. Yalom (1985) strongly advocates that potential group psychotherapy leaders participate in groups as a part of their training. He notes that "the accreditation committee of the American Group Psychotherapy Association has recommended a minimum requirement of 60 hours of participation in group" (p. 523) for those in training to become leaders. Jacobs et al. (1994) also point out the importance of conducting groups in order to fine-tune skills.

In addition to this experiential base, group leaders must have specialized knowledge in the theories, dynamics, interpersonal, ethical, research, and stage components of group work (Association for Specialists in Group Work, 1990). As noted in the previous chapter, group work differs from that conducted with individuals and families. One way of obtaining the specialized training necessary for working with groups is group-based training (Pearson, 1985). In this model, specific skills used in groups are first identified and defined by trainers. Examples are given in which this skill might be used. The flexibility of using various skills is stressed in this presentation. Next, both videotapes and role plays are used to show trainees how a particular skill is employed.

The third step in this procedure is structured practice where each trainee demonstrates how he or she would use the skill that has been previously demonstrated. This enactment is then critiqued. Finally, group leader trainees, after learning all the group skills, are asked to demonstrate their group facilitation skills in 20-minute unstructured practice sessions. They are observed leading a group and given feedback on the use of skills they implemented during this time, as well as those that they did not use. The way this training model works is represented in Figure 3.6.

Another way of preparing group facilitators is a five-step method outlined by Anderson (1982). In this procedure, which is intended to be used in training group generalists, the following stages occur:

Figure 3.6
Major components of the
group-based skills training
format.

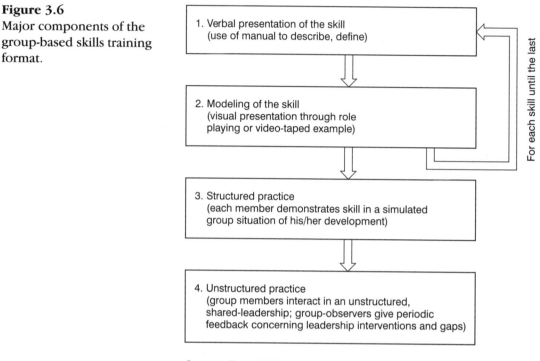

Source: From "A Group-Based Training Format for Basic Skills of Small-Group Leadership" by R. E. Pearson, 1985, *Journal for Specialists in Group Work, 10,* p. 152. Copyright ACA. Reprinted by permission of the American Counseling Association.

1. the trainer models leader behavior for the total group
2. the group is broken down into subgroups of five or six, and each subgroup member practices leading a small group discussion
3. after each discussion, some aspect of the subgroup's behavior is processed (e.g., anxiety)
4. the subgroup critiques the leader's behavior
5. following practice by each trainee, the total group shares observations and conclusions about the activity. (p. 119)

A third model for training group leaders is also educational and developmental. It consists of four components: (a) content, (b) decision making, (c) eventual leadership style, and (d) dual process (Tollerud, Holling, & Dustin, 1992). All of these components are connected to a supervisor "whose role is to make timely decisions as to how and when these components are implemented into the training" (p. 97). The focus of content is on factual information. Decision making involves the process of choosing how and what to do based on an understanding of group dynamics and self-knowledge. Leadership style deals with the complex set of expectations and tasks that face new group leaders. Finally, dual process is the idea that the group leader in training is a member of two groups at once. The first group is composed of those the trainee is leading; the second is that of peers. The experiences from each group can be utilized in the other (see Figure 3.7).

GROUP LEADERSHIP AND SUPERVISION

Regardless of what method is used in the training of group leaders, supervision is required in addition to formal didactic instruction. Yalom (1985) emphasizes that "without ongoing supervision and evaluation, original errors may be reinforced by simple repetition" (p. 520). One way to minimize problems and processes in group supervision is to make it developmental and comprehensive. "At any particular moment, the supervisor must consider the level of cognitive complexity of the supervisee, the developmental level of the group, the level of training of group members, and the interactive effects of these variables with one another" (Hayes, 1990, p. 235).

The American Group Psychotherapy Association recommends a minimum of 180 hours of supervision for group leaders in training. Trotzer (1989) states that one good way of being supervised is to have two potential group leaders co-lead a group under the supervision of a more experienced leader. This type of super-

Figure 3.7
An educational model for
teaching in group leadership.

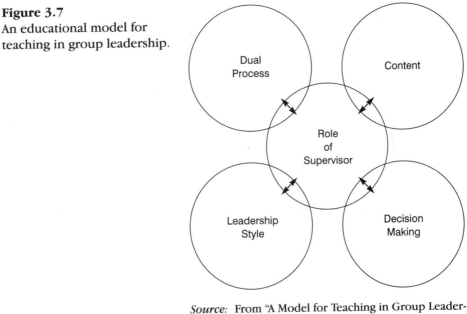

Source: From "A Model for Teaching in Group Leadership: The Pre-Group Interview Application" by T. R. Tollerud, D. W. Holling, and D. Dustin, 1992, *Journal of Specialists in Group Work, 17*(2), p. 97.

vision is less threatening to a novice group leader than trying to co-lead with an experienced group leader. It also requires less time on the supervisor's part and allows him or her to be more objective in critiquing the new group leaders. This technique may also lead to videotaping and observations by a group team behind a one-way mirror. Overall, supervision methods add to the overall learning experience of the group leader(s) in training.

SUMMARY AND CONCLUSION

This chapter has focused on the complex nature of group leadership. The concept of leadership is often misunderstood, but some of its common factors include multiple relationships in which there are reciprocity, legitimate influence, motivation, and cooperation for the achievement of beneficial goals. In order to be an effective group leader, a person must show some versatility and realize different styles of leadership are appropriate in certain situations. Leaders who are too rigid and use one style (e.g., authoritarian, democratic, or laissez-faire) may be less helpful than those who are flexible and developmental.

The personal qualities of group leaders are also important. There is no one trait that is essential for leaders to possess. However, the display of some personal qualities (e.g., support, warmth) in certain quantities will facilitate the movement of the group and the growth of members. What qualities and quantities are vital depend on the dynamics of a particular group. The way theories and theoretical skills are employed is also linked to the nature of the group being led. Some theories are helpful and advantageous to the leader and members; others are not. Some skills are unique to certain groups, whereas others are universal to all areas of human relations. No one skill is crucial for a group leader to possess, but knowing what to do and when to do it is essential. Leadership is developed through experience, course work, and supervision. Skills, if properly applied, can help group members and the group as a whole reach individual and overall goals. Knowing when and how to use a particular skill separates successful and unsuccessful group leaders.

Group leaders function in a variety of ways, for example, as traffic directors, catalysts, and managers of conflict. Therefore, leaders must be sensitive to themselves and their constituents. Sometimes working with a co-leader can be helpful in learning how to integrate personal and professional skills, especially if the experience is under supervision. Group leadership training is a must for those who expect to work on more than a one-to-one basis. Such training will often be composed of three elements: telling, doing, and showing. It is important that group leaders get a feel for what working with a group is like before they actually direct one. The process of updating leadership skills is continuous.

In summary, groups are a unique way to work with individuals in resolving problems or accomplishing tasks. Group leadership involves not only being knowledgeable about group operations but also being skilled through an integrative experience on how to help members and the group as a whole move in productive directions.

CLASSROOM EXERCISES

1. Why do you think the terms *leader* and *leadership* are so misunderstood? Discuss your thoughts as a class. What qualities do you consider essential for a group leader? If possible, tell about a leader who has personally influenced you and how you were affected. What did that person do with the group you were in that you admired most?

2. Make a list of personal and professional qualities and skills you possess that would help you lead a group of your choosing. What qualities and skills do you think you need to cultivate more? Discuss your self-assessment with two other class members. Notice how your ideas and theirs change or remain the same in this process.

3. Find an article on the supervision of group leaders (Hint: consult the *Journal for Specialists in Group Work, Small Group Behavior,* or *Counselor Education and Supervision*). Share the content with the class and with your instructor. Other class members will do the same. From the ideas presented, discuss what the process of supervision entails in group work.

4. Discuss how you feel about conflict in a group with another class member. After you have identified your feelings, look at the five ways of managing conflict suggested in this chapter. Which ones are you most uncomfortable with and why? Describe a specific way you can work to improve your management of group conflict.

REFERENCES

Alfred, A. R. (1992). Members' perceptions of co-leaders' influence and effectiveness in group psychotherapy. *Journal for Specialists in Group Work, 17,* 42–53.

Anderson, W. (1982). A training module for preparing group facilitators. *Journal for Specialists in Group Work, 7,* 119–124.

Association for Specialists in Group Work. (1990). *ASGW Professional Standards for Group Counseling.* Alexandria, VA: ACA Press.

Bates, M., Johnson, C. D., & Blaker, K. E. (1982). *Group leadership: A manual for group counseling leaders* (2nd ed.). Denver: Love Publishing.

Blocher, D. H. (1987). On the uses and misuses of the term *theory. Journal of Counseling and Development, 66,* 67–68.

Burns, J. M. (1978). *Leadership.* New York: Harper.

Childers, J. H., Jr., & Couch, R. D. (1989). Myths about group counseling: Identifying and challenging misconceptions. *Journal for Specialists in Group Work, 14,* 105–111.

Claiborn, C. D. (1987). Science and practice: Reconsidering the Pepinskys. *Journal of Counseling and Development, 65,* 286–288.

Corey, G. (1990). *Theory and practice of group counseling* (3rd ed.). Pacific Grove, CA: Brooks/Cole.

Corey, G., Corey, M. S., Callanan, P. J., & Russell, J. M. (1992). *Group techniques* (2nd ed.). Pacific Grove, CA: Brooks/Cole.

Corey, M. S., & Corey, G. (1992). *Groups: Process and practice.* Pacific Grove, CA: Brooks/Cole.

Forsyth, D. (1990). *Group dynamics* (2nd ed.). Pacific Grove, CA: Brooks/Cole.

French, J. R. P., Jr., & Raven, B. (1960). The bases of social power. In D. Cartwright & A. Zander (Eds.), *Group dynamics* (2nd ed., pp. 607–623). Evanston, IL: Row, Peterson.

Gardner, J. W. (1990). *On leadership.* New York: The Free Press.

Gazda, G. M. (1989). *Group counseling: A developmental approach* (4th ed.). Boston: Allyn & Bacon.

Gladding, S. T. (1989). In anticipation. Unpublished poem.

Hansen, J. C., Warner, R. W., & Smith, E. J. (1980). *Group counseling: Theory and practice* (2nd ed.). Chicago: Rand McNally.

Hayes, R. L. (1990). Developmental group supervision. *Journal for Specialists in Group Work, 15,* 225–238.

Hersey, P., & Blanchard, K. H. (1969). Life-cycle theory of leadership. *Training and Development Journal, 23,* 26–34.

Hersey, P., Blanchard, K, & Natemeyer, W. (1979). *Situational leadership, perception, and the impact of power.* Escondido, CA: Center for Leadership Studies.

Hulse-Killacky, D. (1994, April). *Effective group leadership.* Presentation at American Counseling Association annual convention, Minneapolis, MN.

Jacobs, E. E., Harvill, R. L., & Masson, R. L. (1994). *Group counseling: Strategies and skills* (2nd ed.). Pacific Grove, CA: Brooks/Cole .

Johnson, D. W., & Johnson, F. P. (1991). *Joining together* (4th ed.). Englewood Cliffs, NJ: Prentice Hall.

Korchin, S. J. (1976). *Clinical psychology.* New York: Basic Books.

Kormanski, C. (1982). Leadership strategies for managing conflict. *Journal for Specialists in Group Work, 7,* 112–118.

Kottler, J. A. (1983). *Pragmatic group leadership.* Pacific Grove, CA: Brooks/Cole.

Kottler, J. A. (1994). *Advanced group leadership.* Pacific Grove, CA: Brooks/Cole.

Latham, V. M. (1987). Task type and group motivation. *Small Group Behavior, 18,* 56–71.

Lewin, K. (1944). The dynamics of group action. *Educational Leadership, 1,* 195–200.

Lewin, K. (1951). *Field theory in social science.* New York: Harper.

Lieberman, M., Yalom, I., & Miles, M. (1973). *Encounter groups: First facts.* New York: Basic Books.

McClure, B. A. (1990). The group mind: Generative and regressive groups. *Journal for Specialists in Group Work, 15,* 159–170.

McClure, B. A. (1994). The shadow side of regressive groups. *Counseling and Values, 38,* 77–89.

McGregor, D. (1960). *The human side of enterprise.* New York: McGraw-Hill.

Mullan, H., & Rosenbaum, M. (1978). *Group psychotherapy: Theory and practice* (2nd ed.). New York: Free Press.

Myers, I. (1962). *Myers-Briggs Type Indicator.* Princeton, NJ: Educational Testing Service.

Napier, R. W., & Gershenfeld, M. K. (1989). *Groups: Theory and experience.* Boston: Houghton Mifflin.

Nolan, E. J. (1978). Leadership interventions for promoting personal mastery. *Journal for Specialists in Group Work, 3,* 132–138.

Ohlsen, M. M., Horne, A. M., & Lawe, C. F. (1988). *Group counseling* (3rd ed.). New York: Holt, Rinehart & Winston.

Ouchi, W. (1981). *Theory Z.* Reading, MA: Addison-Wesley.

Parsons, T., & Shils, E. A. (1951). *Toward a general theory of action.* Cambridge, MA: Harvard University Press.

Patterson, C. H. (1985). New light for counseling theory. *Journal of Counseling and Development, 63,* 349–350.

Patterson, C. H. (1986, April). *Gimmicks in groups.* Paper presented at the annual convention of the American Association for Counseling and Development, Los Angeles.

Pearson, R. E. (1985). A group-based training format for basic skills of small-group leadership. *Journal for Specialists in Group Work, 10,* 150–156.

Peterson, J. V., & Nisenholz, B. (1987). *Orientation to counseling.* Boston: Allyn & Bacon.

Polcin, D. L. (1991). Prescriptive group leadership. *Journal for Specialists in Group Work, 16,* 8–15.

Posthuma, B. W. (1989). *Small groups in therapy settings: Process and leadership.* Boston: College-Hill.

Rogers, C. R. (1970). *Carl Rogers on encounter groups.* New York: Harper & Row.

Ruitenbeek, H. M. (1970). *The new group therapies.* New York: Avon.

Sampson, E. E., & Marthas, M. (1981). *Group process for the health profession* (2nd ed.). New York: Wiley.

Shaffer, J., & Galinsky, M. D. (1989). *Models of group therapy* (2nd ed.). Englewood Cliffs, NJ: Prentice Hall.

Shapiro, J. L. (1978). *Methods of group psychotherapy and encounter: A tradition of innovation.* Itasca, IL: Peacock.

Simpson, D. (1977). Handling group and organizational conflict. In J. Jones & J. W. Pfeiffer (Eds.), *1977 Annual handbook for group facilitators* (pp. 120–122). La Jolla, CA: University Associates.

Slavson, S. R. (1962). Personality qualifications of a group psychotherapist. *International Journal of Group Psychotherapy, 12,* 411–420.

Starak, Y. (1988). Confessions of a group leader. *Small Group Behavior, 19,* 103–108.

Stockton, R., & Morran, D. K. (1982). Review and perspective of critical dimensions in therapeutic small group research. In G. M. Gazda (Ed.), *Basic approaches to group psychotherapy and group counseling* (3rd ed.). Springfield, IL: Charles C. Thomas.

Stockton, R., Morran, D., & Velkoff, P. (1987). Leadership of therapeutic small groups. *Journal of Group Psychotherapy, Psychodrama & Sociometry, 39,* 157–165.

Stogdill, R. M. (1969). Personal factors associated with leadership: A survey of the literature. In C. A. Gibb (Ed.), *Leadership* (pp. 91–133). Harmondsworth, England: Penguin.

Stogdill, R. M. (1974). *Handbook of leadership.* New York: Free Press.

Tollerud, T. R., Holling, D. W., & Dustin, D. (1992). A model for teaching in group leadership: The pre-group interview application. *Journal of Specialists in Group Work, 17,* 96–104.

Trotzer, J. P. (1989). *The counselor and the group* (2nd ed.). Muncie, IN: Accelerated Development.

Tuckman, B. W. (1965). Developmental sequences in small groups. *Psychological Bulletin, 63,* 384–399.

Vander Kolk, C. J. (1985). *Introduction to group counseling and psychotherapy.* Columbus, OH: Merrill.

Wolf, A. (1963). The psychoanalysis of groups. In M. Rosenbaum and M. Berger (Eds.), *Group psychotherapy and group function* (pp. 273–327). New York: Basic Books.

Yalom, I. D. (1985). *The theory and practice of group psychotherapy* (3rd ed.). New York: Basic Books.

CHAPTER 4

Beginning a Group

Knowing that most beginnings are awkward
we wait anxiously for words or actions
to break the silence of this gathering
and give our group its genesis.
Strangers to each other,
and to ourselves at times,
we slowly move into awareness
of our own uniqueness. *

There are many beginnings in the formation of a group. The most obvious is when group members and leaders assemble for the first session. However, before the initial meeting, many processes have already been completed, for example, the formulating of the idea for the group, the screening of members, and the selecting of preliminary individual and group goals. Even after the group meets, it continues to evolve and can be conceptualized as forever forming, with certain issues returning from time to time to be explored in greater depth—the so-called **cyclotherapy process** (Yalom, 1985). Some of the issues with which groups continually struggle are anxiety, power, norms, interpersonal relationships, and personal growth (Cohen & Smith, 1976).

In this chapter, the focus will be on what is considered to be the **forming or orientation stage of the group** (Tuckman & Jensen, 1977; Ward, 1982). This stage is characterized by initial caution associated with any new experience. During this time, there is an attempt by group members to avoid being rejected by others, the leader, or even themselves. This feature of the group is particularly strong in groups where individuals do not know each other very well, but it can also be part

*Source: Gladding, 1993.

of a task/work group where members have a common shared history. The forming stage of the group begins conceptually with ideas generated by group leaders and ends after the newness of the group experience wears off and group members start working together. When the group settles down after the forming stage, more productive issues can be addressed individually and collectively.

Tuckman and Jensen (1977) identify the stages that follow the initial one of *forming* as *storming, norming, performing,* and *adjourning.* Ward (1982) characterizes them as *power, cohesiveness, working,* and *termination,* whereas Kormanski and Mozenter (1987) state that groups develop out of *awareness* and then move on to *conflict, cooperation, productivity,* and finally *separation.* Not all group theorists agree that "stages do or must exist," at least in a progressive fashion (Yalom, 1985, p. 310). However, developmental stages have been identified in learning groups (e.g., Lacoursiere, 1974), therapy groups (e.g., Brabender, 1985), and training groups (e.g., Dunphy, 1968).

By understanding a group's stage/phase, it is possible to assess the group's and its members' goals and progress (Zimpfer, 1986). For those who view groups as developmental, the generally agreed-on number of stages in their evolvement is between four and five (Hansen, Warner, & Smith, 1980; Yalom, 1985). Regardless of how many stages a group completes, its beginning is a clearly identifiable, important, and multidimensional event.

STEPS IN THE FORMING STAGE

Forming is a process that involves several steps. Although some of these steps may be completed concurrently, none may be skipped if the group is going to form properly.

The First Step in Forming: Developing a Rationale for the Group

Behind every successful group is a *rationale* for its existence. The more carefully the reasons for conducting a group are considered, the more likely there will be a positive response to the idea and a positive outcome as well. Therefore, a clear rationale and focus are of uppermost importance in planning. Group leaders who are unclear of their purpose will end up being nonproductive at best and possibly harmful.

For example, school counselors may wish to make sure that all members of a sixth-grade class learn appropriate ways of interacting with the opposite gender. One counselor decides to run a series of guidance/psychoeducational groups with the sixth-grade students based on the rationale that students first need knowledge before they can act properly. This counselor plans a sequential series of interactive presentations. Another counselor at the same school does not think through the process and impulsively decides to conduct counseling groups with the sixth graders to deal with this situation. There is no rationale for such groups—they are not well suited for children who have not expressed a concern about this subject, and they take considerable time to conduct. Needless to say, the outcome of the two groups run by these counselors would vary greatly because of the initial thought processes of each counselor.

The Second Step in Forming: Deciding on a Theoretical Format

In addition to developing a rationale on what type of group to conduct, group workers must consider the theoretical format from which they will work. Some group leaders pretend not to work from a theoretical basis. They claim they will let groups decide how to develop. Yet, even this type of purported atheoretical stance is really a theoretical statement about how the leader thinks and conducts himself or herself in a group. It basically states that the best way to conduct a group is to let members decide what to do and when in a behavioral or existential manner.

Ward (1982, 1985) notes that each major theory of group work has limitations and strengths. Leaders who are most aware of these areas before groups begin can choose a format appropriate to their group even if it is eclectic (i.e., a composite of theoretical approaches). In choosing a theoretical format, the limitations and strengths of such an approach must be considered. All types of groups (e.g., task/work, counseling, psychoeducational, and psychotherapeutic) deal with individual, interpersonal, and group focus levels. A theoretical format should function on intrapersonal, interpersonal, and extrapersonal levels, but in varying degrees. Ideally, the theoretical base of the group will match the needs of participants and the group as a whole (see Table 4.1).

Waldo (1985) has conceptually described levels of functioning in a group as I/We/It. "I" is the individual, intrapersonal focus on beliefs, attitudes, and feelings. "We" is the interpersonal dimension, that is, the relationship between group members. "It" is the extrapersonal emphasis on issues, tasks, or group concerns. Leaders who wish to facilitate interpersonal ("We") development of members might choose a theoretical format that promotes this process, such as a person-centered counseling group, whereas those emphasizing individual ("I") development might plan to employ an active psychoeducational group. Despite the approach chosen, the planning for a group must consider that groups contain many variables, such as people, processes, and products. "Group work is challenging and complex because groups are complex" (Ward, 1985, p. 59).

The Third Step in Forming: Practical Considerations

After deciding on a clear, convincing rationale and theoretical format, group proposals should stress specific, concrete, and practical objectives and procedures.

Table 4.1
Characteristics of counseling groups according to focus.

Characteristics Variables	Group Focus		
	Extrapersonal	**Interpersonal**	**Intrapersonal**
Type	Task	Process	Therapy
Expectation	Action	Development	Remediation
Time Focus	Future	Present	Past
Leader Role	Directive	Facilitative	Responsive
Structure	High	Variable	Low
Stigma	Very low	Low	Moderate
Confidentiality	Not necessary	Desirable	Necessary
Size	3–30+ members	6–20 members	5–10 members
Member Consistency	Frequent changes	Occasional changes	Few changes
Duration	1–30+ sessions	5–20 sessions	12–30+ sessions

Source: From "A Curative Factor Framework for Conceptualizing Group Counseling" by M. Waldo, 1985, *Journal of Counseling and Development, j64,* p. 53. Copyright AACD. Reprinted by permission of the American Association for Counseling and Development.

Considerations, such as meeting time, place, and frequency of meetings, cannot be overlooked if the group is to be successful (Jacobs, Harvill, & Masson, 1994; Sadock, 1983). Group leaders must be sensitive to political and practical realities as well. There are some good group ideas that never get implemented because colleagues fear, misunderstand, or disapprove of the group leader's plans. For example, a high school guidance group focusing on understanding opposite-sex relationships might be prohibited or canceled if the principal of the school thinks sex is to be the main agenda item of the group. In a case like this, the group leader should first thoroughly brief the principal to prevent a negative reaction.

Overall, the formulation of a group proposal will be influenced by the setting in which the leader works. For instance, an employee assistant professional might propose an adjustment group for recent retirees in a community center, whereas a college counselor might focus on offering a series of guidance presentations on careers in the student university center. Counselors and therapists in private practice will generally have more flexibility and fewer administrative procedures than those in the public domain. However, private practitioners who conduct groups are not protected by institutions. They must be as careful and meticulous as other group practitioners in their proposals. A partial secret of success in all cases is detailed preparation. A good model that reflects adequate preparation is a proposal that includes the broad range of information presented in Table 4.2. This model can be adapted to meet the needs of group leaders interested in serving other populations.

The Fourth Step in Forming: Publicizing the Group

Corey and Corey (1992) note that "how a group is announced influences both the way it will be received by potential members and the kind of people who will join" (p. 77). Some of the best ways of announcing the formation of a group are through word of mouth with professional colleagues, personal contact with potential members, and written announcements to a targeted audience. There are advantages and disadvantages to each of these ways of **publicizing a group**. For example, announcing a group through word of mouth to professional colleagues may personalize the information but fail to reach a large number of individuals who might wish to participate. The same is true if a group leader simply contacts those he or she thinks might benefit from the experience. Written announcements to select audiences are likely to reach the most people. However, the drawback to this method is that the announcements may not be clear enough to specify who should be a member of the group. Therefore, some persons who are not suited for the group may apply, and/or too many persons may apply, requiring the group leader to spend a large amount of time screening them.

The American Psychological Association (1973) and the Association for Specialists in Group Work (1989) have published two statements—*Guidelines for Psychologists Conducting Growth Groups* and *Ethical Guidelines for Group Leaders,* respectively—that provide guidelines on the proper conduct expected of those who lead groups, including preparation procedures. Professional group workers have also focused on specific issues regarding content that should be addressed. Among the best of these checklists is one by Tollerud, Holling, and Dustin (1992). Another checklist on specific issues reguarding content is found in Table 4.2.

The Fifth Step in Forming: Pretraining and Selection of Members and Leaders

Pretraining.   The maturity, readiness, and composition of members plays a major role in determining the success of a group. Therefore, potential group members should be **screened** (interviewed prior to the group in regard to their suitability for the group) and carefully chosen whenever possible. (Exceptions to choosing members are likely to occur in psychoeducational and work/task groups.) One way to ensure that members are ready for the group is by **pretraining** them, i.e., orienting them on what to expect of the group before it ever meets. "Such an investment should enhance the functioning of the group, speed its work, reduce dropouts, and increase the positive outcomes (Zimpfer, 1991, p. 264).

Pretraining can be done on an individual or group basis. When conducted individually, there is always the possibility that a leader will accidentally leave out some vital details about the group. The advantage of such a process, however, is to increase the rapport of the member and leader.

A pregroup session is a more uniform and less personalized way of pretraining. Such a session focuses on topics that might be explored in the group and gives

Table 4.2
Checklist of specific issues on content.

Proposal for a group

I. Type of Group

This will be a (task/work, psychoeducational, counseling, psychotherapy) group for people between the ages of (____ and _____) or with the following interests or aspirations (_____). The group will specifically focus on _____. It will not concentrate on _____. The group will meet for a (limited, unlimited) time starting with a meeting on (fill in specific date, length of meeting, and place).

During the initial session, the leader will give specific suggestions to participants in getting the most from their group experience.

The fee (if any) for this group will be _____.

II. Rationale, Goals, and Objectives

The rationale for conducting this type of group is as follows:

1.

2.

3.

Goals and objectives for the group are as follows:

1.

2.

3.

III. Rights and Expectations of Group Members

Group members have rights as well as responsibilities. It is expected that group members will be active participants. However, members will decide at what level they participate, how much they reveal about themselves, and when they wish to share information. Ethical guidelines of _____ will be followed.

IV. Group Leader

Name(s) of the group leader(s), degrees, professional and personal backgrounds and experiences, qualifications for leading groups, and other pertinent information.

V. Basic Ground Rules

In order to obtain the most from the group, members will be asked to suggest ways of conducting it. However, these generic rules will be followed:

1.

2.

3.

VI. Topics for the Group

Certain topics will be given emphasis, but group members will have the opportunity to discuss the aspects of those topics that are most meaningful to them. Following is a sample of some possible topics for the group to explore. Other topics of concern to group participants can be developed.

1.

2.

3.

members an opportunity to assess whether they wish to invest themselves in this particular group. It is a final screening procedure for the leader and the potential members. A pregroup screening session and pretraining are not required, but the more thoroughly prepared potential members and the group leader are, the more likely the dropout rate will be low, the communication clearer, and the cohesion of the group as a whole greater (Sadock, 1983; Yalom, 1985).

Two examples of pretraining will illustrate the essence of it. In a group that is voluntary and therapeutic, potential members should be informed of what techniques and procedures will be used, the qualifications of the leader, fees (if any), types of records kept, member responsibility, personal risks involved, and the types of services that can realistically be provided (Gazda, 1989). If the group is more information focused and nonvoluntary, such as a college freshmen orientation group, this information may not need to be presented in quite as much detail. However, a schedule of events and what they are focused on accomplishing should accompany individuals who are selected for such groups.

When in doubt about how specific to be, the group leader should err on the side of caution and give group members a thorough explanation of group and administrative procedures. In no case should the leader make promises or guarantees. Facts concerning the formation and procedure of a group are preferably put in writing (ASGW, 1989).

Selection of Group Members.   The selection of group members is usually a two-way process. The exceptions are in some guidance/psychoeducational groups, where material is presented to a captive audience such as in schools or the armed forces, and in work/task groups, where individuals are grouped with each other because they work in the same office. When potential group members and the leader are mutually involved in the selection process, both have input into deciding who will be included or excluded. Most experts in the group field endorse an **individually conducted screening procedure,** that is, an intake interview, as a way of determining who will join a particular group (Sadock, 1983). In such a session, the group leader and potential member can interview each other about different aspects of the group process and about themselves (Corey & Corey, 1992; Yalom, 1985). The goal is to determine if a particular group is right for a particular person at a specific time.

Pertinent questions to ask potential group members vary, but queries that are open ended and elicit personal responses and interpersonal styles seem to work best (Gladding, 1994). For example, a prospective member of a group might be asked:

"What has been your past experiences with groups?"
"What has led you to want to be a part of this group?"
"What can you contribute to this group?"
"How do you express your emotions, especially your negative ones?"

Individuals who do not appear likely to contribute to the growth of the group or who lack personal maturity are prime candidates for exclusion from it. These persons include those who are extremely hostile, self-centered, mentally unbalanced, fragile, or crisis-oriented (Corey, 1990). Other individuals who may be excluded from a particular group are those who are either too different or too similar to other potential group members. Extremely heterogeneous group members may not relate well to each other (Melnick & Wood, 1976), whereas extremely homogeneous group members may relate too well, not work hard on individual or group tasks, and stay on a superficial level. Over time, heterogeneous groups may be most effective for intensive group therapy procedures in which the emphasis is on personality change (Kellerman, 1979), whereas homogeneous groups may be most appropriate for individuals who need support or have more focused problems such as solving a dilemma on a job-related task. Clearly, there are advantages and disadvantages to both heterogeneous and homogeneous groups (Furst, 1953).

A potential group member should never be coerced to join a group (ASGW, 1989). Likewise, if a potential group member and group leader determine that group work "does not show promise as a source of help," the group leader should work with the interviewee in looking for other sources of assistance (Ohlsen, Horne, & Lawe, 1988, p. 37).

Selection of a Group Leader.   Certain qualities distinguish an effective group leader. Some of these features were discussed in chapter 3 and will not be reiterated here. What will be emphasized is the selection of a leader by a potential group member. The selection process hinges partly on professional qualities and partly on personal qualities. It is easier to deal with professional issues because, in the pregroup screening procedure, the potential group member can ask about the group leader's qualifications. The group leader can voluntarily offer information about his or her educational preparation and experience in conducting groups. Such professional disclosure is considered a must at this point in group formation (ASGW, 1989).

Personal information about the group leader's style in sessions is also important (George & Dustin, 1988; Napier & Gershenfeld, 1989). The leader's style may incorporate humor, self-disclosure, confrontation, or other helping modalities. The leader's style and personality will be an important aspect of the group for the potential member to consider. If the potential group member does not think that the group leader is one with whom he or she can comfortably work, it is best to find another group to join.

TASKS OF THE BEGINNING GROUP

Group leaders and group members have tasks to accomplish during the first sessions of a group. These tasks are varied but include:

1. dealing with apprehension
2. reviewing members' goals and contracts
3. specifying more clearly or reiterating group rules

4. setting limits
5. promoting a positive interchange among members so they will want to continue. (Weiner, 1984)

A failure to accomplish any of these tasks may result in the failure of the group to function properly. Each of these tasks will be examined individually.

✳ Apprehension

Apprehension is synonymous with anxiety. Too much or too little anxiety inhibits performance of the group and its members (Yalom, 1985). Therefore, it is appropriate that group members and leaders have a moderate amount of apprehension when they begin a group. It helps them key in on what they are experiencing and what they want to do. Apprehension differs in psychotherapeutic and psychoeducational groups where there is an individual focus to the apprehension and task/work groups where there is a group focus to the apprehension. For example, in a therapy group, Ellen may be anxious about whether others will see her as capable, whereas in a task group, Ellen may be anxious about whether the group can perform the assignment it has been given.

It is helpful, and sometimes necessary, after each group session for group leaders to deal with any misunderstandings that may have arisen due to anxiety. For example, if James is berating himself in front of his counseling group for being defensive when asked a question about his attitudes toward race, the leader may say: "James, I hear you are concerned about two aspects related to the question Jan asked you about race. One is your verbal answer; the other, your failure to live up to your own expectations. I wonder what feelings got in the way of your handling Jan's question." Such an observation and invitation give James a chance to deal with his emotions, especially his apprehension about saying the right words and being perfect. By clarifying what has happened, James and the group as a whole are able to move on.

ice breakers can be used later in therapy before a crucial sessions

Goals and Contracts

Goals are specific objectives that individuals or the group wish to accomplish. Group goals are announced at the time a group proposal is formulated and again during the pregroup interview. Group members should keep these objectives in mind throughout the group process. Likewise, individual goals are worked out in the pregroup screening session and are consistent with the group's overall goals. In counseling, guidance, and task/work groups, such goals may have a universal quality about them, for example, understanding careers. In psychotherapeutic groups, especially with individuals in severe distress, the goals and contracts may vary widely. For example, such groups may contain members who are trying to resolve grief as well as those who are attempting to overcome depression.

A thorough way of clarifying group and individual goals is to have the group leader restate the purpose of the group during the first session and have each member elaborate on his or her goals. In some cases and with some theories (e.g. , Gestalt, behaviorism, transactional analysis), members are asked to formulate a **contract** (i.e., an agreement of what will be done and when) (Corey, 1990; Donigian & Malnati, 1987). A written contract helps members to specify what, how, when, and where they will work to make changes related to their goals (see Figure 4.1).

Group Rules

Rules are the guidelines by which groups are run. They are established both before and during the group process. In pregroup screening sessions, leaders take the initiative in setting up rules. For example, most groups contain rules set by the leader, such as no physical violence, no drugs, and attendance at all meetings (Vander Kolk, 1985). Rules should be stated in a positive, rather than a negative, way. "No physical violence" is better expressed as "Members will respect the physical and psychological space of others at all times."

During the first session of the group and afterward, members make contributions to rules by which the group will abide, for example, "Smoking will be per-

---

As a member of this group, I, John Smith, make this contract to achieve the following goals.

What (i.e., goal)	How	When	Where
(1) share my thoughts	verbal	each session	in group
	verbal	each day	home
	verbal	each class	school
(2) eat healthy	choice	each meal	everywhere
(3) exercise	discipline	each day	home
(4) control anger	choice	each time	home
	choice	each time	in group

John Smith	*January 31, 1995*
signature	date

Figure 4.1
Sample contract on goals for an individual group member.

mitted outside the group room but not during the group session." It is important to formulate a rationale behind every group rule, rather than set rules in an arbitrary and "thou shall not" manner that invites violations and game playing (Yalom, 1985). One rule that is usually agreed to, but difficult to enforce, is confidentiality.

Confidentiality is the explicit agreement that what is said in the group will stay in the group. It will be covered in more detail in chapter 8 on ethical and legal aspects of group work. However, it should be noted here that confidentiality is the "ethical cornerstone" of group counseling and psychotherapy (Plotkin, 1978). It is also a valued component of many work/task and psychoeducational groups for it is "a prerequisite for the development of group trust, cohesion, and productive work" (Gazda, 1989, p. 303). However, confidentiality is sometimes violated, either intentionally or unintentionally. At the beginning of the group, members and leaders should review possible ways that confidentiality might be violated, including revealing identification information about group members and/or talking about group interactions outside the group.

Leaders also need to be sure of their responsibilities regarding confidentiality, for example, protecting group members' files and/or computer records and erasing or destroying audiotapes and videotapes after they have been used to critique group progress. Leaders often take responsibility for keeping confidence by reviewing group codes of ethics and legal precedents. They usually do so outside the presence of the group. However, the extent to which leaders go to maintain confidence may be productively discussed in the group itself, especially if members raise issues pertaining to it.

When breaches of confidentiality occur, they disrupt the functioning of the group and promote distrust among group members. Therefore, it is crucial that group rules or procedures be in place to deal with such possibilities. The group that can agree in the initial session on the nature of rules and the consequences for breaking them is far ahead of the group that bypasses this procedure.

Setting Limits

Limits are the outer boundaries of a group in regard to behaviors that will be accepted within the group. They are set explicitly and implicitly in group settings. Explicitly, these limits take the form of rules regarding acceptable behaviors and procedures related to time (Napier & Gershenfeld, 1989). When members violate an explicit limit, they are corrected by either the group as a whole, individual members, the leader, or the outside community. For example, if Kathy tells Connie what Louise said in confidence in a group counseling session, Kathy may be ostracized by the group and members of her sorority when they find out what occurred.

Implicit limits are more subtle and involve such actions as the attention of the leader to a particular member or the verbal reinforcement or discouragement of certain content topics (Jacobs et al., 1994). For example, group members, such as Jeff, who ramble on about their families may be instructed by the leader, "Keep your comments about past family matters brief and to the point so the group can help you." Eye contact may also be employed by the leader to encourage or suppress dialogue. Skilled group leaders use their power of facilitating and setting limits in both direct and indirect ways.

Promoting a Positive Interchange Among Members

Promoting a positive interchange among members of a group is initially the task of the group leader. If positive interchanges among group members can be facilitated, group members will begin to share openly with one another. "The leader can establish a positive tone by drawing out members; by holding the focus on interesting topics; by shifting the focus when the topics are irrelevant or only interesting to a couple of members; by cutting off any interactions that are hostile or negative; and by being enthusiastic. . . ." (Jacobs et al., 1994, p. 84). If such a productive tone is not created, group members may drop out, close up, or attack one another.

RESOLVING POTENTIAL GROUP PROBLEMS IN FORMING

There are a number of problems that can occur during the formation of the group and afterward. Some of these difficulties deal with people; others are related to the process. One of the best ways of handling potential group problems is to prevent them. Prevention involves following the steps for forming the group already mentioned in this chapter. When prevention is not possible, the leader and group can work to bring about resolution. Member interaction patterns that are particularly troublesome will be dealt with first in this section, then initial group procedures.

People Problems

Despite careful screening, some group members display difficult behaviors early on in the group process. Those who cause the most concern, especially in counseling groups, are individuals in the group who monopolize, withdraw, intimidate, verbally ventilate, focus on others, seduce, or show intolerance (Edelwich & Brodsky, 1992). **Subgroups** (cliques of members who band together) may also be troublesome. Sometimes, group leaders will become too involved in the content of what is being expressed in the group and not notice interactional patterns. By concentrating on the styles of different group members, however, leaders are better able to plan and lead future sessions (Jacobs et al., 1994). Six common membership roles often displayed during the first session will be covered here, along with the problem of subgroups. In dealing with people problems, group leaders are well advised to avoid labeling individuals. The tendency that goes with labels is to stereotype individuals and to perceive situations as always falling within a certain behavioral range (Kline, 1990).

Manipulators.   Members who are **manipulators** are characterized by their subtle and not-so-subtle use of feelings and behaviors to get what they want. Often they are angry and bring into the group unresolved life problems centering on control. For example, Joe, in his manipulator role, may say to the group, "If you are not going to give me what I want, I am leaving this group."

Manipulative individuals may be helped by "reframing" their potentially destructive acts in a positive way (e.g., "Sounds like what you really want from this group is specific help in dealing with trust"). The group leader or members may also intervene by blocking manipulating actions, such as threatening or pleading. At the beginning of a group, manipulators will often struggle with group leaders for control of the group. They should not be allowed to usurp the leader's function or the group will fail.

Resisters.   **Resisters** are also often angry or frustrated and bring these feelings with them. They do not participate in group exercises or tasks and act as barriers to helping the group form. For example, Babs may say to the group, "I do not see any sense in telling you how I feel. That won't really help me."

Leaders can help resistant group members build trust in the group by inviting them to participate, but not insisting that they do. This is an affirmation approach and allows resisters and leaders a chance to explore this behavior later (Larrabee, 1982). A second way of working with these individuals is to confront and interpret in a reflective manner what is happening with them (Vriend & Dyer, 1973). For instance, a group leader may say to Babs in the previous example, "I hear you have been disappointed with the groups you have previously been in. They have not been very productive for you." Often the feelings of resistant members are dealt with best in the working stage of the group.

Monopolizers.   People who are **monopolizers** dominate the conversation in a group and do not allow other members a chance to verbally participate. Monopolizers initially offer group members relief because they focus attention on themselves and away from everyone else. These individuals are dealing with underlying anxiety but often become sources of irritation for other group members. One soliloquy does not a monopolizer make, so anxious members should not be characterized as exhibitors of this behavior too early. At the same time, members who display this pattern from the beginning need the help of the leader and other members to realize how certain behaviors hurt their interpersonal relationships and what other actions they could take to improve. The sooner the nonproductive talk of the monopolist is addressed, the more productively an outcome can be reached (Ohlsen et al., 1988). The technique of "cutting off" is an excellent way to deal with monopolists and will be highlighted later in this chapter.

Silent Members.   **Silent members** may or may not be involved with the group. Sometimes, silence is used to cover hostility (Ormont, 1984). Members who are silent are often nonassertive, reflective, shy, or just slow in assessing their thoughts and feelings. The best way to determine the meaning of silence is to give a person a chance to respond, such as answering a question, and notice what happens. A simple question such as "What do you think about what other group members have been saying?" is often enough to draw a silent member into the group.

Acceptance of silence by the group leader and the creation of opportunities by the leader for silent members to become more involved usually rectifies any negative impact that may be associated with these individuals or this behavior. If a group member remains silent throughout the group experience, he or she will probably not get as much from the process as more active members (Coyne & Silver, 1980).

Users of Sarcasm.   Persons who express themselves through **sarcasm** differ from those who are outwardly angry. They mask their feelings through the use of clever language that has a biting humor. For instance, the sarcastic member may say, "Oh joy, now I get to tell you about how I feel. Isn't that just thrilling!"

The group leader can help the sarcastic member work on expressing anger more directly by identifying what is happening in his or her life, by having the group member explore what the behavior means for him or her now and where it was learned, and by inviting other group members to give the sarcastic member feedback on how they respond to sarcastic ways of relating.

Focusers on Others.   This final category of behavior—**focusers on others**—involves those who become self-appointed group "assistant leaders" by questioning others, offering advice, and acting as if they did not have any problems. These individuals are often challenged by group members and can be helped to overcome this other-focused behavior by being taught that self-disclosure is more helpful to most people than a style devoid of personal involvement. They may also be given permission during this stage of the group to make wishes for themselves. For instance, the leader may say, "Jane, if you could have some new traits for yourself, what would they be?" In essence, other-focused group members must be helped to realize the value of becoming personally committed to the group.

Overall, it is important that group members be given time to express themselves and not be labeled or stereotyped early in the group process. Leaders must also trust their feelings and reactions in regard to difficult group members. In some instances, a difficult group member may have to be removed from the group, but this measure is a last-resort strategy (Kline, 1990). Such a process creates anxiety in other members about whether they might also be removed. Before such a step is ever taken, the leader needs to try to help the group help itself by working through their thoughts and feelings about certain behaviors. Allowing group members to give and receive feedback enables them to obtain insight and change from the troublesome and disruptive behavior.

In regard to *subgroups*, group leaders may help prevent their formation by focusing on the uniqueness of each individual and his or her connectedness with the group as a whole. Leaders may also discourage the formation of subgroups by making their expectations known in regard to such groups in the screening interview, pregroup training, and in the initial group session. When subgroups do develop, however, they must be dealt with directly, or they may have a deleterious effect on the group member interaction (Vander Kolk, 1985; Yalom, 1985). Three ways of handling subgroup behavior (outside of prevention) are given by Trotzer (1989):

1. Bring all coalescing, colluding, and subgrouping behavior that occurs in the group to the group's attention. For example, point out that John, Jim, and Mary seem to be acting as a team on their own and not with the other members of the group.
2. Establish a guideline and expectation that the group be informed about extra group activities among members. In such a case, one of the group rules can be that all meetings of group members outside the regular schedule of the group be reported to the group at large before sessions begin.
3. As a group leader, do not collude with subgroups overtly or covertly by not disclosing what you perceive and/or know about the subgroup. If a group leader remains silent when he or she realizes a subgroup has formed, the leader is hurting the group as a whole. Speaking out may risk alienating members of the subgroup for awhile but to not do so possesses an even greater risk of losing the group as a whole. (p. 300)

Group Procedural Problems

An initial group session is often filled with anxiety, awkwardness, and anticipation by both the group leader and members (Vander Kolk, 1985). Even veterans of group experiences may feel some apprehension because every group is different. Most group members will try to put on their best behavior and be friendly and positive, but potential problems may arise at certain points. The best way to deal with these areas is to prevent them from developing. At other times, however, corrective measures may need to be taken.

Opening the Group.   Beginning the first group session is often a difficult experience, especially for the novice leader. It is what Donigian and Malnati (1987) describe as a **critical incident in the life of the group** (i.e., an event that has the power to shape or influence the group positively or negatively). How it is handled can make a major difference in what happens later in the group. Some practitioners, such as Coulson (1972, 1974), choose to begin a group in silence, but most group leaders are more structured. There are several options available for beginning the first group session. Jacobs et al. (1994, pp. 77–81) suggest seven different ways. Each is dependent on the style of the leader and purpose of the group.

1. "Start with an opening statement about the group and its purpose and then do an introduction exercise." This type of procedure is usually

employed with psychoeducational or task/work groups, although it may be used in therapeutic groups. It involves the leader taking about five minutes to describe the format and purpose of the group and to introduce himself or herself. This process is followed by a brief exercise, such as members introducing themselves.

2. "Start with a very brief statement about the group and then do an introduction exercise." In this style, the leader only talks for about one or two minutes. He or she then quickly gets group members involved by having them participate with each other, such as introducing themselves to each other in some way such as saying their names and what animals they feel like today.

3. "Start with a long opening statement and then get right into the content of the group." This procedure is used when the group's focus is on accomplishing a task. In the long opening statement, the leader reminds group members of their purpose and then helps the group get down to business by describing what the group is going to do.

4. "Start with a brief statement about the group and then get into the content." This opening is ideal for task/work groups where members know each other and the purpose of the group is clear. In this opening, members freely exchange ideas and suggestions at the initial group meeting.

5. "Start with a brief statement about the group and then have the members form dyads." In this type of opening, the purpose of coming to the group is clear, and members have some comfort in being in the group. Breaking into dyads helps group members focus more on content and/or purpose associated with the group experience.

6. "Start with a brief statement about the group and then have members complete a short sentence-completion form." The sentence-completion format is useful in helping members focus on the purpose of the group. It is employed in task/work, psychoeducational, and therapy/counseling groups when no introductions are needed.

7. "Start with an introduction exercise." This final type of introduction is employed when members have a strong idea of the purpose of the group. It helps members introduce themselves and immediately focus on the content of the group. There are a number of creative exercises that can be utilized, but texts, such as Jacobs (1992) *Creative Counseling Techniques*, are excellent resources in picking or modifying a procedure with which to begin. For example, Jacobs points out that props, such as cups and chairs, can often illustrate to group members what words alone cannot convey.

Overall, there is no one single type of introduction that will work consistently for every group or every group leader. The style of introduction is largely determined by the interpersonal skill of the leader and the nature of the group.

Other aspects of the group at its beginning that will be problematic if not addressed are structure, involvement, cohesion, hope, and ways of terminating the initial session. Therefore, these processes will be examined more thoroughly here.

Structuring.   Group leaders in the initial stage of a group must make decisions on **structuring the group** (i.e., running the group according to a prescribed plan or agenda). Those conducting task/work and psychoeducational groups will be much more direct than leaders of counseling and psychotherapy groups. The advantages of structuring a group are that it promotes group cooperation, lessens anxiety, highlights individual performance, and facilitates the inclusion of everyone in the group (Bach, 1954). Structuring may also give leaders more confidence and help them concentrate on group goals (Landreth, 1973; Trotzer, 1989). The disadvantages of structuring are that it may discourage personal responsibility and may restrict freedom of expression. Unstructured groups, while promoting more initial anxiety and discontent, also ultimately create high group cohesiveness and morale (Trotzer, 1989).

Regardless of who promotes involvement, the structuring of a group is inevitable. As Corey and Corey (1992) state, "The proper question is not whether a group leader should provide structure but, rather, what degree of structure" (p. 134). A major guideline for the amount of structure will be the theoretical stance of the leader. "Overtly and covertly, members look to the leader for structure and answers, as well as for approval and acceptance" (Yalom, 1985, p. 302). It is important that the leader not over- or understructure the group experience during the beginning sessions.

Some guidelines for proper structuring in the initial stage of group development have been given by Dies (1983). These ideas include an awareness by leaders that directly structuring the group in its early stages facilitates the group's development and may promote the establishment of trust and the accomplishment of goals. However, structuring depends on the type of group being led. It can include indirect modeling of behaviors by the leader, as well as confrontation of actions. Once the group begins to work well, leaders who use a lot of structure ease up on this process.

Involvement.   **Involvement** of group members, in which they actively participate with each other and invest themselves in the group, is necessary for first sessions to work best. Structured exercises, such as those proposed by Lessner (1974) and Johnson and Johnson (1991), are excellent in bringing people together in a creative and enjoyable way. For example, Lessner gets members involved by first having them center on who they are. This process is accomplished by the leader reading the group a nondidactic poem and then having members describe how they are like an image in the poem, such as a leaf, a rock, a tree. However, there is no instant intimacy or involvement of group members with one another.

During the first sessions, group leaders need to facilitate member interaction. The use of structured activities is one way to accomplish this goal. By discussing specific concerns related to the exercises, group members are able to stop concentrating on group acceptance issues and start focusing on individual goals. Therefore, there is a place in some groups for these activities on a limited basis. In deciding how to get members involved, leaders need to focus on the primary purpose of the group before they decide on a strategy for achieving this goal. Groups that are most productive are composed of members who realistically deal with themselves, others, and issues.

Group Cohesion.   "The effective development of any group requires that members share an image of the group" (Hansen et al., 1980, p. 492). Unfortunately, in the initial stage of group work, "members bring individual images of the group" (Hansen et al., 1980, p. 492). Not only is a common identity lacking, but often many group members resist any directions from the group leader and are reluctant to join with others (Corey & Corey, 1992).

To combat this problem and build **group cohesion,** that is, a sense of "we-ness," individuals should be allowed to voice their concerns freely and fully. By participating in this way, members gain a sense of ownership in the group because they have invested in it. The participatory process also promotes a sense of openness, trust, and security in the group as a whole as well as in its members. These perceptions lead to positive group member interactions, such as cooperation on tasks, resolution of differences, and agreement of group goals (Corey & Corey, 1992; Johnson & Johnson, 1991). Although group cohesion usually does not manifest itself fully until the norming (or identity) stage of the group, the seeds for its development are planted early in the group process.

Promoting Hope and Engendering Risks.   **Promoting hope** is one of the basic "therapeutic" factors described by Yalom (1985). If members are hopeful that their situations can be different and better, they are likely to work hard within the group. There are a number of ways leaders can instill hope during the initial sessions of the group. For instance, they can convey information to members about group process, validate commonalties among members, and accentuate the positive (Couch & Childers, 1987). They can also use humor or give general examples of how hope has been conveyed in other groups (Gladding, 1994).

If members are able to experience a sense of **universality** (i.e., commonness with others) within the group, they will feel more cohesive (MacKenzie & Livesley, 1983). They are then more likely to take risks that, when successfully completed, add to their sense of accomplishment and their attractiveness to the group. "The degree of risk should not be excessive at this point, or the disclosure too threatening to other members" (MacDevitt, 1987, p. 79). Therefore, leaders must strive for balance in the area of self-disclosure. Those leaders who can facilitate the disclosure by members of limited and nonthreatening information in the early stages of the group are appropriate in what they are doing and on their way to conducting a successful group.

Closing the Group.   The termination of a group session is filled with many feelings—anxiety, relief, sadness, and joy. It is just as important to end a group session appropriately as it is to begin it correctly. Too often, not enough attention is focused on closing a session; a group leader may simply announce time is up. Corey and Corey (1992) recommend that at least ten minutes be set aside at the end of a group for reflection and summarization. Otherwise, group members may become frustrated and fail to gain insight into themselves and others. They also suggest that, at the end of weekly sessions, group members leave with

some unanswered questions
some reflection about their involvement in the group
some self-report about what they are learning
some concentration of what they would like to explore during the next session
some feedback from others about positive changes in their behaviors

The initial sessions of a group are crucial in establishing such a pattern. Even if a group does not make it through more than a few sessions, many group members may experience "considerable relief" because they are able to release repressed feelings (catharsis), experience themselves as possessing commonalities with others (universality), find themselves caring about the fate of others (altruism), and experience hope about their personal futures (Zimpfer, 1986, personal communication, December 1989).

USEFUL PROCEDURES FOR THE BEGINNING STAGE OF A GROUP

There is no one way or technique that is appropriate for all aspects of a group as it begins. The reason is simple: each group is unique. Yet, there are some universal group procedures that seem to work well in most groups, especially at the beginning of the group. Following are a few of these.

Joining

Joining is the process by which members connect with one another psychologically and physically. Joining requires that leaders and members exert some effort to meet one another and find out more about each other. Joining can occur in several ways. Probably the most common is for members to introduce themselves stating their names and some brief background information. A more exciting way of joining is through an **icebreaker**, that is, an activity designed to promote communication between two or more people. Such an activity can take many forms. For instance, members can simply go around and state their name and a favorite food or activity. Such a superficial icebreaker is appropriate in most task/work and psychoeducational groups. Counseling and psychotherapy groups, on the other hand, are better served when members go into more depth about themselves and their reasons for becoming a part of the group.

Linking

Linking is the process of connecting persons with one another by pointing out to them what they share in common. It strengthens the bonds between individuals and the group as a whole. For example, the leader may point out how two participants are dealing with issues involving loss or transition. The leader may also help the group realize through linking sentences that one of the issues during the session has been the establishment of trust. In such a case, the leader might say, "I have observed today that some of you are struggling with a common problem. Henry, Alice, Alicia, and Timothy, you have all talked about being unsure of whether you can say what you really feel in the group. The issue of trust seems important and one that is shared."

Linking is employed throughout the life of a group, but it is especially powerful at the beginning stage. Through linking, group cohesion is developed. Some group workers consider linking to be development because, as the group progresses, more themes, interpersonal relationships, and issues tie the group together and facilitate a sense of interrelatedness (Trotzer, 1989). This developmental quality of linking is more likely to occur if the process is utilized from the start of the group.

Cutting Off

Cutting off is defined two ways. First, it is making sure that new material is not introduced into the group too late in the session for the group to adequately deal with it. For instance, if a member relates that he or she would like to share an important secret with the group and only five minutes remain in the session, the leader may cut the member off by noting the time left, the importance of the information, and the atmosphere needed to deal with such material. In such a procedure, the member is invited to bring this information with him or her next time and introduce it at the start of the session.

The leader might phrase a cutoff statement this way, "Carole, I think the group is receptive to hearing from you but are unable to because of the time. I regret that what you wished to share has surfaced so late in the session. I need you to save this material until next session so we can deal with it properly and give it, and you, the consideration you are due."

Cutting off is also preventing group members from rambling. For instance, if Mark begins to relate his life history to the group, when all he has been asked to do is briefly introduce himself, the group leader may cut him off by saying something such as, "Mark, we will go into more depth about our backgrounds as the group goes on. Now we need to move on to the next person to make sure everyone has an opportunity to be introduced." By cutting Mark off, the leader keeps the group on task and teaches proper conduct to Mark and others in the group.

Drawing Out

The opposite of cutting off is **drawing out,** in which the leader purposefully asks more silent members to speak to anyone in the group, or to the group as a whole, about anything. For example, the leader might say, "Andy, we haven't heard from you about this matter." By using the drawing-out technique, the leader helps members feel more connected with each other. Drawing out also helps members invest more in the group as well as recognize their thoughts. At the same time, other group members receive valuable information about the person who is being drawn out. This technique is particularly appropriate for group members who tend to be introverted or reflective.

Clarifying the Purpose

Sometimes, members unintentionally bring up material that is not appropriate for a beginning session or for the overall purpose of the group. In such situations, the leader should **clarify the purpose** of the group with the individuals and the group as a whole, the stage the session has reached, and/or what behavioral interactions are appropriate. For example, the group leader may say, "Frank, your comments are quite interesting, but I am not sure where you are going with them in regard to the topic we have been dealing with. Remember, in this group we are focusing on improving our interpersonal communication skills."

SUMMARY AND CONCLUSION

Beginning a group is a major undertaking filled with complex tasks. Group leaders can be overwhelmed by all the demands associated with this responsibility if they are not prepared properly. Therefore, carefully prepared proposals and selection of group members are a must if the group is to be successful. These processes take time and effort but are likely to pay off for the leader in such ways as obtaining approval from colleagues, obtaining appropriate group members, gaining clarity on group and individual goals, and ensuring as much as possible confidentiality and proper procedure. Groups that begin well are more likely ultimately to do well.

Group leaders need to be prepared for developmental and unexpected events within the group, such as members who play certain roles and processes that contribute positively or negatively to group and individual growth. Structuring the group and confronting problems when they occur are important for an overall successful outcome. There is no way to know exactly what will happen when, but group leaders who have a knowledge about how to open and close first group sessions, as well as how to help group members get what they both want and need, are valuable resources whose importance cannot be underestimated.

CLASSROOM EXERCISES

1. Draw up a proposal for a group you would like to lead following the model presented in this chapter. Present your proposal to three other people in a

small group of four and elicit their feedback about ways to improve your ideas. Take turns listening to others in the group and making positive suggestions to them on ways to refine what they are proposing.

2. Using seven volunteer class members, assign one to play the role of the group leader who will screen the others as potential group members for a personal growth group. Have the leader interview members individually and in subgroups of two or three. Notice what questions are asked and how the interview process differs on an individual and small-group basis. Then have the leader screen members for a task-oriented group. How do the questions differ? Discuss what you observed as a class.

3. Invite a group leader to speak to your class about how he or she conducts the initial sessions of groups and gets them off to "good beginnings." Specifically focus in on how the leader deals with the matter of confidentiality and troublesome group procedures such as those discussed in this chapter.

4. What ground rules do you consider essential for conducting an initial group session? How would these rules differ if the group was therapy oriented as opposed to task oriented?

REFERENCES

American Psychological Association. (1973). Guidelines for psychologists conducting growth groups. *American Psychologist, 28,* 933.

Association for Specialists in Group Work. (1989). *Ethical guidelines for group leaders.* Alexandria, VA: Author.

Bach, G. R. (1954). *Intensive group psychotherapy.* New York: Ronald Press.

Brabender, V. (1985). Time-limited inpatient group therapy: A developmental model. *International Journal of Group Psychotherapy, 3,* 373–390.

Cohen, A. M., & Smith, R. D. (1976). *Critical incidents in growth groups: Theory and techniques.* La Jolla, CA: University Associates.

Corey, G. (1990). *Theory and practice of group counseling* (3rd ed.). Pacific Grove, CA: Brooks/Cole.

Corey, M. S., & Corey, G. (1992). *Groups: Process and practice* (4th ed.). Pacific Grove, CA: Brooks/Cole.

Couch, R. D., & Childers, J. H., Jr. (1987). Leadership strategies for instilling and maintaining hope in group counseling. *Journal for Specialists in Group Work, 12,* 138–143.

Coulson, W. R. (1972). *Groups, gimmicks and instant gurus.* New York: Harper & Row.

Coulson, W. R. (1974). *A sense of community.* Columbus, OH: Merrill.

Coyne, R., & Silver, R. (1980). Direct, vicarious, and vicarious-process experiences. *Small Group Behavior, 11,* 419–429.

Dies, R. R. (1983). Clinical implications of research on leadership in short-term group psychotherapy. In R. R. Dies & K. R. MacKenzie (Eds.), *Advances in group psychotherapy: Integrating research and practice* (pp. 27–78). New York: International Universities Press.

Donigian, J., & Malnati, R. (1987). *Critical incidents in group therapy.* Pacific Grove, CA: Brooks/Cole.

Dunphy, D. (1968). Phases, roles, and myths in self-analytic groups. *Journal of Applied Behavioral Science, 4,* 195–225.

Edelwich, J., & Brodsky, A. (1992). *Group counseling for the resistant client.* New York: Lexington.

Furst, W. (1953). Homogeneous versus heterogeneous groups. *International Journal of Psychotherapy, 3,* 59–66.

Gazda, G. M. (1989). *Group counseling: A developmental approach* (4th ed.). Boston: Allyn & Bacon.

George, R. L., & Dustin, D. (1988). *Group counseling: Theory and practice.* Englewood Cliffs, NJ: Prentice Hall.

Gladding, S. T. (1993). *Beginnings.* Unpublished manuscript.

Gladding, S. T. (1994). *Effective group counseling.* Greensboro, NC: ERIC/CASS.

Hansen, J. C., Warner, R. W., & Smith, E. J. (1980). *Group counseling: Theory and process* (2nd ed.). Chicago: Rand McNally.

Jacobs, E. (1992). *Creative counseling techniques: An illustrated guide.* Odessa, FL: Psychological Assessment Resources, Inc.

Jacobs, E. E., Harvill, R. L., & Masson, R. L. (1994). *Group counseling: Strategies and skills* (2nd ed.). Pacific Grove, CA: Brooks/Cole .

Johnson, D. W., & Johnson, F. P. (1991). *Joining together* (4th ed.). Englewood Cliffs, NJ: Prentice Hall.

Kellerman, H. (1979). *Group psychotherapy and personality: Intersecting structures.* New York: Grune & Stratton.

Kline, W. B. (1990). Responding to "problem" members. *Journal for Specialists in Group Work, 15,* 195–200.

Kormanski, C. L., & Mozenter, A. (1987). A new model of team building: A technology for today and tomorrow. In J. W. Pfeiffer (Ed.), *The 1987 annual: Developing human resources* (pp. 255–268). San Diego: University Associates.

Lacoursiere, R. (1974). A group method to facilitate learning during the stages of a psychiatric affiliation. *International Journal of Group Psychotherapy, 24,* 114–119.

Landreth, G. L. (1973). Group counseling: To structure or not to structure. *School Counselor, 20,* 371–374.

Larrabee, M. (1982). Working with reluctant clients through affirmation techniques. *Personnel and Guidance Journal, 60,* 105– 109.

Lessner, J. W. (1974). The poem as a catalyst in group work. *Personnel and Guidance Journal, 53,* 33–38.

MacDevitt, J. W. (1987). Conceptualizing therapeutic components of group counseling. *Journal for Specialists in Group Work, 12,* 76–84.

MacKenzie, K., & Livesley, W. (1983). Developmental model for brief groups. In R. E. Dies & K. R. MacKenzie (Eds.), *Advances in group psychotherapy: Integrating research and practice* (pp. 101–116). New York: International Universities Press.

Melnick, J., & Wood, M. (1976). Analysis of group composition research and theory for psychotherapeutic and growth-oriented groups. *Journal of Applied Behavioral Science, 12,* 493–512.

Napier, R. W., & Gershenfeld, M. K. (1989). *Groups: Theory and experience* (4th ed.). Boston: Houghton Mifflin.

Ohlsen, M. M., Horne, A. M., & Lawe, C. F. (1988). *Group counseling* (3rd ed.). New York: Holt, Rinehart & Winston.

Ormont, L. J. (1984). The leader's role in dealing with aggression in groups. *International Journal of Group Psychotherapy, 34,* 553–572.

Plotkin, R. (1978, March). Confidentiality in group counseling. *APA Monitor,* p. 14.

Sadock, B. J. (1983). Preparation, selection of patients, and organization of the group. In H. I. Kaplan & B. J. Sadock (Eds.), *Comprehensive group psychotherapy* (2nd ed., pp. 23–32). Baltimore: Williams & Wilkins.

Tollerud, T. R., Holling, D. W., & Dustin, D. (1992). A model for teaching in group leadership: The pre-group interview application. *Journal for Specialists in Group Work, 17,* 96–104.

Trotzer, J. P. (1989). *The counselor and the group* (2nd ed.). Muncie, IN: Accelerated Development.

Tuckman, B. W., & Jensen, M. A. C. (1977). Stages of small-group development revisited. *Group and Organizational Studies, 2,* 419–427.

Vander Kolk, C. J. (1985). *Introduction to group counseling and psychotherapy.* Columbus, OH: Merrill.

Vriend, J., & Dyer, W. W. (1973). Counseling the reluctant client. *Journal of Counseling Psychology, 20,* 240–246.

Waldo, M. (1985). A curative factor framework for conceptualizing group counseling. *Journal of Counseling and Development, 64,* 52–58.

Ward, D. E. (1982). A model for the more effective use of theory in group work. *Journal for Specialists in Group Work, 7,* 224–230.

Ward, D. E. (1985). Levels of group activity: A model for improving the effectiveness of group work. *Journal of Counseling and Development, 64,* 59–64.

Weiner, M. F. (1984). *Techniques of group psychotherapy.* Washington, DC: American Psychiatric Press, Inc.

Yalom, I. D. (1985). *The theory and practice of group psychotherapy* (3rd ed.). New York: Basic Books.

Zimpfer, D. G. (1986). Planning for groups based on their developmental phases. *Journal for Specialists in Group Work, 11,* 180–187.

Zimpfer, D. G. (1991). Pretraining for group work: A review. *Journal for Specialists in Group Work, 16,* 264–269.

CHAPTER 5

The Transition Stage in a Group

In the midst of struggles, stagnation, and stress
  we gather as pilgrims on a journey
    to explore the territories of our minds
      and the spaces that separate us from others.
The air is tense with anxiety
  as we venture into the unknown.
Like the settlers of yesterday's time
  we strive to take in all we encounter.
Enlivened by a new awareness
  we are moved to consider change.*

G roups and their members seldom stay the same. The enthusiasm that is prevalent in the initial group meeting, for instance, usually wanes by the second or third meeting, and participants may experience a letdown. This type of behavior is to be expected. Another predictable development is the movement of members from talking about past history to concentrating on the "here and now." The movement to an emphasis on the present may not occur without guidance from the leader, but in most groups, it takes place on two levels—the personal and the group as a whole (Sklare, Keener, & Mas, 1990; Yalom, 1985). It is this event, in which members are willing to risk more and move past the superficial, that signals the end of the forming stage and the beginning of transition.

The **transition stage** is the period after the forming process and prior to the working stage. In groups that last 12 to 15 sessions, this stage begins in the second or third group session and usually extends for one to three meetings. In other words, the transition stage in a group takes up an average of 5% to 20% of

*Source: Gladding, 1979, pp. 126–127. Copyright ACA. Reprinted by permission of the American Counseling Association.

the group's time. This stage, which is a two-part process, is characterized by the expression of a number of member emotions and interactions.

Transition begins with a **storming** period in which members start to compete with others in the group to find their place in the group. This unsettling aspect of the group involves struggles over power and control that may be both overt and covert (Carroll, 1986). Anxiety, resistance, defensiveness, conflict, confrontation, and transference are frequent feelings that surface at this time (Corey & Corey, 1992; Gladding, 1994a). If the group successfully weathers this turbulence, it moves on to a **norming** period in which there are resolutions, cohesiveness, and the opportunity to move forward in growth (Ward, 1982). The purpose of the group and the theoretical orientation of its leader influence the general ebb and flow of these processes, but the personalities and needs of members and their levels of trust, interest, and commitment also play a major part (Gordon & Liberman, 1971; Jacobs, Harvill, & Masson, 1994; Zimpfer, 1986). Because every group is unique, leaders and members have to pay special attention to group dynamics and personal feelings in order to maximize the benefits from these two experiences.

In this chapter, attention is concentrated on how the qualities displayed in the storming and norming periods of a group (i.e., the transition) are influenced (Tuckman, 1965; Tuckman & Jensen, 1977). Each group and group experience is different, but the development of the group involves the interdependence of task goals and interpersonal relationships (Napier & Gershenfeld, 1989). Characteristics associated with transitions in the group follow some general universal patterns whether they are stage (development) or theme (issue) oriented (Cohen & Smith, 1976; Vander Kolk, 1985). The overall patterns must be taken into consideration if the group is to effectively negotiate through this stage and eventually be productive. The two predictable processes in the group's transitions—storming and norming—have characteristics uniquely their own.

STORMING

Storming is a time of conflict and anxiety when the group moves from **primary tension** (awkwardness about being in a strange situation) to **secondary tension** (intragroup conflict) (Bormann, 1975). During this period, the group works out its "threshold for tension" and reaches a balance between too little and too much tension (see Figure 5.1). Group members and leaders struggle with issues related to structure, direction, control, catharsis, and interpersonal relationships (Hershenson & Power, 1987; Maples, 1988). Although frustration and noise increase during this substage, it is often a productive time as members work through past nonproductive ways of relating, create new repertoires, and establish their place in the group.

Each group experiences the storming process differently. Some may encounter all the problems associated with this period, whereas others may have few difficulties. A group may become arrested here by either dwelling on conflict or ignoring it (Forsyth, 1990) and never move on to the working stage of development. The group leader must help members recognize and deal with their

Figure 5.1
Primary and secondary tension in groups.

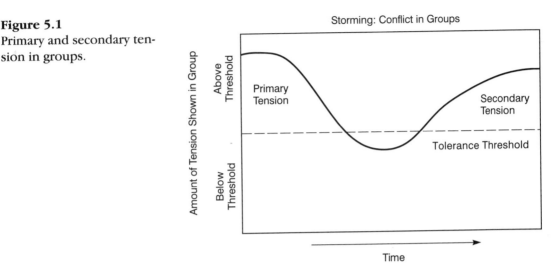

Source: From *Discussion and Group Methods: Theory and Practice,*
2nd ed. (p. 186) by E. G. Bormann, 1975, New York: Harper & Row.
Copyright 1975 by Harper & Row, New York. Reprinted by permission.

anxiety and resistance at this time (Gladding, 1994a; Mahler, 1969). Several features are central characteristics of storming, specifically those related to peer
relationships, resistance, and task processing.

Peer Relationships

During the storming period, group members are initially more anxious in their
interactions with each other. Their anxiety is related to the fear of losing control,
being misunderstood, looking foolish, or being rejected (Corey & Corey, 1992).
Some members avoid taking a risk by remaining silent at this time. On the other
hand, other members who want to establish their place in the group deal with
their anxiety by being more open and assertive (Bach, 1954; Yalom, 1985). For
instance, Cheryl may remain quiet during storming and simply observe the group
members' interactions. However, Tony may be verbally aggressive and express his
thoughts on every idea raised in the group.

The concern for power is also prevalent during storming. **Power** is "the capacity
to bring about certain intended consequences in the behavior of others" (Gardner,
1990, p. 55). The struggle for power occurs soon after group members have oriented
themselves to the group formation (Yalom, 1985). Attitudes toward power become
important because the ways in which group members deal with this issue influence
how conflictual or cooperative a group will become (Johnson & Johnson, 1991).

There are several forms of power within a group, for example, informational,
influential, and authoritative. **Informational power** is premised on the idea that

those who know more are able to exert control over situations, including those involving people. **Influential power** is based on the idea of persuasion and manipulation of others through convincing them that a certain course of action is correct. **Authoritative power** is predicated on social position or responsibility in an organization. Authoritative means, such as "pulling rank," may be employed to try to influence members of groups that include individuals of unequal status, such as in task/work groups.

The principles that operate in dealing with power are similar regardless of the type of power being expressed. At first, members will attempt to resolve power concerns in ways that resemble those they have used outside the group, for example, by fighting or fleeing. If these strategies work, they will continue to be employed. If not, new ways of handling potentially conflictual situations will be formulated. For example, when Tracy finds that yelling at other group members does not influence them to respect her, she may try one-to-one conversations, or she may try to persuade the group that she should be respected by telling members stories about what she has done in the past.

Members' attitudes about trusting the group and its leader are also an issue during storming. There is usually a good deal of mistrust in others during the storming period. Part of this mistrust is based on inexperience in dealing with the group. Another part of this mistrust involves resolving anxiety and power issues while moving from a superficial group toward becoming a unified one. Too much mistrust will hinder people in the group from becoming cohesive. However, blind trust that is uninformed by experience, such as telling group members intimate thoughts before one gets to know them fully, is also inappropriate.

Connected to the issues of anxiety, power, and trust among peers is the question of the quality of verbal interaction. Negative comments, judgments, and criticisms are frequent during storming as members deal with issues of control, conflict, and dominance in the establishment of a hierarchy (Maples, 1988; Schutz, 1971; Yalom, 1985). For instance, during the storming part of a counseling group, members may focus on the content of the message. In such situations, their responses would most likely be statements such as:

"I cannot understand why you allowed that to happen to you,"
"I don't think you were very smart in letting that occur," or
"If I were you, I would have . . . "

If all goes well during the storming period, group members come to understand themselves and each other better. They begin to develop empathy for one another, too. However, in order to make progress, the group must work collectively through its resistance to change.

Resistance

Resistance is best defined as any behavior that moves the group away from areas of discomfort, conflict, or potential growth. Resistance appears to increase especially during the early part of the storming period (Higgs, 1992). Forms of resistance are multidirected and aimed at

discussion material (e.g., "I don't want to talk about that"),
the leader (e.g., "You're the leader, you show me how to change"),
other members (e.g., "I think Jenny doesn't like me. I'm leaving"),
questions of control (e.g., "I don't feel safe in here and I'm not going to say anything until I do"), or
the group in general (e.g., "You guys are a bunch of losers. I don't have anything in common with you")

Group leaders who are unprepared for such experiences may be put on the defensive when this kind of behavior happens. In such situations, the group is thrown into chaos, and the leaders may feel personally attacked or insulted. When this behavior occurs, responses by members and leaders are usually in the form of anger and are unproductive. For example, Helen may say, "June, if you don't like this group and what is being discussed here you can quit and find another group." June may reply by yelling, "You are not in charge and have no right to tell me what to do!"

Some forms of resistance are more subtle than others. For example, group member behaviors may appear accepting on the surface but be resisting underneath. Among the most prevalent forms of subtle *indirect resistance* are the following:

Intellectualization—This behavior is characterized by an emphasis on abstraction with a minimal amount of affect or emotion (Clark, 1992). The person uses thoughts and a sophisticated vocabulary to avoid dealing with personal feelings. Such a process helps the member become detached from the group. For example, a psychotherapy group member displaying intellectualization might say to the group in general, "Many people think they are being threatened when others disagree with them." Unless this comment contains some personal feelings, such as "I feel that this group is rejecting me when members disagree with me," it is hard to make a meaningful response.

Questioning—In interpersonal relationships, a question is often a disguise for a statement (Benjamin, 1981). If members are constantly questioning each other, they are safe from exposing their true selves. Questions also keep the group focused on why something occurred in the past and thereby prevent members from concentrating on what is happening now. In a resistant counseling group, members may use questions such as, "Do we really have to talk about how we feel?" or "How come John is not saying as much as Susan about his past group experience?"

In order to counter questions, group leaders need to take corrective actions. One of the best strategies is for leaders to ask members to use the word "I" before beginning a sentence, such as "I feel nervous." A complementary strategy is for leaders to simply say to the group, "Since most questions are really statements, I wonder if each of you would rephrase your query as such?" (Sklare et al., 1990). Thus, in the examples just given, statements would be: "I do not want to talk about my feelings" and "I wish John would say as much as Susan about his past group experience." Through such approaches, members and the group as a whole are invited to examine their thoughts and feelings in a productive way.

Advice giving—This behavior involves instructing someone on what to do in a particular situation. Advice is seldom appropriate or needed in most groups (Sack, 1985). It prevents members from struggling with their own feelings and keeps the advice giver from having to recognize shortcomings in his or her own life. In a resistant group member, advice may be general or specific, but it is usually not helpful. For example, Jan may say to Wanda, "I think what you need to do is to exercise more. Until you feel better about your body, you will never feel good about yourself." This advice may have merit, but because the members do not know each other well at this time, it will probably be seen as criticism and separate the individuals involved even further apart than they were.

Band-aiding—This cleverly named concept involves the misuse of support. It is the process of preventing others from fully expressing their emotional pain through ventilating their feelings, i.e., catharsis. Band-aiders soothe wounds and alleviate feelings when just the opposite would be more appropriate. For example, in a psychotherapy group, Ralph may try to calm Jason physically and psychologically when Jason is shouting about the way he was treated by his parents. If Ralph succeeds in his effort, he prevents Jason from releasing his feelings and thereby dealing with them. Jason may then continue to be angry and, at times, project his emotions onto others. This may result in extending the storming period of the group.

Dependency—Group members who display dependent behavior encourage advice givers and band-aiders. They present themselves as helpless and incapable but refuse to listen to feedback. They are "help-rejecting complainers" (Yalom, 1985). For example, Joyce may say to Tom, "What would you do in my situation? You are more experienced than I am. I need your help." If Tom responds, neither he nor Joyce are helped because Joyce becomes more dependent on Tom, and the two begin to relate as unequals in a one-up/one-down position.

Other forms of resistance are more direct and potentially more destructive.

Monopolizing. **Monopolizing** occurs when a person or persons within the group dominate the group's time through excessive talking or activity. Often their conversation or behavior is irrelevant to the group's task. At other times, their points are pertinent but so full of unimportant details or movement that the group is unable to process what they have heard. In any case, this form of resistance keeps the group from working on either individual or group projects.

Monopolizers may be helped by (a) confronting them, (b) teaching them new skills to deal with anxiety (such as progressive relaxation), and/or (c) giving them feedback on how their old or new behaviors affect interpersonal communications (Krieg, 1988; Yalom, 1985). In some cases, the group leader may display a hand signal to the monopolizer to remind him or her that they are monopolizing and need to change behaviors.

Attack on the Leader.   This is probably the most direct form of resistance that causes groups difficulty. Many theories view an **attack on the group leader** as "an opportunity to shape new norms and enhance group movement" (Donigian & Malnati, 1987, p. 213). Regardless, it is vital that the group leader does not ignore an attack. Sometimes attacks are justified, especially if the group leader has been insensitive to the needs of members. However, such is not always the case.

Processes that contribute to leader attacks in almost all groups are subgrouping, fear of intimacy, and extra-group socializing. For example, if subgroups develop in the group, isolated thoughts and ideas may germinate in regard to the leader's competence. It does not take long for such negative thoughts to surface and be expressed. These difficulties and attacks can be prevented if members are screened, there is pregroup training, and if rules for the group are clearly defined in the beginning. For example, in a psychotherapy group, Zack may be asked to wait to participate in the next group being offered because he appears unable to think through situations by himself. When the leader has doubts about whether someone is ready for a group, it is probably better to err on the side of caution and deny the person a particular group experience.

When an attack on the leader comes, however, it must be addressed and dealt with immediately. Otherwise, the group will become unsafe for any risk-taking behavior and will disintegrate into a series of attack sessions in which members feel threatened and drop out (Yalom, 1985). In other words, *perpetual storming* will prevail. One of the best strategies for group leaders to use in dealing with attacks is to face them directly and attempt to determine the underlying variables that have led to them, such as unresolved feelings. It is best that the leader do this in a nondefensive and open manner. For example, if Ben is being attacked for not creating a safe and trusting atmosphere, he may state, "As I listen to what you are saying, I am aware that you would like for me to do more. I would like to know what you have specifically in mind. I would also like to know how you would like others in the group to act so that you would feel safer and more trusting."

Task Processing

During the storming period, **task processing** (i.e., ways of accomplishing specific goals) appears to regress. No longer do members or leaders concentrate as directly on objectives as they did at the beginning of the group. Rather, there is a great deal of attention on personal matters, such as group safety, leader competence, trust, and ways of interacting. It is healthy that this "pause" in the group takes place, for it allows everyone the opportunity of reevaluating goals and directions. More importantly, it provides a chance for group participants to "look" before they "leap" toward the process of change.

A potential problem in this suspension of effort to accomplish a task is that someone in the group may be blamed, or scapegoated, for the group's lack of achievement (Rugel, 1991). To **scapegoat** is to project the group's problems onto a single individual instead of the group taking responsibility for creating and resolving its difficulties. If such an event occurs, the group spends additional time and energy working on interpersonal issues that must be resolved before the group as a whole can get back on task. It is crucial that members and leaders take responsibility for their own actions at this point in the life of the group. For example, in response to Marc being blamed by several group members for present problems, Jean may say, "I think the situation we are currently in is the result of more than one person's actions. We have all contributed in our own unique ways to this situation. If we are going to help each other, we need to explore what we have done up to this point and try to do some things differently."

If members can be helped by the leader and each other to express their feelings in relationship to individual or collective goals, scapegoating is less likely to happen, and greater awareness will most likely evolve (Saidla, 1990). This process is helpful in the eventual achievement of selective tasks and the healthy growth of the group and its members.

Working Through Storming

Several methods for working through particular forms of problematic intrapersonal and interpersonal group issues during storming have already been mentioned. However, there are global and uniform means of helping the group as a body during this time as well. One way to help group members work through their feelings in storming is to use the process of **leveling** where members are encouraged to interact freely and evenly (Kline, 1990; Kottler, 1994). In leveling, group members who are under-participating are drawn out by the leader, and those who are excessively active are helped to understand the impact of their actions through group feedback. For instance, if Tonya is always making a comment after each group member voices a concern or makes a statement, the leader may intervene by saying, "Tonya, do you realize how your active participation in the group affects other members' abilities to get involve?" If Tonya does not acknowledge any awareness, the leader may ask the group to help Tonya become more sensitive to how her actions are preventing others from becoming involved in the group. A slightly different strategy would work for Al who is not speaking up in the group. An open invitation by the group leader might be, "Al, we have not heard from you today. What's on your mind?" If leveling works well, there is a modification in the verbal behavior within the group so that members participate evenly. By having everyone in the group interact, issues that have the potential to cause conflict may surface and be resolved sooner.

Another method for working through storming is for group members to acknowledge it is occurring. If group leaders or group members deny that the group is in unrest or even in conflict, confusion will arise in the group. In addition, members will not trust themselves, take risks, or believe the leader. In most groups, members can handle honesty better than they can handle denial or deception (Gladding, 1994a). They may agree with Walter who says, "I wish you guys would get your acts together so we can move on toward working on our goals." Yet, by facing the fact that storming is happening, members and leaders know what they are up against and can thereby give themselves permission to be less frustrated and display greater tolerance of what is happening. Acknowledgment also enables members to make plans and develop a greater sensitivity to the situation so that it can be improved.

A final global way of dealing with the storming part of transition is to get feedback from members on how they are doing and what they think needs to be done (Ponzo, 1991). The process of **feedback** can take place in a formal or informal way. Using **informal feedback**, the leader may ask members to give their reactions to a group session in an unstructured way at any time they wish. Such an invitation is likely to increase spontaneity and sensitivity. For instance, Bettie may say, "Oh, I just realized something I'm doing. Every time Patricia talks, I tune her out. She reminds me of someone in my life I had real trouble with. Yet, just now, Patricia, I heard your comments about your own pain, and I suddenly became aware that you are your own person." **Formal feedback** is structured. It may be set up, for example, through the use of a *time-limited round* at any appropriate point in the group. In this type of round, each individual has the same amount of time, usually one or two minutes each, to say whatever he or she wishes. Through using a time-limited round, everyone gets equal "air time," and the views of the group as a whole are heard.

Results of Working Through Storming

When the group works through storming, especially in regard to resistance, the group will be characterized by members making emotional space for each other and being accommodating to one another. Additional changes will include "more plain talk, open risk taking, overt agendas, increased intimacy, greater appreciation for one another, more intense emotions, and an emphasis on the present" (Ormont, 1988, p. 44). Members may also decide to revise their goals or alter their style of interpersonal relationships as a result of working through storming.

Altering interpersonal relationship style is especially important to the future development of the group. Often members enter a group with a limited response range. For example, in the area of conflict management, members may only know or feel comfortable using one or two of five dominant **conflict-management orientations** (i. e., competing, accommodating, collaborating, sharing, or avoiding) (Thomas & Kilmann, 1974). This limited range of responses may restrict their ability to relate to all members of the group. Such a case would occur if Kenneth constantly challenged other members of his work group to "put up or shut up." By altering their style of conflict management, members increase their flexibility and increase the probability that the conflicts they have with other members will have a more positive than negative outcome (e.g., provide vivid feedback, motivate individuals to search for creative alternatives) (Mitchell & Mitchell, 1984) (see Figure 5.2).

Figure 5.2
Five conflict-handling modes.

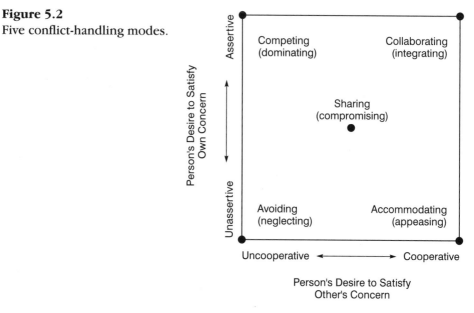

Source: From "Constructive Management of Conflict in Groups" by R. C. Mitchell and R. R. Mitchell, 1984, *Journal for Specialists in Group Work, 9,* p. 141. Copyright ACA. Reprinted by permission of the American Counseling Association.

Different types of groups will vary in the length and depth of their experience in storming and the amount of conflict they may have (Jacobs et al., 1994). For psychotherapy groups, the impact of the storming period on the group itself will be greater and last longer than for psychoeducational groups. In fact, psychoeducational groups are usually low in interpersonal conflict, and the amount of time that such conflict occurs is relatively brief if it occurs at all. Psychotherapy groups, on the other hand, are generally intense, and the storming period can be quite long. Regardless of the time and intensity, storming provides a time for group members to become realistic and active in examining their goals and working out relationships in their interactions with others. For most groups, the interdependency among group members and the stability of the group as a whole cannot deepen until intragroup hostility has surfaced, been acknowledged, and dealt with (Bennis & Shepard, 1956). Therefore, the work done during storming is the foundation on which most groups will be built (Mahler, 1969).

NORMS AND NORMING

There is both a distinction and a relationship between the concept of norms and the group experience of norming. **Norms** are expectations about group members' behaviors that should or should not take place (Forsyth, 1990). "Group norms function to regulate the performance of a group as an organized unit, keeping it on the course of its objectives" (Napier & Gershenfeld, 1989, pp. 117–118). Words that are commonly associated with norms are "ought, should, must, or better" (Shepherd, 1964, p. 123). In some groups, especially those that are open ended, group norms may be unclear, confusing, ambiguous, arbitrary, and restrictive. In most groups, however, norms are clear and "are constructed both from expectations of the members for their group and from the explicit and implicit directions of the leader and more influential members" (Yalom, 1985, p. 117). Therefore, most norms are based on input from everyone involved in the group and ensure group predictability and survival.

At the beginning of a group, norms may not be as clear or as well defined as later in the life of the group. As the group develops, group members and leaders become more aware of the verbal and nonverbal rules they wish to follow to achieve their goals (Vander Kolk, 1985). They also become better acquainted with one another.

Group norming is the feeling of "we-ness," identity, groupness, or cohesiveness that comes when individuals feel they belong to an association or organization larger than themselves. The process of "norming" is often characterized as one of the major aspects of groups (Tuckman, 1965; Tuckman & Jensen, 1977). Like storming, norming is a crucial part of the group process because it sets the pattern for the next stage: performing (i.e., working). In the norming period, there is often enthusiasm and cooperation (Hershenson & Power, 1987). In many ways, it parallels the forming stage in its emphasis on positive emotions. However, because group members are more informed and experienced with each other, they can concentrate on themselves and each other better in the group. Although some groups experience norming as a distinct stage in their development, others find the process continuously evolving. Two main aspects of norming are peer relations and task processing.

Peer Relations

During the norming period, several important changes occur in peer relationships. Among these are outlook and attitude. Group members usually have a positive attitude toward others in the group and the experience itself during norming. They feel a newfound sense of belongingness and groupness (Saidla, 1990). This positive mindset is likely to result in learning, insight, and feelings of support and acceptance. Members are willing to give of themselves and are committed to taking needed actions. They expect to be successful (Gazda, 1989). Peer interactions are manifested through identification, here-and-now experiences, hope, cooperation, collaboration, and cohesion.

Identification.   A sense of **identification** is a "normal" developmental process in which individuals see themselves as being similar to one another (Freud, 1949).

For example, in a counseling group, Allison and Lynn may come to realize they have many similar tastes, from food to clothes to reading materials. Identification explains why group members often become emotionally attached to their leaders and give them power. It also explains why many strong friendships begin as a result of working in a group. Identification must be taken into account when considering the behavior of groups of all sizes. Those groups in which there is more identification with the leader or other members will be more cohesive and less resistant to change than those that are not. In norming, identification with others grows.

Existential Variables.   Although group progress can be charted on a session-by-session basis, the best way to help individuals and the group make progress is to deal with immediate feelings and interactions, i.e., existential variables. Conflict, withdrawal, support, dominance, and change all need to be acknowledged as they occur. Feelings from ecstasy to depression also must be addressed as they surface. Group leaders and members can link the present with past trends, but it is crucial that behaviors and emotions be recognized and worked on when they arise (Kelman, 1963). Some individual and group experiences will focus on what Yalom (1985) describes as personal issues about one's own life and death; others will be directed at obtaining specific goals, such as learning to accept others who differ or finding new ways to interact with members of the opposite sex that are appropriate (Carkhuff, 1971; Rose, 1982; Watson & Tharp, 1981).

Hope.   The experience of **hope** occurs on both a cognitive and emotional level in groups. Cognitively, hope is the belief that what is desired is also possible and that events will turn out for the best. Emotionally, hope is the feeling that what one believes will occur. The importance of hope is that it energizes group members and the group as a whole. Furthermore, hope helps groups envision meaningful, but not yet realized, possibilities (Gladding, 1994b).

In norming, groups and their members need to hope and usually do so. Psychotherapeutic group members may hope, for instance, that they have the courage to overcome past tragedies, whereas counseling group members may hope they can purposefully plan a future different from their past. Work/task group members may also express hope in combining their talents so that new products can be marketed. Likewise, psychoeducational group members may hope they can learn to integrate new life skills into their daily lives.

Cooperation.   **Cooperation** is when group members work together for a common purpose or good. During norming, group participants become relaxed and work better together. The vying for position, so prevalent in storming, diminishes. In some task/work groups, cooperation increases because there is increased awareness of a group goal and members realize more fully what each can do for the other (Johnson & Johnson, 1991). In psychotherapeutic groups, cooperation is often the result of better understanding and communication worked out in the storming period. In such cases, it is based on a hope for change (Weiner, 1984).

Collaboration.   **Collaboration** goes hand in glove with cooperation. Members who think they can work in a harmonious, cooperative manner are likely to share facts and feelings about themselves and other matters with other group members, i.e., they collaborate. Furthermore, they are prone to work together with other group members in sharing a vision and in making that goal a reality. Collaboration is probably seen most clearly in work/task groups where members have a tangible product on which to work. However, in counseling groups, collaboration is also expressed when members assist one member in obtaining a personal goal even when there is no observable reward for the rest of the group.

Cohesion. The last factor in the interpersonal process of norming, **cohesion,** has received a great deal of attention. Cohesion can be thought of as a sense of "groupness" or "we-ness." Groups that establish such a spirit (and keep it) run harmoniously. When group cohesiveness develops, the group functions as a unit. Morale, trust, and solidarity increase, as do actions involving self-disclosure. The "chief concern" of the group at this time "is with intimacy and closeness" (Yalom, 1985, p. 309). In a cohesive atmosphere, emotional closeness becomes acceptable.

There is a difference between "total group cohesiveness and individual member cohesiveness (or, more strictly, the individual's attraction to the group)" (Yalom, 1985, p. 49). Yet, there is often a positive correlation between the two with members of groups attracted to a particular group contributing to it. Group and individual cohesion can be measured by behaviors such as attendance, punctuality, risk taking, self-disclosure, and dropout rates (Hansen, Warner, & Smith, 1980). Cohesive groups are more effective in their communication patterns, and members communicate with each other frequently. Cohesive groups also appear to have considerable fun together and yet are achievement oriented, especially on difficult tasks (Johnson & Johnson, 1991). They are able to express their hostilities and conflicts openly and come to some resolutions.

The advantages and limitations of group cohesion are notable. On the positive side, it has generally been demonstrated that members of cohesive groups "(1) are more productive; (2) are more open to influence by other group members; (3) experience more security; (4) are more able to express hostility and adhere more closely to group norms; (5) attempt to influence others more frequently; and (6) continue membership in the group longer" (Bednar & Lawlis, 1971, pp. 822–823).

However, cohesion can be problematic. Among the potential problems with cohesion is that group participants may decide they like the positive atmosphere so much that they are unwilling to talk about anything that might be upsetting. In such groups, harmony is stressed over everything, and a type of **pseudo-acceptance** (i.e., false acceptance) prevails. This type of atmosphere prevents anxiety (Miles, 1957), but it keeps the group from progressing. Groups that finally settle down into the performing or working stage are those that can discuss negative, as well as positive, material.

Task Processing

One main task objective in the norming stage is for members to reach an agreement on the establishment of *norms,* that is, rules and standards from which to operate the group. Some norming is done on a nonverbal, mostly unconscious, level, but other aspects of norming are conducted verbally. Through norms, group members learn to regulate, evaluate, and coordinate their actions (Gibbs, 1965). Groups typically accept both *prescriptive norms,* which describe the kinds of behaviors that should be performed, and *proscriptive norms,* which describe the kinds of behaviors that are to be avoided (Forsyth, 1990).

Norms are value laden and give a degree of predictability to the group that would not be there otherwise (Luft, 1984). Often, they evolve so gradually that they are never questioned until violated. Basically, norms allow the group to begin to work, although not all norms are productive (Wilson & Hanna, 1986).

Another main, task-related goal of the norming group is **commitment** (Maples, 1988). The commitment is to the group as a whole and its rules, as well as to individual goals. The group and its members begin to operate on a higher level than previously when commitment is a central part of the group. Eventually, participants come to "evaluate their performances and the performances of others in terms of accomplishment of the group's goals" (Napier & Gershenfeld, 1989, p. 204). This sense of commitment carries over and intertwines with the group at work (Schutz, 1958). It is at this point the group and its members can begin to see the tangible results from their dreams and efforts. Groups where members are most committed to each other are more likely than not to be productive in achieving tasks, as well as successful in feeling good about the group experience.

Examining Aspects of Norming

Norming is generally characterized in terms of behaviors and feelings expressed by group members toward each other. Although it is difficult to measure the impact of emotion on the group, there are ways of examining behaviors during this period that are both concrete and scientific. One way involves peer relationships. This method uses a research-based theory of personality and group dynamics that is referred to by the acronym **SYMLOG** (System for the Multiple Level Observation of Groups) (Bales, 1980; Bales, Cohen, & Williamson, 1979) (see Figure 5.3).

The SYMLOG model yields a field diagram that pictures how members of a group are rated on three dimensions: dominance versus submissiveness, friendliness versus unfriendliness, and instrumentally versus emotionally expressive. In addition, it yields a total of 26 roles found in groups. One way to use this instrument is to rate each group member's tendency to engage in any of the 26 roles on the instrument and then to summarize the scores along the three dimensions already described. For instance, an industrialist such as Lee Iacocca might be classified as UF (assertive and businesslike) whereas a talk-show host such as David Letterman might be UPB (entertaining, sociable, smiling, and warm). By using SYMLOG, the interactional dynamics and personality of the group can be better understood because the homogeneous or heterogeneous nature of the group is clearer.

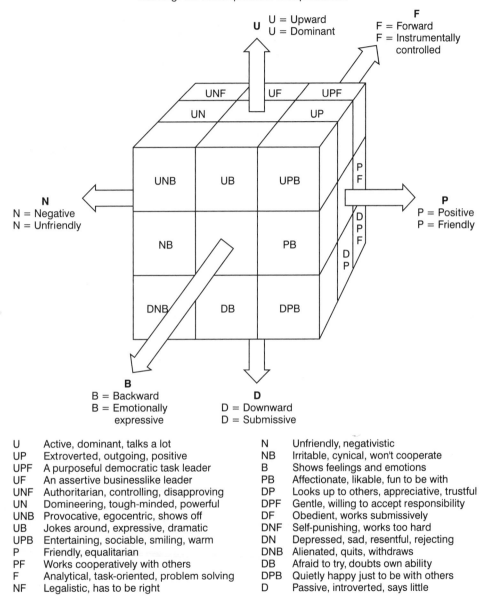

Norming: The Development of Group Structure

U = Upward
U = Dominant

F = Forward
F = Instrumentally controlled

N = Negative
N = Unfriendly

P = Positive
P = Friendly

B = Backward
B = Emotionally expressive

D = Downward
D = Submissive

U Active, dominant, talks a lot	N Unfriendly, negativistic
UP Extroverted, outgoing, positive	NB Irritable, cynical, won't cooperate
UPF A purposeful democratic task leader	B Shows feelings and emotions
UF An assertive businesslike leader	PB Affectionate, likable, fun to be with
UNF Authoritarian, controlling, disapproving	DP Looks up to others, appreciative, trustful
UN Domineering, tough-minded, powerful	DPF Gentle, willing to accept responsibility
UNB Provocative, egocentric, shows off	DF Obedient, works submissively
UB Jokes around, expressive, dramatic	DNF Self-punishing, works too hard
UPB Entertaining, sociable, smiling, warm	DN Depressed, sad, resentful, rejecting
P Friendly, equalitarian	DNB Alienated, quits, withdraws
PF Works cooperatively with others	DB Afraid to try, doubts own ability
F Analytical, task-oriented, problem solving	DPB Quietly happy just to be with others
NF Legalistic, has to be right	D Passive, introverted, says little

Figure 5.3

The SYMLOG model.

Source: Reprinted with the permission of The Free Press, a Division of Simon & Schuster from *SYMLOG: A Case Study Kit* by Robert F. Bales. Copyright © 1980 by The Free Press.

Promoting Norming

Norming can be promoted through actions by either the group leader or group members. Several human relations and specific group skills can be utilized in this process. Chief among these skills are supporting, empathizing, facilitating, and self-disclosure.

Supporting.   **Supporting** is the act of encouraging and reinforcing others. Its aim is to convey to persons that they are perceived as adequate, capable, and trustworthy. Through the act of supporting, group members feel affirmed and are able to risk new behaviors because they sense a backing from the group. The result is often creative and surprising actions that are novel and positive. For example, in a counseling group, Trip (speaking for the group) may say to Burgess, "I, and we as a group, really think you can be more assertive in letting your spouse know what you want." The results are that Burgess comes into the group the following week and presents a one-person play called "How to Be Assertive" in which she humorously, yet sensitively, shows how she used the group's support to ask her husband for what she wanted.

Empathizing.   **Empathizing** means putting oneself in another's place in regard to subjective perception and emotion and yet keeping one's objectivity (Brammer, 1993). It demands a suspension of judgment and a response to another person that conveys sensitivity and understanding. Again, during the norming period, expressing empathy takes on special significance. Members need to listen to both the verbal and nonverbal messages of others in the group and be responsive. For instance, in a psychotherapy group, Nancy may say to Fred, "It seems to me you are sad. Your voice is low, and your eyes are focused on the floor." Such a message reflects an understanding of another person's voice and body signals and opens up potential dialogue and problem-solving avenues.

Facilitating.   The act of facilitation is one that involves using clear and direct communication channels between individuals. It is an activity usually assumed by a group leader, although members of the group may engage in this process at select times. Part of facilitation is to make sure messages are sent and received accurately. The leader may say, for instance, "Tammy, when Mark said he was glad you had resolved your differences, you looked a bit perplexed. I wonder what you were thinking?" In this case, Tammy may shrug off the suggestion that anything was bothering her, or she may confess that it feels unusual for her not to be at odds with Mark. In either case, Mark, Tammy, and the group as a whole get the benefit of making sure these two group members are feeling connected so that underlying problems do not arise later to the detriment of the group as a whole.

Self-Disclosure.   One of the strongest signs of trust in a group is **self-disclosure,** i.e., revealing to group members information about oneself of which they were previously unaware (Jourard, 1971). Self-disclosure is enhanced when members feel safe. Through self-disclosure, barriers that inhibit communication between individuals are torn down. A sense of community and camaraderie is established. Leaders may model disclosure behaviors in order to show what materials should be revealed and how. It is best to first disclose materials related to individuals and experiences in the group. Through such a process, members' bonds become stronger.

Results of Norming

If the process of norming goes well, the group will be ready for the next step in its developmental process—working. Members will feel connected with the group and will be able to concentrate on being productive rather than protecting themselves. Just as Maslow's (1962) hierarchy of personal needs builds from the basics on up, such is also the case in groups. When members feel secure and linked with others, they are free to begin cooperating and coordinating their efforts in achieving specific goals.

Norming gives group members guidelines under which to operate. They are, therefore, able to gauge how well they are doing individually and as a group. If there is discomfort in the group, members may realize that they and/or the group as a whole are regressing instead of progressing. It is from the baseline of norming that the group is measured or referenced.

Overall, norming has the effect of helping members in the group feel good about themselves and the group as a whole. Norming is like a breath of fresh air after the turmoil of successfully resolving the difficulties of the storming period. Norming allows members to clear their minds, reassess their goals from a realistic perspective, feel good about themselves and the group's progress, and make new plans for the working stage of the group. Such processes help group members and groups as a whole renew their efforts toward achievement.

SUMMARY AND CONCLUSION

The transition stage of groups is multifaceted and complex. If it is successful, this stage will be a takeoff point for the work of the group. Ideally, in the two-part transition stage, group members resolve conflict through a stormy but predictable period, i.e., storming, and are able to set up and follow rules (i.e., norms) as well as form a cohesive bond with each other (norming). In such cases, the group ends the transition stage ready to get down to work collectively and personally and be productive.

In practice, groups are unique and differ in the way they develop because of their members, leaders, climates, and goals. A number of procedures can be enacted to facilitate the group's development and that of its members during this time. Some of these activities are as simple as recognizing what is happening, i.e., promoting awareness. Others are more complicated and require that the leader learn appropriate skills and/or enlist members' help and participation, e.g., empathy and support.

In this chapter, common aspects and problems of the transition stage of group work have been discussed, particularly in regard to personal and task-related consequences. In the processes of storming and norming, group leaders and members must be cognizant and emotionally attuned at all times to each other's intrapersonal and interactional patterns. If the overall outcome of groups is to be productive, individuals and the group as a whole must make a transition from the more superficial stage of forming to the more demanding stage of working. To do so, they must learn to relate to each other as well as to plans and purposes.

CLASSROOM EXERCISES

1. Under the direction of your classroom instructor, have group members enact resistant roles, for example, withdrawing, monopolizing, attacking the group leader, and so on. After about 15 minutes of role playing, ask group members what they think would be helpful to them in overcoming resistance to specific situations. Discuss their ideas and the ideas of the class as a whole in regard to dealing with resistance.

2. Discuss with a classmate and then with the class as a whole how you would promote cohesion as a group leader. Refer to different techniques mentioned in this chapter as well as to other ideas or procedures you think would be beneficial.

3. What types of self-disclosure have you seen in groups to which you have belonged? What impact did these revelations have on you? Discuss your experiences in a group of four. Then talk about how the act of self-disclosure differs for individuals in task/work groups as opposed to counseling, psychotherapy, and psychoeducational groups.

4. What part do you think hope and commitment play in the storming aspect of the transition stage of group work? What other factors have you seen successfully employed in helping individuals reach a settlement of conflict or differences? Discuss with two other members of the class and then the class as a whole your ideas and experiences in this regard.

REFERENCES

Bach, G. (1954). *Intensive group psychotherapy.* New York: Ronald Press.

Bales, R. F. (1980). *SYMLOG: A case study kit.* New York: Free Press.

Bales, R. F., Cohen, S. P., & Williamson, S. A. (1979). *SYMLOG: A system for the multiple level observation of groups.* New York: Free Press.

Bednar, R. L., & Lawlis, G. F. (1971). Empirical research in group psychotherapy. In S. L. Garfield & A. Bergin (Eds.), *Handbook of psychotherapy and behavior change* (pp. 812–838). New York: Wiley.

Benjamin, A. (1981). *The helping interview* (3rd ed.). Boston: Houghton Mifflin.

Bennis, W. G., & Shepard, H. A. (1956). A theory of group development. *Human Relations, 9,* 415–437.

Bormann, E. G. (1975). *Discussion and group methods: Theory and practice* (2nd ed.). New York: Harper & Row.

Brammer, L. M. (1993). *The helping relationship* (5th ed.). Boston: Allyn & Bacon.

Carkhoff, R. (1971). *Helping and human relations* (Vols. 1 & 2). New York: Holt, Rinehart & Winston.

Carroll, M. R. (1986). *Group work: Leading in the here and now* [Film]. Alexandria, VA: American Counseling Association.

Clark, A. J. (1992). Defense mechanisms in group counseling. *Journal for Specialists in Group Work, 17,* 151–160.

Cohen, A. M., & Smith, R. D. (1976). *Critical incidents in growth groups: Theory and techniques.* La Jolla, CA: University Associates.

Corey, M. S., & Corey, G. (1992). *Groups: Process and practice* (4th ed.). Pacific Grove, CA: Brooks/Cole.

Donigian, J., & Malnati, R. (1987). *Critical incidents in group therapy.* Pacific Grove, CA: Brooks/Cole.

Forsyth, D. R. (1990). *Group dynamics* (2nd ed.). Monterey, CA: Brooks/Cole.

Freud, S. (1949). *Group psychology and the analysis of the ego.* New York: Hogarth.

Gardner, J. W. (1990). *On leadership.* New York: The Free Press.

Gazda, G. M. (1989). *Group counseling: A developmental approach* (4th ed.). Boston: Allyn & Bacon.

Gibbs, J. (1965). Norms: The problems of definition and classification. *American Journal of Sociology, 70,* 586–594.

Gladding, S. T. (1979). A restless presence: Group process as a pilgrimage. *School Counselor, 27,* 126–127.

Gladding, S. T. (1994a). *Effective group counseling.* Greensboro, NC: ERIC/CASS.

Gladding, S. T. (1994b, January). The place of hope in the group. Presentation at the Second ASGW National Conference, St Petersburg, FL.

Gordon, M., & Liberman, N. (1971). Group psychotherapy: Being and becoming. *Personnel and Guidance Journal, 49,* 611–617.

Hansen, J. C., Warner, R. W., & Smith, E. J. (1980). *Group counseling: Theory and process* (2nd ed.). Chicago: Rand McNally.

Hershenson, D. B., & Power, P. W. (1987). *Mental health counseling.* New York: Pergamon Press.

Higgs, J. A. (1992). Dealing with resistance: Strategies for effective group. *Journal for Specialists in Group Work, 17,* 67–73.

Jacobs, E. E., Harvill, R. L., & Masson, R. L. (1994). *Group counseling: Strategies and skills* (2nd ed.). Pacific Grove, CA: Brooks/Cole.

Johnson, D. W., & Johnson, F. P. (1991). *Joining together* (4th ed.). Englewood Cliffs, NJ: Prentice Hall.

Jourard, S. M. (1971). *The transparent self* (2nd ed.). New York: Van Nostrand.

Kelman, H. C. (1963). The role of the group in the induction of therapeutic change. *International Journal of Group Psychotherapy, 13,* 399–442.

Kline, W. B. (1990). Responding to "problem" members. *Journal for Specialists in Group Work, 15,* 195–200.

Kottler, J. A. (1994). *Advanced group leadership.* Pacific Grove, CA: Brooks/Cole.

Krieg, F. J. (1988). *Group leadership training and supervision manual for adolescent group counseling in schools* (3rd ed.). Muncie, IN: Accelerated Development.

Luft, J. (1984). *Group processes* (3rd ed.). Palo Alto, CA: Mayfield.

Mahler, C. A. (1969). *Group counseling in the schools.* Boston: Houghton Mifflin.

Maples, M. F. (1988). Group development: Extending Tuckman's theory. *Journal for Specialists in Group Work, 13,* 17–23.

Maslow, A. H. (1962). *Toward a psychology of being.* Princeton, NJ: Van Nostrand.

Miles, M. B. (1957). Human relations training: How a group grows. *Teachers College Record, 55,* 90–96.

Mitchell, R. C., & Mitchell, R. R. (1984). Constructive management of conflict in groups. *Journal for Specialists in Group Work, 9,* 137–144.

Napier, R. W., & Gershenfeld, M. K. (1989). *Groups: Theory and experience* (4th ed.). Boston: Houghton Mifflin.

Ormont, L. R. (1988). The leader's role in resolving resistances to intimacy in the group setting. *International Journal of Group Psychotherapy, 38,* 29–45.

Ponzo, Z. (1991). Critical factors in group work: Clients' perceptions. *Journal for Specialists in Group Work, 16,* 16–23.

Rose, S. D. (1982). Group counseling with children: A behavioral and cognitive approach. In G. M. Gazda (Ed.), *Basic approaches to group psychotherapy and group counseling* (3rd ed.). Springfield, IL: Charles C. Thomas.

Rugel, R. P. (1991). Closed and open systems: The Tavistock group from a general system perspective. *Journal for Specialists in Group Work, 16,* 74–84.

Sack, R. T. (1985). On giving advice. *AMHCA Journal, 7,* 127–132.

Saidla, D. D. (1990). Cognitive development and group stages. *Journal for Specialists in Group Work, 15,* 15–20.

Schutz, W. (1958). *FIRO: A three dimensional theory of interpersonal behavior.* New York: Rinehart.

Schutz, W. C. (1971). *Here comes everybody.* New York: Harper & Row.

Shepherd, C. R. (1964). *Small groups.* Scranton, PA: Chandler.

Sklare, G., Keener, R., & Mas, C. (1990). Preparing members for "here-and-now" group counseling. *Journal for Specialists in Group Work, 15,* 141–148.

Thomas, K. W., & Kilmann, R. H. (1974). *Thomas-Kilmann Conflict Mode Instrument.* Tuxedo, NY: XICOM.

Tuckman, B. (1965). Developmental sequence in small group. *Psychological Bulletin, 63,* 384–399.

Tuckman, B. W., & Jensen, M. A. (1977). Stages of small group development revisited. *Group and Organizational Studies, 2,* 419–427.

Vander Kolk, C. J. (1985). *Introduction to group counseling and psychotherapy.* Columbus, OH: Merrill.

Ward, D. E. (1982). A model for the more effective use of theory in group work. *Journal for Specialists in Group Work, 7,* 224–230.

Watson, D. L., & Tharp, R. G. (1981). *Self-directed behavior: Self-modification for personal adjustment* (3rd ed.). Pacific Grove, CA: Brooks/Cole.

Weiner, M. F. (1984). *Techniques of group psychotherapy.* Washington, DC: American Psychiatric Press.

Wilson, G. L., & Hanna, M. S. (1986). *Groups in context.* New York: Random House.

Yalom, I. D. (1985). *The theory and practice of group psychotherapy* (3rd ed.). New York: Basic Books.

Zimpfer, D. G. (1986). Planning for groups based on their developmental phases. *Journal for Specialists in Group Work, 11,* 180–187.

CHAPTER 6

The Working Stage in a Group

In the calmness of reflection
    we examine the depths of our lives
        and the purposes for which we have come together.
I am amazed that out of silence
    and through a sharing of support
        a whole new group has evolved.
In the process of working
    we have welded an identity
        from where we shall stand
            and likewise be moved.*

Members of successful, ongoing groups usually undergo a number of adjustments and changes before they begin to work. However, after a group makes the transition from forming to resolving conflicts and norming, the **working stage** begins. This stage focuses on the achievement of individual and group goals and the movement of the group itself into a more unified and productive system (Maples, 1988).

The working stage of the group is also described as its "performing stage" (Tuckman & Jensen, 1977) and the "action stage" (George & Dustin, 1988). It is a time of problem solving which usually lasts longer than any of the other group stages. In groups of all types, somewhere between 40% to 60% of the total group time will be spent in the working stage. Task/work groups will generally spend a higher percentage of their time in this stage than will counseling, psychotherapy, or psychoeducational groups. The working stage is often regarded as the most productive stage in group development and is characterized by its constructive nature and the achievement of results.

*Source: Gladding, 1993.

During the working stage, group leaders and group members feel more free-dom and comfort in trying out new behaviors and strategies because the group is settled and issues, such as power and control, have been worked through enough for members to trust each other (Hansen, Warner, & Smith, 1980). At this stage in the group's development, "therapeutic forces" such as openness to self, others, and new ideas "are well-established" (Ohlsen, Horne, & Lawe, 1988, p. 88). The group, regardless of its purpose, displays a great amount of intimacy, self-disclosure, feedback, teamwork, confrontation, and humor, if it is healthy. These positive behaviors are expressed in interpersonal relationships among members, that is, in peer relations. Other behaviors of the group during this stage are primarily focused on task-related endeavors, such as achieving specific goals. Both peer- and task-related dimensions of a group in the working stage will be considered in this chapter along with generic core skills.

PEER RELATIONSHIPS

There appears to be genuine concern on a deep, personal level by members for each other in the working stage of most groups. Participants are more *intimate* after problems of control have been resolved (Schutz, 1973). Feelings of empa-thy, compassion, and care abound, and groups gradually grow closer emotionally. This bonding or cohesiveness usually increases, even in work/task groups, as group members interact and understand each other better. Emotional closeness is especially likely to grow if group members can identify with each other and have been successful in working through their struggles together. Whereas the previous two stages of the group were characterized by concerns of being *"in and out"* (i.e., forming, becoming a member of the group, as opposed to being an outsider) and *"top to bottom"* (i.e., transition, establishing one's place in the group structure), the working stage of the group focuses on *"near and far"* (Schutz, 1966). Participants establish how physically and psychologically close they wish to be to others and behave accordingly.

Along with positive feelings about the group and the constructive behaviors of its members comes a greater willingness to **self-disclose,** i.e., reveal informa-tion about oneself to the group. Society generally discourages self-disclosure (Jourard, 1971), and in some groups, such as task/work groups or psychoeduca-tional groups, members can sometimes be too open. For example, if members talk extensively about family secrets in psychoeducational groups, they most likely have overstepped appropriate limits. However, self-disclosure has a place in most groups.

Self-disclosure involves more than simply talking about oneself. It is a multi-dimensional activity. It involves listening and receiving feedback as well as speak-ing. It is related to many other factors such as the type of group in which one is in, the level of others' disclosures, group norms, and timing (Morran, 1982; Stockton & Morran, 1980; Wilson & Hanna, 1986).

The **Johari Awareness Model**, sometimes called the *Johari Window,* is a good representation of what happens in the arena of self-disclosure when a group is in the working stage (Luft, 1969). This model also illustrates how appropriate disclosure develops. The process occurs as shown in Figure 6.1.

The first quadrant (the **open quadrant**) is one that contains information that is generally known to self and others. For example, Flo knows that the group is aware that she chews her nails. In the working stage, this quadrant expands. Members learn names, stories, and likes/dislikes of other group members. With an expansion of knowledge, participants are able to interact more fully and freely with one another. Exchanges of thoughts and feelings move to a deeper and more personal level. What was previously hidden to others and even to oneself is now exposed and dealt with openly.

The second quadrant (the **hidden quadrant**) contains undisclosed information known only to oneself. During the working stage, this quadrant shrinks. The process by which this shrinkage occurs is through self-disclosure. For example, group members become aware of the experiences others have had, such as travel or study, that would not be apparent unless revealed. Members become increasingly comfortable with each other as a result of finding out more about each other. This comfort leads them to take further risks in revealing hidden secrets to the group as a whole. When this process happens, members who have opened up, and the group as a whole, are both freer to explore other personal and interpersonal dimensions of relationships that were previously limited to them.

The third quadrant (the **blind quadrant**) is originally unknown to oneself but known to others when the group began. For instance, Tom may be unaware that his face twitches slightly before he speaks in the group, but everyone else

Figure 6.1
Johari Window.

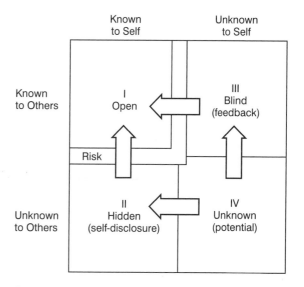

Source: From *Group Processes: An Introduction to Group Dynamics,* 3rd ed., by Joseph Luft, 1984, Palo Alto, CA: Mayfield Publishing Company. Reprinted by permission of Mayfield Publishing Company, copyright 1984, 1970, and 1963 by Joseph Luft.

sees it. In the working stage, the personal unknown area diminishes. Feedback is a key ingredient in this process, as members share their impressions and observations of one another. There is a risk in giving and receiving feedback of this nature, for all comments may not be positive. Nevertheless, through sharing, members come to know about how they are seen and are able to interact on a deeper and more authentic level in the group.

The fourth quadrant (**the unknown quadrant**) is full of potential because it contains material hidden from self and others due to a lack of opportunity. As the group progresses, this quadrant shrinks. It may be developed in the group because of crises or opportunities. Basically, the possibilities and potentials that individuals possess lie dormant until there are opportunities to express them. In the working stage of the group, some situations develop where, unknown to the group or the person, an untapped talent emerges. For example, a shy group member may suddenly take the lead when the group is in the midst of a dilemma, such as searching for ways to deal with a rival group in a positive way. Though unexpected, this type of emergent behavior is usually welcomed by all within the group because it represents growth.

Overall, in the working stage of the group, there is increased awareness in the group about individual participants and the world of each person. There is increased sharing of past and present experiences and perceptions. In addition, risk taking increases. What the group and its members achieve are growth and freedom. New discoveries open the group and its members to other insights and actions as well (Gladding, 1994a). A long-term, closed group membership is especially prone to display the behaviors just described.

TASK PROCESSES DURING THE WORKING STAGE

The major emphasis in the working stage is productivity, whether the results are tangibly visible or not. Group members focus on improving themselves and/or in achieving specific individual and group goals. One way productivity may be increased is by encouraging equal member air time through making the **rounds** (Yalom, 1985). This procedure has been elaborated on previously, but its importance as a process in a group that is working cannot be overestimated. Members who are given time during the group to discuss issues of concern to them will invest more deeply in the group with each session and will do the type of work that can be of benefit to themselves and the group as a whole. For example, if in a counseling group, Timothy realizes the group will help him in finding new ways to overcome his shyness with women, he is likely to faithfully attend all group meetings and participate actively. The only problem with the technique of rounds is having enough time for all members to articulate and work on situations to the extent they wish.

A second way tasks are accomplished at the working stage is through **role playing.** In role plays, members are given a chance to assume an identity that differs widely from their present behavior. "Role playing is a tool for bringing a specific skill and its consequences into focus, and thus is vital for experiential learning" (Johnson & Johnson, 1991, p. 47). This psychodramatic technique can be powerful in helping group members see and feel how certain actions will be experienced before they actually occur outside the group.

Trust and caring are vital in the role-playing process, and specific ideas about what the group member wants to accomplish are helpful. In a role play, the participants set up an imaginary life situation and ask others in the group to play certain parts while they respond in a prescribed way, such as remaining calm. After the action is completed, the member and the group discuss benefits, consequences, and alternative ways of behaving in the given situation.

A group member can have a frustrating experience in a role play and still benefit from the experience. For instance, Helen asked her psychoeducational group members to role play a situation with her in which she confronted her boss about his rude and demeaning behavior to her. Although group members tried to assist Helen in their enactment of roles, Helen was not sure after the role play ended that she had found a way to address her boss or not. However, as she continued talking, Helen began to realize that, although she had not achieved all that she wished, she did feel some relief and confidence about the situation and had a base from which to continue.

Another task process that is prevalent in the working stage is **homework,** or working outside the group itself (Gazda, 1989). Group members often find that they need to carry behaviors they practice within the group to situations outside the group. Although they may not be given a specific assignment by the group, they will often try out new skills and bring their experiences back to the group to process. In this way, participants receive twice the benefits they would otherwise, that is, they get to practice skills in a real-life situation and they get to interact with the group about the experience.

An example of homework is when a member practices being calm when his colleagues in a work setting make demands on him. In returning to the group, he can relate not only how his homework went but receive support and suggestions from other group members on future homework assignments. Homework generally varies as to its intensity and importance. Sometimes, simple and less noticeable acts, such as making phone calls to friends, going to a meeting, or inviting someone over for refreshments, are vital homework tasks.

A final dimension that must be considered in the working stage of the group is **incorporation** (i.e., a personal awareness and appreciation of what the group has accomplished both on an individual and collective level). When the working stage of a group ends, members should have a feeling and knowledge of what was achieved and how. Through incorporation, members realize the value of the group in their lives and remember critical times in the group regarding what they or other members of the group said or did. Incorporation prepares members to move on to the termination stage. For example, in thinking about the group as it progressed, Elaine was able to realize that she took risks in the group by disclosing information she had never revealed before. Instead of being devastating, this experience gave her a sense of relief and direction. She was able to take satisfaction in what she did and begin to see that she could accomplish goals outside the group. Her gratitude for the group and for what she learned as a result of being in the group increased.

TEAMWORK AND TEAM BUILDING
DURING THE WORKING STAGE

Teamwork and team building are vital in the working stage of groups. A **team** is "a number of persons associated together in work or activity" (Webster's New Collegiate Dictionary, 1987, p. 1210). The outcome of a team effort is seen most graphically in athletic or artistic competition in which members of a group act and perform in a coordinated way to achieve a goal, such as scoring points or dancing in a unified and coordinated manner.

Groups sometimes function as teams whether planned or not. However, promoting a team spirit increases the likelihood that a group will work together constructively. This is done through encouraging **teamwork** (i.e., all members of a group working together cooperatively) through team building. The process of **team building** takes time and may take different patterns over time (Kormanski, 1990). For example, some teams may build through completing tasks together whereas others may do so through extended group discussions. Groups that work to achieve consensus, promote interpersonal relationships, and minimize conflict perform best. In psychoeducational groups, teamwork and learning are promoted by emphasizing how tasks can be achieved by the group that cannot be accomplished by an individual alone (Gough, 1987). For instance, if an academic class is given a long reading assignment that could not be covered by one class member in the time allotted, a study group, as a team, could come together and distribute the reading so that each member could become an expert on an area that he or she would later teach the group when they reassembled (Light, 1994).

Teamwork is considered so important to many organizations that teachers from graduate business schools to elementary schools often break their classes into teams at the beginning of a term both to help them master material and to learn how to work cooperatively with others. A team can be a socializing as well as a productive experience. The founder of reality therapy, William Glasser (1986), considers teams to be an essential part of his theory especially as the theory relates to control within self and others. Teamwork and the team building that goes with it can also be applied to counseling and psychotherapy groups in stressing the importance of the interpersonal dimension in one's own growth and development.

Effective development of a team (i.e., team building) can take other forms as well. One model of developing a group into a team has been proposed by Maples (1992). She premises her model on the assumption that group members trust one another and are motivated for success. Basic components of this model involve choice and ownership. Groups that make positive choices that lead to success do so from a stance of openness, honesty, compassion, enthusiasm, integrity, and a commitment to communication. The ownership of the group is achieved in such cases through patience, objectivity, personal responsibility, and investing energy in the group. Keeping focused in the present, being sincere, and at times being introspective or humorous are other factors that help the group achieve a sense of unity as a team. Maples suggests groups need icebreaking exercises (introductory activities that link people together), too. Such exercises increase the group's awareness of each other and/or remind members of what they did in previous sessions.

PROBLEMS IN THE WORKING STAGE OF GROUPS

Despite good intentions, some groups are more productive than others. The reason is due to a variety of factors, including pregroup preparation, the makeup of group members, the focus of the group, and group leadership/followership interactions. Among the specific problems that arise during the working stage are fear and resistance, challenges to leaders, and a lack of focus on achieving individual and group goals. These problems are expressed in numerous ways such as intense emotionality in members, projection or scapegoating of a member, and lack of constructive participation. Focusing on issues outside the group, such as gender/race or turning inward as a group to be protective (collusion), are also problematic and will be considered here.

Racial and Gender Issues

Matters pertaining to race and gender are manifest in some groups more than others. However, race and gender issues occur in the vast majority of all types of groups in subtle and blatant ways. The thoughts and feelings surrounding these descriptors of persons reflect societal attitudes in general. In regard to race, Rokeach, Smith, and Evans (1960) proposed that racial prejudice is based on assumptions about the beliefs and attitudes of persons of a given race. Some groups may struggle and/or engage in high conflict because of racial prejudices among members. Other groups deal with racial issues through denial (Lanier & Robertiello, 1977). Individuals who hold stereotyped views and act accordingly are **culturally encapsulated** (Wrenn, 1985) and behave in a rigid and stereotyped manner (Pedersen, 1988). Contact with others from different cultures in a group context often helps members become more aware of their racial feelings. It can have "the healthy effect" of making them realize their ethnocentric assumptions and limiting beliefs, "thus leading to a broader view of human nature" (Walsh, 1989, p. 547).

The same dysfunctional/functional and nonproductive/productive dynamic of prejudice and stereotypes may occur in regard to gender, too (Sullivan, 1983). In such cases, the words *male* and *female* are highlighted at the expense of the concept *person.* The result is that males and females must learn new roles within the group that give them greater freedom to be flexible and competent. Sometimes this new learning is hampered by others, but it has a good chance of success if begun early in the group's development. Leaders must work with the group to prevent or limit negative outcomes between members by increasing sensitivity and decreasing the escalation of conflict (Korda & Pancrazio, 1989). Generally, the issue of gender is highly visible and dealt with constructively by group leaders and members as part of larger issues in the working stage.

Group Collusion

Group collusion involves cooperating with others unconsciously or consciously "to reinforce prevailing attitudes, values, behaviors, or norms" (Butler, 1987, p. 1). The purpose of such behavior is self-protection. Its effect is to maintain the status quo in the group. For example, in work groups, when subordinates agree with their boss to keep from being fired, they are engaging in a collusion process. The same is true in psychoeducational groups when students concur with their professors to receive a good grade.

There is some degree of collusion in most groups, but in extremes, group collusion prevents open discussion, critical thinking, and problem solving. Such closedness, and the conformity promoted by it, may lead to a destructive process that is regressive in nature. Janis (1972, 1982) has called this phenomenon **groupthink**. In a groupthink situation, there is a "deterioration of mental efficiency, reality testing, and moral judgment that results from in-group pressures" (Janis, 1972, p. 9). Forms of groupthink may become destructive and even deadly as evidenced in the Bay of Pigs invasion of the Kennedy administration, the Watergate cover-up of the Nixon administration, the mass suicide that occurred in Jonestown, Guyana, under the leadership of the Reverend Jim Jones, and the Branch Davidian tragedy in Waco, Texas. In less severe cases, groupthink inhibits growth and represses individual and group development. For example, in some work groups, criticism of a new or existing product may be suppressed because of groupthink. Ignoring the groupthink attitude and expressing criticism may cause talented individuals to lose their jobs and influence in a company.

To prevent group collusion from occurring to any great extent, group membership should be diversified. In addition, open discussion should be promoted, and goals and purposes should be continuously clarified. As a precautionary measure, some type of **devil's advocate procedure** should be actively implemented. This procedure is where one or more members in the group are asked to question group decisions with a firm skepticism before the group reaches a conclusion (Forsyth, 1990; Tjosvold, 1986). Interpersonal relationship skills should be strengthened as well.

THE WORKING STAGE OF THE GROUP AND GROUPS THAT WORK

Just as there is a difference in the dynamics that underlie the working stage of a group's development, there is also a difference in working and nonworking groups. For instance, working groups have a sense of cohesion and trust with one another. They work in the present and are willing to take risks in self-disclosing or sharing ideas. When there is disagreement in the group, members acknowledge it and deal with it in an open and overt manner. Communication is clear and direct, and members use each other as resources. In addition, working groups are aware of the group progress and process. They accept responsibility for doing their part within the group in relation to either their own or group goals. They give honest feedback to one another without fear of reprisal. They are hopeful and secure within the group and are, therefore, able to maximize their thinking, feeling, and behaving capabilities. Corey and Corey (1992, pp. 194–196) have identified some 20 characteristics that compare working versus nonworking groups (see Figure 6.2).

It is evident from examining their list that the Coreys believe leaders and members both play a vital, interactional part in the success or failure of the group. Research confirms such a view. Leaders who have prepared themselves and their members adequately beforehand are more likely than not to be successful. However, despite preparation, incidents may happen within a group in the working stage that cause problems. For example, the death of a loved one may influence a group member to focus on his or her internal agendas rather than the group's task. Likewise, an unresolved conflict between group members may break down the harmony and constructive nature of the group.

STRATEGIES FOR ASSISTING GROUPS IN THE WORKING STAGE

When groups are not doing well in the working stage, there are several approaches that can be employed to rectify the situation. These include modeling by the leader (Borgers & Koenig, 1983); exercise experiences (Corey, Corey, Callanan, & Russell, 1992); group observing group (Cohen & Smith, 1976); brainstorming (Osborn, 1957); nominal-group technique (NGT) (Delbecq & Van de Ven, 1971); synectics (Gordon, 1961), written projectives (Hoskins, 1984), and group processing (Jerry Donigian, personal communication, July 8, 1994).

Modeling

The **modeling** method is used to teach group members complex behaviors in a relatively short period of time by copying/imitating. Modeling depends on timing, reinforcement, the amount of positive feedback received, the view of the group leader, the degree of trust, and the amount of motivation for imitation. Borgers and Koenig (1983) stress that group members borrow from leaders and other members what they need in order to function better and become more their own persons. Leaders can promote working in the group by displaying behaviors congruent with this stage, such as self-disclosure, or by having a core of group members with whom others can readily identify display such actions.

The following lists represent our view of some basic differences between productive and nonproductive groups. As you study the lists, think of any other factors you could add. If you are or have been in a group, think about how these characteristics apply to your group experience.

Working Group	**Nonworking Group**
Members trust other members and the leaders, or at least they openly express any lack of trust. There is a willingness to take risks by sharing meaningful here-and-now reactions.	Mistrust is evidenced by an undercurrent of unexpressed hostility. Members withhold themselves, refusing to express feelings and thoughts.
Goals are clear and specific and are determined jointly by the members and the leader. There is a willingness to direct ingroup behavior toward realizing these goals.	Goals are fuzzy, abstract, and general. Members have unclear personal goals or no goals at all.
Most members feel a sense of inclusion, and excluded members are invited to become more active. Communication among most members is open and involves accurate expression of what is being experienced.	Many members feel excluded or cannot identify with other members. Cliques are formed that tend to lead to fragmentation. There is fear of expressing feelings of being left out.
There is a focus on the here and now, and participants talk directly to one another about what they're experiencing.	There is a "there-and-then" focus; people tend to focus on others and not on themselves, and storytelling is typical. There is a resistance to dealing with reactions to one another.
The leadership functions are shared by the group; people feel free to initiate activities or to suggest exploring particular areas.	Members lean on the leader for all direction. There are power conflicts among members as well as between members and the leader.
There is a willingness to risk disclosing threatening material; people become known.	Participants hold back, and disclosure is at a minimum.
Cohesion is high; there is a close emotional bond among people, based on sharing of universal human experiences. Members identify with one another. People are willing to risk experimental behavior because of the closeness and support for new ways of being.	Fragmentation exists; people feel distant from one another. There is a lack of caring or empathy. Members don't encourage one another to engage in new and risky behavior, so familiar ways of being are rigidly maintained.
Conflict among members or with the leader is recognized, discussed, and often resolved.	Conflicts or negative feelings are ignored, denied, or avoided.

Figure 6.2
Contrasts between a working group and a nonworking group.

Working Group	Nonworking Group
Members accept the responsibility for deciding what action they will take to solve their problems.	Members blame others for their personal difficulties and aren't willing to take action to change.
Feedback is given freely and accepted without defensiveness. There is a willingness to seriously reflect on the accuracy of the feedback.	What little feedback is given is rejected defensively. Feedback is given without care or compassion.
Members feel hopeful; they feel that constructive change is possible—that people can become what they want to become.	Members feel despairing, helpless and trapped, victimized.
Confrontation occurs in such a way that the confronter shares his or her reactions to the person being confronted. Confrontation is accepted as a challenge to examine one's behavior and not as an uncaring attack.	Confrontation is done in a hostile, attacking way; the confronted one feels judged and rejected. At times the members gang up on a member, using this person as a scapegoat.
Communication is clear and direct.	Communication is unclear and indirect.
Group members use one another as a resource and show interest in one another.	Members are interested only in themselves.
Members feel powerful and share this power *with* one another.	Members or leaders use power and control over others.
There is an awareness of group process, and members know what makes the group productive or nonproductive.	There is an indifference or lack of awareness of what is going on within the group, and group dynamics are rarely discussed.
Diversity is encouraged, and there is a respect for individual and cultural differences.	Conformity is prized, and individual and cultural differences are devalued.
Group norms are developed cooperatively by the members and the leader. Norms are clear and are designed to help the members attain their goals.	Norms are merely imposed by the leader. They may not be clear.
There is an emphasis on combining the feeling and thinking functions. Catharsis and expression of feeling occur, but so does thinking about the meaning of various emotional experiences.	The group relies heavily on cathartic experiences but makes little or no effort to understand them.
Group members use out-of-group time to work on problems raised in the group.	Group members think about group activity very little when they're outside the group.

Source: From *Groups: Process and Practice,* 4th ed. (pp. 194–196) by M. S. Corey and G. Corey, 1992, Pacific Grove, CA: Brooks/Cole. Copyright © 1992 by Wadsworth, Inc. Reprinted by permission from Brooks/Cole Publishing Company, Pacific Grove, CA.

The latter strategy of having peers help peers is especially effective if the members that are modeling behaviors are similar to those they are helping in regard to age, gender, and background.

Exercises

Exercise experiences involve less direct showing and more an experiential integration. "The term **exercise** is used among group leaders to refer to activities that the group does for a specific purpose" (Jacobs, Harvill, & Masson, 1994, p. 214). There are different views about whether preplanned exercises should be used in groups and when. On one end of the spectrum is a group represented by Carl Rogers (1970) who advocates the avoidance of "any procedure that is planned" (p. 56). On the other end of this continuum are leaders who simply employ a series of exercises in their groups from group exercise books (e.g., Pfeiffer & Jones, 1972–1980).

A more moderate approach is using exercises in groups at specific times for specific reasons. As Jacobs et al. (1994) point out, group exercises can be employed by a leader for at least seven reasons:

1. Generate discussion and participation
2. Focus the group
3. Shift the focus
4. Provide the opportunity for experiential learning
5. Provide the leader with useful information
6. Increase the comfort level
7. Provide fun and relaxation (p. 215)

All of these reasons make it likely that sometimes group leaders will employ a prestructured exercise during the working stage of the group. Preplanned exercise experiences should not be used indiscriminately or even employed frequently in the working stage of most groups. However, interventions such as these, when well planned and tailored to a particular situation, can increase member awareness and responsiveness to self and others. Whether exercises are used in group work depends on the need for these devices, the comfort of the group and its leader with such a method, and the potential benefits and liabilities of utilizing such procedures (Wenz & McWhirter, 1990).

As previously discussed, an icebreaker at the beginning of a group can be a potent stimulant as can a well-timed intervention at a critical moment in the group's development. For instance, if a counseling group appears to be anxious and overly concerned about one of its members, Michelle, and is talking *about* her instead of *with* her, the leader might simply ask the group to gather in a tight circle with arms interlocked. Michelle would then be invited to try to break through the circle which, even if successful, would be frustrating and aggravating. From this brief exercise, the leader could help the group focus on its dynamics and the group processes that keep the group from discussing their anxiety about Michelle with her.

In addition to their benefits, exercises have disadvantages, too (Gladding, 1992). They may make group members overly dependent on the leader if used too often. They may make some group members angry or resentful because members may feel a lack of control over what will happen next. Finally, exercises can disrupt the natural development of a group if employed too frequently.

Group Observing Group

Group observing group requires that the group break up into two smaller groups in any way the leader directs and that each observe the other function (as outsiders) for about 10 minutes each. This process is sometimes called a "fishbowl procedure" (see Figure 6.3).

After the group observations are completed, the group reunites, and members give each other and the group as a whole feedback on what was observed. The intent of this activity is to help members focus on common concerns that outweigh differences and to begin working harder (Cohen & Smith, 1976).

For example, Carolyn might notice that the group she is observing struggles with the problem of making sure everyone gets heard who wants to contribute. This awareness helps her realize that her own group is not unique in its quest to be fair to all members and make sure they have a say. She also realizes from this experience some things she could do differently in her own group such as being an encourager of those who are most reflective and less likely to overtly participate.

Figure 6.3
Group observing group.

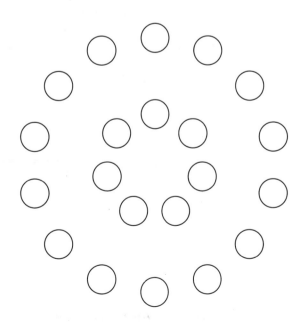

Brainstorming

Brainstorming, a way to stimulate divergent thinking, requires an initial generating of ideas in a nonjudgmental manner (Osborn, 1957). The premise of this approach is that creativity and member participation are often held back because of the critical evaluation of ideas and actions by other group members. Therefore, in this procedure, the ideas of every person are recorded first before any comments are made. Quantity is emphasized in this process—the more ideas the better. Only after a large number of ideas have been written down do members go back and evaluate the feasibility of what they have contributed. This results in an increase in group activity and responsibility as well as an emphasis on reality. However, by the time ideas are judged along qualitative lines, many thoughts have been contributed that would not have been voiced otherwise.

Nominal-Group Technique

Another helpful procedure for getting the group to work is the **nominal-group technique** (NGT). This process has up to six steps (Delbecq, Van de Ven, & Gustafson, 1975). In the first step, the group leader introduces the problem or issue with a brief statement and then asks members to silently, and individually, generate a number of ideas/solutions connected with the statement. Members are given 10 to 15 minutes to complete this exercise and are asked to do it in writing. The second step involves members' sharing of ideas, with each person stating an idea in a round-robin fashion and the group leader writing that idea and an identification code on a blackboard or flip chart before the next person speaks.

The third step requires a discussion of ideas for clarification, with "What did you mean when you said . . .?" dialogue. The fourth step has members write their top five ideas/solutions on an index card. The cards are then collected by the leader, a vote is tallied, and the information is fed back to the group as a whole. In the fifth step, a short discussion of the vote follows. At this time, members can again raise points, seek clarification, or solicit comments. The final step is possible revoting. A revote takes place usually if the discussion on the original vote has brought out new information that members want to consider in light of their earlier decision.

The nominal-group procedure does not require the open exposure of members as much as brainstorming. However, it is quite useful in getting group members to think and to work on problematic situations, especially in task/work groups. Overall, the nominal task group places more objectivity in the group decision-making process than almost any other type of method.

Synectics

A novel way of helping groups in the working stage become more productive is **synectics**. The word "synectics," from the Greek, means the joining together of different and apparently irrelevant elements. Synectics theory applies to the integration of diverse individuals into "a problem-stating, problem-solving group" (Gordon, 1961, p. 1). In general, synectics follows the general pattern of group discussions—problem statement, discussion, solution generation, and decision (Forsyth, 1990). There are several important differences, however.

First, throughout the discussion, members are asked to analyze all sides of an issue by adopting a spectrum policy. This policy is the recognition that few ideas are totally good or bad. Next, members are encouraged to express their wishes and hopes throughout this process. Although they may not receive what they wish for, members are able to clarify what they want better through this process and to relieve some pent-up frustrations. A very refreshing and stimulating part of synectics is called **excursions**. In these activities, members actually take a break, a vacation, from problem solving and engage in exercises involving fantasy, metaphor, and analogy. The idea is that the material generated in these processes can be reintegrated into the group later, specifically to issues that are of individual and group importance.

Written Projections

Written projections are yet another means to help a group during the working stages. In these processes, members are asked to see themselves or their groups in the future having been successful and to describe what the experience was like. Group members are able to play with their fantasies at times as well as be realistic. An example of projection that captures the spirit of this approach is the writing of a **therapeutic fairy tale** (Hoskins, 1984). In this activity, members are asked to write a fairy tale in a 6- to 10-minute time frame. They are to begin their story with "Once upon a time" and in it they are to include (a) a problem or predicament, (b) a solution, even if it appears outlandish, and (c) a positive, pleasing ending. The time limit helps members focus on the task and prevents resistance.

In response to being asked to write a therapeutic fairy tale, a group member in a therapeutic group once wrote,

> *"Once upon a time, there was an old woman who had managed, like the woman in the shoe, to raise a number of children. The only problem was that the children now knew what they wanted to do with their lives and the old woman did not. At first she got depressed and thought if she got sad enough the children would come back to her. They did, but they were angry and put her in a mental health facility. She tried getting even more down, but her strategy just didn't seem to help.*
>
> *"One day the old woman woke up and said to herself, 'Today, I'll wear purple, a healing color, and I will go out in the wards and say hello to everyone I meet.' She did and to her amazement most of those she encountered responded back in a positive way. She felt better, they felt better, and as a result she realized all the world could now be her surrogate children.*

*So she left the hospital with a good feeling and a great plan and lived hap-
pily both with her children and her neighbors."*

Group Processing

A final strategy for helping groups maximize their resources in the working stage
is through group processing. **Group processing** is when a neutral third party
observes and feeds back to the group what is occurring between members and in
the group itself. In order to do group processing, there must be a **process
observer**, i.e., a professional human services person who is neutral in regard to
the group agenda and personalities and who can observe and feedback to the
group what they are doing and how (Jerry Donigian, personal communication,
January 26, 1994). The job of the process observer is not to judge but to objectively inform the group about the dynamics that are occurring. For instance, in a
task group, the observer might say something like the following:

> *"I noticed during this portion of the group that Beverly was trying to make
> sure the group was aware of the ramifications of investing money in the
> foundation. She did this through providing the group with a lot of facts.
> Bree, you were most supportive of Beverly and encouraged her. Chuck,
> you were also supportive but you seemed to grow impatient as Beverly's
> presentation continued. Michael, on the other hand, I observed you
> wanted to end the discussion and kept asking the group if there were other
> agenda items to cover. I'm not sure exactly what that was about."*

Having made an observation, group members are then free to discuss and
process what the observer has presented. They may do so through talking with
each other, owning their feelings, or asking the observer for more detailed or
clearer information. In any case, through process observation, the work of the
group is enhanced because members begin to see patterns in themselves and
others and to address issues related to who they are with each other as well as
the content on which they are focusing. It is prudent for most groups, regardless
of their emphases, to have the process observer "report" either right before or
after they take a break or when they seem to be getting bogged down. Process
observing energizes the group as well as gives it useful information.

OUTCOMES OF THE WORKING STAGES

The end result of the working stage on a group is usually tangible. Goals have
been worked on and achieved. Some of these goals take the form of personal
objectives. For example, in counseling and psychotherapy groups, members are
usually involved in improving particular areas in their lives. Other goals evolve as

the result of a combined group vision and effort. Group members often gain a clearer idea of what they have accomplished in the working stage when they put their group session goals down on paper before each session (see Table 6.1).

One of the most productive aspects of the group in the working stage is the learning and sharing of ideas and information between members. As a result, the entire group membership is enriched. The ability some groups achieve to generate new thoughts spontaneously is another benefit. "Group stuckness" cannot remain the same if the group is really working.

An important aspect to realize about any group is its cyclical nature between task and social/emotional vectors (Bales, 1951). There are certain roles that are primarily task oriented and others that are either positive or negative in regard to the creating of social/emotional atmospheres. Leaders and members must be vitally aware of roles, because by being so, they can best promote strategies and resolutions.

Other procedures used in the working stage of a group overlap with techniques previously described in prior group stages. For instance, in counseling and psychotherapy groups, as participants make discoveries about themselves, they experience an emotional *catharsis*—a release of pent-up feelings. In such cases, they may cry, laugh, become angry, or tap into any other feeling state that

Table 6.1
Group session goals chart.

Group Session Goal Chart			
Your Name:_____		Date:_____	Group Session:_____
What I want to accomplish today	What I need to do to accomplish it	The resources in the group that can help me	How I will know if I accomplished my goal for today

Source: Adapted from *The Theory and Practice of Group Psychotherapy* (3rd ed.) by I. D. Yalom, 1985, New York: Basic Books.

has been released. For example, in a psychotherapy group, Irene found herself still mad at her childhood siblings for teasing her about matters over which she had no control. Her awareness and release of bottled-up feelings were therapeutic as was the discussion she had later with her group members.

Sometimes, group members will add actions to the emotions they are experiencing during the working stage. It is hoped participants can gain insight and become more cognitively aware of themselves and their options during this stage through such means. If this developmental process occurs, members **cognitively restructure** their lives, i.e., they begin to think and perceive of themselves differently. They see that although change is difficult, they are not helpless and the situation is not necessarily hopeless (Ellis, 1977, 1986; Watzlawick, 1983). Expressing negative emotions without cognitive restructuring only reinforces such feelings.

With this increased awareness comes increased inter-member exchanges and a giving and receiving of honest, direct, and useful information. Group members seem to genuinely care how their behaviors are perceived by others in the working stage. What impact their actions have in promoting or inhibiting relationships becomes valued. The focus is on the present and it may include confrontation. The idea behind **confrontation** is for members to challenge one another to examine the discrepancies between their words and actions. For example in a counseling group, Paul may say to Allison, "I hear that you really want to make your own decisions, but I see that you are constantly asking your mother for advice. Help me understand how these two behaviors relate." Confrontation does not usually lead to conflict or withdrawal. Instead, members become more thoughtful about what they are doing and why.

Feedback is also utilized in the working stage as it is throughout the group. Feedback is sharing relevant information with other people, such as how they are perceived, so they can decide whether to change or not. Information should be given in a clear, concrete, succinct, and appropriate manner. Feedback is not uni-dimensional (e.g., Bednar & Kaul, 1985; Morran, Robison, & Stockton, 1985). Timing and the type of feedback given are important variables on its impact. Positive feedback is generally received more willingly and has a greater impact than negative feedback (Dies, 1983; Morran et al., 1985). Likewise, specific feedback about behaviors is rated more effective by group members than general or non-specific feedback (Rothke, 1986; Stockton & Morran, 1980).

In giving feedback, it is important to "carefully assess" a recipient's readiness to receive a corrective message (Stockton, Morran, & Harris, 1991, p. 253). It is also essential to allow enough time for processing feedback messages. If adequate time is not allowed, group members may rationalize or forget the messages they receive. Overall, the quality of feedback is higher during the latter stages of the group at work and is likely to be more accepted by members then. Regardless, it is important that feedback be given within the group throughout the entire group experience (Morran et al., 1985).

In addition to increased intimacy, openness, and feedback, another quality that is useful, important, and likely to be helpful during the working stage is **humor**—the ability to laugh at oneself or a situation in a therapeutic and nondefensive manner (Watzlawick, 1983). Groups that last make more frequent and longer use of humor than those that are short lived (Scogin & Pollio, 1980). In a successful working stage, seriousness may be interspersed with laughter as members gain better insight into themselves, others, and the dynamics of life inside and outside the group. Humor may have a potential benefit on a group by easing tension, distilling hostility, promoting positive communication bonds, and fostering creativity (Baron, 1974; Fine, 1977; La Gaipa, 1977; Murstein & Brust, 1985).

The exact role humor plays in a group is not always easy to determine. Certainly, it may distract members from their work or be used to make put-downs. Therefore, it is important for groups to notice when and how humor is used in order to determine its impact. There are always opportunities in groups to cultivate humor "by taking advantage of paradoxes within the group, discrepancies, the unpredictable, the unanticipated, universal truths, the absurd, and the familiar" (Napier & Gershenfeld, 1989, p. 408). For example, in a round, the group leader asked members to remember a funny experience in their lives that made them more aware of their humanness. Sam related that because of his cultural background, he had not understood that a "Danish" was a sweet pastry as well as a person from Scandinavia. When he was invited by his group to "go get a Danish," he just looked at them in amazement and questioned why they would want to do something like that. It was only when his peers escorted him to a bakery that he fully understood what they were talking about and with them laughed at the misinterpretation (Gladding, 1994b).

Well-conducted counseling, psychotherapeutic, work/task, and psychoeducational groups often make use of humor. Sharing a lighter moment from one's personal experience or enjoying an illustration that makes a point while being amusing helps people remember and enjoy a laugh together at no one's expense. Humor also helps individuals and group members as a whole bond and gain insight (Fry & Salameh, 1993). It influences them positively about working together.

SUMMARY AND CONCLUSION

In this chapter the dynamics of groups during the working stage have been examined. Particular attention has been focused on personal and task issues of this stage. In addition, the difference between a group that is working and a group in the working stage was examined. These two concepts are not necessarily the same, although they could be.

As previously pointed out, the working stage is where the group should be most productive in resolving or solving personal, task, or educational issues. If for some reason this stage of the group does not go well, group members may leave the group frustrated and disheartened. In addition, attempts at termination will be impeded. Members who have had a bad experience in the group during this stage are less likely to want to participate in collective efforts again. On the other hand, when the group functions well in the working stage, members are positively influenced.

In order to assist groups to help themselves, some of the factors of which group leaders and members must be aware and execute have been highlighted. Among these important elements in assisting the group to be productive are modeling, using structured exercises, group observing groups, brainstorming, the nominal-group technique, synectics, written projects, and group processing. When groups are successful in the working stage, they achieve goals and move toward termination. Members of such groups increase their insight and utilization of basic therapeutic devices, such as feedback, confrontation, and humor. Overall, in successful groups, the working stage is one that is remembered fondly and proudly by its members.

CLASSROOM EXERCISES

1. Divide into groups of four. Discuss the use of humor in groups for facilitating the group process. What are the advantages and limitations of using humor in task, guidance, and therapy groups?

2. Write a "therapeutic fairy tale" about some aspect of your life. In groups of two, discuss how you reacted to this exercise and for which populations you think it would be appropriate and inappropriate. Share your fairy tales with one another if you wish.

3. How does a representation such as the Johari Window help you understand the similarities and differences between working and nonworking groups? Talk with another classmate and then the group as a whole.

4. Discuss in a group of five the nominal-group technique (NGT). Use the technique, as explained in this chapter, to generate ideas on how, when, and with whom the NGT would be most effective.

REFERENCES

Bales, R. F. (1951). *Interaction process analysis.* Chicago: University of Chicago Press.

Baron, R. A. (1974). The aggression-inhibiting influence of nonhostile humor. *Journal of Experimental Social Psychology, 10,* 23–33.

Bednar, R. L., & Kaul, T. J. (1985). Experiential group research: Results, questions, and suggestions. In S. L. Garfield & A. Bergin (Eds.), *Handbook for psychotherapy and behavior change* (3rd ed.). New York: Wiley.

Borgers, S. B., & Koenig, R. W. (1983). Uses and effects of modeling by the therapist in group therapy. *Journal for Specialists in Group Work, 8,* 133–138.

Butler, L. (1987). Anatomy of collusive behavior. *NTL Connections, 4,* 1–2.

Cohen, A. M., & Smith, R. D. (1976). *Critical incidents in growth groups: Theory and techniques.* La Jolla, CA: University Associates.

Corey, G. (1990). *Theory and practice of group counseling* (3rd ed.). Pacific Grove, CA: Brooks/Cole.

Corey, G., Corey, M. S., Callanan, P. J., & Russell, J. M. (1992). *Group techniques* (2nd ed.). Pacific Grove, CA: Brooks/Cole.

Corey, M. S., & Corey, G. (1992). *Groups: Process and practice* (4th ed.). Pacific Grove, CA: Brooks/Cole.

Delbecq, A. L., & Van de Ven, A. H. (1971). A group process model for problem identification and program planning. *Journal of Applied Behavioral Science, 7,* 466–492.

Delbecq, A. L., Van de Ven, A. H., & Gustafson, D. H. (1975). *Group techniques for program planning.* Glenview, IL: Scott, Foresman.

Dies, R. R. (1983). Clinical implications of research on leadership in short-term group psychotherapy. In R. R. Dies & K. R. MacKenzie (Eds.), *Advances in group psychotherapy: Integrating research and practice* (pp. 27–78). New York: International Universities Press.

Ellis, A. (1977). Fun as psychotherapy. In A. Ellis & R. Grieger (Eds.), *Handbook of rational-emotive therapy* (Vol. 1, pp. 262–270). New York: Springer.

Ellis, A. (1986). Rational-emotive therapy approaches to overcoming resistance. In A. Ellis & R. Grieger (Eds.), *Handbook of rational-emotive therapy* (Vol. 2, pp. 246–274). New York: Springer.

Fine, G. A. (1977). Humour in situ: The role of humour in small group culture. In A. J. Chapman & H. C. Foot (Eds.), *It's a funny thing, humour* (pp. 315–318). New York: Pergamon.

Forsyth, D. R. (1990). *Group dynamics* (2nd ed.). Monterey, CA: Brooks/Cole.

Fry, W. F., & Salameh, W. A. (Eds.). (1993). *Advances in humor and psychotherapy.* Sarasota, FL: Pro Resources.

Gazda, G. M. (1989). *Group counseling: A developmental approach* (4th ed.). Boston: Allyn & Bacon.

George, R. L., & Dustin, D. (1988). *Group counseling: Theory and practice.* Englewood Cliffs, NJ: Prentice Hall.

Gladding, S. T. (1992). *Counseling as an art: The creative arts in counseling.* Alexandria, VA: American Counseling Association.

Gladding, S. T. (1993). *In reflection.* Unpublished manuscript.

Gladding, S. T. (1994a). *Effective group counseling.* Greensboro, NC: ERIC/CASS.

Gladding, S. T. (1994b, January). *Hope and the group.* Presentation made at the Second National ASGW Conference, St. Petersburg, FL.

Glasser, W. (1986). *Control theory in the classroom.* New York: Perennial Library.

Gordon, W. (1961). *Synectics: The development of creative capacity.* New York: Harper & Row.

Gough, P. B. (1987). The key to improving schools: An interview with William Glasser. *Phi Delta Kappa, 68,* 656–662.

Hansen, J. C., Warner, R. W., & Smith, E. J. (1980). *Group counseling: Theory and process* (2nd ed.). Chicago: Rand McNally.

Hoskins, M. (1984, April). *Guidelines for writing therapeutic fairy tales.* Paper presented at the Fourth Annual Conference of the National Association for Poetry Therapy, Hempstead, NY.

Jacobs, E. E., Harvill, R. L., & Masson, R. L. (1994). *Group counseling: Strategies and skills* (2nd ed.). Pacific Grove, CA: Brooks/Cole.

Janis, I. L. (1972). *Victims of groupthink.* Boston: Houghton Mifflin.

Janis, I. L. (1982). *Groupthink: Psychological studies of policy decisions and fiascos* (2nd ed.). Boston: Houghton Mifflin.

Johnson, D. W., & Johnson, F. P. (1991). *Joining together* (4th ed.). Englewood Cliffs, NJ: Prentice Hall.

Jourard, S. M. (1971). *The transparent self* (2nd ed.). New York: Van Nostrand.

Korda, L. J., & Pancrazio, J. J. (1989). Limiting negative outcome in group practice. *Journal for Specialists in Group Work, 14,* 112–120.

Kormanski, C. (1990). Team building patterns of academic groups. *Journal for Specialists in Group Work, 15,* 206–214.

La Gaipa, J. (1977). The effects of humour on the flow of social conversation. In A. J. Chapman & H. C. Foot (Eds.), *It's a funny thing, humour* (pp. 421–427). New York: Pergamon.

Lanier, E., & Robertiello, R. C. (1977). A small group of patients discuss their experiences and feelings about working with therapists of different races. *Journal of Contemporary Psychotherapy, 9,* 42–44.

Light, R. (1994, March). *Effective teaching.* Presentation made at Faculty Development Seminar, Wake Forest University, Winston-Salem, NC.

Luft, J. (1984). *Group processes: An introduction to group dynamics* (3rd ed.). Palo Alto, CA: Mayfield.

Maples, M. F. (1988). Group development: Extending Tuckman's theory. *Journal for Specialists in Group Work, 13,* 17–23.

Maples, M. F. (1992). STEAMWORK: An effective approach to team building. *Journal for Specialists in Group Work, 17,* 144–150.

Morran, D. K. (1982). Leader and member self-disclosing behavior in counseling groups. *Jour-

nal for Specialists in Group Work, 7, 218–223.

Morran, D. K., Robison, F. F., & Stockton, R. (1985). Feedback exchange in counseling groups: An analysis of message content and receiver acceptance as a function of leader versus member delivery, session, and valence. *Journal of Counseling Psychology, 32*(5), 7–67.

Murstein, B. I., & Brust, R. G. (1985). Humor and interpersonal attraction. *Journal of Personality Assessment, 49,* 637–640.

Napier, R. W., & Gershenfeld, M. K. (1989). *Groups: Theory and experience* (4th ed.). Boston: Houghton Mifflin.

Ohlsen, M. M., Horne, A. M., & Lawe, C. F. (1988). *Group counseling* (3rd ed.). New York: Holt, Rinehart & Winston.

Osborn, A. F. (1957). *Applied imagination.* New York: Scribner.

Pedersen, P. (1988). *A handbook for developing multicultural awareness.* Alexandria, VA: American Association for Counseling and Development.

Pfeiffer, J. W., & Jones, J. E. (1972–1980). *A handbook of structured exercises for human relations training* (Vols. 1–8). San Diego, CA: University Associates.

Rogers, C. (1970). *Carl Rogers on encounter groups.* New York: Harper & Row.

Rokeach, M., Smith, P. W., & Evans, R. I. (1960). Two kinds of prejudice or one? In M. Rokeach (Ed.), *The open and closed mind* (pp. 132–168). New York: Basic Books.

Rothke, S. (1986). The role of interpersonal feedback in group psychotherapy. *International Journal of Group Psychotherapy, 36,* 225–240.

Schutz, W. (1966). *FIRO-B: Interpersonal underworld.* Palo Alto, CA: Science & Behavior Books.

Schutz, W. (1973). Encounter. In R. Corsini (Ed.), *Current psychotherapies.* Itasca, IL: Peacock.

Scogin, F., & Pollio, H. (1980). Targeting and the humorous episode in group process. *Human Relations, 33,* 831–852.

Stockton, R., & Morran, D. K. (1980). The use of verbal feedback in counseling groups: Toward an effective system. *Journal for Specialists in Group Work, 5,* 10–14.

Stockton, R., Morran, D. K., & Harris, M. (1991). Factors influencing group member acceptance of corrective feedback. *Journal for Specialists in Group Work, 16,* 245–254.

Sullivan, M. (1983). Introduction to women emerging: Group approaches. *Journal for Specialists in Group Work, 8,* 3–8.

Tjosvold, D. (1986). Constructive controversy: A key strategy for groups. *Personnel, 63,* 39–44.

Tuckman, B. W., & Jensen, M. A. (1977). Stages of small group development revisited. *Group and Organizational Studies, 2,* 419–427.

Walsh, R. (1989). Asian psychotherapies. In R. J. Corsini & D. Wedding (Eds.), *Current psychotherapies* (4th ed.) (pp. 546–559). Itasca, IL: Peacock.

Watzlawick, P. (1983). *The situation is hopeless, but not serious.* New York: Norton.

Webster's New Collegiate Dictionary. (1987). Boston: Merriam.

Wenz, K., & McWhirter, J. J. (1990). Enhancing the group experience: Creative writing exercises. *Journal for Specialists in Group Work, 15,* 37–42.

Wilson, G. L., & Hanna, M. S. (1986). *Groups in context.* New York: Random House.

Wrenn, C. G. (1985). Afterward: The encapsulated counselor revisited. In P. Pedersen (Ed.), *Handbook of cross-cultural counseling and therapy* (pp. 323–329). Westport, CT: Greenwood Press.

Yalom, I. D. (1985). *The theory and practice of group psychotherapy* (3rd ed.). New York: Basic Books.

CHAPTER 7

Termination of a Group

I travel back to the land of my genesis
as a different man in a changing world,
like Joseph, after his stay in Egypt.
At the end of night, I will begin,
by exploring the light and hope of dawn,
recalling the length of just past days,
and feeling the warmth of lasting friendships.
Amid the abundance of still fresh memories
I will journey on a path of transition
into the unknown and ever evolving
as I experience the fullness of time
that leads to closure and permanent growth.

The termination of a group member, a group session, or an entire group experience received relatively little attention in professional publications until the 1970s. For example, it was not until the late 1970s that Tuckman and Jensen (1977) added the stage "adjourning" to the developmental model of groups devised by Tuckman in 1965. Part of the reason for the neglect of termination in group work was the assumption that ending a group experience on any level is a natural phenomenon that most leaders and participants know how to do.

Yet, termination is never simple, and it is often handled ineptly by group leaders who have not made proper preparations (Shapiro, 1978). It is filled with thoughts and feelings that tend to influence individuals long after the group experience is just a memory. According to Corey (1990), the termination stage is equally as important as the beginning stage of a group. During the initial forming

*Source: Gladding, 1994a.

stage of a group, members come to know one another better. During the termination stage, participants come to know themselves on a deeper level. If properly understood and managed, termination can be an important force in promoting change in individuals (Yalom, 1985).

Primary activities of group members in termination are

to reflect on their past experiences,
to process memories,
to evaluate what was learned,
to acknowledge ambivalent feelings, and
to engage in cognitive decision making (Wagenheim & Gemmill, 1994)

Through their participation in these activities, group members are helped to integrate and use information gleaned from the group experience in outside situations (Lieberman, Yalom, & Miles, 1973; Woody, Hansen, & Rossberg, 1989). They are able to generalize learning from one situation to another (Shulman, 1992). For instance, if Maria realizes in the group that she has the ability to confront individuals and not placate them, she can utilize this skill in her work situation where individuals are constantly making demands on her.

Overall, **termination** is a transition event that ends one set of conditions so that another experience can begin (Cormier & Hackney, 1993). It is considered the last stage of the group process, but in reality it marks the start of a new beginning. Termination provides group members an opportunity to clarify the meaning of their experiences, to consolidate the gains they have made, and to make decisions about the new behaviors they want to carry away from the group and apply to their everyday lives. It is influenced in a positive or negative way by the action and direction of the group leader. It differs for members in closed versus open groups because members of closed groups prepare for and experience termination collectively, whereas members of open groups prepare for and experience termination individually.

Within termination, there are many issues and processes. One concern is **emotional ambivalence**. Often there are feelings of loss, sadness, and separation (Gladding, 1994b; Hulse-Killacky, 1993; MacKenzie & Livesley, 1984). Frequently, these feelings are mixed with those of hope, joy, and accomplishment (Schutz, 1967). Almost always, there are issues involving "unfinished business," transference, and countertransference (Kauff, 1977). How to solidify and translate learning accomplished within the group to outside experiences is still another aspect of termination. Therefore, it is crucial to the health and well-being of everyone in a group that termination be handled correctly.

In this chapter, several different aspects of group termination are covered. First, proper preparation for termination is examined. Second, the effect of termination on the individual is explored. Next, ways of handling premature termination are discussed, especially when the ending is involuntary. Fourth, proper methods of ending single group sessions are noted, along with appropriate ways of ending the group as a whole. Finally, the issues of problems in termination and of group member follow-up are addressed. In each of these situations, the responsibilities of leaders and members are highlighted.

PREPARING FOR TERMINATION

Proper preparation for terminating a group begins in the planning stage. Leaders should have in mind not only what type of group they wish to conduct but also how long it will meet and how it will end. They are guided in these decisions by theoretical and pragmatic considerations, such as what approach has shown positive results with certain populations and problems as well as what facilities are available and when (Cormier & Hackney, 1993).

To ensure proper group procedures from start to termination, leaders must establish appropriate boundaries. **Boundaries** are physical and psychological parameters under which a group operates, such as starting and ending on time or sitting in a certain configuration like a circle. Leaders who do not keep these dimensions of a group in mind basically "are abdicating their responsibility and reinforcing a perception many group members may already have—that people often don't mean what they say, that they cannot be trusted" (Bates, Johnson, & Blaker, 1982, p. 88). Therefore, planning for termination should go hand in glove with other theoretically based group procedures and be a coordinated process. The impact of termination is both direct and subtle on the growth of individuals and the group as a whole.

Termination occurs on two levels in groups:

at the end of each session, and
at the end of a certain number of group sessions

Both types of termination have step processes within them that are predictable. In considering termination, group leaders should make plans accordingly. One of the best guidelines for making plans to terminate is based on a model for ending family therapy sessions. The main idea in this model is that regardless of theory, termination is a four-step process:

1. orientation,
2. summarization,
3. discussion of goals, and
4. follow-up (Epstein & Bishop, 1981)

During orientation, the subject of termination is raised. At times during the process, group members are reminded when a session or a group will end. During summarization, material and processes that have occurred in the group are reviewed. Ideally, both the group leader and group members participate in this summary. During the discussion of goals, the focus of the group centers on what members will do after the session or the group ends. In the final step, follow-up, group members inform each other of what progress they have made in obtaining their objectives. Through reminding themselves of these steps and procedures, group leaders help themselves, group members, and the group as a whole end successfully.

In open-ended therapy groups such as those for psychiatric patients, termination is highly individualized, but even in these situations, there is some predictability. For example, Yalom (1985) states that most psychiatric patients in outpatient groups "require approximately twelve to twenty-four months to undergo substantial and durable change" (p. 368). Working though issues in these types of groups takes time. Therefore, trying to end a group before its members are ready for closure is ill-advised and can be detrimental.

In closing a group session, a leader will usually inform members that the group is ending about 5 to 30 minutes before its conclusion. Such an announcement (i.e., orientation) does not have to be elaborate. Rather, the leader can simply say during a pause or a brief interruption, "I see we have about 15 minutes left. What do we need to do collectively or individually in order to end on time?" In a therapy group, the amount of time needed to bring about closure is almost always greater than in a task/work or psychoeducational group. Regardless, this orientation to the end makes it possible for the group to summarize, set goals, and plan for follow-up if they wish.

In ending a total group experience, the orientation to termination involves a planned number of sessions that are devoted to the topic of closure. In closed counseling and psychotherapy groups, at least two to four sessions should be focused on the ending (Gazda, 1989; Maples, 1988). Task/work groups may decide to disband more rapidly, but they also need time to get used to the idea of no longer being a group. In guidance/psychoeducational groups, members are usually aware in advance that the group will be time limited. However, a reminder is often appreciated and keeps the group on task and mentally prepared for the final ending. A straightforward orientation to termination followed by the other steps in the termination process helps members accomplish their pregroup goals and clarify any questions they have of themselves or others. As in other environments, members who gain the most from a group experience are informed in advance what will happen during the time they are together and what is expected of them. The process of termination is no exception to this rule.

EFFECTS OF TERMINATION ON INDIVIDUALS

The effects of termination on individuals depends on many factors. Some of the more pertinent include whether the group was opened or closed, whether members were, in fact, prepared in advance for its ending, and whether the speed and intensity of work within sessions was at an appropriate level to allow participants to properly identify and resolve concerns or problems. If handled inappropriately, termination may have an adverse effect on persons and inhibit their growth. "If handled adequately, the process of termination in itself can be an important role in helping individuals develop new behaviors" (Hansen, Warner, & Smith, 1980, p. 539). Often from the death of relationships, whether physical or psychological, comes a new understanding of who one was with others and who one is now as a result (Hulse-Killacky, 1993).

The behavior of group members at the end of the group indicates how they think and feel as well as what they have experienced (Luft, 1984; Shulman, 1992). Members who are anxious at or during termination may feel they cannot function without the support of the group. Participants who are sad may be afraid they will not see others in the group again. Those who are angry may think they have not accomplished what they should have done (Ellis, 1988). For example, if Jane says to the group that she is "upset" about its ending and wishes to continue longer, she may be indirectly stating that she wants reassurance from group members that she is competent to deal with situations by herself.

Usually the range of feelings in individual members of groups is wide. In some cases, group members emphasize only the positive aspects of what has occurred in the group instead of what they have learned. This type of focus is known as the **"farewell-party syndrome"** and tends to avoid the pain of closure (Shulman, 1992, p. 205). However, the most likely overriding emotion at the end of a group is one that can best be described as mixed or bittersweet (Goodyear, 1981).

The best way for individuals to end a group is to reflect on what they have experienced and make way for new beginnings outside the group, but the achievement of this ideal is not always possible. Therefore, group leaders may have to focus special attention on the issue of separation with some people more than others (Corey, Corey, Callanan, & Russell, 1992). For example, the leader may have to spend more time with Jason at the end of a therapy or counseling group because of his unstable background. Simultaneously, the leader may spend less time with Jacob because of his emotionally secure past. For Jason, the fear that he will be unable to find supportive relationships in other settings can be countered by a leader who helps him remember the risks he took in the present group and ways he achieved his group goal in a personal and satisfactory way. The leader can help Martha, who has unfinished business involving anger and regret, review how she combated these negative feelings in the counseling or therapy group and what steps she might take in the future.

Regardless of how careful and thorough the leader is during the termination stage, a few group members may on occasions need more help. For these people, three options are productive:

1.   individual counseling—where unique concerns can be given greater attention,
2.   referral to another group or organization—where more specific or specialized assistance can be rendered, or
3.   **recycling,** where the individual can go through a similar group experience again and learn lessons missed the first time

In all of these cases, the focus is on helping group members maximize their capabilities and obtain their goals. Through these procedures, group members discover more about themselves, try to better understand others, and take steps toward creating the types of communities or organizations they need.

PREMATURE TERMINATION

Sometimes, individuals quit a group abruptly or the group experience ends suddenly because of actions by the leader. Both cases are examples of **premature**

termination and may result in difficulties for the participants (Donigian & Malnati, 1987). Various theoretical perspectives and practitioners handle such situations differently. For example, a person-centered group and leader may trust a group member's judgment that leaving before the group is scheduled to end is the best action, whereas a reality-therapy orientation may concentrate on trying to persuade a member not to leave. A psychodynamic perspective may explore intrapersonal reactions associated with premature termination.

There are ethical guidelines (e.g., Association for Specialists in Group Work, 1989) to follow in premature termination cases regardless of the reason for the action or the group leader's theoretical persuasion. Most of these guidelines apply to guidance/psychoeducational, counseling, and psychotherapy groups because the impact of premature endings is greatest on these types of groups. Task/work group members and leaders, however, may also make use of these guidelines.

Generally, three types of premature termination must be dealt with:
the termination of the group as a whole,
the termination of a successful group member, and
the termination of an unsuccessful group member (Yalom, 1985)

Premature Termination of the Group as a Whole

Premature termination of the whole group may occur because of a group leader or group member action. Group leaders may appropriately terminate the group prematurely if they become sick, move, or are reassigned to other duties. In all of these situations, group members may feel incomplete and try to reestablish contact with the leader (Pistole, 1991).

To handle these types of premature termination properly, leaders need to have at least one group session to say good-bye to the group as a whole, or they need to be able to contact group members directly. The logistics of making such arrangements is difficult. Inappropriate premature group termination, however, is even more stressful. Group leaders who prematurely terminate groups because they feel personal discomfort, fail to recognize and conceptualize problems, or feel overwhelmed by member problems do themselves and the group a disservice by leaving the group and its members with unresolved issues (Bernard, 1979).

Premature Termination Initiated by Group Members

For individuals, premature termination may be due to appropriate or inappropriate reasons, and the experience may be successful or unsuccessful. Yalom (1985) lists a number of reasons that are often given by individuals who leave psychotherapy and counseling groups prematurely:

1. "external factors" (e.g., scheduling conflicts or external stress)
2. "group deviancy" (members who do not "fit in" with others)

3. "problems of intimacy"
4. "fear of emotional contagion" (i.e., a negative personal reaction to hearing the problems of other group members)
5. "inability to share the doctor" (i.e., wanting individual attention from the group leader)
6. "complications of concurrent individual and group therapy"
7. "early provocateurs" (i.e., overt, strong rebellion against the group)
8. "inadequate orientation to therapy"
9. "complications arising from subgrouping" (p. 233)

Of these reasons, those involving external factors, not fitting in, and complications of concurrent individual and group therapy are most likely to be appropriate factors in deciding to end a group experience early. It should be cautioned, however, that group members may rationalize reasons for premature endings.

The other reasons given by Yalom, with the exception of inadequate orientation, are associated most often with immaturity of group participants. These individuals, who are usually unsuccessful in the group process, avoid dealing with loss by physically removing themselves from the group. They deny their need for self-exploration and understanding. They often prevent themselves from experiencing deep personal growth by making a few changes in behavior and then leaving (McGee, Schuman, & Racusen, 1972). At other times, if such group members do not remove themselves but consistently and disruptively act out, the leader may have to ask them to leave. This type of behavior is in marked contrast to successful group members who terminate prematurely for legitimate reasons and take the time to say good-bye to others in the group before they go.

Preventing Premature Termination

If a group appears to have a high potential for premature termination, there are steps that can be taken to prevent it. For instance,

groups should start and end on time,
members should commit to attend a number of sessions,
members should be treated in a personal and professional way,
clarity and conciseness should be used in talking about individual and group issues, and
reminders should be sent to members if there are long intervals between group sessions (Young, 1992)

Other steps that can be taken to soften or alleviate premature termination and its potential negative impact are as follows:

The first action is for the leader or members to inform the group as soon as possible about their departure from the group. Individuals need time to prepare for transitions and loss. The more time available the better, especially if the departure is unexpected. For example, a leader who is forced to move because of a spouse relocation to another city may telephone group members to prepare them for this event before the next session, especially if the move is unforeseen.

A second procedure group leaders can follow when faced with a member wanting to leave prematurely is to discuss thoroughly the ramifications of such a move with the member and the group in a safe, protected atmosphere (Corey & Corey, 1992). Often, members will not leave a group prematurely if they are given a chance to talk things out and explore their feelings more thoroughly. For instance, Peter may think he has been slighted but may feel differently once he has had a chance to face the issue in the group. Through this type of contact, he may recognize his tendency to flee situations when he is uncomfortable and acknowledge that he may have to change his lifestyle if he stays in the group.

Finally, in the case of premature termination, members should be helped to realize what they have gained from the group and what positive steps they can take in the future to build on these achievements. Giving members feedback is one valuable way to help them adjust to an abrupt ending (Wagenheim & Gemmill, 1994). If Penny, for instance, decides she wants to work on a project on her own without input from the group, members can tell her before she leaves what she has meant to them or the group as a whole. In such a situation, Dick might say, "Penny, I have really benefitted from the energy you have generated in this group," while Robin might respond, "Penny, I find what you want to do is refreshing and inspiring." When this feedback procedure is utilized, all members leave on a positive note and are more likely to benefit from the group.

Occasionally, a member will drop out of the group with no warning and without saying good-bye. In such cases, the group leader should follow up and ask the absent member why he or she left the group prematurely. The member should be invited back to discuss his or her thoughts and feelings with the group as a whole and to say good-bye and achieve closure when appropriate. Ethical guidelines (Association for Specialists in Group Work, 1989) state that no undue pressure should be used to force a member to return or remain in a group. However, the benefits and liabilities of staying in the group can and should be explored openly.

TERMINATION OF GROUP SESSIONS

There are numerous ways to end group sessions when the group has come to its planned conclusion. For each group session, the appropriate format for closing will depend on the type of group that was conducted, the purpose of the particular session, and the content of the session. It is best for the leader to vary the ending of the group whenever possible so members do not get bored with the same routine. Among the most effective formats for closing a group session are "having the members summarize, having the leader summarize, using a round, using dyads, and getting written reactions" (Jacobs, Harvill, & Masson, 1994, p. 335). The use of rating sheets is also recommended, as is homework (Wagenheim & Gemmill, 1994).

Member Summarizations

In member summarization, one or more members of the group summarize what has transpired during the session. The idea is to have members state what has happened to them individually and how they have gained from the particular session. If done regularly, "it challenges members each week to think about what they are both giving and getting from the group" (Corey, Corey, Callanan, & Russell, 1992, p. 152). At least ten minutes should be allotted to this exercise, but it is important that group members not become bored. Thus, each member who speaks must keep his or her summary brief. For example, member comments at the end of a session might go as follows:

Manuel:	"I've learned a lot just by listening today. I have found out I share many of the same feelings about taking risks that Russell does."
Mary Grace:	"I was surprised that the focus of the group today centered on risks. I expected we would talk about past events, not present challenges. This session has got me thinking about what I will do in regard to my work situation."
Russell:	"It was a risk for me to speak up today and talk about my feelings in regard to taking risks, such as moving to a new city. While I still have mixed emotions about what I am going to do in the future, I'm glad I spoke up."
Chip:	"I'm glad you initiated our focus on risk-taking, Russell. There are some situations in my own life that involve risks that I want to talk about next time."

Leader Summarizations

When leaders summarize, they give a personal reaction to what they perceive to have occurred in the group. Leaders may comment on "the cohesion of the group, the degree to which members freely brought up topics for work, the willingness of members to take risks and talk about unsafe topics, the degree to which members interacted with one another, and the willingness of members to discuss negative concerns or feelings" (Corey, Corey, Callanan, & Russell, 1992, p. 154). For example, the leader may say on such occasions,

"I like the way Julie confronted Joe on the issue of anger. I don't know that you resolved how anger should be handled, but at least you started a dialogue. I was also pleased to see Sally assert herself. Sally, I have wondered about your silence, so it was good to see you come out. Mark, I was impressed with your comments, too, in regard to trying new behaviors when in a different environment. I'll be interested in what you do this week in that regard. Tom, it seemed to me that you were avoiding con-

frontation with Diana today. It might be productive for you and Diana to talk about that next session."

The leaders' advantage in summary situations is the emphasis they can place on certain points and comments. The disadvantage is that leaders may neglect some important developments during the session or fail to mention the contributions of one or two members. Also, leaders may misinterpret behaviors or interchanges.

Rounds

The exercise of *rounds* (sometimes called *go-rounds*) is a variation on member summarization, except in this procedure every group member comments briefly (usually a sentence or two) about highlights of the group session. Rounds are a way of completing loose thoughts, ending on a positive note, and ensuring that each member feels involved in the group (Trotzer, 1989). In a round, each group member gets equal air time and leaves with a feeling of having participated in the group.

Dyads

By having members form into groups of two, or dyads, at the end of a session, group leaders make sure all members are involved in termination, and at the same time, the group is energized. Often, group leaders may decide to pair participants up at the end of a session if they are working on similar concerns or problems. For example, if Tom and Jean are both striving to be better listeners and more empathetic, they may be put together to talk and practice skills connected with their concerns. If there are no obvious pairings, members are free to choose their partners or work with those assigned to them.

Written Reactions

Several forms of written reactions can be used at the end of group sessions. One is an exercise in which members are asked to take a few minutes during the closing of a session and write their reactions to what has happened. This procedure is conducted infrequently, and members may or may not share their writing, depending on the time left in the session and the instructions of the leader.

A second form of this procedure is for group members to write regularly at the end of each session in a **journal,** or **log** (Carroll, 1970; Lifton, 1967). In this process, group members are required to write their reactions to the events of each session. This process enables them to spot inconsistencies in their reactions more quickly than if they simply talked about them. A paper trail is established that group members and the group leader may later consult in charting the personal effect of the group. "Logs written immediately following the session will tend to reflect more accurately the emotions experienced within the session, while those written following a reasonable time lapse will present observations digested and organized in a fashion compatible with the self-concept . . ." (Riordan & Matheny, 1972, p. 381).

A third form of writing is to combine the written word with either music or drawings (Wenz & McWhirter, 1990). For example, in summing up a session or a group, members may be invited to draw logos that represent their lives or to bring in music that symbolizes through lyrics or a melody who they are. In the case of Elaine, she drew a tree that was green and full as her logo. Underneath the tree she wrote the words shown.

I have grown to be me,
All that I hoped in the group I could be.
Now I am moving on.

Logos can be created by first asking members of groups to doodle. After they have engaged in doodling for a few minutes, they are then invited to find part of the doodle to expand on in making their logo. They are, furthermore, encouraged to think of words and phrases that come to mind as they embellish their drawings and to jot these descriptors down for when they write about what they have drawn.

Finally, the group leader can make written notes about or to members at the end of each session, which may or may not be shared with the group or individuals (Yalom, 1985). When the leader chooses to write notes about members, this usually takes the form of a private, clinical record. When the leader writes notes to group members on their logs, the response is aimed at promoting insight and communication with individuals. In some group exercises, written responses are given to the group as a whole by the leader or other members.

Rating Sheets

Another way of closing a group and obtaining an accurate picture of how the group assessed the session is by having the leader distribute a **rating sheet** to members that they fill out and return before they leave. Members can rate themselves, other members, and the leader on a number of dimensions including involvement, risk taking, goals, emotional involvement, feedback, and productivity (Corey, Corey, Callanan, & Russell, 1992). They can give their opinions on how satisfactory the group was for them and how they think it could be improved. In order to be effective, a group session rating sheet should be brief. Sometimes it can be set up in the form of incomplete sentences, as follows:

End-of-Group-Session Rating Sheet

1. The thing I liked most about today's group was _____.
2. My best and most productive time in today's group was _____.
3. The thing I will remember most about today's group is _____.
4. I think that today's group could have been improved if _____.
5. My suggestions for making the group even better are _____.

Homework

The closing of a group may often occur with the assignment of *homework*. Such "real-world," nongroup experiences can include thinking, feeling, or behavior experiences (Vander Kolk, 1985). Homework may be especially important in work/task groups where members need to complete assignments so the group can complete a project. Homework is also important in counseling/therapy groups because it helps members find ways of transferring learning in the group to events in their everyday life. Getting homework assignments at the close of the session allows group members to be more concrete in determining their between-group goals.

TERMINATION OF A GROUP

The termination of a group is filled with a mixture of emotions and tasks. It is a time when there are noticeable changes in the behavior of members (Davies & Kuypers, 1985). In successful groups, there is an increase in positive feedback and a certain amount of distancing as members anticipate change. In unsuccessful groups, anger and frustration may emerge along with distancing as members realize they will not obtain individual or group goals. "Embedded in the process of termination are issues of the individual's separateness, autonomy, and independence from the group" (Ohlsen, Horne, & Lawe, 1988, p. 93). Leaders and members who successfully complete this stage of the group work hard and employ certain interpersonal and process skills. These interpersonal and process skills will be concentrated on here because they serve as a model to emulate.

Movement into the stage of termination rests squarely on the shoulders of group leaders. Although members of all groups realize the group will end, it is the leader who provides the type of guidance that will make this process positive and productive. One way leaders do this, as previously noted, is through setting a time limit for the group (i.e., a number of meeting times that are announced in advance). A second way they help the group terminate is through **capping**—easing out of emotional interaction and into cognitive reflection (Bates et al., 1982). Skilled group leaders realize that if members leave groups stirred up emotionally they may not remember much, if any, of what they learned within the group. Therefore, there is a purposeful attempt to promote more cognitive interpersonal and intrapersonal interactions as the group moves into disbanding.

A third way group leaders can ease termination is to model appropriate termination skills and call the group's attention to what needs to be done in bringing about closure. This means that group leaders will approach the group from a more matter-of-fact and reflective manner and help focus group members in such a direction. Finally, there are a number of capping (i.e., closure) skills that enable the group to close appropriately. In their interactions with the group as a whole, leaders must utilize these skills to the maximum. Since time and modeling processes have been covered previously, capping skills, especially as they relate to affective aspects of the group, will be focused on here.

Capping Skills in Terminations

Some groups need less time to close than others. For instance, task/work and guidance/psychoeducational groups usually end when they have completed their mission. There may be **summarizing** reflections by group members that recall significant events or learning experiences in the group at its end. However, other procedures are not utilized. On the other hand, psychotherapy and counseling groups may struggle with multiple issues during closure because of the personal nature of material covered. In actuality, all types of groups can benefit from capping skills in closure. When these skills are employed properly, group members gain a sense of completeness that the group has ended and a new time in their lives has begun. Some of the most important capping skills for groups to employ at the termination of the group as a whole are

1. reviewing and summarizing the group experience
2. assessing members' growth, change [or achievement]
3. finishing business
4. applying change to everyday life (implementing decisions)
5. providing feedback
6. handling good-byes
7. planning for continued problem resolution (Jacobs et al., 1994, p. 347)

Reviewing and summarizing the group experience is the first way to ask members to cap the group. This procedure involves having members recall and share special moments they remember from the group. One way to implement this review is by asking members to recollect their most salient memories from each of the group sessions. Giving the members copies of their feedback sheets on individual sessions may enhance this experience, but it is not absolutely necessary. At review and summary times, group leaders or other group members may guide participants through the process in ferreting out important points they wish to remember or contribute to the group.

For example, in her review of the group, Carolyn became stuck in remembering exactly when she made her first major contribution to the group.

Carolyn:	"I think it was during the fifth session that I noticed how we all shared a common concern about not being recognized for the work we do and pointed it out to the group as a whole. I was pleased that I did that, and I think you, as members of the group, were, too. I just wish I could remember when I did that."
Group Leader	(politely interrupting):"Carolyn, although you cannot remember the exact session, what would you like for us as a group to remember?"
Carolyn:	"Two things—First, I made a contribution, and second, I helped us all realize more clearly a common bond— concern over not being recognized. I think the second contribution was important to the group as a whole in what eventually happened here."

Assessing is a similar technique to that of reviewing, but in **assessing members' growth and change,** the emphasis is on individuals' memories of themselves at the beginning of the group and now. The idea of such a capping exercise is to have members see and share significant gains with themselves and others. If group logs have been used, they may be consulted before members share with one another. The important point of this exercise is for members to recognize their own growth. For instance,

Marge: "When I came here, I was scared. I felt I was the only
              one who was self-conscious about how she looked
              physically. Through this group, I have grown to under-
              stand that everyone, including really attractive people
              like you, Betsy, worry about how you present yourself. I
              am more confident than I was when we began this
              group that I can overcome my feelings. I have also
              learned, through my conversations with you, some
              things that I can do to enhance my appearance."

Completing unfinished business is a crucial task at the end of a group.
Unfinished business is basically "when someone hurts another, or is hurt by
someone, and fails to resolve (the) problems with the relevant person" (Ohlsen
et al., 1988, p. 128). Unfinished business may develop in groups because of their
fast pace and lack of time to process all of the material that is brought up. If not
resolved, unfinished business festers like an untreated wound and can hamper
personal functioning. The "hurt" may distract a person from concentrating on
what he or she needs to do and has a negative impact on the group itself. In
either case, clear communication, congruence, and direct confrontation of the
event with the significant person are needed to make resolution and start the
healing process. During termination, group members are encouraged to complete this process, feel relief, and start mending and growing. Different theoretical approaches will direct exactly how this may be done, but sometimes the
learning of a new behavior is required. In completing this task, it is crucial not to
bring up new business.

For example, if Tamara thinks Wendy has put her down in the group, she
needs to voice her concern during the termination stage, if not before. Then, if
shy, she may need to assert herself and ask for what she wants or thinks she
needs, such as an apology. From that point, there is clarification, negotiation, and
if successful, resolution. When the process is over, Tamara and Wendy should be
able to move on with their lives, each other, and the group.

The process of *applying change to everyday life* involves rehearsal, role play,
and homework. **Rehearsal** can be done in the group setting with members
showing others in the group how they plan to act in particular situations. This
type of demonstration can be made more concrete and meaningful when others
in the group play the roles of significant people in such environments. Some
common mistakes that members make in rehearsals and role plays are focusing
on the change in others instead of self, becoming impatient with the slowness of
others' change, and relying too much on the jargon of the group (Corey, Corey,
Callanan, & Russell, 1992; Shulman, 1992). Usually, rehearsals and role plays will
occur in the working part of the group and only be reviewed at termination.

Sharing homework is a transitional exercise that often follows rehearsal and
role playing where group members actually practice in public what they have
done experientially in the group. Homework is usually specific and allows group
members to report their results to the group, decide more clearly what they wish
to change, and make a transition from group to personal norms. Homework has

been covered before, and in reviewing it here, the important points that should be remembered are (a) homework is a continuous technique that may be employed in many different types of group sessions, and (b) homework of group members should always be processed.

Providing feedback is crucial to the closure of a group and is often an integrating experience. It provides an opportunity for leaders and members to reinforce each other for the progress they have made, as well as to deal with their thoughts and feelings about making meaningful changes. Feedback should be honest, specific, sincere, and as positive as possible, although leaders and members occasionally can use it "to confront members who are still denying problems or who have not taken responsibility for their behavior" (Jacobs et al., 1994, p. 350). It is helpful for members to write down specific feedback, otherwise they tend to forget what was said (Wagenheim & Gemmill, 1994). After the group has ended, members can use written records of feedback to see if they are continuing to make progress toward being the type of person they were becoming when the group ended.

Expressing farewells allows the group to wrap up, at least on an affective/cognitive level. By **saying good-bye,** members are encouraged to own their feelings and express their thoughts at this time, especially in regard to what others in the group have meant to them. Members may reminisce about significant group events at this time, "remind each other of the way they were, and give personal testimonials about how much they have been helped" (Hansen et al., 1980, p. 546). The group leader may also deal with feelings about separation if they come up.

Sometimes there is a resistance to saying good-bye, for this is the final capping experience. Group leaders can set the tone for the closing moments in such cases by sharing their feelings of satisfaction with the work the group has done and by inviting members to express themselves in a farewell. For some members, there is a need for touching, shaking hands, or hugging. Depending on the type of group, one or more of these demonstrative ways of saying good-bye may be appropriate, but it is best for leaders and members to error on the side of caution if they are ever in doubt as to how to say good-bye. This means using a verbal approach. The important thing in good-byes is that thoughts and feelings be expressed in a constructive manner.

Often, especially in closed groups, structured exercises can be used in this farewell process (Cohen & Smith, 1976; Pfeiffer & Jones, 1969–1975; Schutz, 1967; Trotzer, 1989). These exercises can help bring a ceremonial close to the group and bring it to a climactic and conclusive ending. One such structured exercise is the awarding of certificates for attending the group. Another is a **pat on the back** where members draw the outline of their hand on a piece of white paper that is then taped on their back. Other group members then write closing comments on the hand outline or the paper itself that are positive and constructive about the person.

The final step in closing a group is *developing a specific plan for continuing each member's progress* after the group ends. This **planning for continued problem resolution** may be completed before or after individual good-byes are said. It should include when and how certain activities will be carried out, but "others' expectations should not be part of the plan" (Vander Kolk, 1985, p. 204). In essence, this activity is a variation on what Corey et al. (1992) describe as **projecting the future,** in which group members are asked to imagine what changes they would like to make in the short term and long term. However, this planning process is more concrete and may involve the use of a written contract between the group member and the group that spells out in a realistic way how the member will implement the plan. Such a procedure can be quite productive in a work/task group as well as a therapeutic group. For example, Bob may state to the group and to himself that within the next three months he will complete his survey to find out how customers in his department like the services they are being offered. He will then send group members the data he collects.

PROBLEMS IN TERMINATIONS

Sometimes group members (and occasionally group leaders) have difficulty with the stage of termination. In such cases, they will attempt to deny that they are close to ending and will not do work connected with closure and transition (Hansen et al., 1980). At other times, they will encounter difficulties in transference issues with the leader or other members. Another scenario may be the group leader's countertransference in relationship to one or more members. Finally, there are the issues of closure and transition, which may or may not be handled correctly. Each of these four possible problem areas will be examined here.

Denial

Denial is acting as if an experience, such as a group, will never end. It can be expressed in a group on a limited or mass level (Donigian & Malnati, 1987; Yalom, 1985). Usually the denial of termination is an individual matter, although there are some groups at times that act as if the group experience will continue indefinitely. In cases of denial, the group leader must remind participants, especially in closed groups, when the last session will be and encourage them to prepare accordingly. In cases where the group or individuals refuse to deal with termination issues, the leader needs to focus specifically on these areas. This focus may involve consultation with another professional, individual sessions with denying members, or a special session or two with the group as a whole.

For example, when John led a six-part psychoeducational group on home repairs, members of the group told him after the fourth session that they would not let him end the group. Collectively, they insisted they wanted more and would not stop learning. To John's credit, he thanked the group for its confidence in him and compliments to him, but at the beginning of the fifth session, he also stated firmly and matter-of-factly that the group would end in one more session. He gave group members additional information on other courses they might find of interest and referred them to the community college's director of continuing education for information on what other classes were available.

Transference

Transference is the "displacement of affect from one person to another" (Ohlsen et al., 1988, p. 179). It has many sources but basically operates on an unconscious level and is manifest most directly when individuals attempt to relate to other persons in ways inappropriate for the situation (Glatzer, 1965). Group leaders and members in counseling and psychotherapy groups are often the objects of multiple transferences, that is, distorted perceptions (Shaffer & Galinsky, 1989). However, transference can occur in task/work and psychoeducational groups, too. For example, at various times in the group, leaders and members may be perceived by other participants as experts, authority figures, superpersons, friends, and/or lovers. There is a natural tendency for many group participants, especially adult children of alcoholics, to interact in the group as they did in their family of origin (Brown & Beletsis, 1986).

One way of dealing with these perceptions is to recognize them for what they are initially in the group and encourage participants to give both positive and negative feedback to others throughout the group process. This is a tricky process to keep in balance, and group leaders may be wise to seek consultation or supervision in such situations. At the end of the group, if transference is still present, the group may be used as a whole to help individuals deal with their unresolved issues, including the revealing of feelings and the realistic exploration of them. Individual counseling for the person with transference problems, after the group terminates, may also be appropriate.

Countertransference

Countertransference is usually thought of as the leader's emotional responses to members that are a result of the leader's own needs or unresolved issues with significant others. However, in addition to leader/member interactions, countertransference can occur between members of unequal status. The first step in dealing with it is to recognize how it is being manifest. Watkins (1985) states that countertransference is being exhibited when leaders are oversolicitous, distant, protective, nonconfrontational, overly identified with, or romantically and/or socially attracted to group members. To combat these feelings and actions, the group leader may need help in the form of direct supervision and/or individual therapy. It is crucial in ending a group that countertransference issues be resolved.

Handling Termination Correctly

As evidenced from the literature on termination, there is no one way to handle it correctly. However, there are some specific signs that termination is being conducted incorrectly. For example, if a group is closed in an abrupt manner and issues about ending are not processed, the group is being closed improperly. "More often than not, this problem is observed when the group is of the short-term, weekend encounter variety where there is no follow-up period built into the process," or where the group leader is "from out-of-town and conducts a combination training-therapy workshop" (Gazda, 1989, p. 307).

Another sign that the group is being terminated incorrectly is when members are left with a number of unresolved issues. In open-ended groups, this problem may be handled by extending the number of sessions in the group (Yalom, 1985). In closed and time-limited groups, leaders must try to resolve as many of these issues in the time left in the group and make appropriate referrals or offer individual counseling to those who still have difficulties when the group ends.

Overall, termination is a gradual process, and group leaders who handle it properly "give it time" to evolve (Hansen et al., 1980). "Embedded in the process of termination are issues of the individual's separateness, autonomy, and independence from the group" (Ohlsen et al., 1988, p. 93). The pain and anxiety of separating from the group (if they occur) are best dealt with at this time by using capping techniques such as sharing of past experiences, remembering meaningful group events, reminiscing about the way one entered the group as opposed to how one is now, and talking about present and future plans (Gladding, 1994b; Yalom, 1985). The sharing of this information can be done on an individual basis through a brief leader/member exit interview prior to the final session of the group or within the confines of the last few sessions of the group itself.

FOLLOW-UP SESSIONS

Follow-up is the procedure of reconnecting with group members after they have had enough time to process what they experienced in the group and work on their goals/objectives. Usually follow-up is planned for three to six months after a group ends, either with the group as a whole or with the leader and a group member. There are several ways to follow up with group members once a group has ended. The first is "to arrange for a private interview with each group member a few weeks to a few months after the group terminates" (Corey, Corey, Callanan, & Russell, 1992, p. 163). These interviews focus on the achievement of individual goals of group members and give leaders and members a way of assessing what has happened to members since the group terminated. At these times, the impact of the group on members can be examined more closely, and any unresolved business can be discussed. Leaders also have an opportunity at such sessions to suggest other resources or opportunities for group members.

A second variation on the follow-up of group members is to hold a follow-up session, a reunion of the group, about three to six months after its termination (Cormier & Hackney, 1993; Gladding, 1994b). These sessions may take the form of parties/ celebrations or may be conducted in a business-style manner. Regardless, it is important that leaders and members are given the opportunity to reconnect with one another and share their unique experiences. The best way to plan for reunions is to announce them before the group officially ends. In this way, group members are more motivated to follow through on changes to which they have committed during the group.

Another way that is utilized in follow-ups is the employment of an evaluation questionnaire. An evaluation questionnaire serves the purpose of helping group members be concrete in assessing the group in which they have participated. These questionnaires can take many forms but is best if kept brief. An evaluation questionnaire should cover at least three aspects of the group:

the leadership of the group,
the facilities in which the group was held, and
the effectiveness of the group in achieving its objectives

Leadership can be assessed by asking such questions as whether the leader (or co-leaders) were personally and professionally responsible and whether they were effective in helping the group and its members. Questions related to whether the group began and ended on time are also appropriate.

Queries related to facilities should focus on the location, comfort, and usefulness of the room in conducting a group. If a room is too noisy or cold, or even if it is the wrong shape, the group will be affected.

Final inquiries on a follow-up questionnaire should deal with the effectiveness of the group. If the individuals involved got their personal and collective needs met through the group, the group was successful. It may take months before such an assessment can accurately be made.

A final frequently used method to evaluate a group is through writing a journal. A *journal*, or log, may be a valuable document for later examining what actually happened and when within the group (Adams, 1993). Individuals who keep journals may discover through reading their writings how they progressed during the group. Leaders may especially benefit by sharing their journals with other professionals as a means of supervision and feedback. In such a process, they may gain insight into their own strengths and weaknesses in handling particular group stages, difficult group members, and forms of group behavior.

Among the benefits of keeping a journal are its immediacy and availability for the group member or leader. A journal is a paper trail that can be kept in a special place so that it is always accessible. Journals also allow group members to release their emotions and check the reality around them. By recognizing themes within one's journal, a person can examine predominant ways of reacting toward a person or situation. If such expression is irrational or irresponsible, the group member can work within or after the group to become more skilled in making another response. Finally, journals help group members clarify their thoughts. For example, by journal writing, Jill may discover she is mad at herself for not taking risks rather than angry at Amy for taking up too much "air time."

SUMMARY AND CONCLUSION

Termination is an important stage in groups, both on an individual session basis and as an overall process. The impact of termination on group participants and on the group as a whole can either be positive or negative. Thus, it is crucial that group leaders and members have an awareness of termination and its importance even before the group starts.

Up until the late 1970s, termination was not given much attention because it was assumed that group leaders would know how to close off groups. Since that time, however, termination has increasingly been recognized as a distinct process in group work, and has been the subject of numerous research studies. On an individual level, group members may either resist or gradually move toward termination. Some members, who have not been properly screened or who are immature, may leave the group early. Leaders and members must deal with these situations as well as with unavoidable premature exits due to circumstances beyond a leader's or member's control. Ways of handling these situations vary, but general guidelines exist. One of these guidelines is to recognize that major theoretical positions deal with premature termination differently. Another guideline is to be aware that termination is a gradual and stepwise process.

Appropriate ways of ending individual sessions and the group as a whole exist. Group leaders must take precautions and necessary steps to see that groups run on time and that members realize the importance of participating within the group while there is time. Ways of encouraging members to do so include structured exercises, such as making the rounds, as well as setting up parameters and focus. It is the leader's responsibility to make sure the group stays on track in closing and to help members who have unfinished business or other problems at the time of termination. Follow-up on either an individual or group basis is a way of helping members concentrate on what they have achieved within the group as well as what they wish to accomplish. Structured exercises used throughout the termination process, such as journal keeping or feedback questionnaires, will help leaders and group members end a group positively and productively.

CLASSROOM EXERCISES

1. As a class studying groups, bring in song lyrics, poems, or short stories that deal with the theme of termination. Examine how writers treat the subject, and discuss those whom the class feels personify these themes.

2. In a group of three, think of an exercise you could use to help a group terminate, for example, the making of a group collage. As a triad, formulate directions to do your exercise and conduct it before the class as a whole. Try to make your exercise as concrete and creative as possible.

3. Discuss in a group of three what you would do as a group leader in the following situations:
    a. A group member at the last session angrily attacks you as the leader and says his experience in the group has been worthless.
    b. Five out of eight group members ask you during the last session to extend the group for at least four more sessions.

c. After the close of an individual group session, a member lingers and tells you she must talk about something she did not reveal in the group today. Share your strategies for dealing with these situations with the class as a whole.

4. Role play a group session in which one member gets up and leaves the group (during the second session). Have group members and the leader react in ways they feel at the moment. Then have other class members who have been on the outside of this demonstration give the inside group feedback about what they observed and what they might do.

REFERENCES

Adams, K. (1993). *The way of the journal.* Lutherville, MD: Sidran Press.

Association for Specialists in Group Work. (1989). *Ethical guidelines for group counselors.* Alexandria, VA: Author.

Bates, M., Johnson, C. D., & Blaker, K. E. (1982). *Group leadership: A manual for group counseling leaders* (2nd ed.). Denver: Love Publishing.

Bernard, J. M. (1979). Supervisor training: A discrimination model. *Counselor Education and Supervision, 19,* 60–68.

Brown, S., & Beletsis, S. (1986). The development of family transference in groups for adult children of alcoholics. *International Journal of Group Psychotherapy, 36,* 97–114.

Carroll, M. R. (1970). Silence is the heart's size: Self-examination through group process. *Personnel and Guidance Journal, 48,* 546–551.

Cohen, A. M., & Smith, R. D. (1976). *The critical incident in growth groups: A manual for group leaders.* La Jolla, CA: University Associates.

Corey, G. (1990). *Theory and practice of group counseling* (3rd ed.). Pacific Grove, CA: Brooks/Cole.

Corey, G., Corey, M. S., Callanan, P. J., & Russell, J. M. (1992). *Group techniques* (2nd ed.). Pacific Grove, CA: Brooks/Cole.

Corey, M. S., & Corey, G. (1992). *Groups: Process and practice.* (4th ed.). Pacific Grove, CA: Brooks/Cole.

Cormier, L. S., & Hackney, H. (1993). *The professional counselor: A process guide to helping* (2nd ed.). Boston: Allyn & Bacon.

Davies, D., & Kuypers, B. (1985). Group development and interpersonal feedback. *Group and Organizational Studies, 10,* 184–208.

Donigian, J., & Malnati, R. (1987). *Critical incidents in group therapy.* Pacific Grove, CA: Brooks/Cole.

Ellis, A. (1988). *How to stubbornly refuse to make yourself miserable about anything—Yes, anything!* Secaucus, NJ: Lyle Stuart.

Epstein, N. B., & Bishop, D. S. (1981). Problem centered systems therapy of the family. *Journal of Marital and Family Therapy, 7,* 23–31.

Gazda, G. M. (1989). *Group counseling: A developmental approach* (4th ed.). Boston: Allyn & Bacon.

Gladding, S. T. (1994a). *Transitions.* Unpublished manuscript.

Gladding, S. T. (1994b). *Effective group counseling.* Greensboro, NC: ERIC/CASS.

Glatzer, H. T. (1965). Aspects of transference in group psychotherapy. *International Journal of Group Psychotherapy, 15,* 167–176.

Goodyear, R. K. (1981). Termination as a loss experience for the counselor. *Personnel and Guidance Journal, 59,* 347–350.

Hansen, J. C., Warner, R. W., & Smith, E. J. (1980). *Group counseling: Theory and process* (2nd ed.). Chicago: Rand McNally.

Hulse-Killacky, D. (1993). Personal and professional endings. *Journal of Humanistic Education and Development, 32,* 92–94.

Jacobs, E. E., Harvill, R. L., & Masson, R. L. (1994). *Group counseling: Strategies and skills* (2nd ed). Pacific Grove, CA: Brooks/Cole .

Kauff, P. F. (1977). The termination process: Its relationship to separation–individuation phase of development. *International Journal of Group Psychotherapy, 27,* 3–18.

Lieberman, M., Yalom, I., & Miles, M. (1973). *Encounter groups: First facts.* New York: Basic Books.

Lifton, W. M. (1967). *Working with groups.* New York: Wiley.

Luft, J. (1984). *Group processes* (3rd ed.). Palo Alto, CA: Mayfield.

MacKenzie, K., & Livesley, W. (1984). Developmental stages: An integrating theory of group psychotherapy. *Canadian Journal of Psychiatry, 29,* 247–251.

Maples, M. F. (1988). Group development: Extending Tuckman's theory. *Journal for Specialists in Group Work, 13,* 17–23.

McGee, T., Schuman, B., & Racusen, F. (1972). Termination in group psychotherapy. *American Journal of Psychotherapy, 22,* 3–18.

Ohlsen, M. M., Horne, A. M., & Lawe, C. F. (1988). *Group counseling* (3rd ed.). New York: Holt, Rinehart & Winston.

Pfeiffer, J. W., & Jones, J. E. (Eds.). (1969–1975). *A handbook of structured experiences for human relations training* (5 vols.). La Jolla, CA: University Associates.

Pistole, M. C. (1991). Termination: Analytic reflections on client contact after counselor relocation. *Journal of Counseling and Development, 69,* 337–340.

Riordan, R. J., & Matheny, K. B. (1972). Dear diary: Logs in group counseling. *Personnel and Guidance Journal, 50,* 379–382.

Schutz, W. (1967). *Joy: Expanding human awareness.* New York: Grove.

Shaffer, J., & Galinsky, M. D. (1989). *Models of group therapy* (2nd ed.). Boston: Allyn & Bacon.

Shapiro, J. L. (1978). *Methods of group psychotherapy and encounter: A tradition of innovation.* Itasca, IL: F. E. Peacock.

Shulman, L. (1992). *The skills of helping* (3rd ed.). Itasca, IL: F. E. Peacock.

Trotzer, J. P. (1989). *The counselor and the group* (2nd ed.). Muncie, IN: Accelerated Development.

Tuckman, B. W. (1965). Developmental sequence in small groups. *Psychological Bulletin, 63,* 384–399.

Tuckman, B. W., & Jensen, M. A. (1977). Stages of small group development revisited. *Group and Organizational Studies, 2,* 419–427.

Vander Kolk, C. J. (1985). *Introduction to group counseling and psychotherapy.* Columbus, OH: Merrill.

Wagenheim, G., & Gemmill, G. (1994). Feedback exchange: Managing group closure. *Journal of Management Education, 18,* 265–269.

Watkins, C. E. (1985). Countertransference: Its impact on the counseling situation. *Journal of Counseling and Development, 63,* 356–359.

Wenz, K., & McWhirter, J. J. (1990). Enhancing the group experience: Creative writing exercises. *Journal for Specialists in Group Work, 15,* 37–42.

Woody, R. H., Hansen, J. C., & Rossberg, R. H. (1989). *Counseling psychology: Strategies and services.* Pacific Grove, CA: Brooks/Cole.

Yalom, I. D. (1985). *The theory and practice of group psychotherapy* (3rd ed.). New York: Basic Books.

Young, M. E. (1992). *Counseling methods and techniques.* New York: Macmillan.

CHAPTER 8

Ethical and Legal Aspects of Group Work

I am taken back by your words—
To your history and the mystery of being human
*   in an all-too-often robotic world.*
I hear your pain
*   and see the pictures you paint*
*   so cautiously and vividly.*
The world you draw is a kaleidoscope
*   ever changing, ever new, encircling, and fragile.*
Moving past the time and through the shadows
*   you look for hope beyond the groups you knew*
*   as a child.*
I want to say: "I'm here. Trust the process."
But the artwork is your own
*   so I withdraw and watch you work*
*   while occasionally offering you colors*
*   and images of the possible.* *

G roup leaders are constantly making decisions. Much of what they decide is guided by the ethical guidelines of the professional organizations to which they belong and the legal codes of local, state, and federal governments. At times, practitioners are confused about whether their decision making is based on ethical guidelines, legal standards, or both. *Ethics* and the *law* are not one and the same. Rather, "they can probably be best conceptualized as two over-lapping circles which share a common intersection" (Kitchener, 1984a, p. 16). Ethical and legal opinions complement and contradict each other. Group leaders who make the best and wisest decisions are those who are informed by as many sources as possible.

Information is not enough, however. Knowledge in and of itself does not guarantee proper ethical behavior (Baldick, 1980; Welfel & Lipsitz, 1984). Group leaders and members must also practice what they learn. "Conduct and character are correlated" (Hayes, 1991, p. 24). It is only with practice that those who work in groups become skilled at discerning the rationale for their behaviors and the consequences of them (Foltz, Kirby, & Paradise, 1989). Therefore, ethical and legal decision making is a dynamic activity that needs careful attention if group leaders are to stay current and act in the best interest of their group members. "It becomes every group leader's responsibility to attempt to think ethically and behave professionally" (Gumaer & Scott, 1986, p. 149).

In this chapter, the nature of professional and personal ethics will be examined, along with some specific ethical guidelines for group leaders. Potential problems related to ethics in group work will be examined, along with issues involving the training of group leaders in ethics. In addition, the nature of law and legal codes will be explored as they affect the field of group work. Potential legal problems in groups will be discussed. Although many ethical and legal matters are fairly straightforward and clear-cut, others are not. Group work is a complex process, and those who are most involved in it must be multifaceted.

THE NATURE OF ETHICS AND ETHICAL CODES

In group work, **ethics** may best be defined as "suggested standards of conduct based on a set of professional values" (George & Dustin, 1988, p. 124). To behave in an ethical way is to act in a professionally acceptable manner based on these values (Hayes, 1991). Ethics deal with what is right and correct and are deduced from values. All ethical issues involve values as grounds for decision making. Some of the dominant values underlying the practice of ethics are based on the virtues of autonomy, beneficence, nonmaleficence, and justice (i.e., fairness) (Kitchener, 1984b).

Autonomy is the promotion of self-determination or the power to choose one's own direction in life. In groups, it is important that members feel they have a right to make their own decisions.

Beneficence is promoting the good of others. It is assumed in groups that leaders and members will work hard for the betterment of the group as a whole.

Nonmaleficence means avoiding doing harm. In order to act ethically, members of groups must be sure the changes they make in themselves and the help they offer others are not going to be damaging.

Justice (i.e., fairness) refers to the equal treatment of all people. This virtue implies that everyone's welfare is promoted and that visible differences in people, such as gender or race, do not interfere with the way they are treated.

At first glance, the practice of ethics does not appear difficult. Indeed, individuals who are sheltered from complex interpersonal relationships may find it relatively easy to behave ethically. However, when behavior is considered in the multifaceted world of a group of people, the matter of ethics and acting ethically may become complicated. A uniform code of ethics is sometimes needed as a guide in such situations. A **code of ethics** is a set of standards and principles that organizations create to provide guidelines for their members to follow in working with the public and each other. Codes of ethics are constantly evolving and thus do not refer to all possible situations. In a field such as group work, where practitioners come from diverse backgrounds, there is often some question as to which codes of ethics to follow and when. The reason is that within each specialty (e.g., counseling, medicine, nursing, psychology, social work), codes of ethics have been developed, some of which do not deal with aspects of group conduct and some of which contradict each other (Corey, Corey, & Callanan, 1993).

The two documents that most clearly address ethical issues in group work in detail are *Ethical Guidelines for Group Counselors* by the Association for Specialists in Group Work (1989) and "Guidelines for Psychologists Conducting Growth Groups" by the American Psychological Association (1973). These guidelines and their standards are based on years of group experience by members of these associations. They were developed as a result of the need to outline proper behaviors and correct questionable practices within the group field, especially when group work was virtually unmonitored and growing rapidly in the late 1960s and early 1970s (Olsen, 1971; Zimpfer, 1971).

It is important that group leaders be aware of these codes in some detail. Although codes of ethics are not entirely satisfactory because "in many situations no one behavior seems entirely ethical," ethical codes such as the two just mentioned give group workers a starting place to find answers and resolutions (Post, 1989, p. 229). Therefore, codes of ethics should be studied and discussed throughout a professional's career. "The advanced group leader is expected to operate much more ethically than those with less experience" (Kottler, 1982, p. 182).

MAJOR ETHICAL ISSUES IN GROUP WORK

There are a number of major ethical issues involved in most kinds of group work. For some types of groups, such as task/work groups, a few of these issues will not be as prevalent as for other types of groups, such as psychotherapy or counseling groups. Among the most important issues are those involving:

1. training of group leaders
2. screening of potential group members
3. the rights of group members
4. confidentiality
5. personal relationships between group members and leaders
6. dual relationships
7. personal relationships among group members
8. uses of group techniques
9. leader's values
10. referral
11. termination and follow-up

Training of Group Leaders

There are certain personal characteristics of group leaders that are vital. These include such qualities as self-awareness; genuineness; ability to form warm, caring relationships; sensitivity and understanding; self-confidence; a sense of humor; flexibility of behavior; and a willingness to self-evaluate (George & Dustin, 1988, p. 33). Without these traits, potential group leaders would have difficulty in their interpersonal relationships and would not be effective. Usually, individuals wishing to become group leaders will go for further training, but if they do not, it is the responsibility of professional education programs to be sure that the persons whom they graduate are personally integrated and competent to engage in leading a group.

In addition to personal qualities, the training of group leaders involves selected coursework and experience. For example, individuals who intend to lead groups need courses in personality, deviant behavior, counseling theory, systematic human relations, and assessment, as well as instruction on the theory and practice of group work (Vander Kolk, 1985). They also need to be involved in different types of group experiences, both as participants and as leaders or co-leaders (Corey, et al., 1993; Yalom, 1985). The Association for Specialists in Group Work (ASGW) (1990) has published its *Professional Standards* (see Appendix B), which outlines knowledge competencies, skill competencies, and suggested clinical group experience for leaders of four types of groups: psycho-educational, counseling, psychotherapy, and task/work. The American Group Psychotherapy Association (AGPA) (1978) has also published a standards document for the training of group psychotherapists: *Guidelines for the Training of Group Psychotherapists.* Both the ASGW and the AGPA recommend personal-growth experiences as part of the total program for aspiring group leaders.

Regardless of the standards followed, group leaders must recognize their limitations. Those who do not possess professional credentials in an area in which they wish to practice must either not practice or be supervised by a professionally qualified person (Gazda, 1989). It is essential that leaders and members have a clear conception of the type of group to which they belong and the kind of goals they wish to achieve (Gumaer & Martin, 1990; Ohlsen, Horne, & Lawe, 1988). One way for beginning group leaders to gain clarity and experience, in addition to those ideas mentioned previously, is to join a **training group** (Corey & Corey, 1992). In such a group, beginning leaders can learn to recognize and work out major personal and professional issues that affect their ability to conduct groups, for example, criticism, anxiety, jealousy, or the need for control.

Screening of Potential Group Members

A second major issue in group work is screening potential members. This process is more difficult than it seems, and it becomes even more complicated when the group is composed of nonvolunteers.

The task of **screening** is actually a three-part process. It begins when group leaders formulate the type of group they would like, and are qualified, to lead. Next is the process of recruitment, in which the leader must make sure not to misrepresent the type of group that is to be conducted. In the recruiting process, potential members have a right to know the goals of the group, the basic procedures to be used, what will be expected of them as participants, what they can expect from the leader, and any major risks as well as potential values of participating in the group (Corey, Corey, Callanan, & Russell, 1992). Recruiting is often conducted in a number of ways, including the distribution of flyers as well as direct, personal contact with potential group members and helping professionals who may know of individuals appropriate for such an experience.

Finally, there is the task of screening applicants by the leader to be sure they are able to benefit from and contribute to the group (Vander Kolk, 1985). This type of screening, which is conducted on a one-to-one or small-group basis, is valuable because it provides an opportunity for the group leader to establish rapport, to clarify norms and expectations of group behavior, and to answer any questions the individual may have about the group (George & Dustin, 1988, p. 89).

An important aspect of screening, besides the personal contact it provides, is finding out whether a potential group member is currently in any other kind of mental health treatment. If a person is, it is essential for the group leader to contact the other mental health services provider and inform him or her about the potential member's desire to participate in the group (Gazda, 1989). The potential group member ultimately must decide in collaboration with these professionals about whether to join the group or not. He or she needs as much information as possible about the benefits and liabilities of such action. It is advisable at the end of the screening process, and before accepting a member into the group, that the leader obtain a member's signature on an **informed consent statement** (acknowledging that the individual is aware of the group activity he or she is about to participate in and is doing so voluntarily) (Gazda, 1989) (see Figure 8.1).

The Rights of Group Members

Group members have rights that must be respected and protected if the group is going to work well. These rights are similar to the rights of others who are consumers of professional services. In some types of groups, such as in counseling groups, recipients of services can be especially alerted to their rights through the distribution of prepackaged materials such as those produced by Chi Sigma Iota (International Academic and Leadership Counseling Honor Society) and the National Board of Certified Counselors (see Figure 8.2).

Specific guidelines pertaining to rights in particular group situations should be covered, too. According to the *Ethical Guidelines for Group Counselors* (Association for Specialists in Group Work, 1989), group members should be told before the group begins that their participation in the group is voluntary and that they can leave the group whenever they choose. Furthermore, group

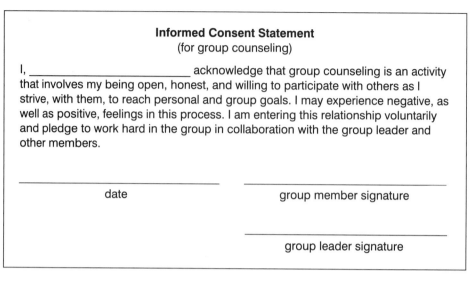

Informed Consent Statement
(for group counseling)

I, _____ acknowledge that group counseling is an activity that involves my being open, honest, and willing to participate with others as I strive, with them, to reach personal and group goals. I may experience negative, as well as positive, feelings in this process. I am entering this relationship voluntarily and pledge to work hard in the group in collaboration with the group leader and other members.

_____
date

_____
group member signature

_____
group leader signature

Figure 8.1
An informed consent statement.

members have the right to resist following the instructions or suggestions of leaders and other members. They should expect to be treated individually and respectfully and to be protected from physical and psychological threats and intimidation. They should also be informed as clearly as possible about what the group leader can and cannot do. Basically, group members have the right to know as realistically as possible what type of group procedures will be used and what the risks are in their participation.

Confidentiality

Confidentiality is the right of group members "to reveal personal thoughts, feelings, and information to the leader and other members of the group and expect that in no way will nonmembers of the group learn of this" (Jacobs, Harvill, & Masson, 1988, p. 302). Not keeping confidences is like gossiping and is destructive to the group process (Poppen & Thompson, 1974). Underlying the keeping of confidence is the matter of trust. If groups of any kind are going to be productive, members must trust each other (Vander Kolk, 1985).

Group leaders should deal with the importance and reality of confidentiality during the pregroup screening process. It should be stressed to potential group members that confidentiality is expected of everyone in the group in order to promote trust, cohesiveness, and growth (Hansen, Warner, & Smith, 1980). At the same time, the leader must acknowledge that he or she cannot guarantee confidentiality and that there may be certain cases in which ethical and/or legal considerations may force the leader to break confidentiality (Gazda, 1989). For

Counseling Services:
Consumer Rights and Responsibilities
Consumer Rights

- Be informed of the qualifications of your counselor: education, experience, and professional counseling certification(s) and state license(s).
- Receive an explanation of services offered, your time commitments, and fee scales and billing policies prior to receipt of services.
- Be informed of limitations of the counselor's practice to special areas of expertise (e.g., career development, ethnic groups, etc.) or age group (e.g., adolescents, older adults, etc.).
- Have all that you say treated confidentially and be informed of any state laws placing limitations on confidentiality in the counseling relationship.
- Ask questions about the counseling techniques and strategies and be informed of your progress.
- Participate in setting goals and evaluating progress toward meeting them.
- Be informed of how to contact the counselor in an emergency situation.
- Request referral for a second opinion at any time.
- Request copies of records and reports to be used by other counseling professionals.
- Receive a copy of the code of ethics to which your counselor adheres.
- Contact the appropriate professional organization if you have doubts or complaints relative to the counselor's conduct.
- Terminate the counseling relationship at any time.

Consumer Responsibilities

- Set and keep appointments with your counselor. Let him/her know as soon as possible if you cannot keep an appointment.
- Pay your fees in accordance with the schedule you pre-established with the counselor.
- Help plan your goals.
- Follow through with agreed-upon goals.
- Keep your counselor informed of your progress toward meeting your goals.
- Terminate your counseling relationship before entering into arrangements with another counselor.

nbcc

This statement was prepared jointly by the National Board for Certified Counselors and Chi Sigma Iota to help you understand and exercise your rights as a consumer of counseling services. NBCC and CSI believe that clients who are informed consumers are able to best use counseling services to meet their individual needs.

Figure 8.2

Counseling Services: Consumer Rights and Responsibilities.

Source: National Board for Certified Counselors, Greensboro, NC, and Chi Sigma Iota (International Academic and Leadership Counseling Honor Society), Greensboro, NC. Reprinted by permission.

example, if a group member is dangerous to himself or herself or others, such as being suicidal or threatening others with violence, confidentiality may have to be broken (Kaplan, Sager, & Schiavi, 1985).

When group leaders find or suspect that confidentiality has been broken by members, they need to address the matter quickly and directly. For instance, if Paul learns in a counseling group that Beverly has told her closest friends about Jill's reactions to her failed marriage, Paul needs to raise the issue before the group for discussion and suggestions. The atmosphere surrounding such an experience is tense and should be serious.

In order to try to prevent breaks in confidentiality, leaders "need to periodically reaffirm to group members the importance of not discussing with others what occurs in the group" (Corey et al., 1993, p. 339). This approach keeps the matter of confidentiality constantly before the group and may serve a preventive function. Unfortunately, leaders and members cannot prevent breaks of confidentiality after a group ends, and this reality must also be addressed.

Personal Relationships Between Group Members and Leaders

The amount and kind of relationship between group members and leaders will vary from group to group. In task/work groups, for instance, casual contact between group members and leaders is usually unavoidable and may be productive. However, in therapeutic groups, such contact is likely to be inappropriate and could be destructive to the persons involved as well as to the group as a whole. It is more likely that relationships between group members and leaders will be detrimental to the group as a whole if they are not carefully handled. Such relationships can lead to favoritism and/or a failure to focus on important personal topics within the context of the group itself. Usually, outside personal contact between group leaders and members in therapeutic or counseling groups is discouraged or prohibited because this behavior may foster dependency—a violation of the ASGW (1989) *Ethical Guidelines*.

Dual Relationships

Dual relationships occur when group leaders find themselves in two potentially conflicting roles with their group members (Donigian, 1993). For instance, in a counseling setting, a group leader might also be a member's teacher. In a work setting, a group leader might be a member's supervisor. Regardless, of the exact setting, dual relationships can negatively affect the people involved in subtle and obvious ways. Therefore, they are best avoided.

In academic settings, Remley advises counselor educators to avoid "dual relationships" such as requiring or allowing students to participate in a group experience led by them as a part of a course, since such situations involve a conflict of interest (Remley & Reeves, 1989). Ways of resolving such situations include (a) using faculty-supervised postmaster's students to lead groups for entry-level students, (b) using a blind-grading system, (c) requiring students to participate in externally supervised groups, and (d) employing role-play techniques (Forester-Miller & Duncan, 1990).

If a dual relationship cannot be avoided, it should be carefully explored by all parties concerned and strictly monitored on a regular basis by an outside neutral party. Such an arrangement is preventive, but it is a second-best solution to ending such a relationship.

Personal Relationships Among Group Members

The matter of personal relationships among group members is another ethically gray area. Context is one of the major deciding factors. In some settings, such as work environments, schools, or mental hospitals, it is inevitable that group members will interact with each other outside the group. In other settings, such as outpatient treatment groups or special task forces, there is little likelihood of this type of interaction occurring naturally. Most group leaders do not make hard and fast rules about personal relationships among group members because this type of rule is impossible to enforce (Jacobs et al., 1994). In some cases, as in self-help groups, contact with members outside the structured group may be therapeutic.

If member-to-member contact outside the group results in the formation of subgroups and becomes detrimental, the group leader will have to deal with the situation. Overall, the focus of the group should be on open relationships within the group setting. "There is a rich and subtle interplay between the group member and the group environment, and each member at once shapes and responds to his or her social microcosm. The more spontaneous the interaction, the more varied will be the environment and the greater the likelihood that problematic issues will, for all the members, be touched upon" (Yalom, 1985, p. 39).

Uses of Group Techniques

Group techniques or exercises are structured ways of getting members to interact with one another. They can have a powerful impact on group members and positively affect how people work together or change. They can also inhibit the natural ebb and flow of a group and be ethically questionable. There are specific techniques for different stages or situations in a group (Pfeiffer & Jones, 1972–1980).

Corey (1990) believes that structured exercises are best when they are focused on group goals and/or group members' achievements. Group leaders face ethical problems when they lack either the skill or sensitivity to use exercises properly (Jacobs et al., 1994). In such cases, leaders may generate more feelings or nonverbal expressions than they or the group can handle (Corey & Corey,

1992). In choosing an exercise for a group, the leader should always have a rationale and should tailor the exercise to fit the particular needs of the group. The use of techniques isolated from relationships and theories amounts to the employment of "gimmicks" which is an unprofessional and unethical way to work (Patterson, 1985).

There are at least 12 different kinds of exercises group leaders can employ: "written; movement; touching; dyads and triads; rounds; arts and crafts; fantasy; common reading; feedback; trust; moral dilemma; and group decision" (Jacobs et al., 1988, p. 166). Whenever an exercise is used in a group, it should be processed so that it allows group members to become better informed about themselves and the group. Therefore, at least twice as much time should be allowed for the processing of exercises than for completing the exercises. Ways of processing including sharing in small groups, sharing in the group as a whole, sharing through writing, utilizing rounds, or some combination of these methods (Jacobs et al., 1994).

Leaders' Values

Group leaders have values, and, for better or worse, values influence the goals, methods, and ultimately the success of group work and counseling (Mitchell, 1993; Patterson, 1958; Williamson, 1958). Leaders who try to hide their values may actually do more harm than good in certain situations. However, leaders must be careful not to impose their values on group members. Such action short-circuits members' exploration, especially in counseling and psychotherapy groups and results in confusion and chaos (Corey, Corey, & Callanan, 1990; Patterson, 1989).

It is the ultimate responsibility of group members to make their own decisions. However, leaders help members explore their values more thoroughly while maintaining their own. If group leaders and members have conflicts about values, leaders are responsible for making referrals (Corey et al., 1993). It is important that leaders stay attuned and be aware of the impact of values in a group of any kind.

Referrals

Referrals, that is, transfers of members to another group, are made when group leaders realize they cannot help certain members achieve designated goals or when there is a conflict between leaders and members that is unresolvable. The group leader is responsible for making appropriate referrals when necessary since he or she cannot be all things to all people (Jacobs et al., 1994). The process of making a referral involves assessing one's own values and limitations as a group leader, as well as listening to individual group members concerning their particular needs.

It is imperative that group leaders maintain an extensive and current list of referral sources. The referral process itself involves four steps: "(1) identifying the need to refer; (2) evaluating potential referral sources; (3) preparing the client for the referral; and (4) coordinating the transfer" (Cormier & Hackney, 1987, p. 254). For instance, if Dorothy realizes in her psychotherapy group that she cannot help Martha, she may first arrange to meet with Martha after a group session and discuss the situation with her. Prior to meeting, she should have prepared a list of potential referral sources and have these ready for Martha to see during their session together. If Martha is not ready for a referral, Dorothy may have to meet with her again. After Martha has been persuaded of the wisdom of the referral, Dorothy will work with her to help her make arrangements.

Termination and Follow-up

"Termination and follow-up become ethical issues more because of errors of omission rather than errors of commission" (Gazda, 1989, p. 307). Groups need to reach some form of closure before ending. For long-term groups, this may mean several sessions devoted to winding down and tying up loose ends, whereas for short-term groups, a few hours devoted to this activity will be all that is necessary. Issues related to attachment and loss are primarily dealt with in termination (Cormier & Hackney, 1987; Patterson & Eisenberg, 1983). The important point is that these issues involving separation be addressed.

The ethical issue in follow-up usually centers around its neglect rather than its inclusion. ASGW's (1989) *Ethical Guidelines for Group Counselors* states that group leaders should make themselves available to group members for between-session consultation as well as follow-up after the termination of the group. If group leaders are negligent about this important procedure, group members may not adequately assess the impact the group has had on them and are unlikely to continue working on their goals as specifically as they would otherwise. Besides providing for the welfare of group members, follow-up after termination also has the added benefit of helping group leaders evaluate the effectiveness of what they did in the group and improve their group leadership styles. "Perhaps the most meaningful evaluation material can be gained by a group leader 30 days or more after a group ends. At that time the members are more independent of the leader and perhaps can be more honest" (George & Dustin, 1988, p. 115).

MAKING ETHICAL DECISIONS

Since group leaders face such a wide variety of issues, it is crucial that they know beforehand how they will make ethical decisions. Although such decisions can be made in many ways, some approaches to ethical decision making can make the process operate more smoothly. For example, in the case of promoting benefi- cence and enhancing ethical decision making, a mnemonic device that reminds group leaders and members of what they should do can be helpful. One device created for these situations is the **A-B-C-D-E Worksheet** (Sileo & Kopala, 1993) (see Figure 8.3). The letters of this worksheet stand for Assessment, Benefit, Con- sequences and Consultation, Duty, and Education. Some of its points are more applicable in certain situations than in others, but it gives practitioners an idea of what they can use to enhance the group's good.

In addition to this type of worksheet on a particular aspect of group ethical decision making, there are general steps members can take in the overall process. For example, in ethical decision making, Thomas (1992) poses several actions to follow in a sequential fashion. First, she attempts to define a situation. Once this is done and the situation is better defined, ethical codes are consulted for informa- tion and guidance. After this procedure, a continuum of alternative actions is gen- erated. At either ends of the spectrum will be choices ranging from "take radical action" to "take no action" with more moderate suggestions in the middle part of the choice curve. The next part of the process is to evaluate all suggested actions in regard to other persons' welfare and professional responsibilities. After the con- sequences of each alternative action is examined, some tentative decision is made and finally implemented. Records should be kept, at least of the final outcome.

PROMOTING ETHICAL PRINCIPLES IN GROUP WORK

The promotion and implementation of ethical conduct in groups occur on two lev- els: training and practice. There is an opportunity in educational settings to instill in prospective group leaders a knowledge of and feel for ethics (Hayes, 1991; Par- adise & Siegelwaks, 1982). Indeed, such a procedure is crucial to the welfare of group leaders and other helping professionals in general. For those individuals already in practice, training in the ethics of working with groups can best be achieved through continuing educational opportunities and peer supervision.

Training Group Leaders

The training of group leaders to address ethical issues is a multidimensional process. On one level, group leaders must become familiar with ethical codes and standards. On another level, they must become familiar with their own ethics and values. On a third level, prospective group leaders must practice rec- ognizing ethical dilemmas and making ethical decisions. Finally, individuals need to become aware of the development of ethical decision making over time so they can assess their own development as practitioners.

All of these different aspects need integrating if individuals are to be properly educated. Indeed, as Kitchener (1986) points out, the training of potential group

An A-B-C-D-E Worksheet for Ethical Decision Making.

A = Assessment

    1. What is the client's mental state?

        a. What are his/her strengths, support systems, weaknesses?

        b. Is a psychiatric/medical consult necessary?

    2. How serious is the client's disclosure? Is someone at risk for physical harm?

    3. What are my values, feelings, and reactions to the client's disclosure?

B = Benefit

    1. How will the client benefit by my action?

    2. How will the therapeutic relationship benefit?

    3. How will others benefit?

    4. Which action will benefit the most individuals?

C = Consequences and Consultation

    1. What will the ethical, legal, emotional, and therapeutic consequences be for:

        a. The client?

        b. The counselor?

        c. Potential clients?

    2. Have I consulted with colleagues, supervisors, agency administrators, legal counsel, professional ethics boards, or professional organizations?

D = Duty

    1. To whom do I have a duty?

        a. My client?

        b. The client's family?

        c. A significant other?

        d. The counseling profession?

        e. My place of employment?

        f. The legal system?

        g. Society?

E = Education

    1. Do I know and understand what the ethical principles and codes say regarding this issue?

    2. Have I consulted the ethical case books?

    3. Have I recently reviewed the laws that govern counseling practice?

    4. Have I been continuing my education through journals, seminars, work shops, conferences, or coursework?

Figure 8.3

An A-B-C-D-E Worksheet for ethical decision making.

Source: From "An A-B-C-D-E Worksheet for Promoting Beneficence When Considering Ethical Issues," by F. J. Sileo and M. Kopala, 1993, *Counseling and Values, 37,* 89–95.

leaders requires sensitizing them to ethical standards and issues; helping them learn to reason about ethical situations; developing within them a sense of being morally responsible in their actions; and teaching them tolerance of ambiguity in ethical decision making.

To become familiar with ethical codes and standards in group work is initially as simple as reading pertinent documents and articles. This type of approach has often been used, and although it may expose persons to the basics of what are commonly accepted guidelines in the practice of group work at a particular time, it does not teach them that ethics are normative rather than factual (Huber, 1994). Ethics "inevitably change both as new scientific evidence dictates new approaches and as our culture changes" (Gazda, 1989, pp. 297–298). A prime example of the rapid change in ethics is the revision of the 1980 ASGW *Ethical Guidelines for Group Counselors* in 1989. Therefore, training group leaders in ethical decision making involves examining particular codes of ethics while simultaneously exposing prospective group leaders to case vignettes related directly to the guidelines (Gumaer & Scott, 1985). Casebooks, such as the one developed by Corey, Corey, and Callanan (1982), are essential in this procedure.

On a second level, ethical training requires individuals to examine and understand their own personal codes of ethics (Van Hoose & Kottler, 1977; Van Hoose & Paradise, 1979). Group discussion related to general dilemmas can increase ethical awareness and help individuals gain more self-understanding (Paradise & Siegelwaks, 1982). For example, in a classroom situation, a teacher may use a values scale, like the Rokeach Value Survey (Rokeach, 1973), to help class members assess the values they hold most closely. The teacher may also, or in addition to such an experience, present controversial group case histories to the class and ask members to focus on ways they would handle these situations.

A third way to emphasize ethics is on an integrated level. Prospective group leaders can gain a greater exposure to dealing with ethical dilemmas from a practical viewpoint through role plays in simulated groups and by direct participation in practitioner training groups, (Corey et al., 1993). Using these methods, group leaders-to-be get a feel for decision making and group dynamics.

Finally, as a last part of training, individuals who aspire to be group leaders need to be exposed to developmental theories of ethical reasoning so they can gauge their own professional growth. Models, such as those developed by Van Hoose and Paradise (1979), hold promise for helping persons in training gain a clearer understanding of their own level of functioning (see Figure 8.4).

Continuing Education and Peer Supervision

For practitioners already in the field of group work, the matter of keeping up with ethical codes and growing as an ethically based professional can be met by taking continuing education courses and by peer supervision. Almost all professional associations offer programs on ethics at their national, regional, and state conventions. **Continuing Education Units** (CEU) credits for participating in

---

***Stage I.* Punishment Orientation**

Counselor decisions, suggestions, and courses of action are based on a strict adherence to prevailing rules and standards, i.e., one must be punished for bad behavior and rewarded for good behavior. The primary concern is the strict attention to the physical consequences of the decision.

***Stage II.* Institutional Orientation**

Counselor decisions, suggestions, and courses of action are based on a strict adherence to the rules and policies of the institution or agency. The correct posture is based upon the expectations of higher authorities.

***Stage III.* Societal Orientation**

The maintenance of standards, approval of others, and the laws of society and the general public characterize this stage of ethical behavior. Concern is for duty and societal welfare.

***Stage IV.* Individual Orientation**

The primary concern of the counselor is for the needs of the individual while avoiding the violation of laws and the rights of others. Concern for law and societal welfare is recognized, but is secondary to the needs of the individual.

***Stage V.* Principle or Conscience Orientation**

Concern is for the legal, professional, or societal consequences. What is right, in accord with self-chosen principles of conscience and internal ethical formulations, determines counselor behavior.

Figure 8.4

Stages of ethical behavior.

Source: From *Ethics in Counseling and Psychotherapy* (p.117) by W. H. Van Hoose and L. V. Paradise, 1979, Cranston, RI: Carroll Press. Reprinted by permission.

professional programs help group workers stay attuned to the latest developments in areas related to group work. For example, programs on group dynamics, group leadership, and group standards are frequently offered at helping relationship conventions. Many professional associations require that their members participate in such activities (Corey, Corey, & Callanan, 1993).

Continuing education can be supplemented with **peer supervision** where practitioners meet on a regular basis to consult with each other about particularly difficult group situations (Ohlsen et al., 1988). Through this type of experience, practitioners, especially those in private practice, become more informed, establish support, avoid burnout, and stay more aware of the ethical dimension of working with clients in particular cases. It is interesting to note that peer supervision is conducted in a group environment which can also provide information on dealing with, among other topics, issues in running groups (Greenburg, Lewis, & Johnson, 1985).

Both continuing education and peer supervision can be helpful to professionals who practice group work in subtle and blatant ways. Besides giving them more knowledge and procedures to use in groups, these educational methods can create new awareness of even minor misconduct in the group leader or in the group. Through this awareness, such behavior can be eliminated. For example, in some groups, a promise is made that no pressure will be put on a participant, but then nonactive members are encouraged to be involved in the group in subtle ways (Kottler, 1994). In helping themselves and their groups make ethical decisions about incidents like this, group workers increase the safety and efficiency of their groups as well as their own self-knowledge.

LEGAL ISSUES IN GROUP WORK

Ethics and the law are separate but sometimes overlap. *Law* refers to "a body of rules recognized by a state or community as binding on its members" (Shertzer & Stone, 1980, p. 386). There are some ethical issues, such as telling the truth, that have legal ramifications when violated. Therefore, group leaders are well advised to have a knowledge of both ethical codes and legal precedents. Often, when persons feel wronged by professional helpers, the helpers' actions will be judged according to the standards of the group with which their services are most identified (Woody, Hansen, & Rossberg, 1989). The conduct of group leaders, for example, would likely be compared to the type of behavior considered appropriate in *Ethical Guidelines for Group Counselors* (Association for Specialists in Group Work, 1989) or a similar definitive document. Thus, group workers must keep up with professional and legal developments on a very regular basis. This means staying abreast primarily with community, state, and national standards and knowing what to do in the case of legal action.

Community, State, and National Standards

Group leaders who function successfully are aware of "community standards, legal limitations to work, and state laws" governing the practice of groups, especially those that directly affect counseling or psychotherapy (Ohlsen et al., 1988, p. 391). This type of information may be best obtained from these sources:

1. civic, religious, and business leaders of the community in which the group worker resides
2. professional state counseling boards
3. state departments of education
4. persons involved in the state or national divisions of major professional counseling associations
5. liaison personnel in national professional associations
6. local attorneys
7. members of the state attorney general's office

It is not unusual for helping professionals, such as group workers, to fail in their practices because they have not paid enough attention to community, state, and national standards (Woody, 1988). Knowing theories and techniques of group work is not enough to make practitioners successful, especially those who operate in diversified settings or who wish to operate as private practitioners (Paradise & Kirby, 1990).

The best procedure to employ in preventing legal difficulties is to do one's professional "homework" beforehand. This means reading and studying major references on legal decisions that have an impact on conducting groups. For example, major sources explaining the relationship between the law and mental health practices include those by Cohen and Mariano (1982), Hopkins and Anderson (1985), Hummel, Talbutt, and Alexander (1985), Sidley (1985), Van Hoose and Kottler (1985), and Woody and Associates (1984). Primary sources for researching legal opinions include the *United States Supreme Court Report* (for Supreme Court decisions), the *Federal Reporter* (for U.S. Courts of Appeals decisions), and the *Federal Supplement* and *Federal Rules* (for U.S. District Court decisions). State court decisions are usually disseminated by an official state reporter, such as *Connecticut Reports* or *Alabama Reports.* A frequently used legal research source is *Shepard's Case Citations,* which follows "the judicial history of a targeted case" (Woody & Mitchell, 1984, p. 32).

Bibliographies on group work, such as the one compiled by Zimpfer (1984), are a rich source of obtaining information on all professional aspects of groups. Reading journal articles, books, and monographs and attending workshops on trends and issues in human services should all be included in group workers' schedules. Consultation with professional peers on landmark legal decisions, such as *Tarasoff v. Board of Regents of the University of California* (1969) or *Grant v. National Training Laboratories* (1970) is also vital.

Legal Action

Legal action is most likely to be taken against a group worker, especially in a psychotherapy or counseling group, if members think they have suffered physical harm, emotional trauma, or psychological/financial damage as a result of participating in a group experience (Shaffer & Galinsky, 1989). This legal action usually is in the form of a **malpractice suit** that implies the group leader has failed to render proper service due to either negligence or ignorance. "The word '**malpractice**' means bad practice" and "the claim against the professional is made by a 'plaintiff' who seeks a monetary award based on a specific amount of damages physical, financial, and/or emotional" (Gazda, 1989, p. 299). Practitioners can best avoid these suits by "maintaining reasonable, ordinary, and prudent practices" (Corey & Corey, 1992, p. 60).

Specific practices that are most likely to prevent law suits include

1. screening to reject inappropriate potential group members
2. spending extra time at the beginning of the first group session to discuss group rules and group members responsibilities

3. following the ethical codes of professional organizations to which one belongs

4. practicing only those theories and techniques in which one has actual expertise

5. obtaining consent or contracts in writing from members (or in the case of minors, their parents)

6. warning members about the importance of confidentiality and the exceptions in which member confidentiality will have to be broken

7. staying abreast of recent research, theory, and practice techniques within one's specialty

8. empowering members to evaluate their own progress and be in charge of their own progress

9. obtaining regular peer supervision of one's work

10. following billing regulations and record-keeping practices to the letter of the law (Hopkins & Anderson, 1985; Hummel et al., 1985; Paradise & Kirby, 1990; Van Hoose & Kottler, 1985).

If a malpractice suit is filed, especially as a result of a counseling or psychotherapeutic experience, plaintiffs must show that

1. a therapist-client relationship was established

2. the therapist's conduct fell below the minimal acceptable standard for the case

3. the conduct of the therapist was the cause of injury to the client

4. an actual injury was sustained by the client (Schultz, 1982).

Although the therapist-client relationship may be established easily (e.g., through producing a bill or receipt for services), other criteria in malpractice suits are more difficult to prove. In suits charging that the group leader's conduct fell below minimum standards, the measure usually used in such cases is what other practitioners in the same geographical area would do under similar circumstances (Huber, 1994). Group workers who are in contact with and in line with other practitioners in their area are less likely to be affected by this criterion, although local standards are increasingly being replaced with those on the national level.

The question of whether the conduct of the group leader caused injury to a person is easiest to prove if the acts and injury are closely related in time (Huber, 1994). Finally, in deciding whether an actual injury was sustained by a group member, one or more of the following effects must be shown:

1. exacerbation of a previous symptom

2. appearance of a new symptom

3. client misuse or abuse of therapy, for example, increased intellectualization or dependency

4. client overextension of self, for example, taking on inappropriate tasks

5. disillusionment with therapy, for example, feelings of hopelessness and depression (Strupp, Hadley, & Gomes-Schwartz, 1977).

Most malpractice suits in group work will center on **unintentional civil liability**, i.e., a lack of intent to cause injury. However, there are cases where "intentional" harm becomes the issue in question. Intentional civil liability cases include situations in which there are issues regarding

1. *battery* (the unconsented touching of a person)
2. *defamation* (injury to a person's character or reputation either through verbal *[slander]* or written *[libel]* means)
3. *invasion of privacy* (violation of the right to be left alone)
4. *infliction of mental distress* (outrageous behavior on the part of the therapist) (Huber, 1994).

These types of cases are usually more clear-cut than those involving unintentional actions. In all cases, group specialists, especially those who work in psychotherapeutic or counseling groups, are advised to study their professional standards and codes of ethics carefully before, during, and after group sessions. In all cases, professionals who work with groups should carry **professional liability insurance**, i.e., insurance designed specifically to protect a group worker from financial loss in case of a civil suit. Any court litigation can be costly and even the most careful group leader may be the subject of legal action. Thus, purchasing liability insurance (usually available through professional associations) and carefully keeping up to date on ethical/legal matters may be two of the best practices that group leaders can employ in helping themselves operate on the highest possible level.

SUMMARY AND CONCLUSION

In this chapter, various aspects of ethical and legal issues regarding group work have been covered. Many of the topics focus on group leaders' responsibilities to their members and themselves. However, some material in this chapter is specifically targeted at the rights and responsibilities of group members. It is assumed by most individuals who join a group that their leaders will be ethical and professional. However, that is not always the case, and some group members become casualties of their experience (Shaffer & Galinsky, 1989). To ensure against this, most professional associations, particularly the Association for Specialists in Group Work and the American Group Psychotherapy Association, have constructed ethical codes and professional standards by which group leaders and groups should operate. These documents are probably more relevant to leaders of psychotherapy and counseling groups, but they also apply to those who work in group educational settings and with task groups. By adhering to such codes and standards, group leaders tend to maximize the benefits and minimize the harm that a group can have on individuals (Lakin, 1985).

Group leaders must pay attention to these specific ethical issues: their training and qualifications; screening potential members; informing members about the group and the rights they have; ensuring confidentiality, to the extent possible; establishing appropriate relationships among group members and between the leader and members; owning but not imposing their own values; using group exercises properly; making appropriate referrals; and employing termination and follow-up procedures correctly. Group leaders and members must also scrutinize how they make ethical decisions. None of these are simple tasks that are easily accomplished on a one-time basis. Therefore, group leaders must constantly monitor their behavior and keep current on ethical codes. "A combination of good personal character and virtue with sound thinking and good decision-making skills . . . ensures the best solution to an ethical dilemma (Sileo & Kopala, 1993, p. 90). Prospective group leaders may receive cognitive and experiential training in ethics while they are still in training, whereas more experienced leaders (who are supposed to be more knowledgeable about ethics) will have to rely on continuing education experiences and peer supervision.

Legal aspects of group work are similar to those involving ethics. It is important that group specialists do their homework in researching legal cases that affect human services professionals and that they consult with others about ways to behave within the limits and spirit of the law. Getting to know community, state, and national standards for the practice of their profession is a major way to do this. If practitioners encounter legal difficulties, they need to know the difference between unintentional and intentional malpractice suits and what they need to do in such cases. It is crucial that all group leaders carry professional liability insurance.

CLASSROOM EXERCISES

1. Compare the ethical codes of as many professional associations as you can in regard to the practice of group work. Once codes are collected, have half of the class note the similarities within them and the other half of the class highlight their differences. Discuss your findings and their implications for working with groups.

2. Pretend you are a group leader. Think of what you would do in the following two situations and then role play these scenes with fellow classmates:
   a. A group member of the opposite sex, whom you find attractive, asks to meet with you outside the confines of the group. The purpose of such a meeting is stated in very vague terms by the member, but he or she assures you that it is important.
   b. It comes to your attention that several of the group members are talking about group activities and individuals to their friends. This is the fourth meeting of the group, and everyone is present.
      How did your thinking change and/or stay the same after these role-playing situations?

3. Have each member of the class write down a potential ethical dilemma within a group context in which they are currently involved. Collect the situations,

and as a class, discuss with your instructor some strategies that might be employed to deal with these situations.

4. As a class, visit the reference librarian of your library. Have him or her show you the resources most readily available for tracking down legal information on counseling cases. If possible, have the librarian follow a case through its introduction and appeals. Discuss with a classmate how you could make use of the resources you have at your disposal for keeping up with the legal aspects of group work.

REFERENCES

American Group Psychotherapy Association. (1978). *Guidelines for the training of group psychotherapists.* New York: Author.

American Psychological Association. (1973). Guidelines for psychologists conducting growth groups. *American Psychologist, 28,* 933.

Association for Specialists in Group Work. (1989). *Ethical guidelines for group counselors.* Alexandria, VA: Author.

Association for Specialists in Group Work. (1990). *Professional standards for training of group work generalists and of group work specialists* (revised). Alexandria, VA. Author.

Baldick, T. (1980). Ethical discrimination ability of intern psychologists: A function of training in ethics. *Professional Psychology, 11,* 276–282.

Cohen, R. J., & Mariano, W. E. (1982). *Legal guidebook in mental health.* New York: The Free Press.

Corey, G. (1990). *Theory and practice of group counseling* (3rd ed.). Pacific Grove, CA: Brooks/Cole.

Corey, G., Corey, M., & Callanan, P. (1982). *A casebook of ethical guidelines for group leaders.* Monterey, CA: Brooks/Cole.

Corey, G., Corey, M. S., & Callanan, P. (1990). Role of group leader's values in group counseling. *Journal for Specialists in Group Work, 15,* 68–74.

Corey, G., Corey, M. S., & Callanan, P. (1993). *Issues and ethics in the helping professions* (4th ed.). Pacific Grove, CA: Brooks/Cole.

Corey, G., Corey, M. S., Callanan, P. J., & Russell, J. M. (1992). *Group techniques* (2nd ed.). Pacific Grove: CA: Brooks/Cole.

Corey, M. S., & Corey, G. (1992). *Groups: Process and practice* (4th ed.). Pacific Grove, CA: Brooks/Cole.

Cormier, L. S., & Hackney, H. (1987). *The professional counselor: A process guide to helping.* Englewood Cliffs, NJ: Prentice Hall.

Donigian, J. (1993). Duality: The issue that won't go away. *Journal for Specialists in Group Work, 18,* 137–140.

Foltz, M-L., Kirby, P. C., & Paradise, L. V. (1989). The influence of empathy and negative consequences on ethical decisions in counseling situations. *Counselor Education and Supervision, 28,* 219–228.

Forester-Miller, H., & Duncan, J. A. (1990). The ethics of dual relationships in the training of group counselors. *Journal for Specialists in Group Work, 15,* 88–93.

Gazda, G. M. (1989). *Group counseling: A developmental approach* (4th ed.). Boston: Allyn & Bacon.

George, R. L., & Dustin, D. (1988). *Group counseling: Theory and practice.* Englewood Cliffs, NJ: Prentice Hall.

Gladding, S. T. (1990). Journey. *Journal of Humanistic Education and Development, 28,* 142.

Greenburg, S. L., Lewis, G. J., & Johnson, J. (1985). Peer consultation groups for private practitioners. *Professional Psychology: Research and Practice, 16,* 437–447.

Gumaer, J., & Martin, D. (1990). GROUP ETHICS: A multimodal model for training knowledge and skill competencies. *Journal for Specialists in Group Work, 15,* 94–103.

Gumaer, J., & Scott, L. (1985). Training group leaders in ethical decision making. *Journal for Specialists in Group Work, 10*, 198–204.

Gumaer, J., & Scott, L. (1986). Group workers' perceptions of ethical and unethical behavior of group leaders. *Journal for Specialists in Group Work, 11*, 139–150.

Hansen, J. C., Warner, R. W., & Smith, E. J. (1980). *Group counseling: Theory and process* (2nd ed.). Chicago: Rand McNally.

Hayes, R. L. (1991). Group work and the teaching of ethics. *Journal for Specialists in Group Work, 16*, 24–31.

Hopkins, B. R., & Anderson, B. S. (1985). *The counselor and the law* (2nd ed.). Alexandria, VA: American Counseling Association.

Huber, C. H. (1994). *Ethical, legal and professional issues in the practice of marriage and family therapy* (2nd ed.). New York: Merrill/Macmillan.

Hummel, D. L., Talbutt, L. C., & Alexander, M. D. (1985). *Law and ethics in counseling.* New York: Van Nostrand Reinhold.

Jacobs, E. E., Harvill, R. L., & Masson, R. L. (1988). *Group counseling: Strategies and skills.* Pacific Grove, CA: Brooks/Cole.

Jacobs, E. E., Harvill, R. L., & Masson, R. L. (1994). *Group counseling: Strategies and skills* (2nd ed). Pacific Grove, CA: Brooks/Cole.

Kaplan, H. S., Sager, C. J., & Schiavi, R. C. (1985). Editorial: AIDS and the sex therapist. *Journal of Sex and Marital Therapy, 11*, 210–214.

Kitchener, K. S. (1984a). Ethics and counseling psychology: Distinctions and directions. *The Counseling Psychologist, 12*, 15– 18.

Kitchener, K. S. (1984b). Intuition, critical evaluation, and ethical principles: The foundation for ethical decisions in counseling psychology. *The Counseling Psychologist, 12*, 43–55.

Kitchener, K. S. (1986). Teaching applied ethics in counselor education: An integration of psychological processes and philosophical analysis. *Journal of Counseling and Development, 64*, 306–310.

Kottler, J. A. (1982). Unethical behaviors we all do and pretend we do not. *Journal for Specialists in Group Work, 7*, 182–186.

Kottler, J. A. (1994). *Advanced group leadership.* Pacific Grove, CA: Brooks/Cole.

Lakin, M. (1985). *The helping group: Therapeutic principles and issues.* Reading, MA: Addison-Wesley.

Mitchell, C. L. (1993). The relationship of clinicians' values to therapy outcome ratings. *Counseling and Values, 37*, 156–164.

Ohlsen, M. M., Horne, A. M., & Lawe, C. F. (1988). *Group counseling.* New York: Holt, Rinehart & Winston.

Olsen, L. C. (1971). Ethical standards for group leaders. *Personnel and Guidance Journal, 50*, 288.

Paradise, L. V., & Kirby, P. C. (1990). Some perspectives on the legal liability of group counseling in private practice. *Journal for Specialists in Group Work, 15*, 114–118.

Paradise, L. V., & Siegelwaks, B. J. (1982). Ethical training for group leaders. *Journal for Specialists in Group Work, 7*, 162–166.

Patterson, C. H. (1958). The place of values in counseling and psychotherapy. *Journal of Counseling Psychology, 5*, 216–223.

Patterson, C. H. (1985). *Gimmicks in groups.* Paper presented at the annual convention of the American Association for Counseling and Development, Los Angeles.

Patterson, C. H. (1989). Values in counseling and psychotherapy. *Counseling and Values, 33*, 164–181.

Patterson, L. E., & Eisenberg, S. (1983). *The counseling process* (3rd ed.). Boston: Houghton Mifflin.

Pfeiffer, D. C., & Jones, J. E. (1972–1980). *A handbook of structured experiences for human relations training* (Vols. I–VIII). San Diego: University Associates.

Poppen, W. A., & Thompson, C. L. (1974). *School counseling: Theories and concepts.* Lincoln, NE: Professional Educators Publications.

Post, P. (1989). The use of the ethical judgment scale in counselor education. *Counselor Education and Supervision, 28*, 229–233.

Remley, T. P., Jr., & Reeves, T. G. (1989). *Beyond the formal classroom: Faculty/Graduate student relationships.* Paper presented at the annual meeting of the American Association for Counseling and Development, Boston.

Rokeach, M. (1973). *Rokeach values survey.* Sunnyvale, CA: Halgren Tests.

Schultz, B. (1982). *Legal liabilities in psychotherapy.* San Francisco: Jossey-Bass.

Shaffer, J., & Galinsky, M. D. (1989). *Models of group therapy* (2nd ed.). Englewood Cliffs, NJ: Prentice Hall.

Shertzer, B., & Stone, S. (1980). *Fundamentals of counseling* (3rd ed.). Boston: Houghton Mifflin.

Sidley, N. T. (Ed.). (1985). *Law and ethics: A guide for the health professional.* New York: Human Sciences Press.

Sileo, F. J., & Kopala, M. (1993). An A-B-C-D-E worksheet for promoting beneficence when considering ethical issues. *Counseling and Values, 37,* 89–95.

Strupp, H. H., Hadley, S. W., & Gomes-Schwartz, B. (1977). *Psychotherapy for better or worse: The problem of negative effects..* New York: Jason Aronson.

Thomas, M. B. (1992). *An introduction to marital and family therapy.* New York: Macmillan.

Van Hoose, W., & Kottler, J. (1977). *Ethical and legal issues in counseling and psychotherapy.* San Francisco: Jossey-Bass.

Van Hoose, W., & Kottler, J. (1985). *Ethical and legal issues in counseling and psychotherapy* (2nd ed.). San Francisco: Jossey-Bass.

Van Hoose, W., & Paradise, L. V. (1979). *Ethics in counseling and psychotherapy: Perspectives in issues and decision-making.* Cranston, RI: Carroll Press.

Vander Kolk, C. J. (1985). *Introduction to group counseling and psychotherapy.* Columbus, OH: Merrill.

Welfel, E. R., & Lipsitz, N. E. (1984). The ethical behavior of professional psychologists: A critical analysis of the research. *The Counseling Psychologist, 12,* 31–41.

Williamson, E. (1958). Value orientation in counseling. *Personnel and Guidance Journal, 36,* 520–528.

Woody, R. H. (1988). *Protecting your mental health practice.* San Francisco: Jossey-Bass.

Woody, R. H. and Associates (Eds.). (1984). *The law and the practice of human services.* San Francisco: Jossey-Bass.

Woody, R. H., Hansen, J. C., Rossberg, R. H. (1989). *Counseling psychology: Strategies and services.* Pacific Grove, CA: Brooks/Cole Publishing.

Woody, R. H., & Mitchell, R. E. (1984). Understanding the legal system and legal research. In R. H. Woody and Associates (Eds.), *The law and the practice of human services.* San Francisco: Jossey-Bass.

Yalom, I. (1985). *The theory and practice of group psychotherapy* (3rd ed.). New York: Basic Books.

Zimpfer, D. (1971). Needed: Professional ethics for working with groups. *Personnel and Guidance Journal, 50,* 280–287.

Zimpfer, D. G. (1984). *Group work in the helping professions: A bibliography* (2nd ed.). Muncie, IN: Accelerated Development.

PART TWO

GROUPS THROUGHOUT THE LIFE SPAN

CHAPTER 9

Groups for Children

I watch the children line up like ducks
all in a row, except one.
Noisily they ramble past concrete walls
follow-the-leader style
behind a blond-haired woman
in a light yellow dress
who quietly talks to them through her motions.
Today is picture day in the school
with a jolly old man who says: "Cheese"
tossing tidbit compliments before boys and girls
as they fix their smiles at him.
In just a flash roles are caught,
a moment recorded, and lines form again.
Straight and precise the children walk
all except one, who in dimly-lit halls,
rapidly steps in a zigzag manner
defying a rule and defining himself.*

Group work with children, defined here as groups for children below the age of 14, requires a special knowledge of child development and group theory. Group specialists must adapt their approaches to the social, emotional, physical, and intellectual levels of this population or face being inefficient and ineffective (Johnson & Kottman, 1992; Ohlsen, Horne, & Lawe, 1988). Children, as opposed to adults, need more structure in their groups. They usually

*Source: Gladding, 1975, p. 28.

respond better to nonverbal techniques than they do to verbal exercises because of their limited vocabularies and their dispositions to display feelings through play instead of words (Thompson & Rudolph, 1988).

When children face natural age and stage developmental tasks together (e.g., learning how to work cooperatively, learning how to express emotions appropriately), they frequently master more than the specifically targeted skills. Their social interactions with other children and the adult group leader often promotes within them a sense of well-being and leads to the prevention of future problems as the children develop human resources and models to go with their already formed cognitive and behavioral skills (Boutwell & Myrick, 1992). Through the process of being exposed to new people and ways of handling situations, growth is enhanced on all levels. Timing as well as content in children's groups is crucial, and learning occurs best at what Havighurst (1972) describes as a **teachable moment**, a time when children are ready and able to learn. Since the late 1960s, small-group work, especially in school settings, has proven its efficacy and has become a major model by which children are helped (Bowman, 1987; Stamm & Nissman, 1979). This type of work concentrates on the promoting of life-skills and the correction of faulty assumptions.

In elementary and middle schools (where most children under 14 are educated), psychoeducational/guidance groups are used to help children not only learn new skills but also become aware of their values, priorities, and communities. Small groups give students the opportunity to "explore and work through their social and emotional challenges with others who are experiencing similar feelings" (Campbell & Bowman, 1993, p. 173). For example, group counseling is often employed with children who have special life-event concerns, such as the loss of a parent through divorce (Gwynn & Brantley, 1987; Yauman, 1991) or failing grades (Boutwell & Myrick, 1992). Group counseling is also appropriate for children who have behavior problems "such as excessive fighting, inability to get along with peers, violent outbursts, chronic tiredness, lack of supervision at home, and neglected appearance" (Corey, 1990, p. 9). For some children with severe problems, family therapy outside or inside the school environment will be necessary (Hinkle, 1993; Whiteside, 1993).

In almost all their daily environments, children spend a great deal of time interacting in groups, so these settings are ideal places to conduct both preventive guidance work as well as remedial counseling (Campbell, 1993; Gumaer, 1984). The most basic underlying principle of dealing with children in groups stresses that groups are natural childhood environments and, therefore, have the power to hurt or heal (March, 1935). Care must be exercised in working with children in group settings in order to prevent harm and promote health. Readiness for group guidance and psychoeducational experiences "is determined by the developmental level of individuals and their corresponding need system" (Gazda, 1989, p. 33). Readiness for group guidance and counseling is determined by the amount of dissonance children feel between how they are acting and what they see others their age doing. Overall, the key to working with children in groups is readiness on the part of both the leader and the children.

TYPES OF GROUPS FOR CHILDREN

Developmental and nondevelopmental factors determine what types of groups are set up for children. **Developmental factors** include variables such as the age, gender, and maturity level of those involved. **Nondevelopmental factors**, on the other hand, encompass less predictable qualities such as the nature of the problem, the suddenness of its appearance, the intensity of its severity, and the present coping skills of children and their families.

As mentioned previously, groups for children generally take the form of guidance and psychoeducation (i.e., learning a new skill or experience) or counseling and psychotherapy (i.e., rectifying or resolving problematic behaviors, assumptions, or situations). Interventions vary depending on the children (and/or parents and teachers) with whom the group worker is interacting. However, there are some generalizations that can be made. First, group guidance and psychoeducation usually involves the group worker in the role of an information giver with a large group of children. In such situations, the group worker functions as a teacher and may work directly with teachers. For example, a group worker and teacher may jointly present information on ways of communicating effectively. The teacher may read excerpts from stories on good communication skills while the group worker uses discussions and role plays to help the class apply the examples to their daily lives.

It is "not . . . easy to give individual attention to all members" of a guidance/psychoeducational group (Myrick, 1987, p. 234). Consequently, the experience is usually less personal and more limited in scope than a counseling or psychotherapy group. However, group guidance/psychoeducation, like group counseling and psychotherapy, can be an effective way to help children "unlearn inappropriate behaviors and learn new ways of relating more easily through interaction and feedback in a safe, practice situation with their peers" (Thompson & Rudolph, 1988, p. 257).

Second, group guidance and psychoeducation primarily focuses on improving skills and awareness in personal and interpersonal areas such as values, attitudes, beliefs, social maturity, and career development (Franks, 1983), but it is not limited to these general growth topics. Group counseling and psychotherapy, on the other hand, are more remediation based and deal with such personal and interpersonal concerns as "self-concept, social skills, interpersonal relationships, problem solving, academic skills, communication skills, and values" (Franks, 1983, p. 201). Therefore, when the fifth-grade class participates in a group guidance/psychoeducational experience, it is assumed they are generally healthy but uninformed about a subject area, not distraught and in need of personally reconstructing their lives.

Third, although there is often an overlap in the subject areas covered in the activities of the groups just mentioned, the number of children involved in group guidance/psychoeducation and group counseling and psychotherapy usually differs. The latter types of groups focus on more specific concerns and in greater depth. Not as many individuals can be included.

Finally, the amount of risk taking and the overall process of these ways of working with groups tend to be distinct. Greater personal risks are taken in group counseling and psychotherapy and in a less structured environment than is found in group guidance and psychoeducation (Myrick, 1987). In addition, learning is more cognitively based in guidance and psychoeducational groups whereas it is more emotionally based in counseling and psychotherapeutic groups.

GROUP GUIDANCE FOR ELEMENTARY/ MIDDLE SCHOOL CHILDREN

Group guidance for children of elementary and middle school age may be conducted either in school or community agencies (Corey & Corey, 1992). **Preschool and early school-aged children** include ages 5 through 9, and **preadolescents** are defined as children in the latency period ranging in age from 9 to 13 years (Gazda, 1989). Children below the age of 5 are usually not included in groups because of the egocentristic nature of their development (Flavell, 1963; Havighurst, 1972). However, exceptions can be made for more mature 3- and 4-year-olds, and children below age 5 may successfully be included in prosocial learning groups (Golden, 1987).

Because group guidance in the schools is a preventive approach, counselors usually act as group leaders. Traditionally, they have presented their lessons to groups of children within a regular classroom environment. These offerings are varied and can range from a puppet show on friendship for preschoolers to realistic portrayals of preteen situations, such as those shown in the award-winning Public Broadcast System's "DeGrassi Junior High," for older children. Other lessons center on a variety of subject areas such as personal or mental hygiene, boy/girl relationships, getting along with parents, and cooperation. One interesting group guidance/psychoeducational activity for helping third graders contain their anger is known as the "Get Along Gang" (Bond, 1993). In this experience, the counselor presents name calling as a game. Name callers win if another person gets angry at being called a name. To win the game, students who are called names must not get angry or show their anger.

Group guidance works best when counselors know what they want the group to achieve. One model for reaching this goal is known as **SIPA** (Structure, Involvement, Process, and Awareness) (Tyra, 1979). In *structuring*, counselors ask children to listen and/or do new activities according to certain guidelines. *Involvement* consists of getting the group to be active participants. (Even children who do not wish to participate may report back to the group as observers after an activity is over.) *Processing* is composed of sharing ideas, and *awareness* is consolidating what was learned in the guidance time.

Many guidance groups revolve around activities and are subsequently called **activity group guidance** (AGG) (Hillman & Reunion, 1978). These activities are developmental in nature and typically include coordinated guidance topics. For example, in promoting self-understanding and understanding of others, puppets and music are often used (Egge, Marks, & McEvers, 1987; Harper, 1985). These activities are nonthreatening and enhance interaction and motivation in ways that language alone cannot do. For some children who are not in contact with their emotions, songs that they have written and sung to different tunes can give them an awareness of themselves not possible otherwise (Miles, 1993). Because of the inherent power of active developmental media, they are often packaged in commercial classroom guidance programs, such as **Developing Understanding of Self and Others—Revised** (DUSO–R) (Dinkmeyer & Dinkmeyer, 1982). A typical AGG session has three stages:

1. a 10-minute warm-up time in which the group and leader discuss an appropriate guidance principle
2. a planned activity that attempts to implement the guidance principle for the day
3. a follow-up discussion, lasting about 5 to 10 minutes, in which the group discusses the impact of the guidance principle activity on themselves (Hillman & Reunion, 1978).

At other times, group workers implement group activities on their own, sometimes in various formats. For example, they may decide to have the group express a variety of feelings through making rhythmic sounds on their knees to represent the emotions at different times of the day or in different situations. In cases such as these, children may sound out in a group a variety of feelings such as sad, mad, unsure, happy, and satisfied. Then, as in the more structured methods, group discussions take place (Gladding, 1992).

In guidance and psychoeducational groups, a variety of techniques usually works best. For example, Campbell (1991) gives four techniques for working with undermotivated students including (a) using guided fantasy, (b) focusing on specific behaviors to be improved, (c) creating of positive affirmations (positive statements about oneself), and (d) employing visualizations. One or more of these techniques may not work with some children, but probably some of the procedures will. The point is that variety is the essence of group guidance and psychoeducational lessons.

GROUP COUNSELING WITHIN THE SCHOOLS

Group counseling within the schools is essential to the healthy growth of elementary and middle school students. "Small group counseling is becoming the preferred counselor intervention. It enables a counselor to see more students and to use counselor time to its maximum" (Boutwell & Myrick, 1992, pp. 65–66). In group counseling, the affective as well as the cognitive and behavioral domains of students are emphasized.

Sometimes group counseling is structured, such as in the *Fresh Start Club* for elementary school children who have been retained at grade level (Campbell

& Bowman, 1993). In situations where the group is structured, the emphasis is placed on positive aspects of an experience as well as group support. In group counseling, opportunities are also provided for learning about self and others through less structured interactions (Dyer, 1979). Group counseling usually takes one of three approaches in dealing with persons and problems: (a) crisis-centered, (b) problem-centered, and (c) growth-centered (Myrick, 1987).

Crisis-centered groups are formed due to some emergency, such as conflict between student groups. These groups usually meet until the situation that caused them to form has been resolved. Group counseling provides individuals with "a means to examine their situation and to think together about some possible solutions" (Myrick, 1987, p. 235). Sometimes, groups formed because of a crisis continue meeting after the crisis has passed and develop into either problem-centered or growth groups. For example, after a fight between some fourth and fifth graders, children in one school formed a "peace group." The purpose of the group was originally to promote ways to resolve problems between the children who had been in open conflict. As the group continued to develop, however, its purpose was enlarged to finding ways to spot problematic situations in the school and correct them in a productive way.

Problem-centered groups are small groups set up to focus on one particular concern, for example, coping with stress. They are useful to students who have one major difficulty, such as being under too much pressure. Like the members of crisis-centered groups, those involved with problem-centered groups are usually highly motivated and committed to working on their situations and themselves.

Clark and Seals (1984) describe a three-phase open group counseling approach for ridiculed children that provides support "to children who long for acceptance" (p. 161). In the initial phase, the focus is on establishing a relationship based on trust and encouragement. Children who get involved in the group feel a sense of **universalization** realizing they are not the only ones who face being ridiculed (Dinkmeyer & Muro, 1979). In the second phase, erroneous thoughts and distorted cognitions are challenged. (See Table 9.1.)

The final phase of the group serves to promote positive behaviors, including the working out of strategies to deal with peers who ridicule. Role plays are often used in this phase, and interpersonal interaction and cooperation are encouraged.

Another problem-centered group is the *friendship group* (Coppock, 1993). This group is for students who have been referred to a school counselor for specific problems such as misbehavior, lack of social skills, or poor academic performance. It is closed ended and lasts from 6 to 8 weeks. In it, students are invited to "develop and practice friendship skills" (p. 152). These skills revolve around nonthreatening activities such as introducing oneself or another, playing games (e.g., receiving compliments), making up adventures (e.g., imagining oneself in a new place and time), and solving problems, especially those that are of a personal nature. This last part of the group is done only if students are developmentally ready to work with the group on a problem and only after problem-solving skills have been discussed and demonstrated in the group.

"**Growth-centered groups** focus on the personal and social development of students" (Myrick, 1987, p. 236). Their purpose is to enable children to explore

Table 9.1
Basic mistakes of ridiculed children.

Erroneous Statement	Type	Corrected Statement
"Everyone hates me."	Overgeneralizations	"I do have one friend."
"They're all out to get me."	False or impossible goals of security	"Six children make fun of me."
"There's nothing I can do about it."	Misperceptions of life and life's demands	"I can avoid some of the teasing."
"I can't do anything right."	Minimization or denial of one's worth	"I am very good with computers."
"I'll get them all back someday."	Faulty values	"Why waste my time on getting revenge?"

Source: From "Groups Counseling for Ridiculed Children" by A. J. Clark and J. M. Seals, 1984, *Journal for Specialists in Group Work, 9*, p. 160. Copyright ACA. Reprinted by permission of the American Counseling Association.

their feelings, concerns, and behaviors about a number of everyday subjects. For instance, Rose (1987) describes a time-limited group for children ages 6 to 12 that promotes social competence. Although the group is behaviorally based and uses a number of behavioral principles, such as rehearsal, instruction, modeling, feedback, coaching, assignments, and social rewards, the basic format of the group could be modified to work with children who are not in distress but who wish to improve their social functioning. Although personal skills may be taught to children in group guidance classes, growth-centered groups allow a more personal touch to be added to the learning process and give the group worker an opportunity to get to know children more deeply and help them in specific ways.

GROUP GUIDANCE AND COUNSELING IN COMMUNITY SETTINGS

The basic dynamics of group guidance and counseling for children in settings outside of school environments do not differ substantially from those conducted within. Community settings with groups for children, such as churches, clubs, and mental health centers, basically structure and run their groups in a manner similar to that used in educational institutions. A major difference, however, between schools and community agencies is the populations of children served. Community organizations will usually have more homogeneous groups than will schools. This difference occurs because children group themselves in organizations according to interests and because mental health professionals in agencies often start groups for certain "types" of children, for example, the shy, low achievers, or those with conduct disorders.

Nevertheless, this occasional lack of diversity can be overcome through group exercises. For example, a structured technique, such as the *Human Rainbow*, makes it possible for children to recognize unique, as well as universal, qualities in themselves and others. In this structured activity, children first create masks and then form a circle—a human rainbow—around the room. Afterward, they discuss similarities and differences among people and address areas in human relations in which they have a major concern (Buban, McConnell, & Duncan, 1988).

It is important in community settings, as well as educational institutions, that group guidance or counseling activities be presented in an appealing way. One means to do so is to advertise groups as "clubs" (Boutwell & Myrick, 1992). By forming clubs instead of guidance or counseling groups, children avoid any stigmas attached to mental health activities. In the process, they can become more involved in the group and, thereby, get more from the experience.

SETTING UP GROUPS FOR CHILDREN

In designing group experiences, group workers must consider the maturity of the children with whom they are working and the purpose for the group. Assessing children's maturity is most frequently accomplished by establishing regular contacts with them. Determining topics for the group to explore can be accomplished through the use of "sociograms, self-concept inventories, incomplete sentence activities, and children's drawings" (Gerler, 1982, p. 87). Decisions can also be made when counselors conduct needs assessments with students, teachers, parents, and other related school personnel, or when counselors hear several students voicing similar concerns over a short period of time. Regardless of how the decision is made, many questions must be answered before the group begins, including

1. What medium will be most utilized in group communication?
2. What structure will be employed?
3. What materials will be used in the group?
4. How will group members be recruited and screened?
5. How long will group sessions meet?
6. How many children will be in the group?
7. What will the gender mix be?

Nonverbal Versus Verbal Communication

Gazda (1989), in concurrence with other authorities in the field of children's group counseling such as Dinkmeyer and Muro (1979), Keat (1974), and Slavson (1945, 1948), states that children under 12 years of age should participate primarily in groups that involve play and action, using techniques such as sociodrama, child drama, and psychodrama. Ginott (1968) also recommends the use of active play therapy for young children (under age 9) in groups. He advocates the use of water colors, finger paints, clay, and sand in these groups. As Campbell (1993, p. 10) states, "Toys have been referred to as the words children use to express emotions." Opposed to this action-centered view of groups are theorists, such as Ohlsen et al. (1988), who believe that children can be taught the proper ways to express themselves verbally and that verbal-oriented groups are viable with even very young children.

"In practice most counselors should combine a mixture of verbalization and activity in a manner that will be most helpful to their clients" (Kaczkowski, 1979, p. 45). Those who advocate verbal interaction believe the interplay of words and roles will "change the cognitive map and action patterns of a group member," whereas those who are activity oriented "believe that personality modifications occur through activity" (Kaczkowski, 1979, p. 45). There is some truth in both points of view.

Group Structure and Materials

Besides deciding on the primary way of obtaining information from children, professionals who conduct such groups must also formulate how groups will be structured (Leland & Smith, 1965). **Highly structured groups** have a "predetermined goal and a plan designed to enable each group member to reach this identified goal with minimum frustration" (Drum & Knott, 1977, p. 14). Such groups are usually used for teaching skills that may be transferred "to a wide range of life events" (Drum & Knott, 1977, p. 14). Often, groups are highly structured at their beginning and become less structured as group members get to know each other better. Unstructured groups, on the other hand, are used in more experientially based situations in which there is an emphasis on process rather than product. It is rare for a children's group of any kind to be totally unstructured.

In addition to how the group will be formed structurally, group workers must decide how materials used in the groups will be employed (Leland & Smith, 1965). If the emphasis of the group is on completing a project (e.g., drawing a figure) as opposed to experiencing a feeling (e.g., freehand drawing), the materials that are distributed and instructions given should reflect this. There are basically four approaches to this process: (a) unstructured material, unstructured approach; (b) unstructured material, structured approach; (c) structured material, unstructured approach; and (d) structured material, structured approach (Kaczkowski, 1979). Each approach has its advantages and limitations. (See Table 9.2)

The key to making the group a productive vehicle for helping children is for the counselor to use a leadership style that will enable him or her to blend meaningful materials with an appropriate degree of verbalization and activity (Kaczkowski, 1979, pp. 50–51). For instance, in group counseling, a leader may employ a democratic style that encourages sharing and openness. By creating such an atmosphere and modeling appropriate behaviors, group leaders establish trust within the group and concrete examples of how change can be accomplished.

Table 9.2
Relationships among key elements in group work.

Group	Goal	Leader	Child	Materials
Unstructured material, unstructured approach	Recognition of self Understanding that impulse can be controlled Living within social boundaries Self-responsibility	Cognitive stimulant Rewards Intrudes (approves, disapproves, etc.) Provides materials but not goals	Forced to think Free to use material	Conducive to creation, control, and change No end product Freedom of action
Unstructured material, structured approach	Improved self-concept Improved impulse control Improved social interaction	Preselects activity Acts as participant Helps child manipulate things and people in acceptable manner	Forced to think about something Tests reality Learns basic interaction with others	Designed to place limits on action Develops some skill Process rather than product emphasis
Structured material, unstructured approach	Reduce egocentric behavior Build relationship between things and people Deal effectively with social realities Evaluation of personal goals	Selects materials with child Facilitates interpersonal relations Active in skill presentation (minimal emphasis) Identification figure Rewards behavior	Learns practical working relationships Externalizes hostility Respects properly	May facilitate skill development Used to develop relations and cooperation No end product Has an acceptable standard of performance
Structured material, structured approach	Improved social reality Development of acceptance Reality relationships	Selects materials with child Provides for success Formal Teaches skill Facilitator	Completes project Tries to exhibit selective behavior Independent	Conducive to generating a product Cognitive or creative skill development Enhances reality relations

Source: From "Group Work with Children" by H. Kaczkowski, 1979, *Elementary School Guidance and Counseling, 14,* p. 47. Copyright ACA. Reprinted by permission of the American Counseling Association.

Recruiting Members and Screening

Once preliminary decisions about form, structure, and materials are made, the group worker begins the task of recruiting members. One of the best ways to accomplish this is to provide teachers and students with an "information statement" that describes what the group is all about and what is expected of its members (Thompson & Rudolph, 1988). Children who are potential group members, especially for topic-focused group counseling, will often ask to join a group. Others are referred by teachers.

Not all children who volunteer or are referred are appropriate for a group. Therefore, a pregroup screening process must be used. One way to screen potential participants is through individual or small-group intake interviews. In these sessions, group workers talk with children about the group and its purpose (Corey & Corey, 1992; Moore, 1969). If the counselor thinks certain children can benefit from the group and these children display an interest, the children are invited to join (Kochendofer & Culp, 1979; Silverman, 1976). Selection is crucial to the group's success, because group member satisfaction and identity with the group will influence group cohesion and ultimately affect personal outcomes.

When group workers and children decide that the group is appropriate, letters to parents requesting permission for participation must be sent out. Group work with children is more difficult to set up than group work with adults because of ethical and legal considerations in protecting children's rights (Corey, Corey, & Callanan, 1993).

Group Session Length and Number in Group

Opinions vary on how long the group sessions should last and how many children should be included. One general guideline is the younger the children, the shorter the session and the smaller the group (Myrick, 1987; Vinson, 1992). When groups become too large (e.g., nine or over), members do not get an opportunity to participate as much with one another and the dynamics of the group change (Castore, 1962). In such situations, subgroups may form or "in groups" and "out groups" may develop.

There is virtually no limit to the number who can be included in large group guidance activities. However, most counselors "think in terms of 25 to 30 students. This enables the group to be conveniently subdivided into five or six small working teams with about five or six students each" (Myrick, 1987, p. 282). Small groups within the group can be further subdivided, if necessary, into triads and dyads.

In group counseling, numbers are of more concern. "Group size should always be determined after examining the purpose of the counseling group, the developmental needs of the students, and the time available" (Gumaer, 1986). When working with children ages 5 to 6, sessions may be held for only 20 minutes, two or three times a week, and the number of children allowed to participate may be limited to three or four (Thompson & Rudolph, 1988). As children mature, the time allotted for each session and the numbers included go up. For example, preadolescent children (ages 9 to 13) may meet in groups of five to seven for as long as a regular classroom period (45 to 50 minutes) (Gazda, 1989).

Gender and Age Issues

A final consideration in setting up a group is a decision regarding the sex and age range of the participants. On the issue of gender, there is considerable disagreement (George & Dustin, 1988). For example, Ginott (1968) believes that children of different sexes should be mixed in preschool group settings but that school-age children should be separated. Gazda (1989) also believes that school-age children should be segregated by sex but not until the ages of 9 or 10. Gazda contends that around the time of puberty, girls begin to mature more rapidly than boys, and the two genders do not mix well in groups. On the other hand, Ohlsen (1977) advocates that groups include both girls and boys because he feels that group counseling is the safest place for girls and boys to learn to cope with each other regardless of social/sexual development. This same point of view is held by Thompson and Rudolph (1988), who stress a balance of both sexes in a group "unless the problem to be discussed is such that the presence of the opposite sex would hinder discussion—sex-education topics, for example" (p. 261).

In regard to age, a general rule of thumb is to group children with those who are within about one chronological year of one another (Gazda, 1989). Exceptions are made when more aggressive children are grouped with older children and less mature children are grouped with younger children. Some children with severe problems may be better candidates for individual counseling.

ROLE OF THE LEADER IN CHILDREN'S GROUPS

The role of the leader in children's groups varies. In group guidance, the leader is a teaching facilitator who encourages self-exploration. Guidance lessons are planned in cooperation, and often participation, with classroom teachers. Sometimes a counselor and teacher will co-lead a group and map out their developmental curriculum far in advance. At other times, they will make use of **timely teaching**, when a particular event stimulates thinking and discussion among students (Faust, 1968). Many group guidance leaders operate from an atheoretical base in regard to the process of change. They stress developmental learning. Others are more integrative or holistic. Yet a third group of leaders concentrate solely on a single area of change such as in the affective, behavioral, or cognitive domain.

In relationship to the approach taken, leaders of children's guidance and psychoeducational groups also influence what happens in the groups by the way they arrange chairs. Myrick (1993) states that there are five basic arrangements in which students can be seated (see Figure 9.1). When the classroom is arranged in

Figure 9.1
Managing large groups: Seating arrangements.

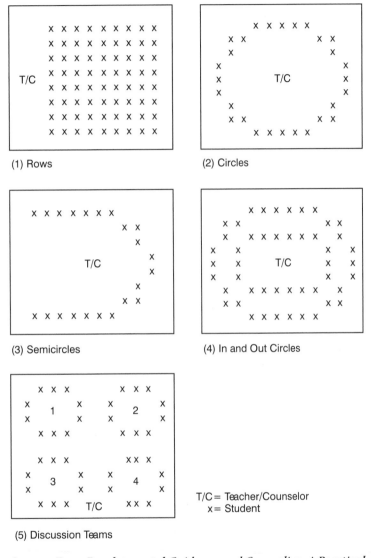

Managing Large Groups:
Seating Arrangements

(1) Rows

(2) Circles

(3) Semicircles

(4) In and Out Circles

(5) Discussion Teams

T/C = Teacher/Counselor
x = Student

Source: From *Developmental Guidance and Counseling: A Practical Approach,* Second Edition (p. 236) by R. D. Myrick, 1993, Minneapolis: Educational Media Corporation. Copyright 1993 Educational Media Corporation. Reprinted with permission.

a **row formation,** attention is focused toward the front. This arrangement is good for making a presentation, but it limits, and even inhibits, group interaction. In the second formation, a **circle**, student eye contact is increased and equality is promoted, but if the class group is too large (e.g., above 20), students may lose a sense of connectedness with others. In the **semicircle arrangement**, students can see each other and discussion is likely to involve almost everyone. However, if the group is too large (e.g., above 20), students may not feel that they are a group.

The fourth arrangement, **in and out circles**, is often referred to as the *fishbowl.* The inner circle promotes a sense of closeness, but those in the outer circle may feel left out and become bored. To help promote participation by everyone, group leaders can assign tasks for the outside group members to do while they observe the inside group, such as taking notes on group interactions. They can also rotate groups in and out of the inner circle on a regular timely basis. Another way to encourage participation by everyone is for leaders to leave an empty chair in the inner circle where those in the outer circle can sit and observe directly on a one-by-one basis what is happening in the inner circle.

Finally, the group guidance leader can use another structured arrangement known as **discussion teams** to promote involvement in guidance and psychoeducational activities. In this arrangement, students are divided into four or five teams that are then seated in semicircles around the room. This formation has the advantage of getting students involved with one another and raising the level of excitement among the children. The disadvantage is that interaction is mainly limited to a small number of individuals and other group members get to participate in only one group.

In group counseling, there is more of a tendency than in group guidance for leaders to have a theoretical orientation and act accordingly (Long, 1988). For example, the Adlerian group leader functions as an open, democratic individual who is based in the here and now. These leaders vary in their techniques, but in working with children's groups, they are prone to emphasize encouragement and the law of natural consequences (Dinkmeyer, Dinkmeyer, & Sperry, 1987; Hansen, Warner, & Smith, 1980). Leaders who are psychoanalytically based (and work more in group psychotherapy rather than group counseling) focus on the release of feeling through catharsis and the analysis of transference and interpretation (Corey, 1990). On the other hand, group counselors who take a Rogerian approach in their group work with children "put far greater emphasis on the facilitative quality of the counselor as a person. . . . The counselor's personhood [is] the basic catalyst that prompts group participants to make progress or not" (Boy & Pine, 1982, p. 179).

Leaders in rational-emotive therapy groups with children stress the teaching of rational thinking (Ellis, 1974). However, leaders in transactional analysis prefer to work with children in groups in order to promote the confrontation of games and help children learn basic TA concepts by seeing them demonstrated in themselves and others (Harris, 1969; Thompson & Rudolph, 1988). In a similar way, leaders who adhere to Gestalt theory work in groups in order to promote awareness and promote personality change from within (Corey, 1990). Leaders of behavioral groups focus on teaching children appropriate prosocial skills and helping them eliminate dysfunctional behavior (Rose, 1987). A critical component in bringing about behavioral change is promoting behavioral awareness, that is, "increasing students' ability to identify socially inappropriate behaviors, antecedents, and consequences and to use self-selected contingencies positively" (Safran & Safran, 1985, p. 91).

Basically, the "principles of group counseling apply to all ages. However, the group counselor (leader) must adapt his or her techniques to the clients' social, emotional, and intellectual development, as well as their ability to communicate verbally" (George & Dustin, 1988, p. 136).

RESEARCH ON THE OUTCOME OF CHILDREN'S GROUPS

Because group guidance and counseling have been conducted with elementary and middle school children for years, there are numerous studies on their effectiveness. Only a few of those will be highlighted here, but as Bowman (1987) discovered in a national survey, counselors who work with all age levels consider groups to be vital in reaching some students whom they would otherwise miss.

In elementary schools, Allan and Bardsley (1983) report that group counseling may be used to help **transient children** (i.e., those children who have moved to a new community and a new school) adapt to their environments. They describe a six-session group counseling format that positively affected students, teachers, parents, and a principal.

In working with fourth and fifth graders whose parents divorced, an 11-session support group was found helpful (Tedder, Scherman, & Wantz, 1987). In this group, a developmentally appropriate introductory activity, the *caterpillar,* was used. Students filled in the eight sections of their caterpillar by drawing an expressive face in the first segment, writing three words that described themselves in segment two, listing two of their hobbies in segment three, writing three present feelings in segment four, identifying where they were born in segment five, describing where they would like to be at the present time in segment six, listing an activity they would like to do in segment seven, and writing about a unique special personal quality in segment eight (see Figure 9.2).

Figure 9.2
Caterpillar introductory activity.

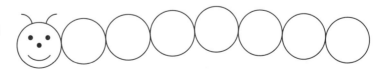

Source: From "Effectiveness of a Support Group for Children of Divorce" by S. L. Tedder, A. Scherman, and R. A. Wantz, 1987, *Elementary School Guidance & Counseling, 22,* p. 105. Copyright ACA. Reprinted by permission of the American Counseling Association.

The most important outcome of this research was its use of objective instruments to verify positive outcomes. Parents especially noted the impact of the group on the behavior of their children.

A *Disruptive Child's Play Group (DCPG)* for third-grade children in an elementary school has also been found to have positive results (Bleck & Bleck, 1982). After participating in this ten-session program, the self-concept scores for the children involved improved significantly compared to a similar control group. In another study on self-concept, Durbin (1982) found that self-concept for a sixth-grade girls' group improved significantly at the end of nine 35-minute sessions. Durbin's group followed a multimodal format based on Keat's (1979) **HELPING** framework—Health, Emotions, Learning, Personal Interactions, Imagery, Need to Know, and Guidance. HELPING is an alternative model to Lazarus's (1976, 1981) **BASIC ID**—behavior, affect, sensation, imagery, cognition, interpersonal relations, drugs. The HELPING model has been found to be a motivator for increasing daily attendance at school of third-grade boys (Keat, Metzgar, Raykovitz, & McDonald, 1985). It includes developmentally stimulating activities within it, such as *"Feelings Bingo,"* in which participants use "I-messages" after a feeling is called and "win" by filling out their feeling card horizontally, diagonally, or any way the caller decides beforehand (see Figure 9.3).

In two studies involving *learning disabled (LD) children,* who comprise 2% to 10% of the school-age population (Humes, 1974), group counseling was found to improve self-concept, social behavior, and locus of control (Omizo, Cubberly, & Longano, 1984; Omizo & Omizo, 1988). One of the studies (Omizo & Omizo, 1988) included participants from various ethnic backgrounds in grades four to six and compared the ten-session treatment group with a control group. The other study, which also included a control group, was conducted with predominantly white middle-class children from ages 8 to 11 years and lasted for a total of eight sessions. Both studies have significant implications for educators in helping LD children learn.

Happy	Afraid	Worried	Free Space
Sad	Timid	Mad	Lonely
Joyful	Excited	Scared	Smart
Angry	Tired	Good	Overwhelmed

Figure 9.3
Feelings bingo game.
Source: From "Multimodal Counseling: Motivating Children to Attend School Through Friendship Groups" by D. B. Keat, K. L. Metzgar, D. Raykovitz, and J. McDonald, 1985, *Journal of Humanistic Education and Development, 23,* p. 170. Copyright ACA. Reprinted by permission of the American Counseling Association.

One of the most promising research studies on groups with children is a replication study conducted by Lee (1993) of classroom guidance on student achievement. In her work, Lee followed the *Succeeding in School* lessons created by Gerler and Anderson (1986). This series of ten lessons deals with modeling after successful people in school while learning to feel comfortable and responsible. It focuses on promoting cooperative efforts, enhancing student self-concept, and learning appropriate school skills such as listening and asking for help. Although her research was not without some flaws, Lee found that fifth and sixth graders who took part in this experience significantly improved their academic achievement in mathematics over a control group. The group also made gains in language and conduct.

In addition to the studies cited, there are many others that either statistically or anecdotally report positive results on the use of groups with elementary and middle school children. Some studies are now investigating the strengths and weaknesses of specific packaged group guidance kits, such as DUSO-R, in order to help counselors maximize the effectiveness of these tools in working with children (Morse, Bockoven, & Bettesworth, 1988). Overall, research is making strides in informing potential group workers with children about what types of groups and experiences are effective with certain populations and when.

ADVANTAGES AND LIMITATIONS OF USING GROUPS WITH CHILDREN

There are a number of advantages and limitations of using guidance/psychoeducational, counseling, and psychotherapy groups with children. How successful a particular group will be depends on many variables, such as how well prepared the leader and members are, the composition of members, the amount of time allotted, and the focus of the group.

Children who profit most from group counseling and psychotherapy share the following characteristics. They volunteer, are committed to discussing what genuinely concerns them, are committed to learning new behaviors, are interested in helping other group members learn new behaviors, and believe that their counselor/group leader, parents (and even teachers) have confidence in their ability to learn and implement new behaviors (Ohlsen et al., 1988). The opposite may be said for children who do not benefit.

Myrick (1987) lists a number of advantages and limitations for both group guidance and group counseling with children. Among the advantages of group guidance and psychoeducational activities are the following:

1. It allows the counselor/group leader to see a large number of students in a brief amount of time and work in a preventive fashion.
2. It allows the counselor/group leader to use inside (i.e., teachers) and outside (i.e., community personnel) resources to help children learn to help themselves.

3. It promotes security and comfort in children, promotes peer interaction, and enhances learning of practical ways to handle problem situations.

Among the limitations of group guidance and psychoeducational activities are the following:

1. It may be too impersonal at times and fail to help children in a practical way.
2. It may include too many individuals and prohibit general discussion or the exploration of certain subjects.
3. It may stereotype the counselor as a presenter of knowledge and inhibit the counselor from being more spontaneous.

Group counseling with children has advantages and limitations also. Among the advantages listed by Myrick (1987) are the following:

1. It is more efficient than individual counseling because more children can be seen at any one time.
2. It is more realistic than individual counseling. Because of its social inter- action base, it allows group members to share with each other frequently and learn through peer modeling and feedback (Hoffman, 1976).
3. It promotes support, acceptance, relaxation, risk taking, and resources for involved members.
4. It may free the counselor/group leader to make strategic intervention with members of the group.

Limitations of group counseling with children are the following:

1. It takes more time to develop trust and closeness because of the increased number of individuals involved in the counseling process.
2. It is more difficult to safeguard confidentiality and to include all mem- bers actively in group discussions/activities.
3. It is more difficult to organize group counseling activities than it is to see select children on a one-on-one basis, that is, some group counseling formats may require school system and/or parental permission/approval.
4. It requires leaders and members to be sensitive to topics that are inap- propriate for the group and to be aware of, and counteract, nonproduc- tive behavior of select group members.

Gumaer (1986) states that experienced middle school counselors can imple- ment group work by recognizing its value, improving their involvement with teachers, discussing the rationale for more group work with their principals, obtaining additional training if necessary, and becoming self-motivating through initiating groups in cooperation with principals, faculty, and students. Ways in which new counselors can begin group work include selling the principal on the value of it and explaining that it is an integral part of counseling, offering in-ser- vice training to teachers, setting up a time to conduct a group, implementing one group at a time, publicizing groups, leading growth-centered groups initially, and evaluating all group experiences.

SUMMARY AND CONCLUSION

This chapter has examined the use of guidance/psychoeducation, counseling, and psychotherapy groups with elementary and middle school children. Group workers, both inside and outside schools, frequently conduct groups for children in this age range (under 14 years). In order to be effective, leaders must have a knowledge of group dynamics, group process, and human development. They must target their activities either toward guidance and psychoeducational groups, where learning and prevention are the chief targets, or toward group counseling and psychotherapy, where resolution and growth are the primary concerns. Developmental and nondevelopmental situations are dealt with in these groups.

Setting up groups for children is contingent on many factors. Certainly the matter of structure is of central concern. Structure involves how much control the group leader allows members to have and how materials are used. Another important aspect of setting up a group is related to how long it will meet and with whom. A general rule of thumb seems to be that the younger the children, the shorter the time of the meeting, although frequency of meetings may be increased. The debate about mixing genders is fairly evenly split . There are some advantages and disadvantages of conducting groups for just one gender. On the other hand, there seems to be agreement among clinicians and researchers that children should be developmentally within a chronological year of one another in most cases.

The role of the leader will vary in children's groups depending on the purpose of the group and the theoretical model advocated. Generally, leaders will be more active at first. Leaders use both nonverbal and verbal ways of learning depending on the maturity of the children involved. Research supports the employment of groups in many settings with children including those who have suffered loss, need support, or are deficient in social skills. Multimodal group counseling and guidance seem especially appropriate because children respond to a number of stimuli at different times in their lives. Although group guidance, counseling, and psychotherapy are not without limits, counselors/group leaders often limit the effectiveness of group work by failing to utilize their resources sufficiently. Thus, various ways of advocating for and implementing groups have been discussed.

CLASSROOM EXERCISES

1. Poppen and Thompson (1975) have suggested that one way to begin a group on an elementary/middle school level is to have children engage in

activities that focus on their strengths. For example, children may be asked to draw something they do well and wear it after they have shared it in the group. In groups of five, pretend you are under age 14, and try this activity. Discuss with your group, and then the class as a whole, your reaction to this exercise. As a class, devise five other activities to use in group guidance and counseling with children. List the pros and cons of each.

2. In a group of four, create an activity for a group guidance class in each of the areas listed by Keat et al. (1985) in the HELPING model. Discuss the advantages and limitations of multimodal guidance and counseling as developed by Keat and Lazarus.

3. Compare problem-centered counseling with growth-centered counseling. Discuss with another student in class how problem-centered counseling might become more growth oriented. Continue the discussion by listing strategies that a group leader could use in keeping a growth-oriented group from becoming problem centered. Share your ideas with the class as a whole.

4. Find a current research article on using groups with children. Share the results with the class as a whole in a reaction report giving the strengths and limitations of the study as you see them and how you might use this information later in working with a children's group.

REFERENCES

Allan, J., & Bardsley, P. (1983). Transient children in the elementary school: A group counseling approach. *Elementary School Guidance & Counseling, 17,* 162–169.

Bleck, R. T., & Bleck, B. L. (1982). The disruptive child's play group. *Elementary School Guidance & Counseling, 17,* 137–141.

Bond, K. (1993). Classroom guidance: The get along gang. *Elementary School Guidance & Counseling, 27,* 303–304.

Boutwell, D. A., & Myrick, R. D. (1992). The go for it club. *Elementary School Guidance & Counseling, 27,* 65–72.

Bowman, R. P. (1987). Small-group guidance and counseling in schools: A national survey of school counselors. *School Counselor, 34,* 256–262.

Boy, A. V., & Pine, G. J. (1982). *Client-centered counseling: A renewal.* Boston: Allyn & Bacon.

Buban, M. E., McConnell, S. C., & Duncan, B. L. (1988). Children's fears of nuclear war: Group intervention strategies. *Journal for Specialists in Group Work, 13,* 124–129.

Campbell, C. A. (1991). Group guidance for academically undermotivated children. *Elementary School Guidance & Counseling, 25,* 302–307.

Campbell, C. A. (1993). Play, the fabric of elementary school counseling programs. *Elementary School Guidance & Counseling, 28,* 10–16.

Campbell, C., & Bowman, R. P. (1993). The 'fresh start' support club: Small-group counseling for academically retained children. *Elementary School Guidance & Counseling, 27,* 172–185.

Castore, G. (1962). Number of verbal interrelationships as a determinant of group size. *Journal of Abnormal and Social Psychology, 64,* 456–457.

Clark, A. J. & Seals, J. M. (1984). Groups counseling for ridiculed children. *Journal for Specialists in Group Work, 9,* 157–162.

Coppock, M. W. (1993). Small group plan for improving friendships and self-esteem. *Elementary School Guidance & Counseling, 28,* 152–154.

Corey, G. (1990). *Theory and practice of group counseling* (3rd ed.). Pacific Grove, CA: Brooks/Cole.

Corey, G., Corey, M. S. & Callanan, P. (1993). *Issues and ethics in the helping professions* (4th ed.). Pacific Grove, CA: Brooks/Cole.

Corey, M. S., & Corey, G. (1992). *Groups: Process and practice* (4th ed.). Pacific Grove, CA: Brooks/Cole.

Dinkmeyer, D., & Dinkmeyer, D., Jr. (1982). *Developing understanding of self and others, D-2* (rev. ed.). Circle Pines, MN: American Guidance Service.

Dinkmeyer, D., Dinkmeyer, D., Jr., & Sperry, L. (1987). *Adlerian counseling and psychotherapy* (2nd ed.). Columbus, OH: Merrill.

Dinkmeyer, D., & Muro, J. J. (1979). *Group counseling: Theory and practice* (2nd ed.). Itasco, IL: Peacock.

Drum, D. J., & Knott, J. E. (1977). *Structured groups for facilitating development: Acquiring life skills, resolving life themes, and making life transitions.* New York: Human Science Press.

Durbin, D. M. (1982). Multimodal group sessions to enhance self-concept. *Elementary School Guidance & Counseling, 16,* 288–295.

Dyer, W. W. (1979). The case for group counseling as the means for eliminating erroneous zones. *Elementary School Guidance & Counseling, 14,* 145–148.

Egge, D. L., Marks, L. G., & McEvers, D. M. (1987). Puppets and adolescents: A group guidance workshop approach. *Elementary School Guidance & Counseling, 21,* 183–192.

Ellis, A. (1974). Rational-emotive therapy in groups. *Rational Living, 9,* 15–22.

Faust, V. (1968). *The counselor-consultant in the elementary school.* Boston: Houghton Mifflin.

Flavell, J. N. (1963). *The developmental psychology of Jean Piaget.* New York: Von Nostrand Reinhold.

Franks, J. C. (1983). Children. In J. A. Brown & R. H. Pate, Jr. (Eds.), *Being a counselor: Directions and challenges* (pp. 195–206). Pacific Grove, CA: Brooks/Cole.

Gazda, G. M. (1989). *Group counseling: A developmental approach* (4th ed.). Boston: Allyn & Bacon.

George, R. L., & Dustin, D. (1988). *Group counseling: Theory and practice.* Englewood Cliffs, NJ: Prentice Hall.

Gerler, E. R., Jr. (1982). *Counseling the young learner.* Englewood Cliffs, NJ: Prentice Hall.

Gerler, E. R., & Anderson, R. F. (1986). The effects of classroom guidance on success in school. *Journal of Counseling and Development, 65,* 78–81.

Ginott, H. (1968). Group therapy with children. In G. Gazda (Ed.), *Basic approaches to group psychotherapy and group counseling.* Springfield, IL: Charles C. Thomas.

Gladding, S. T. (1975). Still life. *North Carolina Personnel & Guidance Journal, 4,* 28.

Gladding, S. T. (1992). *Counseling as an art: The creative arts in counseling.* Alexandria, VA: American Counseling Association.

Golden, L. B. (1987). Prosocial learning groups with young children. *Elementary School Guidance & Counseling, 22,* 31–36.

Gumaer, J. (1984). *Counseling and therapy for children.* New York: Free Press.

Gumaer, J. (1986). Working in groups with middle graders. *School Counselor, 33,* 230–238.

Gwynn, C. A., & Brantley, H. T. (1987). Effects of a divorce group intervention for elementary school children. *Psychology in the Schools, 24,* 161–164.

Hansen, J. C., Warner, R. W., & Smith, E. J. (1980). *Group counseling: Theory and process* (2nd ed.). Chicago: Rand McNally.

Harper, B. L. (1985). Say it, review it, enhance it with a song. *Elementary School Guidance & Counseling, 19,* 218–221.

Harris, T. A. (1969). *I'm ok—You're ok.* New York: Harper & Row.

Havighurst, R. J. (1972). *Developmental tasks and education.* New York: David McKay.

Hillman, B. W., & Reunion, K. B. (1978). Activity group guidance: Process and results. *Elementary School Guidance & Counseling, 13,* 104–111.

Hinkle, J. S. (1993). Training school counselors to do family counseling. *Elementary School Guidance & Counseling, 27,* 252–257.

Hoffman, L. R. (1976). Peers as group counseling models. *Elementary School Guidance and Counseling, 11,* 37–44.

Humes, C. (1974). The secondary school counselor and learning disability. *School Counselor, 21,* 210–215.

Johnson, W., & Kottman, T. (1992). Developmental needs of middle school students: Implications for counselors. *Elementary School Guidance & Counseling, 27,* 3–14.

Kaczkowski, H. (1979). Group work with children. *Elementary School Guidance and Counseling, 14,* 44–51.

Keat, D. B. (1974). *Fundamentals of child counseling.* Boston: Houghton Mifflin.

Keat, D. B. (1979). *Multimodal therapy with children.* New York: Pergamon.

Keat, D. B., Metzgar, K. L., Raykovitz, D., & McDonald, J. (1985). Multimodal counseling: Motivating children to attend school through friendship groups. *Journal of Humanistic Education and Development, 23,* 166–175.

Kochendofer, S. A., & Culp, D. (1979). Relaxation group—Intake procedure. *Elementary School Guidance & Counseling, 14,* 124.

Lazarus, A. A. (Ed.). (1976). *Multimodal behavior therapy.* New York: Springer.

Lazarus, A. A. (1981). *The practice of multimodal therapy.* New York: McGraw-Hill.

Lee, R. S. (1993). Effects of classroom guidance on student achievement. *Elementary School Guidance & Counseling, 27,* 163–171.

Leland, H., & Smith, D. (1965). *Play therapy with mentally subnormal children.* New York: Grune & Stratton.

Long, S. (1988). The six group therapies compared. In S. Long (Ed.), *Six group therapies* (pp. 327–338). New York: Plenum.

March, L. C. (1935). Group therapy and the psychiatric clinic. *Journal of Nervous and Mental Disorders, 32,* 381–392.

Miles, R. (1993). I've got a song to sing. *Elementary School Guidance & Counseling, 28,* 71–75.

Moore, L. (1969). A developmental approach to group counseling with seventh graders. *School Counselor, 16,* 272–276.

Morse, C. L., Bockoven, J., & Bettesworth, A. (1988). Effects of DUSO-2 and DUSO-2 revised on children's social skills and self-esteem. *Elementary School Guidance & Counseling, 22,* 199–205.

Myrick, R. D. (1987). *Developmental guidance and counseling: A practical approach.* Minneapolis: Educational Media Corporation.

Myrick, R. D. (1993). *Developmental guidance and counseling: A practical approach* (2nd ed.). Minneapolis: Educational Media Corporation.

Ohlsen, M. M. (1977). *Group counseling* (2nd ed.). New York: Holt, Rinehart & Winston.

Ohlsen, M. M., Horne, A. M., & Lawe, C. F. (1988). *Group counseling* (3rd ed.). New York: Holt, Rinehart & Winston.

Omizo, M. M., Cubberly, W. E., & Longano, D. M. (1984). The effects of group counseling on self-concept and locus of control among learning disabled children. *Humanistic Education and Development, 23,* 69–79.

Omizo, M. M., & Omizo, S. A. (1988). Group counseling's effects on self-concept and social behavior among children with learning disabilities. *Journal of Humanistic Education and Development, 26,* 109–117.

Poppen, W., & Thompson, C. (1975). *School counseling: Theories and concepts.* Lincoln, NE: Professional Educators.

Rose, S. R. (1987). Social skill training in middle childhood: A structured group research. *Journal for Specialists in Group Work, 12,* 144–149.

Safran, J. S., & Safran, S. P. (1985). Teaching behavioral awareness in groups. *Elementary School Guidance & Counseling, 20*(9), 1–96.

Silverman, M. (1976). The achievement motivation group: A counselor-directed approach. *Elementary School Guidance and Counseling, 11,* 100–106.

Slavson, S. R. (1945). Different methods of group therapy in relation to age levels. *Nervous Child, 4,* 196–210.

Slavson, S. R. (1948). Group therapy in child care and child guidance. *Jewish Social Service Quarterly, 25,* 203–213.

Stamm, M. L., & Nissman, B. S. (1979). *Improving middle school guidance: Practical procedures for counselors, teachers, and administrators.* Boston: Allyn & Bacon.

Tedder, S. L., Scherman, A., & Wantz, R. A. (1987). Effectiveness of a support group for children of divorce. *Elementary School Guidance & Counseling, 22,* 102–109.

Thompson, C. L., & Rudolph, L. B. (1988). *Counseling children* (2nd ed.). Pacific Grove, CA: Brooks/Cole.

Tyra, R. P. (1979). Group guidance and the SIPA model. *Elementary School Guidance & Counseling, 13,* 269–271.

Vander Kolk, C. J. (1985). *Introduction to group counseling and psychotherapy.* Columbus, OH: Merrill.

Vinson, A. (1992). Group counseling with victims of abuse/incest. In D. Capuzzi & D. R. Gross (Eds.), *Introduction to group counseling* (pp. 165–181). Denver: Love Publishing.

Whiteside, R. G. (1993). Making a referral for family therapy: The school counselor's role. *Ele-mentary School Guidance & Counseling, 27,* 273–279.

Yauman, B. E. (1991). School-based group counseling for children of divorce: A review of the literature. *Elementary School Guidance & Counseling, 26,* 130–138.

CHAPTER 10

Groups for Adolescents

Out of the depth of your mind come the secrets
   rough diamond-shaped forms
      slowly pressured in pain and cut with hope.
With inner strength
   you mine repressed memories
      and change your expressions
         as crystallized anger is slowly released.
Privately, I wish for more of your story
   but the struggle is deep and the thoughts are too heavy
      to be quickly lightened with insight.
So with the group I patiently listen
   and silently applaud your emergence.*

Adolescence (defined here as the age span from 13 to 19 but extended to include some individuals up to age 25) is a difficult period in the life of many young people. It is a time of unevenness and paradoxes marked by extensive personal changes (Hamburg & Takanishi, 1989). Young adults during this time grow up physically and mature mentally, but they struggle with psychological and social issues related to their growth and development. "Adolescents must cope with crises in identity, extraordinary peer pressures, dramatic physical changes, impending career decisions, the desire for independence, and self doubt . . ." (Vander Kolk, 1985, p. 308). They are expected to behave as adults and are given some adult privileges, such as obtaining a driver's license and registering to vote.

However, for most adolescents, there is frustration and stress in being dependent on their parents and school/community authorities and being offi-

*Source: Gladding, 1990, p. 141.

cially denied some of the most tempting status symbols of adulthood, such as sanctioned sex and the legal consumption of alcohol. Often, "they seem to have to wait for circumstances to make their decisions for them, because they are not really free to decide for themselves" (Harris, 1967, p. 176).

Yet, despite frustrations, adolescents continuously reach out for growth and change and become the "cultural pioneers" of each generation (Dinkmeyer, Dinkmeyer & Sperry, 1987, p. 144). In their search for identity, they frequently create new fashions and trends. Many adolescent identities are relatively short-lived and discarded with maturity, for example, wearing one's hair long or not trusting adults. Yet, the fads in clothing, music, language, and dance, while isolating some adolescents from general society, unite them with peers and in many cases help them constructively break away from their families of origin and establish a sense of individuation from others.

Overall, *adolescence* (a term originated by G. Stanley Hall) is a time of rapid changes. It is characterized by some or all of the following: "storm and stress" (Hall, 1904), heightened emotionality (Gesell, Ilg, & Ames, 1956), experimentation (McCandless, 1970), and a desire for independence (Ohlsen, Horne, & Lawe, 1988). Some of the "normal expectations" of late childhood and middle-grader adolescence have been summarized by Gumaer (1984) (see Table 10.1). These

Table 10.1

Normal expectations for children's social and emotional development.

Developmental Stage	Social Development	Emotional Development
Late childhood (8–11 years)	Peer group extremely influential. Bias and prejudice developed. Independence from family and adults developed. Team games and competition enjoyed. Opposite sex may be excluded in play. Interest in sex education and sexual differences developed.	Need to receive reinforcement and approval from peers. Strong bond, attachment to same sex. May antagonize and be hostile toward opposite sex. More willing to accept constructive criticism. Accepts responsibility for behaviors and consequences of actions.
Middle-grader adolescence (11–14 years)	Status among peers predominates behavior. Dating begins. Personal appearance becomes important. Very interested in sex and body development. Sexual experimentation begins.	Anxiety present related to acceptance by peers, status in group, personal appearance, dating, and body development. Growing need to express independence from parents. Antagonism in home may develop over "control."

Source: Reprinted with the permission of The Free Press, a Division of Simon & Schuster from *Counseling and Therapy for Children* by Jim Gumaer. Copyright © 1980 by The Free Press.

expectations differ widely but increase with each age group. The rapidity of transition associated with adolescence helps explain why many individuals in this category have difficulties in adjustment.

Groups can be especially helpful to adolescents in making a successful transition from childhood to adulthood. They can provide support, facilitate new learning, help ease internal and external pressures, and offer hope and models for change. A group context allows open questioning and/or modification of values and an opportunity to practice communication skills with peers and adults. In a group setting, adolescents can safely experiment with reality, test their limits, express themselves, and be heard (Corey, 1990). By participating in groups, adolescents may develop a greater sense of identity and intimacy (Erikson, 1963, 1968). Using the processes of increased self-awareness and self-disclosure to others in the group (Jourard, 1971), along with having the opportunity to prove that they can translate their ideas into actions in the context of a community (Erikson, 1968), enables adolescents to achieve these personal and interpersonal skills. Within groups, adolescents often find "genuine acceptance and encouragement" from peers, and "a trustworthy adult who seems to trust and respect" them (George & Dustin, 1988, p. 142).

TYPES OF GROUPS FOR ADOLESCENTS

Adolescents spend a great deal of their time in groups on a typical day (Bates, Johnson, & Blaker, 1982). There is the family group at home, the learning group at school, a possible work group, and, of course, a social group. Peers with whom adolescents associate are especially important and influence the developing young person for better or worse. Society labels such groups as the "right" or "wrong" crowd, and adolescents strongly identify with the values generated by their primary peer groups. In addition to these natural groups are at least two other main types of groups to which adolescents may belong and to which adults may have input. One is the developmental psychoeducational/guidance group, which is primarily voluntary and self-focused; the other is the nondevelopmental counseling or psychotherapy group, which is usually nonvoluntary and often focused on others' concerns. Both can have a powerful impact on the adolescents who participate in them.

Developmental Psychoeducational/Guidance Groups

Developmental psychoeducational/guidance groups usually focus on common concerns of young people such as identity, sexuality, parents, peer relationships, career goals, and educational/institutional problems. Individuals join these groups out of a sense of need and a desire to gain knowledge and experience that will help them better handle their concerns (Carty, 1983). Such groups are conducted in community and school settings and traditionally have an adult leader.

Within the schools, Bowman (1987) found that the top five group topics for adolescents described by a national sample of high school counselors were career, communication skills and peer helping, decision making, study skills, and self-concept (see Table 10.2). These topics differ somewhat in popularity from those found in elementary and middle schools and reflect the developmental issues most relevant to these different age groups.

Most of the counselors surveyed by Bowman believed that small-group guidance and counseling services are "vital and practical to implement in their programs" (p. 261), but high school counselors, in particular, believed setting up such groups was less practical than did counselors on the elementary and middle school levels. Consequently, they did not lead groups as often and confirmed Carroll's (1979) observation about the lack of group work at this level.

When developmental psychoeducational/guidance groups are offered to adolescents, however, they seem to have positive results. For example, group discussion can facilitate the process of examining careers that adolescents may not have considered before (Glaize & Myrick, 1984). In addition, cognitive restructuring groups can help students learn skills related to resolving problematic situations before they arise and thereby avert major crises (Baker, Thomas, & Munson, 1983). Likewise, communication skills groups can effectively help high school

Table 10.2
Percentages of counselors who led each group topic.

Small Group Topics	Elementary		Middle or Junior High		High School	
	%	Rank	%	Rank	%	Rank
Decision Making	10.0	3	12.9	3	14.1	3
Communication Skills and Peer Helping	6.8	7	20.8	1	19.7	2
Self-Concept	12.0	1	9.6	5	9.2	5
Study Skills	8.0	5	14.5	2	12.0	4
Career	6.0	9	11.9	4	20.4	1
Behavior	11.6	2	7.9	6	7.0	7
Family	8.4	4	4.3	9	5.6	8
Drugs	4.8	11	5.9	7	7.7	6
Single Parent and Divorce	7.6	6	2.3	12	1.4	9
Death	5.2	10	5.0	8	0.7	10
Truancy	6.0	9	3.3	10	1.4	9
Fears	6.4	8	2.0	13	0.0	11
Sex	2.8	12	3.0	11	0.7	10

Source: From "Small-Group Guidance and Counseling in Schools: A National Survey of School Counselors" by R. P. Bowman, 1987, *School Counselor, 34,* p. 259. Copyright ACA. Reprinted by permission of the American Counseling Association.

students improve their interpersonal relationships with peers in sending and receiving verbal and nonverbal messages. This improvement is especially likely if role-playing exercises are included as a part of the small-group experience (Hudson, Doyle, & Venezia, 1991). Small-group work in adolescent sexuality education has also proven effective both in and out of school settings. "Some adolescents' lives will be immediately and dramatically improved by sexuality education" in a group setting, while for others the impact will be more subtle (McMurray, 1992, p. 389). The actual and potential results for employing developmental guidance and psychoeducational groups with adolescents are great.

An exemplary school district's model of offering structured developmental groups has been summarized by Phillips and Phillips (1992). The groups set up in this model focused on personal concerns of students. Groups of 8 to 16 met for 50 minutes (i.e., one class period) a week. They were conducted for ten weeks during school hours, with the periods being rotated each week. All groups were co-led, with some teachers serving as co-leaders with counselors and other mental health staff. During the sessions, the group leaders used basic group counseling skills such as reflecting content and feeling, clarifying messages, helping members recognize their own strengths and outside resources, and encouraging members to take actions that could help them resolve situations by themselves. Students were reminded of group rules each session, such as confidentiality, but otherwise were allowed to talk freely and openly about their concerns. The outcome was both personal growth and prevention.

Nondevelopmental Counseling/Psychotherapy Groups

In contrast to developmental guidance and psychoeducational groups, **nondevelopmental counseling and psychotherapy groups** tend to focus mainly on concerns of adults and society, such as drug use, school problems (e.g., poor grades, truancy), or deviant behavior. Usually, these groups are established by a school, agency, or court, and troubled adolescents are forced to attend (Jacobs, Harvill, & Masson, 1994). These nonvoluntary groups generate many negative feelings among those required to participate, yet the groups themselves may be nurturing and supportive (Napier & Gershenfeld, 1989; Zimpfer, 1992).

When potential members are not given a choice of participating, the result is usually dissatisfaction and reluctance to participate in the group. Although some of the hostility of these members may be overcome prior to the beginning of the group by talking to the participants and inviting them to share their thoughts and feelings, leaders of such groups face an uphill battle to create cohesion. They must be creative and innovative to turn the negative energy around. Starting with a formal presentation of the rules is not the way to begin a nonvoluntary group of adolescents. Initially, just listening to the adolescents' complaints about having been referred to the group is a good place to start such a group. After such feelings have been ventilated, members and leaders can begin to talk about common concerns and goals (O'Hanlon & Weiner-Davis, 1989). Several constructive ways of handling participants' negative feelings and resistance are suggested by Corey and Corey (1992):

1. *Meet with these adolescents individually before the group starts*—This pregroup meeting gives the counselor/group leader and the adolescents a chance to explore feelings connected with participation in a required group and alternatives connected with the choice of nonparticipation. Such a meeting also provides the counselor/group leader with an opportunity to explain the nature of the group and how it will be conducted and to find out if the adolescents have had any previous therapy experiences. Rapport may be established at this time, too.

2. *Work with the resistance that uncooperative adolescents bring rather than fighting it*—Working with resistance includes listening in an understanding and nondefensive way to adolescents' stories about the reasons they have been forced to come to a group. The experience of being heard is helpful in breaking down hostility and building up trust. The group leader may also work with resistance by inviting certain adolescents to try the group for a few sessions and then decide whether they will continue. This type of option gets adolescents into the group and yet gives them a choice. If this technique does not work, an adolescent may be invited to the group as an observer for a session. After seeing the group in action, the adolescent can then make a decision of whether to participate or choose another consequence imposed by others.

3. *Respond to adolescents' sarcasm or silence with honest, firm, and caring statements*—By so doing, group leaders can help nonvoluntary adolescents become less emotionally upset in regard to the group, the leader, and the process. For example, leaders may tell adolescents who call them names, "I really care about you as a person, but I care about myself, too, and name calling will not be permitted in this group. I would like for you to be able to talk about your anger and other feelings but in a direct and clear manner. That will mean using 'I' before you make a statement." Responding in this manner shows concern and care. It also establishes rules that are clear and firm. It helps the group leader and the group take care of themselves and function in a direct and nondefensive way.

Overall, developmental psychoeducational/guidance and nondevelopmental counseling/psychotherapy groups are two of the primary ways adolescents receive help from adults. Although such groups are found in both schools and agencies, the ways they are conducted may differ because schools have more internal control than most agencies. Developmental guidance and psychoeducational groups are almost always choice oriented, whereas developmental counseling/psychotherapy groups are almost always geared toward change. As a rule, leaders of nondevelopmental counseling/psychotherapy groups face more of a challenge in helping participants get involved in the group than do those in developmental psychoeducational/guidance groups (O'Hanlon & Weiner-Davis, 1989). An excellent resource for working with young adolescents in developmental and nondevelopmental groups is Morganett's (1990) *Skills for Living,* which covers topics pertinent to the needs of this age population, such as developing self-esteem, managing stress, making friends, and coping with grief and loss.

SETTING UP GROUPS FOR ADOLESCENTS

Determining how a group will be set up is based on the type of group to be led. In some groups, the material to be presented may have general applicability to a wide range of individuals. In other groups, the focus of the group is more narrow and deals with specific and sometimes troublesome aspects of life such as sexuality (McMurray, 1992) or grief (Moore & Herlihy, 1993). Regardless of the topic, group leaders may still need to be careful in selecting members to make sure they are mature and motivated enough to benefit from the group and be of benefit to the group. Various factors that must be considered in working with adolescents in groups include the use of verbal versus nonverbal behavior, group structure and materials, recruiting members, screening, group session length, number of members, and gender/age issues.

Nonverbal Versus Verbal Communication

Whereas groups for children and middle schoolers are activity focused, groups for adolescents are more verbally oriented (Gazda, 1989). The reason is that the majority of individuals ages 13 and older are developmentally ready and prefer to interact through speech. Sometimes adolescents, out of fear of being rejected or ridiculed, will withdraw or hold back on topics they wish to discuss (Bates et al., 1982; George & Dustin, 1988). In such cases, nonverbal cues, such as body posture or facial expression, will take on added significance. For instance, if Paula begins to frown when the subject of group rules comes up but does not say anything, the group leader may say, "Paula, you are frowning. I wonder if it is in connection to what we are now discussing?" Structured exercises may be introduced into adolescent groups, especially at the beginning, to facilitate trust, cohesion, and eventually more open and honest verbal communication. For example, in the introductory session of a counseling group, members might be asked to begin by comparing themselves to an animal, body of water, or machine (Paisley, Swanson, Borders, Cassidy, & Danforth, 1994). Participants could first make a drawing and then talk about their ideas, or they could just discuss their comparisons in a go-round warm-up experience. For example, if a group is asked to compare themselves to a body of water, statements might be made as follows:

Jill:	"I am like a babbling brook. I flow in an even way most times."
Derrick:	"I am a raging stream. I have a lot of anger that spills over into my life and interactions with others."

Russs: "I am a lake. Placid on the outside with a lot that waits
                  to be discovered underneath."
Allison: "I am a mountain river. Flowing hard but as yet undis-
                  covered."

In groups for adolescents, just as in groups for adults, members should be free to decide whether to talk or not, but the leader should work at setting up conditions that promote positive exchanges. Sometimes these conditions involve teaching basic communication skills in a very structured manner (Goldstein, Sprafkin, Gershaw, & Klein, 1980; Leaman, 1983).

Certain theories, such as Gestalt and psychodrama, will focus on the congruence between verbal and nonverbal messages. Yet, even leaders from primarily talk-oriented traditions, such as psychoanalysis, will be more efficient when they concentrate on noticing how congruent members' words and behaviors are. Nonverbal behavior, such as inattentiveness, conveys a great deal and may be as important as verbal messages for all groups for adolescents, even task groups.

Another way to help adolescent group members unify their thoughts and actions is to use action-oriented group techniques, such as role playing and "I" statements (Corey & Corey, 1992). For example, a leader may say to Joe, "I want you to show the group what happens when you are being rejected by Sal. By role playing this situation, I think both you and the group can get a better handle on it. Would you pick someone in the group to help us all see what is happening in the situation you just described?" Appropriate behaviors that are modeled by the counselor and prestigious peers may also be useful in showing members what other options are available to them (Gazda, 1989).

Group Structure and Materials

Many adolescent groups work best when they are structured around themes (Corey & Corey, 1992). **Themes** should relate to the genuine interests of the participants, thereby holding their interest and inviting their participation. Themes can vary from those that are very serious, such as dealing with loss, to those that are very pragmatic, such as explaining how to lead a discussion group. Flexibility can be built into theme structures, too. In a flexible theme format, the group decides week by week on the topic to be addressed. Too much choice can result in the group becoming bogged down and members losing interest. Therefore, limited flexibility is recommended. One way to achieve this goal is to have adolescents check off a list of the interests/problems on which they would like to concentrate. Corey, Corey, Callanan, and Russell (1992) have devised such an instrument, although any checklist of this type should be modified to reflect local concerns (see Figure 10.1).

The materials needed in a group for adolescents will vary according to the type of group to be led and the personalities of the members and leaders. For some highly verbal groups, few, if any, materials will be needed. For other less

Directions: Rate each of the following problems as they apply to you at this time and indicate the degree to which you'd like help from the group with them.

1. This is a major problem of mine, one I hope will be a topic for exploration in the group.

2. This is a problem for me at times, and I could profit from an open discussion of the matter in this group.

3. This is not a concern of mine, and I don't feel a need to explore the topic in the group.

   • Feeling accepted by my peer group

   • Learning how to trust others

   • Getting along with my parents (or brothers, sisters, etc.)

   • Getting a clear sense of what I value

   • Worrying about whether I'm "normal"

   • Being fearful of relating to the opposite sex

   • Dealing with sexual feelings, actions, and standards of behavior

   • Being too concerned about doing what is expected of me to the extent that I don't live by my own standards

   • Worrying about my future

   • Wondering whether I will be accepted into a college

   • Trying to decide on a career

Additional problems I'd like to pursue:

Figure 10.1
Problem checklist for adolescent group.

Source: From *Group Techniques,* 2nd ed. (pp. 45–46) by G. Corey, M. S. Corey, P. J. Callanan, and J. M. Russell, 1992, Pacific Grove, CA: Brooks/Cole. Copyright © 1992 by Wadsworth, Inc. Reprinted by permission of Brooks/Cole Publishing Company, Pacific Grove, CA 93950.

motivated and primarily nonverbal groups, many materials, in the form of activities, will be crucial. Structured activities (i.e., exercises) and associated materials will generate discussion and participation, help the group focus, promote experiential learning, provide the group leader with useful information, increase group comfort, and facilitate fun and relaxation (Jacobs et al., 1994). Some materials in these activities are used passively, for example, having members imagine themselves as certain objects that the counselor has; other materials are employed in a more active arts-and-crafts fashion.

Regardless of how materials are used, it is crucial that groups for adolescents do not focus on the materials to the exclusion of the meaningful process. For example, if a group used video feedback (Stoller, 1968), the emphasis should be on how viewing certain segments of the video is helpful to members in planning alternative behaviors, not on how everyone looked or how the equipment worked.

Recruiting Members and Screening

Not all members of groups for adolescents are recruited. For example, the members of mandatory groups may be assigned to, or drafted into, a group whether they wish to be involved or not (Leaman, 1983; Taylor, Adelman, & Kaser-Boyd, 1986). However, in voluntary groups for adolescents, recruitment is of major importance. Leaders wishing to reach as many potential members as possible should publicize the group by putting up announcements on bulletin boards and making contact with students, organizations, and teachers. Members for groups can also be recruited through using questionnaires (Kochendofer, 1975) and making informal contacts (Corey & Corey, 1992).

Public relations is a very crucial part of the recruitment process (Huey, 1983). Potential members and referral sources must be courted and sold on the idea that what the group is designed to do can be effective, if properly supported. Thus, the group leader must include as much information as possible on material sent to key individuals, such as administrators. However, it is also important that the group not be oversold (Deck & Saddler, 1983).

Once a pool of potential members is recruited, screening takes place as it would with any other age group. Leaders look for members who will fit together well in regard to maturity, purpose, and background. A key component of the screening interview is to keep it from becoming too formal (Jacobs et al., 1994). Leaders must develop systems that help them screen potential candidates in a minimum amount of time and yet promote two-way interaction so that the potential group members become more informed about the leader and structure of the group. One way to establish such an interactional process is to discuss a potential situation in a group with a group member candidate. The situation could be about any subject related to the type of group for which he or she is being screened: psychoeducational, counseling, psychotherapy, or task. For example, for a task group, a member might be questioned about a situation in which the group strayed from its task and did not seem willing or able to get back to it.

Ohlsen et al. (1988) state that attraction is a key component to the final selection of adolescents for a group. **Attractiveness** is a multidimensional concept, but basically it refers to members positively identifying with others in the group. Leaders must be careful in selecting members who can relate well to one another, not just to the leader. For example, Steve may have interests that are similar to the group leader's, but in his peer group, he is considered to be abrasive. Unless the group is to focus on improving peer relationships, Steve would probably not be a good choice as a group member.

Group Session Length and Number in Group

Sessions with adolescents usually last between one and two hours (Gazda, 1989; Jacobs et al., 1994). They may be extended, however, and even include mini-marathons lasting all day (Corey & Corey, 1992). Task groups that are charged with completing an assignment, such as decorating for an event, may especially benefit from longer group meetings.

In educational settings, the number of group sessions is usually dictated by divisional times in the school year, such as quarters or semesters. For instance, if a semester lasts 16 weeks, a guidance/psychoeducational group might be geared toward a similar time table, such as 14 weeks. Yet, "the frequency of the group sessions and also the duration of the . . . sessions are directly related to the intensity of group involvement and growth" (Gazda, 1989, p. 153). If group members have major problems or deficits, the group sessions may last longer and be more frequent. Psychotherapeutic groups may especially benefit from these enlarged parameters.

The number in a group ultimately affects its outcome and rate of progress. With increased size, member interaction and relationships decrease, and the group becomes more leader centered (Gladding, 1994; Goldstein, Heller, & Sechrest, 1966). Therefore, small groups of five to ten members may be ideal in working with adolescents. Gazda (1989) states that the number of adolescents he includes in a group is based on duration and frequency. When both are brief, for example, three months, he prefers to work with a group of from five to seven. If both are longer, for example, six months, the group may include from seven to ten members. He notes that "as a rule, the smaller the group, the more frequently it meets, and the longer it meets, the greater the opportunity for intensity of group involvement and growth" (p. 152).

Gender and Age Issues

Whether to include both males and females in a group for adolescents depends on the purpose of the group. There are occasions when groups for one gender or another will be more appropriate. For instance, in a counseling or psychotherapy group dealing with the trauma and recovery from rape, it may be in the best interest of the group that only girls be included. In one-gender groups, a key to the success of the group is the identity associated with gender and the topic. This type of identity comes through early socialization patterns. In summing up the research on the socialization of boys and girls in groups, Gigliotti (1988, p. 277) states that the most reliable differences show that boys play in large groups whereas girls play in small ones; boys' friendship groups are more extensive or broadly accepting; girls' friendship groups are more stable and exclusive; and boys in a group show more outward competitive behavior than girls.

While not dismissing gender socialization differences, Jacobs et al. (1994) believe the value of a coed group "is that there is a lot to learn about the opposite sex during the adolescent years, and the group can serve as a very good place to do so" (p. 288). Myrick (1987) also does not think gender makes a difference in how groups run "unless a boy and girl who are 'going together' are in the same group" or unless "a topic related to physical growth" or other sensitive sex-related issues are discussed (p. 245).

In running *mixed-gender groups,* especially those that focus on social relationships and interaction with others in dating, it may be necessary for counselors/group leaders to develop methods to get young adolescent males involved so they will get the maximum benefit from the experience (LeCroy, 1986). Adolescent boys, as compared with adolescent girls, are usually less comfortable, less involved, and less likely to achieve as positive an outcome in groups that emphasize interpersonal relationships. Adolescent girls are more interested as a group in social relationships and are more at ease in sharing. "Adolescent females also perceive counselors and counseling 'as significantly more attractive and trustworthy,' than do adolescent males" (LeCroy, 1986, p. 505).

In regard to age, Gazda (1989) has found that certain adolescent ages do not blend well together. For example, high school freshmen and sophomores do not mix well with juniors and seniors. On the other hand, he reports that there is little difficulty mixing college undergraduates, although undergraduates and graduate students are not easily combined. Age in the adolescent years may not be quite as sensitive a variable as during childhood. Nevertheless, it appears that older adolescents are less affected by age differences than are younger adolescents.

PROBLEMS IN ADOLESCENTS' GROUPS

As with other types of groups, there are problematic areas that can arise in adolescent groups. McMurray (1992) discusses these difficulties in regard to an educational group, but these problem behaviors are not limited to just one type of group. Among the problems that can arise are outright disruptiveness, a hesitancy or reluctance to engage with others, polarization, attempting to monopolize, inappropriate risk taking, and overactivity. Each of these behaviors will be briefly discussed.

Outright Disruptiveness

Cases of outright disruptiveness in adolescent groups are more common than in adult groups. The reason is the level of group member maturity. Disruptiveness can range from verbally yelling at other group members to attempting to pick a fight.

Ways of combatting this behavior include going over the rules of the group so that the inappropriate member is better informed, having the group leader talk with the member directly after the meeting, or allowing members of the group to discuss the situation and decide what to do with the member. As a final measure, the disruptive person can be dropped from the group if nothing else can be done.

Hesitancy to Engage with Others

A reluctance or hesitancy to engage with others can be a result of underdeveloped verbal or social skills. Sometimes, members want to act productively but simply do not know how. In such cases, engaging the problematic member either within the group context or in a leader/member conference can help correct the situation. During these encounters, the motivation of the member can be determined. For members who wish to become more appropriate and productive, times of modeling and encouragement are recommended.

Polarization

Polarization is when a group becomes divided into different and opposing subgroups or camps. The reasons for such divisiveness may be caused by accidental circumstances, such as chance encounters of members outside the group setting, or by premeditated plans. In the first case, polarization is more easily corrected because the group and its leader can help members to understand how their behavior outside of the group affects the functioning of the group. On the other hand, if polarization is a result of planned actions, a member or members may have to be dismissed for the group as a whole to work well again.

Monopolizing

The activity of monopolizing is not unique to adolescent groups. Reasons for it, which have been discussed previously, are related to anxiety of a group member or members. Monopolizing may also be used as an attention getter and a way of avoiding people or situations. In task groups, monopolizing may be handled by delegating tasks or asking for limited responses. In other types of groups, timed methods may help cut down or eliminate monopolizing behaviors.

Inappropriate Risk Taking

Sometimes, group members share information too soon or reveal inappropriate information. This type of behavior is not unusual with adolescents, especially those who have limited awareness of themselves and others. In such cases, structured group exercises that help individuals understand themselves better in relationship to others may be helpful. Reviewing group rules, talking privately with the person involved, cutting off the person's behavior, or redirecting the group as whole may be appropriate strategies for handling such a situation.

Overactivity or Giddiness

When adolescents are overactive or giddy in a group, it is attributable to several factors: the natural energy of individuals in this age group, embarrassment, failure of the leader or the group to set limits, or boredom with the group or the topic being discussed.

In order to respond to this type of behavior, leaders can simply acknowledge it and continue with group activities. Leaders can also discuss their feelings about the behavior with the group, or they can talk privately and individually with the member(s) most responsible for it. Another corrective action that can be taken in such a situation is to process with the group what is happening and how they as a group would like to handle the matter.

Overall, adolescent groups have unique problematic behaviors that those who work with such groups need to know about to be effective. Such information is helpful, if not vital, for leaders who plan to enter group work with adolescents .

ROLE OF THE LEADER IN ADOLESCENTS' GROUPS

The role of leaders in groups for adolescents is multidimensional. In addition to keeping up with the interpersonal and intrapersonal dynamics of group members, leaders must be extremely sensitive to themselves. They must be willing and courageous enough to explore, and perhaps relive, much of their own adolescent experience so that it will not interfere with their work and result in countertransference (Corey & Corey, 1992). Adolescents respond well to leaders who are open with them, enthusiastic, and caring. These types of leaders are true to themselves first and are good role models for those whom they lead.

The role of leaders is determined by the type of group they lead. In evaluating the literature on child, preadolescent, and adolescent groups (CPAGs), Denholm and Uhlemann (1986) have devised a three-dimensional model with several components under each dimension. The first dimension, developmental level, includes three age groupings: children, preadolescents, and adolescents. The second dimension is approach, which is composed of four approaches to group work: activity, discussion, counseling, and therapy. The third dimension, inquiry theme, includes three components: theory, research and practice (see Figure 10.2).

The classification scheme that Denholm and Uhlemann have devised has a utilitarian as well as a conceptual function. From it, the authors have classified select journals so that leaders can learn more about the types of groups they are conducting by consulting these periodicals. For example, by using the Denholm and Uhlemann chart, a leader looking for ideas for a counseling group for adolescents would find that issues of *The School Counselor* and the *Journal of Counseling and Development* would provide the best information. This saves the leader time and energy in finding practical ideas. A complete list of periodicals related to this model is shown in Table 10.3.

In general, group leaders for adolescents in high school are usually more active than are leaders for groups of college students and adults (Ohlsen et al., 1988). Both

Figure 10.2
The three-dimensional model of child, preadolescent, and adolescent groups.

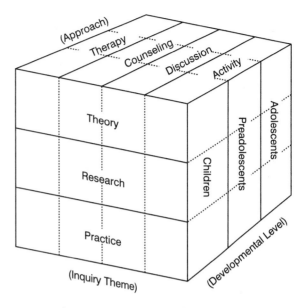

Source: From "Organizing the Child, Preadolescent, and Adolescent Group Literature: A Pragmatic Teaching Tool" by C. J. Denholm and M. R. Uhlemann, 1986, *Journal for Specialists in Group Work, 11,* p. 165. Copyright ACA. Reprinted by permission of the American Counseling Association.

activity level and structure are related to the maturity of the groups. The theoretical persuasion of leaders also plays a vital part, as does whether the group is voluntary or not.

One way that leaders can promote group cohesiveness and the acquisition of skills in adolescent groups is through modeling the types of behaviors they wish to encourage. "Good models have a tremendous impact on adolescents and can teach them how to relate openly and to help others" (Ohlsen et al., 1988, p. 279). By matching the gender between leaders and adolescents, the acquisition of modeled social skills may be enhanced (LeCroy, 1986). Leaders can also use influential peers, as well as themselves, in modeling. Peer leaders in adolescent groups are usually more persuasive than adult leaders in bringing about change (Bates et al., 1982; Frank, Ferdinand, & Bailey, 1975).

As in groups for other special populations, it is the leader's responsibility to stress the importance of confidentiality. Adolescents may use personal information gathered in a group for gossip or simply to be vindictive (Jacobs et al., 1994). In either case, the information is harmful, and such action must be prevented. One preventive measure is for leaders to state rules about confidentiality during the first session and every session afterward. Leaders must also deal immediately with any potential breach in confidentiality and determine what has occurred. Finally, if confidentiality is broken, leaders must either enforce rules (e.g., remove a member from the group) or have the group itself deal with the problem. In any case, leader responsibility must be exercised.

Table 10.3
Selected journals for each developmental area.

	Approach			
Inquiry Theme	**Therapy**	**Counseling**	**Discussion**	**Activity**
Practice	(C) American Journal of Orthopsychiatry. Child Welfare.	(C) Elementary School Guidance & Counseling. Journal of Counseling and Development.	(C) Elementary School Guidance & Counseling. Young Children.	(C) Child Care, Health and Development. Childhood Education.
	(P) Journal of Child Psychiatry. Child Care Quarterly.	(P) Elementary School Guidance & Counseling. International Journal of Group Psychotherapy.	(P) Elementary School Guidance & Counseling. Child Welfare.	(P) Child Care Quarterly. Childhood Education.
	(A) Child Welfare. Adolescence.	(A) School Counselor. Journal of Counseling and Development.	(A) Adolescence. Social Work.	(A) Adolescence.
Research	(C) Group Psychotherapy, Psychodrama and Sociometry. International Journal of Group Psychotherapy.	(C) Elementary School Guidance & Counseling. Journal of School Psychology.	(C) Education and Treatment of Children. Elementary School Guidance & Counseling.	(C) Child Care, Health and Development. Child Development.

(P) International Journal of Group Psychotherapy. Child Care Quarterly.	(P) Elementary School Guidance & Counseling. School Counselor.	(P) School Counselor. Psychology in the Schools.	(P) Child Development. Runner.
(A) American Journal of Orthopsychiatry. International Journal of Group Psychotherapy.	(A) Adolescence. School Counselor.	(A) Journal of Counseling Psychology. Journal for Specialists in Group Work.	(A) Adolescence. Youth and Society.
Theory (C) International Journal of Group Psychotherapy. Child Welfare.	(C) Elementary School Guidance & Counseling.	(C) The Journal: Canadian Association for Young Children. Journal for Specialists in Group Work.	(C) Child Care Quarterly: Young Children.
(P) Social Work. Adolescence.	(P) Child Welfare. Journal of Counseling and Development.	(P) School Counselor. Journal for Specialists in Group Work.	(P) Runner. The Physical Educator.
(A) Adolescence. International Journal of Group Psychotherapy.	(A) Adolescence. Journal of Counseling and Development.	(A) School Counselor. The School Guidance Worker.	(A) The School Guidance Worker.

Note: C = Children, P = Preadolescents, A = Adolescents.

Source: From "Organizing the Child, Preadolescent, and Adolescent Group Literature: A Pragmatic Teaching Tool" by C. J. Denholm and M. R. Uhlemann, 1986, *Journal for Specialists in Group Work, 11*, pp. 169–170. Copyright ACA. Reprinted by permission of the American Counseling Association.

Overall, leaders of groups for adolescents face a number of challenges. Some of these include being understanding, yet firm; facilitative, yet controlling; and active, yet trusting of the group process. How the group leader acts will depend on the composition, focus, and maturity of the group, as well as the background of the leader. Myrick (1987, p. 153) states that there are six basic responses that make leaders more effective facilitators:

1. using feeling-focused responses (e.g., "You seem to have some real feelings about what happened in this situation.")
2. clarifying or summarizing responses (e.g., "So instead of responding to Laura's words, you found yourself getting depressed and withdrawing from the group.")
3. employing **open-ended questions** (e.g., questions that invite more than a one- or two-word response—"What?" or "How?")
4. giving **facilitative feedback** (i.e., telling another person the effect they have on you) as a compliment or confrontation (e.g., "Leon, I find you easy to talk with.")
5. providing a simple acknowledgment (e.g., "Thanks" or "All right")
6. presenting **linking** (when the leader identifies similarities and sometimes differences that are occurring among group members in order to help them join together)

It is important that leaders of groups for adolescents be skilled and flexible in the use of these responses to avoid what Myrick (1987, p. 168) describes as **low facilitative responses**:

1. advice/evaluation (telling people how to behave or judging them)
2. analyzing/interpreting (explaining the reasons behind behavior without giving the adolescent an opportunity for self-discovery)
3. reassuring/supportive (trying to encourage someone, yet dismissing the person's real feelings)

Leaders of groups for adolescents may help themselves and their groups even more if they also make use of peer counselors and/or use parents as consultants, when appropriate. In either case, leaders receive information and feedback they might not get otherwise.

RESEARCH ON THE OUTCOME OF GROUPS FOR ADOLESCENTS

Even though groups are not as widely used with adolescents as with younger children, there are numerous studies on the impact of such groups. Some of these reports are in the form of case studies, but many have used well-controlled research designs. Groups have been found effective with adolescents in promoting an exploration of participants' life-style patterns and relationships with parents (Dinkmeyer et al., 1987). Group work has also been used in helping adolescents deal with major changes in their lives, such as moving to a new school as freshmen or transfer students (Deck & Saddler, 1983; Strother & Harvill, 1986; Valine & Amos, 1973) and in reducing conflict among students in racially tense situations (Dragoon & Klein, 1979).

Groups are important ways to help adolescent refugees from other cultures, such as the Vietnamese, learn about the United States's customs and prevent adjustment difficulties and/or psychological disturbances related to the resettlement experience (Tsui & Sammons , 1988). In addition, groups have a long tradition of being helpful experiences for students trying to make career decisions (Barkhaus, Adair, Hoover, & Bolyard, 1985; Glaize & Myrick, 1984). Groups may also be used in school settings to attract and hold students in school through graduation (Blum & Jones, 1993). In five schools cited by the American School Counselor Association as being exemplary in practice, there were deliberate attempts by counselors in these institutions to achieve specific goals through group work (Carroll, 1981).

Likely candidates for group counseling among adolescents are potential high school dropouts (Krivatsy-O'Hara, Reed, & Davenport, 1978) and high-risk adolescents with divorced parents (Coffman & Roark, 1988). The group approach for those with divorced parents takes a systems perspective in that it focuses on helping adolescents realize they are not alone in their experience and that a change in the family structure, such as divorce, has an impact on many facets of adolescents' lives. A triangle represents the three dimensions in the divorce system: the person ("I"), others ("We"), and the divorce ("It") (see Figure 10.3).

In a group for adolescents with divorced parents, information about the effects of divorce ("It") are highlighted first. For instance, the legal, adversarial, and prolonged nature of divorce might be discussed along with the stages most people go through in coming to terms with a divorce. After enough information is provided by the group leader, "I" and "We" interaction is focused on. Discussion of these areas may include topics such as dealing with friends, extended family members, and the separating parents, as well as strategies for coping with depression, anger, and grief. In general, Omizo and Omizo (1988) have found that young adolescents who participate in divorce groups have higher self-esteem and possess a more internally based locus of control than those who do not.

In regard to groups for adolescents who have low motivation for learning, Thompson (1987) formulated the "Yagottawanna" (you have to want to) group. The group relies heavily on the following concepts: "positive thinking, positive reinforcement, modeling, shaping, skill development, self-responsibility, self-discipline, and cognitive restructuring" (pp. 134–135). It consists of nine sessions of 45 minutes each spread over nine weeks. The sessions are both didactic and experiential, and students are followed up on individually two months after the group ends. When pre- and posttest results have been compared for the group, it was found that participants viewed the group favorably and their abilities more positively.

In the area of juvenile delinquency, Zimpfer (1992) found group treatment for this population international in scope. "By far the most frequently reported treatment approach involves the delinquents' peers for therapeutic leverage" (p. 117). Treatment groups for juvenile delinquents seem to fall most often into the category of long-term psychotherapy. However, cognitive, behavioral, psychoeducational, psychodrama, family, and even music therapy have been employed in working with this population. Bringing about change in the treatment of juvenile

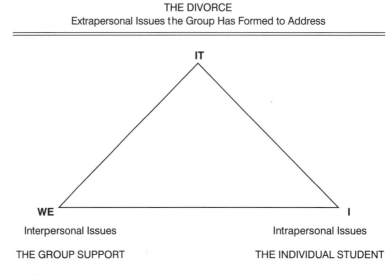

Figure 10.3

Conceptual model.

Source: From "Likely Candidates for Group Counseling: Adolescents with Divorced Parents" by S. G. Coffman and A. E. Roark, 1988, *School Counselor, 35,* p. 250. Copyright ACA. Reprinted by permission of the American Counseling Association.

delinquents in groups seems to be most productive with youth who are first-time offenders, those who were less abused as children, and those who are from better social and economic backgrounds.

Overall, it appears that groups have a powerful potential for helping many adolescents change and develop new social and academic skills. Studies with these groups need to use control groups more and refine their research methods. Nevertheless, the use of groups with adolescents in preventive and remedial ways is promising, especially in the schools. In the 21st century, Larrabee and Terres (1984) predict that the "secondary school counselor will certainly be group work oriented" (p. 261). The picture they paint is one where counselors will "coordinate and supervise an extensive program of peer-led counseling groups" (p. 261). They also envision that counseling groups at the secondary school level will be organized and initiated using computers and that "groups will be an integral part of the curriculum" (p. 262).

ADVANTAGES AND LIMITATIONS OF USING GROUPS WITH ADOLESCENTS

Many of the advantages and limitations of using groups with children are also those found in using groups with adolescents. Among the advantages of such groups are the following:

1. Groups are a "natural" environment in which adolescents can learn because adolescents spend a great deal of their time every day in groups (Bates et al., 1982; Trotzer, 1980). Therefore, groups feel familiar to many adolescents who look forward to participating in them.

2. Life-skills may be taught to adolescents in groups through modeling, role playing, group discussions, and brief lectures (Dennis-Small, 1986; Gazda, 1989). Many adolescents have behavioral deficits. Through groups, they can learn important ways of coping and dealing with life stressors.

3. In groups, a sense of belonging is created, and adolescents are given opportunities to learn through direct interaction or observation (Trotzer, 1989). Often this learning is carried over (**generalization**) from the group experience to the adolescent's daily life.

4. Groups provide for multiple feedback that can help adolescents in their personal growth and development. In addition to having the advantage of the leader's input, adolescents in groups also receive peer feedback (Myrick, 1987). Many times, the power of the peer group can be used constructively to promote needed change.

5. A final advantage of groups for adolescents is the opportunity they provide for members of the group to help one another (Trotzer, 1980). It is often through helping others that an individual's own self-esteem and self-confidence are increased.

Among the disadvantages of groups for adolescents are the following:

1. Unless potential members are carefully screened, the group may not have enough appeal to motivate the participants (Vander Kolk, 1985). Many adolescents deny they have any type of problem and feel there is a stigma in discussing problems with others. This is especially true with adolescent boys (LeCroy, 1986).

2. Some adolescents may feel pressured to conform to behaviors in which they do not believe. Peer group pressure is extremely strong in the adolescent years and may be misused in a group of adolescents unless carefully monitored (Corey & Corey, 1992; Ohlsen et al., 1988).

3. Individuals within the groups may not be given enough attention. Because of their backgrounds or maturity levels, some adolescents need individual counseling or programmed learning. The group is not a suitable environment initially for some troubled young adults, for example, the suicidal.

4. Poor group communication and interaction may result if the group is not screened carefully. Often adolescents tend to "scapegoat" (i.e., blame) others for their problems (Vander Kolk, 1985). At other times, they will disrupt, criticize, and/ or ignore others because they are so engrossed in themselves. Properly run adolescent groups screen out adolescents who are not ready to work on themselves or who are too self-centered, immature, and unhelpful (Yalom, 1985).

5. A final limitation of doing group work with adolescents concerns legal and ethical issues (Corey, Corey, & Callanan, 1993). In order to work

with minors, group leaders almost always have to obtain parental consent. In addition, if leaders want their groups to succeed, they must obtain the consent of the adolescent as well. Leaders may need to consult professional colleagues and associations more when working with adolescents than when working with adults. This process is time consuming and may slow down progress.

SUMMARY AND CONCLUSION

In leading groups for adolescents, a number of variables must be taken into consideration. First, the age and stage of adolescents must be appreciated. Adolescence as a period of life is filled with rapid changes and a number of paradoxes. It is a time of transition in which the developing young person's focus is on achieving a solid sense of identity. There is much experimentation and periods of progression and regression during this time. Adolescents often look more mature than they are and get themselves into situations for which they are not developmentally ready. Older adolescents usually are more mature than younger adolescents, but in screening these individuals for groups, each case must be considered individually.

Because adolescents spend a great deal of their lives in groups (Bates et al., 1982), working with them in a group setting is usually beneficial. Voluntary, developmental/guidance groups contain adolescents who are concerned about particular situations. Individuals in these groups are generally quite motivated. Adolescents in nonvoluntary counseling/psychotherapy groups, which often focus on issues that are of low priority to them, are much less motivated and involved. In setting up either type of group, leaders must remember to pay attention to the verbal and nonverbal behavior of participants, to focus the group structure around themes, and to make sure that participants, regardless of how recruited, find the group attractive. When working with adolescents who are forced into a group situation, leaders are wise to spend time talking with them about their feelings on an individual level before the group begins. Regardless of what type of group is led, the number of sessions, lengths of sessions, and other ground rules for the group experience should be spelled out before the group officially begins. Potential problematic behaviors should also be kept in mind.

The leader of a group for adolescents, although a facilitator, is also an authority figure because of his or her adult status. Therefore, effective group workers make the most of peers within the group and model behaviors frequently. They also make themselves sensitive to age and gender issues that may affect the development of the group. When conducted properly, groups for adolescents can help them become more aware of their values and life styles. Groups can also help young people overcome or cope with situational concerns, such as moving, dealing with divorce, choosing a career, and becoming motivated to learn and make good grades. More long-term problems involving adolescents, such as juvenile delinquency, can also be handled through group work, although with limited success.

The advantages of groups for adolescents are that groups are a natural way for adolescents to relate to each other, they emphasize the learning of life-skills, they focus on generalizing behaviors practiced in the group to real-life situations, and they provide multiple feedback and an increase in self-esteem that comes about through helping others. The drawbacks to working with adolescents in groups include legal and ethical considerations, the stigma of talking to others about one's problems (especially for boys), the lack of attraction the group may have for some, and the pressure of the group to force some of its members to conform to behaviors that are against their beliefs.

CLASSROOM EXERCISES

1. Reflect on your own life as an adolescent. What were your major concerns? List the top five. In a group of three, compare your list with that of the other members. Which are similar, and which are different? To what do you attribute the commonalities and differences? Discuss how working in a group was (or would have been) helpful to you at this stage of life. Be specific. Share your results with the class as a whole.

2. Discuss with another class member how you would go about setting up a nonvoluntary group for adolescents in a school or agency in which you work or hope to work. How would this procedure differ from setting up a voluntary group for adolescents? Focus particular attention in your assessment on screening processes, motivational issues, verbal/nonverbal exchanges, and results. Share your ideas with the class as a whole.

3. Critique a recent journal article on group work with adolescents. How did the group leader set up the experience? What made it successful or unsuccessful? Discuss your results in a group of four. As a group, make a list of factors that you obtained from reading these articles that promote or inhibit the success of groups for adolescents.

4. Pair up with another class member and talk to him or her about the different types of groups you participated in as an adolescent (e.g., Boy or Girl Scouts, Key Club, athletic teams). Discuss how you think each group affected your development as a person and what carryovers from these experiences still have an impact on you.

REFERENCES

Baker, S. B., Thomas, R. N., & Munson, W. W. (1983). Effects of cognitive restructuring and structured group discussion as primary prevention strategies. *School Counselor, 31,* 26–33.

Barkhaus, R. S., Adair, M. K., Hoover, A. B., & Bolyard, C. W. (1985). *Threads* (3rd ed.). Dubuque, IA: Kendall/Hunt.

Bates, M., Johnson, C. D., & Blaker, K. E. (1982). *Group leadership* (2nd ed.). Denver: Love Publishing.

Blum, D. J., & Jones, L. A. (1993). Academic growth group and mentoring program for potential dropouts. *School Counselor, 40,* 207–217.

Bowman, R. P. (1987). Small-group guidance and counseling in schools: A national survey of school counselors. *School Counselor, 34,* 256–262.

Carroll, M. R. (1979). Group counseling: The reality and possibility. *School Counselor, 26,* 91–96.

Carroll, M. R. (1981). End the plague on the house of guidance—Make counseling part of the curriculum. *NASSP Bulletin, 65,* 17–22.

Carty, L. (1983). Shalom: A developmental group model for young adults. *Journal for Specialists in Group Work, 8,* 205–210.

Coffman, S. G., & Roark, A. E. (1988). Likely candidates for group counseling: Adolescents with divorced parents. *School Counselor, 35,* 246–252.

Corey, G. (1990). *Theory and practice of group counseling* (3rd ed.). Pacific Grove, CA: Brooks/Cole.

Corey, G., Corey, M. S., & Callanan, P. (1993). *Issues and ethics in the helping professions* (4th ed.). Pacific Grove, CA: Brooks/Cole.

Corey, G., Corey, M. S., Callanan, P. J., & Russell, J. M. (1992). *Group techniques* (2nd ed.). Pacific Grove, CA: Brooks/Cole.

Corey, M. S., & Corey, G. (1992). *Groups: Process and practice* (4th ed.). Pacific Grove, CA: Brooks/Cole.

Deck, M. D., & Saddler, D. L. (1983). Freshmen awareness groups: A viable option for high school counselors. *School Counselor, 30,* 392–397.

Denholm, C. J., & Uhlemann, M. R. (1986). Organizing the child, preadolescent, and adolescent group literature: A pragmatic teaching tool. *Journal for Specialists in Group Work, 11,* 163–173.

Dennis-Small, L. (1986). *Life skills for adolescents.* Ann Arbor, MI. ERIC/CAPS(ED 278883).

Dinkmeyer, D. C., Dinkmeyer, D. C., Jr., & Sperry, L. (1987). *Adlerian counseling and psychotherapy* (2nd ed.). Columbus, OH: Merrill.

Dragoon, M., & Klein, R. (1979). Preventive intervention to reduce conflicts among students. *School Counselor, 27,* 98–100.

Erikson, E. H. (1963). *Childhood and society* (2nd ed.). New York: Norton.

Erikson, E. H. (1968). *Identity: Youth and crisis.* New York: Norton.

Frank, M., Ferdinand, B., & Bailey, W. (1975). Peer group counseling: A challenge to grow. *School Counselor, 22,* 267–272.

Gazda, G. M. (1989). *Group counseling: A developmental approach* (4th ed.). Boston: Allyn & Bacon.

George, R. L., & Dustin, D. (1988). *Group counseling: Theory and practice.* Englewood Cliffs, NJ: Prentice Hall.

Gesell, A., Ilg, F. L., & Ames, L. B. (1956). *Youth: The years from ten to sixteen.* New York: Harper & Row.

Gigliotti, R. J. (1988). Sex differences in children's task-group performance. *Small Group Behavior, 19,* 273–293.

Gladding, S. T. (1990). Secrets—Revised. *Journal of Humanistic Education and Development, 28,* 141.

Gladding, S. T. (1994). *Effective group counseling.* Greensboro, NC: ERIC/CASS.

Glaize, D. L., & Myrick, R. D. (1984). Interpersonal groups or computers? A study of career maturity and career decidedness. *Vocational Guidance Quarterly, 32,* 168–176.

Goldstein, A. P., Heller, K., & Sechrest, L. B. (1966). *Psychotherapy and the psychology of behavior.* New York: Wiley.

Goldstein, A., Sprafkin, R., Gershaw, N. J., & Klein, P. (1980). *Skillstreaming the adolescent: A structured learning approach to teaching prosocial skills.* Champaign, IL: Research Press.

Gumaer, J. (1984). *Counseling and therapy for children.* New York: Free Press.

Hall, G. S. (1904). *Adolescence.* New York: Appleton.

Hamburg, D. A., & Takanishi, R. (1989). Preparing for life: The critical transition of adolescence. *American Psychologist, 44,* 825–827.

Harris, T. A. (1967). *I'm ok–You're ok.* New York: Harper & Row.

Hudson, P. E., Doyle, R. E., & Venezia, J. F. (1991). A comparison of two group methods of teaching communication skills to high school students. *Journal for Specialists in Group Work, 16,* 255–263.

Huey, W. C. (1983). Reducing adolescent aggression through group assertive training. *School Counselor, 30,* 193–203.

Jacobs, E. E., Harvill, R. L., & Masson, R. L. (1994). *Group counseling: Strategies and skills* (2nd ed.). Pacific Grove, CA: Brooks/Cole.

Jourard, S. M. (1971). *The transparent self* (2nd ed.). New York: Van Nostrand.

Kochendofer, S. A. (1975). Group preparation: Interview vs. questionnaire. *School Counselor, 23,* 38–42.

Krivatsy-O'Hara, S., Reed, P., & Davenport, J. (1978). Group counseling with potential high school dropouts. *Personnel and Guidance Journal, 56,* 510–512.

Larrabee, M. J., & Terres, C. K. (1984). Group: The future of school counseling. *School Counselor, 31,* 256–264.

Leaman, D. R. (1983). Group counseling to improve communication skills of adolescents. *Journal for Specialists in Group Work, 8,* 144–150.

LeCroy, C. W. (1986). An analysis of the effects of gender on outcome in group treatment with young adolescents. *Journal of Youth and Adolescence, 15,* 497–508.

McCandless, B. R. (1970). *Adolescence: Behavior and development.* Hinsdale, IL: Dryden.

McMurray, D. (1992). When it doesn't work: Small-group work in adolescent sexuality education. *School Counselor, 39,* 385–389.

Moore, J., & Herlihy, B. (1993). Grief groups for students who have had a parent die. *School Counselor, 41,* 54–59.

Morganett, R. S. (1990). *Skills for living: Group counseling activities for young adolescents.* Champaign, IL: Research Press.

Myrick, R. D. (1987). *Developmental guidance and counseling: A practical approach.* Minneapolis: Educational Media Corporation.

Napier, R. W., & Gershenfeld, M. K. (1989). *Groups: Theory and experience* (4th ed.). Boston: Houghton Mifflin.

O'Hanlon, B., & Weiner-Davis, M. (1989). *In search of solutions: A new direction in psychotherapy.* New York: Norton.

Ohlsen, M. M., Horne, A. M., & Lawe, C. F. (1988). *Group counseling* (3rd ed.). New York: Holt, Rinehart & Winston.

Omizo, M. M., & Omizo, S. A. (1988). The effects of participation in group counseling sessions on self-esteem and locus of control among adolescents from divorced families. *School Counselor, 36,* 54–60.

Paisley, P., Swanson, L., Borders, S., Cassidy, N., & Danforth, C. (1994, March). *Counseling children using play media and the expressive arts.* Presentation at the North Carolina Counseling Association Conference, Charlotte, NC.

Phillips, T. H., & Phillips, P. (1992). Structured groups for high school students: A case study of one district's program. *School Counselor, 39,* 390–393.

Stoller, F. H. (1968). Focused feedback with video tape: Extending the group's function. In G. M. Gazda (Ed.), *Innovations to group psychotherapy.* Springfield, IL: Charles C. Thomas.

Strother, J., & Harvill, R. (1986). Support groups for relocated adolescent students: A model for school counselors. *Journal for Specialists in Group Work, 11,* 114–120.

Taylor, L., Adelman, H. S., & Kaser-Boyd, N. (1986). Exploring minors' reluctance and dissatisfaction with psychotherapy. *Professional Psychology: Research and Practice, 16,* 418–425.

Thompson, E. C., III. (1987). The "Yagottawanna" group: Improving student self-perceptions through motivational teaching of study skills. *School Counselor, 35,* 134–142.

Trotzer, J. P. (1980). Develop your own guidance group: A structural framework for planning and practice. *School Counselor, 27,* 341–349.

Trotzer, J. P. (1989). *The counselor and the group* (2nd ed.). Muncie, IN: Accelerated Development.

Tsui, A. M., & Sammons, M. T. (1988). Group intervention with adolescent Vietnamese refugees. *Journal for Specialists in Group Work, 13,* 90–95.

Valine, W. J., & Amos, L. C. (1973). High school transfer students: A group approach. *Personnel and Guidance Journal, 52,* 40–42.

Vander Kolk, C. J. (1985). *Introduction to group counseling and psychotherapy.* Columbus, OH: Merrill.

Yalom, I. D. (1985). *The theory and practice of group psychotherapy* (3rd ed.). New York: Basic Books.

Zimpfer, D. G. (1992). Group work with juvenile delinquents. *Journal for Specialists in Group Work, 17,* 116–126.

CHAPTER 11

Groups for Adults

Now matured to adulthood
    embers from our past times glow
    waiting to burst forth in the presence of others
    like kindling and feelings when heated and flamed.
As we grow, so does our light,
    a spark that spreads like friendship in a circle,
    a blaze that brightens but does not consume.
So in the warmth and reality of a group we become
    stronger in reflection,
    people who are openly aware of the gift that is life
        and the bittersweet insight that cycles,
        *like fires, have endings . . .**

Adulthood is a somewhat nebulous term. It implies that a person has reached physical, mental, social, and emotional maturity. Yet, as numerous researchers (e.g., Levinson, Darrow, Klein, Levinson, & McKee, 1978) note, adulthood is a multidimensional stage of growth often characterized by a certain unevenness and unpredictability (Neugarten, 1979). There is little uniformity to it (Merser, 1987). Indeed, as Allport (1955) states, human beings are "always becoming" and what may be appropriate behavior in one period of adulthood may be considered inappropriate at a later time.

For purposes of this chapter, adulthood will be conceptualized as the age period between 20 and 65 years. It includes individuals in the traditional college years and in **young adulthood** (20–40 years), in which identity and intimacy are two intense primary issues, as well as adults in **midlife** (40–65 years), in which

Source: Gladding, 1986, p. 3.

needs related to generativity become the main focus (Erikson, 1963). Men and women experience this stage of life differently (Gilligan, 1982; Miller, 1976), as do single, married, divorced, and widowed people, and individuals with special needs related to abuse, parenting, and nondevelopmental problems.

Wrenn (1979) advises counselors to "learn to work more effectively with adults" (p. 88). This means understanding their life-stage issues and transitional experiences. As Nichols (1986) points out, the **aging process** is as much a mental process of considering one's self older, as it is a biological phenomenon composed of physiological changes. The reaction to the total process of being an adult and issues related to it may be facilitated in a group setting in which people talk about and identify with others in similar situations. Psychoeducational and counseling groups are primarily used in exploring issues of adulthood and the transitions that go with them. "Group counseling with adults is essentially a process of using group facilitation to help adult group members deal with transitions relevant to their life-cycle changes" (Ohlsen, Horne, & Lawe, 1988, p. 301).

Although it is somewhat artificial to divide adulthood into age, gender, marital status, and problem concerns, this chapter will focus on these four areas because many groups for this population are conducted around these themes and center on issues related to particular ages and stages in life (Corey & Corey, 1992). Specific topics covered here include groups for college students and young adults, for individuals in midlife, for men and women, and for singles, couples and families.

GROUPS FOR COLLEGE STUDENTS AND YOUNG ADULTS

Characteristics of the Population

College students and young adults (those in their twenties and thirties) struggle with many issues. Major concerns involve matters related to autonomy (independence/dependence), choosing a career, deciding about marriage, developing a life style, finding meaning in life, and dealing with loneliness, disappointment, and potential (Corey & Corey, 1992; Havighurst, 1972; Worth, 1983). Early in one's adult life, the focus is on personal promise. Young adults are expected to live up to their potential through making good decisions, working hard, adjusting, and achieving proper roles and status. It is a time of maturation and transition.

Many of the tasks dealt with at this age, such as intimacy, continue over the life span and influence future life outcomes. Therefore, young adults are under considerable pressure to do well. Although society will tolerate some delays in making adult commitments, young adults who do not respond appropriately are discounted, disregarded, severely criticized and/or ostracized (Worth, 1983).

It is no wonder that many young adults try to avoid entering this stage of life by staying at home in a delayed adolescence. Others fail to take risks and do not progress in forming a new or expanded identity. Yet, a third group physically separates from their families of origin but simply flounders vocationally and interpersonally. A final unproductive strategy at this time is to short-circuit the developmental process of independence by premature marriage and the assumption of new family responsibilities (Aylmer, 1988).

Group Work with College Students and Young Adults

Groups may play a key role in helping individuals in the college or young adult part of life maximize their efforts and focus their energy on appropriate developmental tasks. In college settings, groups are used in a number of preventive and remedial ways. For instance, to aid young people in separating from their families and in becoming independent adults, family-of-origin groups have been found to help students "leave home" and become more self-sufficient (Valdes & McPherson, 1987). In such groups, students explore the family context from which they came by drawing a type of family tree (i.e., a **genogram**) (see Figure 11.1).

Ideally, a genogram will represent three generations in the student's life. By examining the vocational, intergenerational, and marital patterns of men and women in their families, students can gain insight into their own behaviors and make positive changes based on present needs rather than inherited patterns. In the process, nonproductive behavior (such as striving to be a physician when one's aptitude and desire is to be an artist) can be altered, and the young person can gain a stronger identity as a person.

In addition to helping students gain a better sense of self, groups have also been used to help undergraduates and graduate students master course material (Ender, 1985). These **study groups**, a type of task group, typically involves three to four students who meet at least on a weekly basis to "share information, knowledge, and expertise about a course in which they are all enrolled" (p. 469). The idea is that each group member will support and encourage the others, and will obtain insight and knowledge through the group effort. A variation of this type of peer group has been successfully employed to assist college students with learning disabilities to deal with personal and academic needs (Orzek, 1984).

For students high in test anxiety, groups may be used to help them manage their fears (Stevens, Pfost, & Bruyere, 1983). These psychotherapeutic groups concentrate on assisting students to reduce somatic tension and modify disruptive cognitions. The groups use some of the rational-emotive methods of Ellis (1962) and some of the cognitive-behavioral modifications of Meichenbaum (1977). This combination seems to work well, and student responses at Illinois State University, where these types of groups were first tried, have been highly favorable. Another psychotherapeutic type of group for college students is for adult children of alcoholics who may suffer anxiety, depression, substance abuse, and psychosomatic disorders as a result of growing up in a home in which one or both parents were alcoholics (Harman & Withers, 1992). These types of groups are usually structured so that potential group members will feel safe and members will be able to address issues readily.

Groups may also be helpful to college students in becoming more aware of what careers they wish to pursue and becoming more decisive about an occupation (Cooper, 1986; McWhirter, Nichols, & Banks, 1984). In **career awareness**

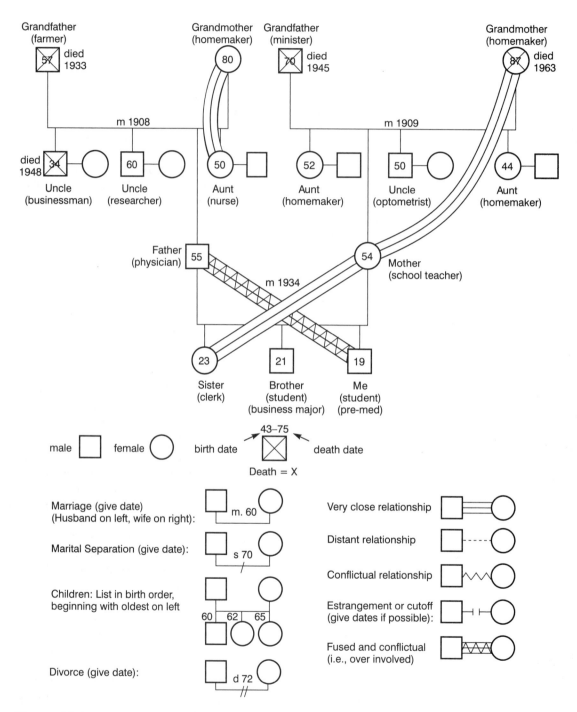

Figure 11.1

Genogram: Three generations of the Smith family (as of 1965).

and self-exploration (CASE) groups, McWhirter et al. (1984) have found that brief lectures on particular subjects, such as self-disclosure, trust, self-esteem, and communications, combined with small-group interaction give undergraduates an opportunity to evaluate more carefully what they wish to do vocationally.

Sometimes college students need information (but not necessarily **group guidance and psychoeducation**) and want some support (but are not seeking personal counseling). For these individuals, an **educational growth group (EGG)** may be beneficial. This type of group, composed of 8 to 15 students who meet for a total of five sessions, "incorporates the best parts of teaching with the best parts of group work" (Cerio, 1979, p. 399). It covers specific topics chosen by students and helps them assimilate and personalize this information. The goals of the model are represented in Figure 11.2.

For adult college students (i.e., those outside of the traditional 18- to 21-year-old range), groups may be used to help them find information and resources about academic life, obtain emotional support from peers, interact socially, and meet developmental and remedial needs (Wilcoxon, Wilcoxon, & Tingle, 1989). Such groups are longitudinal in nature and provide both an

Figure 11.2
The goals of the EEG model.

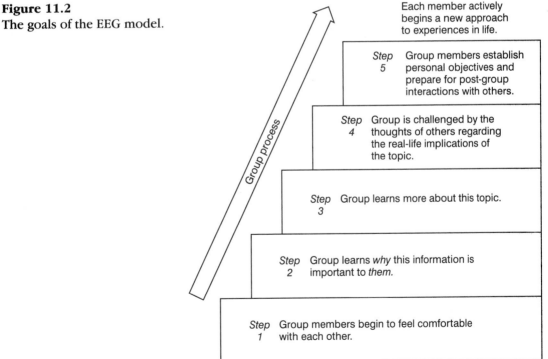

Source: From "Structured Experiences with the Educational Growth Group" by J. E. Cerio, 1979, *Personnel and Guidance Journal, 57,* p. 400. Copyright ACA. Reprinted by permission of the American Counseling Association.

emphasis on topics of particular concern to these students and emotional support and growth. More limited groups for adult college students can focus on other concerns such as reentry problems, dealing with spouses or family, and competing successfully in the classroom. At the end of the college experience, a job support group can help these individuals become more easily launched into the job market and find a proper fit between their skills and employers' needs (Arp, Holmberg, & Littrell, 1986). These types of groups meet for a limited time, for example, six sessions, but provide older students a wealth of information on how to set goals, evaluate their assets, use placement centers, write resumes, and conduct themselves in interviews.

In order to assess the needs of all persons in campus communities, a *nominal-group process* (a structured small-group technique) may be used by college officials. In such a procedure, five to nine people from different campus settings identify specific issues related to the mental health and personal needs of students, faculty members, and staff (Skibbe, 1986). Ideas are written down and discussed in a round-robin format with minimum attention devoted to relationships among group members. Ideas are then prioritized and sometimes discussed and reranked. The session takes between 45 to 90 minutes, after which the group is disbanded and the members thanked for their participation. Although this group procedure does not lend itself to statistical analysis and may not yield a representative sample of opinion, it is an enjoyable process for those involved and is a fairly quick and efficient way for counselors to obtain a good idea of major issues within the campus community.

GROUPS IN MIDLIFE

Characteristics of the Population

Early adulthood ends and **middle adulthood** (ages 40–65) begins somewhere between the late thirties and early forties. Individuals at this time realize that "life is half over and death is a reality" (Worth, 1983, p. 240). It is a time for evaluating, deciding, and making adjustments. This process is known as the **midlife transition**. It is a difficult time for many individuals as they give up the dreams of adolescence and come to terms with their own mortality (Marmor, 1982). Once they get through the thought process of having reached midlife, they typically settle down and enjoy themselves (Nichols, 1986; Sheehy, 1976). However, those who do not successfully integrate the reality of this period into their lives will often try these ways of coping:

1. *denial by escape* (frantically engaging in activities)
2. *denial by overcompensation* (engaging in sexual adventures)
3. *decompensation* (being depressed and angry) (Marmor, 1982)

Overall, there is some physical decline in men and women during middle adulthood, including losses in hearing, sight, hormonal level, height, and attractiveness. Yet, there are some gains, too, including an improvement in crystallized intelligence (the ability to do something as a result of experience and education) and freedom from early child-rearing responsibilities and/or novice job demands. Women as a group become more assertive and achievement oriented, whereas men as a group become more nurturant and emotional (Neugarten, 1968). These behavioral changes support Jung's (1971) idea that men and women achieve a more nearly balanced personality during this time. A prime developmental task for all individuals at this stage is to increase interest in **generativity** (creativity in their lives and work for the benefit of others) and to work toward **self-actualization** (realistically living up to their potential). A failure to do so results in stagnation and self-absorption (Erikson, 1963; Maslow, 1962).

Predictable crises that occur in midlife include coping with aging parents; launching children; reestablishing and evaluating one's work career; and bereavement (Kimmel, 1976; McCullough & Rutenberg, 1988). Midlifers are often sandwiched between caring for the needs of their children (if any), themselves, and their parents. They must constantly readjust to losses and gains in a manner secondary only to the rapid changes of adolescence (Nichols, 1986). "For most people the middle years are quite busy, which may explain why some arrive at the end of this period with surprise that the journey is finished so quickly" (Worth, 1983, pp. 242–243).

Groups for Adults in Midlife

There are many types of groups for adults in midlife. In fact, adults in this age range probably have the widest choice and greatest freedom in determining what type of groups they will join and how much they will become involved. Most groups for adults are either psychoeducational and preventive (and geared toward learning and wellness) or counseling and psychotherapeutic (and focused toward change). Some of the groups mentioned in this section may be used by individuals of almost any age, but they especially tend to attract midlife adults.

In the area of psychoeducation and prevention, Parker (1975) reports on the use of systematic desensitization within a leadership group for the purpose of helping adult members become less anxious about public speaking. The results of the five-session group were that participants noticed improvements in their relaxation about public speaking and a more relaxed attitude in their personal lives in general. Bisio and Crisan (1984) used a one-day group workshop with adults to focus on nuclear anxiety and hidden stress in life. They emphasized principles of Victor Frankl's (1962) logotherapy and helped participants create a renewed sense of hope and purpose in life. In neither of these groups did members want counseling, yet both were therapeutic in addressing areas of immediate concern.

An interesting, interdisciplinary, positive-wellness model of group work for self-selected adults that is more long-term (16 weeks) is the **jogging group** (Childers & Burcky, 1984). This approach is built on the premise that physical exercise is an important element that contributes to people's abilities to perform better in all areas of life (Freund & Seligman, 1982; Gerler, 1980). The jogging group itself combines an hour of exercise in the form of walking, jogging, or running, with another hour of group process. The group is co-led by a counselor and a health facilitator (e.g., a physician or an exercise physiologist) and follows Lazarus's (1976, 1981) multimodal *BASIC ID* concept, which focuses on behavior, affect, sensation, imagery, cognition, interpersonal relationships, and drugs/biological factors. Jogging seems to speed up the group's developmental growth, and although research is lacking, the authors report that jogging groups function more like marathon groups than extended groups because of the high energy invested in the physical exercises before the group experience.

For adults who have grown up in families where at least one parent abused alcohol, heterogeneous groups based on Yalom's (1985) therapeutic factors, especially altruism and imitative behavior, can be empowering (Corazzini, Williams, & Harris, 1987). Such groups allow them to question and change any of the four common roles (i.e., hero, scapegoat, lost child, and mascot) that **adult children of alcoholics (ACoAs)** tend to play out in order to survive the instability, confusion, and fear they experienced growing up (Wegscheider, 1981). Groups of this nature also increase the support and reference network these individuals have within their lives.

Because alcoholic families tend to be rather isolated (Steinglass, 1982), this extended system of group support is invaluable for ACoAs who wish to continue their growth toward more functional behavior. These individuals need help in learning to break the three rules that Black (1981) has identified as being universal for them: (a) don't trust, (b) don't talk, and (c) don't feel. Corazzini et al. (1987) recommend that groups of this nature work best when conducted in an open versus a closed format. Whitfield (1987) further notes that "many clinicians who work with ACoAs or other troubled or dysfunctional families believe that group therapy is the major choice for recovery work" (p. 142). Such work should be combined with a psychoeducational approach to the dynamics related to addiction, dysfunction, and recovery, as well as individual and family counseling.

Groups may also be used to help grown-ups who were abused as children (Courtois & Leehan, 1982). *Victims of abuse* (whether physical, psychological, sexual, or neglect) have a number of common characteristics, such as low self-esteem, self-blame, unresolved anger, and an inability to trust. Groups help them share their stories with others and feel emotional relief. In addition, group members can help each other focus on resolving present, problematic behaviors that would be difficult to do individually. "The sharing and empathy derived from common experiences and reactions, as well as the analysis of the interactions between members, are of great therapeutic value" (Courtois, 1988, p. 244).

In short, **groups for victims of abuse** help them break the cycle of isolation so common to this population and interrelate in a healthy, dynamic way. "Many survivors come to view the group as a new family in which they are reparented as they help to reparent others" (Courtois, 1988, p. 247). Courtois and Leehan (1982) recommend that no more than six members be included in such groups in order to give everyone adequate "air time" (p. 566).

A final type of group for adults in midlife that is both psychoeducational and psychotherapeutic in nature is the **career change group** (Zimpfer & Carr, 1989). There are pressures within and outside the middle-aged adult to advance in their life's work. Some midlife adults, especially those at the middle management level, think the best way to advance is to change careers. Persons who usually consider such a strategy have the following personal characteristics as a group: high achievement motivation, a steady and successful work record, high need for advancement, career challenge and individual satisfaction, positive self-image, high energy level, and a sense of limited chances for advancement in their present position (Campbell & Cellini, 1980). They may also face increased pressure for different behavior from their spouses (McCullough & Rutenberg, 1988). Career change groups help participants sort out the reasons for pursuing a new career and whether some alternative course of action may be more healthy for them. An effective career change group is holistic in nature, exploring personal and professional aspects of individuals' lives.

Related to career change groups are group career programs for **displaced homemakers**, i.e., those who have lost their source of economic support and are now forced back into the work force after spending a number of years at home caring for their families (McAllister & Ponterotto, 1992). Short-term, psychoeducational groups for this population can do much to assist them in discovering their abilities and ways to apply their talents and skills. For a displaced homemaker who has experienced a recent divorce, entering a psychoeducational *separation group* to deal with the psychological difficulties of divorce may first be in order (Addington, 1992).

GROUPS FOR MEN AND WOMEN

Men and women share many common concerns and experiences as adults. For example, "autonomy and attachment are functional adult goals, in love and work, for both men and women" (Aylmer, 1988, p. 192). Yet, socialization patterns dramatically influence the ways men and women perceive themselves and how they function in society. In this section, some general and basic characteristics of adult men and women are considered, along with how personal behavioral factors contribute to the needs of each gender for group work. How the genders participate in groups is discussed also.

General Characteristics of Men as a Group

Men have special needs and ways of interacting that are heavily dependent on socialization patterns (Moore & Haverkamp, 1989; Scher, 1981). Values learned by boys during early socialization are often "based on rigid gender role stereotypes and beliefs about men and masculinity" (O'Neil, 1981, p. 205). For many boys "masculinity" becomes synonymous with what is known as the "**masculine mystique**"—"men are superior to women and therefore have the right to devalue and restrict women's values, roles and life-styles" (O'Neil, 1981, p. 205). Therefore, many men work to hide their more feminine side from others and from themselves. This side is exhibited in acts of care, sensitivity, and affect. Instead of behaving in such a way, many men focus on playing competitive sports, being independent, getting a good job, and not being intimate. They pay a high cost in their own personal growth and development as a result, such as internal and external conflict, an inability to relax, and a shorter life expectancy (Jourard, 1974; Jung, 1971). Six negative outcomes of traditional male sex-role socialization that have been well documented are (a) restrictive emotionality, (b) a high preference for and prevalence of control, competition, and power, (c) homophobia, (d) restrictive sexual behavior, (e) obsession with success, and (f) health care problems (Croteau & Burda, 1983; O'Neil, 1981). This pattern of gender-role conflict and strain is conceptualized by O'Neil (1981) as shown in Figure 11.3.

The socialization consequences of the traditional masculine role are such that adult men, as a group, have fewer choices in the behaviors they display than women do. For example, men have very limited options about dropping out of careers or being dependent on others (Carter & McGoldrick, 1988). They are expected to fit into more rigid behavioral categories than women are and to be relatively unemotional.

Working with Men in Groups

Groups can help men in identifying personal and general concerns of being male and ways of constructively dealing with men's issues. They can also help men

Figure 11.3
Patterns of gender-role conflict and strain emanating from men's gender-role socialization, the masculine mystique, and the fear of femininity.

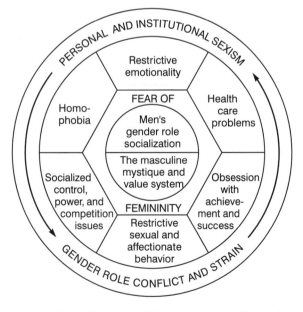

Source: From "Patterns of Gender Role Conflict and Strain: Sexism and Fear of Femininity in Men's Lives" by J. M. O'Neil, 1981, *Personnel and Guidance Journal, 60,* p. 206. Copyright ACA. Reprinted by permission of the American Counseling Association.

become more attuned to the realities of their worlds as well as find validity, confirmation, or suggestions in how they are handling situations (DeAngelis, 1992). Furthermore, groups can help men integrate and appreciate both their masculine and feminine sides and realize more fully the transformational aspect of their lives. As O'Neil and Egan (1992) have shown, there are at least 30 gender role transitions for men over their life span. These "role transitions are interactive and not mutually exclusive. This means that changes in one may affect the other" (p. 312) (see Table 11.1).

Getting men to participate in groups, although usually beneficial, is often difficult because traditional sex-role stereotypes hinder many males from even thinking they could benefit from a group experience (Washington, 1979; Wilcox & Forrest, 1992). However, if groups are set up in certain ways, men are attracted to them and will participate actively in them. One of the first types of groups set up specifically for men in the early 1970s was the all-male **consciousness-raising (C-R) group** (Farrell, 1974). It is interesting to note that C-R groups became popular at a time of turmoil and rapid change and paralleled one of the peaks of the women's movement. These groups did not maintain their popularity during the more conservative 1980s, yet the variations of them that remain today are a viable way of helping men begin to see how they have been affected by culturally prescribed roles and how they have inhibited their own growth by following these roles.

"In addition to C-R groups, a diverse set of group formats, such as encounter therapy, and structured growth groups, are applicable for helping men with their specific needs" (Heppner, 1981, p. 250). For instance, support and psychoeducational groups for single, custodial fathers have been implemented and found to be effective. One study (Tedder, Scherman, & Sheridan, 1984) revealed that men who participate in *custodial father support group* meetings make more changes in the desirable direction of learning how to take better care of their children and themselves than those who do not. A commonality of experience and purpose unites these individuals and leads to greater cohesion more quickly than is usually the case in groups for men.

Groups have also been used to work with bisexual men (Wolf, 1987). These groups allow bisexual men to share experiences and gain support from each other. The matter of confidentiality is of uppermost importance in groups for bisexual men. A weekly 90-minute, open-ended format allows participants to use the group as long as they need.

Other approaches to working with men in groups include using mixed-sex groups to help men receive more varied input on who they are and what they are experiencing as males (DeAngelis, 1992). This information is compared with other group members, especially females. Groups contribute to the interpersonal growth of men, too, and help sanction the employment of unused skills, such as emotions. Further, groups for men help participants observe new role models and practice what they learn within a safe environment (Heppner, 1981). When leaders use social learning principles, men in groups increase their levels of affective expressiveness and ultimately their flexibility and overall functioning (Moore & Haverkamp, 1989). Many men do best in groups when they have a chance to participate in a physical or mental exercise before the group's work actually begins. Therefore, specific exercises for this population have been developed (Karsk & Thomas, 1989).

Table 11.1
Men's gender role transitions over the life span.

Approximate Life Stage	Gender Role Transition	Definition
Toddlerhood and Early School Age	1. Oedipal conflicts	Separation from mother and identification with father
	2. Early childhood gender role identification, learning in family	Internalization of masculine norms from father, mother, and other models
	3. Development of masculine gender role standards	Internalization of masculine expectancies and roles that govern behavior
	4. Rejection of mother and all that is feminine	Devaluation of and distancing from mother and the feminine
	5. Entering school	Formal learning where boys experience evaluation from others and self-evaluation
Middle School Age	6. Same-sex gender role preferences	Strong desire to have male companions and play activities reinforcing internalized masculine norms and standards
	7. Peer group identification— early male bonding	Internalization of male peer group gender role values and standards
	8. Heterosexual antagonism	Rejection and devaluation of girls and femininity to establish superiority of masculinity
	9. Physical maturation	Biological growth that produces changes in body and mind
	10. Interaction with female peer group norms	Contact with girls' different views of masculinity and femininity
Adolescence	11. Puberty	Physical development where the reproductive system matures and secondary sex characteristics appear, causing changes in gender role identity
	12. Teenage gender role identification and learning	Internalization of adult expectations and norms for masculinity and manhood
	13. Tentative career choice	Early expressed interests and aspirations about chosen area of work as it relates to masculine gender role norms
	14. Dating	Social interaction with females where gender role norms and standards are expressed
	15. Initiating heterosexual or homosexual relations	Sexual activity that validates one's masculinity and value as a man

Approximate Life Stage	Gender Role Transition	Definition
Early Adulthood	16. Leaving home—going to school	Departure from primary family where the man is independent and on his own
	17. Developing capacity for intimacy	Process of being personal, disclosive, and vulnerable in a relationship
	18. First job or work experience	Initial work commitment where the man's success, power, and competence are tested
	19. Marriage	Personal and legal relationship where gender role norms and standards are expressed
	20. Procreation	Sexual act where the man produces children with a woman
	21. Parenting	Becoming a father, protector, and nurturer of children
Middle Adulthood	22. Managing career and family life	The man's ability to coordinate work and home life
	23. Maintaining intimacy	The man's ability to continue being personal, disclosive, and vulnerable in a relationship
	24. Divorce	Legal and emotional processes of dissolving a marriage contract, relationship, and union
	25. Career change/transition	Events and nonevents that cause changes in the man's work status, self-assumptions, and meaning of a career
	26. Unemployment	Losing one's primary employment and sense of masculinity
	27. Aging	Becoming older, affecting a man's physical appearance and self-concept
Later Adulthood and Old Age	28. Retirement	A man's decision to withdraw from his primary occupation, work, or career
	29. Loss of stamina	A man's decreasing energy to work and live life
	30. Facing death	A man's capacity to deal with the end of his life and give up ultimate control

Source: From "Men's Gender Role Transitions over the Life Span: Transformations and Fears of Femininity" by J. M. O'Neil and J. Egan, 1992, *Journal of Mental Health Counseling, 14,* pp. 313–315. Copyright ACA. Reprinted by permission of the American Counseling Association.

The men's movement, exemplified in the mythopoetic approach of Robert Bly (1990) can be a power adjunct to traditional therapeutic groups for men. "**Mythopoetic** refers to a process of ceremony, drumming, storytelling/poetry reading, physical movement, and imagery exercises designed to create a 'ritual process.' Through this process, the participants explore individually and in groups their intuitive sense of masculinity, which differs from socially mediated male gender roles" (Williams & Myers, 1992, p. 395).

General Characteristics of Women as a Group

Until the late 1960s, the unique development of women was largely ignored by personality theorists. Socialization patterns of girls were noted, but healthy adult behavior was associated with maleness (Broverman, Broverman, Clarkson, Rosenkrantz, & Vogel, 1970). "Developmentally women have been expected from the point of early adulthood to 'stand behind their men,' to support and nurture their children, and, paradoxically, to be able to live without affirmation and support themselves. Adaptability has probably been the major skill required of women" (McGoldrick, 1988, p. 33).

The lack of study on women led to the creation of a new psychology of women and a greater emphasis on such personality variables as attachment and affiliation (Miller, 1976). Popular books, such as *Against Our Will* (Brownmiller, 1975) and *Women Who Love Too Much* (Norwood, 1985), increased the awareness of the general public about the special and particular concerns of women as a group. These works and other more scholarly tomes also sparked interest in empirical studies on women, such as that by Hall (1978), which found women better as a group than men in identifying nonverbal cues of others.

Overall, women in general seek help more than men, are more verbally skilled, and are more likely to form and maintain strong social network systems (McGoldrick, 1988). They exhibit certain behaviors and problems more often than men because of specific socialization processes and biological differences. For example, many of the behaviors women learn as girls, such as being dependent and passive, can actually hinder the development of their full potential as adults (Sullivan, 1983a). In addition, on a biological level, "females have the unique ability to menstruate, lactate, and parturate, leading to unique problems related to sexuality" (Thames & Hill, 1979, pp. 17–18). Many special concerns of women can be handled effectively in groups that are both educational and therapeutic. The caregiver characteristics of many women make them good candidates for group work (Pearson, 1988).

Working with Women in Groups

Although all-women groups were initially controversial (Halas, 1973), they are now employed frequently, along with mixed-gender groups. Some of the most focused issues in groups for women center around sexuality, relationships, self-concepts, and work. Groups can provide "a special environment in which women may resocialize themselves" (Sullivan, 1983a, p. 4).

For example, until the 1970s, women who were the victims of sexual assaults were often blamed by society for such attacks. Through forming a **rape survivors' group**, Sprei and Goodwin (1983) found women from ages 18 to 60 who had been raped were able to decrease their sense of isolation and stigma while learning to model effective coping strategies. The group they set up was open-ended and addressed issues related to information, anger, feelings of helplessness, and rape trauma. On the whole, the group offered support to women in the midst of crisis and helped them "to explore behaviors, attitudes, and life choices" (p. 45). A variation of this type of group, combining rape and incest victims, has also worked well over an 8-week, 2-hour session format (Sharma & Cheatham, 1986). In both cases, consciousness raising and learning new coping behaviors have been stressed. Because of groups like the ones just mentioned, psychoeducational and task groups have been formed by women and men to bring the subject of incest and rape before the general public's attention and to develop programs to combat these demeaning and dehumanizing behaviors.

Relationship dependency groups for women have also been found to be useful (Pearson, 1988). In such groups, based on a socioprocess model, relationships are formed for learning and examining personal beliefs and values. The groups are short-term (6 weeks) and goal oriented. The benefits of participating include the formation of new friendships, the expression of emotions, and the changing of destructive patterns.

Eating disorders groups for women who have obsessive and distorted ideas in regard to thinness and body image have also proved helpful (Enright & Tootell, 1986; Gerstein & Hotelling, 1987; Zimpfer, 1990). These groups may be geared toward self-help, support, or be professionally led. Each has advantages and disadvantages in regard to group dynamics and recovery. Self-help groups by themselves do not seem to be adequate to deal with the complex nature of eating disorders (Enright, Butterfield, & Berkowitz, 1985). Yet, participation in any of these groups can help individuals make initial contact with organized help and demystify the nature of the eating disorder (Enright & Tootell, 1986). Often, relatively short-term treatment (four months) can alter participants' behaviors and help them develop more effective coping mechanisms. "A group therapy program combining therapeutic orientations (psychodynamic, group process, and feminist)" can increase "the independence, ego strength, degree of personal control, and ability of bulimic women to form healthy interpersonal relationships" (Gerstein & Hotelling, 1987, p. 172). Cognitive-behavioral groups also are useful in the treatment of eating disorders (Mines & Merrill, 1986).

A final type of popular group for women focuses on work, either inside or outside the home. For women who work primarily as homemakers, a support group, especially when they are located in another community, is useful (Olson & Brown, 1986). The functions of such a group center on addressing common concerns, sharing, and goal setting. For women who work outside the home, group activities may be particularly helpful in overcoming internal barriers, such as sexism or discrimination based on gender (Sullivan, 1983b). Activities used in these groups are nonsequential in nature, designed for a group of 6 to 12 persons, and usually begin with some stimulus activity, such as a film, a brief reading, or a paper/pencil exercise. The results have been positive in increasing self-awareness and changing self-defeating behaviors. Some groups initially formed for psychotherapeutic reasons have evolved into task groups to combat destructive work practices.

GROUPS FOR THE MARRIED AND UNMARRIED

Groups for the married and the unmarried generally take the form of psychoeducation, counseling, or psychotherapy. Those that are psychoeducational are growth oriented. They are aimed toward helping their members take preventive steps before a crisis arises. Groups that are counseling and psychotherapy oriented are geared toward remediation. In this section, groups for married and unmarried adults that focus on both orientations will be discussed. The specific types of groups addressed are marriage enrichment, couple group therapy, groups for the divorced and widowed, parenting groups, and singles groups.

Marriage Enrichment

Marriage enrichment is the chief form of a psychoeducational and growth group for marrieds. Such groups, which began in the early 1960s, are proactive in nature (Mace, 1986). They attempt to assist couples who want to enhance their relationship and move toward greater fulfillment of their potential as a trusting, loving couple (Worthington, Buston, & Hammonds, 1989). There is a preventive aspect to these groups that usually takes one of several forms from a highly structured and couple-centered focus to one that is relatively nonstructured and couple-group centered.

On the highly structured end are programs, such as L'Abate's (1985) *Structured Enrichment (SE),* in which the leader makes a presentation to a group of couples but limits group interaction. Discussion is centered on individual couples. On the relatively unstructured end are programs such as the *Association for Couple and Marriage Enrichment (ACME),* in which the leader facilitates the establishment of goals for the five to eight couples present and emphasizes couple sharing, feedback, and support (Mace, 1986; Mace & Mace, 1975). The main drawback to this second type of approach is that little information is given by the leader on a topic. In the middle of this continuum are enrichment programs, such as *Marriage Encounter* (Doherty, McCabe, & Ryder, 1978) and *Conjugal Relationship Enhancement* (Guerney, 1977), in which a combination of information and sharing is conducted within the group format and by the couples themselves. Writing exercises are often a part of this experience.

All marriage enrichment groups make use of some form of group process. The therapeutic factors outlined by Yalom (1985), especially imparting information, instilling hope, creating a sense of universality, catharsis, and having an opportunity to help others in the group, seem to be particularly important. The leaders within this preventive movement vary in background from being nonprofessional married couples with training in a particular program to being professional individuals with specialized training (Waring, 1988). Although research on these programs is limited, marriage enrichment seems to work, especially with couples who are not in psychological distress (Worthington et al., 1989; Zimpfer, 1988).

Couple and Family Group Therapy

Couple group therapy began in the 1970s and has had an uneven history (Ohlsen, 1979; Piercy & Sprenkle, 1986). Proponents of couple group therapy list many advantages for it including

1. identification by group members of appropriate and inappropriate behaviors and expectations by others
2. development of insight and skills through observing other couples
3. group feedback and support for the ventilation of feelings and changed behavior
4. cost

Framo (1981) recommends that couple group therapy be used when preparing couples to do family-of-origin work, in which they meet with their families and work through difficulties not resolved in childhood. Couple groups are limited to three couples in this approach, all of whom have some similarity in background. Ohlsen (1979) includes five couples in his groups. He believes that having this number of couples makes the group easier to handle and provides an enriched learning environment for members.

Hendrix (1988) also uses five or more couples in his workshops known as **Imago (i.e., Image) Relationship Therapy**, an eclectic approach that includes elements of psychoanalysis, transactional analysis, Gestalt psychology, cognitive therapy, and systems theory. Hendrix's approach, popularized in his book, *Getting the Love You Want,* is the most structured of the couple group therapies and has revived interest in psychotherapy workshops for couples. Hendrix suggests couples go through specific exercises in a uniform manner and encourages observation of others and participation by the individual couple.

Multiple-family group therapy involves treating several families together at the same time. It requires the use of co-leaders and has many of the same advantages that couple group therapy has, including the fact that families can often serve as co-therapists for each other (Piercy & Sprenkle, 1986). Working with multiple families in groups is probably the most demanding form of group work, for it requires leaders to have a solid, working knowledge of both group and family theories and dynamics.

Groups for the Divorced and Widowed

Most individuals (95%) marry at some point in their lives. Yet, approximately half of all marriages in the United States end in divorce. Another large percentage are terminated through death. In 1986, for example, the U.S. Bureau of the Census (1988) reported 2,400,000 marriages and 1,159,000 divorces. In that same year, the Bureau estimated that approximately 16% of the adult population of the nation were divorced and another 15% were widowed. Whether a marriage is cut short by divorce or death, survivors must relearn skills of singlehood after they work through the similar processes of coping with grief and trauma (DiGiulio, 1992; Kitson, Babri, Roach, & Placidi, 1989).

The divorced and widowed can best make use of groups in the process of working through their pain. In groups specifically designed to deal with their situations, the divorced and widowed can share experiences with one another, as well as obtain emotional support, receive feedback on one's perceptions and behaviors, gain advice and information on dealing with problems, and get tangible assistance (Addington, 1992; DiGiulio, 1992). One model of a specific group for those who have separated has been devised by Addington (1992) who focuses the group on both the emotional impact and emotional response of such an experience. The **emotional impact of separation** includes dealing with loss, putting the separation in perspective, becoming aware of the limited value of searching for causes of separation, becoming more cognizant of systems interactions (family, work, social network), using the past as a guide to the future, and moving from a dyadic to a monadic identity. The **emotional response of separation** focuses on continuing relationships with an ex-spouse; recognizing the influence of the separation on family, friends, and children; working and dating; and sexual adjustment. Addington's model also includes a diagram of the grief process to help participants assess where they are and to chart their progress in recovery (see Figure 11.4).

Outside of structured groups offered by professionals, most *groups for the divorced and widowed* tend to be of a psychoeducational or self-help nature. **Parents Without Partners (PWP)** is probably the best known and most organized of such groups on a national level. PWP offers a variety of activities to its members including interest groups, educational presentations and discussions, and recreational/social activities. Members and their children become linked to one another through these formal and informal group activities.

Parent Education Groups

One of the major concerns of many adults is parenting. Most adults who become parents do not receive any training in how to parent and have to learn how to

Figure 11.4
Grief process.

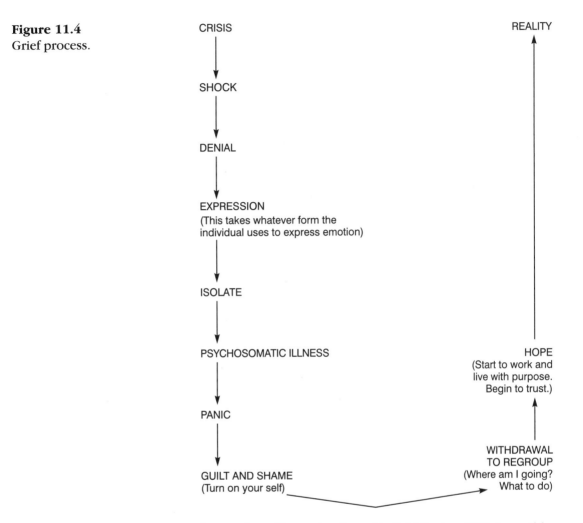

Source: From "Separation Group" by J. Addington, 1992, *Journal for Specialists in Group Work, 17,* p. 25. Copyright ACA. Reprinted by permission of the American Counseling Association.

work with children on a trial-and-error basis. In order to help parents acquire knowledge and evaluate their beliefs and attitudes, **parent education groups** were organized beginning in the late 1800s by the Child Study Association of America (Resnick, 1981). These groups initially focused on a discussion orientation format about the needs of parents (usually mothers) and children. However, parent education groups are now considered "a form of consultation in which the consultant (leader) is assisting the consultee (parent) by teaching effective child-rearing techniques" (White & Riordan, 1990, p. 201). They are more theoretically based and skill focused then ever before. Groups based on Rogerian, Adlerian, rational-emotive, Transactional Analysis, and eclectic theories are available (Lamb & Lamb, 1978). In the 1990s, three theoretical approaches to parent education have become most dominant.

The first, **Adlerian parent education**, stresses the cooperation among family members as a goal and emphasizes the use of logical and natural consequences in order to avoid power struggles. There is a democratic emphasis to this orientation, and regular family council meetings are held in order for all members to voice concerns and needs. The Adlerian approach stresses parent discussion groups with a trained leader and a set curriculum. One variation of these types of groups is the **C group** (Dinkmeyer, 1973). Each component of the group—collaboration, consultation, clarification, confrontation, concern, confidentiality, and commitment—begins with a *c.* The group is primarily psychoeducational. It emphasizes developmental and preventive aspects of parenting. Furthermore, it focuses on empowering parents to consider the dynamics and purposes of their children's behaviors and encourages group members' discussion and interaction. Change in parental behaviors is expected before a change will occur in children. Since the 1970s, Dinkmeyer has updated his C group approach and now packages variations of it under the label, **Systematic Training for Effective Parenting (S.T.E.P.)**.

A second model of parent education is based on Rogerian theory. Thomas Gordon's (1970) **Parent Effectiveness Training (PET)** is an example of one such program that follows this model. In PET, there is an emphasis on communication skills, and parents are encouraged to recognize their positive and negative feelings toward their children and come to terms with their own humanness. A major hypothesis of this approach is that *active listening* (i.e., hearing what is implied as well as what is actually said) and *acceptance* (acknowledging what is happening as opposed to evaluating it) will decrease family conflicts and promote individual growth (Resnick, 1981).

A final theoretical approach, **behavioral parent education**, is most associated with direct change and manipulation. In it, parents are trained to be change agents and to record and reinforce certain behaviors in their children (Lewis, 1986). "Evaluative studies of the behavioral approach indicate significant changes in parental attitudes and behaviors with concomitant modifications in children's behavior" (Resnick, 1981, p. 57). Many behavioral programs of parent education are targeted toward specific behaviors and come with training manuals for parents to follow.

Overall, there are literally dozens of parenting programs across the United States, in which single parents or couples work in groups to develop healthy strategies for dealing with each other and their children as the family develops. Some of these parenting programs include those for abusive and neglectful parents, adoptive parents, foster parents, minority-group parents, single parents, and parents of children with special needs (LeMasters & DeFrain, 1989). Most take an eclectic approach and train their leaders to understand and promote positive group dynamics in order to bring about constructive changes in parent/child and family interactions.

Regardless of the approach followed, White and Riordan (1990) state there are common aspects to all parent education groups. For instance, parents are "usually sensitive to almost any issue that relates to their relationship with their child" (p. 205). They are also initially resistant to change. When leading a parent education group, a leader is wise to anticipate issues that parents might raise and be prepared to address these concerns in a productive manner. For example, parents will frequently inquire about the use of physical punishment (i.e., spanking), the importance of heredity in determining behavior, gender role appropriateness, religious beliefs as a basis for parenting, peer influences, guilt over parental decisions, and feelings about school. Overall, parents are best served in parenting groups when they are listened to, helped to sort through their options, and newly empowered to make decisions regarding their children.

Singles Groups

In the United States, the percentage of individuals either delaying marriage, not getting married, or divorcing after a few years of marriage with no children is growing. The proportion of single adults in the United States (i.e., those 18 years and over) is rising according to the U.S. Census Bureau from approximately 5% to 10% of the total population, a level last reached in the 1940s. For instance, in 1991 approximately 64% of women and 80% of men ages 20-24 were unmarried (Usdansky, 1992). That compares to a 1970 figure for these two groups of 36% and 55% respectively.

There are many advantages to being single, such as being able to set one's own schedule and not being encumbered by demands or stresses from a spouse or children. However, there are drawbacks to singlehood, too. Coping with being a single adult is not always easy. Physical or psychological crises can be detrimental and dealing with the daily stress from one's regular work can be difficult to handle. For example, in a national survey of women in academic settings, Fong and Amatea (1992) found that single, never-married women tended to have higher stress levels than other women and were, as a group, more passive in their coping strategies for handling stress. The mental health and overall well-being of single, never-married men has been a topic of concern, also. It appears that these individuals do not do as well as a group in regard to mental and physical health as their female counterparts.

Therefore, groups for *singles adults,* whether never married or not, can be a major resource in helping this portion of the population stay healthy. Psychoeducational groups and counseling/psychotherapeutic groups are essential in meeting the needs of singles. The opportunity to socialize and form friendships and support networks is essential for singles. They can meet others with whom they can connect in groups for singles. They can practice new behaviors in some of these groups, too, and feel affirmed for who they are by themselves. Overall, groups for singles can take many forms, but the ones that are most likely to be popular and helpful are those with an initial psychoeducational emphasis that allows for maximum interaction in a nonthreatening environment, such as a church or community center.

GROUPS FOR ADULT OFFENDERS AND PERSONS WITH LIFE-THREATENING ILLNESSES

In addition to the other types of groups already discussed, there are two more that are prevalent in adulthood but do not neatly fit a category. The first of these is groups for *adult offenders*. The second is groups for those who have *life-threatening illnesses*, such as cancer.

Groups for Adult Offenders

In examining the literature on adult offenders, Zimpfer (1992) found that group work in prisons for those who have committed a crime has been around since the late 1950s. Potential problematic areas in working with adult offenders is their low level of trust and their high level of anger, frustration, and sense of deprivation. Therefore, a number of approaches and types of groups have been reported in the professional literature. Some have focused on helping inmates adjust to prison life; others have concentrated on trying to help prisoners re-adjust to the outside world.

Among the specific types of adult offenders targeted for treatment in groups have been those found guilty of sex offenses, driving while intoxicated, shoplifters, domestic violence perpetrators, and crack cocaine users. Success with this population in general has been mixed, but there is some consensus that group psychotherapy and group counseling for sex offenders is much more effective than individual treatment for this population (DeAngelis, 1992). The reasons have to do with the manipulative nature of such offenders and the power of the group to prohibit seductive or illusive behavior. Zimpfer (1992) points out that research in the area of treating adult offenders is growing. The importance of self-image as a variable in treatment is increasingly being noted.

Groups for Persons with Life-Threatening Illnesses

The concept of group work initially originated from Joseph Hersey Pratt's idea of treating tuberculosis outpatients in a group context (see chapter 1). More recently, psychotherapeutic groups have also been employed as a way of treating persons with other life-threatening illnesses. In a review of the literature on groups for cancer patients, Harman (1991) notes the results of outcome studies with this population.

One of the most interesting of Harman's findings is that groups are still a preferred method of working with cancer patients and their families. Such groups offer education, support, and release from stress and emotion that has built up. Further, they help all involved in experiencing the therapeutic factors described by Yalom (1985) as essential to good psychotherapeutic groups: universality, cohesiveness, and the instillation of hope. Groups for those with terminal illnesses are a way to impart information, too, in a quick and efficient manner.

SUMMARY AND CONCLUSION

The period of adulthood ranges from the early twenties to the mid-sixties. Such a wide span in life is filled with many problems and possibilities. In young adulthood (ages 20–40), major concerns center on identity and intimacy, whereas in midlife (ages 40–65), attention is focused on generativity and fulfillment. Group work can help individuals in all stages of adulthood to clarify their focus and maximize their potential. In this chapter, groups for different ages and stages, genders, marital statuses, and problems have been considered.

College students and young adults, for example, are faced with major decisions involving learning, relationships, and career choices. Groups for them, especially on college campuses, are relatively short term in nature and focus on specific agenda items. Groups can help college students and young adults become better oriented toward their environments and tasks in life, may facilitate growth, and prevent problems. However, when members of this population become stuck, they may also use groups for psychotherapy purposes.

Adults in midlife struggle to come to grips with the reality of their aging. Groups are especially helpful to midlifers in evaluating themselves in regard to family and career. Many individuals do not fully realize how their childhood influences their adulthood until midlife. For people who have grown up in families with alcohol addiction or other forms of abuse, groups can be supportive, educational, and therapeutic. Many self-help groups, such as those sponsored by Adult Children of Alcoholics (ACoA), can help them break out of isolation and learn how to change dysfunctional behavioral patterns. Groups for midlifers may also focus on positive wellness, such as jogging groups, or potential change, such as those that emphasize careers.

Because men and women are socialized differently, and because biological differences often result in unique concerns, groups for one gender or the other are sometimes helpful. Through group work, men may realize the strict limitations of traditional roles for males and make changes that allow them greater flexibility and growth. Particular problems related to work and stress may be dealt with from a psychotherapeutic and psychoeducational perspective. The mythopoetic movement is an appropriate adjunct to working in groups with men. Women may use groups to help free themselves from socialized roles that are not productive for them as adults, such as always being dependent or passive. Furthermore, they may work in groups to overcome traumatic events in their lives, such as rape, or to concentrate on self-concept issues, such as those involved in eating disorders or careers inside or outside the home.

Groups are also helpful for adults in midlife who are married and unmarried. Marriage enrichment may help married adults improve their couple relationship. Marriage enrichment takes many forms, from being extremely structured to being very unstructured. Research indicates it works regardless of structure. Couple and family groups are another form of group work for midlife married adults in need of a psychotherapeutic rather than a psychoeducational approach. Groups for the divorced and widowed, especially self-help groups such as Parents Without Partners, can offer much for this population. Parent education groups, which focus on skill development, support, and discussion, are useful for parents of all types. In these groups, parents learn to concentrate on their own behaviors as well as those of their offspring.

CLASSROOM ACTIVITIES

1. In groups of three, investigate the number of groups that operate on your college campus. These groups may vary from those that emphasize learning to those that are psychotherapeutically oriented. Each group in the class should concentrate on either a particular type of group or a particular organization which offers groups. Have each class group report back to the class as a whole and discuss what they have found out about the campus community and group work.

2. The transition to midlife is sometimes filled with apprehension. Have each member of the class draw a picture depicting himself or herself at young adulthood and midlife. In dyads, talk with another class member about the differences you anticipate or have experienced. What are the advantages and drawbacks of aging as you perceive them, and how might a group be helpful in this process?

3. Divide the class into two groups based on gender. Each group will review articles from professional periodicals within the past three years on the use of groups with men and women. The males will review only articles on females in groups, while the females in the class will do the opposite. Each group will then tabulate the results of its findings and present this information to the whole class. After the presentation, discuss what has been found and how it might be used.

4. Interview a panel of parents (other class members, if possible) about parenthood. List top concerns and explore how a parent education group leader might address these difficulties. Consult your parent panel about which interventions seem most constructive for them and why. Then discuss as a class the merits and limitations of parent education groups.

REFERENCES

Addington, J. (1992). Separation group. *Journal for Specialists in Group Work, 17,* 20–28.

Allport, G. W. (1955). *Becoming: Basic considerations for a psychology of personality.* New Haven: Yale University Press.

Arp, R. S., Holmberg, K. S., & Littrell, J. M. (1986). Launching adult students into the job market: A support group approach. *Journal of Counseling and Development, 65,* 166–167.

Aylmer, R. C. (1988). The launching of the single young adult. In B. Carter & M. McGoldrick (Eds.), *The changing family life cycle* (2nd ed.) (pp. 191–208). New York: Gardner.

Bisio, T. A., & Crisan, P. (1984). Stress management and nuclear anxiety: A structured group experience. *Journal of Counseling and Development, 63,* 108–109.

Black, C. (1981). *It will never happen to me.* Denver: M.A.C. Printing.

Bly, R. (1990). *Iron John: A book about men.* Reading, MA: Addison-Wesley.

Broverman, I. K., Broverman, D. M., Clarkson, F. E., Rosenkrantz, P., & Vogel, S. R. (1970). Sex-role stereotypes and clinical judgments of mental health. *Journal of Consulting Psychology, 43,* 1–7.

Brownmiller, S. (1975). *Against our will: Men, women, and rape.* New York: Bantam Books.

Campbell, R. E., & Cellini, J. V. (1980). Adult career development. *Counseling and Human Development, 12,* 1–8.

Carter, B., & McGoldrick, M. (1988). Overview: The changing family life cycle: A framework for family therapy. In B. Carter & M. McGoldrick (Eds.), *The changing family life cycle* (2nd ed.) (pp. 3–28). New York: Gardner.

Cerio, J. E. (1979). Structured experiences with the educational growth group. *Personnel and Guidance Journal, 57,* 398–401.

Childers, J. H., Jr., & Burcky, W. D. (1984). The jogging group: A positive-wellness strategy. *AMHCA Journal, 6,* 118–125.

Cooper, S. E. (1986). The effects of group and individual vocational counseling on career indecision and personal indecisiveness. *Journal of College Student Personnel, 27,* 39–42.

Corazzini, J. G., Williams, K., & Harris, S. (1987). Group therapy for adult children of alcoholics: Case studies. *Journal for Specialists in Group Work, 12,* 156–161.

Corey, M. S., & Corey, G. (1992). *Groups: Process and practice* (4th ed.). Pacific Grove, CA: Brooks/Cole.

Courtois, C. A. (1988). *Healing the incest wound.* New York: W. W. Norton.

Courtois, C. A., & Leehan, J. (1982). Group treatment for grown-up abused children. *Personnel and Guidance Journal, 60,* 564–566.

Croteau, J. M., & Burda, P. C., Jr. (1983). Structured group programming on men's roles: A creative approach to change. *Personnel and Guidance Journal, 62,* 243–245.

DeAngelis, T. (1992, November). Best psychological treatment for many men: Group therapy. *APA Monitor, 23,* 31.

DiGiulio, J. F. (1992). Early widowhood: An atypical transition. *Journal of Mental Health Counseling, 14,* 97–109.

Dinkmeyer, D. C. (1973). The parent "C" group. *Personnel and Guidance Journal, 52,* 252–256.

Doherty, W. J., McCabe, P., & Ryder, R. G. (1978). Marriage encounter: A critical appraisal. *Journal of Marriage and Family Counseling, 4,* 99–107.

Ellis, A. (1962). *Reason and emotion in psychotherapy.* New York: Lyle Stuart.

Ender, S. C. (1985). Study groups and college success. *Journal of College Student Personnel, 26,* 469–471.

Enright, A. B., Butterfield, P., & Berkowitz, B. (1985). Self-help and support groups in the management of eating disorders. In D. M. Garner & P. Garfinkel (Eds.), *Handbook of psychotherapy for anorexia nervosa and bulimia* (pp. 419–512). New York: Guilford.

Enright, A. B., & Tootell, C. (1986). The role of support groups in the treatment of eating disorders. *AMHCA Journal, 8,* 237–245.

Erikson, E. H. (1963). *Childhood and society* (2nd ed.). New York: W. W. Norton.

Farrell, W. (1974). *The liberated man.* New York: Random House.

Fong, M. L., & Amatea, E. S. (1992). Stress and single professional women: An exploration of causal factors. *Journal of Mental Health Counseling, 14,* 20–29.

Framo, J. L. (1981). The integration of marital therapy with family of origin sessions. In A. S. Gurman & D. P. Kniskern (Eds.), *Handbook of family therapy.* New York: Brunner/Mazel.

Frankl, V. (1962). *Man's search for meaning: An introduction to logo-therapy.* New York: Washington Square Press.

Freund, P., & Seligman, M. (1982). Group jogging and emotionally disturbed clients. *Journal for Specialists in Group Work, 7,* 194–198.

Gerler, E. R., Jr. (1980). Physical exercise and multimodal counseling groups. *Journal for Specialists in Group Work, 5,* 157–162.

Gerstein, L. H., & Hotelling, K. (1987). Length of group treatment and changes in women with bulimia. *Journal of Mental Health Counseling, 9,* 162–173.

Gilligan, C. (1982). *In a different voice: Psychological theory and women's development.* Cambridge, MA: Harvard University Press.

Gladding, S. T. (1986). Circles. *ASGW Newsletter, 14,* 3.

Gordon, T. (1970). *Parent effectiveness training.* New York: Peter Wyden Press.

Guerney, B. G., Jr. (Ed.). (1977). *Relationship enhancement.* San Francisco: Jossey-Bass.

Halas, C. (1973). All women's groups: A view from inside. *Personnel and Guidance Journal, 52,* 91–95.

Hall, J. A. (1978). Gender effects in decoding nonverbal cues. *Psychological Bulletin, 85,* 845–857.

Harman, M. J. (1991). The use of group psychotherapy with cancer patients: A review of recent literature. *Journal for Specialists in Group Work, 16,* 56–61.

Harman, M. J., & Withers, L. (1992). University students from homes with alcoholic parents: Considerations for therapy groups. *Journal for Specialists in Group Work, 17,* 37–41.

Havighurst, R. J. (1972). *Developmental tasks and education.* New York: David McKay.

Hendrix, H. (1988). *Getting the love you want.* New York: Henry Holt & Company.

Heppner, P. P. (1981). Counseling men in groups. *Personnel and Guidance Journal, 60,* 249–252.

Jourard, S. M. (1974). Some lethal aspects of the male role. In J. H. Pleck & J. Sawyers (Eds.), *Men and masculinity.* Englewood Cliffs, NJ: Prentice Hall.

Jung, C.G. (1971). The stages of life. In J. Campbell (Ed.), *The portable Jung.* New York: Viking.

Karsk, R., & Thomas, B. (1989). *Working with men's groups.* Duluth, MN: Whole Person Press.

Kimmel, D. C. (1976). Adult development: Challenges for counseling. *Personnel and Guidance Journal, 55,* 103–105.

Kitson, G. C., Babri, K. B., Roach, M. J., & Placidi, K. S. (1989). Adjustment to widowhood and divorce. *Journal of Family Issues, 10,* 5–32.

L'Abate, L. (1985). Structured enrichment (SE) with couples and families. *Family Relations, 34,* 169–175.

Lamb, J., & Lamb, W. A. (1978). Parent education and elementary counseling. In G. Walz & L. Benjamin (Eds.), *New vistas in counseling series* (Vol. 5). New York: Human Science Press.

Lazarus, A. A. (1976). *Multimodal behavior therapy.* New York: Springer.

Lazarus, A. A. (1981). *The practice of multimodal therapy.* New York: Holt, Rinehart & Winston.

LeMasters, E. E., & DeFrain, J. (1989). *Parents in contemporary America* (5th ed.). Belmont, CA: Wadsworth Publishing Co.

Levinson, D. J., Darrow, C. N., Klein, E. B., Levinson, M. H., & McKee, B. (1978). *The seasons of a man's life.* New York: Alfred Knopf.

Lewis, W. M. (1986). Group training for parents of children with behavior problems. *Journal for Specialists in Group Work, 11,* 194–199.

Mace, D. (1986). Marriage and family enrichment. In F. Piercy & D. Sprenkle (Eds.), *Family therapy sourcebook* (pp. 187–212). New York: Guilford Press.

Mace, D. R., & Mace, V. C. (1975). Marriage enrichment—Wave of the future? *Family Coordinator, 24,* 131–135.

Marmor, J. (1982). Transition to the empty nest. In L. Allman & D. Jaffe (Eds.), *Reading in adult psychology: Contemporary perspectives.* New York: Harper & Row.

Maslow, A. (1962). *Toward a psychology of being.* New York: Van Nostrand.

McAllister, S., & Ponterotto, J. G. (1992). A group career program for displaced homemakers. *Journal for Specialists in Group Work, 17,* 29–36.

McCullough, P. G., & Rutenberg, S. K. (1988). Launching children and moving on. In B. Carter & M. McGoldrick (Eds.), *The changing family life cycle* (2nd ed.) (pp. 285–309). New York: Gardner.

McGoldrick, M. (1988). Women and the family life cycle. In B. Carter & M. McGoldrick (Eds.), *The changing family life cycle* (2nd ed.) (pp. 29–68). New York: Gardner.

McWhirter, J. J., Nichols, E., & Banks, N. M. (1984). Career awareness and self-exploration (CASE) groups: A self-assessment model for career decision making. *Personnel and Guidance Journal, 62,* 580–582.

Meichenbaum, D. H. (1977). *Cognitive-behavioral modifications: An integrative approach.* New York: Plenum.

Merser, C. (1987). *Grown-ups: A generation in search of adulthood.* New York: Putnam.

Miller, J. B. (1976). *Toward a new psychology of women.* Boston: Beacon.

Mines, R. A., & Merrill, C. A. (1986). The group treatment of bulimia: Assumptions and recommendations. *AMHCA Journal, 8,* 229–236.

Moore, D., & Haverkamp, B. E. (1989). Measured increases in male emotional expressiveness following a structured group intervention. *Journal of Counseling and Development, 67,* 513–517.

Neugarten, B. L. (Ed.). (1968). *Middle age and aging.* Chicago: University of Chicago Press.

Neugarten, L. (1979). Time, age and the life cycle. *American Journal of Psychiatry, 136,* 887–894.

Nichols, M. (1986). *Turning forty in the '80s.* New York: Norton.

Norwood, R. (1985). *Women who love too much.* Los Angeles: Jeremy P. Tarcher.

Ohlsen, M. M. (1979). *Marriage counseling in groups.* Champaign, IL: Research Press.

Ohlsen, M. M., Horne, A. M., & Lawe, C. F. (1988). *Group counseling* (3rd ed.). New York: Holt, Rinehart & Winston.

Olson, S. K., & Brown, S. L. (1986). A relocation support group for women in transition. *Journal of Counseling and Development, 64,* 454–455.

O'Neil, J. M. (1981). Patterns of gender role conflict and strain: Sexism and fear of femininity in men's lives. *Personnel and Guidance Journal, 60,* 203–214.

O'Neil, J. M., & Egan, J. (1992). Men's gender role transitions over the life span: Transformations and fears of femininity. *Journal of Mental Health Counseling, 14,* 305–324.

Orzek, A. M. (1984). Special needs of the learning disabled college student: Implications for interventions through peer support groups. *Personnel and Guidance Journal, 62,* 404–407.

Parker, C. L. (1975). A desensitization group for adult community leaders. *Personnel and Guidance Journal, 54,* 48–49.

Pearson, J. E. (1988). A support group for women with relationship dependency. *Journal of Counseling and Development, 66,* 394–396.

Piercy, F., & Sprenkle, D. (1986). *Family therapy sourcebook.* New York: Guilford.

Resnick, J. L. (1981). Parent education and the female parent. *The Counseling Psychologist, 9,* 55–62.

Scher, M. (1981). Men in hiding: A challenge for the counselor. *Personnel and Guidance Journal, 60,* 199–202.

Sharma, A., & Cheatham, H. E. (1986). A women's center support group for sexual assault victims. *Journal of Counseling and Development, 64,* 525–527.

Sheehy, G. (1976). *Passages: Predictable crises of adult life.* New York: E. P. Dutton.

Skibbe, A. (1986). Assessing campus needs with nominal groups. *Journal of Counseling and Development, 64,* 532–533.

Sprei, J., & Goodwin, R. A. (1983). Group treatment of sexual assault survivors. *Journal for Specialists in Group Work, 8,* 39–46.

Steinglass, P. (1982). The roles of alcohol in family systems. In J. Oxford & J. Harwin (Eds.), *Alcohol and the family* (pp. 127–150). New York: St. Martin's Press.

Stevens, M. J., Pfost, K. S., & Bruyere, D. (1983). Managing test anxiety: A group approach. *Journal of College Student Personnel, 24,* 88–89.

Sullivan, M. (1983a). Introduction to women emerging: Group approaches. *Journal for Specialists in Group Work, 8,* 3–8.

Sullivan, M. (1983b). Women and career development: Group activities to overcome internal barriers. *Journal for Specialists in Group Work, 8,* 47–55.

Tedder, S. L., Scherman, A., & Sheridan, K. M. (1984). Impact of group support on adjustment to divorce by single, custodial fathers. *AMHCA Journal, 6,* 180–189.

Thames, T. B., & Hill, C. E. (1979). Are special skills necessary for counseling women? *The Counseling Psychologist, 8,* 17–18.

U.S. Bureau of the Census. (1988). *Statistical abstract of the United States: 1988* (108th ed.). Washington, DC: U.S. Government Printing Office.

Usdansky, M. L. (1992, July 17). Wedded to the single life. *USA Today,* p. 8A.

Valdes, T. M., & McPherson, R. H. (1987). "Leaving home": A family of origin group for college students. *Journal of College Student Personnel, 28,* 466–467.

Waring, E. (1988). *Enhancing marital intimacy through cognitive self-disclosure.* New York: Brunner/Mazel.

Washington, C. S. (1979). Men counseling men: Redefining the male machine. *Personnel and Guidance Journal, 57,* 462–463.

Wegscheider, S. (1981). *Another chance: Hope and health for the alcoholic family.* Palo Alto, CA: Science & Behavior Books.

White, J., & Riordan, R. (1990). Some key concerns in leading parent education groups.

Journal for Specialists in Group Work, 15, 201–205.

Whitfield, C. L. (1987). *Healing the child within: Discovery and recovery for adult children of dysfunctional families.* Pompano Beach, FL: Health Communications.

Wilcox, D. W., & Forrest, L. (1992). The problems of men and counseling: Gender bias or gender truth? *Journal of Mental Health Counseling, 14,* 291–304.

Wilcoxon, S. A., Wilcoxon, C. W., & Tingle, C. M. (1989). Enriching the adult student environment (EASE): A counseling group for adult students. *Journal for Specialists in Group Work, 14,* 40–45.

Williams, R. C., & Myer, R. A. (1992). The men's movement: An adjunct to traditional counseling approaches. *Journal of Mental Health Counseling, 14,* 393–404.

Wolf, T. J. (1987). Group counseling for bisexual men. *Journal for Specialists in Group Work, 12,* 162–165.

Worth, M. R. (1983). Adults. In J. A. Brown & R. H. Pate, Jr. (Eds.), *Being a counselor: Directions and challenges* (pp. 230–252). Pacific Grove, CA: Brooks/Cole.

Worthington, E. L., Jr., Buston, B. G., & Hammonds, T. M. (1989). A component analysis of marriage enrichment: Information and treatment modality. *Journal of Counseling and Development, 67,* 555–560.

Wrenn, C. G. (1979). Proposed changes in counselor attitudes: Toward your job. *School Counselor, 27,* 81–90.

Yalom, I. D. (1985). *The theory and practice of group psychotherapy* (3rd ed.). New York: Basic Books.

Zimpfer, D. (1988). Marriage enrichment programs: A review. *Journal for Specialists in Group Work, 13,* 44–53.

Zimpfer, D. (1990). Group work for bulimia: A review of outcomes. *Journal for Specialists in Group Work, 15,* 239–251.

Zimpfer, D. (1992). Group work with adult offenders: An overview. *Journal for Specialists in Group Work, 17,* 54–61.

Zimpfer, D. G., & Carr, J. J. (1989). Groups for midlife career change: A review. *Journal for Specialists in Group Work, 14*(2), 43–250.

CHAPTER 12

Groups for the Elderly

When you wake up one morning
and feel you've grown old
Take this poem down from your shelf
And slowly read its well-wrought lines
which fade like memories of our youth.
Those were the days on the knolls of Reynolda
when times were measured in looks not words,
Those were the moments we wrote in our memories
and now, like fine parchment, though faded they remain
clear impressions in the calmness of age,
bringing warmth and smiles to the chill of the season:
brightness in a world full of grey.*

A ging is an inevitable process. Despite mythical and historical searches for the fountain of youth, everyone who lives grows older. Many individuals begin to acknowledge the inevitable decline in their physical powers somewhere between ages 35 and 50 (Peck, 1968). Others continue to deny any changes.

In previous generations, working in groups with the elderly was not a priority because the number of individuals over the age of 65 years was relatively small (2% of the population in 1776; 4% in 1900) (American Association of Retired Persons, 1986). In the 1990s, the percentage of those over age 65 was 12% and rising, with those 85 and older being the fastest growing subgroup population in the United States (Hern & Weis, 1991; Myers, 1989; Williams & Lair, 1988). By the year 2000, the number of Americans over the age of 65 will be 35 million and will almost double to 64 million by the year 2050 (Wrenn, 1989).

*Source: Gladding, 1968/1989.

Although the elderly are of interest to mental health professionals, existing services for this population have not kept up with demand (Myers, 1989). There are many reasons for this deficiency. One is that the number of people in this category has grown dramatically. Since 1900, persons above age 85 have increased eightfold, whereas the population in general has increased only threefold (Hern & Weis, 1991). Another reason is that mental health services have traditionally not been geared toward serving those past middle age. Further complicating the situation are the limitations some helpers place on themselves and the elderly by accepting many of the myths, misconceptions, and stereotypes about the aged, for example, old people cannot change or be creative (Corey & Corey, 1992; Greene, 1986). The acceptance of these myths creates an "attitude bias" against working with the elderly (Vander Kolk, 1985). This bias is often called **ageism**, which is basically discrimination against older people (Butler, 1975). In actuality, many characteristics of the old make them excellent candidates for numerous helping services, especially group work.

CHARACTERISTICS OF THE ELDERLY

There are benefits and liabilities that come with any age. Growing old is no exception. On the positive side, most people past the traditional retirement age of 65 (used as a marker event to separate midlifers from old age) still enjoy a high quality of life and have many years to live (about a quarter of their lives) (Myers, 1989). Often they exemplify what Erikson (1963) describes as **"wisdom"**—the ability to make effective choices among alternatives—and **"integrity"**—the total integration of life experiences into a meaningful whole. If married, older people frequently experience increased marital satisfaction and intimacy (Walsh, 1988).

Because approximately 70% of persons over age 65 are grandparents, they often find great meaning and enrichment through interacting with their grandchildren (Mead, 1972; Streib & Beck, 1981). Others find significance in their lives through becoming foster grandparents or doing volunteer work. Most keep in contact with their children and are able to resolve some issues of earlier family life. A significant percentage (95%) maintain their own households and seem to value their independence. Up to age 75, the majority of individuals are, as a rule, relatively free from disabling physical impairments, view themselves as basically middle-aged, and generally enjoy a variety of physical exercises and activities, including sex (Masters & Johnson, 1970; Okun, 1984). Persons in this age range are known as the **young-old**.

On the negative side, the elderly as a group share many common psychological and physiological concerns. For instance, loneliness, loss, fear, or hopelessness are often prevalent among members of this group (Corey & Corey, 1992; France, 1984). Individuals over the age of 76 are considered the **old-old** and are more likely to experience declines in health and overall functioning (Myers, 1989). A majority of the old have chronic health problems that require increased attention as they age (Walsh, 1988). In addition, numerous individuals, especially older men, have difficulty adapting to retirement and mourn the loss of meaningful roles outside the household. Sometimes this adjustment can lead to conflict and dysfunctioning.

Loss of spouse and widowhood is another down side to aging. Because women traditionally marry older men and live longer than men, this possibility is of special concern to them (Neugarten, 1970). Ageism may be a painful societal force that tarnishes one's sense of pride in age. Finally, there is the prospect of facing one's own mortality and death. The inevitable end of life is an event some individuals in old age have difficulty accepting.

Changes required of most individuals at the "old" stage of life include making adjustments for less physical strength, retirement, death of friends and/or spouse, and declines in income and health (Cox, 1988; Havighurst, 1972). New social roles, such as being a grandparent, must be learned, and establishing different relationships with peers and children must be managed. The requirements of the elderly, though not as numerous as those in adolescence, are still demanding. Not everything happens at once, however, and most older individuals have time to make the transition gradually (Lorton & Lorton, 1984). The " 'density of time'—its fullness and eventfulness—seems to lessen with age" (Schlossberg, 1981, p. 13).

Many of the problems associated with living over 65 years "are the result of limited socialization and interpersonal activities; others involve damaged self-image and self-esteem" (Vander Kolk, 1985, p. 286). Almost all of these difficulties can be constructively addressed through some form of group work. In fact, just the interpersonal nature of groups can be therapeutic for the elderly, especially those who are isolated and lonely (Brandler, 1985; Capuzzi & Gross, 1980; France, 1984; Zimpfer, 1987).

BENEFITS OF GROUPS FOR THE ELDERLY

Being a member of a group has numerous benefits for older people. The benefits, however, are related to both the quantity and quality of interpersonal relationships that older adults have (Horswill, 1993). As a group, the elderly have many of "the same needs, interests, and fears as persons of other ages" (Myers, 1989, p. 96). They become more aware of their needs, communalities, uniquenesses, and possibilities through sharing in a group. They are also able to find support and resolutions. Although the major needs of the elderly may not always be addressed in all groups, it is crucial that the needs and interests of both men and women are considered in setting up groups (Horswell, 1993). For example, activities that center around both social and task-related opportunities should be included. This may mean setting up groups that focus on quilting bees, crafts, dances, and woodwork as well as those that attend to seminars on travel, social security policies, and health insurance benefits.

Myers (1984) divides needs for older adults into four interrelated and independent areas: environmental concerns, activity needs, personal concerns, and interpersonal concerns. Effective groups will accomplish some or all of the following in regard to these needs.

First, an effective group will help its members gain a sense of the universality of their concerns (Hawkins, 1983). Elderly members of society often lose natural groups, such as those promoted through work and the family. These social losses, combined with those that are physical or psychological, often drain the vitality of these individuals and make them more vulnerable to stress-related disorders, such as depression and physical disease (O'Brien, Johnson, & Miller, 1979). Belonging to a group, especially with people who are around the same age, assists participants in realizing they are not alone in their focus on "body image, physical ailments, and fear of mental deterioration" (Hawkins, 1983, p. 187). Through sharing, they come to develop a sense of community and a feeling of belongingness (Thomas, 1991). This type of atmosphere contributes to their overall wellness.

A second benefit of joining a group involves trying out different responses and initiating new behaviors. Older persons often engage in **growing times** when fresh learning occurs on an individual and interpersonal level (Wrenn, 1989). This process may involve merely a better appreciation of what they encounter or where they have been, or it may involve a physical action, such as talking or taking on a different life role. Within a group, especially if it is psychoeducational older individuals can experiment with behaviors they never had an opportunity to try before. It can help them fulfill their sense of what is ideal and give them a more positive view of themselves.

A third advantage of group membership involves the process of formal and applied learning. A popular movement in the United States since the 1970s is the **elder hostel**, where older individuals live and study together for a select period of time (Ganikos & Benedict, 1982). This way of learning helps members reinforce one another and promotes social cohesion while making the acquisition of knowledge fun. Often the older person who is the student becomes the teacher on occasions in these types of situations because of life experiences. Learning groups are not just for the young (Johnson & Johnson, 1991).

A fourth advantage of groups for the elderly centers on enhancing self-concept (O'Brien et al., 1979). Through groups, the elderly can be helped to focus on some of the advantages of growing old. For instance, many older individuals find comfort in integrating different aspects of their lives and discovering that their life experiences can help others. Such reflection and ongoing involvement foster hope and ward off depression. Persons in such situations become contributors to society.

Finally, groups for the elderly provide a series of checks and balances for those who participate in them. They shift responsibility for growth and development from caretakers or relatives to the persons in the group (Mardoyan & Weis, 1981). Participants in groups are empowered to take control of their present lives and to resolve past difficulties as best they can. This type of emphasis promotes growth in a way not usually possible in other one-to-one relationships.

TYPES OF GROUPS WITH THE ELDERLY

Groups for those age 65 and over are geared toward the needs of the persons involved and the expertise of the group leader(s) (Corey & Corey, 1992). Basically, there are six major types of groups that are appropriate for different segments of the older population: (a) reality oriented, (b) remotivation therapy, (c) reminiscing, (d) psychotherapy and counseling, (e) topic-specific, and (f) member-specific (Beaver, 1983; Burnside, 1984; Capuzzi & Gross, 1980; Wellman & McCormack, 1984). The first four types are aimed at helping mentally impaired older people through psychotherapeutic means, whereas the last two are more psychoeducational and preventive in nature (Myers, 1989). Each will be briefly described here.

Reality-oriented groups are set up for older individuals who have become disoriented to their surroundings. (Reality-oriented theory is unrelated to the theory of reality therapy developed by William Glasser.) These groups, while educationally focused, are therapeutically based in that they emphasize helping group members to become more aware of their present surroundings in terms of time, place, and people (Burnside, 1984). Group membership is limited to three or four participants when the circumstances are severe, but groups for less disoriented individuals may involve seven or eight people. Groups meet daily, and if basic information is mastered, members progress to more creative and practical activities (Capuzzi & Gross, 1980). Because reality-oriented groups are conducted at such a low level, helping professionals with minimal training in human relationship skills are able to lead them.

Normally, these types of groups are established in institutional settings and meet every day. Group sessions can include sensory training, group exercises, or practical skills (Taulbee, 1978). The process of orientation, however, cannot be limited to group sessions. It must be conducted on a 24-hour-a-day basis, with accurate records kept daily. The empirical evidence for the success of reality-orientation groups is not strong, possibly due to the limited nature of the clients who compose the groups or to the low level of leadership skill required of facilitators (Zimpfer, 1987).

Remotivation therapy groups are aimed at helping older clients become more invested in the present and future. Their membership is composed of individuals who have "lost interest" in any time frame of life except the past. The groups were originally set up in mental hospitals and nursing homes in the early 1950s by Dorothy Smith, a hospital volunteer. Participation in such groups is usually limited to 15 members, who are selected for their ability to relate to others, their willingness to join the group, and their lack of distorted memories (Dennis, 1978). Sessions focus on nonpathological topics, such as gardening, art, or the holidays, and participants are encouraged to respond to others and to materials presented in an appropriate verbal or nonverbal manner. The goal of this process is for participants to become more cognitively organized and to increase their socialization skills through interacting with others.

According to Beaver (1983, p. 240), remotivation therapy groups follow five basic steps:

1. "The climate of acceptance"—establishing a warm, friendly relationship in the group.
2. "A bridge to reality"—reading literature, keeping up with current events, investigating ideas.

3. "Sharing the world"—developing a specific topic through leading questions, use of props, planned activities.
4. "An appreciation of the work of the world"—stimulating the participants to think about themselves in relationship to work or avocational interests.
5. "The climate of appreciation"—finding joy through getting together.

Often remotivation groups are preliminary to other types of group experiences, such as those involving family problems or individual concerns. Studies show positive empirical results for remotivation therapy groups (Burnside, 1984; Zimpfer, 1987).

Reminiscing groups, which originated in the 1960s, are based on the importance of "life review" (Butler, 1961; Ebersole, 1978). They help individuals who are at the older life stage to comprehend and appreciate more fully who they are and where they have been. Persons in these groups share memories, increase personal integration, and become more aware of their lives and the lives of those their age. Insight gained from this process helps these persons realize more deeply their finiteness and prepare for death (Lewis & Butler, 1984).

A major therapeutic value of the reminiscing group process lies in the sense of affiliation it creates among its members. Reminiscence groups provide "an opportunity for social intimacy with others" (Singer, Tracz, & Dworkin, 1991, p. 167). Further beneficial aspects of these groups include a more positive mood among members, increased self-esteem, and enhanced life satisfaction (Goldwasser, Auerbach, & Harkins, 1987). In addition, members feel more competent and in greater control of their lives. Their memories give them a vehicle for communicating with others who are at their same age and stage. Isolation and loneliness are eliminated in group interactions. Through sharing, the processes of creativity and pleasure are enhanced as the individual, the group, and the group leader gain insight into a person's psychological history (Berghorn & Schafer, 1987). In short, the reminiscing group can be the springboard for conducting other groups or be an end in itself.

Reminiscing groups are usually conducted once or twice a week for about an hour and consist of six to eight members. They may be relatively long-term (more than a year) or short-term (ten weeks or less) (Beaver, 1983). The content of the group sessions is often chosen by group members but may be selected at times by the group leader(s). Whatever the case, content is often highlighted through the use of poetry, music, bright visual aids, and other memorabilia. Leaders for such groups need to be skilled in group dynamics and interpersonal communication responses. They should be inquiring, but not intrusive. Patience and flexibility are key ingredients that leaders must master (Capuzzi & Gross, 1980).

A model of a reminiscence group in an adult day-care center has been provided by Singer, Tracz, and Dworkin (1991). In establishing their group, these leaders decided on a closed, voluntary group format. They screened their prospective members beforehand to ensure they were mentally alert as well as motivated for the experience. Goals for the group included decreasing social and emotional isolation, depression, and loneliness; increasing social skills and self-esteem; and enabling members to develop a social network by the end of the group. After ten weekly one-hour sessions, the staff of the center and members themselves noticed significant advancements in the achievement of the group's goals. Life for participants became more meaningful and enjoyable because of the respect and understanding they found in the group. The main drawback to this particular group was that ten sessions did not provide enough time for the members to process fully all of the material they wanted to discuss.

Psychotherapy and counseling groups are geared toward the remediation of specific problems faced by the elderly, such as role changes, social isolation, physical decline, and fear of the future (Altholz, 1978; Weisman & Schwartz, 1989). "Elderly clients who are referred to group psychotherapy are very often depressed, highly agitated and disruptive, or unable to do reality testing" (Maynard, 1980, p. 232). Those who are referred to counseling have fewer problems but are still in need of help. The important therapeutic value of these two types of groups was recognized in the 1950s and has continued (Capuzzi & Gross, 1980).

Generally, psychotherapy and counseling groups for the elderly are composed of between 6 and 12 members. Psychotherapy groups are usually long-term (a year or more). Counseling groups tend to be briefer. Both psychotherapy and counseling are mostly unstructured and seldom make use of predetermined group exercises (Maynard, 1980). Leaders of such groups need a background in gerontology as well as experience in group work with the elderly. Two leaders may be needed in order to sustain enthusiasm and interest.

Leaders of psychotherapy groups for the elderly must be knowledgeable about and skilled in the treatment of major mental disorders. Although group counseling leaders should also have this type of background, it is vital that they recognize and be able to deal with developmental and transitional factors connected with aging. Both types of leaders must also be encouraging of group members and willing to self-disclose when appropriate (Altholz, 1978). Overall, psychotherapy and counseling groups help their members gain a greater appreciation of themselves and where they are developmentally.

Two such counseling groups for dealing with the problems of the aged were studied. The first group focused on expressing anger and alleviating depression (Johnson & Wilborn, 1991), and the other concentrated on ways of handling stress and promoting the mental health of the elderly (Stone & Waters, 1991). In the group dealing with anger, Johnson and Wilborn did not find that a six-week group counseling experience lowered anger significantly in a group of older women. However, they did find that the women seemed to value the opportunity to talk about the expression of anger and its importance in their lives. They suggested a longer period of time be allocated to anger groups for the elderly in replication studies.

In the group set up to help older adults manage stress, Stone and Waters (1991) used peer facilitators in a format of four sessions, each lasting two hours. They emphasized the importance of personal sharing, participant control, and enhancement of self-esteem. The peer counselors who worked with this small group of eight to ten individuals had instant credibility because of their age, and they were perceived as strong role models and reinforcers of group members' actions. Although no formal measures of change were taken in this group, members and the peer counselors did report the group to be helpful in increasing members' abilities to handle stress, change perceptions, and realize that others shared their concerns.

Topic-specific groups are centered around a particular topic, such as widowhood, bibliotherapy, sexuality, health, or the arts. "They are designed ultimately to improve the quality of daily living for older people" (Beaver, 1983, p. 241). They also assist the aged to find more meaning in their lives and to establish a support group of like-minded people. Because the focus of these groups is psychoeducational, their leaders must have topic-specific knowledge of the issues being covered (Myers, 1989). Membership is voluntary, and improved self-esteem and encouragement through significant social interaction is often the result of such experiences (Burnside, 1984; Capuzzi & Gross, 1980).

An example of an open-ended, topic-specific group is a support group for widowed persons in Orange County, Florida, called "The Talk Group." The idea behind this group, which has been in existence since 1983, is that a *"therapeutic alliance"* is formed between individuals in grief and those who are helping them. The result is "bereaved individuals who enjoy a high level of social support suffer fewer depressive symptoms and somatic complaints than those who are not so well supported" (Folken, 1991, p. 173). The Talk Group is an extension of one-to-one support and benefits both the newly widowed as well as the group volunteers who work in it.

Member-specific groups are related to topic-specific groups, but they focus more on particular transitional concerns of individual members, such as grief, hospitalization, or institutionalized day-care. Basically, member-specific groups may be conducted for older adults or for members of their families (Capuzzi & Gross, 1980). When these types of groups are conducted for the aged, they are aimed at helping all participants recognize and face particular concerns that are common to people who grow older, such as loss of physical strength (Peck, 1968) or the effects of physical illnesses (Sullivan, Coffey, & Greenstein, 1987). In a similar way, member-specific groups that concentrate on families assist them in dealing with common themes related to how a group member's well-being and adjustment will affect each person in the family (Sullivan et al., 1987).

The same leadership skills required to lead a topic-specific group are necessary in conducting a member-specific group, but leaders must focus more on individual concerns than those of the group as a whole. For example, a family group with a member who has Alzheimer's disease may all have different areas on which they wish to concentrate (Glosser & Wexler, 1985; Hinkle, 1991). There is no simple way to personalize a member-specific group.

SETTING UP GROUPS FOR THE ELDERLY

Just as with other groups, those involving the elderly must be carefully and thoughtfully proposed. This means that goals should be clearly established before the group begins. "Elderly people generally need a clear, organized explanation of the specific purpose of a group and why they can benefit from it" (Corey & Corey, 1992, p. 419). The establishment of any group for the elderly involves pregroup screening, especially if the group is therapeutically oriented.

Most groups for the elderly are conducted on an outpatient or outreach basis, but in some cases, they are carried out in institutional settings. In outreach environments, task-oriented psychotherapy groups are beneficial because of a sense of accomplishment that these groups foster among their members through the achievement of tangible products (Zimpfer, 1987). Regardless of the setting or the focus, there are certain procedures to follow when preparing to work with a group of individuals aged 65 and older.

The first consideration is the physical environment in which the group will be conducted. The meeting room should be functional, geared for comfort, and in a quiet area. The ideal location is a ground-floor room, with upholstered chairs, good lighting, space for wheelchairs, near a bathroom, away from steps, and with a constant temperature of about 75 degrees with no drafts—but this is usually hard to find (Capuzzi & Gross, 1980; Hendrix & Sedgwick, 1989). In this setting, a tight circle works best for accommodating the hearing impaired and creating a sense of cohesiveness (Stone & Waters, 1991).

A second matter of importance is scheduling. There are certain times of the day that do not work well for meetings. For example, early evening is not good for many older group members who may have difficulty with night driving or like to go to bed early. Therefore, the group should be set up to maximize participation. This usually means finding out the schedules of potential participants and building time for group meetings around them. Once a good time is established, most groups for the elderly are closed in order to build trust and develop empathy (Capuzzi & Gross, 1980; Hendrix & Sedgwick, 1989). The major exceptions to this procedure are psychotherapy groups in institutional settings or support groups such as those for the widowed that may benefit from an open-ended format (Folken, 1991).

A third matter that must be considered is the physical ability of group members. Physical disabilities and sensory impairment can contribute to a feeling of social isolation in the elderly and can also inhibit their participation in a group (Myers, 1990). Some members who have lost sensory and mobility functions may require special treatment. One way to take care of their needs is to employ a **multimodal method** (i.e., using verbal and nonverbal means) for conveying information. A warm-up activity or brief informational presentation before the group actually gets down to work can help members to understand the focus of the group for the day (Capuzzi & Gross, 1980).

ROLE OF THE GROUP LEADER

Almost all major theoretical approaches can be used to work with the elderly (Storandt, 1983). Therefore, the role of the leader in groups for the elderly depends on his or her knowledge of theory, the type of group to be led, the leader's previous experience, and the abilities and level of readiness of participants. Hawkins (1983) suggests the following steps for prospective leaders, especially those with little experience:

1. *Read.* It is critical to separate fact from fiction when working with members of an older population. Reading books and articles specifically geared toward the developmental and nondevelopmental issues of the aged will help leaders be more objective. Excellent reviews of the literature on groups for the elderly are often published in scholarly journals (e.g., Myers, Poidevant, & Dean, 1991).

2. *Examine.* Along with reading, leaders need to examine their own prejudices and stereotypes of the old. Some leaders who grew up in a culture or subculture that stressed youth or staying young, such as the "baby boom generation," may have particular difficulty in dealing with the elderly and their concerns (Folken, 1991). Leaders with negative ideas about older adults will probably be detrimental to the group and should be replaced.

3. *Meet.* It is crucial to the group's success that leaders become aware of their own perspectives on the lives of older individuals. One place such an encounter can occur is through remembering major exchanges with the elderly within the leaders' families of origin. Other opportunities for such meetings are found in present settings, such as retirement homes, where leaders visit older individuals and learn more about them as persons.

4. *Fantasize.* Leaders should imagine their own lives in the future and become more aware of what their wishes, hopes, and fears might be then. For instance, leaders may envision themselves as lonely or economically destitute after retirement. If such is the case, they can empathize more with actual group members they may meet in these circumstances. By fantasizing, leaders can face their future and avoid projecting any undesirable characteristics onto those with whom they work.

5. *Learn.* Those who lead groups for the elderly need to learn what social and political organizations, such as the American Association of Retired Persons (AARP), are available on the national, state, and local level. These groups are often rich resources for group members.

6. *Care.* It is important, and indeed critical, that the elderly realize that others, such as group leaders, sincerely care about them. Such caring adds to the self-esteem of everyone. It promotes rapport and enriches the process of being in a group (Myers et al., 1991).

Overall, group leaders for the elderly must be verbally and nonverbally active, personally and professionally concerned, as well as clear and direct. By performing in such a fashion, leaders can help move their groups away from a self-centeredness to a healthy group-centeredness (Hendrix & Sedgwick, 1989). Group leadership skills in such cases do not differ significantly from those used with other populations, but the emphases of leaders vary. Their alertness to certain key issues, such as religion, economics, intergenerational conflict, or loss, is usually greater than would be the case in other age groups.

In summary, leaders working with older persons in groups "must be sensitive to relevant issues such as concerns with aging and death as well as to real constraints such as waning physical health and vitality and fewer social outlets" (Jacobs, Harvill, & Masson, 1994, p. 391). They must come to terms with their own aging and eventual death in a way that enables them to face life energetically and realistically. Therefore, personal integration of one's own life, professional knowledge of aging, and the familiarity with the psychotherapeutic processes that will best help them relate to the aged are the key variables to becoming an effective group leader for the elderly.

ISSUES IN CONDUCTING GROUPS FOR THE ELDERLY

There are many issues to consider when conducting groups for the elderly. A great number of these involve the difference between working with the elderly and working with other age groups. Burnside (1978) lists a number of factors that make groups for the aged distinct from other types of groups.

1. Groups for the elderly, as a rule, tend to be smaller in size (e.g., four to eight members) than groups with other age populations, except for elementary school children. Remotivation therapy groups, which may be as large as 15 members, are a notable exception to the rule of having small-sized groups for the elderly.
2. The pace of a group for the elderly is usually slower and the goals are more limited. To compensate for this slower pace and to reduce frustration, group leaders need to be accepting, remind members of positive changes, and encourage continued participation (Myers et al., 1991).
3. Common themes in groups for the elderly are loss and loneliness, death and dying, concern about physical changes, increased dependency, relationships with adult children, grandparenting, and finding meaningful and enjoyable activities in which to participate (Myers, 1989).
4. Sensory deficits in group members who are elderly must be taken into consideration in structuring and conducting group meetings. For example, physical limitations such as loss of hearing, are frequent; selecting a meeting room in a quiet location and seating members close together are essential in these situations.
5. The physical environment of the group is more important to the well-being of the group and its members than is true with other age groups. The elderly have greater difficulties with physical body systems than do other age groups due to life-style factors such as **hypokinesis** (physical inactivity) (Burlew, Jones, & Emerson, 1991). For some groups, physical exercise along with group activities is an excellent combination.
6. Leaders need to share impressions and experiences in their lives within the group to keep it focused and moving. One of the most important mistakes new group leaders make when working with the elderly is not self-disclosing (Myers et al., 1991).

7. Unlike the norms for some other groups, elderly group members are encouraged to socialize with one another outside of the group setting. This type of socializing helps break down barriers that isolate the elderly from one another and is, therefore, therapeutic.

8. The rhythmicity of individual members needs to be considered, and meetings should be scheduled to accommodate members' preferences. Usually, certain times of the day, for example, after lunch, are not acceptable because some group members may take an early afternoon nap.

9. Transportation and economic considerations are also very important because the elderly are usually limited in their accessibility to both.

10. Growth and enhancement are meaningful themes for groups for the elderly. Encouragement is more appropriate than confrontation in working with this population.

Other issues and potential obstacles for conducting groups for the elderly include matters such as trust. Older adults take longer to build up trust than do those in other age groups (Waters, McCarroll & Penman, 1987). The reasons for this gap vary, but they often reflect socialization patterns, such as believing that negative secrets should be kept private or feeling that no one will really understand them.

A second concern is the use of certain words and processes that are normally discussed in groups for other populations. *Long-term goal* and *termination,* for instance, should be avoided (Ekloff, 1984; Waters et al., 1987). These words have a tendency to arouse anxiety in some older persons, especially those who are frail or sick. Members may become fearful that they will not be able to attain goals or that they may suffer yet another loss. In general, a less stringent criteria for success is appropriate when working with groups for the elderly. A relaxed atmosphere is also important.

Overall, although the issues involved in conducting groups for the aged are similar in form to those for other particular populations, there are certain methods that work best. By implementing these methods, acquired through knowledge and skill, leaders will find group work with these individuals to be truly special. A major issue that most group workers face in dealing with the elderly is their inexperience in knowing what that stage of life is like. Therefore, they must accept this reality and be open to being a learner, as well as a facilitator, within these groups.

GROUPS FOR CARETAKERS OF THE ELDERLY

The phenomena of groups for caretakers of the elderly is a recent development. It stems from the "advancements in medical science, technology, and health care" that enable human beings to live longer (Dobson & Dobson, 1991, p. 178). With this increased life span, middle-aged adults, the children of the elderly, are often finding themselves as caretakers of this population with limited information and few role models. The result is often frustration, resentment, and physical/emotional strain. In order to address these concerns, groups for caretakers have been formed.

There are a number of different kinds of caretaker groups ranging from those for direct relatives to those for nursing home staffs. The common denominator for these groups is that they primarily attempt to provide their members with information and support. Therefore, caretaker groups are mainly psychoeducational and psychotherapeutic in nature. Often they are short-term, closed, and meet at nontraditional hours, such as early evening. Through the caretaker group, a bond is formed among participants that helps them realize the universal nature of their situations (Dobson & Dobson, 1991; Hinkle, 1991). For nonrelative caretakers, especially those concerned with providing services to the dying, groups help them ventilate their feelings and revitalize themselves and their efforts (Smith & Maher, 1991).

Overall, groups for caretakers are preventive in nature. They affirm, support, and educate. They help link caretakers with others who can help them handle unique and universal problems (Myers et. al., 1991). They provide a means for participants to renew their mental health and concentrate on the interactional tasks ahead of them. As the elderly population increases, groups for caretakers of the elderly will become more prevalent and more necessary.

SUMMARY AND CONCLUSION

It has only been since the late 1950s that aging and the aged have been rigorously studied in the United States. With a growing number of individuals reaching age 65 and over, however, the importance of studying and working with this population has increased rapidly. The elderly have unique concerns and potentials that are often denied or overlooked. They bring to any situation a wealth of experience and talent, as well as life circumstances unique to their time and informative to others.

Group work with the elderly is still basically in its infancy. Prior to 1980, there was almost no professional literature on working with groups of older people (Myers, 1989). In the 1990s, research and approaches are more refined (Myers et al., 1991). However, questions still remain about what works best with which populations and when, even though Zimpfer (1987) has stated, "When the elderly client's needs are diagnosed correctly, the treatment often seems to work no matter what it is" (p. 91). There are six major types of groups most frequently used with the elderly: reality orientation, remotivation therapy, reminiscing, psychotherapy and counseling, topic-specific, and member-specific. Each type of group has advantages and limitations.

In general, groups are quite appropriate and useful for the elderly by helping them to integrate their lives better and find support and a sense of universality. Groups help older people to combat loneliness and a sense of isolation by forming friendships and by providing information, a sense of orientation in time and place, and an opportunity to continue to grow and develop.

Setting up a group for the elderly depends on the leader's background and the needs of participants. Basically, many of the procedures for establishing groups are those found in working with other populations. However, group leaders need to be sensitive to time factors, foci, and themes that are especially appropriate for the elderly. By directing their attention to these matters and by coming to terms with their own prejudices about age and their own sense of aging, leaders can promote positive interactions and development within groups of elderly.

As the qualitative and quantitative aspects of groups for the elderly grow, so will other activities connected with them. Among the most important of these related occurrences will be groups for caretakers of the aged. Such groups can help relatives and professionals of the elderly maintain their own mental health and give optimal care through psychoeducational and psychotherapeutic means.

CLASSROOM EXERCISES

1. Divide into teams and investigate the most recent professional literature on any of the six primary types of groups mentioned in this chapter. Report back to the class as a whole on your findings and what approaches seem to work best with which populations of the elderly.

2. Draw a picture of yourself at age 80. Then work backward and make a drawing of yourself for each preceding decade until you reach your present age decade. After you have finished the drawings, role play one of the ages you have drawn with a classmate and talk with him or her about how it feels to be that age and what concerns you have.

3. Collect data for a week from popular media, such as television, magazines, and newspapers, that demonstrate ageism or a lack of ageism. Share your findings with classmates in a group of four. Make recommendations to the class as a whole from your groups on three ways that ageism can be positively countered.

4. Think of your experiences with older people when you were a child. Talk with other classmates in a group of three about what your experiences taught you about the aged and what impressions they still make on your life. How would your past affect your present performance as a leader for an elderly group?

REFERENCES

Altholz, J. A. S. (1978). Group psychotherapy with the elderly. In I. M. Burnside (Ed.), *Working with the elderly: Group process and techniques* (pp. 354–370). North Scituate, MA: Duxbury.

American Association of Retired Persons. (1986). *A profile of older Americans.* Washington, DC: Author.

Beaver, M. L. (1983). *Human service practice with the elderly.* Englewood Cliffs, NJ: Prentice Hall.

Berghorn, F. J., & Schafer, D. E. (1987). Reminiscence intervention in nursing homes: What and who changes? *International Journal of Aging and Human Development, 24,* 113–127.

Brandler, S. M. (1985). The senior center: Informality in the social work function. In G. S. Getzel & M. J. Mellor (Eds.), *Gerontological social work practice in the community* (pp. 195–210). New York: Haworth Press.

Burlew, L. D., Jones, J., & Emerson, P. (1991). Exercise and the elderly: A group counseling approach. *Journal for Specialists in Group Work, 16,* 152–158.

Burnside, I. M. (1978). Responsibilities of the preceptor. In I. M. Burnside (Ed.), *Working with the elderly: Group processes and techniques* (pp. 88–100). North Scituate, MA: Duxbury.

Burnside, I. M. (1984). *Working with the elderly: Group processes and techniques* (2nd ed.). Monterey, CA: Wadsworth.

Butler, R. N. (1961). The life review: An interpretation of reminiscence in the aged. *Psychiatry, 26,* 65–76.

Butler, R. N. (1975). *Why survive? Being old in America.* New York: Harper & Row.

Capuzzi, D., & Gross, D. (1980). Group work with the elderly: An overview for counselors. *Personnel and Guidance Journal, 59,* 206–211.

Corey, M. S., & Corey, G. (1992). *Groups: Process and practice* (4th ed.). Pacific Grove, CA: Brooks/Cole.

Cox, H. G. (1988). *Later life: The realities of aging.* Englewood Cliffs, NJ: Prentice Hall.

Dennis, H. (1978). Remotivation therapy groups. In I. M. Burnside (Ed.), *Working with the elderly: Group processes and techniques* (pp. 219–235). North Scituate, MA: Duxbury.

Dobson, J. E., & Dobson, R. L. (1991). Changing roles: An aging parents support group. *Journal for Specialists in Group Work, 16,* 178–184.

Ebersole, P. P. (1978). A theoretical approach to the use of reminiscence. In I. M. Burnside (Ed.), *Working with the elderly: Group processes and techniques* (pp. 139–154). North Scituate, MA: Duxbury.

Ekloff, M. (1984). The termination phase in group therapy: Implications for geriatric groups. *Small Group Behavior, 15,* 565–571.

Erikson, E. H. (1963). *Childhood and society* (2nd ed.). New York: W. W. Norton.

Folken, M. H. (1991). The importance of group support for widowed persons. *Journal for Specialists in Group Work, 16,* 172–177.

France, M. H. (1984). Responding to loneliness: Counselling the elderly. *Canadian Counsellor, 18,* 123–129.

Ganikos, M. L., & Benedict, R. C. (1982). Aging and the schools: An introduction to issues and ideas for school counselors. *School Counselor, 29,* 263–274.

Gladding, S. T. (1968/1989). *A poem in parting.* Unpublished manuscript.

Glosser, G., & Wexler, D. (1985). Participants' evaluation of educational/support groups for families of patients with Alzheimer's disease and other dementias. *The Gerontologist, 25,* 232–236.

Goldwasser, A. N., Auerbach, S. M., & Harkins, S. W. (1987). Cognitive, affective, and behavioral effects of reminiscence group therapy on demented elderly. *International Journal of Aging and Human Development, 25,* 209–222.

Greene, R. R. (1986). *Social work with the aged and their families.* New York: Aldine DeGruyter.

Havighurst, R. J. (1972). *Developmental tasks and education* (3rd ed.). New York: McKay.

Hawkins, B. L. (1983). Group counseling as a treatment modality for the elderly: A group snapshot. *Journal for Specialists in Group Work, 8,* 186–193.

Hendrix, F. G., & Sedgwick, C. (1989). Group counseling with the elderly. In G. M. Gazda (Ed.). *Group counseling: A developmental approach* (pp. 195–211). Boston: Allyn & Bacon.

Hern, B. G., & Weis, D. M. (1991). A group counseling experience with the very old. *Journal for Specialists in Group Work, 16,* 143–151.

Hinkle, J. S. (1991). Support group counseling for caregivers of Alzheimer's disease patients. *Journal for Specialists in Group Work, 16,* 185–190.

Horswill, R. K. (1993). Are typical senior center group activities better suited for women than for men? *Journal for Specialists in Group Work, 18,* 45–48.

Jacobs, E. E., Harvill, R. L., & Masson, R. L. (1994). *Group counseling: Strategies and skills* (2nd ed.) Pacific Grove CA: Brooks/Cole.

Johnson, D. W., & Johnson, F. P. (1991). *Joining together* (4th ed.). Englewood Cliffs, NJ: Prentice Hall.

Johnson, W. Y., & Wilborn, B. (1991). Group counseling as an intervention in anger expression and depression in older adults. *Journal for Specialists in Group Work, 16,* 133–142.

Lewis, M. I., & Butler, R. N. (1984). Life-review therapy: Putting memories to work. In I. M. Burnside (Ed.), *Working with the elderly: Group processes and techniques* (2nd ed.) (pp. 50–59). Monterey, CA: Wadsworth.

Lorton, J. W., & Lorton, E. L. (1984). *Human development.* Pacific Grove, CA: Brooks/ Cole.

Mardoyan, J. L., & Weis, D. M. (1981). The efficacy of group counseling with older adults. *Personnel and Guidance Journal, 60,* 161–163.

Masters, W. H., & Johnson, V. E. (1970). *Human sexual inadequacy.* Boston: Little, Brown.

Maynard, P. E. (1980). Group counseling with the elderly. *Counseling and Values, 24,* 227–235.

Mead, M. (1972). *Blackberry winter.* New York: William Morrow.

Myers, J. E. (1984). *Counseling older persons.* Ann Arbor, MI: ERIC/CAPS (ED 250 648).

Myers, J. E. (1989). *Infusing gerontological counseling into counselor preparation.* Alexandria, VA: American Counseling Association.

Myers, J. E. (1990). Aging: An overview for mental health counselors. *Journal of Mental Health Counseling, 12,* 245–259.

Myers, J. E., Poidevant, J. M., & Dean, L. A. (1991). Groups for older persons and their caregivers: A review of the literature. *Journal for Specialists in Group Work, 16,* 197–205.

Neugarten, B. (1970). Dynamics of transition of middle age to old age: Adaptation and the life cycle. *Journal of Geriatric Psychiatry, 4,* 71–87.

O'Brien, C. R., Johnson, J. L., & Miller, B. (1979). Counseling the aging: Some practical considerations. *Personnel and Guidance Journal, 57,* 288–291.

Okun, B. F. (1984). *Working with adults.* Pacific Grove, CA: Brooks/Cole.

Peck, R. (1968). Psychological development in the second half of life. In B. Neugarten (Ed.), *Middle age and aging.* Chicago: University of Chicago Press.

Schlossberg, N. K. (1981). A model for analyzing human adaptation to transition. *The Counseling Psychologist, 9,* 2–18.

Singer, V. I., Tracz, S. M., & Dworkin, S. H. (1991). Reminiscence group therapy: A treatment modality for older adults. *Journal for Specialists in Group Work, 16,* 167–171.

Smith, D. C., & Maher, M. F. (1991). Group interventions with caregivers of the dying: The 'Phoenix' alternative. *Journal for Specialists in Group Work, 16,* 191–196.

Stone, M. L., & Waters, E. (1991). Accentuate the positive: A peer group counseling program for older adults. *Journal for Specialists in Group Work, 16,* 159–166.

Storandt, M. (1983). *Counseling and therapy with older adults.* Boston: Little, Brown.

Streib, G., & Beck, R. (1981). Older families: A decade review. *Journal of Marriage and the Family, 42,* 937–956.

Sullivan, E. M., Coffey, J. F., & Greenstein, R. A. (1987). Treatment outcome in a group geropsychiatry program for veterans. *The Gerontologist, 27,* 434–435.

Taulbee, L. R. (1978). Reality orientation: A therapeutic group activity for elderly persons. In I. M. Burnside (Ed.), *Working with the elderly: Group processes and techniques* (pp. 206–218). North Scituate, MA: Duxbury Press.

Thomas, M. C. (1991). Their past gives our present meaning—Their dreams are our future. *Journal for Specialists in Group Work, 16,* 132.

Vander Kolk, C. J. (1985). *Introduction to group counseling and psychotherapy.* Columbus, OH: Merrill.

Walsh, F. (1988). The family in later life. In B. Carter & M. McGoldrick (Eds.), *The changing family life cycle* (2nd ed.) (pp. 311–332). New York: Gardner Press.

Waters, E., McCarroll, J., & Penman, N. (1987). *Training mental health workers for the elderly: An instructor's guide.* Rochester, MI: Continuum Center.

Weisman, C., & Schwartz, P. (1989). Worker expectations in group work with the frail elderly: Modifying the model for a better fit. *Social Work with Groups, 12,* 47–55.

Wellman, F. E., & McCormack, J. (1984). Counseling with older persons: A review of outcome research. *Counseling Psychologist, 12,* 81–93.

Williams, W. C., & Lair, G. S. (1988). Geroconsultation: A proposed decision-making model. *Journal of Counseling and Development, 67,* 198–203.

Wrenn, C. G. (1989). Preface. In J. E. Myers (Ed.), *Infusing gerontological counseling into counselor preparation* (pp. 9–15). Alexandria, VA: ACA.

Zimpfer, D. G. (1987). Groups for the aging: Do they work? *Journal for Specialists in Group Work, 12,* 85–92.

PART THREE

LEADING GROUPS FROM A THEORETICAL PERSPECTIVE

CHAPTER 13

Psychoanalytic and Adlerian Groups

We sit like strangers in hard-backed chairs
   at right angles from each other—
On the corners our sentences meet
   reflecting our thoughts and lives.
Slowly, messages in our minds
   make a move, a personal process
      whose destination is undetermined
But develops as we detect
   a crowd of quick-passing, open questions
That linger in our conversations
   after the sights of people
      have vanished with the light
And self-understanding has broken through
   as we travel from dusk into night. *

The aftereffects of a group are often long lasting. Individuals usually enter groups as strangers but leave with a different understanding of themselves and others. These changes can be positive or negative, but rarely neutral. Conducting a group from a theoretical position is one factor that can influence a group for better or for worse (Gladding, 1994).

In this chapter, psychoanalytic and Adlerian theory will be examined as they pertain to group work. Although Alfred Adler was not a disciple of Sigmund Freud, he did interact with Freud from 1902 to 1911 (Sweeney, 1989). Some of Adler's ideas and concepts were developed more fully because of his reaction to

*Source: Gladding, 1978, p. 148. Copyright ACA. Reprinted by permission of the American Counseling Association.

and interaction with Freud and his psychosexual theory. Likewise, Freud's positions were strengthened as a result of his contact and conversations with Adler. The historical connection between these two men is unique. Although their approaches and emphases differ, the overlap in time and professional relationships link the two theorists and their work.

PSYCHOANALYTIC GROUPS

Psychoanalytic theory assumes that in-depth change takes years to produce. Therefore, it is usually oriented toward individuals with deep underlying psychological problems. However, this theory has changed from its original individual orientation to include groups. Psychoanalytic group work has several historical roots.

Freud (1959), although never interested in conducting groups, applied his psychoanalytic theory to groups in 1922 in his book *Group Psychology and the Analysis of the Ego.* In this work, Freud examined the nature of groups and how they influence individuals' lives. He concluded that a "group" is similar to a **primal horde** and that leaders of both function as substitute *"parental figures"* (Slavson, 1964). Freud also stressed the importance of ego development within a group context and the reconstruction of the family unit among group members (Hansen, Warner, & Smith, 1980).

Several physicians in the United States began using psychoanalytic theory as a basis for group psychotherapy prior to World War I. Among the most notable was E. W. Lazell (1921), who conducted group psychotherapy with schizophrenics. Trigant Burrow (1927) was the first to apply the term **group analysis** to the treatment of individuals in psychoanalytically oriented groups. He emphasized that social forces affect individuals' behaviors. Paul Schilder and Louis Wender were also pioneers in experimenting with group psychotherapy from a psychoanalytical perspective in New York in the 1930s (Shaskan & Roller, 1985). Both worked with psychotic, hospitalized adults, but Schilder also used group psychotherapy with prisoners while Wender employed the approach with discharged patients (Gazda, 1968).

It was not until 1938, however, that a psychoanalytic model of group work was implemented on a sustained basis. Alexander Wolf, a psychiatrist and psychoanalyst, is generally credited with being the first to systematically apply psychoanalytic principles and techniques to groups (Corey, 1990; Hansen et al., 1980; Ruitenbeek, 1970). He developed his analytical approach based more on economic reasons (i.e., the financial strain of clients to pay for individual services in the 1930s) than on an interest in groups. He quickly realized the utility of psychoanalytic groups, however, and became an enthusiastic supporter of them. Another early contributor to the psychoanalytic group work model was Samuel Slavson, who formed activity groups for children ages 8 to 15 based on psychoanalytic principles. He described his approach as **situational therapy** (Mullan & Rosenbaum, 1978).

One of the interesting outcomes of the psychoanalytic group movement is that at least two models for conducting groups have developed. Alexander Wolf created a model that stresses psychoanalysis in groups. In this model, the focus is on the individual, and the major tools of the psychoanalytic method are used: transference, dreams interpretation, historical development analysis, interpretation of resistance, and free association. On the other hand, George Bach (1954) and W. R. Bion (1959) developed models totally different from Wolf's, referred to as **group psychoanalysis.** These models emphasize that the whole group is the client and that group dynamics are an essential feature to analyze. Bion's point of view is similar to general systems theory (von Bertalanffy, 1968) whereas Bach's view is based on field theory (Lewin, 1951). Both practitioners maintained that groups may manifest healthy or unhealthy influences on those within them. Generally, the most practiced form of psychoanalytically oriented group work emphasizes individual therapy in a group context, i.e., psychoanalysis in groups (Seligman, 1982).

Premises of Psychoanalytically Oriented Groups

Regardless of the model, there are basic premises that underlie all psychoanalytically oriented groups. These common denominators deal with the major tenets of classic psychoanalytic theory, as well as the belief that psychoanalysis is possible in a group setting. The importance of freeing unconscious thoughts, making the unconscious more conscious, and the use of specific techniques to do so (e.g., free association, transference, and interpretation) are universally emphasized. Individuals who undergo psychoanalysis, regardless of the setting, should function better as a result of the experience since they have resolved intrapsychic conflicts.

The major assumptions of classic psychoanalytic theory are premised on the importance of the interaction between the id, ego, and superego. The **id** is the first system within the personality to develop and is primarily "where human instincts reside" (Nye, 1981, p. 7). It is amoral, functions according to the pleasure principle, and contains the psychic energy (*libido*) of the person.

The **ego** is the "executive of the mind," works according to the reality principle, and tries to reduce the tension of the id. A strong ego is necessary for a healthy personality to develop.

The **superego** represents the values of parents and parental figures within the individual. It operates on the moral principle by punishing the person when he or she disobeys parental messages through the *conscience,* and by rewarding the person through the *ego ideal* when parental teachings are followed. "The superego strives for perfection and is seldom satisfied with less" (Nye, 1981, p. 16). In this regard, it is as unrealistic as the id.

Equally important as the interaction of these three ego states is the classic psychoanalytic theory hypothesis that individuals pass through **four stages of psychosexual development** during the first 20 years of life: oral, anal, phallic, and genital, with a period of latency between the phallic and genital stages. Each of these stages is named for a zone of pleasure at a particular age in a person's growth (see Table 13.1).

Failure to resolve the development tasks associated with these stages by being overindulged or excessively frustrated results in **fixation** (a tendency to cope with the outside world in a manner similar to that employed in the stage in which one is stuck). To overcome fixation requires that people regress to that time and come to terms with themselves and significant others who were involved in the fixation process. Ideal development can then go on and result in an ability to interrelate well with the self (with the ego in control of the id and superego) and with others. A number of **defense mechanisms** (ways of protecting a person from being overwhelmed by anxiety), such as repression or denial, are overutilized when a person is not coping adequately (see Table 13.2). The main task of classic psychoanalysis is to undo fixation and to help people gain insight.

As implied earlier, a major premise espoused by a number of psychoanalytic theorists (Foulkes & Anthony, 1965; Locke, 1961; Wolf & Schwartz, 1962) is that psychoanalysis is possible in a group setting. Any objections to its use in such a context, they imply, can easily be overcome. Group psychoanalysis as well as psychoanalysis in a group is more a modification of individual analysis than a distinct school of thought (Slavson, 1964). However, group psychoanalysis and psychoanalysis in a group differs from Freud's original opinions about group members. In groups that are psychoanalytically oriented,

1. group members do not necessarily view the group leader as an ego ideal
2. group members are not necessarily passive and dependent
3. group standards are not always those of the leader

Table 13.1

Psychosexual stages of development.

Stage	Age	Emphasis
Oral	Birth to 1 year	Gratification through sucking, biting; chief zone of pleasure is the mouth.
Anal	1st to 2nd year	Gratification through the withholding or eliminating of feces; chief zone of pleasure is the anus.
Phallic	3rd to 5th year	Gratification through stimulation of the genital area, sexual fantasy; resolution comes in giving up wish to possess opposite-sex parent and identifying with same-sex parent.
Latency	6th to 11th year	This is a period devoted to activity and achievement with peers; it is a quiet time sexually.
Genital	12th year on	This is the time of relating to persons of the opposite gender in an appropriate manner if previous stages have been resolved successfully.

Table 13.2
Psychoanalytic defense mechanisms.

• **Repression**	The most basic of the defense mechanisms, repression is the unconscious exclusion of distressing or painful thoughts and memories. All other defense mechanisms make some use of repression.
• **Denial**	In this process, a person refuses to see or accept any problem or troublesome aspect of life. Denial operates at the preconscious or conscious level.
• **Regression**	When individuals are under stress, they often return to a less mature way of behaving.
• **Projection**	Instead of stating what a person really thinks or feels, he or she attributes an unacceptable thought, feeling, or motive onto another.
• **Rationalization**	This defense mechanism involves giving an "intellectual reason" to justify doing a certain action. The reason and the action are only connected in the person's mind after the behavior has been completed.
• **Reaction Formation**	When an individual behaves in a manner that is just the opposite of how he or she feels, it is known as a "reaction formation." This type of behavior is usually quite exaggerated, such as acting especially nice to someone whom one dislikes intensely.
• **Displacement**	This defense is a redirection of an emotional response onto a "safe target." The substitute person or object receives the feeling instead of the person directly connected with it.

4. group members' reactions to the group and to its leader are not the same
5. group members do not repress their aggression in deference to the group leader (Durkin, 1964).

Two other points regarding the differences between conducting psychoanalysis in a group and doing so individually are stressed by Scheidlinger (1952) and Spotnitz (1961). They emphasize that certain processes, such as transference, are more intense in groups because of the interaction of members. Furthermore, factors stressed in individual psychoanalysis, such as individual differences and genetic factors, are not emphasized as much in a group setting.

Basically, psychoanalytically oriented groups can be practiced on either a regressive-reconstructive or a repressive-constructive basis. The first approach (the **regressive-reconstructive model**) emphasizes that participants will become responsible for themselves and for society. It stresses the importance of being a creator of society as well as a transmitter of patterns. Therefore, it pushes participants to continue to change after the group has ended. The **repressive-**

constructive model puts more focus on adaptation and adjustment of participants without stressing the creation of newness within culture (Mullan & Rosenbaum, 1978). Both approaches emphasize that a major change in personality is the goal of the group, which comes about only if there is sufficient regression followed by reconstruction.

Practice of Psychoanalytic Theory in a Group

The practice of psychoanalytic theory in a group is related to the premises of the theory in general. Because the theory emphasizes regression and resolution of previously unresolved stages of psychosexual development, membership in the group is usually restricted to either psychiatric patients or analytically oriented individuals. Therefore, the practice of psychoanalysis in groups is mainly applicable to counseling and psychotherapy groups. Although aspects of psychoanalytic theory may be included in a psychoeducational group, these same factors are not prevalent in a work/task group.

Most psychoanalytic groups are heterogeneous by design. The reason for this is that such groups are more reflective of the world at large and promote transference and interaction while discouraging conformity (Wolf & Schwartz, 1962). Psychoanalytic groups should have about six to nine members and meet once or twice a week for at least 90 minutes (Mullan & Rosenbaum, 1978; Shaffer & Galinsky, 1989). There is no fixed number of sessions, but some groups of this type will meet over 200 times (i.e., 300 hours).

The most important techniques used in the psychoanalytical approaches to groups parallel those employed in individual analysis. Each technique will be examined separately here, although in practice they are used together.

Free Association.   **Free association** in individual psychoanalysis is aimed at uncovering unconscious materials that have never been revealed or that have been repressed because they are too painful to keep in the conscious mind. In group psychoanalysis, the purpose of free association is similar, but the technique is also used to promote spontaneity, interaction, and feelings of unity in the group (Corey, 1990). In a group, free association works as a type of "freefloating discussion" (Foulkes & Anthony, 1965) in which group members report their feelings or impressions immediately.

One way to promote group-free association is through the "go-around technique" (Wolf, 1963). This procedure encourages all members to share their feelings and impressions about others in the group by saying whatever they think. In this way, members become more active within the group process and not only give personal impressions but receive interpersonal information as well. Interpersonal perceptions are very important in the development of the human personality (Mead, 1934).

Dream Analysis.   **Dream analysis** is just as essential in group psychotherapy as it is in individual psychoanalysis. In both cases, individuals must be prepared to share. In an early session, the group leader asks members to describe a recent dream, a recurring dream, or even a daydream (Hansen et al., 1980). Through sharing, group members get to know each other better and, at the same time, are able to be more concrete in handling their feelings associated with the dream and in managing themselves in general (Corey, 1990).

Dream content is manifest (conscious) and latent (hidden). *Manifest* content is the obvious and recallable features of the dream, such as who was in it. *Latent* content is the symbol features of the dream that escape first analysis, such as water being a symbol for life. Psychoanalytic groups work on dreams at both levels. By giving their interpretations and free associations to others' dreams, those within the group gain insight into themselves and to the group process as a whole. Dreams work on an interpersonal as well as an intrapersonal level in group psychotherapy (Kolb, 1983).

Interpretation.   **Interpretation** focuses on helping clients gain insights into their past or present behavior. Interpretations are generally made by group leaders in the earliest stages of the group, because group members seldom possess the sophistication to do so adequately and appropriately (Stoller, 1968). Some group leaders who follow Melanie Klein's psychoanalytic method will make interpretations at the beginning of the group to try to make contact with an individual's unconscious (Mullan & Rosenbaum, 1978). Most will wait, however, until they are sure that a therapeutic alliance has been formed with group members and that members are able to work productively with the interpreted material. In the later stages of the group, members interpret and give feedback to each other.

There are generally three levels of interpretation: thematical, constructional, and situational (Clark, 1993). *Thematical* interpretation is broad based and covers the whole pattern of a person's existence, such as self-defeating behavior. A leader might say, for instance, to a person who displays this behavior, "Pat, you seem to keep shooting yourself in the foot." *Constructional* interpretation focuses on thought patterns and the way group members express themselves, such as "I just can't win." *Situational* interpretation is context centered and emphasizes the immediate interactions within the group, such as members talking about trivia rather than meaningful or relevant issues. For example, the leader might observe, "This group is having a hard time getting down to work. Everyone seems to want to avoid real issues."

There are several drawbacks to the use of interpretation in group settings. One of the biggest is that the group leader will become overly involved with one member of the group and not give needed attention to others (Posthuma, 1989). Interpretation may also be rejected by group members and make them defensive, thereby halting the progress of the group. Finally, interpretation may divert the group's attention from the individual goals of members. Therefore, interpretation should be used with caution.

Resistance.   **Resistance** works in overt and covert ways to keep the group from making progress. Overtly, it may take the form of rebellion by group members against the leader (Saravay, 1978). Covertly, it is demonstrated when group members get bogged down in details and become preoccupied with the unimportant (Corey, 1990). If the group is to make progress, resistance must be confronted. Although the group leader may take the initiative in doing this, group members may also confront one another about the behaviors being displayed in the group. For example, Walter may say to Skip, "I sense you are reluctant for us to talk about our past histories. Every time the subject comes up, you say 'Let's wait and discuss that later.'" Psychoanalytically oriented group work is an especially good approach to use with very resistant clients.

Transference.   **Transference** is the projection of inappropriate emotions onto the leader or group members. It usually occurs when members have come to know each other fairly well. A manifestation of transference might be when Jill says to Randy, "You really don't like me. I can just tell it from the way you look at me."

In psychoanalysis, transference is encouraged, and clients are helped to work through unresolved experiences of the past and gain insight into their present patterns of interaction. Group members can often help each other in this process that Wolf (1975) describes as the most important work in psychoanalytic groups.

Participants in groups that are psychoanalytically oriented are helped to see patterns of transference when the group leader directs their attention to present interactions and invites them to examine how much they are investing in relationships with each other and the leader (Hansen et al., 1980). Transference in group psychoanalysis has broader dimensions than in individual psychoanalysis (Thompson & Kahn, 1970).

Role of the Psychoanalytically Oriented Group Leader

The role of the psychoanalytically oriented group leader varies with the characteristics and emphases of the groups he or she is leading. The stage of the group's development is an important variable as well. As a rule, psychoanalytic group leaders should be objective, warm, and relatively anonymous (Corey, 1990). They should strive to conceal, rather than reveal, information about themselves, while at the same time attempt to foster transference. The group leader should promote a positive atmosphere within the group to help members feel free to explore and express themselves. They should have directional and stimulational skills, too, to keep the group moving and revitalize it if it gets bogged down in resistance (Slavson, 1964).

The psychoanalytic group leader is of necessity not a member of the group, but at the same time, he or she must avoid taking a dictatorial attitude toward group members. Those leaders who function most effectively make efforts to transfer some leadership responsibility to the group when appropriate (Wolf, 1963; Wolf & Schwartz, 1962). They should recognize each participant's potential to contribute to the good of the group and recognize the potential power of the group as a whole.

Psychoanalytic group leaders should acknowledge their mistakes, while making every effort to guide members toward their fullest development by encouraging transference and by discouraging destructive alliances. Wolf (1963) believes that effective psychoanalytic group leaders promote members' interpersonal relationships above member and group leader relationships. Foulkes (1964) believes that because psychoanalytically oriented group leaders do not wish to be the main attention of the groups they facilitate, they should be referred to as **conductors**.

Desired Outcome of Psychoanalytically Oriented Groups

Psychoanalytic group theory emphasizes stages of individual development in the group rather than the group itself (Hansen et al., 1980). Therefore, psychoanalytically oriented group work differs from other therapeutic systems that concentrate attention on the growth of the group. Wolf (1963) notes that not all clients pass through the same stage of treatment at the same time, but for those who do, the desired stages they go through are as follows:

1. *Preliminary individual analysis*—In this stage, all individuals in the psychoanalytically oriented group are interviewed individually by the group leader. Their suitability for the group experience is assessed along with their diagnostic difficulty. Those persons found to be too anxious or potentially unsettling for a group experience are referred for individual treatment. Ground rules for conducting group sessions are explored at this time.

2. *Establishment of rapport through dreams and fantasies*—Group members are asked to discuss a recent dream, recurring dream, or a fantasy they have. The idea is to encourage group participation by having all members report on themselves and help others interpret or free-associate on their experience. This second stage usually begins around the second or third session of the group.

3. *Analysis of resistance*—This stage manifests itself when group members become reluctant to share themselves with others. At such times, individual defenses are examined and handled. Resistance may take many forms, but it is usually recognized when group participants are either too cooperative or reluctant. For example, if Sue says to the leader, "I am ready to do anything you ask me to do," she may be essentially resisting initiatives to change and is passing control of the group to the leader instead of to herself. The task of the group leader is to uncover and correct these barriers to therapeutic growth .

4. *Analysis of transference*—Transference occurs when participants project feelings onto the group leader, group members, or significant others. Transference basically gets in the way of reality testing. In this stage, then, the focus is on discovering and breaking up of "irrelevant, repetitious, and irrational ways of viewing others" (Hansen et al., 1980, p. 49). In this process, transference interactions are examined as close to the time of their occurrence as possible. Individual members are also asked

to examine their feelings and involvement with other members of the group. For example, Paula may be asked to look at how she always blames others when she does not get her way. Her "your fault" way of dealing with failure is thereby challenged when group members respond to her accusations by making her examine what she might be doing that contributes to failures.

5. *Working through*—In this stage, individuals are required to accompany insight with action (Wolf, 1949). In Paula's case, if she realizes she is her own worst obstacle to accomplishing goals, she will be challenged by the group to start acting differently. The process of working through involves the participants' resolution of transference investments. The ability to deal with transference appropriately enables clients to terminate from the group.

6. *Reorientation and social integration*—The last stage of psychoanalytically oriented group treatment is reached when clients demonstrate they are able to deal with the realities and pressures of life in an appropriate fashion. This means they do not become overanxious or overcompliant when requests are made of them.

Hansen et al. (1980) note that the six-stage model of psychoanalytic group change is not as distinct as presented here. Participants develop at different levels and may regress at different times in the group. Nevertheless, it is desirable that they pass through all six stages. It is usually the group leader who decides when a person has made a good adjustment and is ready to leave the group.

Evaluation of Psychoanalytically Oriented Groups

As with other methods, there are assets and liabilities in using a psychoanalytical orientation in groups. By realizing these factors before a group begins, leaders and members will be able to benefit most from this orientation to group work.

Advantages. Psychoanalytically oriented groups have a major advantage when compared to individual psychoanalysis in that group members can experience transference feelings with others in the group as well as with the group leader, i.e., **multiple transferences**. The broad range of feelings that are generated and worked through in a group enables individuals to learn more about themselves than they might otherwise.

A second advantage of this approach is that members have an opportunity to work with others in the group to resolve current problems, as well as problems in their past. Therefore, therapeutic progress can be made more rapidly.

A third plus for psychoanalytically oriented groups is that group members learn they experience and express a wide range of feelings. Members within the group demonstrate different feelings, and all who are within the setting learn that uncomfortable emotions can be released without unduly upsetting the group or its members.

Another advantage of this type of group is its emphasis on long-term personality change through the group process. For individuals who need major changes in the ways they interact with others at a basic level, psychoanalytically oriented groups may be beneficial. They are usually conducted in psychiatric hospital settings and are complementary to other long-term change treatments being utilized in such environments. They are often open ended, so members can take maximum advantage of the help they can offer.

Limitations.   The limitations of psychoanalytically oriented groups are pointed out by those with and without an analytic background. One contention is that free association is not possible in a group setting. Group members tend to be interrupted in groups and may be unable to link their thoughts. Locke (1961) answers this criticism by stating that it is not absolutely necessary that free association come from one person. Comments from others may contribute significantly to the free association of the entire group or the individual.

A second limitation of the psychoanalytic approach to group work is that too often those within the "psychoanalytic establishment" only read and absorb their own papers and thoughts (Ruitenbeek, 1970). This type of inbreeding prevents more creative thinking and innovations. For instance, as noted earlier, psychoanalytically oriented groups are mainly employed in counseling and psychotherapeutic settings. Do they also have potential for psychoeducational and work/task groups? At this point due to the isolation of practitioner/theorists, that question has barely been addressed.

A third criticism of the psychoanalytically oriented groups is that the theory on which they are based is deterministic, biologically biased, and oriented toward a pathological view of the human nature. Those who criticize psychoanalytic groups from this basis point out that the aim of such groups is geared toward "coping" rather than growth; that women may experience bias in these experiences, especially if they are nontraditional; and that group members in general may be perceived as "sick" rather than "stuck" in their development. In general, these critics point out that psychoanalysis as a theory seems to overanalyze everything, even in groups.

Finally, psychoanalytically oriented groups and the theory of psychoanalysis are criticized for a lack of openness to rigorous scientific investigations. Case reports, rather than empirically designed comparison studies, are most often used to document the effectiveness of the theory and its method. Critics of this approach point out the need for more rigor in determining for whom this theoretical group approach is best suited.

ADLERIAN GROUPS

Adlerian theory has always had a group focus. It concentrates on the inherent social interest of persons and emphasizes social development, cooperation, and education. As mentioned in chapter 1, Alfred Adler was an early user of groups for psychotherapeutic and psychoeducational purposes (Manaster & Corsini, 1982). He used groups to counsel with parents as early as 1922. He often employed co-therapists in his work at the Vienna Child Guidance Clinics (Rosenbaum, 1978) and frequently had his groups observed by others. However, he never developed a theory of group work beyond the major principles he advocated in his approach to individual psychology (Donigian & Malnati, 1987). It was left for followers of Adler to develop a group approach based on his principles.

Five such theorists who helped refine Adlerian concepts for group work were Rudolf Dreikurs, Manford Sonstegard, Oscar Christensen, Raymond Corsini, and Donald Dinkmeyer. Dreikurs became the major impetus behind the establishment of group procedures based on Adlerian theory. He introduced group therapy into private practice in 1929 in Vienna and then again in the United States in the late 1930s (Dreikurs, 1950; Terner & Pew, 1978). Christensen, Sonstegard, and Corsini applied Adlerian principles to family counseling groups (Christensen & Marchant, 1983; Dreikurs, Corsini, Lowe, & Sonstegard, 1959). Dinkmeyer and his colleagues (Dinkmeyer, Dinkmeyer, & Sperry, 1987) are most noted for packaging Adlerian group models, including the development of kits for specific populations with step-by-step instructions for leaders.

Premises of Adlerian Groups

Chief among the major tenets of Adlerian theory is the primary concern for social interest (Corsini, 1988; Donigian & Malnati, 1987). **Social interest** has been defined as "not only an interest in others but an interest in the interests of others" (Ansbacher, 1977, p. 57). "From the Adlerian point of view the essence of normality is having a feeling of concern for others" (Corsini, 1988, p. 10). Such a feeling can be developed in a group context.

Other major concerns that undergird the theory are as follows:

1. *The purposefulness of all behavior*—Adlerians believe that individuals do not act randomly. They act with a goal in mind, although they are sometimes not aware of their goal (Dreikurs, 1950). For instance, if Beverly lashes out at Carmen, her intent may be to protect her privacy, although she may say afterward, "I'm not sure why I just did that." The general direction of life is from minus (inferiority) to plus (perfection, i.e., completeness) (Ansbacher & Ansbacher, 1956).

2. *The subjective nature of perception*—Adlerians emphasize the phenomenological nature of human behavior. People perceive the world based on their experiences, not objectively. Therefore, if Eric has only known abuse in his life, he may perceive the world as a hostile place.

3. *The holistic nature of people*—For Adlerians, people are a unified whole, not a collection of parts (Donigian & Malnati, 1987). People are more like trees, which grow from seeds and branch out, than they are like machines, such as automobiles, which are a collection of parts (Corsini,

1988). From this perspective, one answer is usually inadequate to explain even a simple act.

4. *The importance of developing a healthy style of life*—A **style of life** is the way one prefers to live and relate to others. Adlerians stress that a faulty life style is based on competitiveness and a striving to be superior to others. Life styles are often not noticed when a person is in a favorable situation but manifest themselves when the person faces difficulties (Adler, 1956). Life styles are developed early in a person's development (around age 5), but they are open to change.

5. *The self-determinism of the individual to chart a future based on expected consequences of behavior* (Corsini, 1988; Hawes, 1985)—Adlerians stress that people are creative and can choose from among a wide range of possible behaviors (Manaster & Corsini, 1982). All behavioral disorders are based on failures to choose wisely.

Practice of Adlerian Theory in a Group

Adlerian groups follow primarily a psychoeducational, rather than a medical, model. They are "heterodox with respect to procedures" (Corsini, 1988, p. 19), but nevertheless have many unifying aspects. The idea in all Adlerian groups is that people can learn from each other. As Dreikurs (1969) points out, "Since . . . problems and conflicts are recognized in their social nature, the group is ideally suited not only to highlight and reveal the nature of a person's conflicts and maladjustments but to offer corrective influences" (p. 43). Some groups, such as parent groups, are more didactic than others, but there are common aspects to all Adlerian groups.

At least three unifying factors link Adlerian groups together. One is the emphasis on an **interpretation of a person's early history** (Corey, 1990). In order to promote change, it is helpful for group members to recognize and understand the ways they created their own life styles. A second similarity in Adlerian groups is the practice of stressing individual, interpersonal, and group process goals during the duration of the group (George & Dustin, 1988). **Individual goals** may involve developing insight into the creation of a mistaken life style and taking corrective measures. **Interpersonal goals** may involve becoming more socially oriented and involved with other individuals experiencing life difficulties. **Group process goals** may center around promoting and experiencing a cooperative climate within the group.

Another linkage that unifies Adlerian groups in practice is the phases they go through. For instance, Dreikurs (1969) has outlined four phases of Adlerian group counseling:

1. establishing and maintaining a proper therapeutic relationship
2. exploring the dynamics that are operating within the individual
3. communicating to the individual an understanding of self
4. envisioning of new alternatives and choices

An Adlerian counseling group begins, after an initial screening of members, with an emphasis on the leader's part to promote cooperation and an egalitarian spirit. Group members may contract formally or informally to work on areas that have personal meaning to them. After the proper participatory atmosphere has been created, participants are then invited to explore their own life styles and understand more clearly how their present behavior promotes or deters their current functioning in all life tasks (Mosak, 1984). Some of the ways this second phase of the group is conducted include an exploration of family constellations, early recollections, and basic mistakes (Corey, 1990).

After this analysis, group members are ready to move into the **insight and reorientation phases of the group.** The insight phase involves helping individuals understand why they made the choices they did in the past. It often is accompanied by the use of interpretation on the group leader's part. Interpretation is offered as a tentative hypothesis in these groups, such as "Could it be . . .?" or "I wonder if . . .?" For example, "Joan, I wonder if there is a connection with your sister's success and your pattern to abandon projects just when you are doing well in them?"

In the final phase of **reorientation,** counseling group members are encouraged to act differently and take more control of their lives. Such a procedure means taking risks, acting "as if" they were the person they wished to be, and "catching themselves" in old, ineffective patterns and correcting them. For example, Dan may resolve to act as if he does not need the backing of his parents in order to make a successful career choice. In this case, he sets up an appointment with a career counselor and begins exploring vocational possibilities he never considered before.

Role of the Adlerian Group Leader

There are a number of qualities that effective Adlerian group leaders share. The ideal leader is a well-balanced person who possesses certain characteristics, according to Vander Kolk (1985) including sincerity and an acceptance of others, as well as an openness that promotes honest interchange with group members. Adlerian group leaders need a positive attitude that instills hope within others that change is possible. In addition, group leaders must have good knowledge of their clients and be active in attacking in a timely manner the "faulty logic," i.e., irrational ideas their clients hold. They further need to help clients clarify life styles and encourage group members to act.

Both Corsini (1988) and Hansen et al. (1980) state that the personality of the Adlerian group leader is as important as the techniques he or she employs. Mosak (1984) agrees that the personhood of the leader is crucial. He also stresses that for the leader to be effective, he or she must feel free to share opinions and feelings. Therefore, the group leader is a participant in the group process in a collaborative manner. The leader models the behavior that group members should demonstrate (Dinkmeyer et al., 1987) and creates the proper attitude in the group (Donigian & Malnati, 1987).

Overall, Adlerian group leaders focus on understanding present behavioral patterns of group members and challenging them to change. Effective leaders use group dynamics to help groups help themselves (Hansen et al., 1980). For example, the leader may encourage group members to confront each other about specific behaviors with the realization that, in so doing, members learn something about their own beliefs and goals in life. In working with groups of children, Adlerian leaders may primarily use **encouragement** (taking a risk without knowing its final outcome) and **natural consequences** (living with the results of a particular behavior, such as not following instructions). With adult groups, more systematic plans may be employed. In either case, Adlerian leaders are encouraged to stay true to the theory behind the process, yet also be inventive (Corey, 1990).

Desired Outcome of Adlerian Groups

The outcomes of Adlerian group practice focus primarily on the growth and actions of the individual within the group, rather than the group itself. In this respect, Adlerian groups are similar to psychoanalytic groups. Because there is greater variety in the types of groups offered by Adlerians than those offered by psychoanalysts, specific outcomes differ as does the focus of these approaches.

On a global level, individual members of an Adlerian group experience should be more socially oriented, personally integrated, and goal directed. They should have also corrected faulty beliefs, eliminated competitive behavioral stances, and become more in contact with family-of-origin issues. Children in Adlerian groups should recognize more clearly the logical consequences of their actions; parents, teachers, and other adults who work with children should be more cognizant of children's faulty belief systems (i.e., that they must be superior, helpless, powerful, or deficient) and corrective measures to take in helping them eliminate misguided thoughts and behaviors (Dreikurs, 1968). Generally, children in Adlerian groups are worked with more directly than any other age group.

Adolescents in Adlerian groups are specifically helped to deal better with their own and others' perceptions of themselves and to realize they do not have to engage in competitive behaviors to be accepted. There are a number of ways to promote cooperative behaviors among adolescents (see Table 13.3).

With families and adults, Adlerian groups are directed toward social adjustment (Hansen et al., 1980). Members of these groups are helped to understand that the basic problems in families and social relationships are people oriented and that relationships built on democratic principles, which foster healthy interactions, work best.

Although there is not much literature on Adlerian work/task groups, the outcome from these groups should also be one that emphasizes social cooperation and teamwork (Larson & LaFasto, 1989). Through working together, work/task group members should realize anew how much more they can accomplish together than separately.

Table 13.3
Typical faulty goals of adolescents.

Faulty Beliefs	Goals	Examples	Adult Reactions	Peer Group Reactions	Reactions to Corrective Feedback	Alternative Corrective Methods
I am worthwhile and belong only:						
When I am best at everything	Superiority	Super striving for best grades, most honors, first in the class, etc.	Approval	Admiration	Justifies striving	Avoid blanket approval / Promote courage to be imperfect / Encourage social cooperation
When I have widespread peer social acceptance	Popularity (Social climbing)	Constantly attempting to obtain widespread peer social acceptance	Approval	Acceptance / Subgroup envy or annoyance	Superficial compliance / Friendly disagreement	Avoid blanket approval / Encourage independent activity
When I live up completely to all standards of established adult society	Conformity	Constantly tries to please, particularly adults rather than peers, with good behavior, grades, etc.	Approval	Annoyance (with some envy)	Superficial compliance	Avoid blanket approval / Encourage peer social activities / Encourage individuality
When I am in complete control or free from outside control	Defiance: Independence struggle	Arguments over hair, dress, etc.	Annoyance / Irritation / Anger	Acceptance / Approval	Continue to argue / Defiant compliance	Avoid arguing / Suggestions at other times
	Aggression	Vandalism / Fighting / Delinquency	Anger / Hurt / Revenge	Rejection by most / Subgroup acceptance	Strike back	Avoid hurt and anger / Don't strike back / Reasonable limits and use of consequences

			Fear / Alarm	Indifference / Some sympathy	Passive response / No improvement	
	Withdrawal	Runaway / Truancy / Suicide	Fear / Alarm	Indifference / Some sympathy	Passive response / No improvement	Avoid hysterical reaction / Encourage social participation
When I prove and enjoy myself sexually	Sexual promiscuity	High level of intimate sexual activity with others	Disgust / Shock / Disapproval	Rejection by most / Subgroup acceptance	Defiant rejection	Avoid shock and disgust / Encourage desire for self-respect and respect of others
When I am completely supported and consoled in my shortcomings	Inadequacy	Gives up easily / Displays dependence	Pity / Hopelessness	Pity / Indifference	Meager effort, then gives up again	Avoid discouraged reaction or pity / Provide opportunities for small successes and encouragement
When others find me completely charming and pleasing	Charm	Fascinating and pleasing with smooth talk and behavior	Charmed and flattered / Sometimes mixed with annoyance	Charmed / Flattered / Pleased / Envious	Steps up charm / Pouting / Withdrawal	Be unimpressed but friendly / Remain courteous and insist on effort
If I am physically beautiful or strong	Beauty / Strength	Excessive attention to and dependence on physical appearance	Admiration sometimes mixed with envy or irritation	Admiration sometimes mixed with envy	Ignoring	Avoid praise / Encourage non-physical pursuits, e.g., reading, art, music
When I am "super" man or "super" woman	Sexism	Boys: Macho behavior / Girls: Clinging-vine behavior	General approval / Some annoyance	General approval / Some annoyance	Rejection	Avoid blanket approval / Encourage contrasting "feminine" or "masculine" attitudes and behaviors

Table 13.3, *continued*

Faulty Beliefs	Goals	Examples	Adult Reactions	Peer Group Reactions	Reactions to Corrective Feedback	Alternative Corrective Methods
I am worthwhile and belong only:						
When I am completely involved in learning or discussing ideas	Intellectualizing	Very bookish	Approval	Indifference Subgroup acceptance	Argument	Avoid blanket approval Encourage social leisure activities
When I am fully involved in religious ideas and activities	Religiosity	Deep involvement in religious ideas and activities Regular and frequent attendance at church	Approval Sometimes mixed with concern or annoyance	Ignored by most Subgroup acceptance	Pity Defensiveness	Avoid blanket approval or arguments Encourage exploratory thinking and talking

Source: From "Typical Faulty Goals of Adolescents" by E. W. Kelly and T. J. Sweeney, 1979, *The School Counselor, 26,* pp. 239–241. Copyright ACA. Reprinted by permission of the American Counseling Association.

Evaluation of Adlerian Groups

As with psychoanalytically oriented groups, it is crucial to be aware of Adlerian theory and the nature of Adlerian groups before participating in them. The theory and practice of Adler's ideas have distinct strengths and limitations.

Advantages.   An advantage of Adlerian groups is that they are usually non-threatening. They are also generally helpful to participants because of their educational emphasis. Group members often enjoy the experience and feel they come out with concrete ways to handle specific everyday problems, such as children, spouse, or work situations.

A second advantage of Adlerian group theory and practice is that methods associated with this approach are logical and based on "common sense" (Corsini, 1988). Most group participants do not feel put off by the terms or procedures used. In addition, most group leaders are able to learn and use Adlerian concepts in a relatively short time. The fact that this approach encourages democratic participation is useful for both the members and the leader in promoting openness and dialogue.

A third attractive feature of Adlerian groups is that they are holistic. Most Adlerians will typically employ a cognitive method to help participants understand the materials being presented, but they will also address behavioral and affective aspects of the person, too.

A fourth strength of Adlerian group work is its eclectic nature (Corey, 1990). Adlerians are not tied to rigid procedures and methods. They will stress common concepts such as the value of social interests, goal-directed behavior, individual indivisibility, and the importance of family constellations. However, the means by which these qualities are emphasized is left entirely to the individual group leader.

Another strong point of the Adlerian approach is its flexibility in working with varied populations. Different forms of Adlerian groups are used with children (Sonstegard & Dreikurs, 1973), adolescents (Kelly & Sweeney, 1979), parents (Croake, 1983; Dreikurs & Soltz, 1964), and families (Lowe, 1982).

Limitations.   A limitation of Adlerian group work is the style of the leader. Adlerians are unified in respect to their philosophy of equality and theory of personality development, but Adlerians follow their own style in regard to procedure. They "have no guidelines other than their experience" (Corsini, 1988, p. 14). Therefore, if the group leader does not personally and professionally adhere to Adlerian principles, the group may have difficulty.

Another limitation of the groups derived from Adlerian theory is the narrowness of their scope. The Adlerian approach assumes that all problems are socially based. Although many difficulties may be so oriented, there are problems that have different causes that are not addressed in Adlerian groups. For example, in a work group, the processes set up to produce a product may be at fault rather than the people involved. Likewise, an impoverished environment or government regulations may contribute to friction between people whether they wish to be social or not.

A third limitation of Adlerian groups is their lack of uniformity of method. Most notable Adlerian theorists have been dynamic as people and practitioners. They have achieved success because of their ability to translate Adlerian principles into practice. Although some followers of Adler (e.g., Dinkmeyer et al., 1987; Kelly & Sweeney, 1979) have translated Adlerian principles into more unified practice techniques, the Adlerian approach still lacks concreteness of techniques in group work.

Finally, the research on which Adlerian group work is based is relatively weak (Manaster & Corsini, 1982). In response to this deficiency, Corsini (1988) contends that all group-based research lacks support. Yet, if Adlerian groups are to achieve prominence, more data must be generated to document their effectiveness.

SUMMARY AND CONCLUSION

Both psychoanalytic and Adlerian groups have deep historical roots. Practitioners of these approaches began using them around World War I. They continue to be methods of conducting various types of groups today.

Psychoanalytic groups concentrate primarily on the resolving of individuals' unconscious thoughts and psychosexual stages. They are primarily employed in psychotherapeutic and long-term counseling groups. Techniques such as free association, transference, and interpretation of dreams are frequently utilized as in individual analysis. However, the dynamics of groups make analysis quite different. The group leader is seen as the expert and directs group members in revealing repressed materials. Group members may or may not be encouraged to help each other or to look beyond their own needs, depending on the orientation of the leader.

If successful, group members will pass through a number of individual developmental stages, including working toward insight and a reorientation to their environments. They will be more aware of the past, the range of their feelings, and how they function in the present. The psychoanalytic group approach stresses long-term personality change through the group process. Psychoanalytic procedures are still in need of better documentation and more refinement. The debate continues for those in this tradition about how to work best with the individual in a group setting and whether individual techniques can be employed effectively in groups of this type.

Adlerian group work is a social, democratic, relationship-oriented approach to working with individuals. As such, it emphasizes the importance of change in the present, while understanding the development of past faulty beliefs and behaviors based on the influence of the family and peer group. Many Adlerian concepts, such as inferiority complex, encouragement, and empathy, have been absorbed into other theories of helping (Corsini, 1988; Hansen et al., 1980). Nevertheless, Adlerian theory is still a viable way of assisting groups of individuals in a wide range of group settings to grow, change, and achieve. A real strength of the Adlerian approach to working with groups is its flexibility in relationship to children, adolescents, adults, parents, and families. The application of Adlerian theory to different groups is psychoeducationally based and therefore nonthreatening and helpful to most.

Adlerian group work will need a stronger base of research support in the future if it is going to continue to prosper. More uniformity and concreteness of methodology will also have to be employed. For now, however, Adlerian group work offers a viable and positive alternative to psychoanalytical groups. By being shorter in length, more health focused, and more socially oriented, Adlerians have carved out a unique niche in the group work field from which others have borrowed but not superseded.

CLASSROOM EXERCISES

1. Locate three journal articles published within the last five years on Adlerian group work. Discuss with another class member the similarities and differences in each writer's description of what he or she did. Talk about what you observed with other class members in the class as a whole and make a list of common elements that the authors you read used in their work with groups.

2. Compare and contrast psychoanalytic and Adlerian group work in regard to theory, method, group leader's role, and desired outcome. How do they overlap? How are they distinct? Share your impressions with three other classmates in a small-group setting.

3. Divide into groups according to your place in your family-of-origin (e.g., firstborn, last born). Discuss your feelings and thoughts about growing up in this type of environment and how you feel it affected your style of life. Compare your opinions with those of others in your group.

4. What is your favorite part about each of the two theories presented in this chapter? Which aspect did you like least? Discuss your thoughts and feelings concerning these two theories with another class member.

REFERENCES

Adler, A. (1956). *The individual psychology of Alfred Adler.* New York: Basic Books.

Ansbacher, H. L. (1977). Individual psychology. In R. J. Corsini (Ed.), *Current personality theories.* Itasca, IL: Peacock.

Ansbacher, H. L., & Ansbacher, R. R. (Eds.). (1956). *The individual psychology of Alfred Adler.* New York: Basic Books.

Bach, G. (1954). *Intensive group psychotherapy.* New York: Ronald Press.

Bertalanffy, L. von (1968). *General systems theory.* New York: George Braziller.

Bion, W. (1959). *Experiences in groups.* New York: Basic Books.

Burrow, T. (1927). *The social basis of consciousness.* New York: Harcourt, Brace & World.

Christensen, O. C., & Marchant, W. C. (1983). The family counseling process. In O. C. Christensen & T. G. Schramski (Eds.), *Adlerian family counseling* (pp. 29–55). Minneapolis: Educational Media.

Clark, A. J. (1993). Interpretation in group counseling: Theoretical and operational issues. *Journal for Specialists in Group Work, 18,* 174–181.

Corey, G. (1990). *Theory and practice of group counseling* (3rd ed.). Pacific Grove, CA: Brooks/Cole.

Corsini, R. J. (1988). Adlerian groups. In S. Long (Ed.), *Six group therapies* (pp. 1–43). New York: Plenum Press.

Croake, J. W. (1983). Adlerian parent education. *The Counseling Psychologist, 11,* 65–71.

Dinkmeyer, D. C., Dinkmeyer, D. C., Jr., & Sperry, L. (1987). *Adlerian counseling and psychotherapy* (2nd ed.). Columbus, OH: Merrill.

Donigian, J., & Malnati, R. (1987). *Critical incidents in group therapy.* Monterey, CA: Brooks/Cole.

Dreikurs, R. (1950). *Fundamentals of Adlerian psychology.* New York: Greenberg Publishers.

Dreikurs, R. (1968). *Psychology in the classroom* (2nd ed.). New York: Harper & Row.

Dreikurs, R. (1969). Group psychotherapy from the point of view of Adlerian psychology. In H. M. Ruitenbeek (Ed.), *Group therapy today: Styles, methods, and techniques.* New York: Adline-Atherton.

Dreikurs, R., Corsini, R., Lowe, R., & Sonstegard, M. (Eds.). (1959). *Adlerian family counseling.* Eugene: University of Oregon Press.

Dreikurs, R., & Soltz, V. (1964). *Children: The challenge.* New York: Duell, Sloan & Pearce.

Durkin, H. E. (1964). *The group in depth.* New York: International Universities Press.

Foulkes, S. H. (1964). *Therapeutic group analysis.* London: Allen & Unwin.

Foulkes, S. H., & Anthony, E. J. (1965). *Group psychotherapy: The psychoanalytic approach* (2nd ed.). Baltimore: Penguin.

Freud, S. (1959). *Group psychology and the analysis of the ego.* New York: Liveright.

Gazda, G. M. (1968). Group psychotherapy: Its definition and history. In G. M. Gazda (Ed.), *Innovations to group psychotherapy* (pp. 3–14). Springfield, IL: Charles C. Thomas.

George, R. L., & Dustin, D. (1988). *Group counseling: Theory and practice.* Englewood Cliffs, NJ: Prentice Hall.

Gladding, S. T. (1978). In the midst of the puzzles and counseling journey. *Personnel and Guidance Journal, 57,* 148.

Gladding, S. T. (1994). *Effective group counseling.* Greensboro, NC: ERIC/CASS.

Hansen, J. C., Warner, R. W., & Smith, E. J. (1980). *Group counseling: Theory and process* (2nd ed.). Chicago: Rand McNally.

Hawes, E. C. (1985). Personal growth groups for women: An Adlerian approach. *Journal for Specialists in Group Work, 10,* 19–27.

Kelly, E. W., & Sweeney, T. J. (1979). Typical faulty goals of adolescents. *The School Counselor, 26,* 236–246.

Kolb, G. E. (1983). The dream in psychoanalytic group therapy. *International Journal of Group Psychotherapy, 33,* 41–52.

Larson, C. E., & LaFasto, F. M. J. (1989). *Team-Work.* Newbury Park, CA: Sage.

Lazell, E. W. (1921). The group treatment of dementia praecox. *Psychoanalytic Review, 8,* 168–179.

Lewin, K. (1951). *Field theory in social science.* New York: Harper.

Locke, N. (1961). *Group psychoanalysis: Theory and technique.* New York: New York University Press.

Lowe, R. N. (1982). Adlerian/Dreikursian family counseling. In A. M. Horne & M. M. Ohlsen (Eds.), *Family counseling and therapy* (pp. 329–359). Itasca, IL: Peacock.

Manaster, G. G., & Corsini, R. J. (1982). *Individual psychology: Theory and practice.* Itasca, IL: Peacock.

Mead, G. H. (1934). *Mind, self, and society.* Chicago: University of Chicago Press.

Mosak, H. (1984). Adlerian psychology. In R. J. Corsini (Ed.), *Current psychotherapies* (2nd ed.). Itasca, IL: Peacock.

Mullan, H., & Rosenbaum, M. (1978). *Group psychotherapy* (2nd ed.). New York: The Free Press.

Nye, R. D. (1981). *Three psychologies* (2nd ed.). Monterey, CA: Brooks/Cole.

Posthuma, B. W. (1989). *Small groups in therapy settings: Process and leadership.* Boston: College-Hill.

Rosenbaum, M. (1978). The co-therapeutic method in the psychoanalytic group. In H. Mullan & M. Rosenbaum (Eds.), *Group psychotherapy: Theory and practice* (2nd ed.) (pp. 153–173). New York: The Free Press.

Ruitenbeek, H. M. (1970). *The new group therapies.* New York: Avon.

Saravay, S. M. (1978). A psychoanalytic theory of group development. *International Journal of Group Psychotherapy, 28,* 481–507.

Schleidlinger, S. (1952). *Psychoanalysis and group behavior.* New York: W. W. Norton.

Seligman, M. (1982). Introduction. In M. Seligman (Ed.), *Group psychotherapy and counseling with special populations.* Baltimore: University Park Press.

Shaffer, J., & Galinsky, M. D. (1989). *Models of group therapy* (2nd ed.). Englewood Cliffs, NJ: Prentice Hall.

Shaskan, D., & Roller, B. (1985). *Paul Schilder: Mind explorer.* New York: Human Sciences Press.

Slavson, S. R. (1964). *A textbook in analytic group psychotherapy.* New York: International Universities Press.

Sonstegard, M., & Dreikurs, R. (1973). The Adlerian approach to group counseling of children. In M. M. Ohlsen (Ed.), *Counseling children in groups* (pp. 47–78). New York: Holt, Rinehart & Winston.

Spotnitz, H. (1961). *The couch and the circle.* New York: Alfred A. Knopf.

Stoller, F. H. (1968). Focused feedback with video tape: Extending the group's functions. In G. M. Gazda (Ed.), *Innovations to group psychotherapy* (pp. 207–255). Springfield, IL: Charles C. Thomas.

Sweeney, T. J. (1989). *Adlerian counseling: A practical approach for a new decade* (3rd ed.). Muncie, IN: Accelerated Development.

Terner, J., & Pew, W. L. (1978). *The courage to be imperfect: The life and work of Rudolf Dreikurs.* New York: Hawthorn.

Thompson, S., & Kahn, J. H. (1970). *The group process as a helping technique.* New York: Pergamon Press.

Vander Kolk, C. J. (1985). *Introduction to group counseling and psychotherapy.* Columbus, OH: Merrill.

Wolf, A. (1949). The psychoanalysis of groups. *American Journal of Psychotherapy, 3,* 529–557.

Wolf, A. (1963). The psychoanalysis of groups. In M. Rosenbaum & M. Berger (Eds.), *Group psychotherapy and group function.* New York: Basic Books.

Wolf, A. (1975). Psychoanalysis of groups. In M. Berger and M. Rosenbaum (Eds.), *Group psychotherapy and group function* (2nd ed.) (pp. 273–327). New York: Basic Books.

Wolf, A., & Schwartz, E. K. (1962). *Psychoanalysis in groups.* New York: Grune & Stratton.

CHAPTER 14

Person-Centered and Gestalt Groups

In eyes there is beauty
*   not found in words.*
Soft, clear expression
*   surrounded by light*
Slowly contracting in the warmth of our day
*   and growing in the depths of our nights,*
Opening up new worlds before us
*   as vividly as a good camera lens*
*   properly set and focused.*
Your eyes find mine
*   sometimes in our sessions*
Looking with you into the present
*   while catching glimpses of a darkened past*
*   that blurs sometimes in a flash.*
Silently, you expose hidden feelings
*   through unspoken language we share the moment. . . .**

Person-centered and Gestalt theories of group work are primarily affect oriented. They are geared to picking up clients' messages that are conveyed nonverbally, such as with eye movements or hand signals, as well as verbally. Both person-centered and Gestalt groups stress the importance of emotions and congruence in human interactions. They also are existentially based and recognize the impact of subjective experiences in people's lives and in the life of a group. In these models of group work, an emphasis is placed on here-

*Source: Gladding, 1975, p. 429. Copyright ACA. Reprinted by permission of the American Counseling Association.

and-now phenomena and on the creation of personal and interpersonal awareness (Day & Matthes, 1992; George & Dustin, 1988).

Each theory has developed over the years and is continuing to evolve. Many of the techniques of these approaches have been incorporated into other group models, and many of the once-unique features of these theories, such as confrontation and a focus on awareness, have become universally accepted as important dimensions in other ways of conducting groups.

PERSON-CENTERED GROUPS

The growth and development of person-centered group work is linked to the theory and personal influence of Carl Rogers (Rogers, 1967, 1970, 1980). Initially, Rogers developed what he termed a *nondirective* counseling approach in reaction to the directive methods used by psychoanalytic therapists and other counselor-practitioners of the 1940s. E. G. Williamson, for example, placed an emphasis on the role of the counselor as the expert and director of the therapeutic process. Rogers had learned from his clients that when they were in charge of their own therapy and were truly accepted and understood by him as a therapist, they improved faster and better than when he directed their actions. During the 1940s and 1950s, Rogers focused on individual clients and worked to prove his theory of counseling. At the same time he developed a *self theory of personality* (Rogers, 1951, 1957, 1959). The main exception to this emphasis was his use of groups to work with counselors-in-training (Shaffer & Galinsky, 1989).

In the 1960s, Rogers expanded his focus to the small group as well as to the individual. His emphasis away from a strictly individual approach (which he had emphasized in his 1951 book, *Client-Centered Therapy*) was in keeping with the times. The T-group (i.e., training group) model was well established in the 1960s, as a result of the work of the National Training Laboratories. Therapy groups in psychiatry settings were also used widely. For Rogers, the T-group approach was too impersonal because of its primary attention to theory, group dynamics, and strictly social material (Hansen, Warner, & Smith, 1980). Groups in psychiatric settings were not appropriate for the general population with whom Rogers preferred to work. So, Rogers adapted some of the T-group structure and combined it with his own clinical approach and positive humanistic views into what he called the **basic encounter group** where "individuals come into much closer and direct contact with one another than is customary in ordinary life" (Rogers, 1967, p. 270).

In the 1970s, variations of these types of groups went by many names—for example, *personal growth groups, sensory awareness groups, sensitivity groups,* and *human relations groups* (Yalom, 1985). They were very popular and experienced "wild flower growth" (Hansen et al., 1980, p. 158). California became the mecca for those interested in a basic encounter group type of experience, but the phenomenon rapidly spread across the country and gained wide acceptance, especially among college students and the middle class. "In its heyday, the decade between 1962 and 1972, a reasonable estimate would be that several million people participated in some form of encounter group" (Bebout, 1978, p. 323). The publicity of encounter groups during this time among the general public was rarely favorable (Lifton, 1972; Yalom, 1985). This was due to the inappropriate and abusive use of such groups by a few publicity-seeking and untrained individuals. By the 1980s, the popularity of encounter groups had waned, but much of their basic format still survives.

Rogers became interested in large-group phenomena in the 1970s and initiated a new group format—the **community for learning**—in which about 100 people lived and worked together for two weeks at a time. Further, Rogers applied person-centered theory to the more formal and established groups found in couples and families (Rogers, 1972, 1977, 1980). The flexibility of the person-centered approach is truly impressive (Raskin & Rogers, 1989). In this chapter, the focus is on Rogers's work with small groups because his involvement and research with these groups is better documented than with other groups with which he worked.

Premises of Person-Centered Group Therapy

Basic encounter groups, as defined by Rogers (1970), are built on several premises. The first is a trust in the inner resources of persons. As Rogers (1980) puts it,

> Individuals have within themselves vast resources for self-understanding and for altering their self-concepts, basic attitudes, and self-directed behavior; these resources can be tapped if a definable climate of facilitative psychological attitudes can be provided. (p. 115)

A second underlying premise of this approach is a sense of trust in the group to help members develop their potential without being directed in a certain way by a leader. This is essentially a belief that encounter groups will promote the basic positive growth tendency that resides within individuals (Rosenbaum, 1974). Rogers (1970) emphasizes that movement in encounter groups will be positive, even when initially ill-defined. "The group will move—of this I am confident—but it would be presumptuous to think that I can or should direct that movement toward a specific goal" (p. 45).

A third major tenet of Rogers's approach is the idea that certain conditions must be created within the group for the group and its members to maximize their full potential (Frank, 1961). *Communication*—for example, the expression by the group leader and group members of empathy, genuineness (congruence), and acceptance (unconditional positive regard)—is necessary. In addition, group members must **actively listen** (i.e., hear meanings behind words and behind nonverbal gestures), self-disclose and unmask pretensions and facades, deal with immediate issues of concern, and, when needed, **confront** (challenge incongruencies in thoughts and actions). "An underlying assumption of an encounter group is that somewhere along the way, people have lost the art of communication" (Hansen et al., 1980, p. 167).

Finally, encounter groups are based on the understanding that a qualified person, who has special training and experience, will facilitate them. Group leaders must be skilled in allowing group members to struggle to express themselves. Furthermore, they must be integrated personally as well as educated professionally.

As opposed to a T-group (the National Training Laboratory model developed by Lewin and colleagues in the 1940s), basic encounter groups are less structured, theoretical, here-and-now oriented, and task oriented. Members are free to talk about their past and present because encounter groups do not make a distinction between "growth and development goals and psychotherapy goals" (Shaffer & Galinsky, 1989, p. 211). Encounter groups also tend to be more process based and more confrontational in feedback than are T-groups.

As a rule, basic encounter groups are more open to allowing a wider range of expressible behaviors than are T-groups. Those who join them are usually more focused on broadening their own **personal growth** (a global emphasis that stresses development as a result of experiences such as travel or encounter) as opposed to working on personal growth issues (an individual emphasis that springs from a perceived deficit or need) (Hansen et al., 1980). However, both deficit and enhancement issues may be dealt with in the group.

Overall, basic encounter groups are established on the premise that individuals who participate in them are relatively healthy. They were initially referred to as **"group therapy for normals"** (Yalom, 1985). In addition, it is assumed these individuals (usually 8 to 18 in number and strangers to each other) will voluntarily commit to attend a select number of group sessions and work on developing a greater sense of awareness and acceptance of themselves and others. They will help themselves and others become more skilled in using personal and interpersonal assets as the group continues.

Practice of Person-Centered Therapy in a Group

There are certain procedures, i.e., techniques and processes, common to encounter groups. One of the most crucial is the creation of a psychological climate in which group members can risk being themselves. To achieve such a therapeutic climate, Rogers (1970) uses an unstructured format in which members can freely express their thoughts and feelings. Trust must also be established. Group members who do not trust one another do not disclose much about themselves or relate very well to others. They fail to develop within the group (Gibb & Gibb, 1969). Group leaders can facilitate the development of trust by disclosing their own negative and positive feelings as they occur. For instance, if group members are simply describing past events in their lives instead of dealing with present experiences, the group leader may say, "I do not think this group as a whole or you as individual members will make much progress unless or until you focus your attention and remarks to what is occurring now in your life."

Feedback and communication are also critical components in encounter group experiences. No real contact can occur between individuals without the expression of feedback and communication. *Feedback* involves one person giving another his or her perception of a behavior. For example, Claudia may say to Carl, "I really like the way you were honest in telling me how you felt about what I suggested to you." *Communication of thoughts and feelings* are best conveyed when clearly understood language and gestures are used. For instance, Matthew may say to Tom in a serious manner, "I find it frustrating when you close up when I ask you to say more in regard to your opinions."

The process in which these basic techniques are employed and the **Rogerian-oriented encounter group stages** are well defined, although they do not always occur in a clear-cut sequence and may vary from group to group. Rogers (1970) delineates a 15-stage process that includes the following patterns:

1. *Milling around*—In the initial stage of the group, members are often confused about who is responsible for conducting the group and what they are supposed to be doing. This confusion results in frustration, silence, and a tendency to keep conversations on a superficial level. Milling around is largely a warm-up activity that prevents members from getting down to business (Hansen et al., 1980).

2. *Resistance*—Group members enter the group with both a public and private self (Vander Kolk, 1985). They tend to avoid exposing their private selves until they have built trust in other members. Therefore, members try to protect themselves and others from revealing too much too fast.

3. *Revealing past feelings*—As trust begins to develop, group members start to talk about their feelings, but only those that are safe to expose, for example, the past. The talk at this point is on there-and-then experiences (i.e., those that are historical) and those that are nonthreatening to expose. Members often act as if what they are saying is related to the present, but in reality it seldom is.

4. *Expression of negative feelings*—As the group develops, initial here-and-now feelings are expressed, but generally in a negative manner. Most of these feelings are directed toward the leader, and they are generally in the form of blame for not providing enough structure. For example, Ralph may say to Kevin, the group leader, "I wish you would either become more active in this group or find us a new leader." Negative feelings are safer to express than positive ones. Rogers hypothesizes that negative feelings occur first because members (a) want to test the trustworthiness of the group, and (b) are less vulnerable to rejection if they are negative, rather than positive.

5. *Expression of personally meaningful material*—It is at this stage that real trust in the group is established. Group members feel free to explore and talk about important meaningful events in their lives. They usually start off being more negative than positive, but change as other group members accept them more. For instance, Peggy may say to the group, "I want to tell you more about myself than you have heard so

far," and then begin to talk about some experiences in her life that she has made known only to very few people.

6. *Communication of immediate interpersonal feelings*—At this point in the life of the group, members begin to be affected by and respond to other group members. They indicate to others how their comments and actions are perceived. For instance, Russell may say to Steve, "Your comments about your life decisions strike me as those of a man with deep regret." Genuine encounter occurs at this point, and participants are now ready to deal with one another.

7. *Development of a healing capacity in the group*—After members have expressed personal feelings about themselves and others, they begin to reach out to one another. This is accomplished after members offer warmth, compassion, understanding, and caring to others in the group who have shared their concerns. "It is the caring attitude of group members more than the expertise of the group facilitator that Rogers believes is of the utmost importance" (Hansen et al., 1980, p. 170). Therefore, when Tommy tells Jean that he cares about her as a person regardless of her past, Jean can begin to take risks.

8. *Self-acceptance and the beginning of change*—As members are accepted more, they become increasingly aware of their own behaviors and feelings and are consequently less rigid. In the process, they open themselves to changes that will lead to more changes. For instance, when Freddie realizes that other members like him even when he is not perfect, he begins to loosen up in what he says and to whom he directs his words.

9. *Cracking of facades*—There is a tendency in encounter groups for members to drop the masks they have been wearing and become more genuine. This process is known as the "cracking of facades." Group members become less tolerant of facades as the group develops and often demand, rather than ask, that an individual stop relating in a polite or superficial way (Donigian & Malnati, 1987).

10. *Feedback*—Through feedback, group members become more self-aware. For instance, Mark may not realize that he is considered to be authoritarian unless other members of the group tell him in the form of feedback. In this stage of the group, feedback is primarily constructive and greatly enhances the ability of a member to perceive how he or she is seen by others.

11. *Confrontation*—At this stage in the process, confrontations of group members become more pronounced as members realize the group is reaching a climax. Confrontation is in the form of both positive and negative feedback.

12. *Helping relationships outside the group*—This stage is a parallel to stage 7, but group members experience healing and helping relationships with each other outside the formal group experience. This process helps them resolve any misunderstandings and develop new relationships.

13. *The basic encounter*—Genuine person-to-person contact is the overriding characteristic at this point in the group. Members come to realize how satisfactory and meaningful it is to relate to one another in such a way. Therefore, George seeks to become closer to Brenda, Betty, and Jerry than previously because he realizes how much he learns from them about himself and human interaction patterns.

14. *Expressions of closeness*—As the group nears completion, group members express positive feelings about their experience and about one another. A sense of group spirit develops more strongly. Thus, Tod may say to the group as a whole, "I feel as if each of you were a member of my family."

15. *Behavior changes*—Behavior changes, the result of increased congruence, are more pronounced toward the end of a group. Members tend to act in a more open, honest, caring manner, and they carry these behaviors into everyday life experiences after the group terminates. For example, Mickey may be more open with strangers after the group than he ever thought about being before he went through the group experience.

Role of the Person-Centered Group Leader

Group leaders of person-centered groups derive their direction from group members. Usually, such leaders view the groups with which they work as being capable and having the inner resources to direct and develop themselves as individuals and as a group (Raskin & Rogers, 1989). The leadership style of such persons is generally more passive than in many other approaches to group work, although Rogers tended to be more confrontive in groups than in individual counseling sessions. Research (Berenson, Mitchell, & Laney, 1968) indicates that effective facilitators confront their clients more frequently in a positive way using empathy and positive regard than do noneffective leaders.

Generally, leaders of Rogerian-based groups are paradigms "for interpersonal effectiveness, modeling the therapeutic norms of openness, congruence, warmth, genuineness, and acceptance" and creating a climate within the group that promotes the development of relationships (Ohlsen, Horne, & Lawe, 1988, p. 68). Gimmicks and planned procedures are not used by group leaders, who are known as **facilitators**. Interpretation and other expert-oriented procedures are ignored. too. Instead, person-centered group leaders participate as a member of the group and share their struggles with the group. In doing so, they attempt to understand each person within the group on a more personal basis and accept themselves and others genuinely (Bozarth, 1981).

Overall, person-centered group leaders carry out five distinct functions: "(1) conveying warmth and empathy, (2) attending to others, (3) understanding meaning and content, (4) conveying acceptance, and (5) linking" (Posthuma, 1989, p. 57). These functions are expressed through such basic group skill techniques as listening, supporting, reflecting, sharing, affirming, clarifying, summarizing, engaging, and, of course, encountering. Overall, leaders use themselves as instruments of change (Corey, 1990). Their attitude toward the group helps to create a climate that makes a difference in the growth of group members.

Desired Person-Centered Group Outcome

Person-centered encounter groups are intended for group members to develop self-awareness and awareness of others. A related goal is personal growth and what Rogers describes as "self-actualization," i.e., becoming all that one can be (Day & Matthes, 1992). Another goal is more openness to experience, especially as it relates to intimacy and meaningfulness with others. Behavior change is hoped for as group members alter their physical gestures and become more relaxed. Finally, there is the desired goal of becoming less alienated from oneself and others (Donigian & Malnati, 1987; Hansen et al., 1980).

Rogers (1970) reports that the desired outcomes of his approach and actual results have been very consistent. In a systematic follow-up study that he conducted, questionnaires were sent to 500 participants of small groups led by him and his associates. The study was conducted three to six months after the group had ended. Only two individuals felt the group experience had been damaging to them, whereas most surveyed reported the group had a positive and long-lasting impact on their behavior. Although there are some problems in doing survey research, it appears that person-centered encounter group members felt that they benefitted from their experiences.

Other researchers, notably Lieberman, Yalom, and Miles (1973), found less positive results and report that almost 10% of the participants they researched reported that marathon, person-centered encounter groups were damaging to them. It should be noted that Rogerians do not prefer marathons or group experiences that last over 12 hours (Landreth, 1984). Nevertheless, Ohlsen et al. (1988) state that more and better research needs to be conducted on the overall impact of basic encounter groups. The outcome of Rogerian-oriented groups is meant to be positive and hopefully long-lasting.

Evaluation of Person-Centered Groups

Person-centered groups have factors that are beneficial for some individuals in some situations. They also have limitations. The benefits and limits of the approach are connected with who is included in the group as well as how the group is used.

Advantages.   The basic encounter group movement has helped traditional group leaders, especially those working from a psychotherapeutic perspective, to become aware of the importance of enhancing the development of the total individual. Up to the 1960s, the focus of group psychotherapists was on reduction, rather than expansion, of their group participants' experiences. After encounter groups gained popularity, group psychotherapists were inclined to stress patients' assets as well as try to alleviate their deficiencies (Yalom, 1985).

A second strength of the person-centered approach has been its emphasis on the group leader (Corey, 1990). The heart of the basic encounter group is the group facilitator (Donigian & Malnati, 1987; Yalom, 1985). The task of the facilitator is to have a genuine interest in others and be able to set up conditions for personal growth. Few other group approaches concentrate as much on the leader as a person. However, most group models have been positively influenced by the person-centered emphasis on the importance of the leader, and there has been a spillover effect. "The traditional 'blank screen' demeanor (of the group leader) is just not possible anymore with most clients" (Lieberman, 1977, p. 26).

A third positive contribution of the basic encounter group model is the emphasis on improving personal communication skills. Maliver (1973) notes that after an encounter group experience, participants are more aware of irritating mannerisms in their communication patterns and may change their behaviors as a result. The change is often long-lasting and productive (Raskin & Rogers, 1989).

A fourth positive influence of basic encounter groups has been in the area of research technology. Yalom (1985) states that before the basic encounter group movement, research of group psychotherapy sessions was rather "crude and unimaginative" (p. 489). Since then, empirical research has become more sophisticated and is rooted in the encounter group tradition of investigation.

Finally, person-centered encounter groups have made group work acceptable for "normals." Because group participants are not seen as "sick," the group can work with individuals on personal development without the stigma of negative labeling. Such an atmosphere has a beneficial effect on a person's willingness to take risks and try out new behaviors.

Limitations.   Encounter groups may be dangerous to participants who need therapy or structure and who try to use these groups as they would more organized psychotherapy groups (Lieberman, Yalom, & Miles, 1973; Vander Kolk, 1985). The mentally retarded, the severely brain damaged, the multiply handicapped, or the severely emotionally disturbed need greater structure and guidance than basic encounter groups provide. These individuals are not ready for the openness of encounter groups and may regress as a result of such an experience.

A second limitation of basic encounter groups is the way in which members and leaders are chosen. There are generally no rules for the selection of encounter group members (Meador, 1975; Wood, 1982). Some individuals may talk their way into such groups by convincing group leaders they can benefit from the experience. Group leader training is also not stressed in this tradition (Corey, 1990), so encounter group facilitators may end up being too passive or too caught up in a **"crash-program mentality"** in which group experiences are carried out to excess (Yalom, 1975). The ethical issue of not screening members and not requiring rigor in the training of group facilitators is critical. Too many problems can occur when there is a lack of screening and training.

A third criticism of the person-centered approach is that it may not lead anywhere. Rogerians as a group have "had little interest in directing the group's conscious attention to its own processes" (Shaffer & Galinsky, 1989, p. 211). Although the qualities espoused by basic encounter group leaders are quite appropriate for beginning a group, the movement of the group may come to a halt because there is no reliance on techniques to motivate members or stir members in a particular direction (Corey, 1990).

A fourth deficit of basic encounter groups is their history. In the 1960s and 1970s, basic encounter groups became a fad and may have lost some of their influence and power as a result. Participants in basic encounter groups emerged from the experiences talking about "finding themselves" and "discovering others." Although the language and the experiences were valid for the time, they may not be as relevant for individuals in the 1990s. Indeed, as Yalom (1985) points out, it is difficult to find a basic encounter group experience now, although much of the structure and technology of this type of group survives in large group awareness programs, such as est and Lifespring.

Another limitation of basic encounter groups centers around the research methods used to evaluate them and their rate of success. The **self-report research format** used by Rogers (1970), in which participants write out or check off how they are different as a result of the group, is attacked as inadequate by empirically oriented investigators. These researchers state that this type of research does not measure the complexity of personal change in a group of this type. Similarly, the claims of success for basic encounter groups is questionable. There are many variations of person-centered encounter groups, so it is hard to determine exactly what variables contributed to the success of which groups and how.

GESTALT GROUPS

Gestalt group work is attributed to Fritz Perls, whose life is a reflection of the theory he developed. Perls was originally trained as a psychoanalyst, and while a practitioner in his native Germany, he incorporated Kurt Goldstein's holistic theory and Wilhelm Reich's idea of *"body armor"* (a notion that gave substance to Freud's concept of resistance) into his clinical work (Vander Kolk, 1985) . Perls was forced to flee Nazism in the early 1930s because of his Jewish background. He settled in South Africa where he encountered the holistic work of Jan Smuts. Then he immigrated to the United States, where his co-authored book, *Gestalt Therapy* (1951), outlined the major tenets of his theory, which was to gain national prominence after his move to the Esalen Institute in Big Sur, California, in 1963.

"Perls himself never claimed to be doing pure group work" (Frew, 1983, p. 175). In fact, "Perls and his immediate disciples preferred to focus on the group solely as a backdrop for individual work" (Shaffer & Galinsky, 1989, p. 121). In his workshops, Perls would concentrate on one individual at a time. The person who wanted to "work" would sit on the **"hot-seat"** with his or her chair facing that of the therapist or leader. The rest of the group served as a kind of "Greek chorus" in the background of the encounter where they resonated and empathized with the one who was working and thereby gained insights into themselves and others through the process of identification. Work sessions would last from 10 to 30 minutes and end with a mutually decided closure.

Overall, Perls was a deep thinker and concerned about the problems of existence (Perls, 1974), but his unique, unconventional, complex, and eccentric life style contributed to a basic misunderstanding of him and his theory (Perls, 1969b). It was the ideas and processes generated by Perls, however, combined with those of Kepner (1980) and Zinker (1977), that have evolved into what is now known as the Gestalt group process.

Premises of Gestalt Group Therapy

There are four basic underlying assumptions of Gestalt therapy according to Latner (1973). First is the **principle of holism** (integration). Often individuals will carry around emotional debris (i.e., "unfinished business") from their past. These concerns are usually linked to resentment and incomplete separation from a lost love-object (Shaffer & Galinsky, 1989). Through a series of prescribed exercises (such as an **empty chair technique** in which the distressed person is given an opportunity to role play and speak to the missing person, say "good-bye," and feel all sides of a situation), integration occurs, and the person becomes more complete, i.e., more than the sum of his or her individual experiences.

A second assumption involves the **principle of awareness.** People are free to choose only when they are *self-aware,* that is, in touch with their existence and what it means to be alive. The concept of awareness includes all sensations, thoughts, and behaviors that individuals experience. It is the "what" of existence and is always focused in the here-and-now, i.e., the present. Awareness often results in insight when a person "owns" his or her control and responsibility over a situation. Awareness and **dialogue** (i.e., talk between others and oneself or between different aspects of oneself) are "the two primary therapeutic tools in Gestalt therapy" (Yontef & Simkin, 1989, p. 333).

Third is the **principle of figure/ground.** The *figure* in one's personal life is composed of experiences that are most important, such as deciding how one will approach a person who is hostile to them. *Background* is composed of experiences that are less pressing, such as what one will do after dinner. Healthy persons take care of their figural (most important) needs first. As figural needs are met, these individuals become more aware of other background needs, some of which become figural and require work.

The fourth principle of Gestalt therapy is the **principle of polarities**. If people are to meet their needs, they must first differentiate their perceptual field into opposites/poles, for example, active/passive, good/bad. The idea is for clients to express both sides of a polarity or conflict and then integrate this experience holistically. Too often people fail to resolve conflicts within themselves and with others because they are not in contact with the opposite sides of the situation.

For example, if Fran sees her father as only good, she will not be able to deal with her relationship with him realistically, especially given the fact that when growing up she had a "love/hate" experience with him.

Overall, Gestalt group process is a complex phenomenon built on the previously cited premises. It is based on the assumption that groups are multidimensional systems that operate on several levels at once. Groups, and people, are holistic with all of their functions interrelated. It is impossible to understand the person in the group outside of the context of the group. Another assumption is that people are *proactive* (i.e., they take the initiative) in making choices, especially if they are self-aware and living in the present (Passons, 1975). As an approach, Gestalt theory views individuals as neither positive nor negative but as **intrinsically neutral**, that is, without a predetermined set of responses.

In addition, Gestalt therapy is premised on the idea that individuals will experience a certain amount of "elasticity" between their more pressing needs (figure) and their less pressing needs (background). **Elasticity** is the ability to move from one set of needs to another and back. It is the elasticity of the figure-ground formation on which selfhood is rooted as individuals define themselves in regard to the needs of which they are most aware. Another way of explaining this phenomenon is to say that people perceive their selves changing in an expanding and contracting way depending on their needs.

A final major idea of the Gestalt approach is that **awareness** (i.e., a total organismic response) gives people self-cohesiveness and enables them. If individuals are healthily aware of themselves and their environments, they choose an active way of dealing with the polarities of their lives. This usually means they integrate the opposite aspects of these polarities and make a choice based on all the information available. Therefore, Gestalt group process stresses increasing awareness, choice, meaningfulness, integrative wholeness, and closure (Mullan & Rosenbaum, 1978; Vander Kolk, 1985).

Practice of Gestalt Therapy in a Group

Gestalt group process is often misperceived as individual "hot-seat" psychotherapy in a group setting (Shaffer & Galinsky, 1989; Yalom, 1975, 1985), even though Perls (1967) distinguished his workshop style, in which he would often interact with someone in this manner, from other forms of Gestalt groups. Actually, Gestalt groups function in several ways. One typical way is for the Gestalt leader to focus on one person in the presence of other group members and work with him or her. This is more of a traditional West Coast practice, according to Latner (1973), where Gestalt practitioners who have been heavily influenced by Perls "pay attention to the issues of self-awareness, centering, and responsibility" (Corey, 1985, p. 300). The traditional East Coast style of Gestalt group work is more interactive, long-term, and cognitive.

Yet, another style that has no geographic identification is **dual-focused Gestalt group work** (Harman, 1988). In this approach, attention is concentrated on "group process with the power of individual work within the group" (p. 230). One older variation of this model is the so-called **floating hot-seat** (Polster & Polster, 1973; Yontef & Simkin, 1989) in which interaction is promoted by encouraging group members to work on exploring their own personal issues when someone else in the group touches on an issue that has personal relevance for them. A newer form of this approach is Kepner's (1980) Gestalt group process in which attention is systematically focused on (a) the individual at the intrapersonal level, (b) two or more people at the interpersonal level, and (c) the group as a systematic unit. Kepner's **tri-level model of Gestalt group work** illustrates how dynamic Gestalt group work can be. Overall, there is no one style of Gestalt group practice.

Despite a diversity in operating procedures, Gestalt group practitioners share many common beliefs and practices. First, they stay centered on here-and-now (i.e., present) experiences. They do this by asking how and what questions, instead of why. Second, Gestalt group practitioners ask their group members to work on a specific problem in order to help foster greater awareness. Sometimes, group members may be actively involved in helping a member process what is happening in his or her work. At other times, the interaction is between the group leader and the group member with the rest of the group functioning as a background. Regardless, the focus is on individual responsibility and integration (Perls, 1969a).

A third quality that Gestalt practitioners share is their emphasis on behavioral, rather than cognitive, processes (Zinker, 1977). Inviting group members to participate in a therapeutic or growth experience, rather than talk about their problem, is helpful for most. Finally, Gestalt practitioners use a series of experiments and exercises to help their members achieve greater awareness and growth (Resnikoff, 1988). **Experiments** are nonplanned experiences that occur spontaneously in the session. For example, if a group member starts waving her arms when talking about how she wishes to be free of her present life circumstances, the group leader might say to her, "Melody, develop that more," at which time the member might begin to exaggerate the arm movement into a wing-like flapping motion. In response to this motion, the leader might encourage the member to "fly," at which point the member might take off and pretend to fly around the room. The experience would then be processed. **Exercises**, on the other hand, are planned activities that have been used previously to help group members become more aware. For example, having a member role play or fantasize a situation is a type of exercise.

Both experiments and exercises revolve around five main themes: (a) enactment, (b) directed behavior, (c) fantasy, (d) dreams, and (e) homework (Polster & Polster, 1973). They all occur in the present and are chosen for the specific purpose of promoting growth (Vander Kolk, 1985). Some of the better known exercises are explored here.

Making the rounds is a warm-up game in Gestalt groups in which confrontation is heightened. In this exercise, group members are asked to say something they usually do not verbalize. For example, a person might say to all group members, "I am afraid to tell you about myself . . . because. . . ." or "When I try to ask for help from you, I feel. . . ." In such cases, the member who makes the rounds with all other members may become aware and "feel like working through some unfinished materials of the past, in which case rounds would be suspended" (Hansen et al., 1980), and the individual in relationship with the group leader and other members would work together.

Two other types of enactment are *rehearsals* and *role reversals.* In **rehearsals,** group members are invited to say out loud what they are thinking internally. For example, they may note how much they struggle to please others and perform properly. They are then free to decide whether they wish to spend their time and energy in this manner. In **role reversals**, people act the opposite of what they feel. For instance, a person who is feeling inadequate will act adequate, even bold. By doing so, the group member gets a feel for an area he or she previously denied.

Body language is another exercise in which group members are invited to participate. Here the emphasis is placed on what a person's body is doing, such as a hand tapping a chair, or a leg kicking. The leader asks participants displaying such behaviors, "What is your hand saying?" or "What is your leg doing?" Participants are then free to emphasize what their behaviors mean. They may do this through exaggerating the behavior or simply noting its present movement. The result is an integration of mind and body awareness.

Another technique that is often used in Gestalt groups is **changing questions to statements.** This procedure requires a group member who has raised a question to make it into a statement. For instance, the question, "Do you really think that is why you did not succeed?" would be changed to "I do not think that is why you were unsuccessful." Changing questions to statements helps all group members become more aware of their true feelings. It also helps eliminate **condemning questions** that put people down and prevent them from seeing situations more honestly and openly. "Don't you think you should feel differently?" is an example of a condemning question.

The **empty chair** is a technique designed to help group members deal with different aspects of their personalities (Fagan & Shepherd, 1970). This technique is often used in individual Gestalt sessions but is also effective in group settings. Two variations of the technique will be discussed here. In both, an empty chair is placed in front of the group member who wishes to work. In the first variation, the participant is asked to put into the chair all of the feelings that are opposite of the way he or she usually feels—such as anger, aggressive, and impulsive. The individual then switches seats and becomes the feelings put into the chair. A dialogue is promoted between the polar parts of the individual with the person changing chairs every time he or she switches feelings. The idea is to promote an integration of feelings and thoughts.

In the second variation, **unfinished business** (the tendency of a person to relive past thoughts and feelings in the present) is the focus. Unfinished business usually centers on unacknowledged grief, anger, or loss of objects, and remains in the background of people's lives, inhibiting their ability to function realistically in the present. Participants who have unfinished business are often asked to put the object, feeling, or person in the empty chair and say good-bye. Sometimes another group member can play the part of whatever was placed in the chair and say good-bye in return.

A variation of the integrative empty chair technique is the **Top-Dog/Underdog Dialogue.** In this method, group members are asked to examine the *top-dog intro-jections* they have taken in from parents (usually represented by "shoulds" and "you") and their own real feelings about situations (usually represented by "I" statements). For example, "You should always be polite, but sometimes I do not feel that way." They then are asked to carry on a dialogue between these two aspects of themselves before the group or with another group member and try to become more aware of their true self-identity and ways to act that would be appropriate.

Fantasy exercises are another popular method used in Gestalt group work. Corey (1985) notes that fantasy can be employed to help group members (a) be more concrete in assessing their feelings, (b) deal with catastrophic experiences, (c) explore and express feelings of guilt and shame, and (d) become more involved in the group. It is not necessary that group members live out their fantasies, for example, conveying their repressed feelings of resentment to an elderly relative. Just the fact that they are acting as if they were doing what they have hoped for is helpful to most in becoming more integrative and holistic.

Dream work is seen by Perls (1969a) as "the royal road to integration." It is utilized in both individual and group work by having those who dream recreate and relive the dream in the present. By doing so, these individuals become all parts of the dream. They may do this through working alone in the group setting or having others in the group act out different parts of the dream. This latter idea is known as *dream work as theater* (Zinker, 1977). It assumes that there are basic archetypal themes that all group members share and can benefit from experiencing.

Dreams are expressions of the polarities within individuals in Gestalt theory. Therefore, it is important to act out the different parts and become conscious of the forces within. Rainwater (1979) suggests that people explore their dreams by asking themselves certain questions such as "What am I feeling?" "What do I want?" "What am I doing?" and "What is my dream telling me?" By questioning and enacting with others, individuals become more aware, integrated, and empowered to act.

Homework is a technique that primarily involves group members practicing outside the group what they have learned inside the group. For example, members may make statements to their colleagues instead of asking them condemning questions. Homework helps group members achieve closure on unresolved issues.

Role of the Gestalt Group Leader

The group leader is central to the functioning of the Gestalt group (Hansen et al., 1980). The leader is usually the person who "determines much of what will take place, and with whom and when such interaction will occur" (p. 217). One of the leader's jobs is to help group members locate their **impasses** (the places in which they get stuck) and work ways through them so awareness and growth will take place (Corey, 1990). In order to achieve this goal and promote a therapeutic breakthrough, the leader may intentionally frustrate group members by refusing to play their manipulative games, such as being helpless or stupid. Perls (1969a) puts it this way, "My function as a therapist is to help you to the awareness of the here and now, and to frustrate you in any attempt to break out of this" (p. 74). The leader balances the challenging of group members with the support of them.

Zinker (1977) sees the leader's role in this process as an artist. It is up to the leader to create an atmosphere that promotes growth within the group and the group's own creativity. To do so, the group leader must self-disclose and allow things to happen. He or she must be "agenda free" and must block off any attempts by group members or the group as a whole to desert the "now." This may mean that the leader asks group members or the group, "What is happening to you (us) now?" It also means that the group leader makes sure everyone speaks for himself or herself by using "I messages" instead of "you messages" (Donigian & Malnati, 1987), for example, "I feel happy when dancing," rather than "You feel happy when dancing." Whenever possible and appropriate, "should" messages are changed to "want-to" messages.

Overall, as Levin and Shepherd (1974) have pointed out, Gestalt group leaders play several roles over the life span of the group: (a) expert-helper; (b) see-er, communications expert; (c) frustrater; (d) creator; and (e) teacher. Leaders must balance these roles with personal integrity and have the strength to withstand pressures from the group not to stay in the present. They must not rely on gimmicks in order to try to promote growth of group members, yet they cannot be passive (Resnikoff, 1988). They must trust their intuition and play their hunches. In many ways, competent Gestalt group leaders are "catalysts" (Shaffer & Galinsky, 1989). They keep group members focused on "now" issues and help them increase awareness and find personal/interpersonal resolutions for issues that emerge.

Desired Gestalt Group Outcome

As a result of a Gestalt group, members should be more aware of themselves in the here-and-now. They should also change (Flores, 1988). It is hoped they will have shed **layers of neurosis** (i.e., the *phony*—being unauthentic; the *phobic*—being afraid to really see themselves as they are; and the *impasse*—where their maturity is stuck). Then they can come to realize self-growth through *implosiveness*—feeling their deadness—and *explosiveness*—releasing pent-up energy to be authentic and alive to all feelings (Perls, 1970). The bottom line is that members will be more congruent in themselves (mind and body) and with others. They will not be mired down in worrying about the past and will become more self-regulating. The experiential quality of Gestalt groups is especially beneficial for persons who are predominantly cognitive, for it forces them to use other ways of relating.

Thousands of people have experienced favorable results through participating in Gestalt groups (Yontef & Simkin, 1989). In a well-designed study, Lieberman et al. (1973) actually found Gestalt group members rated their experience first among 17 different groups in regard to pleasantness and constructiveness. They felt they had learned a great deal and were enthusiastic. They rated their group leader highly. The key to whether a Gestalt group is beneficial or not is whether the leader is well-trained.

Evaluation of Gestalt Groups

There are advantages and limitations of Gestalt groups that must be recognized before individuals decide to enroll in or conduct such groups. Whether a Gestalt group is right for a person or a situation depends on that particular person or situation.

Advantages.   One strength of Gestalt groups is their particular suitability to group leaders "who have a humanistic, existential approach to helping others" (Vander Kolk, 1985, p. 82). Gestalt group work lends itself well to those who are creative and who strive to bring out the creativity in others. It emphasizes the affective dimension of human existence, which is often neglected in groups.

A second advantage of Gestalt groups is that the focus within the groups is on working through impasses and becoming more integrated. Members may help each other feel more connected and less alone than if Gestalt work were conducted individually. As Frew (1983) points out, there is power in the group that comes from member and group interaction, as well as from leader and member interaction.

A third strong point of Gestalt groups is the variety of exercises and experiences they foster. Gestalt group work is usually intense and active (Day & Matthes, 1992). By participating in planned and spontaneous activities, group members come to realize different aspects about themselves than they might through just talking. The group is also influential in forcing members out of previously unproductive patterns of interacting.

Another strength of the Gestalt groups is the abundance of training institutes available to professionals who wish to learn this approach. There are several publications devoted to this approach too, including *The Gestalt Journal,* which is primarily devoted to articles on Gestalt therapy. Group leaders have a reservoir of rich resources available to them, if they are careful in screening the backgrounds of those with whom they work and study (Yontef & Simkin, 1989).

Limitations.   The limitations of Gestalt theory and practice in groups mirror its strengths. First, the Gestalt approach tends to eschew the cognitive side of human nature. Perls and the Gestalt theory are often accused of being anti-intellectual and concerned only with affective and bodily experiences. Perls's famous statement, "Lose your mind and come to your senses," is often quoted in support of this criticism.

A second limitation of Gestalt groups is that group leaders are sometimes not able to help the group help itself, that is, work through impasses. When this occurs, there is individual leader/member interaction, or there is uncontrolled group pressure on individuals to do things they are not ready to do. Either case is nonproductive at best and can be destructive.

A third limitation of the Gestalt approach is the potential danger of abusing techniques and people (Corey, 1990). Unless the group leader is particularly sensitive to the needs of group members, he or she may become mechanical in showing off techniques and not really be helpful. Ethical questions are of major concern if the group leader opens up members' feelings and then does not help them resolve these emotions in an integrative fashion. There is no national organization of Gestalt therapists, no standards for leaders, and no agreed-upon methods for the practice of this theory (Yontef & Simkin, 1989). Consumers of Gestalt groups must be aware of professionals with whom they work.

Finally, Gestalt groups are extremely difficult to research (Fagan & Shepherd, 1970). Very little empirical research has been conducted on them. Although Simkin (1975) may be correct in saying, "Most Gestalt therapists are busy practicing their art rather than evaluating it" (p.283), more research must be conducted if this approach is to continue within the mainstream of group work (Rudestam, 1982). Yalom (1985), for instance, has already dismissed Gestalt group work by saying, "I feel that Perls's group therapy technique is ill-founded and makes inefficient use of a group's therapeutic potential" (p. 453).

SUMMARY AND CONCLUSION

In this chapter, the various nuances of person-centered and Gestalt groups have been discussed. Person-centered groups, especially their most famous form, the basic encounter group, are both a historical footnote in the group work movement and a present reality. Many individuals participated in basic encounter groups in the 1960s and 1970s. The influence of these groups lives on in these people's memories as well as in some groups that are still conducted according to the basic encounter group model.

Carl Rogers (1970) introduced the concept and format of basic encounter groups in the 1960s. They caught on quickly and were widely imitated, partially due to the transitional nature of the period. As a scientist-practitioner, Rogers investigated the impact of these groups and generally found them to make a positive contribution to the lives of individuals participating in them. True to his theory and belief about human nature, he set up the groups in a largely unstructured way believing that the goodness and growth within people would emerge. He noted how the typical group session went and wrote about his findings.

Today, basic encounter groups primarily survive in a less formal format but are the basis of several religious and self-help groups (Yalom, 1985). The bad publicity and negative findings associated with these groups in the past probably means they will not emerge as a widespread popular movement again. Yet, their legacy in the group field is noteworthy. They contributed to new expectations of members and leaders in groups, as well as fostering attention on how communication patterns change in a group setting and how group research should be conducted.

The influence of Gestalt groups has waned, also. At their zenith in the 1970s, Gestalt groups were perceived as exciting and active places to work. The processes within these groups, when properly conducted, helped group members become self-aware and integrated. The approach worked on an individual, interpersonal, and group level. Most often, it was associated with Fritz Perls and a dynamic one-on-one encounter, but the approach eventually became diversified. More than just gimmicks are now employed in Gestalt groups to help members in their growth (Resnikoff, 1988).

Gestalt group processes have received favorable reviews from their participants (Lieberman et al., 1973), but there is still controversy surrounding the use of these groups. Part of the controversy is based on a lack of empirical evidence to support the effectiveness of Gestalt groups. A second part of the controversy is connected with the perception that the groups are all action and no thought. Gestalt group leaders will have to take more productive steps in the future to set aside these criticisms and form uniform standards for training and the conduct of groups (Yontef & Simkin, 1989).

Overall, person-centered and Gestalt theories are and have been important as ways of conducting groups. Leaders within these approaches are challenged to renew and develop different approaches whereby these theories may be utilized in groups in the future.

CLASSROOM EXERCISES

1. Read a recent article (within the last five years) on a person-centered or a Gestalt group. Discuss the content of the article with three other classmates. What were the major findings?

2. Would you have to change your personal style of interaction in order to become a leader of either a person-centered or a Gestalt group (e.g., become more aware, become more/less active)? Discuss the changes you would have to make, if any, with a classmate and then with the group as a whole.

3. Which of the Gestalt exercises listed in this chapter do you think would be effective if you were leading a counseling group? Would they be the same if you were leading a psychoeducational group or a task group? Discuss your answer with other classmates in the group as a whole.

4. With another classmate, compare either the person-centered or Gestalt approaches to group work with psychoanalytic or Adlerian group work. Keep your remarks focused on the comparisons between the two approaches you choose. Share your remarks with another dyad.

REFERENCES

Bebout, J. (1978). Basic encounter groups: Their nature, method, and brief history. In H. Mullan & M. Rosenbaum (Eds.), *Group psychotherapy: Theory and practice* (2nd ed.) (pp. 305–329). New York: The Free Press.

Berenson, B. G., Mitchell, K. M., & Laney, R. C. (1968). Therapeutic conditions after therapist-initiated confrontation. *Journal of Clinical Psychology, 24,* 363–364.

Bozarth, J. D. (1981). The person-centered approach in the large community group. In G. Gazda (Ed.), *Innovations to group psychotherapy* (2nd ed.). Springfield, IL: Charles C. Thomas.

Corey, G. (1985). *Theory and practice of group counseling* (2nd ed.).Pacific Grove, CA: Brooks/Cole.

Corey, G. (1990). *Theory and practice of group counseling* (3rd ed.). Pacific Grove, CA: Brooks/Cole.

Day, B., & Matthes, W. (1992). A comparison of Jungian, Person-Centered, and Gestalt approaches to personal growth groups. *Journal for Specialists in Group Work, 17,* 105–115.

Donigian, J., & Malnati, R. (1987). *Critical incidents in group therapy.* Monterey, CA: Brooks/Cole.

Fagan, J., & Shepherd, I. (1970). *Gestalt therapy now.* Palo Alto, CA: Science and Behavior Books.

Flores, P. J. (1988). *Group psychotherapy with addicted populations.* New York: Haworth Press.

Frank, J. D. (1961). *Persuasion and healing.* Baltimore: Johns Hopkins Press.

Frew, J. E. (1983). Encouraging what is not figural in the Gestalt group. *Journal for Specialists in Group Work, 8,* 175–181.

George, R. L., & Dustin, D. (1988). *Group counseling.* Englewood Cliffs, NJ: Prentice Hall.

Gibb, J. R., & Gibb, L. M. (1969). Role freedom in a TORI group. In A. Burton (Ed.), *Encounter: The theory and practice of encounter groups* (pp. 42–57). San Francisco: Jossey-Bass.

Gladding, S. T. (1975). Reflections. *Personnel and Guidance Journal, 53,* 429.

Hansen, J. C., Warner, R. W., & Smith, E. J. (1980). *Group counseling: Theory and process* (2nd ed.). Chicago: Rand McNally.

Harman, R. L. (1988). Gestalt group therapy. In S. Long (Ed.), *Six group therapies* (pp. 217–255). New York: Plenum.

Kepner, E. (1980). Gestalt group process. In B. Feder & R. Ronall (Eds.), *Beyond the hot seat: Gestalt approaches to group* (pp. 5–24). New York: Brunner/Mazel.

Landreth, G. L. (1984). Encountering Carl Rogers: His views on facilitating groups. *Personnel and Guidance Journal, 62,* 323–326.

Latner, J. (1973). *The Gestalt therapy book.* New York: Julian Press.

Levin, L. S., & Shepherd, I. L. (1974). The role of the therapist in Gestalt therapy. *The Counseling Psychologist, 4,* 27–30.

Lieberman, M. A. (1977). Problems in integrating traditional group therapies with new forms. *Journal of International Group Psychotherapy, 27,* 19–33.

Lieberman, M. A., Yalom, I. D., & Miles, M. (1973). *Encounter groups: First facts.* New York: Basic Books.

Lifton, W. M. (1972). *Groups: Facilitating individual and societal change.* New York: Wiley.

Maliver, B. L. (1973). *The encounter game.* New York: Stein & Day.

Meador, B. D. (1975). Client-centered group therapy. In G. Gazda (Ed.), *Basic approaches to group psychotherapy and group counseling* (2nd ed.). Springfield, IL: Charles C. Thomas.

Mullan, H., & Rosenbaum, M. (1978). *Group psychotherapy* (2nd ed.). New York: The Free Press.

Ohlsen, M. M., Horne, A. M., & Lawe, C. F. (1988). *Group counseling* (3rd ed.). New York: Holt, Rinehart & Winston.

Passons, W. R. (1975). *Gestalt approaches in counseling.* New York: Holt, Rinehart & Winston.

Perls, F. (1967). Group vs. individual therapy. *A Review of General Semantics, 24,* 306–312.

Perls, F. (1969a). *Gestalt therapy verbatim.* New York: Bantam.

Perls, F. (1969b). *In and out of the garbage pail.* New York: Bantam.

Perls, F. (1970). Four lectures. In J. Fagan & I. L. Shepherd (Eds.), *Gestalt therapy now.* New York: Harper & Row.

Perls, F. (1974). *The Gestalt approach and eye witness to therapy.* Ben Lomond, CA: Science and Behavior Books.

Perls, F., Hefferline, R. F., & Goodman, P. (1951). *Gestalt therapy.* New York: Dell.

Polster, I., & Polster, M. (1973). *Gestalt therapy integrated: Contours of theory and practice.* New York: Brunner/Mazel.

Posthuma, B. W. (1989). *Small groups in therapy settings: Process and leadership.* Boston: College-Hill.

Rainwater, J. (1979). *You're in charge! A guide to becoming your own therapist.* Los Angeles: Guild of Tutors Press.

Raskin, N. J., & Rogers, C. R. (1989). In R. J. Corsini & D. Wedding (Eds.), *Current psychotherapies* (4th ed.) (pp. 154–194) . Itasca, IL: Peacock.

Resnikoff, R. (1988, October). *Gestalt couples therapy.* Paper presented at the 46th Annual Conference of the American Association for Marriage and Family Therapy, New Orleans.

Rogers, C. R. (1951). *Client-centered therapy.* Boston: Houghton Mifflin.

Rogers, C. R. (1957). The necessary and sufficient conditions of therapeutic personality change. *Journal of Consulting Psychology, 21,* 95–103.

Rogers, C. R. (1959). A theory of therapy, personality, and interpersonal relationships, as developed in the client-centered framework. In S. Koch (Ed.), *Psychology: A study of science.* New York: McGraw-Hill.

Rogers, C. R. (1967). The process of the basic encounter group. In J. F. T. Bugenthal (Ed.), *Challenges of humanistic psychology.* New York: McGraw-Hill.

Rogers, C. R. (1970). *Carl Rogers on encounter groups.* New York: Harper & Row.

Rogers, C. R. (1972). *Becoming partners: Marriage and its alternatives.* New York: Delacorte.

Rogers, C. R. (1977). *Carl Rogers on personal power: Inner strength and its revolutionary impact.* New York: Delacorte.

Rogers, C. R. (1980). *A way of being.* Boston: Houghton Mifflin.

Rosenbaum, M. (1974). An overview of group psychotherapy and the present trend. In D. S. Milman & G. D. Goldman (Eds.), *Group process today: Evaluation and perspective* (pp. 15–36). Springfield, IL: Charles C. Thomas.

Rudestam, K. E. (1982). *Experiential groups in theory and practice.* Pacific Grove, CA: Brooks/Cole.

Shaffer, J., & Galinsky, M. D. (1989). *Models of group therapy* (2nd ed.). Englewood Cliffs, NJ: Prentice Hall.

Simkin, J. S. (1975). Gestalt therapy in groups. In G. M. Gazda (Ed.), *Basic approaches to group psychotherapy and group counseling* (2nd ed.) (pp. 265–286). Springfield, IL: Charles C. Thomas.

Vander Kolk, C. J. (1985). *Introduction to group counseling and psychotherapy.* Columbus, OH: Merrill.

Wood, J. K. (1982). Person-centered group therapy. In G. Gazda (Ed.), *Basic approaches to group psychotherapy and group counseling* (3rd ed.). Springfield, IL: Charles C. Thomas.

Yalom, I. D. (1975). *The theory and practice of group psychotherapy* (2nd ed.). New York: Basic Books.

Yalom, I. D. (1985). *The theory and practice of group psychotherapy* (3rd ed.). New York: Basic Books.

Yontef, G. M., & Simkin, J. S. (1989). Gestalt therapy. In R. J. Corsini & D. Wedding (Eds.), *Current psychotherapies* (4th ed.) (pp. 322–361). Itasca, IL: Peacock.

Zinker, J. (1977). *Creative process in group therapy.* New York: Vintage Books.

CHAPTER 15

Rational-Emotive Therapy and Transactional Analysis Groups

In the long-shadowed days of winter
*   when the cold seeps through to the depths of your thoughts*
*   and engraves crystal frost on morning windows,*
You awaken inner dreams—
*   images that have laid dormant since summer*
*   when you, warmed by the August sun,*
*   built sandcastles and called your expectations by name.*
Slowly, with chilled fingers,
*   you handle slow-moving memories,*
*   examining them like slightly blurred pictures,*
Under the light from a nearby lamp
*   that flickers off and on*
*   like the sound of your voice*
*   which flows in broken waves. . . .**

Thoughts may serve a positive role in people's lives by being expressed through memories that remind them of earlier, pleasant times; through awareness by assisting them in becoming more conscious of what they are experiencing in the present; or through projection by helping them envision themselves in the future. Thoughts may also have a negative impact on people, especially when they occur involuntarily and are negative (as in posttraumatic stress syndrome) or when their content is irrational and skewed.

Cognitive theories of group work focus primarily on how thought processes affect the overall functioning of group members. These theories include a wide

Source: Gladding, 1977, p. 184. Copyright ACA. Reprinted by permission of the American Counseling Association.

variety of approaches, from a pure emphasis on cognitive restructuring to a combined cognitive-behavioral emphasis that stresses the importance of integrating thoughts and behavior in a social learning format. Overall, **cognitive approaches to human relations** are "based on a theory of personality which maintains that how one thinks largely determines how one feels and behaves" (Beck & Weishaar, 1989, p. 285). Rational-emotive therapy (RET) and transactional analysis (TA), the two theories examined here, have followed the trend of other cognitive approaches by expanding their strategies and techniques through the years.

Cognitive theories, as a rule, are usually not employed entirely by themselves. The reason is simple. Alone, they do not produce much action outside of thinking. Therefore, RET is often combined with behavioral methods (Weinrach, 1980), whereas transactional analysis is frequently integrated with Gestalt techniques (James & Jongeward, 1971). Besides this shared practical feature, both RET and TA emphasize the importance of **self talk** (i.e., the messages people give themselves internally) in influencing the mental health and actions of individuals. They also share an aversion to psychoanalysis, although the creators of both theories, Albert Ellis and Eric Berne, respectively, were originally trained in this modality. Furthermore, these approaches are nondeterministic and interactional in nature. Thus, it is fitting that RET and TA be considered together.

In this chapter, similarities and differences between rational-emotive therapy and transactional analysis will be highlighted in regard to group work. Like Adlerian, Rogerian, Gestalt, and psychoanalytic theories, these two cognitive models are used with both individuals and groups. They came into prominence at about the same time (the late 1950s and early 1960s), and they have influenced how practitioners have conceptualized and conducted groups, especially those that have had psychoeducational and psychotherapeutic emphases.

RATIONAL-EMOTIVE THERAPY GROUPS

Rational-emotive therapy groups originated in 1958 when Albert Ellis noticed that working in groups was beneficial and economical for his clients (Vander Kolk, 1985). From the beginning, RET groups have been quite varied. Sometimes the groups are as large as 100 and meet for the purpose of demonstrating RET principles. In such cases, the emphasis is on a combination of psychoeducational and psychotherapeutic principles regarding a specific topic (Wessler, 1986).

Other types of groups conducted by RET practitioners include open-ended and closed-ended psychotherapy and counseling sessions which may include group marathons. Most RET groups of this nature usually meet weekly, with open-ended ones being conducted on an indefinite basis over a number of months, and closed-ended ones seldom meeting for more than 10 to 12 sessions. Marathons are conducted on a 12- to 36-hour basis depending on the leader and setting. The numbers in RET groups are usually limited to a dozen. This arrangement allows group members to receive maximum feedback from others and to make contributions to the group as a whole. The dynamic interaction among members in such settings is not possible on a one-to-one level.

Premises of Rational-Emotive Groups

The underlying premises of RET are both stoic and humanistic. RET is based on the idea that it is one's thinking about events that produces feelings, not situations themselves. Individuals who have negative, faulty, or irrational thoughts become emotionally disturbed or upset and act in nonproductive ways, whereas those with more neutral or positive thoughts feel calmer and behave constructively (Ellis, 1962). Therefore, in order to behave rationally, individuals need to first control their thoughts (Ellis, 1962). If persons can change their irrational beliefs to rational ones, they will suffer less and actually enjoy life (Wessler, 1986).

The process of change is built on an **A-B-C model of human interaction** (see Figure 15.1). "A" is the event, "B" is the thought process, and "C" is the feeling state resulting from one's thoughts. To change negative or nonproductive feelings, individuals need to think differently. According to Ellis, there are **four types of thoughts: negative, positive, neutral, and mixed**. Negative thoughts concentrate on painful or disappointing aspects of an event; positive thoughts focus on just the opposite. Neutral cognitions are those that are neither positive nor negative, whereas those that are mixed contain elements of the other three thought processes.

Although people are entitled to feel as much emotion as they want about events, Ellis's approach allows individuals to control their affect by switching the focus of their thoughts, for example, from negative to neutral (Ellis, 1988; Harper & Ellis, 1975). In so doing, people can make better-informed decisions and relate productively with themselves and others.

RET stresses the **dual nature of human beings.** Individuals have both rational and irrational beliefs that can be modified through disputation (Ellis, 1976). Self-rating is discouraged in this approach because no one can live up to a label, such as "good," and individuals tend to become discouraged when they act differently from what they believe is perfect behavior for themselves. Therefore, Ellis advocates that individuals see themselves as "fallible human beings" who act in certain ways in specific circumstances. By avoiding labels and forms of the verb "to be" (e.g., am, are, was), people are able to live more rational lives (Harper & Ellis, 1975).

Overall, RET can be thought of as a philosophy of life as well as a treatment for changing behaviors (Wessler & Hankin, 1988). If individuals can learn to think more rationally, they are more likely to stop inappropriately evaluating themselves, others, and events in the world over which they have no control (Ellis, 1989; Wessler, 1986). By doing so, they can also quit **making wishes into demands,** for example, using "should," "ought," and "must" in regard to an action. They are then released to deal with themselves and their environments realistically.

Figure 15.1
The ABC model of human interaction.

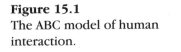 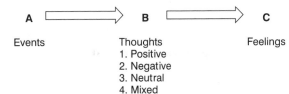

A → B → C

Events   Thoughts   Feelings
             1. Positive
             2. Negative
             3. Neutral
             4. Mixed

Practice of Rational-Emotive Groups

RET groups vary according to the type of group being led. Some groups are open ended with a constant influx of new members, whereas others are closed and limited to the same people who began the group (Wessler & Hankin, 1988). Regardless of the format, RET groups tend to be didactic, philosophical, and skills oriented (Corey, 1990; Hansen, Warner, & Smith, 1980). RET theory is introduced to the group by the leader, and then group members are asked to share troublesome problems or concerns which are usually of a personal nature. These situations are analyzed using the ABCs of therapeutic intervention. Group members, as well as the leader, give feedback and suggestions to the person who initially presented (Ellis, 1984). The feedback is in the form of disputation, which takes three main forms: cognitive, imaginal, and behavioral (Gladding, 1992). The process is most effective if all three forms are used (Walen, DiGiuseppe, & Wessler, 1980).

Cognitive disputation involves direct questioning, reasoning, and persuasion. It may involve asking the question "Why?"—an inquiry seldom employed in helping relationships such as counseling and psychotherapy. For example, group members might ask each other, "Why must that occur?" Cognitive disputation also involves monitoring one's self-talk in regard to giving oneself irrational or absolute messages. Sichel and Ellis (1984) have developed a self-help form to assist clients in identifying irrational beliefs (see Figure 15.2).

Imaginal disputation, a technique first devised by Maxie Maultsby (1984), has participants seeing themselves in stressful situations and examining their self-talk. Then they go through the sequence again, but in the process modifying their self-talk so it is more rational. For example, individuals might imagine themselves taking a major test while initially telling themselves they did not have a chance to pass. The same scene would then be envisioned in which group members would tell themselves more positive or neutral statements, such as "I have studied hard and I am ready" or "I will think each question through before putting down an answer." The RET self-help form can be of value to these individuals, too.

Behavioral disputation involves many forms from reading (bibliotherapy) to role-playing in the group. Often enactment of the problem within the group setting and possible ways of handling it are used. Homework may then be assigned in the form of **shame attacks** (in which the person actually does what he or she dreaded and finds the world does not fall apart regardless of the outcome). For example, a shame attack for Shirley might involve speaking to Ned and confirming in her mind that her self-worth is not based on whether he responds. Ellis actually used such a behavioral exercise in his early adulthood (Dryden, 1989; Ellis, 1989).

Very little attention is paid to past events in the group. It is not that these events are not important, but the focus of the group is on the here-and-now (Wessler & Hankin, 1988). In general, RET groups, which are primarily focused on counseling and psychotherapy, use a "no holds barred approach" (Hansen et al., 1980, p. 243). There are virtually no restrictions placed on the types of subjects that can be discussed. The important point is that members of the group learn to handle themselves better in a variety of difficult situations by thinking rationally

RET SELF-HELP FORM

Institute for Rational-Emotive Therapy
45 East 65th Street, New York, N.Y. 10021
(212) 535-0822

(A) ACTIVATING EVENTS, thoughts, or feelings that happened just before I felt emotionally disturbed or acted self-defeatingly: _____

(C) CONSEQUENCE or CONDITION—disturbed feeling or self-defeating behavior—that I produced and would like to change: _____

(B) BELIEFS—Irrational BELIEFS (IBs) leading to my CONSEQUENCE (emotional disturbance or self-defeating behavior). Circle all that apply to these ACTIVATING EVENTS (A).	(D) DISPUTES for each circled IRRATIONAL BELIEF. Examples: "Why MUST I do very well?" "Where is it written that I am a BAD PERSON?" "Where is the evidence that I MUST be approved or accepted?"	(E) EFFECTIVE RATIONAL BELIEFS (RBs) to replace my IRRATIONAL BELIEFS (IBs). Examples: "I'd PREFER to do very well but I don't HAVE TO." "I am a PERSON WHO acted badly, not a BAD PERSON." "There is no evidence that I HAVE TO be approved, though I would LIKE to be."
1. I MUST do well or very well!		
2. I am a BAD OR WORTHLESS PERSON when I act weakly or stupidly.		
3. I MUST be approved or accepted by people I find important!		
4. I NEED to be loved by someone who matters to me a lot!		
5. I am a BAD, UNLOVABLE PERSON if I get rejected.		
6. People MUST treat me fairly and give me what I NEED!		
7. People MUST live up to my expectations, or it is TERRIBLE!		
8. People who act immorally are undeserving, ROTTEN PEOPLE!		
9. I CAN'T STAND really bad things or very difficult people!		
10. My life MUST have few major hassles or troubles.		
11. It's AWFUL or HORRIBLE when major things don't go my way!		
12. I CAN'T STAND IT when life is really unfair!		
13. I NEED a good deal of immediate gratification and HAVE to feel miserable when I don't get it!		
Additional Irrational Beliefs:		

(F) FEELINGS and BEHAVIORS I experienced after arriving at my EFFECTIVE RATIONAL BELIEFS: _____

I WILL WORK HARD TO REPEAT MY EFFECTIVE RATIONAL BELIEFS FORCEFULLY TO MYSELF ON MANY OCCASIONS SO THAT I CAN MAKE MYSELF LESS DISTURBED NOW AND ACT LESS SELF-DEFEATINGLY IN THE FUTURE.

Joyce Sichel, Ph.D. and Albert Ellis, Ph.D
Copyright © 1984 by the Institute for Rational-Emotive Therapy.

100 forms $10.00.
1000 forms $80.00

(over)

Figure 15.2
RET self-help form.
Source: Used with permission of Joyce Sichel, Ph.D., and Albert Ellis, Ph.D. Copyright © 1984 by the Institute for Rational-Emotive Therapy.

and behaving accordingly. In many ways, RET groups can be conceptualized as psychoeducational both in theory and practice. Members learn a new way of life and, through sharing with each other, reinforce appropriate ideas and behaviors.

The RET approach to group work is not limited to just intellectually bright individuals. It is appropriate for persons functioning at all levels and is used with children, adolescents, adults, and the elderly. Most often, the approach stresses remediation. However, at the *Living School* (a private school for children in New York City) or other similar institutes, the emphasis is on prevention (Ellis & Bernard, 1983). For example, the teacher of the ABCs of RET may illustrate through drawings and other graphic means how emotions develop and what children can do to stay in control of themselves at potentially emotional times (see Figure 15.3).

Regardless of where they participate in a RET group, members are exposed to a wide variety of cognitive and behavioral methods (Corey, 1990). Among the best known of these techniques are actively disputing clients' thoughts, persuad-

Figure 15.3
Jeff's mad thermometer.

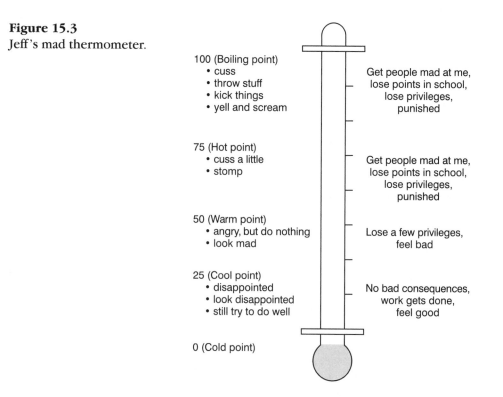

100 (Boiling point)
 • cuss
 • throw stuff
 • kick things
 • yell and scream

Get people mad at me,
lose points in school,
lose privileges,
punished

75 (Hot point)
 • cuss a little
 • stomp

Get people mad at me,
lose points in school,
lose privileges,
punished

50 (Warm point)
 • angry, but do nothing
 • look mad

Lose a few privileges,
feel bad

25 (Cool point)
 • disappointed
 • look disappointed
 • still try to do well

No bad consequences,
work gets done,
feel good

0 (Cold point)

Source: From "Childhood Anxieties, Fears, and Phobias: A Cognitive-Behavioral Psycho-situational Approach by R. M. Grieger and J. D. Boyd, in *Rational-Emotive Approaches to Problems of Childhood* (p. 234) by A. Ellis & M. E. Bernard (Eds.), 1983, New York: Plenum.

ing them to work from a RET viewpoint, teaching clients the ABCs of RET, and giving clients feedback on the rational outcomes of their thoughts. Disputing clients' thoughts has already been covered, so the other three techniques will briefly be discussed.

The RET Viewpoint.   Persuading clients to work from an **RET viewpoint** simply involves getting them to believe that the premises on which RET is based are valid and applicable to their situations. Many RET group specialists spend at least half of their time in initial individual or group sessions highlighting studies that show that the ideas on which RET was founded are valid. For instance, as a group leader, Laurie may talk to group members at length about ancient wisdom as well as modern research on the power of thought to affect a person's way of living.

The ABCs of RET.   The *ABCs of RET* involve group leaders outlining to members how feelings are derived from thoughts. It is one way of persuading clients to work from a rational-emotive viewpoint and teaching them a valuable tool they can use at the same time.

Feedback.   Giving **feedback** on rational outcomes of thoughts requires that the group leader and members suspend judgment and function cognitively. Feedback refers to the final results of rational thinking. Sometimes this feedback is worded in the present; on other occasions, it is projected into the future. For example, Bart may say to Lindsey, "If you keep thinking rationally in regard to your studies, I expect you will be a logical candidate for medical school in the future."

In addition to the techniques already mentioned, group members are encouraged to role-play their situations (often in the group) and to find appropriate models to emulate (or copy). The main focus is not just to teach skills but to promote and foster a way of life. Ellis (1979) states this view as follows:

> Just as skill training enables clients to change their perceptions of their abilities, so does helping them to perceive themselves differently enable them to acquire better skills. (p. 133)

Role of the Rational-Emotive Group Leader

"The Rational-Emotive group is leader-centered. It is the leader's task to make sure that the group is philosophically and cognitively based" (Hansen et al., 1980, p. 246). In RET groups, the leader encourages rational thinking in a number of ways (Ellis, 1974). Some of these methods include

1. teaching group members about the origins of emotions
2. being active in the group process by challenging and probing
3. encouraging group members to help each other think rationally

4. utilizing activity-oriented experiences in the group and homework assignments outside of the group
5. allowing the expression of feelings previously hidden by group members. These emotions are then dealt with in a practical, rational way.

In psychotherapeutic and counseling groups, the group leader encourages members of the group to work as **auxiliary counselors** once someone has presented a problem. When they do, participants benefit from multiple input (Ellis, 1984; Ellis & Dryden, 1987). The group leader also serves as a model for the group and reveals how he or she practices RET in daily life. "The leader's objective is to help participants give up their demands for perfection" (Vander Kolk, 1985, p. 108). Techniques used by the group leader do not vary that much from other group approaches and are usually a combination of cognitive, behavioral, and affective-based interventions, such as confrontation, challenging, persuasion, role playing, and imagining (Hansen et al., 1980; Vander Kolk, 1985).

Desired Outcome of Rational-Emotive Groups

A primary desired outcome of a RET group is for group members to learn how to think rationally. If members are able to learn how to control their thought processes, they will be able to deal more effectively with a wide variety of problems.

A second objective is for group members to achieve a particular goal in their own lives connected with overcoming an irrational belief using RET. Knowing how to implement the theory is not enough; it must be practiced, too. For example, if Dottie knows RET theory but does not apply the process to her own life, she is limiting herself.

A third expected result of a RET group is that members should have a better knowledge of how RET can be employed in situations with which they have no firsthand experience. Knowing this will allow them to be helpful in addressing novel, nondevelopmental problems.

A final payoff from participating in a RET group is that members gain the experience of personally understanding the process of change. Therefore, they can be more empathetic with others who are in the process of trying to modify their thoughts, feelings, and behaviors (Wessler & Hankin, 1988).

Evaluation of Rational-Emotive Groups

As with other types of groups, RET groups have inherent strengths and weaknesses. These groups are primarily of a psychoeducational, psychotherapy, and counseling modality.

Advantages.   A strength of employing RET theory in group work is the focus of the approach on the importance of cognition in influencing people's emotions and actions (Hansen et al., 1980). Many other forms of group work (e.g., psycho-analysis, person-centered) have placed primary emphasis on the role of emotion in helping relationships. RET is one of the few integrative theories used in a group that places primary importance on cognitions as well as behaviors. In this regard, it is very broad based and similar to multimodal theories of clinicians such as Arnold Lazarus (1985) in stressing a multitude of specific treatments (Ellis, 1989).

A second strength of this approach is how Ellis has demystified the process. "The essentials of Rational-Emotive Therapy can be taught quickly to counselors and clients alike" (Hansen et al., 1980, p. 248). It is relatively easy for everyone involved in the group process to learn how to take charge of themselves and help others in the group.

Another advantage of RET groups is that they may be the perfect environ-ment for clients who are phasing out of individual therapeutic counseling (Wessler & Hankin, 1988). The group helps persons in transition see themselves more clearly by giving them feedback. These groups also equip their members further by assisting them in refining their skills in rational thinking.

A fourth advantage of using RET theory in groups is versatility. RET theory is geared toward working with large segments of the population. RET groups emphasize prevention as well as remediation. The basic tenets of this theory are easy to understand and implement with persons from a wide variety of settings and backgrounds, too. For example, RET activities for children have been used in a number of educational and psychotherapeutic environments.

A final strength of RET groups is the opportunities they provide for members to do homework assignments, take verbal and nonverbal risks, and learn from the experiences of others, both inside and outside of the formal group context (Ellis, 1984, 1989). RET groups emphasize action as well as talk. Books, such as *A New Guide to Rational Living* (Harper & Ellis, 1975) and *How to Stubbornly Refuse to Make Yourself Miserable about Anything—Yes, Anything!* (Ellis, 1988), are often assigned reading between sessions.

Limitations.   One limitation of RET is its traditional focus on the individual, not the group (Wessler & Hankin, 1988). Although group members learn a lot about their ability to control thoughts, emotions, and behaviors, they do not usu-ally learn a lot about group dynamics. RET is even more individually oriented than Gestalt group work. Furthermore, RET theory has hardly been applied to groups that deal with work or task situations.

Another limitation of the RET approach is its confrontive and directive stance (Corey, 1990). Group leaders and members may push a member to get rid of faulty beliefs and adopt new thought patterns before he or she is ready. This trade-off may not be in the best interest of the participant because it has not been personalized. Hence, faulty beliefs may not really be discarded, and rational ones may not really be adopted.

A third limitation of RET groups is that borderline disturbed members may actually get worse in them (Wessler & Hankin, 1988). Some individuals, espe-cially those who require a great deal of individual attention or those who have a low intellectual capacity, may do better in individual sessions. Because the emphasis in RET is not on a close client/counselor-leader relationship, these individuals may receive more of the personal and professional attention they need in non-RET settings.

A final limitation of RET groups is the lack of research on them. Ellis (1982) claims that RET groups are effective, but his research is based more on cognitive groups in general than on RET groups in particular. A review of outcome studies of RET by McGovern and Silverman (1986) is more convincing, but greater uniformity in regard to methods and controls is still needed (Wessler, 1986).

TRANSACTIONAL ANALYSIS GROUPS

Transactional analysis (TA) groups are similar to RET groups in their emphases on cognition and participatory learning through interaction and homework assignments. TA has been oriented toward groups since its inception. Eric Berne believed that groups are more efficient in helping individuals understand their personal life scripts than individual counseling or psychotherapy (Barnes, 1977; Berne, 1966). To participate in a group, individuals must master basic TA concepts, such as "ego state," "stroke," and "script." They must also be willing to work on past experiences in a present context.

For the **redecision school of TA** (Goulding, 1987), where the emphasis is on intrapsychic processes, groups are the main choice of treatment. Groups provide a living experience in which members are able to examine themselves and their histories in a precise way. Individuals can then change their life scripts. For the other two schools of TA—**classic**, which emphasizes present interactions, and **cathexis**, which emphasizes reparenting—groups are also employed frequently. Thus, the emphasis of TA groups is on both interpersonal (i.e., the classic model) and intrapersonal (i.e., the cathexis and redecision models) (Barnes, 1977). In addition, TA is geared toward working on work/task group communication processes, such as those between employer–employee and co-workers (Nykodym, Ruud, & Liverpool, 1986).

Premises of Transactional Analysis Groups

There are multiple aspects to TA theory. The basic concepts of TA revolve around the development and interaction of what Eric Berne (1964) called an **ego state**—"a system of feelings accompanied by a related set of behavior patterns" (p. 23). There are three basic ego states—Parent, Adult, and Child—that exist and operate within every individual and can be observed in the dynamic interactions of individuals with each other (Dusay & Dusay, 1989) (see Figure 15.4).

Each ego state functions in its own special way as follows:

1. The **Parent ego state** is dualistic in being both nurturing and critical (or controlling). "The function of the *Critical Parent* is to store and dispense the rules and protection for living. The function of the *Nurturing Parent*

Figure 15.4
TA ego states.

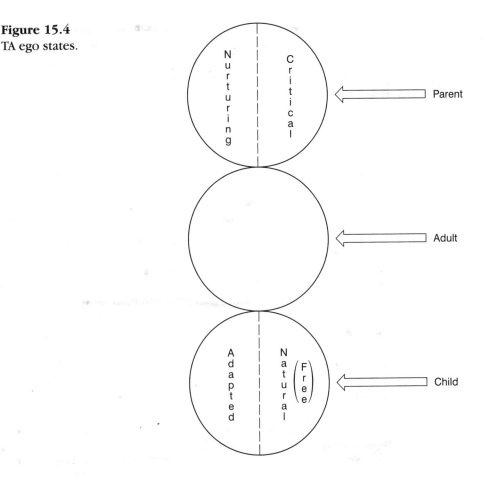

is to care for, to nurture" (Grimes, 1988, p. 53). Typical statements from the Critical Parent are, "Be home by seven" and "Watch what you are doing." Typical statements from the Nurturing Parent are, "Rest for awhile" and "Here, let me take your coat."

2. The **Adult ego state** functions like a computer in that it receives and processes information from the Parent, the Child, and the environment. It then makes the best decision possible. The Adult is the realistic, logical part of the person. A typical statement coming from the adult is, "The appointment is this afternoon. I need to be on time."

3. The **Child ego state** is divided into two parts. The *Adapted Child* conforms to the rules and wishes of Parent ego states within the self and others. It is compliant and easy to get along with. A typical Adapted child statement would be, "I'm going to do what you ask because I am a good boy/girl." The *Free Child* (or *Natural Child*) reacts more spontaneously. It has fun and is curious and playful. It takes care of its needs without regard for others while using its intuition to read nonverbal cues. For instance, the Free Child might say, "Come on. Let's have fun!"

There are four basic ways to identify which ego state individuals are in at a particular moment—behavioral, social, historical, and phenomenological (Woollams, Brown, & Huige, 1977). It is important to be aware of the ego states of people, for it affects the manner in which they interact with themselves and others. For example, a person who is operating from a Parent ego state is more likely to be critical or supportive than is a person who is operating from a Child ego state. Likewise, if an individual utilizes one ego state exclusively, for example, the Adult, he or she is less likely to be flexible in thought and action than is a person who is utilizing all three ego states.

Knowledge of their own ego states empowers individuals and those working with them to assess what types of transactions they are most likely to have and to take corrective measures, if needed. This type of information helps these persons avoid the playing of **"games,"** which Berne (1964) defined as "an ongoing series of complementary ulterior transactions progressing to a well-defined, predictable outcome" (p. 48). Games are played on three levels, and almost all of them are destructive and result in negative payoffs (i.e., *rackets*). *First-degree games* are the least harmful and may even be considered socially acceptable (e.g., "Blemish"). In these games, minor faults are highlighted, such as when Pat says to Suzanne, "You look great except for your hair." *Second-degree games* are more serious and usually result in some physical confrontation (e.g., "Uproar"). The interactive process in second-degree games leaves the people involved feeling negative, such as when Jim is called names by Dick. *Third-degree games* are deadly and often played for keeps (e.g., "Cops and Robbers"). There is nothing socially redeemable about third-degree games, for example, if Ed is caught stealing from the elderly and tries to fight his way free from the police. People who play games operate from three distinct positions: (a) the *victim* (who appears to be innocent), (b) the *persecutor* (who appears to cause problems), and (c) the *rescuer* (who is seen as a problem-solver or hero to the victim). Individuals who play games often switch between these roles as the *drama triangle* (Karpman, 1968) illustrates (see Figure 15.5).

TA also emphasizes several other beliefs about human nature. For instance, it holds that persons are born with positive tendencies to grow and develop, but this potential must be nurtured to become a reality (Dusay & Steiner, 1971). It likewise stresses that individuals structure their time to obtain **strokes** (verbal or nonverbal recognition) in six major ways: (a) withdrawal, (b) ritual, (c) pastimes,

Figure 15.5
Drama (Karpman) triangle.

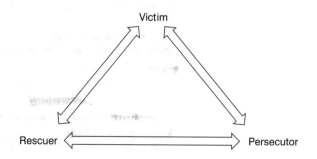

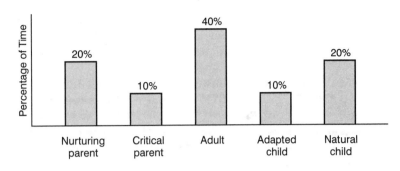

Figure 15.6
An egogram.

(d) work, (e) games, and (f) intimacy (Berne, 1972). These ways of interacting can be represented through the use of an **egogram** (a bar graph) and will not change unless a person actively decides to change the amount of time spent in engaging in certain behaviors (Dusay & Dusay, 1989) (see Figure 15.6).

Over their life span, people gradually develop **scripts**, or habitual patterns of behavior, that influence how they spend their time, for example, as losers, non-winners, or winners (Berne, 1972; Capers, 1975). Most people initially script their lives as a Child in the *I'm Not OK—You're OK* stance (powerless), but change to an Adult stance in later life as they affirm an *I'm OK—You're OK* position (characterized by trust and openness) (Harris, 1967). Other options open to them are *I'm OK—You're Not OK* (projection of blame onto others) and *I'm Not OK—You're Not OK* (hopeless and self-destructive).

Scripts include **transactions** (social action between two or more people). These transactions are manifested in social (overt) and psychological (covert) levels (Dusay & Dusay, 1989). Clear transactions with no hidden agenda are *complementary transactions.* For example,

Person 1:	What time is it?
Person 2:	It is 3 o'clock.

Crossed transactions are those in which a response is returned from an unexpected or inappropriate ego state. When this occurs, the person initiating the conversation often feels hurt and withdraws. Here is an example:

Person 1:	(adult ego state) What time is it?
Person 2:	(critical parent) You are always in such a hurry.

Ulterior transactions (which are often represented by dotted lines) (Dusay & Dusay, 1989) occur when a message appears to be sent on one level but is actually transmitted on another level. Often such transactions will seem to be from an Adult ego state but are actually coming from the Child. They are represented by the designation "Adult/Child."

Person 1:   (adult/child message) "Want to come to my place for
                    some coffee?"
Person 2:   (adult/child message) "I'd really like that."

See Figure 15.7 for an illustration of these three transactions.

Through transactions, individuals receive *strokes* (i.e., physical or psychological recognition). Strokes can be anything from an eye glance to a verbal comment. When positive strokes are not forthcoming, persons will work for negative
strokes by using ulterior means. Games are the result and bad feelings the payoff
in such cases.

Practice of Transactional Analysis in a Group

Transactional analysis is preferably used in groups. "Groups serve as a setting in
which people can become more aware of themselves, the structure of their individual personality, the transactions they have with others, the games they play,
and the scripts they act out. Such awareness enables persons to see themselves
more clearly so that they can change what they want to change and strengthen
what they want to strengthen" (James & Jongeward, 1971, p. 11).

Figure 15.7
Three types of interpersonal
transactions.

1. *Complementary* (both persons are operating from the same ego state)

2. *Crossed* (an inappropriate ego state is activated)

3. *Ulterior* (two ego states operate simultaneously, one disguises the other)

According to Berne (1966), the objective in group treatment settings is to "fight the past in the present in order to assure the future" (p. 250). The past is represented by the Child and Parent ego states, whereas the present is embodied in the Adult. There needs to be appropriate relations among these three ego states for people to function productively. The Adult ultimately needs to be most dominant in deciding which ego state will be displayed.

Therapeutic Contracts.   All TA groups are based on the ability and willingness of participants to make and work on **therapeutic contracts** (Dusay & Dusay, 1989). Contracts are specific, measurable, concrete statements of what participants intend to accomplish during the group. They place responsibility on members for clearly defining what, how, and when they want to change. Contracts can be made in all types of groups: psychoeducational, counseling, psychotherapeutic, and work/task. From the beginning of groups, members should learn that change is a shared responsibility and that they cannot passively wait for the group leader to assume the direction for working in a group. In short, the contract establishes the departure point for group activity (Corey, 1985). Well-written contracts make it clear that participants are getting what they want from the group (Dusay, 1983). They are based on decisions made by the Adult ego state (Dusay & Dusay, 1989).

Generally, "TA contracts have the four major components of a legal contract" (Dusay & Dusay, 1989, p. 428). These aspects include (a) *mutual assent*—clearly defining a goal from an adult perspective and joining with the therapist's Adult as an ally; (b) *competency*—agreeing on what can realistically be expected; (c) *legal object*—an objective; and (d) *consideration*—a fee or price for services. An example of a group contract is an agreement by members of an industrial group to remain together long enough to complete a mutually agreed-on activity, such as eliminating discriminatory language from company contracts (Barnes, 1977). An individual contract includes personal goals, such as giving individuals in one's daily life more compliments than criticisms. Group members usually meet weekly to assess the progress made in pursuing their goals.

Classic Contracts.   *Classic school* contracts are carried out with an emphasis on one or more of the following: (a) structural analysis, (b) transactional analysis, (c) game analysis, and (d) life-script analysis (Berne, 1961). "In order to achieve the most complete treatment, all four need to be accomplished, and since each one is built upon the previous level, it is necessary that they be accomplished in order" (Donigian & Malnati, 1987, p. 75). In *structural analysis,* all group members become aware of the structure of their ego states and how they function. Members are encouraged to "decontaminate" any ego state that is not operating properly. An example of a contaminated ego state is a person who appears to speak from the Adult ego state but is instead speaking from the Parent ego state as in, "Children should be seen and not heard."

Transactional analysis involves the diagnosing of interactions among group members to determine if they are *complementary* (from appropriate and expected ego states), *crossed* (from inappropriate and unexpected ego states), or *ulterior* (from a disguised ego state, such as the Child speaking as if it were an Adult).

Game analysis includes an examination of destructive and repetitive behavioral patterns and an analysis of the ego states and types of transactions involved. Because games prevent intimacy (Berne, 1964), it is crucial that they be eliminated. "The classical TA group devotes considerable time to helping members become aware of the games they initiate and participate in, so that they can come to develop intimate and nonmanipulative relationships" (Corey, 1985, p. 325).

Finally, on the deepest level, classic TA school groups do **life script analyses**, which are people's basic plans involving transactions and games (Steiner, 1974). Typically, scripts are made at an unconscious level when individuals are children (before age 5). They determine life plans, such as living a tragic or happy existence (Berne, 1961). It is said that Berne lived a tragic life script, choosing to die of a "broken heart" at age 60 like his mother, without having known real intimacy (Steiner, 1974). As a general rule, script analysis is difficult to do within a group. Feelings resulting from such an experience, such as depression or discouragement, must be handled carefully and skillfully.

Redecision Contracts.   Groups have within them curative factors because of their social nature (Berne, 1966). When conducted properly, all TA groups give their members knowledge and insight into their lives. A special form of TA, redecision theory (Goulding & Goulding, 1979), helps clients make redecisions while they are in their Child ego state. This task is accomplished by having these individuals reexperience a past event as if it were now present. Persons who engage in the redecision process first make a contract to address significant symptoms they wish to change. Then they take actions that focus on rackets and games they have experienced. They are taught that they are responsible for both their feelings and actions (Goulding, 1975).

The next step of this process is for group members to explore the sources that led them to make a particular life decision. Accountability is stressed as is power for changing. Helpless or so-called cop-out words, such as "can't," "perhaps," and "try" are not accepted. Once members redecide and make a change by actually reliving psychologically an early scene from their past, group members offer them reinforcement and encouragement to continue. Group leaders help such individuals focus on how they will conduct themselves in a new way outside of the group and develop a needed support system to continue the changes they have made. Fantasizing what lies ahead and how they will cope is also a part of this process (Goulding, 1987).

Role of the Transactional Analysis Group Leader

TA group leaders are more than just members of the group they lead. They stand apart as "primarily listeners, observers, diagnosticians, and analysts—and, secondarily, process facilitators" (Donigian & Malnati, 1987, p. 75). TA groups are leader-centered, and although member–member transactions occur, they do not have the same effect as a leader–member interaction.

Overall, transactions in TA groups that take place between the group leader and a member are considered major; those that occur among group members are minor. A group is functioning optimally when there are major and minor transactions involving all members (Hansen et al., 1980) and when there are attitudinal and behavioral changes in group members. By staying detached, the leader is able to see more clearly than group members the games that are occurring and is thereby able to analyze and intervene more dynamically than individual members (Hansen et al., 1980).

It is vital that TA group leaders understand themselves well from a TA perspective and that they adopt an "I'm OK" life position. The reason is that TA leaders are teachers within the group. They must have a thorough understanding of how TA concepts operate in their own lives before they try to help others apply these concepts. They must also think well of themselves most of the time if they are going to be able to establish rapport with group members and help them change.

The leader has four specific roles within the TA group: protection, permission, potency, and operations (Corey, 1990; Grimes, 1988; Hansen et al., 1980). **Protection** involves keeping members safe from psychological or physical harm. **Permission** centers on giving group members directives to behave against the injunctions of their parents. (**Injunctions** are Parent commands recorded by the Child that call for the Child to adopt certain roles, such as "do as you are told.") **Potency** is the use of appropriate counseling techniques in certain situations. For example, making a contract for change or active listening are both appropriate and potent counseling techniques. Finally, **operations** are very specific techniques employed by TA group leaders. These techniques include interrogation, specification, confrontation, explanation, illustration, confirmation, interpretation, and crystallization (Berne, 1966; Gladding, 1992; Hansen et al., 1980). For instance, a group member may be confronted by a group leader about the inconsistencies shown between the member's speech and behavior.

Desired Outcome of Transactional Analysis Groups

If successful, group members will learn about themselves through their analysis of structures, transactions, games, and scripts. The knowledge they acquire from this process will enable them to think, feel, and behave differently if they so choose. They are freed from old Parental messages (injunctions) and early, self-defeating scripts made by their Child. They may adopt an "I'm OK—You're OK" position in life and "get on" with themselves in a positive way.

Woollams and Brown (1978) view the process that leads to this desired outcome as going through seven steps: (a) trust in the other, (b) trust in self, (c) moving into group, (d) work, (e) redecision, (f) integration, and (g) termination. These steps are usually intertwined and rarely can they be distinguished from each other. At the point of termination, however, group members should have accomplished what they set out to do. In many ways, both RET and TA promote the integration of the person in multimodal ways, although the outcome in TA is less likely to be accomplished unless its practitioners borrow behavioral and affective techniques and procedures from other theories.

Evaluation of Transactional Analysis Groups

Transactional analysis groups are potentially powerful ways of helping individuals work together for the good of themselves and others. However, they have their limits as well as their strengths.

Advantages.   There are a number of advantages in employing TA theory in group work. First is the cognitive clarity of the language used to explain TA concepts (Grimes, 1988; Yalom, 1985). TA works in groups by helping members understand how they function intra- and interpersonally and how they came to make the decisions in life they did. The clarity of TA concepts is also useful in helping group members realize what they need to do to change. TA stresses intellectual insight as the initial basis for doing things differently.

A second strength of this approach is its simplicity (O'Hearne, 1977). TA can be readily grasped and used in its most elementary form in just a few hours. The almost immediate applicability of TA makes it popular with group leaders who want their members to gain intellectual understanding quickly.

Another advantage of using TA in groups is that individuals "move faster toward getting well" (Harris, 1967, p. 204). Group members who make progress toward achieving their goals reinforce others in the group to do the same. This dynamic, although not particularly emphasized, occurs in both subtle and overt ways and helps group members achieve results not possible in individual treatment formats.

A final advantage of using TA in groups is that it can be used in work, psychoeducational, and counseling/psychotherapy settings and combined effectively with other more action-centered approaches, such as Gestalt, to produce a dynamic method of change (Goulding & Goulding, 1979; James & Jongeward, 1971). Such combinations help group members put their contracts and thoughts into achievable forms.

Limitations.   A major limitation of TA is its restrictive interpretation of the complexities of human nature by categorizing them "into a limited number of games, ego states, and scripts" (Yalom, 1985, p. 453). People are more complex than the concepts of TA, and group members may find themselves restricted in dealing with complicated situations because of the lack of TA concepts to describe what is happening. There is also the difficulty of using TA language uniformly and correctly.

A second limitation of TA in groups is the strong emphasis in this approach on cognitive understanding. This cognitive focus is further complicated because some TA leaders use the structure and vocabulary of transactional analysis to "avoid genuine contact with their clients or to keep them from revealing their reactions" (Corey, 1990, p. 376). These types of behaviors set up barriers and constitute a misuse of TA theory while lessening the impact of the approach on participants. "If the group becomes immersed in analysis to the exclusion of spontaneous interaction and emotional expression, it has the potential to become merely an intellectual exercise" (Vander Kolk, 1985, p. 66).

Another limitation of TA in groups is its neglect of emphasizing group process (Yalom, 1985). TA is largely member–leader-centered and does not effectively use other group dynamics, for example, interpersonal learning, cohesiveness, and universality. Future research in TA needs to focus on controlled research designs that will allow investigators to contrast and compare TA techniques in groups uniformly (Kapur & Miller, 1987).

A fourth limitation of the use of TA in groups is the lack of empirical evidence to support its effectiveness. Although Dusay and Dusay (1984) cite "hard data gain" as an outcome of TA treatment, there is little research on TA groups per se. The *Transactional Analysis Journal* is interested in publishing such studies but so far has received relatively few.

SUMMARY AND CONCLUSION

Rational-emotive therapy and transactional analysis are both frequently used in group settings, particularly group counseling and psychotherapy. RET, although quite cognitive, makes use of a number of affective and behavioral methods to help its group members bring about change. A primary aspect of this approach is the initial teaching needed to educate group members that feelings are derived from thoughts, not events. After this information is clearly understood, the group proceeds with the leader being in charge, but with other participants acting as "auxiliary counselors."

RET groups stress role-play and homework assignments as well as recognition of thoughts. Affective, behavioral, and cognitive disputations are usually employed to get rid of faulty, irrational thinking and help participants take better control of their lives. Overall, RET groups enable their members to learn from each other and recognize their shortcomings more quickly than is often the case in individual sessions. RET groups are highly structured and didactic and do not stress group dynamics as do other approaches. In many ways, RET groups function in a psychoeducational format even when they are emphasizing psychotherapeutic changes.

Transactional analysis has many parallels to RET in its emphasis on cognitive components. TA has often been used in groups since its inception in the 1950s. It is frequently thought of as a group treatment approach although it has been employed with individuals and families, too (Barnes, 1977; Corey, 1990; Dusay & Dusay, 1989). TA is also utilized in work/task settings. The major thrust of the TA group is to concentrate on analyzing ego states (Parent, Adult, Child) that individuals within the group are using. The group leader helps group members become aware of how they are functioning and how they might change their patterns of interaction. Cognitive understanding is emphasized initially in this process.

When the group is functioning properly, group members interact with one another (minor transactions). However, the major focus of the group is on group leader–member interactions (major transactions). Thus, the TA group is leader-centered and does not take advantage of group dynamics that other theories stress. TA practitioners are still in the process of validating the effectiveness of TA groups. Yet, TA and its 10,000 practitioners stress that TA is "ideally suited for groups" (Corey, 1985, p. 313). The theory is simple, clear, and easily used by group members in coming to better understand their structure, transactions, games, and life scripts.

CLASSROOM EXERCISES

1. Write down your thoughts about working in groups, as opposed to working with individuals. After you have spent about five minutes writing down as many thoughts as you can, pair up with another class member and discuss which of your thoughts are primarily positive, negative, neutral, and mixed. Notice how the tone of the thought affects you as a person and talk to your classmate about what you observe happening to you in discussing your thoughts. How do you think what you experience is similar to that of group members in a cognitively based group?

2. In a group of four, have each person demonstrate to the others how he or she would most likely behave as a group leader and a group member if they were acting from thoughts that were primarily from the following TA ego states: (a) Adult, (b) Parent, and (c) Child. Discuss how you might help members develop other ego states in a group setting.

3. In groups of three, check major periodicals or citation indexes in your library for articles on the use of RET and TA in groups. Refer to the literature of the 1960s, if possible. Report back to the class as a group what you have found and what patterns you have noticed in articles related to these theories.

4. Have a class debate between two teams of five class members each on the pros and cons of using the two cognitive theories covered in this chapter. Poll the class after the debate on which points they remember each side making and why they remember those emphases.

REFERENCES

Barnes, G. (1977). Introduction. In G. Barnes (Ed.), *Transactional analysis after Eric Berne* (pp. 1–31). New York: Harper & Row.

Beck, A. T., & Weishaar, M. E. (1989). Cognitive therapy. In R. J. Corsini & D. Wedding (Eds.), *Current psychotherapies* (4th ed.) (pp. 284–320). Itasca, IL: Peacock.

Berne, E. (1961). *Transactional analysis in psychotherapy.* New York: Grove Press.

Berne, E. (1964). *Games people play.* New York: Grove Press.

Berne, E. (1966). *Principles of group treatment.* New York: Oxford University Press.

Berne, E. (1972). *What do you say after you say hello?* New York: Grove Press.

Capers, H. (1975). Winning and losing. *Transactional Analysis Journal, 5,* 257–258.

Corey, G. (1985). *Theory and practice of group counseling* (2nd ed.). Pacific Grove, CA: Brooks/Cole.

Corey, G. (1990). *Theory and practice of group counseling* (3rd ed.). Pacific Grove, CA: Brooks/Cole.

Donigian, J., & Malnati, R. (1987). *Critical incidents in group therapy*. Pacific Grove, CA: Brooks/Cole.

Dryden, W. (1989). Albert Ellis: An efficient and passionate life. *Journal of Counseling and Development, 67,* 539–546.

Dusay, J. M. (1983). Transactional analysis in groups. In H. I. Kaplan & B. J. Sadock (Eds.), *Comprehensive group psychotherapy* (2nd ed.). Baltimore: Williams & Wilkins.

Dusay, J. M., & Dusay, K. M. (1984). Transactional analysis. In R. Corsini (Ed.), *Current psychotherapies* (3rd ed.). Itasca, IL: Peacock.

Dusay, J. M., & Dusay, K. M. (1989). Transactional analysis. In R. Corsini & D. Wedding (Eds.), *Current psychotherapies* (4th ed.) (pp. 404–453). Itasca, IL: Peacock.

Dusay, J., & Steiner, C. (1971). Transactional analysis in groups. In H. I. Kaplan & B. J. Sadock (Eds.), *Comprehensive group psychotherapy* (pp. 198–240). Baltimore: Williams & Wilkins.

Ellis, A. (1962). *Reason and emotion in psychotherapy*. New York: Lyle Stuart.

Ellis, A. (1974). Rationality and irrationality in the group therapy process. In D. S. Milman & G. D. Goldman (Eds.), *Group process today* (pp. 78–96). Springfield, IL: Charles C. Thomas.

Ellis, A. (1976). The biological basis of irrational thinking. *Journal of Individual Psychology, 32,* 145–168.

Ellis, A. (1979). Rational-emotive therapy. In A. Ellis & J. M. Whitely (Eds.), *Theoretical and empirical foundations of rational-emotive therapy*. Monterey, CA: Brooks/Cole.

Ellis, A. (1982). Rational-emotive group therapy. In G. M. Gazda (Ed.), *Basic approaches to group therapy and group counseling* (3rd ed.). Springfield, IL: Charles C. Thomas.

Ellis, A. (1984). Rational-emotive therapy. In R. J. Corsini (Ed.), *Current psychotherapies* (3rd ed.) (pp. 196–238). Itasca, IL: Peacock.

Ellis, A. (1988). *How to stubbornly refuse to make yourself miserable about anything—Yes, anything!* Secaucus, NJ: Lyle Stuart.

Ellis, A. (1989). Rational-emotive therapy. In R. J. Corsini and D. Wedding (Eds.), *Current psychotherapies* (4th ed.) (pp. 196–238). Itasca, IL: Peacock.

Ellis, A., & Bernard, M. E. (Eds.). (1983). *Rational-emotive approaches to the problems of childhood*. New York: Plenum.

Ellis, A., & Dryden, W. (1987). *The practice of rational-emotive therapy*. New York: Springer.

Gladding, S. T. (1977). Awakening. *The School Counselor, 24,* 184–185.

Gladding, S. T. (1992). *Counseling: A comprehensive profession* (2nd ed.). New York: Macmillan.

Goulding, R. (1975). The formation and beginning process of transactional analysis groups. In G. Gazda (Ed.), *Basic approaches to group psychotherapy and group counseling* (2nd ed.). Springfield, IL: Charles C. Thomas.

Goulding, R. (1987). Group therapy: Mainline or sideline? In J. K. Zeig (Ed.), *The evolution of psychotherapy* (pp. 300–311). New York: Brunner/Mazel.

Goulding, M., & Goulding, R. (1979). *Changing lives through redecision therapy*. New York: Brunner/Mazel.

Grieger, R. M., & Boyd, J. D. (1983). Childhood anxieties, fears, and phobias: A cognitive-behavioral psycho-situational approach. In A. Ellis & M. E. Bernard (Eds.), *Rational-emotive approaches to problems of childhood* (pp. 211–239). New York: Plenum.

Grimes, J. (1988). Transactional analysis in group work. In S. Long (Ed.), *Six group therapies* (pp. 49–113). New York: Plenum.

Hansen, J. C., Warner, R. W., & Smith, E. J. (1980). *Group counseling: Theory and process* (2nd ed.). Chicago: Rand McNally.

Harper, R. L., & Ellis, A. (1975). *A new guide to rational living*. Englewood Cliffs, NJ: Prentice Hall.

Harris, T. A. (1967). *I'm OK—You're OK*. New York: Harper & Row.

James, M., & Jongeward, D. (1971). *Born to win: Transactional analysis with Gestalt experiments*. Reading, MA: Addison-Wesley.

Kapur, R., & Miller, K. (1987). A comparison between therapeutic factors in TA and psychodynamic therapy groups. *Transactional Analysis Journal, 17,* 294–300.

Karpman, S. (1968). Fairy tales and script drama analysis. *Transactional Analysis Bulletin, 7,* 39–43.

Lazarus, A. A. (Ed.). (1985). *Casebook of multimodal therapy*. New York: Guilford.

Maultsby, M. C., Jr. (1984). *Rational behavior therapy*. Englewood Cliffs, NJ: Prentice Hall.

McGovern, T. E., & Silverman, M. (1986). A review of outcome studies of rational-emotive therapy from 1977 to 1982. In A. Ellis & R. Grieger (Eds.), *Handbook of rational-emotive therapy* (Vol. 2). New York: Springer.

Nykodym, N., Ruud, W., & Liverpool, P. (1986). Quality circles: Will Transaction Analysis improve their effectiveness? *Transactional Analysis Journal, 16,* 182–187.

O'Hearne, J. J. (1977). Pilgrim's progress. In G. Barnes (Ed.), *Transactional analysis after Eric Berne* (pp. 458–484). New York: Harper & Row.

Sichel, G., & Ellis, A. (1984). *RET self-help form.* New York: Institute for Rational-Emotive Therapy.

Steiner, C. (1974). *Scripts people live: Transactional analysis of life scripts.* New York: Grove Press.

Vander Kolk, C. J. (1985). *Introduction to group counseling and psychotherapy.* Columbus, OH: Merrill.

Walen, S. R., DiGiuseppe, R., & Wessler, R. L. (1980). *A practitioner's guide to RET.* New York: Oxford University Press.

Weinrach, S. G. (1980). Unconventional therapist: Albert Ellis. *Personnel and Guidance Journal, 59,* 152–160.

Wessler, R. L. (1986). Rational-emotive therapy in groups. In A. Ellis & R. Grieger (Eds.), *Handbook of Rational-Emotive Therapy* (Vol. 2) (pp. 295–315). New York: Springer.

Wessler, R. L., & Hankin, S. (1988). Rational-emotive therapy and related cognitively oriented psychotherapies. In S. Long (Ed.), *Six group therapies* (pp. 159–215). New York: Plenum.

Woollams, S., & Brown, M. (1978). *Transactional analysis.* Dexter, MI: Huron Valley Institute.

Woollams, S., Brown, M., & Huige, K. (1977). What transactional analysts want their clients to know. In G. Barnes (Ed.), *Transactional analysis after Eric Berne* (pp. 487–525). New York: Harper & Row.

Yalom, I. D. (1985). *The theory and practice of group psychotherapy* (3rd ed.). New York: Basic Books.

CHAPTER 16

Behavioral and Reality Therapy Groups

Gazing at you in the midst of change
I am awed by the realization
that beyond the outer calm of appearance
you are not an island.
Stirring within you is transitional growth—
a dynamic resolution of present reality—
struggling to break forth in the now
and join the mainland of the group.
I wait patiently for those moments
and build bridges to connect us,
anticipating each new linking movement
as tides of expectation run high. *

Behaviorally based groups consist of "a series of group methods rather than one cohesive system" (Vander Kolk, 1985, p. 112). Yet, all behavioral- and reality-oriented group approaches concentrate on connecting individuals to themselves and others in a dynamic, observable, and productive manner. The three main behavioral theories that are usually combined when conducting groups are response learning (classical conditioning), operant learning (Skinnerian conditioning), and imitation learning (social modeling). Behaviorists generally focus on what is observable in the group and on what actions may be modified or eliminated. They tend to stress teaching their group members self-enhancing skills, which is one reason their popularity has increased over the years (Corey, 1990; Hansen, Warner, & Smith, 1980).

Source: Gladding, 1984, p. 35. Copyright ACA. Reprinted by permission of the American Counseling Association.

A variation on behavioral group work and a unique approach in its own right is reality therapy, which has "a phenomenological base and an existential heart" (Gladding, 1992, p. 154). Reality therapy within a group setting challenges clients to examine the productivity of their behaviors and change them, when necessary, through making plans and successfully carrying them out (Glasser, 1965, 1986a). Like behavior therapy, transactional analysis, and rational-emotive therapy, reality therapy is an active, directive, and didactic model. It stresses present behavior—not attitudes, insights, one's past, or unconscious motivation (Corey, 1985, p. 399).

BEHAVIORAL GROUPS

Premises of Behavioral Group Therapy

Behavioral theories have a long and diversified history stretching back to the beginning of the twentieth century (Wilson, 1989). John B. Watson (1913) is often credited as being the primary advocate of **respondent conditioning** at the beginning of the 1900s. His views were similar to those of Ivan Pavlov in that he believed all human responses were learned through association. B. F. Skinner (1953) attacked the passivity of respondent conditioning and stressed the need for organisms to be active in the environment in order to learn. His **operant conditioning** model, which led to the development of applied behavioral analysis, emphasizes that behavior is a function of its consequences. Albert Bandura (1969) went even further in stating that much learning is obtained through **social modeling** (i.e., imitation of observation).

Thus, the behaviorist point of view is really a combination of opinions and procedures that since the 1950s has been collectively called **behavior therapy.** Those who consider themselves to be behaviorists emphasize learning and modification of behaviors as opposed to the treatment of underlying symptoms. They are aware that many behaviors are linked to one another. To break the chain of maladaptive responses, practitioners must determine associations and make appropriate interventions (Hollander & Kazaoka, 1988; Wilson, 1989).

Behaviorism includes so-called **radical behaviorists,** such as B. F. Skinner (1974), who avoid any mentalistic concepts and concentrate exclusively on observable actions, to the so-called **cognitive behaviorists,** such as David Meichenbaum (1977, 1986) and Aaron Beck (1976) who believe that thoughts play a major part in determining action and thoughts are behaviors. Behaviorism became popular in counseling and human relations training in the 1960s (Krumboltz, 1966; Krumboltz & Thoresen, 1969) at about the same time groups did. The sophistication of each, alone and in combination, has grown tremendously since then.

In general, **behaviorists** inside and outside of group settings emphasize overt processes, here-and-now experiences, learning, changing of maladaptive actions, defining specific goals, and scientific support for techniques (Rimm &

Cunningham, 1985). As a group, these practitioners offer a wide variety of concrete and pragmatic procedures that are tailored to the needs of particular individuals and empirically verified. A few of the more prevalent techniques are positive reinforcement, extinction, desensitization, and modeling (Hollander & Kazaoka, 1988; Rimm & Cunningham, 1985). These techniques are applied systematically, and a great deal of planning goes into delineating which procedures will be most effective for which clients. Overall, behaviorism can simply be defined as a "learning process" in which helpers "employ a systematic procedure to help clients accomplish a particular change in behavior" (Hosford & deVisser, 1974, p. 15).

In groups, "practically all of the theoretical and conceptual materials drawn from behavior theory and integrated into the area of behavior therapy are germane" (Hollander & Kazaoka, 1988, p. 279). **Behavioral groups** are either interpersonal or transactional depending on the purposes of the leader and members. *Interpersonal groups* are highly didactic and involve specified goals that usually center on self-improvement, such as daily living or study skills. *Transactional groups* are more heterogeneous and focus on broader, yet specific, goals. For example, transactional groups might concentrate on the proper display of a wide variety of social skills in cross-cultural interactions, such as making introductions, accepting compliments, or saying good-bye. They focus on each person in the group as well as the group itself.

Practice of Behaviorism in a Group

Behavioral groups may function in a variety of ways, but Rose (1977, 1983) and Hollander and Kazaoka (1988) give specific stages and principles that universally apply to behavioral groups. The first stage can be labeled *forming the group.* It consists of the organizational details that must be addressed before a group can begin. These details involve the purpose of the group, its membership, and the frequency and length of its meetings. Of these factors, Hollander and Kazaoka (1988) consider the homogeneity or heterogeneity of the problem to be most crucial. Clients with different target behaviors require completely different approaches (Lobitz & Baker, 1979).

Stage two involves *establishing the initial group attraction and identity.* The leader plays a major role in this process by conducting pregroup individual interviews in which members are able to explore their goals more deeply. These interviews also stress the connectedness of group members with each other (Rose, 1980). The third stage can best be described as the *establishment of openness and sharing in the group.* The leader promotes this type of behavior by letting group members know what is expected, by introducing subgroups to each other, and by modeling what he or she is asking group members to do. For example,. if the purpose of the group is to focus on increasing one's comfort speaking in public, the leader may speak out in the group before asking other members to do likewise.

Stage four, *establishing a behavioral framework for all participants,* is really the beginning of the working stage in the group. At this juncture, group leaders introduce their members to the behavioral frame of reference that will directly control the conduct of group members. The **antecedent-response-consequence model of behaviorism** formulated by Bijou, Peterson, and Ault (1968) is an excellent way to present such a concept. This model basically states that "behavior is functionally related to its antecedents and consequent events" (Hollander & Kazaoka, 1988, p. 287). Therefore, all behavior is purposeful, although some behaviors may not be productive. Once group members learn this "A-R-C model," they are better able to assess their own actions and monitor them, especially in regard to prebehavior cues and postbehavior rewards. They can then report more accurately the changes they make inside and outside of the group. In essence, this way of thinking gives the group and its members a tool that can be used to evaluate specific behaviors being tried (Corey, 1990).

Related to this stage is the creation of **positive expectations** within group members. Individuals who expect to be successful are much more likely to achieve their goals. Hollander and Kazaoka (1988) include the establishment of positive expectations as a separate stage, but here it is considered a substage of stage four.

Establishing and implementing a model for change is stage five. At this point, group members become more specific in what they are attempting to do. They identify and pinpoint the behaviors they have targeted to change, keep a baseline on how often they occur, implement appropriate change techniques, and assess their degree of success (Madsen & Madsen, 1970). As highlighted earlier, intervention techniques can take many forms. "There is no 'approved list' of techniques the use of which enables one to call himself (or herself) a behavioral counselor" (Krumboltz & Thoreson, 1969, p. 3).

Some of the most frequently used techniques are reinforcement, extinction, contingency contracts, shaping, modeling, behavioral rehearsal, coaching, cognitive restructuring, and the buddy system (Corey, 1990; Hansen et al., 1980; Posthuma, 1989; Wilson, 1989). They will be briefly described here.

Reinforcement is the key to behavioral groups. Within a group, members reinforce each other for changing specified behaviors. Usually, the reinforcement is positive and takes the form of verbal and nonverbal approval or praise. In some cases, reinforcement will be negative, that is, it will involve the removal of something from the group, such as criticism. In either case, the probability of a response is increased through reinforcement (Nye, 1981). One objective in behavioral groups is to teach individual group members to positively reinforce each other and to learn how to reinforce themselves. For example, Julie may say to Larry: "I like the way you spoke up for yourself in group today. I wonder how you can reward yourself for such behavior?" At that point, Larry would be asked to suggest ways Julie and other group members could reinforce him.

Extinction is the process of lowering the rate at which a behavior occurs through withdrawing the reinforcers that have been maintaining it. Eventually, the targeted behavior will stop altogether. This technique is usually used in combination with other behavioral methods so that group members have a behavior to replace the one being eliminated. Extinction might be used when a group member is talking about irrelevant material. In such a case, the group leader would ignore the behavior and get other group members to ignore it, too. Only when the group member focused on relevant material would he or she receive the attention of the group and its leader (Hansen et al., 1980).

Contingency contracts "spell out the behaviors to be performed, changed, or discontinued; the rewards associated with the achievement of these goals; and the conditions under which rewards are to be received" (Corey, 1990, p. 391). Most often contingency contracts will be used in groups of children rather than with adults because many adults find them offensive. Usually contingency contracts are written out as quasi-formal documents (for example, see Figure 16.1).

Shaping involves teaching behaviors "through successive approximation and chaining" (Hansen et al., 1980, p. 304). This gradual step process allows members to learn a new behavior over time and practice parts of it to perfection. Before undertaking shaping within a group, group leaders need to be aware of the specific response sequence they wish to establish, i.e., what follows what and how, a process known as **(chaining).** Implementing such a procedure, when carefully planned, will usually lead to new and improved behaviors.

Modeling is learning through observing someone else (Bandura, 1965, 1977). Behavioral group leaders often model appropriate behaviors for their members (Trotzer, 1989). Likewise, group members sometimes serve as good models for others in the group. Modeling is an especially powerful tool in group settings when those who are modeling resemble group members (Bandura, 1969, 1977). For example, in a group for shy children, a participant may imitate an assertive behavior if he or she views another child in the group acting in such a manner (Meichenbaum, 1977). Videotape feedback can often be used in the modeling process so that group participants are able to see others like themselves engaging in desired behaviors (Rose & Edleson, 1987).

Behavioral rehearsal consists of practicing a desired behavior until it is performed the way one wishes. The process consists of gradually shaping a behavior and getting corrective feedback. It is frequently used after a person has viewed a model enacting the desired behavior. In such cases, especially with complex behavior, the person who wishes to acquire the behavior will practice what he or she has observed in the presence of other group members and the leader. The person will then receive feedback and suggestions on what was done and make modifications accordingly. The group setting is ideal for such a procedure because it offers safety to the practitioner and a chance to experiment. The more similar the rehearsal is to the actual conditions under which it will take place outside the group, the more likely it is to be performed successfully and generalized (be effective over a wide variety of conditions) in a particular environment (Cormier & Cormier, 1985).

Coaching is a process of providing group members with general principles for performing desired behaviors (Corey, 1990). It works best when the coach sits behind the group member who is rehearsing (see Figure 16.2). If the member forgets what to do next or questions why he or she is doing it, the coach can intervene. Over time, coaching should be diminished, a process known as "fading."

Chocolate Chip Cookie Contract

I, _____Joe Smith_____ , do hereby on this 10th day of June, 1990, commit myself to contract with _____Jane Jones_____ .

_____Joe Smith_____ agrees to forfeit specified monies as outlined below to _____Jane Jones_____ upon failing to comply with the criterion for limited chocolate chip cookie eating as set forth below. Joe Smith will report to Jane Jones each day the number of chocolate chip cookies he has consumed outside her presence. Jane Jones will collect $1.50 for every chocolate chip cookie consumed by Joe Smith above the listed number for the day. Joe Smith will reward himself with a $1.00 in his "tennis ball box" for every day he meets or breaks his target behavior. Joe Smith promises to be honest and accurate in his counting of chocolate chip cookies consumed and report to Jane Jones immediately before Jane's bedtime (11 PM) every night. Jane Jones is free to do with the collected money anything she wishes. Joe Smith will hold no animosity toward her for performing her duties and spending the money in whatever way she wishes. This contract will be in effect for a period of _____8_____ days (until June 18th) after which Joe Smith will be free to eat as many chocolate chip cookies a day as he desires.

Date _____June 10, 1990_____

Signed _____Joe Smith_____

_____Jane Jones_____

Specified number of cookies
allowed to be eaten by
Joe Smith

Date	Maximum # of chocolate chip cookies that can be eaten in a day by Joe Smith
June 11	11
June 12	9
June 13	7
June 14	5
June 15	3
June 16	1
June 17	0
June 18	0

Figure 16.1
Cookie contract.

Figure 16.2
Coaching.

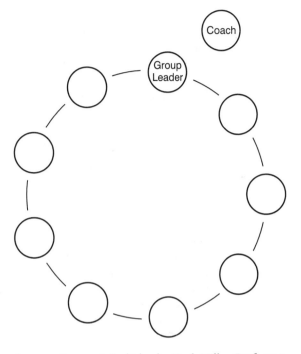

Source: From original idea by Mark Miller, Professor of Counseling, Louisiana Technical University, Ruston, LA. Used with permission.

Cognitive restructuring is a process in which group members are taught to identify, evaluate, and change self-defeating or irrational thoughts that negatively influence their behavior. This process is accomplished by getting group members to vocalize their self-talk before others and change it when necessary from negative to either neutral or positive (Posthuma, 1989). It is similar to what Ellis (1962) and Beck (1976) propose in regard to modifying the way one thinks. One of the best methods for implementing this process is Meichenbaum's (1977) self-instructional training. In this procedure, the group member is trained to become aware of his or her maladaptive thoughts (self-statements). Next, the group leader models appropriate behaviors while verbalizing the reasons behind these strategies. Finally, the group member performs the designated behaviors while verbally repeating the reasons behind the actions and then conducts these behaviors giving himself or herself covert messages.

Rose (1986) has identified a number of cognitive restructuring procedures including corrective information, thought stopping, relabeling, disputing irrational beliefs, imagery, stress inoculation, relaxation exercises, and systematic problem solving. Rose (1983) has also outlined a method of using cognitive restructuring within a group setting that involves the use of teaching, practice, and performance similar to that of Meichenbaum's.

In the *buddy system,* members are paired up in dyadic teams to mutually reinforce and support each other (Hollander & Kazaoka, 1988). This type of learning appears to enhance the change process for each dyad and the entire group.

Stage six, *generalization and transference of treatment to the natural environment,* marks the beginning of group termination. **Generalization** involves the display of behaviors in environments outside of where they were originally learned, for example, at home or at work. It indicates that transference into another setting has occurred. Generalizing behaviors and transferring them to another setting does not happen by chance. Skilled group leaders must ensure that these processes are implemented (Wilson, 1989). They do so by employing a number of procedures including the assignment of behavioral homework, training significant others (e.g., peers or colleagues) in the individuals' environments to reinforce them for appropriate behaviors, and consulting with group members about particular problems they may have in making behavioral switches (Corey, 1990; Rose, 1983).

The seventh and final stage of behavior groups is *maintaining behavior change and fading out of the need for the group's support.* **Maintenance** is defined as being more consistent in doing the actions desired without depending on the group or its leader for support. In this stage, emphasis is placed on increasing group members' self-control and self-management (Mahoney & Thoresen, 1974; Thoresen & Mahoney, 1974). This may be done by **self-monitoring** in which members are simply asked "to keep detailed, daily records of particular events or psychological reactions" (Wilson, 1989, p. 250). For example, in a group for the management of weight control, individuals monitor their calorie intake and their reactions to eating certain foods. They then transfer this behavioral technique outside of the group setting. If they find this technique does not help, they would rejoin another weight management group and try another technique. The results of the chocolate chip cookie contract (Figure 16.3) illustrate the basic components of a detailed self-monitoring program.

Role of the Behavioral Group Leader

Behavioral group leaders have a number of leadership responsibilities. Corey (1990) lists some of their primary functions as follows: screening group members, teaching them about group process, assessing their progress in the group, determining the effectiveness of techniques employed in the group, and reinforcing members' achievements of specific goals. Vander Kolk (1985), while not disagreeing, conceptualizes the behavioral group leader as a systematic planner who identifies problems in behavioral terms and works with group members to achieve their objectives through the employment of appropriate strategies. "The most common strategies are instruction, feedback, modeling, behavioral rehearsal, social reinforcement, and homework assignments" (p. 127).

Overall, the behavioral group leader is a participant-observer (Hansen et al., 1980; Rose, 1983). The leader is much more active and direct at the beginning of

Baseline Chocolate Chip Cookie-Eating Behavior

Date	# of cookies per day	Contract for Treatment
June 1	10	Chocolate chip cookie eating will be
June 2	14	decreased by two cookies a day during
June 3	8	the treatment period. The subject will
June 4	10	either earn or lose money as specified
June 5	11	in the chocolate chip cookie contract
June 6	13	for his behavior.
June 7	9	
June 8	11	
June 9	12	
June 10	10	

Baseline average—11 cookies per day

Treatment Chocolate Chip Cookie-Eating Behavior

Date	Target Behavior # of cookies per day	Actual Behavior # of cookies per day	Difference	Money earned (+) or lost (−)
June 11	11	8	−3	+$1.00
June 12	9	5	−4	+$1.00
June 13	7	4	−3	+$1.00
June 14	5	5	0	+$1.00
June 15	3	3	0	+$1.00
June 16	1	2	+1	−$1.50
June 17	0	0	0	+$1.00
June 18	0	0	0	+$1.00

Total money earned (+) or lost (−) +$5.50

Figure 16.3
Chocolate chip cookie-eating behavior.

the group but delegates more responsibility to group members as sessions go on (Axelrod, 1977). Leaders use as many techniques and instruments as possible, including videos, in helping their group members bring about desired changes. Belkin (1988) describes this leadership style as that of a "manager of contingencies" (p. 391). If the leader performs adequately, group members will help reinforce one another in a positive manner.

Behavioral group leaders may come from any of the major mental health professions (e.g., counseling, social work, psychology, nursing, or psychiatry), or they may come from the business and management domains. Many will need specialized training beyond that which they received in graduate school. Hollander and Kazaoka (1988) recommend two years of postgraduate training as a prerequisite to becoming a behavioral group leader. They also advocate that behavioral groups be co-led by a male and female in order to model a co-equal relationship and show group members that persons of different genders and backgrounds can work together harmoniously. For those wishing to become behavioral therapists, the **Association for Advancement of Behavioral Therapy (AABT)** is the major organization with which to affiliate.

Desired Outcome of Behavioral Groups

As a result of a behavioral group experience, participants should achieve a number of objectives. Many behavioral groups tend to be individually focused, yet goals for the group as a whole may be achieved (Hansen et al., 1980). The magnitude of change and its impact depends on how well the group functions and how dedicated group members are. If all goes well, some or all of the following should occur.

First, they will be more aware of what specific behaviors they and others have that need changing and how to accomplish that. It is highly likely that they will become more sensitive about areas of their lives that they would like to modify. For example, in a behavioral group experience, Blair realized if she was going to be effective in communicating with others, she had to shorten her sentences and focus her ideas in a clearer way.

Second, it is hoped that through the behavioral group, participants will be able to assess how well they have altered their behaviors as well as what they still need to do to generalize them to their daily living environments. For example, in checking her chart on speaking up in the group, Margaret realizes she has improved. However, in monitoring her behavior outside the group, she realizes she has not changed. Therefore, in working with the behavioral group, Margaret asks members for suggestions on how to generalize what she is doing in the group to situations outside of it.

A third outcome of the group is that members will be more cognizant of new models for achieving their desired goals. This outcome objective dovetails with the second outcome focus. Behavioral groups are centered around learning, and one of the primary lessons learned in these settings is that there are many ways to modify behaviors, for example, behavioral rehearsals as well as real-life experiences. Take, for example, an art group in which young novices are beginning to experiment with form and textures. By watching the group leaders and other group members, an individual in such a setting should begin to realize that there are many ways to achieve the end results he or she wants.

Besides individual achievements, behavioral group members may realize more fully the power of group reinforcement. As a result of this psychological and social support, they may structure their life within groups differently. For example, Ed may now say to his friends when he is in doubt, "How am I doing?"

Finally, group members may become more behaviorally oriented in resolving their own difficulties outside of a group setting. In other words, they may make behaviorism more a way of life. As such, they may concentrate on shaping, reinforcing, extinguishing, or modifying behaviors in their immediate environments. For instance, some behaviorally based parent training courses become internalized and integrated into the lives of their participants because of the overall positive effect that takes place in their lives.

Evaluation of Behavioral Groups

Because behaviorism has a long history and strong research methods, groups based on this theory are probably among the easiest to evaluate.

Advantages.   A major advantage of behavioral groups is their focus on helping their members learn new ways of functioning (Corey, 1990; Hollander & Kazaoka, 1988; Vander Kolk, 1985). Many individuals have difficulty in relationships with others because they display excessive or limited behavioral skills (Gladding, 1992). For example, they talk too much or not enough. Behavioral groups directly instruct their members on ways to improve interpersonal and personal skills so that problems are alleviated.

A second strength of the behavioral approach is the impressive research it has generated (Rose, 1983). In 1989, there were at least nine journals devoted exclusively to behavior therapy (Wilson, 1989). In addition, there are a number of researchers investigating behaviorally based groups under controlled conditions (Zimpfer, 1984), and annual reviews on these groups and behavioral methods are constantly being compiled (e.g., Upper & Ross, 1980). Major texts on behavior treatment approaches continue to be published almost every month (Rachman & Wilson, 1980).

Yet, a third advantage of behavioral groups is that they are relatively short-term and focused (Hollander & Kazaoka, 1988). Behavioral psychotherapy and counseling groups, for instance, are seldom conducted more than once a week over an eight- to 12-month period and last 90 to 120 minutes a session. This period of time is relatively brief, especially when compared to psychoanalytic groups. Members have specific goals to work on that are measurable. Psychoeducational and work/task behavioral groups are equally of a short-term duration.

A fourth strength of behavioral groups is their versatility. For example, behaviorally oriented groups can be used to teach specific skills, such as assertion (Alberti & Emmons, 1987), to work on certain problem areas, such as phobic behavior (Wolpe, 1958), and to address holistic issues (Lazarus, 1981). There are very few problems behaviorists do not address. Each group is tailored to the needs of its members (Rose, 1983).

A fifth advantage of the behavioral approach is its emphasis on promoting self-control among its members once the group ends (Corey, 1990). In some ways, the behavioral group is like an incubator that fosters specific growth in its participants and that keeps developing after the group experience terminates.

A final positive about the behavioral group focus is that behavioral theories can be combined with other approaches, for example, cognitive theories, to create a multimodal way of working with groups and their members. Cognitive-behavioral group psychotherapy, for instance, is a very popular way of working with individuals in groups in order to help them integrate their thoughts and behaviors (Sedgwick, 1989).

Limitations. Behavioral groups are not without their disadvantages. One is that group members may become overdependent on the group for support and encouragement. In such cases, these individuals become "group junkies/addicts" and use the group for inappropriate reinforcement. Although this type of behavior is rare, it may occur if the leader and participants do not work hard on generalization and termination issues.

A second limitation of behavioral group work is that some of its methods can be too rigidly applied (Corey, 1990; Vander Kolk, 1985). In such situations, too much emphasis is placed on techniques and not enough on individuals. Groups in which this occurs have leaders who are underinvolved with members and overinvolved in changing behaviors. They work like mechanics instead of human development specialists.

A third limitation of the behavioral approach is its tendency to ignore the past and the unconscious (Rose, 1977). Early history has only so much influence on people, but behaviorally based groups do not consider any influence of early history or repressed thoughts. This theory is not appropriate for those trying to resolve early childhood experiences that are still problematic.

A fourth disadvantage of behavioral groups is their lack of focus on broad life issues (T. M. Elmore, personal communication, 1989). Behavioral groups are much more likely to concentrate on particular events or skills in their members' lives than on members' lives as a whole. In this regard, they are just the opposite from groups with a more existential flavor, such as those with a person-centered base. As a result, some changes brought about in the group may not last because of members' inabilities to see a connection between what they have learned and the rest of their lives.

A fifth limitation of the behavioral approach is its concentration on behavior, whether overt or covert. Behavioral groups are not particularly concerned about feelings but rather the dynamics behind them (T. M. Elmore, personal communication, 1989). In this regard, the behavioral approach is just the opposite of the Gestalt emphasis. Persons who wish to become more aware of their emotions are better served in another setting.

Finally, behavioral groups are not unified theoretically and work best with well-motivated members (Hollander & Kazaoka, 1988). More work is needed in bringing the different theories that underlie this group procedure together and in making it more applicable for low-motivated individuals. To their credit, many behaviorists are actively engaged in trying to rectify these deficits.

REALITY THERAPY GROUPS

Reality therapy has a much briefer history than behavioral theories. However, its growth and development have been phenomenal. Reality therapy was founded by William Glasser, who was initially trained to be a psychoanalyst but grew disenchanted with this approach. Originally, reality therapy "had no systematic theory, only the empirical idea that individuals are responsible for what they do" (Glasser, 1984, p. 320). Since its original development in the 1950s and 1960s, however, reality therapy has evolved. In the 1980s, **control theory,** a complete system for explaining how the brain works, has been added to the base of reality therapy to make it more complete (Glasser, 1985, 1986c; Wubbolding, 1988, 1991).

Like transactional analysis, reality therapy was initially employed more in groups than with individuals. Glasser developed and employed his approach at the Ventura (California) School for Girls, his first employer, but he has since applied his theory to the total population of those seeking mental health services (Glasser, 1969, 1976, 1986b). Reality therapy has also gained a foothold in work/task environments, such as the **total quality movement,** in which there is an emphasis on working cooperatively and productively in small groups.

Premises of Reality Therapy Groups

Reality therapy, as a control theory approach, differs from other common-sense ways of working in groups. It emphasizes that "all behavior is generated within ourselves for the purpose of satisfying one or more basic needs" (Glasser, 1984, p. 323). Unlike most other helping theories, Glasser claims that human behavior is not a reaction to outside events but rather to internal needs. **Reality therapy's four human psychological needs are:** belonging, power, freedom, and fun, whose origin is the "new" human brain. There is also one physiological need, survival, which originated in the "old" human brain (Glasser, 1985). "No matter what the presenting problem, all clients seen in counseling are struggling unsuccessfully to satisfy one or more of these basic needs" (Glasser, 1986c, p. 3) (see Figure 16.4).

Glasser (1965, 1984, 1985) states that reality therapy also differs from other psychotherapeutic systems in the following ways:

1. It rejects the concept of mental illness. People choose to act psychotically or neurotically in an attempt to control the world to some extent and satisfy their needs.

Figure 16.4
Reality therapy as a control
theory therapy.

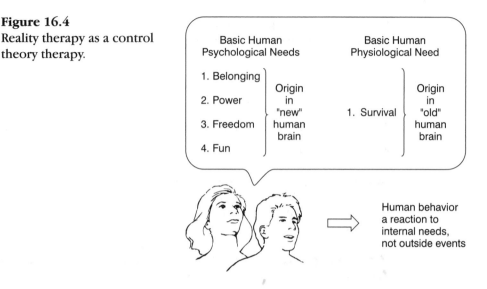

2. It emphasizes the present as the "cutting edge" of peoples' lives and focuses on how individuals can effectively control the world they live in and choose behaviors that are best for them.
3. It does not deal with transference, but relates to clients' perceptions.
4. It does not deal with the unconscious or dreams, but with present awareness and an attempt to make that awareness even greater.
5. It stresses that persons must judge their own behaviors in light of personal and societal values. Contrary to O. Hobart Mowrer's introduction to Glasser's first book, *Reality Therapy* (1965), reality therapists do not take a moral position.
6. It attempts to teach people a better way of fulfilling their needs and taking responsibility for themselves. In essence, Glasser sees all psychotherapy as teaching and all psychoeducation as psychotherapeutic.

Glasser believes that third force psychology with its humanistic emphasis, as represented by the writings of Abraham Maslow, is closely aligned to reality therapy. Mowrer's **integrity therapy**, which stresses helping people live up to their own moral convictions, also has much in common with reality therapy.

Practice of Reality Therapy in a Group

The practice of reality therapy in a group setting is basically a rational process. It emphasizes observable behavior in a here-and-now setting (Hansen et al., 1980), for example, what is someone in the group doing now? If the process goes smoothly, group members will give up unproductive and self-defeating behaviors and commit to new action patterns that they have mutually agreed on with the group leader (Bigelow & Thorne, 1969). There is some variation on how to apply reality therapy concepts, but **reality therapy's eight basic steps** are generally employed both with groups and individuals (Glasser, 1984; Glasser & Zunin, 1973).

1. *Make friends/establish a meaningful relationship*—In this first step, the reality therapist attempts to establish rapport with each group member. People are usually involved in groups because of a need to connect with others. Therefore, the group leader can take the initial step in fulfilling this need. This process is achieved by having the group leader both screen applicants and then engage them in conversation or activity soon after they come to the group. In doing so, the leader also determines with the help of the group member what he or she "pictures" as a way of meeting his or her basic needs. This picture comes from within the internal world of the group member (Glasser, 1986c) and is drawn out by the leader through skillful questioning and interactions (Wubbolding, 1988).

2. *Emphasize present behaviors/Ask what are you doing now?*—This second step focuses in on the process of choice. Reality therapists stress the importance of utilizing thinking and acting, rather than feeling or physiology, to bring about change (Glasser, 1986a). Therefore, group members are asked to concentrate on behaviors they can control in the present. For example, members have choices in the ways they think about and interact with other group members and the group leader.

3. *Stress whether clients' actions are getting them what they want*—The emphasis here is on group members' judging their behaviors and learning that their behaviors are within their control. A part of this process focuses on personal values, whereas a second part underlines reasonable rules by which societal systems live. Persons with difficulties may be acting against their own best judgment or the collected wisdom of society (Glasser, 1986c). For example, if Tess becomes upset every time someone ignores her but her actions do not bring about changes, she may be confronted with the fruitfulness of what she is doing.

4. *Make a positive plan to do better*—This is a critical stage in the group process. It involves "planning, advising, helping, and encouraging" (Glasser, 1984, p. 336). It is based on the accomplishment of the first three stages. The plan of action is the individual's, but group members and the leader can be very effective in providing input and suggestions that will make the plan even more potent. Wubbolding (1988) suggests an effective plan has the following components:
   a.   ties in closely with a member's needs
   b.   is simple and easy to understand
   c.   is realistic and attainable
   d.   includes positive actions
   e.   is independent of other's contributions
   f.   is practicable regularly
   g.   is immediately doable

    h.   is process oriented

    i.   is open to constructive input by group members by being written down and well formulated.

5. *Get a commitment to follow the positive plan*—It is not enough to formulate a plan of action; group members must follow through. "A plan that does not have the client's firm commitment is likely to fail" (Barr, 1974, p. 67). In making a commitment, group members take responsibility for their lives and, in the process, gain more control. For example, if George commits himself to 15 minutes of exercise a day, he achieves control of his body and his time in a new way.

6. *No excuses*—At times, group members will not succeed in their plans of action. In such cases, the group leader and group members simply acknowledge that the person failed. The past is not brought up, and excuses are not discussed. Accepting excuses gives persons in the group the idea that they are weak, cannot change, and are, in effect, unable to control their lives (Wubbolding, 1988, 1991). Instead, individuals are helped to formulate another plan (usually a modification of the original one) and are encouraged to try again. Sometimes the plan is broken down into smaller steps than previously, for as Glasser and Zunin (1973) point out, "It is much better to have client success in small stages than to try to effect a large change and experience failure" (p. 301).

7. *No punishment*—"Punishment is the infliction of pain with no reasonable way to reduce or end the pain no matter what the wrongdoer does" (Glasser, 1984, p. 337). It is the opposite of control and often leads to individuals' acting in negative or self-defeating ways. Therefore, reality therapy (similar to Adlerian-based theory) stresses that persons who do not follow their plans of actions must live with the natural consequences, i.e., the results that follow. This usually means they do not get what they want. This type of response will often motivate them, along with the group's encouragement, to try again.

8. *Never give up*—Change often takes time, especially if the client has a long history of failure. Group leaders persevere with group members who are slow to change. This consistency begins to become internalized by clients. They realize that the leader is like a good friend who does not give up easily. With this realization, they often become more willing to try new behaviors, and the process of change can begin. For example, Betsy may internally remind herself that her group leader still believes she can lose the weight she committed to dropping. Therefore, she renews her commitment and effort.

In addition to the above procedure, Wubbolding (1988, 1991) suggests four special procedures that are applicable to a reality therapy group: (a) skillful use of questioning, (b) self-help procedures, (c) use of humor, and (d) use of paradox.

Skillful use of *questioning* has already been covered. It is crucial that the group leader ask open-ended and inviting questions in order to help members become more explorative. For example, the leader might say, "Claire, what do you hope to get out of this group?"

Self-help procedures are those in which there is a focus on the positive. Behaviors that members would like to have are targeted. There is a real effort on the part of the member and the group to implement actions that will lead to a success identity, such as learning new social skills.

The use of *humor* is a method advocated by Glasser in many of his publications. Wubbolding's emphasis on this procedure is to stress its timing, focus, and the importance of trust in the process. Humor should never put people down. Rather, it should be utilized to help individuals gain an awareness of a situation not easily obtainable in another way. For example, in regard to self, the group leader might say, "Whenever I think I've learned all the answers about groups, the groups change the questions."

Finally, in regard to utilizing *paradox,* Wubbolding stresses that with some group members, change is best brought about indirectly rather than the direct method advocated by Glasser. In these situations, the power of humor (catching someone "off guard") is often effective, but there is the danger of being misunderstood. To be successful, group leaders may employ paradox (asking members to do the opposite of what they want) so that the message they give, such as "go slow," is taken seriously and disobeyed for the good of the group member. Most reality therapy group leaders are not initially able to use paradox successfully.

Role of the Reality Therapy Group Leader

Reality therapy group leaders are active and involved with group members. They strive to be warm, confronting individuals who keep pointing out reality to group members in a direct, caring manner. For example, as the group leader, George may say to June, "Is what you are doing now working?"

Glasser (1965) lists four criteria for effective reality therapy leaders. First, they must be responsible persons who are able to fulfill their own needs. Next, they must be mentally strong and able to resist group members' pleas for sympathy and excuses for nonproductive behavior. A third quality is acceptance of group members for whom they are, at least initially. Finally, reality therapy group leaders must be emotionally involved or supportive of each group member. Fulfilling these criteria is developmental. Leaders must be mentally and emotionally mature and comfortable with themselves before they can work with group members and help them bring about needed changes.

Corey (1990) states reality therapy practitioners must strive to carry out other functions, too. Among the most prevalent of them is serving as a personal model of responsible behavior (i.e., being a success identity). Group members are likely to emulate leaders whether leaders wish them to or not. In addition to working in this way, reality therapy group leaders must also foster the process of self-evaluation in their members. They may do this through modeling the self-evaluation process in themselves. Furthermore, leaders establish a structure and limits for group sessions and assist group members in understanding the scope of the group process and the need to apply what they have learned in the group to their own daily lives. Hansen et al. (1980) state that in carrying out their responsibilities within the group, reality therapy leaders will generally be eclectic in the techniques they employ.

Desired Outcome of Reality Therapy Groups

If the reality therapy group process is successful, members will realize several benefits. Among the most important is the change they will experience in moving past self-defeating patterns of behavior. These individuals will no longer be stuck in repetitive and nonproductive activity. Instead, they will engage in new behaviors designed to help them achieve responsible, present-oriented goals (Glasser, 1984, 1986c). They will realize that just as the group leader did not give up or punish them when they were not successful with their positive plans of action, they too do not have to become discouraged, defeated, or punitive when they do not achieve what they want initially.

Group members come away from the reality therapy experience with a greater awareness of their values. Through the group, they realize they have a choice in what they do (Glasser, 1986a). They are freer to realize the role they play in taking control of their lives. Outside events and past histories lose much of their power if individuals learn one of the basic premises of the reality therapy approach—they are responsible and can choose to change.

Evaluation of Reality Therapy Groups

Reality therapy has been used in a number of different kinds of groups and is among the most versatile of the theories used in groups. Nevertheless, it has its drawbacks as well as advantages.

Advantages.   There are several advantages of reality therapy that make it an attractive and productive method to use in group settings. First, reality therapy emphasizes accountability (Corey, 1990). Individuals are responsible for deciding what they value and wish to change in their lives. They learn that they must work on implementing these changes. Therefore, responsibility is placed squarely where it should be—on the shoulders of group members.

A second strength of this approach is its stress on action and thinking, as opposed to feeling and physiology (Glasser, 1986a). By stressing that group members make plans and carry them out, reality therapy breaks the inertia of the past and makes it more likely that clients will be able to change. Part of this action/thinking process involves refusing to accept excuses and not punishing

(Glasser, 1984). The action/thinking dimension of reality therapy is aimed in a positive direction, i.e., fostering needed and appropriate change.

A third valuable dimension of a reality therapy group is its viability with people in the society on which others have given up (Corey, 1990). For example, delinquents, prisoners, and depressives are but three groups that are often neglected or ineffectively serviced by mental health professionals. Reality therapy groups make it possible to work productively with these populations and others that are viewed as incorrigible or difficult. This approach is also very effective in crisis counseling and in long-term group counseling, such as with victims of rape (McArthur, 1990).

A fourth advantage of this approach is its emphasis on definable procedures for working with individuals in groups (Glasser, 1986b; Wubbolding, 1987). Reality therapy is very straightforward in emphasizing what group leaders need to do and when. It has become more flexible through the years with practitioners other than Glasser adding new techniques to its repertoire, for example, paradoxical methods and the employment of teaching metaphors and stories (Wubbolding, 1991).

A final advantage of using reality therapy in groups is that the treatment continues only until participants are able to resolve difficulties. As a way of promoting positive change, reality therapy is a relatively brief approach (Wubbolding, 1988). Most individuals only have limited time to work on their difficulties, whether therapeutically or in an organizational context. Reality therapy is geared to that reality and helps group members to become involved with others and to reinforce each person's plans that were successful.

Limitations.   One limitation of reality therapy is its emphasis on the exchange of communication, either verbal or written (Glasser, 1984). Many reality therapists use contracts in their groups to have members clarify exactly what their goals are. Individuals who cannot or will not communicate in this way do not benefit very much from this approach.

A second limitation of this method is its simplicity. Glasser's eight-step method of conducting a group may be misapplied by "mechanical" group leaders who do not understand or appreciate the complexity of human nature and change. These individuals are likely to moralize or be too controlling so that group members do not get the opportunity to struggle with their own issues (Corey, 1990).

A third limitation of reality therapy is its extreme position on some issues. Certainly, it can be argued that mental illness diagnoses are overused; however, to deny that there is any such thing as genetically based mental illness, as Glasser does, probably overstates the case (Glasser, 1984; Glasser, 1986a). Likewise, it can be stated that some theories overemphasize the unconscious or the past, but that is different from the reality therapy perspective of refusing to deal with the unconscious and denying the importance of past events except as a way of understanding present behaviors.

A fourth limitation of this theory in group work is its lack of proven effectiveness (Corey, 1990). Glasser argues that reality therapy is one of the most popular theories in educational, correctional, and substance abuse programs (Evans,

1982), but the validity of this theory has seldom been researched thoroughly (Ford, 1982). Until the theory is investigated more thoroughly, its use will continue to be questioned.

A final limitation of reality therapy is its emphasis on conformity and utility. Group members are expected to conform to the reality of those with the most power (Glasser, 1986a). Although this emphasis may be pragmatic, it may also discourage more creative and independent behaviors. It also takes the emphasis away from changing one's environment. Reality therapy is not the only theory that focuses more on individual change within the group than on environmental change. Like other approaches with this emphasis (i.e., most individual theories of counseling), the drawback is that attention to larger and important issues may be bypassed or ignored.

SUMMARY AND CONCLUSION

Behavioral theories and reality therapy are both popular ways of working with groups. The behavioral position, though diverse, focuses on empowering its group members by concentrating on self-improvement skills. Individuals in these groups learn how to manage excessive amounts of behavior or learn new behaviors. The three primary behavior methods for teaching in these groups are respondent learning, operant conditioning, and social learning.

Contracts are often used in behaviorally oriented groups to help members focus on the behaviors they wish to change. As a group, behaviorists employ many techniques to promote and foster change with their group members, including reinforcement, extinction, shaping, cognitive restructuring, coaching, the buddy system, and problem-solving rehearsals. Within groups, members offer support to one another, although this approach is often more leader–member centered than member–member focused. A real strength of the behavioral approach to group work is the solid learning theory base behind it. There is also excellent research to back behavioral approaches to group work.

Reality therapy is a relatively new theory (since the mid-1960s) that is unique, although it does have some similarities to behaviorism. These similarities include its emphasis on changing actions first and its de-emphasis on the past, the unconscious, and emotions. In the 1980s, reality therapy incorporated control theory into its practice, and it has since become more internally focused. At its core, it stresses the employment of action and thoughts.

Reality therapy groups follow a fairly well-formulated eight-stage approach that is specific but may become superficial in the hands of an inexperienced group leader. In the 1980s, there was an emphasis to develop new techniques and incorporate them into this format. An increased emphasis on reality therapy has led to the uniform training of leaders at the Institute for Reality Therapy at Canoga Park, California.

As a result of reality therapy, group members should become more aware of their values and more focused on changing their behaviors instead of trying to change others. It is hoped they will take control of their lives and be responsible and accountable for all they do. Many group leaders, such as those working in education, mental health, and business, find reality therapy effective with the populations they serve. Although popular, reality therapy still needs a more solid research base.

CLASSROOM EXERCISES

1. Pretend that you have been asked to lead a behavioral group. How would your preparation differ if the group were focused on general life skills as opposed to a specific intrapersonal skill? What common dimensions would these two approaches have?
2. How can behavioral groups be used in educational and business settings? List as many ways as you can and compare your list with that of another class member and with the class as a whole.
3. Compare and contrast reality therapy before and after its incorporation of control theory by reading the following two Glasser books, *Reality Therapy* (1965) and *Stations of the Mind* (1981). How has the approach been improved and weakened by this basic change?
4. Examine the many ways reality therapy is used in groups by reading recent periodicals. How does the focus of reality therapy differ with groups when compared to individuals?

REFERENCES

Alberti, R. E., & Emmons, M. L. (1987). *Your perfect right: A guide to assertive behavior.* San Luis Obispo, CA: Impact.

Axelrod, S. (1977). *Behavior modification for the classroom teacher.* New York: McGraw-Hill.

Bandura, A. (1965). Behavioral modifications through modeling procedures. In L. Krasner & L. P. Ullman (Eds.), *Research in behavior modification.* New York: Holt, Rinehart & Winston.

Bandura, A. (1969). *Principles of behavior modification.* New York: Holt, Rinehart & Winston.

Bandura, A. (1977). *Social learning theory.* Englewood Cliffs, NJ: Prentice Hall.

Barr, N. I. (1974). The responsible world of reality therapy. *Psychology Today, 7,* 64–68.

Beck, A. T. (1976). *Cognitive therapy and the emotional disorders.* New York: International Universities Press.

Belkin, G. S. (1988). *Introduction to Counseling.* Dubuque, IA: Wm. C. Brown.

Bigelow, G. S., & Thorne, J. W. (1969). Reality versus client-centered models in group counseling. *The School Counselor, 16*(1), 91–94.

Bijou, S. W., Peterson, R. P., & Ault, M. H. (1968). A method to integrate descriptive and experimental field studies at the level of data and empirical concepts. *Journal of Applied Behavior Analysis, 1,* 175–191.

Corey, G. (1985). *Theory and practice of group counseling* (2nd ed). Pacific Grove, CA: Brooks/Cole.

Corey, G. (1990). *Theory and practice of group counseling* (3rd ed.). Pacific Grove, CA: Brooks/Cole.

Cormier, W. H., & Cormier, L. S. (1985). *Interviewing strategies for helpers.* Pacific Grove, CA: Brooks/Cole.

Ellis, A. (1962). *Reason and emotion in psychotherapy*. New York: Lyle Stuart.

Evans, D. B. (1982). What are you doing? An interview with William Glasser. *Personnel and Guidance Journal, 60,* 460–465.

Ford, E. E. (1982). Reality therapy in family therapy. In A. M. Horne & M. M. Ohlsen (Eds.), *Family counseling and therapy*. Itasca, IL: Peacock.

Gladding, S. T. (1984). Beyond the outer calm. *Journal of Humanistic Education and Development, 23,* 35.

Gladding, S. T. (1992). *Counseling: A comprehensive profession* (2nd ed.). New York: Merrill/Macmillan.

Glasser, W. (1965). *Reality therapy: A new approach to psychiatry*. New York: Harper & Row.

Glasser, W. (1969). *Schools without failure*. New York: Harper & Row.

Glasser, W. (1976). *Positive addiction*. New York: Harper & Row.

Glasser, W. (1981). *Stations of the mind*. New York: Harper & Row.

Glasser, W. (1984). Reality therapy. In R. J. Corsini (Ed.), *Current psychotherapies* (3rd ed.) (pp. 320–353). Itasca, IL: F. E. Peacock.

Glasser, W. (1985). *Control theory: A new explanation of how we control our lives*. New York: Harper & Row.

Glasser, W. (1986a). *The basic concepts of reality therapy* (chart). Canoga Park, CA: Institute for Reality Therapy.

Glasser, W. (1986b). *Control theory in the classroom*. New York: Harper & Row.

Glasser, W. (1986c). *The control theory-reality therapy workbook*. Canoga Park, CA: Institute for Reality Therapy.

Glasser, W., & Zunin, L. M. (1973). Reality therapy. In R. Corsini (Ed.), *Current psychotherapies*. Itasca, IL: Peacock.

Hansen, J. C., Warner, R. W., & Smith, E. J. (1980). *Group counseling: Theory and process* (2nd ed.). Chicago: Rand McNally.

Hollander, M., & Kazaoka, K. (1988). Behavior therapy groups. In S. Long (Ed.), *Six group therapies* (pp. 257–326). New York: Plenum.

Hosford, R. E., & deVisser, L. A. J. M. (1974). *Behavioral approaches to counseling: An introduction*. Washington, DC: AGPA Press.

Krumboltz, J. D. (Ed.). (1966). *Revolution in counseling: Implications of behavioral science*. Boston: Houghton Mifflin.

Krumboltz, J., & Thoresen, C. E. (1969). *Behavioral counseling: Cases and techniques*. New York: Holt, Rinehart & Winston.

Lazarus, A. A. (1981). *The practice of multimodal therapy*. New York: McGraw-Hill.

Lobitz, W. C., & Baker, E. L. (1979). Group treatment of sexual dysfunction. In D. Upper & S. M. Ross (Eds.), *Behavior group therapy*. Champlain, IL: Research Press.

Madsen, C. H., Jr., & Madsen, C. K. (1970). *Teaching/discipline*. Boston: Allyn & Bacon.

Mahoney, M. J., & Thoresen, C. E. (1974). *Self-control: Power to the person*. Monterey, CA: Brooks/Cole.

McArthur, M. J. (1990). Reality therapy with rape victims. *Archives of Psychiatric Nursing, 4,* 360–365.

Meichenbaum, D. H. (1977). *Cognitive-behavior modification: An integrative approach*. New York: Plenum.

Meichenbaum, D. H. (1986). Cognitive-behavior modification. In F. H. Kanfer & A. P. Goldstein (Eds.), *Helping people change*. New York: Pergamon.

Nye, R. D. (1981). *Three psychologies* (2nd ed.). Monterey, CA: Brooks/Cole.

Posthuma, B. W. (1989). *Small groups in therapy settings: Process and leadership*. Boston: College-Hill.

Rachman, S., & Wilson, G. T. (1980). *The effects of psychological therapy*. Oxford: Pergamon Press.

Rimm, D. C., & Cunningham, H. M. (1985). Behavior therapies. In S. J. Lynn & J. P. Garske (Eds.), *Contemporary psychotherapies: Models and methods* (pp. 221–260). Columbus, OH: Merrill.

Rose, S. D. (1977). *Group therapy: A behavioral approach*. Englewood Cliffs, NJ: Prentice Hall.

Rose, S. D. (1980). *A casebook in group therapy: A behavioral-cognitive approach*. Englewood Cliffs, NJ: Prentice Hall.

Rose, S. D. (1983). Behavior therapy in groups. In H. I. Kaplan & B. J. Sadock (Eds.), *Comprehensive group psychotherapy* (2nd ed.). Baltimore: Williams & Wilkins.

Rose, S. D. (1986). Group methods. In F. H. Kanfer & A. P. Goldstein (Eds.), *Helping people change: A textbook of methods* (3rd ed.) (pp. 437–469). New York: Pergamon.

Rose, S. D., & Edleson, J. L. (1987). *Working with children and adolescents in groups.* San Francisco: Jossey-Bass.

Sedgwick, C. (1989). Cognitive-behavioral group therapy. In G. M. Gazda (Ed.), *Group counseling* (4th ed.) (pp. 427–437). Boston: Allyn & Bacon.

Skinner, B. F. (1953). *Science and human behavior.* New York: Macmillan.

Skinner, B. F. (1974). *About behaviorism.* New York: Knopf.

Thoresen, C. E., & Mahoney, M. J. (1974). *Behavioral self-control.* New York: Holt, Rinehart & Winston.

Trotzer, J. P. (1989). *The counselor and the group* (2nd ed.). Muncie, IN: Accelerated Development.

Upper, D., & Ross, S. M. (Eds.). (1980). *Behavioral group therapy, 1980: An annual review.* Champaign, IL: Research Press.

Vander Kolk, C. J. (1985). *Introduction to group counseling and psychotherapy.* Columbus, OH: Merrill.

Watson, J. B. (1913). Psychology as a behaviorist views it. *Psychological Review, 20,* 158–177.

Wilson, G. T. (1989). Behavior therapy. In R. J. Corsini & D. Wedding (Eds.), *Current psychotherapies* (4th ed.) (pp. 241–282). Itasca, IL: Peacock.

Wolpe, J. (1958). *Psychotherapy by reciprocal inhibition.* Stanford, CA: Stanford University Press.

Wubbolding, R. E. (1987). A model for group activities related to teaching reality therapy. *Journal of Reality Therapy, 6,* 23–28.

Wubbolding, R. E. (1988). *Using reality therapy.* New York: Harper & Row.

Wubbolding, R. E. (1991). *Understanding reality therapy.* New York: Harper.

Zimpfer, D. G. (1984). *Group work in the helping professions: A bibliography* (2nd ed.). Muncie, IN: Accelerated Development.

CHAPTER 17

Psychodrama and Self-Help Groups

I remember doing role plays in your group
trying to look cool, while my palms sweated
and my heart beat as fast as a hummingbird's wing.
You were supportive . . . giving me a part of the warmth
you brought with you that summer
while encouraging me to explore the universe
that was myself.
Other classes, other seasons came as quickly as the sound
of laughter and as silently as sorrow.
With you in mind I traveled the road to conventions
and counseling conversations
Sharing all the light and darkness that came to be.*

Psychodrama and self-help groups were specifically designed with the structure and dynamics of groups in mind. Therefore, these approaches to working with others are mainly group focused. Unlike some of the theories examined so far, these ways of working with groups were not derived from individual theories of counseling. At the same time, it should be pointed out that psychodrama includes both individual and group emphases (Moreno, 1946), and some forms of self-help are practiced on an individual as well as group basis. However, like the opening poem of this chapter, these theories generally stress interpersonal interactions.

Psychodrama represents one of the oldest and most dynamic theories yet devised for working with groups (Fine, 1979). Its originator, J. L. Moreno, spent his lifetime developing and refining this theory and practice (Moreno, 1984; Nolte, 1989). Although psychodrama gained notoriety as a therapeutic intervention at Moreno's psychodrama theater in Beacon, NY, and at St. Elizabeth's Hospital in Washington, DC, it is applicable in a number of settings (Blajan-Marcus, 1974; Moreno, 1949). One of the most productive spin-offs of this approach is the common use of role play within psychoeducational, psychotherapeutic, and management groups (Blatner, 1988a, 1989; Corsini, 1966).

Self-help groups are a paradox; they represent one of the earliest as well as latest forms of group work (Balgopal, Ephross, & Vassil, 1986; Fuehrer & Keys, 1988; Katz & Bender, 1976; Wheeler, 1989). The use of peer groups as a medium for change was suggested by such leading therapists as Alfred Adler, Harry Stack Sullivan, and Kurt Lewin (Cole, 1983). Self-help groups grew out of a need for assistance, support, and knowledge that could not be met by professional helpers. It is not surprising, therefore, that mental health workers who are associated with self-help groups even today do so tangentially. Although the once-wide rift between self-help groups and professional group workers has lessened in recent years, it still exists, and the expectations of leaders and members of these groups differ from those of most other kinds of groups (Meissen, Mason, & Gleason, 1991; Powell, 1987). Most of the thousands of self-help groups of the 1990s began developing during and immediately following the late 1960s, but a few, such as Alcoholics Anonymous (AA) and Recovery, have been in existence since the 1930s.

PSYCHODRAMA GROUPS

Psychodrama, a way of exploring the human psyche through dramatic action, was created and developed by J. L. Moreno in the 1920s and 1930s (D'Amato & Dean, 1988; Goldman & Morrison, 1984). The idea for it evolved out of Moreno's creativity, which was fostered by his encounters with children and his love for spontaneity and the theater. In essence, psychodrama became an extension of Moreno's personality. He advocated a group approach in an era of intrapersonal emphasis. Therefore, many of his contributions to the field of group work (e.g., his emphasis for action and his focus on the here-and-now) have never been properly acknowledged.

The main forerunner of psychodrama was the **"Theater of Spontaneity,"** which Moreno originated in 1921 in Vienna. Participants in the theater were "radical young artists" who entertained the Viennese "with dramatic productions which were improvised on the stage. This kind of action took many forms; one was the 'Living Newspaper,' in which recent happenings—sometimes local incidents, sometimes developments in world politics—were spontaneously dramatized" (Anderson, 1974, p. 209). Moreno found that those who played nonscripted and unrehearsed parts, as well as members of the audience, experienced an emotional catharsis (a release of pent-up feelings) as a result of participating in or observing the dramatic enactment. Shortly thereafter, psychodrama as a formal system was conceptualized, with Moreno (1923, 1984) stressing the uniqueness of the approach by having clients relive, instead of retell or analyze, their conflicts.

Premises of Group Psychodrama

Psychodrama is sometimes viewed as "nothing more than a grand extension of the clinical interview" (Greenberg, 1974b, p. 13), but it is actually much more. Psychodrama is similar to psychoanalysis in that it emphasizes a freeing of individuals from the irrational forces that bind them into dysfunctional patterns of behaving. The goals of these two approaches are the same. However, psychodrama differs radically from psychoanalysis in its emphasis on action. The client is removed from the usual one-to-one relationship with the psychotherapist or counselor and given an opportunity to act out and experience various aspects of his or her problem(s) within a group setting. In contrast to psychoanalysis, psychodrama "emphasizes personal interaction and encounter, focus on here and now, spontaneity and creativity, full expression of feelings, and reality testing" (Corey, 1990, p. 223).

A focused emphasis of psychodrama is on the holistic interaction of the protagonist in his or her drama. The group leader is the producer of the drama. In the process, the protagonist reworks his or her life as both a player and playwright (Blatner, 1988b). In action, "habitual verbal defenses are circumvented" (Blatner, 1989, p. 561), and new realizations occur. For instance, a psychodrama leader might say to Bob, a group member, "Show the group how your interactions with your father affected your view of work." Bob would then enact by himself, or with others, scenes that came to mind between his father and him. Such enactments would be based on memories and shown in dramatic form rather than discussed. The result would be new awareness on Bob's part that he could then discuss, and observations from group members on what they noticed in Bob's enactment(s) could be shared. Basically, psychodrama is predicated on the assumption that humans in society are continually evolving and can become aware of matters pertaining to their lives at any developmental stage. Persons who are open to themselves begin to realize their strengths, as well as their liabilities. Such realizations make them more capable of meeting external demands in creative ways.

At the heart of psychodrama is the **encounter,** an existentialist concept that involves total physical and psychological contact between persons on an intense, concrete, and complete basis in the here-and-now. The encounter can relate to past events, anticipated ones, or present circumstances, but it always involves "taking a moment or a particular situation in one's life and expanding it in various dimensions" (Corey, 1990, p. 223). One particular dimension that the encounter deals with is **surplus reality**—"psychological experience that transcends the boundaries of physical reality" (Blatner, 1989, p. 568). These experiences, which include relationships with those who have died or were never born or with God, are often as important to people as their actual experiences with physical entities. For example, Julie may still grieve for the child she lost in childbirth. In the encounter, she can express her feelings through dramatically reliving the scene of loss and the ways she might have handled or dealt with the tragedy at that time. Overall, the encounter is the experience of identity and total reciprocity, summed up by Moreno (1914) in the following poetic way:

> *A meeting of two: eye to eye, face to face. And when you are near I will tear your eyes out and place them instead of mine, and you will tear my eyes out and will place them instead of yours, and I will look at you with your eyes and you will look at me with mine. (p. 3)*

The main concepts (Greenberg, 1974b) that emphasize Moreno's premise on experiencing one's situation fully in the here-and-now are

1. spontaneity and creativity
2. situation
3. tele
4. catharsis
5. insight

Spontaneity is the response people make that contains "some degree of adequacy to a new situation or a degree of novelty to an old situation" (Moreno, 1945, p. xii). The purpose of spontaneity is to liberate one's self from scripts and stereotypes and gain new perspectives on life. Responding in new creative ways is part of this process. For example, Mildred, instead of panicking when she is given a math test, now begins to sit calm and study the whole exam before making a response.

Situation is the emphasis on the present where "natural barriers of time, space, and states of existence are obliterated" (Greenberg, 1974b, pp. 16–17). Under these circumstances, clients are able to work on past problems, future fears, and current difficulties in a here-and-now atmosphere. For instance, Carl plans for his graduation from high school, college, and an entry-level job by confronting his fear of success and his present lack of self-confidence.

Tele is the total communication of feelings between people, "the cement which holds groups together" (Moreno, 1945, p. xi). It is experienced most when it occurs between two people. At its best, it involves complete interpersonal and reciprocal empathy. In a tele, Mitch and Sandy tell each other what qualities they most admire in the other and how it makes them feel when they think they have expressed one or more of these qualities, such as empathy and poise.

Catharsis and insight are the "end-products" of spontaneity and tele (Greenberg, 1974b). **Catharsis** involves an emotional purging, such as when Debra screams out in regard to her mother, "All I ever wanted you to do was love me!!" **Insight,** on the other hand, consists of immediate new perceptions and understandings about one's problems that occur during or after the experience of catharsis. For instance, in the preceding example, Debra might say after her cathartic experience, "I never realized I was so angry." Both catharsis and insight may be experienced by psychodrama participants as well as the audience.

Practice of Psychodrama in a Group

The practice of psychodrama is multidimensional. First, there are physical and personal factors that must be considered, such as a stage, a protagonist, actors, a director, and an audience (Blatner, 1988a, 1989; Haskell, 1973) (see Figure 17.1). Second, there are techniques that must be employed in a methodological manner (Moreno, 1959).

The **stage** is the area where the action takes place. It may be a formal platform, or it may simply be a part of a room. In essence, the stage is wherever the participants want it to be. For instance, Jason says to his psychodrama group, "The corner of the room will be my stage this time." Most groups find it beneficial to have the stage in a separate place from where the group meets to remind members that the enactments are clearly different from verbal interchanges (Blatner, 1989).

Figure 17.1
The psychodrama stage.
Source: Adapted from *Acting In: Practical Applications of Psychodramatic Methods,* 2nd ed., by A. Blatner, 1988, New York: Springer Publishing Company, Inc. Used by permission.

The **protagonist** is the person who is the subject of the psychodrama enact-ment (Blatner, 1988a, 1989). He or she may play many parts. For example, in a psy-chodrama, Laura as the protagonist played different parts of herself, from being sweet and innocent to being mean and spiteful. At times, the protagonist may step out of a scene and observe. Regardless, the goal of the protagonist is to express freely the thoughts, feelings, concerns, and issues relevant to the role he or she plays in the psychodrama. A key element to being a protagonist is spontaneity.

Actors are those who play the parts of other important people or objects in the play. They are called "auxiliaries," and with prompting from the protagonist, they can play the protagonist's double, an antagonist, or even a piece of furni-ture. In the same psychodrama, an auxiliary could play more than one part, such as being the protagonist's best friend and worst enemy.

The **director** is the person who guides the protagonist "in the use of the psy-chodramatic method" in order to help that person explore his or her problem (Blatner, 1988a, p. 8). The director is roughly equivalent to the group leader in other theoretical approaches. Finally, the **audience** is a term used to describe others who may be present during the psychodrama. These individuals may become auxiliaries, but many may not actively participate. "The purpose of the audience is to give feedback regarding what they saw, heard, and felt during the psychodrama" (Ohlsen, Horne, & Lawe, 1988, p. 100). Sometimes the audience will become involved while the psychodrama is being conducted and make sound effects or comments at the request of the director. For example, the audi-ence might be directed to repeat to Paul when he gets angry and makes a mis-take, "Keep cool. Use your head. Keep cool. Use your head." In such cases, the audience becomes a *chorus.*

The techniques employed in psychodrama are dependent on many variables. Among the most important factors that influence which techniques will be used are the situation of the protagonist, the skill of the director, the availability of actors, the size of the audience, the goals of the session, and the phase in which the psy-chodrama is operating. Special situations will require different skills. For example, Blatner (1988a) states that some psychodrama techniques are best employed when the objective is to clarify the protagonist's feelings (e.g., monodrama, soliloquy, or the double). Others are used to facilitate the expression of emotion (e.g., amplifica-tion, asides, and exaggeration of nonverbal actions). Yet other techniques (e.g., role reversal, audience feedback, and nonverbal interaction exercises) are com-pleted in self-awareness situations. The psychodrama process generally goes through three phases: **warm-up** (preaction), **action,** and **integration.**

1. *Warm-up phase*—The warm-up phase is characterized by the director making sure he or she is ready to lead the group and that group mem-bers are ready to be led. This process may involve both verbal and non-verbal activity designed to put everyone in the right frame of mind to conduct the psychodrama and at the same time establish trust and an atmosphere of spontaneity (Blatner, 1989; Moreno, 1940). For instance, the director may walk around arranging furniture while speaking to all

participants. Then he or she may lead the group in some get-acquainted exercises, in which participants are placed in dyads. After these activities, the group as a whole may engage in **action exercises** (e.g., sensory awareness methods or guided imagery), which help members discover common themes within the group as well as focus more on individual concerns. Overall, the warm-up is experiential in nature and allows members to process some of the technical procedures they will experience in the actual psychodrama (Leveton, 1977). The end of the warm-up dovetails into the action phase of psychodrama.

2. *Action phase*—This part of the psychodrama process involves the enactment of protagonists' concerns (Blatner, 1988a; Corey, 1990; Haskell, 1973). The director helps each protagonist who chooses to work "set the stage" for a specific scene in the here-and-now. Group participants are assigned auxiliary ego roles of significant others or things in the protagonist's life. Then the opening scene is portrayed and the protagonist, as well as the auxiliary egos, are given an opportunity to refine their roles and gear their interaction from the surface to the most significant events. The director may encourage the protagonist at this point to do a role reversal so that he or she can feel more empathy or projection of feelings. Other techniques that are often employed are the use of soliloquy, the double technique, and asides. All are targeted toward helping the protagonist elaborate on feelings. Finally, the protagonist is helped to work through the situation by developing other adaptive attitudes and behavioral responses. Working through may mean repeating a scene using new behavioral strategies every time. It may also involve role reversals or even the use of modeling. The crucial thing in the action stage is that protagonists express repressed emotions and find a new, effective way to act.

3. *Integration phase*—This last phase of psychodrama involves discussion and closure. After the action phase, a protagonist is off-balance, vulnerable, and in need of support. The director encourages the group to give the protagonist as much personal, supportive, and constructive feedback as possible during this time. Feedback focuses initially on the affective, rather than intellectual, aspects of the enactment. Toward the end of the group some cognitive aspects of what has been experienced are appropriate to express (Blatner, 1988a; Corey, 1990). At the completion of this phase, there is an emphasis on understanding and integration so the protagonist can act differently if any similar situations arise. Figure 17.2 illustrates how the intensity of emotions in these three phases of psychodrama changes over time.

There are literally hundreds of psychodrama techniques with many variations, so only a few major techniques (**creative imagery, magic shop, sculpting, soliloquy, monodrama, double and multiple double, role reversal,** and **mirror**) will be considered here. Their use varies and is dictated by the circumstances within a particular psychodrama.

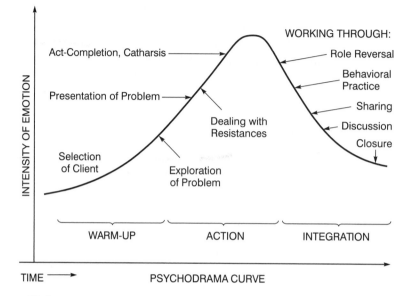

Figure 17.2

Psychodrama curve.

Source: From *Acting In: Practical Applications of Psychodramatic Methods*, 2nd ed., (p. 86), by A. Blatner, 1988, New York: Springer Publishing Company, Inc. Used by permission.

1. *Creative imagery*—This warm-up technique consists of inviting psychodrama participants to imagine neutral or pleasant objects and scenes. The idea is to help participants become more spontaneous (Ohlsen et al., 1988). For instance, Del realizes he can create a picture of a sunrise from a mountain top although he lives on a coastal plain.

2. *The magic shop*—This warm-up technique is especially useful for protagonists who are undecided or ambivalent about their values and goals. It involves a storekeeper (the director or an auxiliary ego) who runs a magic shop filled with special qualities. The qualities are not for sale but may be bartered. Thus, if Willie as the protagonist wants better relationship skills with others, he may have to give up irrational anger in exchange.

3. *Sculpting*—In this exercise, group members use nonverbal methods to arrange others in the group into a configuration like that of significant persons with whom they regularly deal, such as family members, office personnel, or social peers. The positioning involves body posturing and assists group members in seeing and experiencing their perceptions of significant others in a more dynamic way. For example, by arranging her family members with their backs toward her, Jane realizes how shut out of her family of origin she felt growing up.

4. *The soliloquy technique*—This technique involves the protagonist (i.e., the client) giving a monologue about his or her situation, as he or she is acting it out. For instance, the person who is driving home from work alone may give words to the thoughts that are uppermost on his or her mind, such as

"I feel life is unfair." A variation on this activity is the *therapeutic soliloquy* technique, in which private reactions to events in the protagonist's life are verbalized and acted out, usually by other actors (i.e., auxiliary egos). For example, other group members may push and tug at each other, showing Helena her ambivalence in going on to graduate school.

5. *The monodrama (autodrama)*—In this technique, the protagonist plays all the parts of the enactment; no auxiliary egos are used. The person may switch chairs or talk to different parts of the self. The monodrama is a core feature of Gestalt therapy. For instance, Walt becomes the significant thoughts he has about his upcoming marriage and has a dialogue between these expressions in different chairs arranged in a circle.

6. *The double and multiple double technique*—The double is an extremely important technique in psychodrama. It consists of an actor taking on the role of the protagonist's alter ego and helping the protagonist express true inner feelings more clearly (Fine, 1979). In cases where the protagonist has ambivalent feelings, the multiple double technique is used. In these situations, two or more actors represent different aspects of the protagonist's personality. The doubles may speak at once or take turns, but through their input, the protagonist should gain a better idea of what his or her thoughts and feelings are.

   Doubles can emphasize or **amplify** statements made by the protagonist in a number of ways. Examples of amplification include verbalizing nonverbal communications, questioning one's self, interpreting statements for what is being said and not said, contradicting feelings, self-observing, and denial (Blatner, 1988a, 1988b). For instance, referring to Irene's changing jobs, her double says, "I wonder who I am doing this for, myself or my children?"

7. *Role reversal*—In this technique, the protagonist literally switches roles with another person on stage and plays that person's part. For instance, Zelda now becomes Anne and acts like her. Zerka Moreno (1983) states that role reversal encourages the maximum expression of conflict; however, Corey (1990) and Blatner (1989) maintain that role reversal is another core part of psychodrama and one of the most important action techniques within it, especially in the action phase.

8. *Mirror technique*—In this activity, the protagonist watches from offstage while an auxiliary ego mirrors the protagonist's posture, gesture, and words. This technique is often used in the action phase of psychodrama to help the protagonist see himself or herself more accurately. For instance, Tim now knows through watching Roger mirror him that he is not the clearheaded, decisive person he imagined himself to be.

Role of the Psychodrama Group Leader

The director of psychodramas wears many hats. Moreno (1953, 1964) suggests that the **director** serve as a producer, a facilitator, an observer, and an analyzer.

Blatner (1988a) further states that a director should build his or her skills in "three interdependent areas—a) knowledge of methods, principles, and techniques, b) understanding of personality theory and its relationship to developing an evolving philosophy of life, and c) his or her own personality development and maturity" (p. 131). Blatner further points out that in addition to a broad general knowledge of life and human nature, a director is expected to have specific course work in subject areas such as general psychology, group process, humanistic psychology, communication theory, and nonverbal communications.

The director's function is to conduct such tasks as leading the warm-up experience, encouraging the development of trust and spontaneity, establishing a structure so that protagonists can identify and work on significant issues in their lives, protecting members from abuse by others, and bringing some type of closure to group sessions (Haskell, 1973; Ohlsen et al., 1988). To conduct these tasks properly, potential directors should have experienced many psychodramas and received direct supervision from more experienced directors. Overall, Corsini (1966) concludes that effective group directors possess three qualities: creativity, courage, and charisma. These individuals work very hard for the good of the group and often must take risks to help group members begin achieving goals.

Desired Psychodrama Group Outcome

The desired outcome of psychodrama can be described as the creation of catharsis, insight, and emotional resolution (Moreno, 1964). Yablonsky (1976) states that Moreno's goal in psychodrama is "to develop a 'theatrical cathedral' for the release of the natural human spontaneity and creativity that he believed existed naturally in everyone" (p. 274). Through psychodrama, individuals should be able to experience and work through past, present, or anticipated events that have caused them distress. When they have gained emotional and cognitive insight by acting out their difficulties, they will reach a stage of renewed self-awareness, readjustment, integration, acceptance, control, and prevention (Ohlsen et al., 1988).

It is essential, not just desirable, that participants in psychodramas be willing to take risks and be open to constructive feedback from the audience and the director. One of the desirable spin-offs from psychodrama is the learning that takes place when one is not the main protagonist. There is a definite **spillover effect** from this approach for others who are helping or watching a main character reach resolution on important issues. This effect is often that they see themselves as interacting in a new and better way.

Evaluation of Psychodrama Groups

Psychodrama groups can be quite powerful and have much to commend them as ways of working with others. However, they are not without their limitations.

Advantages.   One major advantage of psychodrama is its diversity (Greenberg, 1974a). Psychodrama is appropriately used in psychotherapeutic environments, as well as in psychoeducational and business settings. It can be employed with individuals of all age, educational, and socioeconomic levels. For example, forms of psychodrama are used in family therapy, addiction treatment, the training of theologians, and the sensitizing of leaders (Gendron, 1980).

Another positive aspect of psychodrama is its teaching potential. Group members learn a great deal about themselves through their active participation. Similarly, as Zerka Moreno (1983) points out, professionals in various mental health specialties can also use psychodrama to learn how they interact and resolve matters with difficult clients. Psychodrama gives these professionals a feeling for situations, instead of just thoughts about them.

A third advantage of a psychodrama group is its fostering of creativity and spontaneity within leaders and members. A major problem that people have is their inability to find resolutions to stressful or harmful situations. Psychodrama promotes creative and spontaneous ways to help people find solutions to transitional or permanent problems. By acting on a difficulty in the confines of a safe environment, the protagonist gets a feel for how things can be different and may practice acting accordingly (Moreno, 1987). For example, Peter realizes in the calm atmosphere of the group that he can respond to a negative statement by ignoring it, using humor, becoming negative himself, or using confrontation. Prior to the psychodrama group, he only ignored such statements.

A fourth positive aspect about psychodrama is its integrative and vicarious effect. Psychodrama emphasizes action coupled with emotional release. A by-product of this process is the change in thoughts that accompanies changes in behavior and emotion. This change is not limited to just the protagonist but can extend to members of the audience as well. As the psychodrama concludes, a good psychodrama director "shifts the focus to the audience and discusses the impact of their experiences, parts of the psychodrama with which they identified, issues they got in touch with, and what they learned from the psychodrama in general" (Ohlsen et al., 1988, p. 105).

A final advantage of psychodrama is the input and feedback the audience and actors give the protagonist and each other (Moreno, 1964). Psychodrama promotes interaction and experiential learning among group members. It makes good use of the group format. Many of the dynamics that occur in psychodrama are described regularly in the *Journal of Group Psychotherapy, Psychodrama, and Sociometry* and other periodicals in group work.

Limitations.   A major limitation of psychodrama is the danger of overexposing the protagonist to himself or herself, as well as to the audience (Greenberg, 1974a). A sense of timing and a knowledge of what hidden factors need to be exposed are crucial. The ability of a psychodrama director to know when and what to emphasize is one that takes years to develop and requires both courage and creativity (Corsini, 1966). First attempts at helping are not as polished as later efforts, and sometimes everyone involved struggles in the process.

Another area that is of considerable concern to many professional group workers is the quantity and quality of the research underlying psychodrama (D'Amato & Dean, 1988; Kellermann, 1987). Role playing, one aspect of psychodrama, has the potential to change individual attitudes and behaviors (Janis & Mann, 1954; Mann, 1967). However, psychodrama is more than just role playing. As D'Amato and Dean (1988) point out, there is a need for more controlled research of the factors that make up the approach. Even the "taproot of the theory"—that is, when problems are acted out, the client's mind-set becomes more spontaneous—has never been empirically verified (D'Amato & Dean, 1988, p . 312).

A third limitation of psychodrama is connected with the availability of training (Greenberg, 1974a). As pointed out earlier, it is recommended that directors be involved in a large number of psychodramas and take specific coursework in human development and group work (Blatner, 1988a). At present, there are few training centers for directors. In addition, experience and coursework alone are not enough. Needed qualities of directors go beyond observing/participating and studying to also include intuition and charisma, which vary considerably in human personality. There is the danger that some psychodrama groups may differ radically from others because of self-awareness and knowledge of the director (Corey, 1990). Since 1975, the American Board of Examiners in Psychodrama, Sociometry and Group Psychotherapy has tried to ensure more uniformity in professional standards for directors.

A final criticism of psychodrama is that it may focus too much on expression of feelings, rather than change in behavior. There is a lot of emphasis in psychodrama on affect and present experiences, as opposed to cognitive awareness and exploration of the past. If the group is not carefully constructed, the emotional part of the theory and the here-and-now emphasis will override the integrative aspect of the approach.

SELF-HELP GROUPS

There are more than 500,000 self-help groups in North America with between 12 and 15 million active members (Brown, 1988; Farley, 1988; Squires, 1988). These groups are an effective way of dealing with problems such as stress, hardship, and pain. They may be broadly classified as follows:

1. groups that help individuals and families with any major physical or mental health problem (e.g., groups for families who have members with Alzheimer's disease or who suffer from chronic depression)
2. groups that offer help in behavior modification for addictive disorders (e.g., alcohol abuse, overeating)
3. groups that offer social support for those in the midst of difficult life transitions (e.g., parenthood, bereavement, single parenthood)
4. groups that advocate for special populations (e.g., the handicapped, the elderly, women)

5. groups that work against discrimination (e.g., sexual, ethnic)
6. groups that deal with general problems and conditions (e.g., excessive anxiety, deafness) (Paskert & Madara, 1985).

In this part of the chapter, emphasis will be focused on what self-help groups are and how they differ from support groups and professionally led groups.

Premises of Self-Help Groups

There is no single theory that underlies self-help groups; rather, there are several assumptions. One premise is that there are a large number of individual difficulties. Therefore, persons may be most helped by working with others who have similar backgrounds (Pearson, 1986). This is the age-old assumption that fellow sufferers or **wounded healers** are able to deal most effectively with each other by coming together in a group and sharing through disclosing, listening, and learning (May & Yalom, 1989). In this process, members support each other in making changes (Alcoholics Anonymous World Service, 1984). Members also help themselves by helping one another (Hurley, 1988).

A second theoretical underpinning of self-help groups is the idea that homogeneous membership in a group is most helpful in promoting change. As opposed to most other forms of groups presented in this book, self-help groups do not reflect a social microcosm of the environment in which their members operate (Corey, 1990). The reason for homogeneity is that many self-help groups are composed of members who have been stigmatized or isolated from the mainstream of society, for example, alcoholics, addicts, gamblers, mental patients, and the disabled (Wheeler, 1989).

A third assumption underlying self-help groups is that there are "therapeutic factors" within these groups based on cognitive, behavioral, and affective dimensions (Cole, 1983; Yalom, 1985). For example, on the cognitive and behavioral levels, group members may gain knowledge and skill when effective strategies (e.g., exchanging information, rehearsing an appropriate response) are shared by others. Likewise on the affective level, members may experience a feeling of being among "friends" and being accepted—faults and all—when other members interact with and listen to them. Lieberman and Borman (1979) found that the most commonly chosen factors perceived as most beneficial to self-help group members were a sense within the group of universality, cohesiveness, guidance, and altruism. If, for instance, Gus tells his other group members of his struggle and success in overcoming a disability, those who hear his story and identify with him may begin to hope and expect they will do better just like Gus.

A final premise of self-help groups is that their impact may be positive and pervasive both during and after a person is a member (Pearson, 1986; Yalom, 1985). Many self-help groups stress the imparting of information to their members (Lieberman & Borman, 1979). For example, groups such as Parents Without Partners and Alcoholics Anonymous encourage their members to exchange ideas and remember what works for them, such as the slogan "One day at a time." In addition, these groups may have outside expert professionals speak to them on occasions or provide their members with some basic assistance, such as consultation. This type of psychoeducational effort increases the likelihood of members remembering important information. Through this multitude of endeavors, group members learn more about themselves and their conditions. They also learn how to handle crises that occur in their lives more productively and less stressfully (Thoits, 1986).

Overall, self-help groups are designed to serve as surrogate support systems, providing the kind of help not available in other places in society (Pearson, 1986). Self-help groups that work well are like large, healthy, and accepting families in which honesty and effort are highly valued and reinforcement is given when appropriate.

The Practice of Self-Help in a Group

Each self-help group has some special characteristics, but there are enough universal qualities among self-help groups that specific practices of these groups can be delineated. One of the first noticeable aspects about self-help groups is that members mutually assist one another (Lieberman & Borman, 1979). For that reason, some researchers (e.g., Pearson, 1986; Silverman, 1986) prefer to call these groups **mutual help groups.** Their point is well taken because the concept *self-help* is often associated with individually doing something for one's self, for example, reading a book or joining an organization. It is usually just a first step in the process of obtaining help.

A second quality of self-help groups involves direction. Leaders and members of self-help groups have a purpose. The groups themselves are often described as "non-directive and non-threatening" (Cole, 1983, p. 146). They depend on volunteers for leadership and are definitely member-focused. Peer leadership is a distinguishing quality that separates self-help groups from **support groups** (which have a professional leader) (Wheeler, 1989).

A third quality that influences how self-help groups operate is an emphasis within these groups on the similarities of participants. This focus is a key to change among group members. By being seen as similar, members of self-help groups derive certain benefits, such as cohesiveness and identity. In addition, new members of the group see that changes in perception and behavior are possible as they interact with **old-timers** (i.e., more experienced members of self-help groups). They are given hope or gain renewed hope in this process (Napier & Gershenfeld, 1989). The power of this optimism is centered in the realization that people such as themselves have made progress. Individuals are most influenced by those they see as similar to themselves (Festinger, 1954).

However, not only are new members able to perceive a new possible life style by interacting with those who have already undergone change, they are also able to become "helpers" themselves (Hurley, 1988). This fourth factor aids them in becoming less dependent, becoming more able to see their problems at a distance, and becoming more able to feel they are socially useful (Gartner & Reissman, 1984). In fact, research (Lieberman & Borman, 1979) suggests that participants in self-help groups report enhanced self-esteem and self-respect. Group members also report feeling more empathy for others and a greater sense of self-reliance.

A fifth quality offered through self-help groups is opportunity. Participants in these groups are given the chance, and even encouraged in many cases, to set goals for themselves (Cole, 1983). If they achieve their personal goals, they feel more in control of their lives, and success continues to build on itself. If they do not achieve their goals, they are usually still accepted and encouraged. They feel freer to try again to succeed.

A sixth factor that works to bring about change in self-help groups is ideology. Most self-help groups have an underlying theme that unites members. The theme serves as a rallying point and gives members a "cause" to participate in beyond their own self-interest. For example, a rehabilitation group may have the slogan, "Not there yet, still climbing," with a logo that shows a person climbing a mountain. The sense of connectedness created by themes often helps members feel more a part of a community and likewise more positive about themselves (Gartner & Reissman, 1984).

Role of the Self-Help Group Leader

As stated earlier, leadership in self-help groups is provided by volunteers. A self-help group is usually as strong as those who voluntarily work in it. Many self-help group leaders gain their position from experience and longevity (Riordan & Beggs, 1987) and are often referred to as **pros**. A second, though rare, way that leadership is established is through election. Self-help groups led in this manner are usually short-lived and focused on a single concern, such as overcoming physical barriers in a building. A third model of self-help group leadership is for the position of responsibility to rotate. This type of model may emerge when groups recognize that the task of leading is quite demanding and there are a number of people who can do it. Finally, self-help groups may remain virtually leaderless. In such cases, the leadership emerges as a result of particular concerns. Overall, within self-help groups, "leadership models are diverse" (Vander Kolk, 1985, p. 293). Some self-help groups, such as LaLeche League, have an elaborate screening process for potential leaders; newer and less established groups do not.

Leaders who emerge in self-help groups usually do not receive professional training. Yet, these individuals employ some techniques that are very similar to professional group leaders, such as an emphasis on expression and reflection (Powell, 1987). Similarly, group members are encouraged to talk about themselves, experience their feelings, take responsibility for their behavior, and gain insight into how they can live more productively. The group is usually the medium for events which take place in a self-help organization.

Leaders of self-help groups frequently face difficulty in structuring them. "With too little structure, participants may not realize the importance of performing constructive group member behaviors . . . With too much structure, participants are less likely to feel ownership of group accomplishments" (Fuehrer & Keys, 1988, p. 339). Self-help group leaders face the difficult task of striking a healthy balance between doing too much and doing too little within their groups. Silverman (1980) says that in most cases, leaders of self-help groups must meet the following criteria:

1. They must want to be helpers.
2. They must be able to talk easily about their own experiences, both successes and failures.
3. They must have achieved an accommodation or resolution to their problem.
4. They must offer help from their own personal experience rather than from their formal education or reading.
5. They must have enough time and energy to devote to helping.

Overall, leaders of self-help groups should try to set up an atmosphere within the group that "more closely resembles that of a community meeting than a therapy group" (Cole, 1983, p. 148). This type of balance is not easy to achieve, but if it can be accomplished, the group will function in a give-and-take manner and members will feel more comfortable and benefit.

Desired Outcome of Self-Help Groups

There are at least two desirable outcomes connected with self-help groups. One operates on the global group level; the other, on the personal level. As a group, it is desirable that members identify with and help one another (Stokes, 1983). For instance, in an AA group, it is important that each member be able to say, "I'm an alcoholic." If such an identity can be fostered, the group will function as a system that provides support, encouragement, and educational ideas. It will also be open and interactive for its members. Most members who join self-help groups feel isolated initially. In a properly functioning self-help group, these individuals will come to feel less lonely and more a part of society. They will unify as a part of the group and offer help, as well as receive it (Schubert & Borkman, 1991).

On the personal level, an individual should come to change perceptions and behaviors as a result of the self-help group experience (Gartner & Riessman, 1982). He or she may see their situation as "serious but not hopeless" (Watzlawick, 1983). The situation the individual is in or has experienced takes on a universal quality following a well-run, self-help group. For example, self-help group participants begin to see that no one lives a problem-free life and the way people face adversity is what makes a difference. People also see their uniquenesses through participation in the group. For example, Jen may say, "Although I share a sense of grief, like Randolph and Liz, my feeling is my own." In such a situation, Jen may be able to envision herself differently as well as see the connectedness between herself and the world of others. There is freedom in this change to try out new ideas or behaviors that may have seemed too risky before. In the properly conducted self-help group, a person is also able to release emotions that have been suppressed and relieve physical and psychological tension. The individual may also find new models that are beneficial for dealing with the specifics of a situation.

Overall, for personal growth to occur individuals in self-help groups must accomplish the following (Riordan & Beggs, 1987):

feel attracted to others in the group
feel they are getting help by giving help
be willing to take risks
actively participate as a group member
be self-responsible

There must be a resolution of any discrepancies in individual and group goals, too. Furthermore, leaders must be strong and able to model a number of roles for members.

Evaluation of Self-Help Groups

Although self-help groups are abundant and generally have a good reputation among the public, they are not for everyone. Like other kinds of groups, potential members should evaluate self-help group benefits and limitations before joining.

Advantages.   A major advantage of self-help groups is the mutual support they provide. Through self-help groups, individuals improve and increase their self-esteem and self-identity. They realize they are not alone, and they come to feel more empowered by sharing ideas and giving help, as well as receiving aid (Vander Kolk, 1985; Wheeler, 1989). For example, in a grief group Nic and Patty come to realize they are not the only ones who have struggled in coming to a peaceful resolution with their sorrow.

A second advantage of self-help groups is the way they structure time (Gartner & Riessman, 1984). Often, individuals who seek self-help groups have too much time on their hands, or they do not use their time productively. Self-help groups offer them alternatives to managing their time and resources. Thus, it is not unusual for a recovering alcoholic to attend AA meetings several times a week.

A third positive about self-help groups is that they are specialized (Corey, 1990; Powell, 1987). People need others to work with them on common concerns at specific times. Self-help groups fulfill that need and offer participants support and a sense of community not found elsewhere. For example, Alice realizes through her self-help group that she can deal with her low-self esteem as a special part of her life.

Finally, self-help groups are cost efficient and can be used with other forms of psychotherapy, guidance, psychoeducation, and support to enable people to become more personally integrated and whole (Antze, 1979). In self-help groups, individuals not only gain knowledge and release feelings, but they also make friends (Cole, 1983). Self-help groups assist individuals and communities in achieving greater health by linking people together in multidimensional ways.

Limitations.   One negative aspect of self-help groups is the lack of research on how these groups develop and what interactional processes take place in them (Fuehrer & Keys, 1988). The reason for this lack of research is that mental health professionals and researchers are generally excluded from these groups and that leaders and members are not concerned about researching their groups.

A second criticism of self-help groups is that members of these organizations are removing themselves further from the mainstream of society (Vander Kolk, 1985). By focusing their lives on a self-help group, members may become bogged down in mundane and trivial issues because of a lack of input from outsiders. Furthermore, self-help group members may be unable to influence public opinion in large segments of society because of a lack of contact with members outside the immediate group.

A third criticism of self-help groups is the zealot nature of some members and groups (Silverman, 1980). When there is an overemphasis on identifying with a particular group, a **we/they tendency** may tend to develop, and antagonism may develop between group members and others. This type of tension is most likely to occur between mental health professionals and some leaders of self-help groups.

A fourth negative associated with self-help groups is the ability of some groups to sustain themselves. A tremendous amount of energy and direction must be invested in self-help groups to keep them thriving (Hershenson & Power, 1987; Powell, 1987; Silverman, 1980). Self-help groups that are not properly structured are likely to fail, and individuals with special needs may become even more discouraged than before.

The fifth disadvantage of these groups is the variety and quality of helping skills used by group members. Because some members do not receive any training in the art and science of group dynamics, change, and the helping process, their ability to be helpful to others is limited. In fact, sometimes group members may actually end up hurting each other in the process of trying to be supportive.

A final criticism of self-help groups is that many of them become too absorbed in mundane issues and overlook broad systemic problems that are at the heart of their problem (Vander Kolk, 1985). For example, a self-help group for those with speech disorders may become obsessed with the number of times other members are able to express themselves clearly instead of concentrating on environmental conditions, such as the presence of certain stimuli or people, that contribute to trouble-free speech problems.

SUMMARY AND CONCLUSION

In this chapter, two primary group-oriented therapy approaches have been examined. Psychodrama continues to be one of the most exciting forms of group work around. Although it has largely been used in psychotherapy and counseling settings, aspects of it are quite appropriate in psychoeducational and work/task environments. This approach to groups requires a great deal of action and/or participation on the part of all involved. Within the psychodrama, protagonists work out their problems and are free to release feelings and try new behaviors with the help of others and themselves. The process is exciting and is one of the most powerful group approaches available. Psychodrama goes through stages and needs an expert and experienced director in order to work properly.

Self-help groups, although rooted in the history of groups, have only recently gained widespread popularity. They take advantage of **peer power,** that is, people helping people in a group setting. There are literally thousands of such groups, and their influence is widespread.

There are advantages and disadvantages associated with participation in self-help groups. There seems to be a powerful and positive influence on persons who participate in such groups (Gartner & Riessman, 1984), even though self-helpers can be atheoretical in orientation and practice. Whether these groups will remain as popular as they have been since the 1960s is debatable, but it is almost certain that they will continue. Professional leaders of groups will need to not only acknowledge the presence of self-help groups but also learn to interact with their members effectively if they want to make an impact (Rodolfa & Hungerford, 1982).

CLASSROOM EXERCISES

1. In small groups of four or five, do literature searches in the library on the writings of Jacob Moreno. As a large group, discuss how psychodrama evolved in Moreno's mind and how it now differs from Moreno's conception of it.
2. Discuss in small groups of three how psychodrama has influenced other forms of group work. What techniques have other group approaches borrowed from psychodrama? How do they use these techniques differently? Show, as well as tell, others of your impressions and findings.
3. Invite a member of a self-help group to speak to your class, or obtain information on a major self-help group such as Alcoholics Anonymous. Compare the information you obtain with what you know about self-help groups in general. Discuss in groups of three the similarities and differences you notice. Then report back to the class as a whole.
4. Make a directory of self-help groups in your community. After the task is completed, discuss with other class members how you would use this information.

REFERENCES

Alcoholics Anonymous World Service. (1984). *"Pass it on"—The story of Bill Wilson and how the A.A. message reached the world.* New York: Author.

Anderson, W. (1974). J. L. Moreno and the origins of psychodrama: A biographical sketch. In I. A. Greenberg (Ed.), *Psychodrama: Theory and therapy* (pp. 205–211). New York: Behavioral Publications.

Antze, P. (1979). Role of ideologies in peer psychotherapy groups. In M. A. Lieberman & L. D. Borman (Eds.), *Self-help groups for coping with crisis* (pp. 272–304). San Francisco: Jossey-Bass.

Balgopal, P. R., Ephross, P. H., & Vassil, T. V. (1986). Self-help groups and professional helpers. *Small Group Behavior, 17,* 123–137.

Blajan-Marcus, S. (1974). Psychodrama and its diverse uses. In I. A. Greenberg (Ed.), *Psychodrama: Theory and therapy* (pp. 47–55). New York: Behavioral Publications.

Blatner, A. (1988a). *Acting in: Practical applications of psychodramatic methods* (2nd ed.). New York: Springer.

Blatner, A. (1988b). *Foundations of psychodrama: History, theory, and practice* (3rd ed.). New York: Springer.

Blatner, A. (1989). Psychodrama. In R. J. Corsini & D. Wedding (Eds.), *Current psychotherapies* (4th ed.) (pp. 561–571). Itasca, IL: Peacock.

Brown, P. L. (1988, July 16). Troubled millions heed call of self-help groups. *New York Times*, pp. 1, 7.

Cole, S. A. (1983). Self-help groups. In H. I. Kaplan & B. J. Sadock (Eds.), *Comprehensive group psychotherapy* (2nd ed.) (pp. 144–150). Baltimore: Williams & Wilkins.

Corey, G. (1990). *Theory and practice of group counseling* (3rd ed.). Monterey, CA: Brooks/Cole.

Corsini, R. J. (1966). *Roleplaying in psychotherapy*. New York: Free Press.

D'Amato, R. C., & Dean, R. S. (1988). Psychodrama research-therapy and theory: A critical analysis of an arrested modality. *Psychology in the Schools, 25,* 305–314.

Farley, C. (1988, August 11). Self-helpers find strength in numbers. *USA Today,* p. 4D.

Festinger, L. A. (1954). A theory of social comparison processes. *Human Relations, 7,* 117–140.

Fine, L. (1979). Psychodrama. In R. J. Corsini (Ed.), *Current psychotherapies* (2nd ed.). Itasca, IL: Peacock.

Fuehrer, A., & Keys, C. (1988). Group development in self-help groups for college students. *Small Group Behavior, 19,* 325–341.

Gartner, A., & Riessman, F. (1984). Introduction. In A. Gartner & F. Reissman (Eds.), *The self-help revolution* (pp. 17–23). New York: Human Science Press.

Gartner, A. J., & Riessman, F. (1982). Self-help and mental health. *Hospital and Community Psychiatry, 33,* 631–635.

Gendron, J. M. (1980). *Moreno: The roots and the branches and bibliography of psychodrama, 1972–1980; and sociometry, 1970–1980.* Beacon, NY: Beacon House.

Gladding, S. T. (1989). First thoughts . . . A reflection on professional friendship. *Journal of Humanistic Education and Development, 27,* 190–191.

Goldman, E. E., & Morrison, D. S. (1984). *Psychodrama: Experience and process.* Duquesne, IA: Kendall/Hunt.

Greenberg, I. A. (1974a). Audience in action through simulated psychodrama. In I. A. Greenberg (Ed.), *Psychodrama: Theory and therapy* (pp. 457–486). New York: Behavioral Publications.

Greenberg, I. A. (1974b). Moreno: Psychodrama and the group process. In I. A. Greenberg (Ed.), *Psychodrama: Theory and therapy* (pp. 11–28). New York: Behavioral Publications.

Haskell, M. R. (1973). *The psychodramatic method* (4th ed.). Long Beach: California Institute of Socioanalysis.

Hershenson, D. B., & Power, P. W. (1987). *Mental health counseling: Theory and practice.* New York: Pergamon Press.

Hurley, D. (1988). Getting help from helping. *Psychology Today, 22,* 62–67.

Janis, I. L., & Mann, L. (1954). Effectiveness of emotional role playing in modifying smoking habits and attitudes. *Journal of Experimental Research in Personality, 1,* 84–90.

Katz, A. H., & Bender, E. I. (1976). Self-help groups in western society: History and prospects. *Journal of Applied Behavioral Sciences, 12,* 265–282.

Kellermann, P. F. (1987). Outcome research in classical psychodrama. *Small Group Behavior, 18,* 459–469.

Leveton, E. (1977). *Psychodrama for the timid clinician.* New York: Springer.

Lieberman, M., & Borman, L. (1979). *Self-help groups for coping with crisis* (pp. 202–205). San Francisco: Jossey-Bass.

Mann, L. (1967). The effects of emotional role playing on smoking attitudes and behavior. *Journal of Experimental Social Psychology, 3,* 334–348.

May, R., & Yalom, I. (1989). Existential psychotherapy. In R. J. Corsini & D. Wedding (Eds.), *Current psychotherapies* (4th ed.). Itasca, IL: Peacock.

Meissen, G. J., Mason, W. C. , & Gleason, D. F. (1991). Understanding the attitudes and intentions of future professionals toward self-help. *American Journal of Community Psychology, 19,* 699–714.

Moreno, J. L. (1914). *Einladun zu einer begegnung.* Vienna: Anzuengruber Verlag.

Moreno, J. L. (1923). *Das Stegif Theatre.* Berlin: Gustav Kiepenheur.

Moreno, J. L. (1940). The mental catharsis and the psychodrama. *Sociometry, 3,* 209–244.

Moreno, J. L. (Ed.). (1945). *Group psychotherapy: A symposium.* New York: Beacon House.

Moreno, J. L. (1946). *Psychodrama: Volume 1.* Beacon, NY: Beacon House.

Moreno, J. L. (1953). *Who shall survive?* Beacon, NY: Beacon House.

Moreno, J. L. (1964). *Psychodrama: Volume 1* (rev. ed.). Beacon, NY: Beacon House.

Moreno, J. L. (1984). Reflections on my method of group psychotherapy and psychodrama. In H. Greenwald (Ed.), *Active psychotherapy* (pp. 130–143). New York: Jason Aronson.

Moreno, Z. T. (1949). History of the sociometric movement in headlines. *Sociometry, 12,* 255–259.

Moreno, Z. T. (1959). A survey of psychodramatic techniques. *Group Psychotherapy, 12,* 5–14.

Moreno, Z. T. (1983). Psychodrama. In H. I. Kaplan & B. J. Sadock (Eds.), *Comprehensive group* (2nd ed.). Baltimore: Williams & Wilkins.

Moreno, Z. T. (1987). Psychodrama, role theory, and the concept of the social atom. In J. K. Zeig (Ed.), *The evolution of psychotherapy* (pp. 341–366). New York: Brunner/Mazel.

Napier, R., & Gershenfeld, M. (1989). *Groups: Theory and experience* (4th ed.). Boston: Houghton Mifflin.

Nolte, J. (1989). Remembering J. L. Moreno. *Journal of Group Psychotherapy, Psychodrama, & Sociometry, 42,* 129–137.

Ohlsen, M. M., Horne, A. M., & Lawe, C. F. (1988). *Group counseling* (3rd ed.). New York: Holt, Rinehart & Winston.

Paskert, C. J., & Madara, E. J. (1985). Introducing and tapping self-help mutual aid resources. *Health Education, 16,* 25–29.

Pearson, R. E. (1986). Guest editorial. *Journal for Specialists in Group Work, 11,* 66–67.

Powell, T. J. (1987). *Self-help organizations and professional practice.* Silver Spring, MD: National Association of Social Workers.

Riordan, R. J., & Beggs, M. S. (1987). Counselors and self-help groups. *Journal of Counseling and Development, 65,* 427–429.

Rodolfa, E. R., & Hungerford, L. (1982). Self-help groups: A referral resource for professional therapists. *Professional Psychology, 13,* 345–353.

Schubert, M. A., & Borkman, T. J. (1991). An organizational typology for self-help. *American Journal of Community Psychology, 19,* 769–787.

Silverman, P. R. (1980). *Mutual help groups: Organization and development.* Beverly Hills: Sage.

Silverman, P. R. (1986). The perils of borrowing: Role of the professional in mutual help groups. *Journal for Specialists in Group Work, 11,* 68–73.

Squires, S. (1988, May 17). A group for all reasons. *Washington Post,* pp. 14–17.

Stokes, J. P. (1983). Components of group cohesion: Intermember attraction, instrumental value, and risk taking. *Small Group Behavior, 14,* 163–173.

Thoits, P. A. (1986). Social supports as coping assistance. *Journal of Consulting and Clinical Psychology, 54,* 416–423.

Vander Kolk, C. J. (1985). *Introduction to group counseling and psychotherapy.* Columbus, OH: Merrill.

Watzlawick, P. (1983). *The situation is hopeless but not serious.* New York: W. W. Norton.

Wheeler, I. (1989). Self-help groups. In G. M. Gazda (Ed.), *Group counseling* (4th ed.) (pp. 237–258). Boston: Allyn & Bacon.

Yablonsky, L. (1976). *Psychodrama: Resolving emotional problems through role playing.* New York: Basic Books.

Yalom, I. D. (1985). *The theory and practice of group psychotherapy* (3rd ed.). New York: Basic Books.

CHAPTER 18

Current Trends in Group Work

In the still morning hours as I reflect
  I am aware of the images that I share with you
  of the special feelings and the pictures which I take
  that silently state how much I care for you
  among the many persons in my life.
Out of the group you have emerged
  and with a simple touch and open glance
  you have shaken me to my roots.
Stronger from your presence I emerge
  a new man with a different vision
  of who I am and what can be,
Amid the surprises of human contact
  *I branch out, entwine, and grow.**

C urrent trends for some professionals may be considered passé by others. The status and novelty of a situation is largely dependent on the work settings, background experiences, and present interests of those involved. "Group work in the United States, like other training activities, is a reflection of the culture and the historical moment and is affected by societal, regional, and local concerns (e.g., occupation)" (Klein, 1985, p. 108). Group work appears to be very healthy in the 1990s. As Fannie Cooley, a former president of the Association for Specialists in Group Work (ASGW) stated at the start of the decade, "I see it going everywhere, literally everywhere . . . I believe that groups will be the major modality of the delivery of services in the future" (Hawk, 1991, p. 7).

Source: Gladding, 1989.

60's - "me" —> "we"

The extent to which groups will be utilized in the future is debatable. However, it is clear that group work is becoming more valued by an increasing segment of the American population. Work/task and psychoeducational groups are especially well regarded and accepted by the general public, and counseling and psychotherapeutic groups, including support groups, have found a important niche in society as well. In a special issue of the *Journal for Specialists in Group Work,* a number of leading experts predicted five emphases of group work by the year 2001 (Conyne, Dye, Gill, Leddick, Morran, & Ward, 1985):

1. more emphasis on a comprehensive, life-skills approach that considers the total living and relationship environment of group members
2. more consumer-oriented groups with a greater specialization emphasis and a shorter delivery time
3. increased uses of social support, self-help, and family network groups to enhance the natural systems in society
4. increased employment of group work to promote systematic social change, for example, for aiding oppressed populations or for resolving conflict between systems
5. continued long-term counseling groups that emphasize therapeutic restructuring for members.

In addition, current and future trends in group work will emphasize research on group effectiveness and improved training for group leaders.

Not all of these trends will be covered in this chapter because some, such as self-help groups and theories associated with long-term group work, have been covered in previous sections of this book. Instead, emphasis will be concentrated on the following:

1. life-skills groups
2. consumer-oriented and specialized groups
3. group work in culturally diverse settings
4. groups in business and industry
5. groups for abusers and the abused
6. research on group effectiveness
7. training effective group leaders
8. the future of group work

LIFE-SKILLS GROUPS

The concept of life-skills groups is one that began to emerge in the 1970s when theorists such as Ivey (1973) and Hopson and Hough (1976) started using terms such as *psychoeducation* and *personal and social education.* In the 1980s, the momentum for this approach gained further impetus through the social skills and life-skills training methods advocated by Gazda (1989). **Life-skills training** focuses on helping persons identify and correct deficits in their life-coping skills and learn new appropriate behaviors. Sometimes these corrective measures are achieved in individual counseling, but often they are carried out in a group setting, for example, helping parents to relate effectively to their disabled children (Seligman, 1993). The focus of life-skills training is on immediate remediation and future prevention (Gazda, 1985). The training itself is primarily developmental.

A life-skills emphasis is appropriate for individuals in schools, colleges, families, work settings, clubs, and other natural group environments. Because groups are where many troubling situations arise, they are an excellent place in which to work on resolutions. By focusing on life-skills, such as increasing appropriate interpersonal communications or assertiveness abilities, "the growth process proceeds more comfortably, more observably, and with more precise attention given to the specific ingredients that induce change" (Zimpfer, 1984. p. 204). Through life-skills training, people can be taught how to stop potential problems from occurring and also be reinforced for taking corrective measures on a behavioral and cognitive level if difficulties arise (Alpert & Rosenfield, 1981).

There are a number of steps involved in learning life-skills. Many of these steps are the same as those that Johnson and Johnson (1991) describe in the learning of group skills:

1. Understand why the skill is important and how it will be of value to you.
2. Understand what the skill is, what are the component behaviors you have to engage in to perform the skill, and when it should be used.
3. Find situations in which you can practice the skill over and over again while a 'coach' watches and evaluates how you are performing the skill.
4. Assess how well the . . . skills are being implemented.
5. Keep practicing until the skill feels real and it becomes an automatic habit pattern.
6. Load your practice toward success [i.e., set up practice units that can easily be mastered].
7. Get friends to encourage you to use the skill.
8. Help others learn the . . . skills. (pp. 44–45)

Through implementing these procedures, group members enable both themselves and others. The result is a kind of snowball effect in which skills continue to build on skills in an effective and complementary way.

Groups ideally offer both the opportunity to initially learn new life-skills and the support to continue to exercise them. Leaders and members can learn through each other's feedback and evaluations whether the strategies they employed have been useful and thereby improve their mastery or delivery of skills for future situations. For instance, Paula, as a group leader, may ask her preteen social skills class to inform her which of the methods she is presently employing—role play, lecture, or guided imagery—is working best in mastering the material they are covering. Utilizing such information, she can improve her skills as a leader as well as help group members learn more and in the most effective way.

Like other groups, those groups that are oriented toward life-skills training have a developmental cycle. During the growth stages of the group, "considerable use is made of modeling, role playing and simulation, and homework" (Gazda, 1989, p. 43). Participants who profit most from these experiences are those who have enough time and practice to fully integrate what they have learned in the group into their real-life situations.

CONSUMER-ORIENTED AND SPECIALIZED GROUPS

Consumer-oriented groups are formed on the basis of need and may either be short- or long-term, depending on the problem or concern. For instance, consumer-oriented groups may revolve around long-term themes, such as protection of the environment, civil rights, or the consumption of certain foods. In such cases, they tend to be ongoing, with individuals joining or dropping out of the group depending on the sociopolitical climate and the impact of specific events on their lives. Short-term consumer groups focus on immediate issues, such as highway safety in a particular locale, increased taxation, reassessment of property, or school zone districting in a community. These groups are usually spontaneously organized and less hierarchical than long-term consumer groups. After their issue is settled, for instance, new stoplights are installed or school zones redrawn, short-term groups usually disband.

Consumer groups often follow the group pattern outlined by Tuckman and Jensen (1977) of forming, storming, norming, performing, and adjourning, but they do so differently than in typical psychotherapy-oriented or work-oriented groups. Because there is no immediately recognized leader, the group has to wait for one to emerge. Often there is considerable chaos while members jockey for positions and direction. Consumer groups that are most successful have both *rigor* (i.e., structure and a plan of action) and *vigor* (i.e., constant communication and contact with officials), whereas those that fail primarily have only one of these qualities.

Consumer groups that meet in public and wish to elicit public support need to identify responsible persons who will arrange for a variety of tasks that must be carefully and efficiently carried out if the group is to be successful. Many of these tasks are rather mundane and mechanical but are crucial in promoting the outcome of the group, for instance, arranging for audiovisual equipment and food, if necessary. One of the more important dimensions to planning consumer group meetings is the seating arrangement of the room. There are at least six arrangements that will enhance or detract from the task of the group depending on how they are used (Wilson & Hanna, 1986) (see Figure 18.1). Consumer

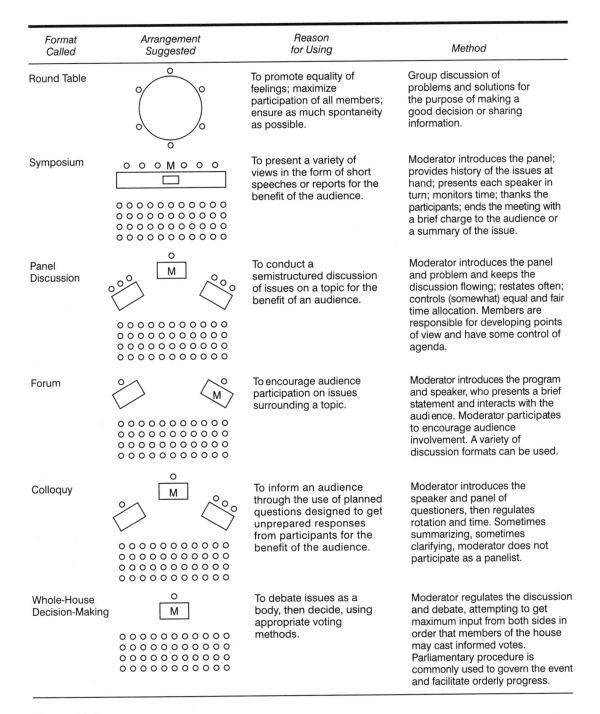

Format Called	Arrangement Suggested	Reason for Using	Method
Round Table		To promote equality of feelings; maximize participation of all members; ensure as much spontaneity as possible.	Group discussion of problems and solutions for the purpose of making a good decision or sharing information.
Symposium		To present a variety of views in the form of short speeches or reports for the benefit of the audience.	Moderator introduces the panel; provides history of the issues at hand; presents each speaker in turn; monitors time; thanks the participants; ends the meeting with a brief charge to the audience or a summary of the issue.
Panel Discussion		To conduct a semistructured discussion of issues on a topic for the benefit of an audience.	Moderator introduces the panel and problem and keeps the discussion flowing; restates often; controls (somewhat) equal and fair time allocation. Members are responsible for developing points of view and have some control of agenda.
Forum		To encourage audience participation on issues surrounding a topic.	Moderator introduces the program and speaker, who presents a brief statement and interacts with the audience. Moderator participates to encourage audience involvement. A variety of discussion formats can be used.
Colloquy		To inform an audience through the use of planned questions designed to get unprepared responses from participants for the benefit of the audience.	Moderator introduces the speaker and panel of questioners, then regulates rotation and time. Sometimes summarizing, sometimes clarifying, moderator does not participate as a panelist.
Whole-House Decision-Making		To debate issues as a body, then decide, using appropriate voting methods.	Moderator regulates the discussion and debate, attempting to get maximum input from both sides in order that members of the house may cast informed votes. Parliamentary procedure is commonly used to govern the event and facilitate orderly progress.

Figure 18.1

A guide for planning group meetings.

Source: From *Groups in Context* by G. L. Wilson & M. S. Hanna, 1986, New York: Random House. Copyright 1986 by McGraw Hill. Reprinted with permission.

group leaders should be aware of these designs when setting up their meetings to enhance the use of their time and the resources of the people involved.

GROUP WORK WITH CULTURALLY DIVERSE POPULATIONS

Group work with culturally diverse populations must take into consideration the collective history of a people as an identified group as well as individual differences (Atkinson, Morten, & Sue, 1983; Harper, 1984; Vacc & Wittmer, 1980). This type of assessment is complex. For some people, their collective history may have a deep impact on them, whereas for others, the influence is minimal. Regardless, there are some cultural groups, such as many Asian-Americans, who do not respond well to traditional group psychotherapy processes because their culture teaches them not to share personal problems or confront others in public (Vander Kolk, 1985). On the other hand, there are cultural groups, such as African-Americans and Hispanic-Americans, who do extremely well in a variety of group settings (Higgins & Warner, 1975; McWhirter, McWhirter, & McWhirter, 1988). It is imperative that group workers understand the cultural backgrounds of their clients before attempting to work with them in group environments. Groups that are composed of people from culturally different backgrounds will have diverse values and world views as well (DeLucia, Coleman, & Jensen-Scott, 1992).

It is important that leaders examine their own thoughts and feelings about people who are culturally distinct from them before they work with groups having minority members. Although groups are usually beneficial to participants and give them an "opportunity to experience open, honest communication and interpersonal intimacy" (Hulse, 1985, p. 92–93), this may not be true for members of culturally diverse groups if leaders are prejudiced toward them. Such leaders may hold stereotypes that impede their ability to truly hear and communicate with the culturally different. Therefore, in conducting groups that include members who are culturally distinct, leaders must sensitize themselves to cultural variables and become more aware of the issues incorporated in their own backgrounds. Only through such a process will differences in group members become assets in the group's development. Such a sensitization process can readily be taught in a group training course (Greeley, Garcia, Kessler, & Gilchrest, 1992).

With the diversity of the United States's population becoming even greater in the future, the need for professional and personal sensitivity to others in groups will continuously increase (DeLucia et al., 1992). Therefore, group workers will need to increase their knowledge about cultural variables regarding African-Americans, Hispanic-Americans, Asian-Americans, and Native American Indians, because these are the four largest cultural minority populations in the nation. Acknowledging, and being sensitive to, the various forms of white ethnic American culture will also be vital for group workers. Examples of issues that need to be addressed before working in groups with culturally distinct persons include matters such as realizing the importance of "saving face" in Asian and Asian-Pacific American culture (Fukuyama & Coleman, 1992; Leong, 1992); the value of cooperation, health, and healing in Native American Indian culture (Dufrene & Coleman, 1992); and the crucial nature of family, creative expression, and spirituality in African-American society (Gainor, 1992; Rollock, Westman, & Johnson, 1992).

GROUPS IN BUSINESS AND INDUSTRY

"Within the business and industrial community, group development theory functions as a guide for effective managers and leaders to use in improving production and quality of work life" (Kormanski, 1988, p. 41). The importance placed on group development theory and groups themselves within business and industry has been growing rapidly since the 1970s. Those within the corporate community increasingly recognize that the morale and mental health of workers is a major factor in the success of their businesses. Therefore, groups within the workplace are often transformed into task groups or teams by management in order to personalize the business environment (Maples, 1992). **Teams** differ from basic groups in four main ways (Reilly & Jones, 1974):

1.   They have shared goals, as opposed to individual goals in most groups.
2.   They stress interdependency more than do groups.
3.   They require more of a commitment by members to a team effort.
4.   They are by design accountable to a higher level within the organization than are groups.

The ultimate example of a team group in business to promote systematic social change is the **quality circle.** The concept of quality circles is American in origin, having been devised by an industrial specialist, W. Edwards Deming, after World War II. Deming's idea became popular in Japan in the form of "quality control circles" and was instrumental in helping the Japanese rebuild their economy following the war. The first quality circles created in the United States were sponsored by the Lockheed Missile Corporation and Honeywell Corporation in 1974. At first, this team-building approach was concentrated on production workers, but now the trend is to include nonproduction workers, such as office support staff, as well.

Quality circles are established on the idea of *participative management*—"a generic term for a broad range of workplace innovations" (Napier & Gershenfeld, 1989, p. 526). The idea is for workers in the same work area to meet on a weekly basis to discuss and try to resolve work-related problems. Quality circles are usually started by management, but they benefit everyone involved because of their emphasis on cooperation and the interdependence of group members on one another. In some ways, they are similar to learning or psychoeducational groups (Johnson & Johnson, 1991). Just like many learning groups, participants in quality circles are volunteers who unite for a particular purpose. The payoff for the time they invest in meetings is found in the increased knowledge they gain of a job or subject area and in intra- and interpersonal enhancement. Overall, there appears to be a direct correlation between quality circle members' self-esteem and group success (Brockner & Hess, 1986). Quality circles that work well improve the quality of participants' work lives and productivity (Lawler & Mohrman, 1985). They concentrate on improving the process of work and interaction rather than focusing on persons or personalities as problems.

Kormanski (1988) suggests that an effective management style in the workplace should differ as groups in business environments progress through the five developmental stages outlined by Tuckman and Jensen (1977). Management style primarily evolves from one that is highly directive to one that is more democratic. In this process, workers have an increasing desire to fulfill higher personal and community needs. Leaders help other workers, themselves, and the process of team-building by changing their leadership pattern as the group develops. Basically, an effective management style evolves from one that is high in **transactional leadership skills** (i.e., helping members to interact) to one that is high in **transformational skills** (i.e., helping members and the group achieve new behaviors) (see Table 18.1). In this way, the power base of the group changes "from position-derived power to personal power" (Kormanski, 1988, p. 41).

The use of group teams and group development theory will continue to increase in the corporate world, especially in large corporations in which a sense of isolation and social alienation is likely to occur without such growth-promoting interventions. It is, therefore, crucial for companies that rely on groups to develop skilled group facilitators and for effective group workers to take their skills into the business domain (Gladding, 1992; Schwarz, 1994).

GROUP WORK WITH ABUSERS AND THE ABUSED

Working with abusers or the abused requires a different approach from that utilized in other forms of group work. Individuals who are abusers, or who have been abused by others, have great difficulty in establishing healthy interpersonal relationships with others (Vinson, 1992). They suffer from a variety of symptoms ranging from poor impulse control in the case of abusers to poor self-concept in the case of the abused. Many individuals in either category have trouble working through their problems on an individual level. In the case of abusers, they "usually have long histories of abuse, extremely strong defenses against change, and relatively little ability to follow through on commitments" (Fuhrmann & Washington, 1984, p. 63). In the case of the abused, especially those who have been sexually molested as children, there is a tendency to shut down, suppress, or distract themselves to the point of not dealing with what happened to them (Emerson, 1988; McBride & Emerson, 1989). In both types of cases, denial is a major means of dealing with present and past situations.

Group methods are often effective with such individuals for at least two reasons. First, many perpetrators of abuse and their victims are socially isolated and welcome a structured experience where they can "tell their story" and become

Table 18.1
Relationship of trends to group development theory.

Group Development Stage	1 Management Style	2 Need Levels	3A Transacting Skills	3B Transforming Skills	4 Team Outcomes	5 Power Bases
1. Forming	High task, low relationship	Physiological, safety and security	Getting acquainted, goal setting, organizing	Values clarification, visioning, communication through myth and metaphor	Commitment, acceptance	Coercive, connective
2. Storming	High task, high relationship	Belonging, social	Active listening, assertiveness, conflict management	Flexibility, creativity, kaleidoscopic thinking	Clarification, belonging	Connective, reward, legitimate
3. Norming	Low task, high relationship	Recognition and esteem	Communication, feedback, affirmation	Playfulness and humor entrepreneurship, networking	Involvement, support	Legitimate, referent, informational
4. Performing	Low task, low relationship	Achievement, self-actualization	Decision making, problem solving, rewarding	Multicultural awareness, mentoring, futuring	Achievement, pride	Informational, expert
5. Adjourning	Low task, high relationship		Evaluating, reviewing	Celebrating, bringing closure	Recognition, satisfaction	Referent, informational

Source: From "Using Group Development Theory in Business and Industry" by C. Kormanski, 1988, *Journal for Specialists in Group Work, 13*, p. 40. Copyright ACA. Reprinted by permission of the American Counseling Association.

more connected with others. Second, groups that are composed of members with similar backgrounds, such as abusers, are more resistant to manipulation.

Almost all groups for abusers and the abused make use of basic group techniques such as role playing, modeling, feedback, and confrontation (Fuhrmann & Washington, 1984; Vinson, 1992). The degree and type of change that occurs in groups is related to both the emphasis in the group and its developmental stage (Wheeler, O'Malley, Waldo, Murphey, & Blank, 1992). Groups that work best are composed of volunteers who are prescreened before being selected. However, due to the seriousness of abusive disorders, some groups are mandated as a part of court-ordered treatment and are filled with openly resistant clients. In such situations, group leaders must know how to work with resistance, such as not opposing it. Because of the volatility in abuse groups, co-leaders are often recommended.

Probably the abusive disorder in which group strategies are most prevalent is with addicts (Vander Kolk, 1985). There are groups for numerous kinds of addicts ranging from "foodaholism" (Stoltz, 1984) to chemical dependency (Clark, Blanchard, & Hawes, 1992). Many such groups are self-help oriented and are part of the reason self-help groups have grown at such a phenomenal rate since the 1970s. Regardless of who leads the group, it is helpful to have members in these settings who have experienced and worked through the abuse involved. A group leader does not have to have been abused or have been an abuser to be effective with such participants, but a thorough understanding of the individual, group, family, and community dynamics that contribute to these disorders is essential.

RESEARCH ON GROUP EFFECTIVENESS

Research on the effectiveness of groups in general has had a relatively brief and uneven history. Indeed, group research is in its infancy when compared to research in the other social sciences (Stockton & Morran, 1982). Three of the leading analysts of what makes groups successful are Gazda (1989), Yalom (1985), and Zimpfer (1984). All have either made extensive reviews of the literature or conducted major group studies. Their findings can be classified in reference to the types of groups they have studied—for example, counseling groups, psychoeducational groups, and work/task groups. Their reporting follows a tradition of cataloging group research dating back to the early 1900s. However, it was not until the 1960s that "formal reviews of the literature on outcome" of groups initially appeared, especially those emphasizing remediation and education (Dies, 1985, p. 68).

Since the 1960s, reviews of the literature have primarily concentrated on short-term groups for adults. The most comprehensive research comparing different theoretical types of groups was conducted by Lieberman, Yalom, and Miles (1973). Although they found some theoretically oriented groups to be more effective overall than others, one of their major findings was that in effective groups, successful members are able to make use of self-disclosure and catharsis.

Another of their more pertinent discoveries was that effective group leaders employed a number of similar effective interpersonal techniques, such as active listening and feedback, regardless of their theoretical orientation.

There are numerous reasons why group research has lagged to the point that relatively few group investigators use "sophisticated research design and statistical analysis" (Conyne et al., 1985, p. 115). One of the primary reasons is the complexity of studying groups. When a group increases by including another member, communication patterns multiply. Therefore, it is harder to trace the interaction among members and the impact of behaviors. Studying dyadic relationships, such as those found in individual counseling, is much simpler than researching a small group.

Another reason that research is difficult in groups is the lack of "process or outcome instruments related specifically to group situations" (Morran & Stockton, 1985, p. 188). There are some tests, such as the Group Attitude Scale (GAS) (Evans & Jarvis, 1986), the FIRO-B (Schutz, 1958), and the Group Satisfaction Scale (Caple & Cox, 1989), that focus on group dynamics and outcome. Other instruments are geared more toward individuals than groups. Examples of these are the Myers-Briggs Type Indicator (MBTI), the Personal Orientation Inventory (POI), and the Tennessee Self-Concept Scale (TSCS) which are frequently employed in reporting group results. An excellent source for beginning group researchers to examine, as they ponder which instruments to use in studying groups, is the CORE Battery published by the American Group Psychotherapy Association (MacKenzie & Dies, 1982).

A third reason why group research has lagged behind relates to the perceptions of potential inquirers. Many researchers perceive their work as a one-time project rather than an ongoing process with study building on study (Morran & Stockton, 1985). Therefore, they fail to enhance their skill in research as they go and do not advance the field of group work. Indeed, as Bednar states, "Researchers have essentially failed to advance knowledge in the last three decades despite inordinate improvements in research methods" (Bednar, Corey, Evans, Gazda, Pistole, Stockton, & Robison, 1987, p. 101). However, the "stuckness" in group research methods may be in the process of changing.

Among the most promising new methods are those that (a) map the complexity of group dynamics (Bales, Cohen, & Williamson, 1980; Hulse-Killacky, 1994) and (b) emphasize a team approach between practitioners and researchers (Morran & Stockton, 1985). One example of the mapping process is **SYMLOG** (System for the Multiple Level Observation of Groups), a systematic way of studying groups developed by Bales et al. (1980) that has been used to analyze group member movement along several dimensions. Poppen and Pruett (1988) employed this instrument to evaluate the Carroll (1986) training tapes on group work in the here-and-now. Their research showed the effect of group member interactions with others and the group leader, as well as the power of members to influence the movement of the group for better or worse.

The practitioner/researcher team approach is well represented in the work of Robison, Morran, and Hulse-Killacky (1989). They advocate using a **single-subject research design** as a way to help the practitioner also be a researcher or work with a researcher. In this procedure, leaders follow one of two methods in evaluating their groups. In the first method, they follow an ABAB design to evaluate the relationship of an intervention on changes that may occur in the group (see Figure 18.2). In the other method, leaders employ a multiple baseline design that randomly measures change across subject, variables, or situations (see Figure 18.3).

Overall, research on the effectiveness of groups needs to be greatly expanded to reach the level of sophistication that has been established on the effectiveness of individual counseling. However, increased concern and attention is being devoted to this area (L. Cuty-Ruiz, 1994, personal communication). For instance, awards for group work research are constantly being given out by professional group work associations. There is also increased emphasis being placed on investigating the effectiveness of interpersonal relationships in other settings, such as families, and relating this research to group work. Models based on observations, such as Yalom's (1985) 12 "therapeutic factors," are further serving to spur on group research efforts.

TRAINING EFFECTIVE GROUP LEADERS

The education of new leaders and the continuing education of current leaders is a strong current trend in group work. New texts as well as scholarly articles and practical exercises for use in groups are being published at an increased rate (e.g., Pfeiffer, 1993). These publications deal with all aspects of groups including feedback, communication skills, trust, process, team building, and closure. In addition, training standards developed by the Association for Specialists in Group Work (1991) have important implications for counselor education programs, the future development of students, and national professional certification organizations such as CACREP (Conyne, Wilson, Kline, Morran, & Ward, 1993). Both the broad scope of group work as well as individual skills are being emphasized in the 1990s. However, such emphasis has not always been the case.

"Perhaps the weakest area of the group work movement throughout the decades has been the lack of attention paid to the training of group leaders"

Figure 18.2
ABAB research design.

(A1)	(B1)	(A2)	(B2)
o o o	o o o	o o o	o o o
Baseline	Intervention	Baseline	Intervention

Source: From "Single-Subject Research Designs for Group Counselors Studying Their Own Groups" by F. F. Robison, D. K. Morran, and D. Hulse-Killacky, 1989, *Journal for Specialists in Group Work, 14,* p. 94. Reprinted by permission of the American Counseling Association.

Group, variable, situation A:	0	0	0	0	0	0	0	0	0	0
Group, variable, situation B:	0	0	0	0	0	0	0	0	0	0
Group, variable, situation C:	0	0	0	0	0	0	0	0	0	0

Figure 18.3

Multiple baseline design.

Source: Robison, Morran, and Hulse-Killacky, 1989, p. 95. Reprinted by permission of the American Counseling Association.

(Shapiro & Bernadett-Shapiro, 1985, p. 86). Until recently, very little was published about training group leaders, although a great deal was written about individual counseling training (Gladding, 1992). Indeed, in the early days of group work (the 1950s and 1960s) before standards for training were established, almost anyone could claim to be a group leader and consequently establish a group. Many such individuals were well-intentioned but used predominantly individual counseling techniques to work with groups. The results were less than desirable and many times were harmful. The self-anointed approach is no longer recognized or considered ethical by major group associations (see ASGW ethical guidelines, Appendix A). Such an approach does not ensure quality or uniformity in treatment.

A second way chosen to select and train group leaders has been the growth experience model that stresses "the value of a group experience for trainees" (Stockton, 1980, p. 58). The idea behind this model is that people must first experience the power of the group as a follower and then become a group leader. Indeed, many self-help group leaders fine-tune their skills in this way. However, being in a group is inadequate instruction for becoming a group leader. Likewise, a sole emphasis on simple didactic instruction or mere observation of a group at work is deficient as the major way to train group leaders (Harvill, West, Jacobs, & Masson, 1985). Rather, leadership skills for conducting groups require input and cultivation of many sources. Only the well-trained professional can make therapeutic moves in a group on a consistent basis (Vriend, 1985).

One of the major trends in group work appears to be the development of methods and courses to emphasize specific training (D. Hulse-Killacky, 1994, personal communication). Among the methods being established to promote the training of future group leaders are (a) a systematic approach (Harvill, Masson, & Jacobs, 1983; Harvill et al., 1985) and (b) a critical incidents and intervention cube model (Childers, 1986).

Systematic group leadership training involves the teaching of basic skills to beginning group leaders. It is a six-step method that includes the videotaping of trainees leading a group before being introduced to the skill they are to learn (steps 1 and 2). Then the trainees read about and see a new skill demonstrated (steps 3 and 4). Finally, trainees critique their original videos and then make new videotapes demonstrating the skill they have just been taught (steps 5 and 6) (Harvill et al., 1983). As first proposed, systematic group leadership training focused on six group leadership skills:

1. *Cutting-off* (i.e., blocking)—to stop group members who continue to speak in a nonfocused way and help them concentrate on a point. For example, as the leader, Milly might say, "Sharon, we have heard a lot about your thoughts on this subject. We need to hear from someone else."

2. *Drawing-out* (i.e., supporting)—to solicit verbalization from one or more group members without putting them on the "hot-seat." For example, Rudy might inquire from Fred and Dee if they have thoughts about the matter before the group.

3. *Holding the focus*—to help members concentrate on a specific topic or person for a set length of time. For example, if the group has been talking about risk taking and Wanda changes the subject, the leader, Alice, may simply say, "Wanda, let's conclude our discussion on risk taking before we deal with anything else."

4. *Shifting the focus*—to move group members to a different topic area or person. For instance, Rusty, as the group leader, may say to the group as a whole, "It appears we have exhausted our ideas about how to take risks. I would like to see us talk about the drawbacks, as well as the advantages, to risk taking."

5. *Use of eyes*—to scan the group and notice nonverbal reactions. For instance, as the leader, Zack notices that Beebee's eyes are focused down on ground instead of on Jean to whom she is talking.

6. *Tying things together* (i.e., linking)—to connect members with one another in regard to their similarities. In linking, Inez and Pablo are connected together by a leader who realizes they both have a passion for computers and software programs.

Research findings support that four of these skills—cutting-off, drawing-out, holding the focus, and shifting the focus—are significantly improved following systematic group leadership training. This procedure for training group leaders in the future holds great promise.

The **critical-incident model** and **intervention cube concept** is a second current way of training group leaders. This model, as first set forth by Cohen and Smith (1976) and later expanded on by Donigian and Malnati (1987), focuses on a number of critical incidents in the life of a group of any type. The trainee, after studying group dynamics, watches a videotape of his or her instructor handling a number of different situations in a group. Then the trainee co-leads a group under the instructor's supervision, where he or she makes strategic interventions geared to the incidents in the particular group (Childers, 1986). Trainees are taught self-management skills, as well as ways to deal with specific group situations. They learn on both a personal and professional level. This type of training, when combined in an integrative way with the type of nonperfectionistic thinking pattern proposed by Miller (1986), can help beginning group leaders to be less rigid and more sensitive, caring, and helpful to others.

Overall, the concepts and methods used in these two approaches to training include the basic prerequisites for an effective group leader as defined by Trotzer (1989): "(1) cognitive knowledge about the group process, (2) involvement as a participant in group interaction, (3) skills and techniques for use in a leadership capacity, and (4) supervised experience in the leadership role" (p. iii). Yalom (1985) concurs with this holistic, research-based, balanced, and multidimensional emphasis in training, and goes beyond techniques in emphasizing the importance of helping "students evaluate their own work in a critical fashion and maintain sufficient flexibility (both technically and attitudinally) so that they can be responsive to their own observations" (p. 534). According to Yalom (1985), "the mature therapist is an evolving therapist, a therapist who regards each patient, each group, indeed his or her whole career as a learning experience" (p. 534). This open and learning attitude is also true for effective and mature group leaders outside the psychotherapeutic and counseling areas, who are constantly growing with each group experience.

THE FUTURE OF GROUP WORK

Group work has come a long way in its brief formal history. There is little doubt that in the future, group work will be robust and permeate almost all segments of society. The main question is how this trend will happen. Some probable tendencies to look for in group work in the future, according to Zimpfer (1984) are

1. more concrete and structured treatments for more precise diagnoses,
2. greater variety in the choice of interventions or their adjuncts,
3. more educative and growth-inducing approaches rather than ameliorative or merely adjustive, and
4. conceiving group participants as collaborators in treatment rather than as passive receivers or as individuals totally responsible for their own change. (p. 207)

Another current and future focus in group work is toward developing and refining standards for specialty areas, including psychoeducation, counseling, psychotherapy, and task/work groups (Association for Specialists in Group Work, 1991). Task and work groups are beginning to receive special attention, since more attention has been paid to counseling and psychotherapy groups in the past (Conyne, 1989). Counselors and human service workers need to know how to conduct such groups in the future if they are going to be effective.

One of the biggest challenges for group workers to resolve in the future is using the power "of the group" more fully than is now the case (Glassman & Wright, 1983). At present, most group leaders concentrate on working with individuals "in the group" and focus their attention on single members rather than the group as a whole. When groups are able to harness the resources within themselves more constructively, a new era of helping will emerge. Group leaders will then have to be better educated and more sophisticated. Yet, the benefits from such an emphasis will be a greater understanding by group members and group workers of what is effective in promoting change or fostering support.

Thus, group experiences may build on each other more precisely and offer participants a better means of achieving their dreams and objectives.

SUMMARY AND CONCLUSION

This chapter has concentrated on current issues in group work, such as general proactive approaches for teaching life-skills, and specific remedial approaches for assisting those who abuse or have been abused. The chapter also contains information on growing trends, such as the emergence of consumer-oriented and specialized groups, and groups to promote systematic change, such as those found in business/industry or those used in various cultural settings. Two other critical issues, research on group effectiveness and the training of competent group leaders, have been covered, too. All of these areas, while diverse in appearance, have a common theme: their development will affect the growth or stagnation of groups and group specialists. For example, group work that is geared toward consumers and personal life-skills is needed if individuals within society, and society as a whole, are to develop in healthy and functional ways. These means of helping people help themselves promote change in a way not possible on a one-to-one basis. Remediation, although always needed in groups, is limited in impact.

Overall, the current state of group work reflects the historical development of this counseling specialty and the future needs of society. Promoting a more humane and effective life and work climate are possible through groups. The simultaneous interest of business/industry and human relations theorists in groups is a positive sign that the dynamics found within such structures can be helpful and influence the makeup of society for the good of all. The emphasis for now and the future is on the training of competent group leaders, who are theoretically driven and ethically based, as well as on research that will uncover more completely the qualities that make groups work well. The tasks of the future are exciting as group work moves toward another plateau of sophistication and promise.

CLASSROOM EXERCISES

1. In a group of three, identify two life-skills, such as applying for a job or making conversation at a party, that you think could easily be taught in a group environment. Outline the ways you would teach these skills. Confer with another group of three about the skills they selected and the approach they decided to use in this process. Select one skill and approach from your now-combined group of six and as a group present it to the class as a whole. The class should then critique the methods and decide which life-skills are easiest to teach in a group and how.

2. Read recent business periodicals in your library to gain a sense for how groups are used in such settings, e.g., quality circles. In a group of three, discuss an article from a business publication, and how the emphasis of groups in business is different from and similar to the use of groups in counseling and psychotherapy. Share your impressions with the class as a whole.

3. In dyads, read and critique a recent research report or article on the effectiveness of psychoeducational groups. Report your findings to the class in a brief oral presentation. Then make a list of the qualities the class believes are most effective in conducting group research.

4. You have been asked to train a group of novice group workers in group theory and dynamics. From what you have read in the last part of this chapter and the rest of the book, what important points about groups would you emphasize and in what order would you present your material? Outline your responses; then compare your approach with that of classmates. Share your outline with the class as a whole and get their feedback.

REFERENCES

Alpert, J. L., & Rosenfield, S. (1981). Consultation and the introduction of social problem-solving groups in schools. *Personnel and Guidance Journal, 60,* 37–41.

Association for Specialists in Group Work. (1991). *Professional standards for the training of group workers.* Alexandria, VA: Author.

Atkinson, D. R., Morten, G., & Sue, D. W. (Eds.). (1983). *Counseling American minorities: A cross cultural perspective* (2nd ed.). Dubuque, IA: Wm. C. Brown.

Bales, R., Cohen, S., & Williamson, S. (1980). *SYMLOG: A system for the multiple level observation of groups.* New York: Free Press.

Bednar, R. L., Corey, G., Evans, N. J., Gazda, G., Pistole, M. C., Stockton, R., & Robison, F. F. (1987). Overcoming obstacles to the future development of research on group work. *Journal for Specialists in Group Work, 12,* 98–111.

Brockner, J., & Hess, T. (1986). Self-esteem and task performance in quality circles. *Academy of Management Journal, 29,* 617–623.

Caple, R. B., & Cox, P. L. (1989). Relationships among group structure, member expectations, attraction to group, and satisfaction with the group experience. *Journal for Specialists in Group Work, 14,* 16–24.

Carroll, M. (1986). *Group work: Leading in the here and now* [Film]. Alexandria, VA: American Counseling Association.

Childers, J. H., Jr. (1986). Group leadership training and supervision: A graduate course. *Journal for Specialists in Group Work, 11,* 48–52.

Clark, J., Blanchard, M., & Hawes, C. W. (1992). Group counseling for people with addictions. In D. Capuzzi & D. R. Gross (Eds.), *Introduction to group counseling* (pp. 103–119). Denver: Love Publishing.

Cohen, A. M., & Smith, D. (1976). *The critical incident in growth groups: Theory and technique.* La Jolla, CA: University Associates.

Conyne, R. K. (1989). *How personal growth and task groups work.* Newbury Park, CA: Sage.

Conyne, R. K., Dye, A., Gill, S. J., Leddick, G. R., Morran, D. K., & Ward, D. E. (1985). A retrospective of "critical issues." *Journal for Specialists in Group Work, 10,* 112–115.

Conyne, R. K., Wilson, F. R., Kline, W. B., Morran, D. K., & Ward, D. E. (1993). Training group workers: Implications of the new ASGW training standards for training and practice. *Journal for Specialists in Group Work, 18,* 11–23.

DeLucia, J. L., Coleman, V. D., Jensen-Scott, R. L. (1992). Cultural diversity in group counseling. *Journal for Specialists in Group Work, 17,* 194–195.

Dies, R. R. (1985). Research foundations for the future of group work. *Journal for Specialists in Group Work, 10,* 68–73.

Donigian, J., & Malnati, R. (1987). *Critical incidents in group therapy.* Pacific Grove, CA: Brooks/Cole.

Dufrene, P. M., & Coleman, V. D. (1992). Counseling Native Americans: Guidelines for group process. *Journal for Specialists in Group Work, 17,* 229–234.

Emerson, S. (1988). Female student counselors and child sexual abuse: Theirs and their clients'. *Counselor Education and Supervision, 28,* 15–21.

Evans, N. J., & Jarvis, P. A. (1986). The Group Attitude Scale: A measure of attraction to group. *Small Group Behavior, 17,* 203–216.

Fuhrmann, B. S., & Washington, C. S. (1984). Substance abuse and group work: Tentative conclusions. *Journal for Specialists in Group Work, 9,* 62–63.

Fukuyama, M. A., & Coleman, N. C. (1992). A model for bicultural assertion training with Asian-Pacific American college students: A pilot study. *Journal for Specialists in Group Work, 17,* 210–217.

Gainor, K. A. (1992). Internalized oppression as a barrier to effective group work with black women. *Journal for Specialists in Group Work, 17,* 235–242.

Gazda, G. M. (1985). Group counseling and therapy: A perspective on the future. *Journal for Specialists in Group Work, 10,* 74–76.

Gazda, G. M. (1989). *Group counseling: A developmental approach* (4th ed.). Boston: Allyn & Bacon.

Gladding, S. T. (1989). *An awareness of Claire.* Unpublished manuscript.

Gladding, S. T. (1992). Total quality and groups. *Journal for Specialists in Group Work, 17,* 3.

Glassman, S. M., & Wright, T. L. (1983). In, with, and of the group: A perspective on group psychotherapy. *Small Group Behavior, 14,* 96–106.

Greeley, A. T., Garcia, V. L., Kessler, B. L., & Gilchrest, G. (1992). Training effective multicultural group counselors: Issues for a group

training course. *Journal for Specialists in Group Work, 17,* 196–209.

Harper, F. D. (1984). Group strategies with black alcoholics. *Journal for Specialists in Group Work, 9,* 38–43.

Harvill, R., Masson, R. L., & Jacobs, E. (1983). Systematic group leader training: A skills development approach. *Journal for Specialists in Group Work, 8,* 226–232.

Harvill, R., West, J., Jacobs, E. E., & Masson, R. L. (1985). Systematic group leader training: Evaluating the effectiveness of the approach. *Journal for Specialists in Group Work, 10,* 2–13.

Hawk, R. S. (1991). Fannie R. Cooley: A humanitarian group worker. *Journal for Specialists in Group Work, 16,* 3–7.

Higgins, E., & Warner, R. (1975). Counseling blacks. *Personnel and Guidance Journal, 53,* 383–386.

Hopson, B., & Hough, P. (1976). The need for personal and social education in secondary schools and further education. *British Journal of Guidance and Counseling, 4,* 16–27.

Hulse, D. (1985). Overcoming the social-ecological barriers to group effectiveness: Present and future. *Journal for Specialists in Group Work, 10,* 92–97.

Hulse-Killacky, D. (1994). *Leadership in groups: Balancing process and content.* Presentation at American Counseling Association Annual Convention, Minneapolis, MN.

Ivey, A. (1973). Microcounseling: The counselor as trainer. *Personnel and Guidance Journal, 51,* 311–316.

Johnson, D. W., & Johnson, F. P. (1991). *Joining together* (4th ed.). Englewood Cliffs, NJ: Prentice Hall.

Klein, E. B. (1985). Group work: 1985 and 2001. *Journal for Specialists in Group Work, 10,* 108–111.

Kormanski, C. (1988). Using group development theory in business and industry. *Journal for Specialists in Group Work, 13,* 30–43.

Lawler, E. E., & Mohrman, S. A. (1985, January-February). Quality circles, after the fad. *Harvard Business Review,* pp. 65–71.

Leong, F. T. L. (1992). Guidelines for minimizing premature termination among Asian American clients in group counseling. *Journal for Specialists in Group Work, 17,* 218–228.

Lieberman, M., Yalom, I., & Miles, M. (1973). *Encounter groups: First facts.* New York: Basic Books.

MacKenzie, K. R., & Dies, R. R. (1982). *The CORE Battery: Clinical outcome results.* New York: American Group Psychotherapy Association.

Maples, M. (1992). STEAMWORK: An effective approach to team building. *Journal for Specialists in Group Work, 17,* 144–150.

McBride, M. C., & Emerson, S. (1989). Group work with women who were molested as children. *Journal for Specialists in Group Work, 14,* 25–33.

McWhirter, B. T., McWhirter, E. H., & McWhirter, J. J. (1988). Groups in Latin America: Comunidades eclesial de base as mutual support groups. *Journal for Specialists in Group Work, 13,* 70–76.

Miller, M. J. (1986). On the perfectionistic thoughts of beginning group leaders. *Journal for Specialists in Group Work, 11,* 53–56.

Morran, D. K., & Stockton, R. (1985). Perspectives on group research programs. *Journal for Specialists in Group Work, 10,* 186–191.

Napier, R. W., & Gershenfeld, M. K. (1989). *Groups: Theory and experience* (4th ed.). Boston: Houghton Mifflin.

Pfeiffer, J. W. (1993). *The 1993 Annual Developing Human Resources.* San Diego: Pfeiffer & Co.

Poppen, W. A., & Pruett, K. S. (1988, October). *Group work: Leading in the here and now—A SYMLOG assessment.* Paper presented at ACES First National Convention, St. Louis, MO.

Reilly, A. J., & Jones, J. E. (1974). Team-building. In J. W. Pfeiffer & J. E. Jones (Eds.), *The 1974 annual handbook for group facilitators* (pp. 227–237). San Diego: University Associates.

Robison, F. F., Morran, D. K., & Hulse-Killacky, D. (1989). Single-subject research designs for group counselors studying their own groups. *Journal for Specialists in Group Work, 14,* 93–97.

Rollock, D. A., Westman, J. S., & Johnson, C. (1992). A black student support group on a predominantly white university campus: Issues for counselors and therapists. *Journal for Specialists in Group Work, 17,* 243–252.

Schutz, W. C. (1958). *FIRO: A three dimensional theory of interpersonal behavior.* New York: Holt, Rinehart and Winston.

Schwarz, R. M. (1994). *The skilled facilitator.* San Francisco: Jossey-Bass.

Seligman, M. (1993). Group work with parents of children with disabilities. *Journal for Specialists in Group Work, 18,* 115–126.

Shapiro, J. L., & Bernadett-Shapiro, S. (1985). Group work to 2001: Hal or haven (from isolation)? *Journal for Specialists in Group Work, 10,* 83–87.

Stockton, R. (1980). The education of group leaders: A review of the literature with suggestions for the future. *Journal for Specialists in Group Work, 5,* 55–62.

Stockton, R., & Morran, D. K. (1982). Review and perspective of critical dimensions in therapeutic small group research. In G. M. Gazda (Ed.), *Basic approaches to group psychotherapy and group counseling* (3rd ed.) (pp. 37–83). Springfield, IL: Charles C. Thomas.

Stoltz, S. G. (1984). Recovering from foodaholism. *Journal for Specialists in Group Work, 9,* 51–61.

Trotzer, J. P. (1989). *The counselor and the group* (2nd ed.). Muncie, IN: Accelerated Development.

Tuckman, B. W., & Jensen, M. A. (1977). Stages of small group development revisited. *Group and Organizational Studies, 2,* 419–427.

Vacc, N. A., & Wittmer, J. P. (Eds.). (1980). *Let me be me: Special populations and the helping professions.* Muncie, IN: Accelerated Development.

Vander Kolk, C. J. (1985). *Introduction to group counseling and psychotherapy.* Columbus, OH: Merrill.

Vinson, A. (1992). Group counseling with victims of abuse/incest. In D. Capuzzi & D. R. Gross (Eds.), *Introduction to group counseling* (pp. 165–181). Denver: Love Publishing.

Vriend, J. (1985). We've come a long way, group. *Journal for Specialists in Group Work, 10,* 63–67.

Wheeler, I., O'Malley, K., Waldo, M., Murphey, J., & Blank, C. (1992). Participants' perception of therapeutic factors in groups for incest survivors. *Journal for Specialists in Group Work, 17,* 89–95.

Wilson, G. L., & Hanna, M. S. (1986). *Groups in context.* New York: Random House.

Yalom, I. D. (1985). *The theory and practice of group psychotherapy* (3rd ed.). New York: Basic Books.

Zimpfer, D. G. (1984). Patterns and trends in group work. *Journal for Specialists in Group Work, 9,* 204–208.

Ethical Guidelines for Group Counselors

PREAMBLE

One characteristic of any professional group is the possession of a body of knowledge, skills, and voluntarily, self-professed standards for ethical practice. A Code of Ethics consists of those standards that have been formally and publicly acknowledged by the members of a profession to serve as the guidelines for professional conduct, discharge of duties, and the resolution of moral dilemmas. By this document, the Association for Specialists in Group Work (ASGW) has identified the standards of conduct appropriate for ethical behavior among its members.

The Association for Specialists in Group Work recognizes the basic commitment of its members to the Ethical Standards of its parent organization, the American Counseling Association (ACA) and nothing in this document shall be construed to supplant that code. These standards are intended to complement the ACA standards in the area of group work by clarifying the nature of ethical responsibility of the counselor in the group setting and by stimulating a greater concern for competent group leadership.

The group counselor is expected to be a professional agent and to take the processes of ethical responsibility seriously. ASGW views "ethical

These guidelines were approved by the Association for Specialists in Group Work (ASGW) Executive Board, June 1, 1989.

process" as being integral to group work and views group counselors as "ethical agents." Group counselors, by their very nature in being responsible and responsive to their group members, necessarily embrace a certain potential for ethical vulnerability. It is incumbent upon group counselors to give considerable attention to the intent and context of their actions because the attempts of counselors to influence human behavior through group work always have ethical implications.

The following ethical guidelines have been developed to encourage ethical behavior of group counselors. These guidelines are written for students and practitioners, and are meant to stimulate reflection, self-examination, and discussion of issues and practices. They address the group counselor's responsibility for providing information about group work to clients and the group counselor's responsibility for providing group counseling services to clients. A final section discusses the group counselor's responsibility for safeguarding ethical practice and procedures for reporting unethical behavior. Group counselors are expected to make known these standards to group members.

ETHICAL GUIDELINES

1. *Orientation and Providing Information*— Group counselors adequately prepare prospective or new group members by providing as much information about the existing or proposed group as necessary.

- Minimally, information related to each of the following areas should be provided.

(a) Entrance procedures, time parameters of the group experience, group participation expectations, methods of payment (where appropriate), and termination procedures are explained by the group counselor as appropriate to the level of maturity of group members and the nature and purpose(s) of the group.

(b) Group counselors have available for distribution, a professional disclosure statement that includes information on the group counselor's qualifications and group services that can be provided, particularly as related to the nature and purpose(s) of the specific group.

(c) Group counselors communicate the role expectations, rights, and responsibilities of group members and group counselor(s).

(d) The group goals are stated as concisely as possible by the group counselor including "whose" goal it is (the group counselor's, the institution's, the parent's, the law's, society's, etc.) and the role of group members in influencing or determining the group's goal(s).

(e) Group counselors explore with group members the risks of potential life changes that may occur because of the group experience and help members explore their readiness to face these possibilities.

(f) Group members are informed by the group counselor of unusual or experimental procedures that might be expected in their group experience.

(g) Group counselors explain, as realistically as possible, what services can and cannot be provided within the particular group structure offered.

(h) Group counselors emphasize the need to promote full psychological functioning and presence among group members. They inquire from prospective group members whether they are using any kind of drug or medication that may affect functioning in the group. They do not permit any use of alcohol and/or illegal drugs during group sessions and they discourage the use of alcohol and/or drugs (legal or illegal) prior to group meetings which may affect the physical or emotional presence of the member or other group members.

(i) Group counselors inquire from prospective group members whether they have ever been a client in counseling or psychotherapy. If a prospective group member is already in a counseling relationship with another professional person, the group counselor advises the prospective group member to notify the other professional of their participation in the group.

(j) Group counselors clearly inform group members about the policies pertaining to the group counselor's willingness to consult with them between group sessions.

(k) In establishing fees for group counseling services, group counselors consider the financial status and the locality of prospective group members. Group members are not charged fees for group sessions where the group counselor is not present and the policy of charging for sessions missed by a group member is clearly communicated. Fees for participating as a group member are contracted between group counselor and group member for a specified period of time. Group counselors do not increase fees for group counseling services until the existing contracted fee structure has expired. In the event that the established fee structure is inappropriate for a prospective member, group counselors assist in finding comparable services of acceptable cost.

2. *Screening of Members*—The group counselor screens prospective group members (when appropriate to their theoretical orientation). Insofar as possible, the counselor selects group members whose needs and goals are compatible with the goals of the group, who will not impede the group process, and whose well-being will not be jeopardized by the group experience. An orientation to the group (i.e., ASGW Ethical Guideline #1) is included during the screening process.

- Screening may be accomplished in one or more ways, such as the following:
  (a) Individual interview,
  (b) Group interview of prospective group members,
  (c) Interview as part of a team staffing, and,
  (d) Completion of a written questionnaire by prospective group members.
3. *Confidentiality*—Group counselors protect members by defining clearly what confidentiality means, why it is important, and the difficulties involved in enforcement.
  (a) Group counselors take steps to protect members by defining confidentiality and the limits of confidentiality (i.e., when a group member's condition indicates that there is clear and imminent danger to the member, others, or physical property, the group counselor takes reasonable personal action and/or informs responsible authorities).
  (b) Group counselors stress the importance of confidentiality and set a norm of confidentiality regarding all group participants' disclosures. The importance of maintaining confidentiality is emphasized before the group begins and at various times in the group. The fact that confidentiality cannot be guaranteed is clearly stated.
  (c) Members are made aware of the difficulties involved in enforcing and ensuring confidentiality in a group setting. The counselor provides examples of how confidentiality can non-maliciously be broken to increase members' awareness, and help to lessen the likelihood that this breach of confidence will occur. Group counselors inform group members about the potential consequences of intentionally breaching confidentiality.
  (d) Group counselors can only ensure confidentiality on their part and not on the part of the members.
  (e) Group counselors video or audio tape a group session only with the prior consent, and the members' knowledge of how the tape will be used.
  (f) When working with minors, the group counselor specifies the limits of confidentiality.

  (g) Participants in a mandatory group are made aware of any reporting procedures required of the group counselor.
  (h) Group counselors store or dispose of group member records (written, audio, video, etc.) in ways that maintain confidentiality.
  (i) Instructors of group counseling courses maintain the anonymity of group members whenever discussing group counseling cases.
4. *Voluntary/Involuntary Participation*—Group counselors inform members whether participation is voluntary or involuntary.
  (a) Group counselors take steps to ensure informed consent procedures in both voluntary and involuntary groups.
  (b) When working with minors in a group, counselors are expected to follow the procedures specified by the institution in which they are practicing.
  (c) With involuntary groups, every attempt is made to enlist the cooperation of the members and their continuance in the group on a voluntary basis.
  (d) Group counselors do not certify that group treatment has been received by members who merely attend sessions, but did not meet the defined group expectations. Group members are informed about the consequences for failing to participate in a group.
5. *Leaving a Group*—Provisions are made to assist a group member to terminate in an effective way.
  (a) Procedures to be followed for a group member who chooses to exit a group prematurely are discussed by the counselor with all group members either before the group begins, during a pre-screening interview, or during the initial group session.
  (b) In the case of legally mandated group counseling, group counselors inform members of the possible consequences for premature self-termination.
  (c) Ideally, both the group counselor and the member can work cooperatively to determine the degree to which a group experience is productive or counterproductive for that individual.

(d) Members ultimately have a right to discontinue membership in the group, at a designated time, if the predetermined trial period proves to be unsatisfactory.

(e) Members have the right to exit a group, but it is important that they be made aware of the importance of informing the counselor and the group members prior to deciding to leave. The counselor discusses the possible risks of leaving the group prematurely with a member who is considering the option.

(f) Before leaving a group, the group counselor encourages members (if appropriate) to discuss their reasons for wanting to discontinue membership in the group. Counselors intervene if other members use undue pressure to force a member to remain in the group.

6. *Coercion and Pressure*—Group counselors protect member rights against physical threats, intimidation, coercion, and undue peer pressure insofar as is reasonably possible.

(a) It is essential to differentiate between "therapeutic pressure" that is part of any group and "undue pressure," which is not therapeutic.

(b) The purpose of a group is to help participants find their own answer, not to pressure them into doing what the group thinks is appropriate.

(c) Counselors exert care not to coerce participants to change in directions which they clearly state they do not choose.

(d) Counselors have a responsibility to intervene when others use undue pressure or attempt to persuade members against their will.

(e) Counselors intervene when any member attempts to act out aggression in a physical way that might harm another member or themselves.

(f) Counselors intervene when a member is verbally abusive or inappropriately confrontive to another member.

7. *Imposing Counselor Values*—Group counselors develop an awareness of their own values and needs and the potential impact they have on the interventions likely to be made.

(a) Although group counselors take care to avoid imposing their values on members, it is appropriate that they expose their own beliefs, decisions, needs, and values, when concealing them would create problems for the members.

(b) There are values implicit in any group, and these are made clear to potential members before they join the group. (Examples of certain values include: expressing feelings, being direct and honest, sharing personal material with others, learning how to trust, improving interpersonal communication, and deciding for oneself.)

(c) Personal and professional needs of group counselors are not met at the members' expense.

(d) Group counselors avoid using the group for their own therapy.

(e) Group counselors are aware of their own values and assumptions and how these apply in a multicultural context.

(f) Group counselors take steps to increase their awareness of ways that their personal reactions to members might inhibit the group process and they monitor their countertransference. Through an awareness of the impact of stereotyping and discrimination (i.e., biases based on age, disability, ethnicity, gender, race, religion, or sexual preference), group counselors guard the individual rights and personal dignity of all group members.

8. *Equitable Treatment*—Group counselors make every reasonable effort to treat each member individually and equally.

(a) Group counselors recognize and respect differences (e.g., cultural, racial, religious, lifestyle, age, disability, gender) among group members.

(b) Group counselors maintain an awareness of their behavior toward individual group members and are alert to the potential detrimental effects of favoritism or partiality toward any particular group member to the exclusion or detriment of any other member(s). It is likely that group counselors will favor some members over others, yet all group members deserve to be treated equally.

(c) Group counselors ensure equitable use of group time for each member by inviting silent members to become involved, acknowledging nonverbal attempts to communicate, and discouraging rambling and monopolizing of time by members.

(d) If a large group is planned, counselors consider enlisting another qualified professional to serve as a co-leader for the group sessions.

9. *Dual Relationships*—Group counselors avoid dual relationships with group members that might impair their objectivity and professional judgment, as well as those which are likely to compromise a group member's ability to participate fully in the group.

(a) Group counselors do not misuse their professional role and power as group leader to advance personal or social contacts with members throughout the duration of the group.

(b) Group counselors do not use their professional relationship with group members to further their own interest either during the group or after the termination of the group.

(c) Sexual intimacies between group counselors and members are unethical.

(d) Group counselors do not barter (exchange) professional services with group members for services.

(e) Group counselors do not admit their own family members, relatives, employees, or personal friends as members to their groups.

(f) Group counselors discuss with group members the potential detrimental effects of group members engaging in intimate inter-member relationships outside of the group.

(g) Students who participate in a group as a partial course requirement for a group course are not evaluated for an academic grade based upon their degree of participation as a member in a group. Instructors of group counseling courses take steps to minimize the possible negative impact on students when they participate in a group course by separating course grades from participation in the group and by allowing students to decide what issues to explore and when to stop.

(h) It is inappropriate to solicit members from a class (or institutional affiliation) for one's private counseling or therapeutic groups.

10. *Use of Techniques*—Group counselors do not attempt any technique unless trained in its use or under supervision by a counselor familiar with the intervention.

(a) Group counselors are able to articulate a theoretical orientation that guides their practice, and they are able to provide a rationale for their interventions.

(b) Depending upon the type of an intervention, group counselors have training commensurate with the potential impact of a technique.

(c) Group counselors are aware of the necessity to modify their techniques to fit the unique needs of various cultural and ethnic groups.

(d) Group counselors assist members in translating in-group learnings to daily life.

11. *Goal Development*—Group counselors make every effort to assist members in developing their personal goals.

(a) Group counselors use their skills to assist members in making their goals specific so that others present in the group will understand the nature of the goals.

(b) Throughout the course of a group, group counselors assist members in assessing the degree to which personal goals are being met, and assist in revising any goals when it is appropriate.

(c) Group counselors help members clarify the degree to which the goals can be met within the context of a particular group.

12. *Consultation*—Group counselors develop and explain policies about between-session consultation to group members.

(a) Group counselors take care to make certain that members do not use between-session consultations to avoid dealing with issues pertaining to the group that would be dealt with best in the group.

(b) Group counselors urge members to

bring the issues discussed during between-session consultations into the group if they pertain to the group.

(c) Group counselors seek out consultation and/or supervision regarding ethical concerns or when encountering difficulties which interfere with their effective functioning as group leaders.

(d) Group counselors seek appropriate professional assistance for their own personal problems or conflicts that are likely to impair their professional judgment and work performance.

(e) Group counselors discuss their group cases only for professional consultation and educational purposes.

(f) Group counselors inform members about policies regarding whether consultation will be held confidential.

13. *Termination from the Group*—Depending upon the purpose of participation in the group, counselors promote termination of members from the group in the most efficient period of time.

(a) Group counselors maintain a constant awareness of the progress made by each group member and periodically invite the group members to explore and reevaluate their experiences in the group. It is the responsibility of group counselors to help promote the independence of members from the group in a timely manner.

14. *Evaluation and Follow-up*—Group counselors make every attempt to engage in ongoing assessment and to design follow-up procedures for their groups.

(a) Group counselors recognize the importance of ongoing assessment of a group, and they assist members in evaluating their own progress.

(b) Group counselors conduct evaluation of the total group experience at the final meeting (or before termination), as well as ongoing evaluation.

(c) Group counselors monitor their own behavior and become aware of what they are modeling in the group.

(d) Follow-up procedures might take the form of personal contact, telephone contact, or written contact.

(e) Follow-up meetings might be with individuals, or groups, or both to determine the degree to which: (i) members have reached their goals, (ii) the group had a positive or negative effect on the participants, (iii) members could profit from some type of referral, and (iv) as information for possible modification of future groups. If there is no follow-up meeting, provisions are made available for individual follow-up meetings to any member who needs or requests such a contact.

15. *Referrals*—If the needs of a particular member cannot be met within the type of group being offered, the group counselor suggests other appropriate professional referrals.

(a) Group counselors are knowledgeable of local community resources for assisting group members regarding professional referrals.

(b) Group counselors help members seek further professional assistance, if needed.

16. *Professional Development*—Group counselors recognize that professional growth is a continuous, ongoing, developmental process throughout their career.

(a) Group counselors maintain and upgrade their knowledge and skill competencies through educational activities, clinical experiences, and participation in professional development activities.

(b) Group counselors keep abreast of research findings and new developments as applied to groups.

SAFEGUARDING ETHICAL PRACTICE AND PROCEDURES FOR REPORTING UNETHICAL BEHAVIOR

The preceding remarks have been advanced as guidelines which are generally representative of ethical and professional group practice. They have not been proposed as rigidly defined prescriptions. However, practitioners who are thought to be grossly unresponsive to the ethical concerns addressed in this document may be subject to a review of their practices by the ACA Ethics Committee and ASGW peers.

• For consultation and/or questions regarding these ASGW Ethical Guidelines or group ethical dilemmas, you may contact the Chairperson of the ASGW Ethics Committee. The name, address, and telephone number of the current ASGW Ethics Committee Chairperson may be acquired by telephoning the ACA office in Alexandria, Virginia at (703) 823-9800.

- If a group counselor's behavior is suspected as being unethical, the following procedures are to be followed:

(a) Collect more information and investigate further to confirm the unethical practice as determined by the ASGW Ethical Guidelines.

(b) Confront the individual with the apparent violation of ethical guidelines for the purposes of protecting the safety of any clients and to help the group counselor correct any inappropriate behaviors. If satisfactory resolution is not reached through this contact then:

(c) A complaint should be made in writing, including the specific facts and dates of the alleged violation and all relevant supporting data. The complaint should be included in an envelope marked "CONFIDENTIAL" to ensure confidentiality for both the accuser(s) and the alleged violator(s) and forwarded to all of the following sources:

1. The name and address of the Chairperson of the state Counselor Licensure Board for the respective state, if in existence.

2. The Ethics Committee
c/o The President
American Counseling Association
5999 Stevenson Avenue
Alexandria, Virginia 22304

3. The name and address of all private credentialing agencies that the alleged violator maintains credentials or holds professional membership. Some of these include the following:

National Board for Certified Counselors, Inc.
3-D Terrace Way
Greensboro, NC 27403

National Council for Credentialing of Career Counselors
c/o NCCC
5999 Stevenson Avenue
Alexandria, Virginia 22304

National Academy for Certified Clinical Mental Health Counselors
3-D Terrace Way
Greensboro, NC 27403

Commission on Rehabilitation Counselor Certification
162 North State Street, Suite 317
Chicago, Illinois 60601

American Association for Marriage and Family Therapy
1100 17th Street, N.W., 10th floor
Washington, D.C. 20036-4601

American Psychological Association
1200 Seventeenth Street, N.W.
Washington, D.C. 20036

American Group Psychotherapy Association, Inc.
25 East 21st Street, 6th Floor
New York, New York 10010

Professional Standards for the Training of Group Workers

PREAMBLE

All counselors should possess a set of core competencies in general group work. These basic knowledge and skills provide a foundation which specialty training can extend. Mastery of the core competencies does not qualify one to independently practice any group work specialty. Specialists in group work must possess advanced competencies relevant to a particular group work type.

The Association for Specialists in Group Work (ASGW) advocates for the incorporation of core group competencies as part of the Masters level training required in all counselor education programs. The Association also supports preparation of group work specialists at the Masters level. ASGW further supports the continued preparation of group work specialists at the post-Masters level (Ed.S. or Certificate, Doctoral, Continuing Education, etc.), recognizing that recommended levels of group work specialty training in many programs will need to be accomplished following completion of the Masters Degree.

This revision of the *Professional Standards for Training of Group Workers* contains two levels of competencies and related training that have been identified by the ASGW Standards Committee: (a) *Core Group Competencies:* The minimum core of group worker competencies and related

These guidelines were adopted by the Association for Specialists in Group Work (ASGW), April 20, 1991.

training necessary for all counselors, including knowledge, skills, and practice (minimum: 10 clock hours; recommended: 20 clock hours); and (b) For Group Work *Specialists:* Advanced competencies that build on the generalist core in the four identified group work specialties of:

- *Task/Work groups,* including knowledge, skills, and supervised practice beyond core group training (additional minimum: 30 clock hours; recommended: 45 clock hours);
- *Guidance/Psychoeducation groups,* including knowledge, skills, and supervised practice beyond core group training (additional minimum: 30 clock hours; recommended: 45 clock hours);
- *Counseling/Interpersonal Problem-Solving groups,* including knowledge, skills, and supervised practice beyond core group training (additional minimum: 45 clock hours; recommended: 60 clock hours);
- *Psychotherapy/Personality Reconstruction groups,* including knowledge, skills, and supervised practice beyond core group training (additional minimum: 45 clock hours; recommended: 60 clock hours).

DEFINITIONS

Group Work

Group work is a broad professional practice that refers to the giving of help or the accomplishment of tasks in a group setting. It involves the application of group theory and process by a capable professional practitioner to assist an interdependent collection of people to reach their mutual goals, which may be personal, interpersonal, or task-related in nature.

Core Training in Group Work for All Counselors

All professional counselors should possess basic, fundamental knowledge and skills in group work. Moreover, this set of competencies provides a basic foundation upon which specialization training in group work is built.

Core training group work competencies does not prepare a counseling professional to independently assume responsibility for conducting any of the specialty groups to be defined in these Standards. Additional focused training is required for independent practice in a specialty, as detailed below.

Group Work Specializations

The trainee may proceed beyond core training in group work to specialize in one or more advanced areas of practice. It is to be expected that all Counseling programs would provide core training in group work to all students and most would offer additional training in at least one of the other specializations. Definitions of each specialization follow.

Task/Work Groups.   Much work in contemporary Western society is accomplished through group endeavor. The task/work group specialist is able to assist groups such as task forces, committees, planning groups, community organizations, discussion groups, study circles, learning groups, and other similar groups to correct or develop their functioning. The focus is on the application of group dynamics principles and processes to improve practice and the accomplishment of identified work goals.

Guidance/Psychoeducation Groups.   Education and prevention are critically important goals for the contemporary counselor. The guidance/psychoeducation group specialist seeks to use the group medium to educate group participants who are presently unaffected about a potential threat (such as AIDS), a developmental life event (such as a transition point), or how to cope with an immediate life crisis (such as suicide

of a loved one), with the goal of preventing an array of educational and psychological disturbance from occurring.

Counseling/Interpersonal Problem Solving Groups.   The group worker who specializes in counseling/interpersonal problem-solving seeks to help group participants to resolve the usual, yet often difficult, problems of living through interpersonal support and problem-solving. An additional goal is to help participants to develop their existing interpersonal problem-solving competencies that they may be better able to handle future problems of a similar nature. Nonsevere career, educational, personal, social, and developmental concerns are frequently addressed.

Psychotherapy/Personality Reconstruction Groups.   The group worker who specializes in psychotherapy/personality reconstruction seeks to help individual group members to remediate their in-depth psychological problems. Because the depth and extent of the psychological disturbance is significant, the goal is to aid each individual to reconstruct major personality dimensions.

TRAINING STANDARDS

A. Core Group Work for All Counselors: Knowledge Competencies

All counselors can effectively:

1. State for the four major group work specializations identified in this document (task groups, guidance groups, counseling groups, psychotherapy groups) the distinguishing characteristics of each, the commonalities shared by all, and the appropriate instances in which each is to be used.
2. Identify the basic principles of group dynamics.
3. Discuss the basic therapeutic ingredients of groups.
4. Identify the personal characteristics of group workers that have an impact on members; knowledge of personal strengths, weaknesses, biases, values, and their effect on others.
5. Describe the specific ethical issues that are unique to group work.
6. Discuss the body of research on group work and how it relates to one's academic prepara-

tion in either school counseling, student personnel education, community counseling, mental health counseling, or other specialized studies.

7. Define the process components involved in typical stages of a group's development (i.e., characteristics of group interaction and counselor roles).
8. Describe the major facilitative and debilitative roles that group members may take.
9. State the advantages and disadvantages of group work and the circumstances for which it is indicated or contraindicated.
10. Detail therapeutic factors of group work.
11. Identify principles and strategies for recruiting and screening prospective group members.
12. Detail the importance of group and member evaluation.
13. Deliver a clear, concise, and complete definition of group work.
14. Deliver a clear, concise, and complete definition of each of the four group work specialties.
15. Explain and clarify the purpose of a particular form of group work.

Core Group Work Training for All Counselors: Skill Competencies

All counselors are able to effectively:

1. Encourage participation of group members.
2. Observe and identify group process events.
3. Attend to and acknowledge group member behavior.
4. Clarify and summarize group member statements.
5. Open and close group sessions.
6. Impart information in the group when necessary.
7. Model effective group leader behavior.
8. Engage in appropriate self-disclosure in the group.
9. Give and receive feedback in the group.
10. Ask open-ended questions in the group.
11. Empathize with group members.
12. Confront group members' behavior.
13. Help group members attribute meaning to their experience.
14. Help group members to integrate and apply learnings.
15. Demonstrate ASGW ethical and professional standards in group practice.

16. Keep the group on task in accomplishing its goals.

Core Group Work Training

Knowledge. Core training in group work should include a minimum of one course. Contained in this course should be attention to competencies in the Knowledge and in the Skills domains.

Skills Through Supervised Practice. The Practice domain should include observation and participation in a group experience, which could occur in a classroom group.

- *Minimum* amount of supervised practice: *10 clock hours.*
- *Recommended* amount of supervised practice: *20 clock hours.*

B. Group Work Specializations: Knowledge, Skill, and Supervised Practice Domains

The counselor trainee, having mastered the core knowledge and skill domains displayed above, can specialize in one or more advanced areas of group work practice. These advanced specialty areas are Task/Work groups, Guidance/Psychoeducation groups, Counseling/Interpersonal Problem-Solving groups, and Psychotherapy/Personality Reconstruction groups. The advanced knowledge and skill competencies associated with each of these specialties are presented below.

Task/Work Groups

Knowledge Competencies. In addition to Core knowledge, the qualified Task/Work group specialist can effectively:

1. Identify organizational dynamics pertinent to task/work groups.
2. Describe community dynamics pertinent to task/work groups.
3. Identify political dynamics pertinent to task/work groups.
4. Describe standard discussion methodologies appropriate for task/work groups.
5. Identify specific ethical considerations in working with task/work groups.
6. Identify program development and evaluation models appropriate for task/work groups.

7. List consultation principles and approaches appropriate for task/work groups.

Skills Competencies.   In addition to Core skills, the qualified Task/Work group specialist is able to effectively:

1. Focus and maintain attention on task and work issues.
2. Obtain goal clarity in a task/work group.
3. Conduct a personally selected task/work group model appropriate to the age and clientele of the group leader's specialty area(s) (e.g., school counseling).
4. Mobilize energies toward a common goal in task/work groups.
5. Implement group decision-making methods in task/work groups.
6. Manage conflict in task/work groups.
7. Blend the predominant task focus with appropriate attention to human relations factors in task/work groups.
8. Sense and use larger organizational and political dynamics in task/work groups.

Specialist Training: Task/Work Groups

Knowledge.   Course work should be taken in the broad area of organization development, management, and/or sociology such that the student understands organizational life and how task groups function within it. Course work also should be taken in consultation.

Skills Through Supervised Practice.   In addition to Core training acquired through observation and participation in a group (10 clock hours minimum; 20 clock hours recommended), practice should include:

- *Minimum* amount of *30 clock hours* should be obtained in co-leading or leading a task/work group in a field-practice setting supervised by qualified faculty or staff personnel.
- *Recommended* amount of *45 clock hours* should be obtained in co-leading or leading a task/work group in a field-practice setting supervised by qualified faculty or staff personnel.

Guidance/Psychoeducation Groups

Knowledge Competencies.   In addition to Core knowledge, the qualified Guidance/Psychoeducation group specialist can effectively:

1. Identify the concepts of primary prevention and secondary prevention in guidance/psychoeducation groups.
2. Articulate the concept of "at risk" in guidance/psychoeducation groups.
3. Enumerate principles of instruction relevant to guidance/psychoeducation groups.
4. Develop a knowledge base relevant to the focus of a guidance/psychoeducation group intervention.
5. List principles involved in obtaining healthy and/or at risk members for guidance/psychoeducation groups.
6. Describe human development theory pertinent to guidance/psychoeducation groups.
7. Discuss environmental assessment as related to guidance/psychoeducation groups.
8. Discuss principles of structure as related to guidance/psychoeducation groups.
9. Discuss the concept of empowerment in guidance/psychoeducation groups.
10. Identify specific ethical considerations unique to guidance/psychoeducation groups.
11. List advantages of guidance/psychoeducation groups and where indicated and contraindicated.

Skills Competencies.   In addition to Core skills, the qualified Guidance/Psychoeducation group specialist can effectively:

1. Plan a guidance/psychoeducation group in collaboration with "target" population members or representatives.
2. Match a relevant guidance/psychoeducation topic with relevant (and currently "unaffected") target group.
3. Conduct a personally selected guidance/psychoeducation group model appropriate to the age and clientele of the group leader's specialty area (e.g., student personnel education).
4. Design a guidance/psychoeducation group plan that is developmentally and practically sound.
5. Present information in a guidance/psychoeducation group.

6. Use environmental dynamics to the benefit of the guidance/psychoeducation group.
7. Conduct skill training in guidance/psychoeducation groups.

Specialist Training: Guidance/ Psychoeducation Groups

Knowledge. Course work should be taken in the broad area of community psychology, health promotion, marketing, consultation, and curriculum design.

Skills Through Supervised Practice. In addition to Core training acquired through observation and participation in a group (10 clock hours minimum; 20 clock hours recommended), practice should include:

- *Minimum* amount of *30 clock hours* should be obtained in co-leading or leading a guidance/psychoeducation group in a field-practice setting supervised by qualified faculty or staff personnel.
- *Recommended* amount of *45 clock hours* should be obtained in co-leading or leading a guidance/psychoeducation group in a practice setting supervised by qualified faculty or staff personnel.

Counseling/Interpersonal Problem-Solving Groups

Knowledge Competencies. In addition to Core knowledge, the qualified Counseling/Interpersonal Problem-Solving group specialist can effectively:

1. State for at least three major theoretical approaches to group counseling the distinguishing characteristics of each and the commonalities shared by all.
2. Identify specific ethical problems and considerations unique to group counseling.
3. List advantages and disadvantages of group counseling and the circumstances for which it is indicated or contraindicated.
4. Describe interpersonal dynamics in group counseling.
5. Describe group problem-solving approaches in relation to group counseling.

6. Discuss interpersonal assessment in group counseling.
7. Identify referral sources and procedures in group counseling.
8. Describe group formation principles in group counseling.

Skills Competencies. In addition to Core skills, the qualified Counseling/Interpersonal Problem-Solving group specialist can effectively:

1. Recruit and screen prospective counseling group members.
2. Recognize self-defeating behaviors of counseling group members.
3. Conduct a personally selected group counseling model appropriate to the age and clientele of the group leader's specialty area(s) (e.g., community counseling).
4. Develop reasonable hypotheses about nonverbal behavior among counseling group members.
5. Exhibit appropriate pacing skills involved in stages of a counseling group's development.
6. Intervene effectively at critical incidents in the counseling group process.
7. Work appropriately with disruptive counseling group members.
8. Make use of the major strategies, techniques, and procedures of group counseling.
9. Use procedures to assist transfer and support of changes by group counseling members in the natural environment.
10. Use adjunct group counseling structures such as homework (e.g., goal setting).
11. Work cooperatively and effectively with a counseling group co-leader.
12. Use assessment procedures in evaluating effects and contributions of group counseling.

Specialist Training: Counseling/Interpersonal Problem-Solving Groups

Knowledge. As much course work in group counseling as possible is desirable, but at least one course beyond the generalist is necessary. Other courses in the Counseling program should provide good support for the group counseling specialty.

Skills Through Supervised Practice. In addition to Core training acquired through observation and participation in a group (10 clock hours minimum; 20 clock hours recommended), practice should include:

- *Minimum amount* of *45 clock hours* should be obtained in co-leading or leading a counseling/interpersonal problem-solving group in a field practice setting supervised by qualified faculty or staff personnel.
- *Recommended* amount of *60 clock hours* should be obtained in co-leading or leading a counseling/interpersonal problem-solving group in a field-practice setting supervised by qualified faculty or staff personnel.

Psychotherapy/Personality Reconstruction Groups

Knowledge Competencies. In addition to Core knowledge, the Psychotherapy/Personality Reconstruction group specialist can effectively:

1. State for at least three major theoretical approaches to group psychotherapy the distinguishing characteristics of each and the commonalities shared by all.
2. Identify specific ethical problems and considerations unique to group psychotherapy.
3. List advantages and disadvantages of group psychotherapy and the circumstances for which it is indicated or contraindicated.
4. Specify intrapersonal and interpersonal dynamics in group psychotherapy.
5. Describe group problem-solving approaches in relation to group psychotherapy.
6. Discuss interpersonal assessment and intervention in group psychotherapy.
7. Identify referral sources and procedures in group psychotherapy.
8. Describe group formation principles in group psychotherapy.
9. Identify and describe abnormal behavior in relation to group psychotherapy.
10. Identify psychopathology as related to group psychotherapy.
11. Describe personality theory as related to group psychotherapy.

12. Detail crisis intervention approaches suitable for group psychotherapy.
13. Specify diagnostic and assessment methods appropriate for group psychotherapy.

Skill Competencies. In addition to Core skills, the qualified Psychotherapy/Personality Reconstruction group specialist can effectively:

1. Recruit and screen prospective psychotherapy group members.
2. Recognize self-defeating behaviors of psychotherapy group members.
3. Describe and conduct a personally selected group psychotherapy model appropriate to the age and clientele of the group leader's specialty area (e.g., mental health counseling).
4. Identify and develop reasonable hypotheses about nonverbal behavior among psychotherapy group members.
5. Exhibit appropriate pacing skills involved in stages of a psychotherapy group's development.
6. Identify and intervene effectively at critical incidents in the psychotherapy group process.
7. Work appropriately with disruptive psychotherapy group members.
8. Make use of the major strategies, techniques, and procedures of group psychotherapy.
9. Provide and use procedures to assist transfer and support of changes by group psychotherapy members in the natural environment.
10. Use adjunct group psychotherapy structures such as psychological homework (e.g., self-monitoring, contracting).
11. Work cooperatively and effectively with a psychotherapy group co-leader.
12. Use assessment procedures in evaluating effects and contributions of group psychotherapy.
13. Assist individual change along the full range of development, from "normal" to "abnormal" in the psychotherapy group.
14. Handle psychological emergencies in the psychotherapy group.
15. Institute hospitalization procedures when appropriate and necessary in the psychotherapy group.
16. Assess and diagnose mental and emotional disorders of psychotherapy group members.

**Specialist Training: Psychotherapy/
Personality Reconstruction Groups**

Knowledge. Course work should be taken in
the areas of group psychotherapy, abnormal psychology, psychopathology, and diagnostic assessment to assure capabilities in working with more
disturbed populations.

Skills Through Supervised Practice. In addition to Core training acquired through observation and participation in a group (10 clock hours
minimum; 20 clock hours recommended), practice should include:

- *Minimum* amount of *45 clock hours* should
  be obtained in co-leading or leading a psy-
  chotherapy/personality reconstruction
  group in a field-practice setting supervised
  by qualified faculty or staff personnel.
- *Recommended* amount of *60 clock hours*
  should be obtained in co-leading or leading
  a psychotherapy/personality reconstruction
  group in a field-practice setting supervised
  by qualified faculty or staff personnel.

Glossary

A-B-C model of human interaction "A" is the event, "B" is the thought process , and "C" is the feeling state resulting from one's thoughts. To change negative or nonproductive feelings, individuals need to think differently (i.e., positive or neutral).

A-B-C-D-E Worksheet an approach to ethical decision making that uses a mnemonic device to remind group leaders and members of what they should do. The letters of this worksheet stand for Assessment, Benefit, Consequences and Consultation, Duty, and Education.

action exercises sensory awareness methods or guided imagery used in psychodrama warm-up phase to help members discover common themes within the group as well as focus more on individual concerns.

action phase second part of the psychodrama process that involves the enactment of protagonists' concerns.

active listening to hear the tone and meanings behind verbal communication and to pick up on messages in nonverbal behaviors.

activity group guidance (AGG) group guidance involving activities that are developmental in nature; typically includes coordinated guidance topics.

actors those who play the parts of other important people or objects in a psychodrama play. They are called *auxiliaries* and with prompting from the protagonist, they can play the protagonist's double, an antagonist, or even a

piece of furniture. In the same psychodrama, an auxiliary could play more than one part, such as being the protagonist's best friend and worst enemy.

Adlerian parent education stresses the cooperation among family members as a goal and emphasizes the use of logical and natural consequences in order to avoid power struggles. There is a democratic emphasis to this orientation, and regular family council meetings are held in order for all members to voice concerns and needs. The Adlerian approach stresses parent discussion groups with a trained leader and a set curriculum.

adolescence the age span from 13 to 19 but extended to include some individuals up to age 25; a time of unevenness and paradoxes marked by extensive personal changes.

Adult ego state (TA) the realistic, logical part of a person; functions like a computer in that it receives and processes information from the Parent, the Child, and the environment.

adult children of alcoholics (ACoAs) adults who grew up in families where one or both parents abused alcohol. These individuals developed coping mechanisms for dealing with their alcoholic family system, such as denial or overcompensation, that are usually not functional for a mature life style. Dealing with feelings about the past as well as learning and behaviors for coping and life skills are therapeutic foci for these persons.

adulthood   a somewhat nebulous term implying that a person has reached physical, mental, social, and emotional maturity.

advice giving   instructing someone what to do in a particular situation. It is seldom appropriate or needed in most groups. It prevents members from struggling with their own feelings and keeps advice givers from having to recognize shortcomings in their own lives.

ageism   discrimination against older people based on their age.

aging process   a biological phenomenon composed of physiological changes as well as a mental process of considering one's self older.

Alcoholics Anonymous (AA)   an organization that helps alcoholics gain and maintain control of their lives by remaining sober; established in the late 1930s.

American Association of Retired Persons (AARP)   a leading group for those age 55 and above to learn what social and political events impact them most.

American Group Psychotherapy Association (AGPA)   a psychoanalytically oriented organization established by Samuel R. Slavson in 1943.

American Society of Group Psychotherapy and Psychodrama (ASGPP)   a professional group association which was established by J. L. Moreno between 1941 and 1942.

amplify   to emphasize statements made by the protagonist in psychodrama. Examples include verbalizing nonverbal communications, questioning one's self, interpreting statements for what is being said and not said, contradicting feelings, self-observing, and denial.

antecedent-response-consequence model of behaviorism   this model basically states that behavior is functionally related to its antecedents and consequent events.

apprehension   anxiety; a moderate amount helps group members key in on what they are experiencing and what they want to do.

assessing members' growth and change   a technique similar to personal reviews, but in assessment, the emphasis is on individuals' memories of themselves at the beginning of the group and now. The idea of such an exercise is to have members see and share significant gains with themselves and others.

Association for Advancement of Behavioral Therapy (AABT)   the major professional organization for behavioral therapists.

Association for Specialists in Group Work (ASGW)   formed in 1973; a division within the American Counseling Association.

attack on the leader   when members of the group become hostile or rebellious in regard to a leader's authority or conduct of the group. Underlying reasons for such attacks are subgrouping, fear of intimacy, and extragroup socializing.

attractiveness   a multidimensional concept, but basically it refers to members positively identifying with others in the group.

audience   a term used to describe others who may be present during the psychodrama. Some may become auxiliaries.

authoritarian group leaders   envision themselves as experts. These leaders interpret, give advice, and generally direct the movement of the group much like a parent controls the actions of a child. They are often charismatic and manipulative. They feed off of obedience, expect conformity, and operate out of the wheel model.

authoritative power   power predicated on social position or responsibility in an organization.

autonomy   the promotion of self-determination or the power to choose one's own direction in life. In groups, it is important that group members feel they have a right to make their own decisions.

auxiliary counselors   RET group leader encourages members of the group to act as types of co-counselors once someone has presented a problem. When they do, participants benefit from multiple input.

avoiding conflict   when the group ignores areas of tension or silences or discounts members who expose the group's disagreements.

awareness   Gestalt term for a total organismic response to the environment so that a person gains insight and control over situations and becomes responsible in achieving a healthy response to life events..

"BA" (basic assumption) activity   a classification devised by Wilfred Bion for the emotional pattern of an antiwork group (as opposed to a "W" [work group]). BA groups can be broken down further into three sub-patterns: *BA Dependency* (where members are overdependent on the group leader); *BA Pairing* (where members are more interested in being with each other than in working on a goal); and *BA Fight-Flight* (where members become preoccupied with either engaging in or avoiding hostile conflict).

band-aiding the misuse of support; process of preventing others from fully expressing their emotional pain.

basic encounter group also known as *encounter group;* first established by Carl Rogers to describe his approach to group work; focuses on individuals' awareness of their own emotional experiences and the behaviors of others; emphasis is placed on the awareness and exploration of intrapsychic and interpersonal issues. Encounter groups are often known as *personal growth groups* because the emphasis in these groups is on personal development.

BASIC ID Lazarus's multimodal model for helping; includes the components of behavior, affect, sensation, imagery, cognition, interpersonal relations, drugs.

Basic Skills Training (BST) approach to groups developed at the National Training Laboratories in the 1940s; predecessor of the *T-group* movement.

behavior therapy the collective behaviorist point of view, a combination of opinions and procedures about behavior and how to influence it.

behavioral disputation rational-emotive therapy treatment that involves many forms from reading (bibliotherapy) to role-playing in the group. Often enactment of the problem within the group setting and possible ways of handling it are used. Homework may then be assigned in the form of *shame attacks* (in which the person actually does what he or she dreaded and finds the world does not fall apart regardless of the outcome).

behavioral groups either interpersonal or transactional groups depending on the purposes of the leader and members. (a) *Interpersonal groups* are highly didactic and involve specified goals that usually center on self-improvement. (b) *Transactional groups* are more heterogeneous and focus on broader, yet specific, goals.

behavioral parent education an approach associated with direct change and manipulation. Parents are trained to be change agents and to record and reinforce certain behaviors in their children.

behavioral rehearsal consists of practicing a desired behavior until it is performed the way one wishes. The process consists of gradually shaping a behavior and getting corrective feedback.

behaviorists inside and outside of group settings, leaders who emphasize overt processes, here-and-now experiences, learning, changing of maladaptive actions, defining specific goals, and scientific support for techniques.

beneficence promoting the good of others. It is assumed in groups that leaders and members will work hard for the betterment of the group as a whole.

blind quadrant information originally unknown to oneself but known to others when the group began.

blocking related to protecting, in which the leader intervenes in the group activity to stop counterproductive behavior. This intervention can be done on a verbal or nonverbal level.

blocking role an anti-group member role. Individuals who take this role act as aggressors, blockers, dominators, recognition seekers, and self-righteous moralists.

body language a Gestalt concept in which emphasis is placed on what a person's body is doing, such as a hand tapping.

boundaries physical and psychological parameters under which a group operates, such as starting and ending on time.

brainstorming a way to stimulate divergent thinking, requires an initial generating of ideas in a nonjudgmental manner. The premise of this approach is that creativity and member participation are often held back because of the critical evaluation of ideas and actions by other group members.

burnout becoming physically and emotionally exhausted.

C group a type of Adlerian parent education group; each component of the group—collaboration, consultation, clarification, confrontation, concern, confidentiality, and commitment—begins with a "c." The group is primarily psychoeducational. It emphasizes developmental and preventive aspects of parenting.

capping the process of easing out of emotional interaction and into cognitive reflection; especially useful during termination.

career awareness and self-exploration (CASE) group a group that combines brief lectures on particular subjects, such as self-disclosure, trust, self-esteem, and communications, with small-group interaction.

career change group a type of group for adults in mid-life that is both psychoeducational and psychotherapeutic in nature.

caring a genuine concern for others.

catharsis a release of pent-up feelings such as anger or joy; a psychoanalytic concept.

cathexis school of TA a branch of TA that emphasizes reparenting.

chain in this group arrangement, people are positioned or seated along a line, often according to their rank. Communication is passed from a person at one end of the configuration to a person at the other end through others. The chain is a popular way to run some group organizations, such as the military. Disadvantages of the chain include the indirectness of communication, the lack of direct contact with others, and the frustration of relaying messages through others.

chaining specific behavioral response sequences linked or chained to each other and used in shaping behavior.

changing questions to statements Gestalt procedure that requires a group member who has raised a question to rephrase it as a statement.

Child ego state (TA) divided into two parts (a) *Adapted Child* conforms to the rules and wishes of Parent ego states within the self and others, (b) *Free Child* (or natural child) reacts more spontaneously, has fun, and is curious and playful. It takes care of its needs without regard for others while using its intuition to read nonverbal cues.

circle in this group configuration, all members have direct access to each other and there is implied equality in status and power. The disadvantage of this arrangement is the lack of a perceived leader in the structure unless the identified leader is active and direct. Overall, the circle is probably the best structured way

to ensure group members have an opportunity for equal "air time."

clarifying the purpose when group leaders remind members and the group as a whole what the appropriate behavioral interactions or foci in the group are and why.

clarity of purpose the first step in the preplanning process, i.e., determining what the group is set up to accomplish.

classic school of TA a branch of TA that emphasizes present interactions.

closed-ended groups groups that do not admit new members after the first session.

coaching a process of providing a group member with general principles for performing desired behaviors. It works best when the coach sits behind the group member who is rehearsing.

code of ethics a set of standards and principles that organizations create to provide guidelines for their members to follow in working with the public and each other.

cognitive approaches to human relations based on a theory of personality which maintains that how one thinks largely determines how one feels and behaves.

cognitive behaviorists behaviorists who believe thoughts play a major part in determining action, and that thoughts are behaviors.

cognitive disputation a process in RET that involves direct questioning, reasoning, and persuasion.

cognitive restructuring thinking and perceiving of oneself differently; a process in which group members are taught to identify, evaluate, and change self-defeating or irrational thoughts that negatively influence their behavior.

cohesion the togetherness of a group; "we-ness."

collaboration sharing facts and feelings with other members in a group; helping a member obtain a personal goal when there is no observable reward for the other members of a group.

co-leader a professional or a professional-in-training who undertakes the responsibility of sharing the leadership of a group with another leader in a mutually determined manner. The use of co-leaders in groups occurs often when membership is 12 or more.

collective counseling Alfred Adler's form of group counseling.

commitment when participants begin to evaluate their performances and the performances of others in terms of accomplishment of the group's goals.

communication facilitator when the group leader reflects the content and feeling of members and teaches them how to do likewise. This process focuses on both the expression of words and the emotion behind these communications. In addition, the leader stresses the importance of speaking congruently, that is, using "I" messages to state what one wants or what one thinks.

community for learning a large-group phenomena in the 1970s initiated by Carl Rogers in which about 100 people live and work together for two weeks at a time.

condemning questions questions that put people down and prevent them from seeing situations more honestly and openly, e.g., "Don't you think you should feel differently?"

conductors the term used to refer to psychoanalytically oriented group leaders who do not wish to be the main attention of the groups they facilitate.

confidentiality the explicit agreement that what is said within a group will stay in the group; the right of group members to reveal personal thoughts, feelings, and information to the leader and other members of the group and expect that in no way will nonmembers of the group learn of this. Not keeping confidences is like gossiping and is destructive to the group process.

conflict-management orientations ways of handling conflict in a group, e.g., competing, accommodating, collaborating, sharing, or avoiding.

confront challenge incongruencies in thoughts and actions.

confrontation challenging group members to look at the discrepancies and incongruencies between their words and actions.

consciousness-raising (C-R) group a group that is set up to help its participants become more aware of the issues they face and choices they have within their environment.

contact-focused group theory a conceptualization of groups in which the purpose of groups is highlighted; three primary contact groups described in this model are group guidance, group counseling, and group psychotherapy.

content functions the actual words and ideas exchanged between leaders and members.

contingency contracts contracts that spell out the behaviors to be performed, changed, or discontinued; the rewards associated with the achievement of these goals; and the conditions under which rewards are to be received.

continuing education units (CEU) credits for participating in professional educational programs.

contract an agreement of what group members or the group as a whole will do and when. Contracts may be verbal or written.

control theory a complete system for explaining how the brain works; added to the base of reality therapy to make it more complete.

cooperation when group members work together for a common purpose or good.

cooperative learning groups study groups established so that assigned tasks can be divided and accomplished; members are responsible for meeting regularly and teaching each other what they have learned.

core mechanisms of group leadership core skills of group leadership, i.e., emotional stimulation, caring, meaning attribution, and executive function.

counseling/interpersonal problem-solving groups groups that focus on each person's behavior and growth or change within the group in regard to a particular problem or concern.

countertransference a leader's emotional responses to members that are a result of the leader's own needs or unresolved issues with significant others.

couple group therapy proponents of couple group therapy list many advantages for it including (a) identification by group members of appropriate and inappropriate behaviors and expectations by others, (b) development of insight and skills through observing other couples, (c) group feedback and support for the ventilation of feelings and changed behavior, and (d) cost.

crash-program mentality when group experiences are carried out to excess.

creative imagery this warm-up technique consists of inviting psychodrama participants to imagine neutral or pleasant objects and scenes. The idea is to help participants become more spontaneous.

crisis-centered groups groups formed due to some emergency, such as conflict between rival groups.

critical incident in the life of the group an event that has the power to shape or influence the group positively or negatively.

critical-incident model this model focuses on a number of critical incidents in the life of a group of any type. The trainee, after studying group dynamics, watches a videotape of his or her instructor handling a number of different situations in a group. Then the trainee co-leads a group under the instructor's supervision and makes strategic interventions geared to the incidents in the particular group. Trainees are taught self-management skills, as well as ways to deal with specific group situations.

culturally encapsulated individuals who hold stereotyped views of others who differ from themselves and act accordingly.

curative (therapeutic) factors within groups 11 group factors (instillation of hope, universality, imparting of information, altruism, corrective recapitulation of the primary family group, development of socialization techniques, imitative behavior, interpersonal learning, group cohesiveness, catharsis, and existential factors) that contribute to the betterment of individuals in the group. First researched by Irvin Yalom.

cutting off another term for blocking; defined two ways: (a) making sure that new material is not introduced into the group too late in the session for the group to adequately deal with it; (b) preventing group members from rambling.

cyclotherapy process the idea that after the group meets, it continues to evolve and can be conceptualized as forever forming, with certain issues returning from time to time to be explored in greater depth.

defense mechanisms ways of protecting a person from being overwhelmed by anxiety, such as repression or denial; overutilized when a person is not coping adequately.

delegating when the group leader assigns a task to the group or one or more of its members.

democratic group leaders group-centered, trust group participants to develop their own potential and that of other group members; serve as facilitators of the group process and not as directors of it. They cooperate and collaborate with the group and share responsibilities with group members.

denial acting as if an experience does not exist or will never end.

density of time the fullness of time and eventfulness, both seem to lessen with age.

dependency group members who present themselves as helpless and incapable, but refuse to listen to feedback. They are help-rejecting complainers and encourage the behavior of advice givers and band-aiders in a group.

Developing Understanding of Self and Others—Revised (DUSO-R) a commercial classroom guidance program based on Adlerian theory.

developmental factors variables such as the age, gender, and maturity level of those involved in a group.

developmental group counseling psychoeducational groups often used for teaching basic life skills.

developmental psychoeducational/guidance groups focus on common concerns of adolescents such as identity, sexuality, parents, peer relationships, career goals, and educational/institutional problems. Individuals who join these groups do so out of a sense of need.

devil's advocate procedure procedure where one or more members in the group are asked to question group decisions with a firm skepticism before the group reaches a conclusion.

diagnosing in this activity, the leader identifies certain behaviors and categories into which a person or group fits. Diagnosing in groups does not usually include psychological instruments but is based more on leader observations.

dialogue talk between others and oneself or between different aspects of oneself; one of the two primary therapeutic tools in Gestalt therapy (along with *awareness*).

director the person who guides the protagonist in the use of the psychodramatic method to help that person explore his or her problem. The director is roughly equivalent to the group leader in other theoretical approaches but serves as a producer, a facilitator, an observer, and an analyzer.

discussion teams small groups used to promote involvement in guidance activities. In this arrangement, a large group is divided into four or five teams that are then seated in semicircles around the room. This formation has the advantage of getting members involved with one another and raising the level of excitement among them. The disadvantage is that interaction is mainly limited to a small number of individuals and other group members do not get the advantage of participating in all the groups, just one.

displaced homemakers women who have lost their source of economic support and are now forced back into the work force after spending a number of years at home caring for their families.

double and multiple double technique the double is an important technique in psychodrama. It consists of an actor taking on the role of the protagonist's alter ego and helping the protagonist express true inner feelings more clearly. In cases in which the protagonist has ambivalent feelings, the multiple double technique is used. In these situations, two or more actors represent different aspects of the protagonist's personality. The doubles may speak at once or take turns, but through their input, the protagonist should gain a better idea of what his or her thoughts and feelings are.

drawing out the opposite of cutting off or blocking; the process whereby group leaders purposefully ask more silent members to speak to anyone in the group, or to the group as a whole, about anything on their minds.

dream analysis in group psychotherapy individuals must first be prepared to share. This preparation can occur through the group leader asking members in an early session to describe a recent dream, a recurring dream, or even a daydream. Through sharing, group members get to know each other better and at the same time are able to be more concrete in handling their feelings associated with the dream, and in managing themselves in gen-

eral. *Dream content* is *manifest* (conscious) and *latent* (hidden). Manifest content consists of the obvious and recallable features of the dream, such as who was in it. Latent content is the symbol features of the dream that escape first analysis.

dream work seen by Perls as "the royal road to integration." It is utilized by having those who dream recreate and relive the dream in the present. By doing so, these individuals become all parts of the dream. They may do this through working alone in the group setting or having others in the group act out different parts of the dream (i.e., *dream work as theater*).

dual-focused Gestalt group work in this Gestalt approach, attention is concentrated on group process with the power of individual work within the group.

dual nature of human beings RET concept that states individuals are both rational and irrational.

dual relationships when group leaders find themselves in two potentially conflicting roles with their group members.

eating disorders group a professionally led psychotherapeutic and support group for individuals who have obsessive and distorted ideas in regard to thinness and body image.

eclectic a composite of theoretical approaches.

educational growth group (EGG) a group, composed of 8 to 15 students who meet for a total of five sessions and cover specific topics chosen by the students. The aim of the group is to help members assimilate and personalize this information.

ego (psychoanalysis) the "executive of the mind"; works according to the reality principle and tries to reduce the tension of the id.

egogram (TA) a bar graph showing how people structure their time in six major ways: (a) withdrawal, (b) ritual, (c) pastimes, (d) work, (e) games, and (f) intimacy.

ego state in TA a system of feelings accompanied by a related set of behavior patterns; three basic TA ego states: Parent, Adult, and Child.

elasticity the ability to move from one set of needs to another and back; a Gestalt term.

elder hostel a place where older individuals live and study together for a select period of time.

emotional ambivalence feelings of loss, sadness, and separation mixed with those of hope, joy, and accomplishment.

emotional impact of separation includes dealing with loss, putting the separation in perspective, becoming aware of the limited value of searching for causes of separation, becoming more cognizant of systems interactions (family, work, social network), using the past as a guide to the future, and moving from a dyadic to a monadic identity.

emotional response of separation focuses on continuing relationships with an ex-spouse, recognizing the influence of the separation on family, friends, and children, working and dating, and sexual adjustment.

emotional stimulation sharing on an affective level as well as intellectual level.

empathizing to put oneself in another's place in regard to subjective perception and emotion and yet keep one's objectivity. It demands a suspension of judgment and a response to another person that conveys sensitivity and understanding.

empty chair technique a Gestalt technique designed to help group members deal with different aspects of their personalities, e.g., a person is given an opportunity to role play and speak to a missing person with whom he/she has unfinished business.

encounter an existentialist concept that involves total physical and psychological contact between persons on an intense, concrete, and complete basis in the here-and-now; a psychodrama concept.

encounter group (see *basic encounter group*).

encouragement an Adlerian technique of having group members examine their life styles in regard to mistaken perceptions and to take note of their assets, strengths, and talents. Encouragement is one of the most distinct Adlerian procedures.

ethics suggested standards of conduct based on a set of professional values.

excursions a part of synectics in which members actually take a break, a vacation, from problem solving and engage in exercises involving fantasy, metaphor, and analogy. The idea is that the material generated in these processes can be reintegrated back into the group later.

executive function the role of the leader to manage the group as a social system that allows the group and its members to achieve specific goals.

exercises planned activities that have been used previously to help group members become more aware; structured activities that the group does for a specific purpose.

existential variables immediate feelings and interactions, such as conflict, withdrawal, support, dominance, and change.

experiments nonplanned experiences that occur spontaneously in the group session.

extinction the process of lowering the rate at which a behavior occurs by withdrawing the reinforcers that have been maintaining it so the targeted behavior will stop altogether.

facilitating leaders facilitate by helping to open up communication between group members.

facilitative feedback telling another person the effect they have on you as a compliment or confrontation.

facilitative/building role a role that adds to the functioning of a group in a positive and constructive way. Members who take on such a role may serve as initiators of actions and ideas, information seekers, opinion seekers, coordinators, orienters, evaluators, or recorders.

facilitators term for Rogerian group leaders.

family councils a form of family group meetings originated by Alfred Adler.

fantasy exercises a method used in Gestalt group work to help group members (a) be more concrete in assessing their feelings, (b) deal with catastrophic experiences, (c) explore and express feelings of guilt and shame, and (d) become more involved in the group. It is not necessary that group members live out their fantasies.

farewell-party syndrome group members emphasize only the positive aspects of what has occurred in the group, instead of what they have learned. This type of focus tends to avoid the pain of closure.

faulty logic irrational ideas that clients hold.

feedback involves one person giving another his or her perception of a behavior, sharing relevant information with other people, such as how they appear to others, so they can make decisions about whether they would like to change or not. Feedback information should be given in a clear, concrete, succinct, and appropriate manner.

field theory Kurt Lewin's approach to groups that emphasizes the interaction between individuals and their environments. It is based on the ideas of Gestalt psychology, in which there is an interdependence of part/whole relationships.

figure/ground Gestalt term, the *figure* in one's personal life is composed of experiences that are most important; *background* is composed of experiences that are less pressing.

fishbowl procedure (see *group observing group*).

fixation a tendency to cope with the outside world in a manner similar to that employed in an earlier stage of development in which one is stuck. To overcome fixation requires that people regress to that time and come to terms with themselves and significant others who were involved in the fixation process.

floating hot-seat Gestalt technique in which interaction is promoted by encouraging group members to work on exploring their own personal issues when someone else in the group touches on an issue that has personal relevance for them.

focus groups temporary groups composed of representative samples of individuals concerned with issues, products, and/or outcomes, increasingly utilized by businesses and politicians.

focusers on others those who become self-appointed group "assistant leaders" by questioning others, offering advice, and acting as if they did not have any problems.

follow-up reconnecting with group members after they have had enough time to process what they experienced in the group and work on their goals/objectives.

formal feedback structured; may be set up through use of a *time-limited round.*

forming (orientation) stage of the group This stage is characterized by initial caution associated with any new experience. During this time, there is an attempt by group members to avoid being rejected by others, the leader, or even themselves.

four stages of psychosexual development oral, anal, phallic, and genital.

four-step process of termination orientation, summarization, discussion of goals, follow-up.

four types of thoughts: negative, positive, neutral, and mixed RET concept; (a) negative thoughts concentrate on painful or disappointing aspects of an event, (b) positive thoughts focus on just the opposite, (c) neutral cognitions are those that are neither positive nor negative, (d) mixed thoughts contain elements of the other three thought processes.

free association in group psychoanalysis, used to promote spontaneity, interaction, and feelings of unity in the group. In a group, free association works as a type of "free-floating discussion" in which group members report their feelings or impressions immediately.

game analysis (TA) an examination of destructive and repetitive behavioral patterns and an analysis of the ego states and types of transactions involved.

games (TA) an ongoing series of complementary ulterior transactions progressing to a well-defined, predictable outcome. Games are played on three levels and almost all of them are destructive and result in negative payoffs (i.e., *rackets). First-degree* games are the least harmful, minor faults are highlighted. *Second-degree* games are more serious; interactive process in second-degree games leaves the people involved feeling negative. *Third-degree* games are deadly and often played for keeps; there is nothing socially redeemable about third-degree games. People who play games operate from three distinct positions: (a) the *victim* (who appears to be innocent), (b) the *persecutor* (who appears to cause problems), and (c) the *rescuer* (who is seen as a problem-solver or hero to the victim). Individuals who play games often switch between these roles.

general systems theory a theory that emphasizes circular causality as opposed to linear causality.

generalization the display of behaviors in environments other than where they were originally learned.

generativity a goal of mid-life according to Erikson in which people seek to be creative in their lives and work for the benefit of others and the next generation.

genogram   a type of family tree.

goals   specific objectives that individuals in the group or the group as a whole wish to accomplish.

Greek chorus   (see *hot-seat*).

group   a collection of two or more individuals who meet in face-to-face interaction, interdependently, with the awareness that each belongs to the group and for the purpose of achieving mutually agreed-upon goals.

group analysis   a term first applied to the treatment of individuals in psychoanalytically oriented groups by Trigant Burrow. He emphasized that social forces affect individuals' behaviors.

group-centered group   focuses on members and interpersonal processes.

group cohesion   a sense of "we-ness."

group collusion   involves cooperating with others unconsciously or consciously to reinforce prevailing attitudes, values, behaviors, or norms. The purpose of such behavior is self-protection, and its effect is to maintain the status quo in the group.

group dynamics   a term originally used by Kurt Lewin (1948) to describe the interrelations of individuals in groups.

group exercises   (see *exercises*).

group interaction   the way members relate to each other with nonverbal and verbal behaviors and the attitudes that go with them. Group interaction exists on a continuum, from extremely nondirective to highly directive.

group observing group   when a group breaks up into two smaller groups and each observes the other function (as outsiders) for a set amount of time; sometimes called a *fishbowl procedure*.

group process   the interactions of group members as the group develops.

group process goals   in Adlerian groups, goals center around promoting and experiencing a cooperative climate within the group.

group processing   when a neutral third party observes and feeds back to the group what is occurring between members and in the group itself.

group psychoanalysis   a model that emphasizes the whole group is the client and that group dynamics are an essential feature to analyze.

group psychotherapy   sometimes referred to as a group that specializes in remediation or personality reconstruction. It is meant to help people who have serious psychological problems of a long-term duration. As such, this type of group is found most often in mental health facilities, such as clinics or hospitals.

group setting   the group's physical environment.

group structure   the way a group is set up physically as well as how the group members interact or structure themselves in relationship to others.

group techniques   exercises that are structured so that group members interact with one another.

group therapy for normals   premise of basic encounter groups that states individuals who participate in them are relatively healthy.

group work   a broad professional practice that refers to the giving of help or the accomplishment of tasks in a group setting. It involves the application of group theory and process by a capable professional practitioner to assist an interdependent collection of people to reach their mutual goals, which may be personal, interpersonal, or task related (ASGW definition).

groupthink   a group situation in which there is a deterioration of mental efficiency, reality testing, and moral judgment that results from in-group pressures.

groups for victims of abuse   groups set up to help victims of abuse break the cycle of isolation so common to this population and interrelate in a healthy, dynamic way.

growing times   when fresh learning occurs on an individual and interpersonal level.

growth-centered groups   groups that focus on the personal and social development of people and are set up to explore feelings, concerns, and behaviors about a number of everyday subjects.

"guidance hour"   also called *"guidance room"*; the term used for a homeroom at school in the 1930s; responsibilities of the teacher in the room were to establish friendly relationships with students, to discover their abilities and needs, and to develop right attitudes with them toward school, home, and the community.

guidance/psychoeducational group   originally developed for use in educational settings, specifically public schools. Primary function of the group is the prevention of personal or societal disorders through the conveying of information and/or the examining of values. Guidance/psychoeducational groups stress growth through knowledge. Content includes, but is not limited to, personal, social, vocational, and educational information.

Hawthorne effect changes in behavior as a result of observation/manipulation conditions under which a person or group works.

HELPING Keat's multimodal framework for helping—Health, Emotions, Learning, Personal Interactions, Imagery, Need to Know, and Guidance.

heterogeneous groups groups composed of dissimilar persons. Such groups can broaden members' horizons and enliven interpersonal interactions.

heuristic dimension research component.

hidden quadrant contains undisclosed information known only to oneself.

highly structured groups have a predetermined goal and a plan designed to enable each group member to reach an identified goal with minimum frustration. Such groups are usually used in teaching skills that may be transferred to a wide range of life events.

holding the focus to help members concentrate on a specific topic or person for a set length of time.

homework working outside the group itself, members implement behaviors they have addressed or practiced within the group. These real-life situations help them realize more fully what they need to work on in the group.

homogeneous groups groups composed of similar persons.

hope both a cognitive and emotional experience in groups. Cognitively, the belief that what is desired is also possible and that events will turn out for the best. Emotionally, the feeling that what one believes will occur. The importance of hope is that it energizes group members and the group as a whole.

hot-seat the place in Gestalt group therapy where the person who wants to work sits with his or her chair facing that of the therapist or leader; the rest of the group serves as a kind of "Greek chorus" in the background of the encounter where they resonate and empathize with the one who is working and gain insights into themselves and others through the process of identification.

humor the ability to laugh at oneself and the group in a therapeutic and nondefensive manner; an especially important quality during the working stage of the group.

hybrid groups groups that defy fitting any category. They encompass multiple ways of working with their members and may change their emphasis frequently. For example, some groups that are instructive are also simultaneously or consequentially therapeutic. The prototype for a hybrid group is a *self-help* group.

hypokinesis physical inactivity.

I/We/It a conceptualization of the group process in which attention is given to personal, interpersonal, and product outcomes.

icebreaker an activity designed to promote communication between two or more people in a group.

id (psychoanalysis) the first system within the personality to develop; primarily where human instincts reside. It is amoral, functions according to the pleasure principle, and contains the psychic energy *(libido)* of the person.

identification a "normal" developmental process in which individuals see themselves as being similar to one another.

imaginal disputation a technique that has participants see themselves in stressful situations and examine their self-talk.

Imago Relationship Therapy image therapy; an eclectic approach to work with couples that includes elements of psychoanalysis, transactional analysis, Gestalt psychology, cognitive therapy, and systems theory.

impasses in Gestalt theory, the places where group members get stuck.

in and out circles often referred to as the *fishbowl*. The inner circle promotes a sense of closeness, but those in the outer circle may feel left out and become bored. To help promote participation by everyone, group leaders can assign tasks for the outside group members to do while they observe the inside group.

incorporation a personal awareness and appreciation of what the group has accomplished both on an individual and collective level.

individual goals in Adlerian groups, involves developing insight into the creation of a mistaken life style and taking corrective measures.

individually conducted screening procedure intake interview used to determine who will join a particular group.

influential power based on the idea of persuasion and manipulation of others through convincing them that a certain course of action is correct.

informal feedback when the group leader asks members to give their reactions to a group session in an unstructured way at any time they wish. Such an invitation is likely to increase spontaneity and sensitivity.

informational power premised on the idea that those who know more are able to exert control over situations including those involving people.

informed consent statement a document a group member signs acknowledging that the individual is aware of the group activity in which he or she is about to participate and is doing so voluntarily.

injunctions (TA) parent commands recorded internally by a child that call for the child to adopt certain roles.

insight consists of immediate new perceptions and understandings about one's problems, often occurs during or after the experience of catharsis.

insight and reorientation phases of the group in Adlerian groups, involves helping individuals understand why they made the choices they did in the past, often accompanied by the use of interpretation on the group leader's part which is offered as a tentative hypothesis.

integrating conflicting ideas to form new solutions the idea behind integration is consensus. In using this strategy, group leaders try to get all parties to reexamine a situation and identify points of agreement.

integration phase last phase of psychodrama; involves discussion and closure.

integrity one of Erikson's virtues; the total integration of life experiences into a meaningful whole.

integrity therapy stresses helping people live up to their own moral convictions, has some commonality with reality therapy.

intellectualization behavior that is characterized by an emphasis on abstraction with a minimal amount of affect; the use of thoughts and a sophisticated vocabulary to avoid dealing with personal feelings.

intentional civil liability cases include situations such as (a) *battery* (the unconsented touching of a person); (b) *defamation* (injury to a person's character or reputation either through verbal *[slander]* or written *[libel]* means); (c) *invasion of privacy* (violation of the right to be left alone); (d) *infliction of mental distress* (outrageous behavior on the part of the therapist or group leader).

interactional catalyst when group leaders promote interaction between group members without calling attention to themselves. It is a functional process that continues throughout the group and can take various forms such as questioning whether two or more group members have something to say to one another and then being silent to see what happens.

interpersonal goals in Adlerian groups, involves becoming more socially oriented and involved with other individuals experiencing life difficulties.

interpersonal style of group leadership leadership that focuses on transactions between individuals in the group.

interpretation a psychoanalytic technique that focuses on helping group members gain insights into their past or present behavior; generally made by group leaders in the earliest stages of the group, because group members seldom possess the sophistication to do so adequately and appropriately at this time. Three levels of interpretation: *thematical* interpretation—broad based, covers the whole pattern of a person's existence such as self-defeating behavior; *constructional* interpretation—focuses on thought patterns and the way group members express themselves; *situational* interpretation—context centered, emphasizes the immediate interactions within the group.

interpretation of a person's early history in Adlerian groups, when group members recognize and understand the ways they created their own life styles.

intervention cube concept model for training group leaders (see *critical-incident model*).

intrapersonal style of group leadership leadership that concentrates on the inward reactions of individual members of the group.

intrinsically neutral as an approach, Gestalt theory views individuals as neither positive nor negative, i.e., without a predetermined set of responses.

involvement when group members actively participate with each other and invest themselves in the group.

jogging group approach built on the premise that physical exercise is an important element that contributes to people's abilities to perform better in all areas of life. The jogging group itself combines an hour of exercise in the form of walking, jogging, or running, with another hour of group process.

Johari Awareness Model also known as *Johari Window;* a representative square with four quadrants that is often used to show what happens in group interactions when the group and its members are working or not working.

joining the process by which leaders and group members connect with one another psychologically and/or physically.

journal also known as *log;* in this experience, group members are required to write their reactions to the events of each session. This process enables them to spot inconsistencies in their reactions more quickly than if they simply talked about them.

justice i.e., fairness; refers to the equal treatment of all people. This virtue implies that everyone's welfare is promoted and that visible differences in people, such as gender or race, do not interfere with the way they are treated.

laissez-faire leaders leaders in name only. They do not provide any structure or direction for their groups. Members are left with the responsibility of leading and directing.

law a body of rules recognized by a state or community as binding on its members.

Law of Triviality the time a group spends discussing any issue is in inverse proportion to the consequences of the issue.

layers of neurosis in Gestalt theory, those aspects of people that keep them from being healthy, i.e., the phony—being unauthentic; the phobic—being afraid to really see themselves as they are; and the impasse—where their maturity is stuck.

leader-centered group autocratic; the leader instructs the followers in the "right" way. The leader-centered group is based on obedience from followers.

leaderless groups groups that rotate the leadership role among their members, e.g., self-help groups.

leveling a process in which group members are encouraged to interact freely and evenly with each other. In leveling, group members who are underparticipatory are drawn out and those who are excessively active are helped to modify their behavior.

life script analyses (TA) an examination of people's basic life plans involving transactions and games.

life-skill development groups a type of guidance/psychoeducational group, especially designed for those who have a deficit of behavior. Emphasis is on a "how-to" approach to learning new behaviors; may include the use of films, plays, demonstrations, role plays, and guest speakers (see *developmental group counseling*).

life-skills training focuses on helping persons identify and correct deficits in their life-coping skills and learn new appropriate behaviors.

limits the outer boundaries of a group in regard to behaviors that will be accepted within the group.

linking the process of connecting persons with one another by pointing out to them what they share in common. Linking strengthens the bonds between individuals and the group as a whole.

log (*see journal*).

low facilitative responses (a) *advice/evaluation* (telling people how to behave or judging them); (b) *analyzing/interpreting* (explaining the reasons behind behavior without giving the person an opportunity for self-discovery); (c) *reassuring/supportive* (trying to encourage someone, yet dismissing the person's real feelings).

magic shop   a warm-up technique in psychodrama that is especially useful for protagonists who are undecided or ambivalent about their values and goals. It involves a storekeeper (the director or an auxiliary ego) who runs a magic shop filled with special qualities. The qualities are not for sale but may be bartered.

maintenance   in this stage, an emphasis is placed on increasing group members' self-control and self-management, e.g., when a behavioral group member is consistent in doing the actions desired without depending on the group or its leader for support.

maintenance role   a person who contributes to the social–emotional bonding of members and the overall well-being of the group. When interpersonal communication in the group is strained, there is a need to focus on relationships. Persons who take on such roles are social and emotionally oriented. They express themselves by being encouragers, harmonizers, compromisers, commentators, and followers.

making the rounds   a warm-up technique where each member is given a chance to speak about a particular topic. In Gestalt groups, confrontation is heightened as group members are asked to say something they usually do not verbalize.

making wishes into demands   using "should," "ought," and "must" in regard to a desired action.

malpractice   bad practice; implies the group leader has failed to render proper service due to either negligence or ignorance.

malpractice suit   a claim against a professional made by a "plaintiff" who seeks a monetary award based on a specific amount of damages—physical, financial, and/or emotional.

manipulators   group members who use feelings and behaviors to get their way regardless of what others want or need. Often they are angry.

marathon groups   originally originated by George Bach and Fred Stoller in 1964 as a way of helping people become more authentic with themselves; usually held for extended periods of time, such as 24 or 48 hours; group members are required to stay together. As time passes, members become tired and experience a breakdown in their defenses and an increase in their truthfulness.

marriage enrichment   a psychoeducational and growth group for marrieds aimed at helping them have healthier relationships.

masculine mystique   the belief that men are superior to women and therefore have the right to devalue and restrict women's values, roles, and life styles.

meaning attribution   refers to the leader's ability to explain to group members in a cognitive way what is occurring in the group.

mediation   having a third party hear arguments about a situation and then render a decision.

member-specific groups   related to topic-specific groups; focus on particular transitional concerns of individual members, such as grief, hospitalization, or institutionalized daycare. Basically, member-specific groups may be conducted for older adults or for members of their families.

middle adulthood   ages 40 to 65, begins somewhere between the late 30s and the early 40s. Individuals at this time realize that life is half over and death is a reality.

mid-life   ages 40 to 65 years.

midlife transition   a time for evaluating, deciding, and making adjustments at midlife. It is a difficult time for many individuals as they give up the dreams of adolescence and come to terms with their own mortality.

mirror technique   in this psychodrama activity, the protagonist watches from offstage while an auxiliary ego mirrors the protagonist's posture, gesture, and words. This technique is often used in the action phase of psychodrama to help the protagonist see himself or herself more accurately.

modeler of appropriate behavior   when group leaders consciously pick and choose actions they think group members need to learn through passive and active demonstrations; can include deliberate use of self-disclosure, role plays, speech patterns, and acts of creativity.

modeling   a social behavioral method used to teach group members complex behaviors in a relatively short period of time by copying/imitating.

monodrama   also known as *autodrama;* in this technique, the protagonist plays all the parts of the enactment; no auxiliary egos are used.

The person may switch chairs or talk to different parts of the self.

monopolizers   group members who because of their own anxiety dominate conversation by not giving other persons a chance to verbally participate.

monopolizing   when a person or persons within the group dominate the group's time through talking.

multimodal method   using verbal and nonverbal means for conveying information.

multiple-family group therapy   involves treating several families together at the same time. It requires the use of co-leaders and has many of the same advantages that couple group therapy has, including the fact that families can often serve as co-therapists for each other.

multiple transferences   in psychoanalytic groups when group members can experience transference feelings with others in the group as well as with the group leader.

mutual help group   when members mutually assist one another; another term for a self-help group.

mythopoetic   refers to a process of ceremony, drumming, storytelling/poetry reading, physical movement, and imagery exercises designed to create a "ritual process"; a process often used in men's groups.

narcissistic groups   groups that develop cohesiveness by encouraging hatred of an out-group or by creating an enemy. As a result, regressive group members are able to overlook their own deficiencies by focusing on the deficiencies of the out-group.

National Training Laboratories (NTL)   a group training facility in Bethel, Maine, established by Kurt Lewin and associates in the late 1940s.

natural consequences   living with the results of a particular behavior, such as not following instructions (an Adlerian concept).

negative group variables   group action that includes, but is not limited to, avoiding conflict, abdicating group responsibilities, anesthetizing to contradictions within the group, and becoming narcissistic.

nominal-group technique (NGT)   a six-step process involving the generation both verbally and in writing of a number of ideas/solutions connected with a problem statement. This exercise does not require the open exposure of members as much as brainstorming and ends with a vote, discussion, and revote on priorities for resolving a situation. The time period for the group takes between 45 to 90 minutes, after which the group, composed of people from diverse settings, is disbanded and the members thanked for their participation.

nondevelopmental counseling and psychotherapy groups   adolescent groups that tend to focus mainly on concerns of adults and society, such as drug use, school problems (e.g., poor grades, truancy), or deviant behavior. Usually, these groups are set up by a school, agency, or court, and troubled adolescents are forced to attend.

nondevelopmental factors   encompass unpredictable qualities such as the nature of a problem, the suddenness of its appearance, the intensity of its severity, and the present coping skills.

nonmaleficence   avoiding doing harm. To act ethically, leaders and members of groups must be sure the changes they make in themselves and help others to make are not going to be damaging.

nonverbal behaviors   behaviors that make up more than 50% of the messages communicated in social relationships such as in groups and are usually perceived as more honest and less subject to manipulation than verbal behaviors. Four categories of nonverbal behavior are body behaviors, interaction with the environment, speech, and physical appearance.

norming   where members form an identity as a group and a sense of "we-ness" prevails; there is enthusiasm, cooperation, and cohesiveness at this time. In many ways, the norming stage parallels the forming stage in regard to its emphasis on positive feelings. Norming, like storming, lasts only for a few sessions; it sets the pattern for the next stage: performing (i.e., working).

norms   rules and standards of behavior. Groups typically accept both *prescriptive* norms, which describe the kinds of behaviors that should be performed, and *proscriptive* norms, which describe the kinds of behaviors that are to be avoided.

old-old individuals over the age of 76; they are likely to experience declines in health and overall functioning.

old-timers more experienced members of self-help groups (see *pros*).

open quadrant one that contains information that is generally known to self and others.

open-ended groups groups that admit new members at any time.

open-ended questions questions that invite more than a one- or two-word response.

operant conditioning emphasizes that behavior is a function of its consequences.

operations specific techniques employed by TA group leaders, such as interrogation, specification, confrontation, explanation, illustration, confirmation, interpretation, and crystallization.

paradox asking members to do the opposite of what you want in the hope they will disobey.

parent education groups primarily psychoeducational groups focusing on the raising of children. Rudolph Driekurs began setting up these groups in the 1950s using Alfred Adler's theory and ideas.

Parent Effectiveness Training (PET) a Rogerian-based parent education program. In PET, there is an emphasis on communication skills, and parents are encouraged to recognize their positive and negative feelings toward their children and come to terms with their own humanness. A major hypothesis of this approach is that *active listening* (i.e., hearing what is implied as well as what is actually said) and *acceptance* (acknowledging what is happening as opposed to evaluating it) will decrease family conflicts and promote individual growth.

Parent ego state (TA) dualistic in being both nurturing and critical (or controlling). The function of the *Critical Parent* is to store and dispense the rules and protection for living. The function of the *Nurturing Parent* is to care for, to nurture.

Parents Without Partners (PWP) a popular national organization whose groups for the divorced and widowed tend to be psychoeducational or self-help.

pat on the back a closing exercise in which members draw the outline of their hand on a piece of white paper that is then taped on their back. Other group members then write closing comments that are positive and constructive about the person on the hand outline or on the paper itself.

peer power people helping people in a group setting.

peer supervision when practitioners meet on a regular basis to consult with each other about particularly difficult group situations.

permission (TA) centers on giving group members directives to behave against the injunctions of their parents.

personal growth Rogerian term; a global emphasis that stresses development as a result of experiences such as travel or encounter; the opposite of *personal growth issues*—an individual emphasis that springs from a perceived deficit or need.

phyloanalysis the biological principles of group behavior.

physical structure the arrangement of group members in relationship to one another.

planning for continued problem resolution this activity may be completed in a group before or after individual good-byes are said. It involves making a specific plan of what group members will do to continue their progress after the group ends. It should include when and how certain activities will be carried out, but others' expectations should not be part of the plan.

polarization when a group becomes divided into different and opposing subgroups or camps.

positive expectations behavioral theory that individuals who expect to be successful are much more likely to achieve their goals.

positive group variables a collection of favorable group factors such as member commitment; readiness of members for the group experience; the attractiveness of the group for its members; a feeling of belonging, acceptance, and security; and clear communication.

potency the use of appropriate counseling techniques in certain situations to bring about change.

power the capacity to bring about certain intended consequences in the behavior of others.

power to resolve the conflict this strategy involves the imposition of someone's will on someone else. The source of power may either be derived from one's position or one's person. *Position* power is most often used when there are immature relationships between individuals. Position power is derived from the status of people's titles, such as "group leader" or "group facilitator." *Personal* power is employed more frequently in mature relationship situations. The source of power in such a situation is from the individual and his or her ability to persuade others to follow a select course of action. By using power, a leader is able to quickly resolve a crisis, but the use of power often creates *win-lose atmospheres.*

preadolescents children in the latency period with an age range from 9 to 13 years.

premature termination when individuals quit a group abruptly or when the group experience ends suddenly because of actions by the leader. There are three types of premature termination: the termination of the group as a whole, the termination of a successful group member, and the termination of an unsuccessful group member.

preschool and early school-aged children include the ages 5 through 9.

pretraining orienting members of a group on what to expect of the group before it meets.

primal horde Freud's conceptualization of a group; he thought leaders within the group function as *parental figures.*

primary affiliation groups those groups with which people most identify as belonging, such as a family or peers.

primary tension awkwardness about being in a strange situation.

principle of awareness Gestalt assumption that people are free to choose only when they are *self-aware,* that is, in touch with their existence and what it means to be alive; awareness includes all sensations, thoughts, and behaviors of the individual.

principle of figure/ground (see *figure/ground*)

principle of holism Gestalt term for integration.

principle of polarities Gestalt belief that if people are to meet their needs, they must first differentiate their perceptual field into opposites/poles, for example, active/passive, good/bad. People fail to resolve conflicts because they are not in contact with the opposite sides of the situation.

problem-centered groups small groups set up to focus on one particular concern, e.g., coping with stress.

process functions identifiable sequences of events over time that influence the development of a group.

process observer a professional human services person who is neutral in regard to the group agenda and personalities; as part of the procedure of group processing, observes and gives feedback to the group on what and how they are doing.

professional liability insurance insurance designed specifically to protect a group worker from financial loss in case of a civil suit.

projecting the future group members are asked to imagine what changes they would like to make in the short term and long term.

promoting a positive interchange among group members a condition that when created can help members become more honest with themselves and others and promote cohesion in the group.

promoting hope one of the basic "therapeutic" factors described by Yalom. If members believe that their situations can be different and better, they are likely to work harder within the group.

pros self-help group leaders who gain their position from experience and longevity (see *old-timers*).

protagonist the person who is the subject of the psychodrama enactment; may play many parts.

protecting involves the leader safeguarding members from unnecessary attacks by others in the group.

protection involves a group leader keeping members safe from psychological or physical harm.

pseudo-acceptance false acceptance; harmony is stressed over everything; prevents anxiety but also progress in a group.

psychic numbing members anesthetizing themselves to contradictions in the group.

psychoanalysis in groups focus is on the individual; the major tools of the psychoanalytic method uses transference, dreams interpretation, historical development analysis, interpretation of resistance, and free association.

psychodrama   an interpersonal group approach in which participants act out their emotions and attempt to clarify conflicts; a way of exploring the human psyche through dramatic action; created and developed by J. L. Moreno.

psychodrama process   generally goes through three phases: (a) warm-up (preaction), (b) action, and (c) integration.

psychotherapy and counseling groups for the elderly   geared toward the remediation of specific problems faced by the aging, such as role changes, social isolation, physical decline, and fear of the future.

publicizing a group   the way a group is announced, an appropriate activity in the planning substage of forming.

quality circles   groups established in businesses on the idea of participative management; composed of workers in the same work area who meet on a weekly basis to discuss and try to resolve work-related problems.

quality groups   work/task groups first set up and utilized by the Japanese under the direction of W. Edwards Deming to assure work was done correctly the first time and efficiently; today these groups are a major part of many American businesses/industries.

questioning   a query that is sometimes a disguise for a statement. If group members are constantly questioning each other, they are safe from exposing their true selves. Questions keep the group focused on why something occurred and prevent members from concentrating on what is happening now.

radical behaviorists   behaviorists who avoid any mentalistic concepts and concentrate exclusively on observable actions.

rape survivors' group   a group for victims of rape aimed at helping them decrease their sense of isolation and stigma while learning to model effective coping strategies.

rating sheet   an evaluation form members fill out and return before they terminate a group or a group session. Members can rate themselves, other members, and the leader on a number of dimensions including involvement, risk taking, goals, emotional involvement, feedback, and productivity.

rational-emotive therapy   based on the idea that it is one's thinking about events that produces feelings, not situations themselves. Individuals who have negative, faulty, or irrational thoughts become emotionally disturbed or upset and act in nonproductive ways, whereas those with more neutral or positive thoughts feel calmer and behave constructively.

reality-oriented groups   set up for older individuals who have become disoriented to their surroundings. These groups, while educationally focused, are therapeutically based in that their emphasis is on helping group members become more attuned to where they are with respect to time, place, and people.

reality testing   a skill used when a group member makes an important decision, e.g., changing jobs or taking a risk. At such moments, the leader will have other group members give feedback to the one who is contemplating a change on how realistic they see the decision. Through this process, the person is able to evaluate more thoroughly his or her decision.

reality therapy   founded by William Glasser. It emphasizes that all behavior is generated within ourselves for the purpose of satisfying one or more basic needs.

reality therapy's eight basic steps   1. Make friends; establish a meaningful relationship. 2. Emphasize present behaviors; Ask, "What are you doing now?" 3. Stress whether clients' actions are getting them what they want. 4. Make a positive plan to do better. 5. Get a commitment to follow the positive plan. 6. No excuses. 7. No punishment. 8. Never give up.

reality therapy's four human psychological needs   belonging, power, freedom, and fun; one physiological need: survival.

recycling   individuals who have not benefitted from a group experience and go through a similar group to learn lessons missed the first time.

redecision school of TA   emphasis is on intrapsychic processes; groups provide a living experience in which members are able to examine themselves and their histories in a precise way. Individuals can then change their life scripts.

redecision theory a special form of TA, helps clients make redecisions while they are in their Child ego state. This task is accomplished by having these individuals reexperience a past event as if it were now present.

referrals transfers of members to another group; made when group leaders realize they cannot help certain members achieve designated goals or when there is a conflict between leaders and members that is unresolvable. The group leader should make appropriate referrals since he or she cannot be all things to all people. The referral process itself involves four steps: (a) identifying the need to refer; (b) evaluating potential referral sources; (c) preparing the client for the referral; and (d) coordinating the transfer.

regressive-reconstructive model of group psychoanalysis emphasizes that participants will become responsible for themselves and for society. It stresses the importance of being a creator of society as well as a transmitter of patterns. It pushes participants to continue to change after the group has ended.

rehearsal (a) when members show others in the group how they plan to act in particular situations; (b) in Gestalt groups when members are invited to say out loud what they are thinking.

reinforcement any behavior, positive or negative, that increases the probability of a response.

reminiscing groups originated in the 1960s; based on the importance of "life review." They help individuals who are not yet at the older life stage to comprehend and appreciate more fully who they are and where they have been. Persons in these groups share memories, increase personal integration, and become more aware of their lives and the lives of those their age. Insight gained from this process helps these persons realize more deeply their finiteness and thus prepare for death.

remotivation therapy groups aimed at helping older clients become more invested in the present and future. Their membership is composed of individuals who have "lost interest" in any time frame of life except the past.

reorientation in Adlerian groups, members are encouraged to act differently and take more control of their lives. Such a procedure means taking risks, acting "as if" they were the person they wished to be, and "catching themselves" in old, ineffective patterns and correcting them.

repressive-constructive model of group psychoanalysis focuses on adaptation and adjustment of participants without stressing the creation of newness within culture.

resistance any behavior that moves the group away from areas of discomfort or conflict and prevents it from developing; works in overt and covert ways, e.g., rebellion by group members against the leader; getting bogged down in details and becoming preoccupied with the unimportant.

resisters group members who do not actively participate in the group and/or act as barriers to helping the group develop.

respondent conditioning also known as *classical conditioning;* behavioral view that human responses are learned through association.

RET viewpoint involves getting group to believe the premises on which RET is based are valid and applicable to their situations.

Rogerian-oriented encounter group 15-stage process

1. *Milling around*—In the initial stage of the group, members are often confused about who is responsible for conducting the group and what they are supposed to be doing. This confusion results in frustration, silence, and a tendency to keep conversations on a superficial level.

2. *Resistance*—Group members tend to avoid exposing their private selves until they have built trust in other members. Members try to protect themselves and others from revealing too much too fast.

3. *Revealing past feelings*—As trust begins to develop, group members start to talk about their feelings, but only those that are safe to expose, e.g., the past. The talk at this point is on there-and-then experiences (i.e., those that are historical) and that are nonthreatening to expose.

4. *Expression of negative feelings*—As the group develops, initial here-and-now feelings are expressed, but generally in a negative manner. Most of these feelings

are directed toward the leader, and they are in the form of blame for not providing enough structure.

5. *Expression of personally meaningful material*—Real trust in the group is established at this stage. Group members feel free to explore and talk about important meaningful events in their lives.

6. *Communication of immediate interpersonal feelings*—At this point in the life of the group, members begin to be affected by and respond to other group members. They indicate to others how their comments and actions are perceived.

7. *Development of a healing capacity in the group*—After members have expressed personal feelings about themselves and others, they begin reaching out to one another. This is accomplished by offering warmth, compassion, understanding, and caring to group members who have shared their concerns.

8. *Self-acceptance and the beginning of change*—As members are accepted more, they become increasingly aware of their own behaviors and feelings and are consequently less rigid. In the process, they open themselves to changes.

9. *Cracking of facades*—The tendency in encounter groups for members to drop the masks they have been wearing and become more genuine.

10. *Feedback.*

11. *Confrontation.*

12. *Helping relationships outside the group*—This stage is a parallel to stage 7, but group members experience healing and helping relationships with each other outside the formal group experience.

13. *The basic encounter*—Genuine person-to-person contact is the overriding characteristic at this point in the group.

14. *Expressions of closeness*—As the group nears completion, group members express positive feelings about their experience and about one another. A sense of group spirit develops.

15. *Behavior changes*—Behavior changes, the result of increased congruence, are more pronounced; members tend to act in a more open, honest, caring manner; and their behaviors are carried with them into everyday life experiences after the group terminates.

role   a dynamic structure within an individual (based on needs, cognitions, and values) which usually comes to life under the influence of social stimuli or defined positions. The manifestation of a role is based on the individual's expectation of self and others and the interactions one has in particular groups and situations.

role collision   when there is a conflict between the role an individual plays in the outside world (such as being a passive observer) and the role expected within the group (such as being an active participant).

role confusion   occurs when a group member (or members) simply do not know what role to perform. This often happens in leaderless groups where members do not know if they are to be assertive in helping to establish an agenda or to be passive and just let the leadership emerge.

role incompatibility   when a person is given a role within the group (such as being the leader) that he or she neither wants nor is comfortable exercising.

role playing   assuming an identity that differs from one's present behavior. Role playing is a tool for bringing a specific skill and its consequences into focus. It is vital for experiential learning within the group.

role reversal   in this psychodrama technique, the protagonist literally switches roles with another person on stage and plays that person's part; group members act the opposite of what they feel.

role transition   a person is expected to assume a different role as the group progresses, but does not feel comfortable doing so.

rounds   also known as *go-rounds;* the process of giving members of a group an equal chance to participate in the group by going around the circle in which they are sitting and asking each person to make a comment on a subject that is presently before the group.

row formation   a group in which attention is focused toward the front. This arrangement is good for making a presentation, but it limits, and even inhibits, group interaction.

rules the guidelines by which groups are run.

sarcasm masked feelings disguised through the use of clever language such as biting humor.

saying good-bye the final words members exchange with others at the end of a group that wraps it up, at least on an affective/cognitive level. Members are encouraged to own their feelings and express their thoughts at this time, especially in regard to what others in the group have meant to them.

scapegoat to blame others for one's own problems.

screened when potential group members are interviewed prior to the group in regard to their suitability for the group.

screening a three-part process that begins when group leaders formulate the type of group they would like to lead. Next is the process of *recruitment,* in which the leader must make sure not to misrepresent the type of group that is to be conducted and to publicize it properly. Finally, there is the task of interviewing applicants by the leader to determine whether they will benefit from and contribute to the group.

scripts (TA) patterns of behavior that influence how people spend their time. Most people initially script their lives as a Child in the *I'm Not OK—You're OK* stance (powerless), but change to an Adult stance in later life as they affirm an *I'm OK—You're OK* position (characterized by trust and openness). Other options open to them are *I'm OK—You're Not OK* (projection of blame onto others) and *I'm Not OK—You're Not OK* (hopeless and self-destructive).

sculpting in this exercise, group members use nonverbal methods to arrange others in the group into a configuration like that of significant persons with whom they regularly deal, such as family members, office personnel, or social peers. The positioning involves body posturing and assists group members in seeing and experiencing their perceptions of significant others in a more dynamic way.

secondary affiliation groups those groups with which people least identify.

secondary tension intragroup conflict.

self-actualization realistically living up to one's potential; being the best one can be.

self-disclosure revealing to the group personal information of which the group was previously unaware. It involves listening and receiving feedback as well as speaking. One of the strongest signs of trust in a group is self-disclosure.

self-help groups groups that usually do not include professional leaders but are led by paraprofessionals or group members. Examples of such groups are Alcoholics Anonymous (AA) and Compassionate Friends (see *mutual help group*).

self-instructional training in this procedure, the group member is trained to become aware of his or her maladaptive thoughts (self-statements). Next, the group leader models appropriate behaviors while verbalizing the reasons behind these strategies. Finally, the group member performs the designated behaviors while verbally repeating the reasons behind the actions and then conducts these behaviors giving himself or herself covert messages.

self-monitoring behavioral group members keep detailed, daily records of particular events or psychological reactions.

self-report research format research method used by Rogers and non-behaviorists, in which participants write out or check off how they have changed as a result of the group experience.

self-talk the messages people give themselves internally.

semicircle arrangement a half-circle group structure in which members can see each other; discussion is likely to involve almost everyone. However, if the group is too large (e.g., above 20), persons may not feel that they are a group.

sensitivity group (see *basic encounter group*).

settling-down period a time when members test one another and the group collectively, before the group unifies.

shame attack a RET technique in which a person actually does what he or she dreaded and finds the world does not fall apart regardless of the outcome.

shaping teaching behaviors through successive approximation and chaining. This gradual step process allows group members to learn a new behavior over time.

shifting the focus to move group members to a different topic area or person.

silent members   group members who are reticent to speak in the group due to anger, nonassertive, reflection, shyness, or slowness in the assessment of their thoughts and feelings.

single-subject research design   in this procedure, leaders follow one of two methods in evaluating their groups. In the first method, they follow an ABAB design to evaluate the relationship of an intervention on changes that may occur in the group. In the other method, leaders employ a multiple baseline design that more randomly measures change across subject, variables, or situations.

SIPA (Structure, Involvement, Process, and Awareness)   a model for achieving group goals in group guidance.

situational therapy   activity groups for children ages 8 to 15 based on psychoanalytic principles first created by Samuel Slavson.

social ecology   context of a group.

social group work   organizing individuals into purposeful and enriching groups; first began by Jane Addams at Hull House in Chicago for immigrants and the poor.

social influence   how interaction in groups exert an influence on altering actions, attitudes, and feelings of people.

social interest   an Adlerian term defined as not only an interest in others but also an interest in the interests of others.

social modeling   learning as a result of imitation of other's behaviors.

soliloquy technique   psychodrama technique; involves the protagonist (i.e., the client) giving a monologue about his or her situation, as he or she is acting it out. A variation on this activity is the *therapeutic* soliloquy technique, in which private reactions to events in the protagonist's life are verbalized and acted out, usually by other actors (i.e., auxiliary egos).

specialty/standards model   an approach to conceptualizing groups where they are defined according to their purpose, focus, and needed competencies. ASGW has defined standards for four types of groups–guidance/psychoeducational, counseling/interpersonal problem solving, psychotherapy/personality reconstruction, and task/work.

spillover effect   the impact for others who are helping or watching a main character in psy-

chodrama reach resolution on important issues; they see themselves as interacting in a new and better way.

spontaneity   in psychodrama, the response people make that contains some degree of adequacy to a new situation or a degree of novelty to an old situation. The purpose of spontaneity is to liberate one's self from scripts and stereotypes and gain new perspectives on life.

stage   in psychodrama, the area in which the action takes place.

stages of psychoanalytically oriented groups

1. *Preliminary individual analysis*—Individuals in the psychoanalytically oriented group are interviewed individually by the group leader for their suitability for the group experience.

2. *Establishment of rapport through dreams and fantasies*—Group members are asked to discuss a recent dream, recurring dream, or a fantasy they have. The idea is to encourage group participation by having all members report on themselves and help others interpret or free associate on their experience.

3. *Analysis of resistance*—When group members become reluctant to share themselves with others and individual defenses are examined and dealt with.

4. *Analysis of transference*—When transference interactions are examined as close to the time of their occurrence as possible. Individual members are also asked to examine their feelings and involvement with other members of the group.

5. *Working through*—When individuals are required to accompany insight with action.

6. *Reorientation and social integration*—When clients demonstrate they are able to deal with the realities and pressures of life in an appropriate fashion without becoming overanxious or overcompliant when requests are made of them.

storming   a time of conflict and anxiety in a group when it moves from primary tension (awkwardness about being in a strange situation) to secondary tension (intragroup conflict). It is a period when group members and leaders struggle with issues related to structure, direction, control, catharsis, and interpersonal relationships.

strokes (TA) verbal, psychological, or nonverbal recognition.

structured activities (see *exercises*).

structuring the group running the group according to a preset prescribed plan or agenda.

study groups a type of task group, typically involve three to four students who meet at least weekly to share information, knowledge, and expertise about a course in which they are all enrolled. The idea is that each group member will support and encourage the others and will obtain insight and knowledge through the group effort.

style of life Adlerian term; the way one prefers to live and relate to others. Adlerians stress that a faulty life style is based on competitiveness and a striving to be superior to others.

subgroups cliques of group members who band together, often to the detriment of the group as a whole.

Succeeding in School lessons a series of ten lessons created by Gerler and Anderson (1986) that deal with modeling after successful people in school while learning to feel comfortable and responsible. Succeeding focuses on promoting cooperative efforts, enhancing student self-concept, and learning appropriate school skills such as listening and asking for help.

summarizing reflections by group members that recall significant events or learning experiences in the group.

superego a psychoanalytic term, represents the values of parents and parental figures within the individual. It operates on the moral principle by punishing the person when he or she disobeys parental messages through the *conscience* and by rewarding the person through the *ego ideal* when parental teachings are followed. The superego strives for perfection.

support groups a type of self-help group in which members share a common concern and have a professional group leader.

supporting the act of encouraging and reinforcing others. Its aim is to convey to persons that they are perceived as adequate, capable, and trustworthy. Through the act of supporting, group members feel affirmed and are able to risk new behaviors because they sense a backing from the group.

suppression of the conflict a strategy that consists of playing down conflict. It is often used when issues are minor. It keeps emotions under control and helps group leaders build a supportive climate.

surplus reality psychological experience that transcends the boundaries of physical reality. These experiences, which include relationships with those who have died or were never born, or with God, are often as important to people as their actual experiences with physical entities; a psychodrama concept.

SYMLOG System for the Multiple Level Observation of Groups.

synectics from the Greek, means the joining together of different and apparently irrelevant elements. Synectics theory applies to the integration of diverse individuals into a problem-stating, problem-solving group.

systematic group leadership training involves the teaching of basic skills to beginning group leaders. It is a six-step method that includes the videotaping of trainees leading a group before being introduced to the skill they are to learn (steps 1 and 2). Then the trainees read about and see a new skill demonstrated (steps 3 and 4). Finally, trainees critique their original videos and then make new videotapes demonstrating the skill they have just been taught (steps 5 and 6).

Systematic Training for Effective Parenting (S.T.E.P.) an Adlerian-based parent education program.

T-group approach to groups developed at the National Training Laboratories in the 1940s; primary attention to theory, group dynamics, and social material involving groups.

task processing ways of accomplishing specific goals in a group.

task/work groups groups whose emphasis is on accomplishment and efficiency in completing identified work goals. They are united in their emphasis on achieving a successful performance or a finished product through collaborative efforts. Task/work groups take the form of task forces, committees, planning groups, community organizations, discussion groups, and learning groups.

Tavistock Institute of Human Relations   a group research facility in Great Britain.

teachable moment   a time when people are ready and able to learn.

team   a number of persons associated together in work or activity such as in athletic or artistic competition in which members of a group act and perform in a coordinated way to achieve a goal. Teams differ from basic groups in four main ways: (a) They have shared goals, as opposed to individual goals in most groups. (b) They stress an interdependency in working more than do groups. (c) They require more of a commitment by members to a team effort. (d) They are by design accountable to a higher level within the organization than are groups.

team building   effective development of a team through managing conflict, promoting interpersonal relationships, and achieving consensus.

teamwork   all members of a group working together cooperatively.

tele   the total communication of feelings between people; involves complete interpersonal and reciprocal empathy; a psychodrama concept.

termination   a transition event that ends one set of conditions so that other experiences can begin. Termination provides group members an opportunity to clarify the meaning of their experiences, to consolidate the gains they have made, and to make decisions about the new behaviors they want to carry away from the group and apply to their everyday lives.

theater style   a type of group structure where members are seated in lines and rows.

Theatre of Spontaneity   a forerunner of psychodrama formulated by J. L. Moreno in 1921.

themes   specific topics or subjects related to the genuine interests of the participants, thereby holding their interest and inviting their participation. Many adolescent groups work best when they are structured around themes.

theory   a way of organizing what is known about some phenomenon in order to generate a set of interrelated, plausible, and, above all, refutable propositions about what is unknown. A theory guides empirical inquiry and is useful in testing hypotheses.

Theory X leader   an autocratic and coercive leader who basically believes people are unambitious and somewhat lazy.

Theory Y leader   a nondirective and democratic leader who thinks that people are self-starters and will work hard if given freedom.

Theory Z leader   a facilitative leader who helps encourage group members to participate in the group and trust that individual and collective goals will be accomplished through the process of interaction.

therapeutic contracts   in TA groups, specific, measurable, concrete statements of what participants intend to accomplish during the group. They place responsibility on members for clearly defining what, how, and when they want to change. TA contracts have the four major components of a legal contract: (a) *mutual assent,* clearly defining a goal from an adult perspective and joining with the therapist's Adult as an ally; (b) *competency,* agreeing to what can realistically be expected; (c) *legal object,* an objective; and (d) *consideration,* a fee or price for services.

therapeutic factors   (see *curative factors*).

therapeutic fairy tale   a projective group activity meant to help persons focus on the future and renew their effort in the group. In this process, individuals are asked to write a fairy tale in a 6- to 10-minute time frame. They are to begin their story with "Once upon a time," and in it they are to include (a) a problem or predicament, (b) a solution, even if it appears outlandish, and (c) a positive, pleasing ending. The tale is then discussed in regard to personal and group goals.

time-limited round   each individual has the same amount of time, usually one or two minutes each, to say whatever he or she wishes.

timely teaching   when a particular event stimulates thinking and discussion among students.

top-dog/underdog dialogue   in this Gestalt method, group members are asked to examine the *top-dog introjections* they have taken in from parents (usually represented by "shoulds" and "you") and their own real feelings about situations (usually represented by "I" statements). They then are asked to carry on a dialogue between these two aspects of themselves before the group or with another group member and try to become more aware of their true self-identity and ways to act that would be appropriate.

topic-specific groups   centered around a particular topic, such as widowhood, bibliotherapy, sexuality, health, or the arts. They are designed ultimately to improve the quality of daily living for older people. They also assist the aged to find more meaning in their lives and to establish a support group of like-minded people.

total quality movement (TQM)   in work/task environments, an emphasis on working cooperatively and productively in small groups.

TRAC model of groups   a model of groups known by the acronym TRAC (tasking, relating, acquiring, and contacting). Each letter represents an area in the total picture of group work. *Tasking* groups are focused on task achievement. *Relating* groups achieve objectives to increase the options for movement within the life of each person. *Acquiring* groups are directed toward learning outcomes that members can apply to others. In contrast, *contacting* groups are focused on the individual growth of members.

traditional leader   a person who is controlling and exercises power from the top down as an expert; may be appropriate in running a hierarchical group that is diverse and whose members are physically separated.

traffic director   when the group leader helps members become aware of behaviors that open communication channels and those that inhibit communication.

training group   a group for beginning leaders designed to help them recognize and work out major personal and professional issues that affect their ability to conduct groups, e.g., criticism, anxiety, jealousy, need for control.

trait approach   the idea that some persons emerge as leaders because of their personal qualities.

transactional analysis   involves the diagnosing of interactions among group members to determine if they are *complementary* (from appropriate and expected ego states), *crossed* (from inappropriate and unexpected ego states), or *ulterior* (from a disguised ego state).

transactional skills   helping group members interact.

transactions (TA)   social action between two or more people, manifested in social (overt) and psychological (covert) levels.

transference   the displacement of affect from one person to another; the projection of inappropriate emotions onto the leader or group members.

transformational leader   a person who empowers group members and shares power with them in working toward the renewal of a group; may be needed when a group is floundering.

transformational skills   helping members and the group achieve new behaviors.

transient children   children who have moved to a new community and a new school.

transition stage   the stage after the forming process and prior to the working stage; characterized by member anxiety, resistance, defensiveness, conflict, confrontation, and transference.

tri-level model of Gestalt group work   attention is systematically focused on (a) the individual at the intrapersonal level, (b) two or more people at the interpersonal level, and (c) the group as a systematic unit.

tying things together   linking; to connect members with one another in regard to their similarities.

unfinished business   emotional debris from a person's past.

unintentional civil liability   a lack of intent to cause injury.

universality   a sense of commonness that group members feel in regard to their experiences when compared to others.

universalization   one's realization that others may have the same concerns.

unknown quadrant   contains material hidden from self and others due to a lack of opportunity.

unstructured groups   used in experientially based situations and employed where there is an emphasis on process rather than product.

use of eyes   to scan the group and notice nonverbal reactions.

verbal behavior   when group members speak to each other. The content of speech between people along with its tone and emphases.

"W" work groups   (see *task/work groups*).

warm-up phase   in psychodrama, characterized by the director making sure he or she is ready to lead the group and that group members are ready to be led.

we/they mentality   where practitioners of other points of view are seen as "uninformed," "naive," or "heretical."

we/they tendency   when there is an overemphasis on identifying with a particular group, group members may tend to develop an antagonism toward other groups.

wheel   in this group arrangement, there is a center spoke, a leader, through which all messages go. Members have the advantage of face-to-face interaction with the leader, but they may become frustrated by the inability to communicate with another group member directly.

wisdom   one of Erikson's virtues; the ability to make effective choices among alternatives.

withdrawal from the conflict   a strategy that involves group leaders distancing themselves from conflict and postponing interventions.

working out a compromise   where each party involved gives up a little to obtain a part of what they wanted and to avoid conflict. The result is a win-win situation in which cooperative behavior and collaborative efforts are encouraged. This approach is effective in groups when there are limited resources.

working stage   most unified and productive group stage that focuses on the achievement of individual and group goals and the movement of the group itself as a system.

wounded healers   fellow sufferers; it is assumed in self-help groups that these individuals are able to deal most effectively with each other by coming together and sharing through disclosing, listening, and learning.

written projections   a process whereby members are asked to see themselves or their groups in the future as having been successful and to describe what the experience is like. They are able to play with their fantasies at times as well as be realistic.

Y   this group arrangement combines the structural elements of the wheel and chain—there is a perceived leader. The efficiency of the unit is second only to that of the wheel in performance. Like a chain, the Y may frustrate group members who wish to have direct contact and communication with each other. Information is not equally shared or distributed.

young adulthood   ages 20 to 40 years, in which identity and intimacy are two intense primary issues.

young-old   individuals between ages 65 and 75.

Name Index

Subject Index